Turkish Foreign Policy in Post Cold War Era

Edited by

İdris Bal

Turkish Foreign Policy in Post Cold War Era

BrownWalker Press
Boca Raton, Florida
USA • 2004

ISBN: 1-58112-423-6

BrownWalker.com

Editor

İdris Bal was born in Kütahya (Turkey) in 1968. Between 1985-1989, he studied Political Science at Istanbul University. After graduation, he became a research assistant at the Police Academy, Faculty of Security Sciences (a state University) in Ankara and continued his studies in the Politics Department of Nottingham University, UK. He received his MA in International Relations in September 1992. Then, he studies in the Department of Middle Eastern Studies at Manchester University and received his Ph.D. degree in 1998. After he returned to Turkey, he was appointed as Assistant Professor Dr. in 1998. He was deputy editor of Journal of Police Sciences (Polis Bilimleri Dergisi) between 2001- 2003. "Fulbright" awarded him a scholarship and he studied at Center for Middle Eastern Studies, Harvard University in the term 2003-2004. He worked on "Place of Turkey in US Foreign Policy After 11 September Attacks and Cooperation Against Terrorism". He is currently lecturer at Faculty of Security Sciences, Police Academy (a state university) in Ankara. He is also lecturing in Institute of Social Sciences (master courses) in Atılım University (a private university) in Ankara. He has four published books; *Turkey's Relations with the West and the Turkic Republics: Rise and Fall of the Turkish Model*, Aldershot: Ashgate Publications, 2000, 232 pages; (Ed.), *21. Yüzyılın Eşiğinde Türk Dış Politikası (Turkish Foreign Policy at the Threshold of the 21. Century)*, Istanbul: Alfa Publications, 2001, 732 pages; (Co-ed.), *Dünden Bugüne Türk Ermeni İlişkileri (Turkish Armenian Relations from the Past to the Present)*, Ankara: Nobel Publications, 2003, 734 pages; (Ed.), *21. Yüzyılda Türk Dış Politikası (Turkish Foreign Policy in the 21. Century)*, Ankara: Nobel Publications, 2004, 994 pages, (revised and expanded version of the second book). He has several articles on Turkish Foreign Policy, Eurasian social, political and economic developments, World Politics, Turkish-US-EU relations, Islam, Middle East and terrorism. His research interests include world politics, US foreign policy, Turkish foreign policy, global rivalries, hydrocarbon issues, Islam and politics, and global terrorism.

Contents

Foreword

Ersin Onulduran,

Professor of International Relations,
Faculty of Political Science, Ankara University

There is an oft used saying in Turkish, which can be roughly translated as: "It is not easy being a Turk". I think this expression summarizes the feelings of some of the observers of Turkish foreign policy upon hearing about yet another set back for Turkey in the international arena. All has not been bad for Turkey's foreign policy, however. Like the proverbial Phoenix rising from the ashes of the devastated Ottoman Empire, the new Turkish Republic rose in importance and effectives in world affairs through the 80 years of its existence. Looking at Turkish foreign policy from the perspective of 2004, it would not be unfair to say that Turkey's fortunes are on the rise in the world, and that the foreign policy establishment can take much of the credit for this rise in prestige and importance since, especially the end of the Cold War.

This new book, a collection of essays on various aspects of Turkey's foreign policy, has a good balance between theory, diplomatic history and analyses of current Turkish concerns. Its main focus is the post World War II. period, but references are made to the Ottoman past and the first years of the Republic as well.

The emphasis of the book, of course, is on the post-Cold War era. This is one of the first systematic treatments of that period of Turkish foreign policy. As the reader will quickly be able to tell, there are a variety of perspectives among the authors. The geographic areas treated are also wide and far-reaching. The chapter on Turkey and the Far East, for example deals with an area, which is not often seen in books on Turkish foreign policy. I was impressed also by the fact that the subjects treated were diverse. Issues related to Copenhagen Criteria for EU membership were addressed alongside Turkey's relations with countries of the Balkans and the Republics of Central Asia.

It is important that any book on foreign policy that aims to explain the foreign policy of a country not confine itself to a single and narrow geographic perspective. In this book, the regional and global issues are treated with equal breadth and depth. Although Turkey is medium sized regional power, it is in many ways affected by global political happenings and it, in turn, affects global issues. Turkey's ultimate help with the U.S. lead coalition effort in the Iraqi campaign will have far reaching effects for the region and for the image of the U.S. as the leader of the Western Alliance. Here is an example: Turkish - American relations appeared to suffer a small set back when The Turkish parliament failed to pass a resolution to permit the U.S. forces to pass through the country to open a northern front in Iraq in March of 2003. However, this small rift was mended relatively quickly, when Turkish policies began to change smoothly to help the Coalition effort in other ways including permitting logistic and humanitarian help and an offer to send Turkish troops to sent to Iraq, which was not taken up by the United States.

All this and more are competently dealt with by the authors in the various chapters of the book.

I am confident that both the interested general public and the specialists seeking a new perspective on Turkey's recent foreign policy actions will find this book very useful. It will be a reference book on post Cold War Turkish foreign policy matters for some time to come.

Ankara, April 2004

Acknowledgments

This book analyzes Turkish foreign policy in the post Cold War era. There are twenty articles by twenty one authors in the book. I would like to thank all of them for taking part in this comprehensive project. I have received help and encouragement from many people in the preparation of this book. I would like to thaunk Ersin Onulduran for his encouragement and writing a foreword for the book. I would like to thank also Hüseyin Bağcı, Gül Turan, İlter Turan, Victor Panin, Cemal Kafadar, Saziye Gazioğlu, Deniz Ülke Arıboğan, Mustafa Türkeş, Ramazan Gözen, Cengiz Başak, Veysel Karani Bilgiç, Bülent Olcay for their help and encouragement in different stages of the preparation of the book.

Abdullah S. Eyles and his wife Zülfiye Eyles, Fikret Işık and Nejat Kumral provided assistance in the proofreading stage of the work. Hilal Şahin and Zehra Çobanoğlu helped me in typesetting of the book. Mesut Muhammed Solak and Ömer Yılmaz helped me in the preparation of final manuscript as well. I am grateful to all of them. I also would like to thank Brown Walker Press and Jeff Young for their cooperation in the preparation of the book.

I wish this book would be helpful to everyone who is interested in international relations, world politics, the Middle East and Turkey in particular.

İdris Bal
Ankara, April 2004
idrisbal@fulbrightweb.org

Introduction

İdris Bal

With the end of the Cold War discipline the world has entered a new era. Parameters have changed; new handicaps as well as new opportunities have been created for countries. Turkey, as a neighbor of the former USSR, a member of NATO and located at the center of a sensitive region covered by Caucasus, the Balkans and the Middle East, has been radically affected by the end of the Cold War. Turkey has lost some of her bargaining cards in the new era and therefore has needed new arguments. This need encouraged Turkey to take active steps in the post Cold War era. This comprehensive book focuses on Turkish foreign policy in the post Cold War era. However, apart from historical background given at the beginning of most of the chapters, there is a chapter at the beginning of the book that summarises Turkish foreign policy since the Ottoman Empire. Books on Turkish foreign policy usually focus on Turkish relations with the West and the USA. However, all regions including Asia are taken under consideration in this book. This book analyzes Turkey's relations with the US, the EU, the Balkans, the Middle East, Caucasus, Central Asia, Russia and Far East Asian countries. At the same time, effects of economic crises and domestic developments on foreign policy, the Turkish model in Turkish foreign policy, water conflict, the Cyprus question, and the Kurdish problem are all analyzed.

There are twenty chapters in this book. The book begins with a Foreword by Prof. Dr. Ersin Onulduran. The first chapter belongs to Cengiz Okman; *Turkish Foreign Policy: Principles-Rules and Trends, 1814-2003.* The chapter gives a comprehensive framework for Turkish foreign policy from the Ottoman Empire up to present time and serves as a background chapter of the book.

Ramazan Gözen's chapter *Turkish Foreign Policy in Turbulence of the Post Cold War Era: Impact of External and Domestic Constraints*, focuses on the external and internal environment and their implications for foreign policy. Gözen initially analyzes the new characteristics of the external environment as far as its implications for Turkey are concerned. Then, he analyses responses of the domestic environment in so far as their implications for foreign policy. Finally, he focuses on patterns in Turkish foreign policy during the 1990s.

The third chapter, *Impacts of International Capital Flows to Turkish Economy During the 90's*, belongs to Saziye Gazioglu and Erol Bulut. This chapter focuses on economic crises in Turkey. Initially, the authors give an account of the Turkish economy after 1980. Then, they discuss the 1994 economic crisis. Finally they examine the November 2000 and the February 2001 crisis in Turkey.

The following chapter belongs to Faruk Sönmezoğlu, *Turkey and the World in the 21st Century*. Sönmezoğlu initially analyses the basic characteristics of International politics in the 21st Century and then he focuses on the main characteristics of the Turkish Foreign Policy in the 21st Century. He emphasizes in his chapter: "Turkish foreign policy in the 21st century must not be simply reactive, but rather more proactive and more carefully planned. Within the goals of maximum interest and minimum conflict, these are the fundamental elements of a successful foreign policy aiming to reach targets with minimum cost."

The fifth chapter, *Turkish Foreign Policy in Post Cold War Era: New Problems and Opportunities,* belongs to Hüseyin Bağcı and myself (İdris Bal). This chapter analyzes Turkish foreign policy in terms of new problems and opportunities in the post Cold War era. To this end, firstly changing parameters and problems for Turkey are underlined, and then new opportunities for Turkey and Turkey's strategic importance are analyzed.

The following chapter is my own, *Turkey-USA Relations and Impacts of the 2003 Iraq War*. This chapter analyzes factors that encouraged Turkey and the US for further cooperation in the post Cold War era. Then, the role of the 2003 Iraq War (third Gulf War) and its implications for US-Turkish relations are taken under consideration. There is a discussion in the concluding part of the chapter regarding the implications of the Iraq War and the future of Turkish-US relations. In fact although there is one chapter on Turkish-US relations, because of the position of the US in world politics and close relations between Turkey and the US, the impact and role of the US in Turkish relations is also examined in other chapters.

The following three chapters are related with EU-Turkish relations. Turkish Relations with the EU is at the top of the Turkish political agenda. Turkey expects to get a date in this year to begin negations with the EU for full membership. Therefore, relations between Turkey and the EU are examined from three different perspectives in this book. İbrahim Canbolat's chapter *The European Union and Turkey* analyses the formation and the systematic feature of the European Union and then the relationship between Turkey and the EU are considered.

Dirk Rochtus' chapter *"Turkestroika" as Precondition for Turkey's European Dream,* analyzes the Turkish system as well as Turkey's relations with the EU. He initially focuses on the foundations of the State, and some of the handicaps of the present system, then he analyses the Turkish ambition to become a full member of the EU. In doing this, he makes special reference to especially the Kurdish question and political Islam in Turkey.

The third chapter related with the EU belongs to Fulya Kip; *The Role of Turkish Migration and Migrants in Turkey's Relations With the EC/EU*. She analyzes Turkish migration to the EU in detail. She discusses some issues such as basic characteristics of Turkish migration, factors affecting Turkish migration, evaluation of Turkish migration, changing role of migration in Turkey's relations with the EU.

Mustafa Türkeş's chapter *Turkish Foreign Policy towards the Balkans: Quest for Enduring Stability and Security,* sketchs out the underlying factors which played significant roles in the process of the formation of Turkey's Balkan policy, and then identifies and analyzes the foreign policy strategy taken up by the Turkish governments, and finally discerns continuity and change in Turkey's Balkan policy from 1990 to 2003.

Nasuh Uslu's chapter *The Cyprus Question Between 1974 and 2004 and Its Relation to Turkish Foreign Policy* examines the Cyprus problem from the beginning up to the present time. He examines recent events related to the Cyprus issue with constant references to views, interests and interventions of the concerned powers. Especially the Turkish and American actions and approaches are the main focus of the study. Uslu concludes "it has become clear that the Greek Cypriots have expected to dominate the whole island by using their membership in the EU, which they secured regardless of the result of the referendum. The Turkish government and the Turkish Cypriots have accepted to make concessions for the sake of integration with the European Union, but the Greek Cypriots, relying on their secured membership in the EU, have chosen not to solve the problem by making some sacrifices."

Victor Panin and Henry Paniev's chapter *Turkey and Russia,* analayzes Turkish-Russian relations. They focuses on new bases for relationship, the Caucasus, cooperation in the Middle East, role of Islam, perspectives of the Russian Turkish relations on the civilizational level respectively. They emphasises new opportunuties and possibilities of cooperatin between two countries in post Cold War era.

Zeyno Baran's chapter *Turkey and the Caucasus,* focuses on Turkey's relations with Russia and the countries of Caucasus; Azerbaijan, Georgia and Armenia. She focuses on energy issues and the American factor and also US-Turkish cooperation. Her chapter ends with policy suggestion regarding the problems of the region.

The chapter by Gül Turan, İlter Turan and myself (İdris Bal), *Turkey's Relations with the Turkic Republics* focuses on Turkey's relations with the Turkic states. The chapter initially outlines the historical background, then, the evolution of relations between Turkey and the Turkic republics are analyzed. The relations between Turkey and Azerbaijan and the Turkic states of Central Asia are analyzed through three stages. High levels of optimism and expectations about the future mark the first stage. The second comprises the period of the mutual discovery of constraints that helped define the limits of the relationship. The third stage is described as the routinization of the relationship.

The following chapter is my own chapter; *Turkish Model as a Foreign Policy Instrument in Post Cold War Era: The Cases of Turkic Republics and the Post September 11th Era.* The chapter outlines the position of Turkey during and after the Cold War era and identifies what is meant by the term 'Turkish Model'. Then, it focuses on the rise of the Turkic republics with the end of the USSR and analyzes Western support for the Turkish model, Turkish policies towards those republics and their reactions. Finally it makes emphasis on Turkey and the Turkish model in the post September 11 era, and the importance of cooperation between the US and Turkey against terrorism. It concludes, "It is very likely that a successful Turkish model will attract other Islamic countries and serve for peace and cooperation in the world, but not as a model developed around her present-day characteristics - a far cry from the ideal."

Turkey is a European country as well as a Middle Eastern country. The Middle East is famous for its instability and this instability also has several implications for Turkey. Therefore, the following three chapters are related with the Middle East. The chapter *Instability in the Middle East and the Relevant Role of the PKK* is my own chapter. It outlines and analyses the factors that prepare instability in the Middle East. Then, the contribution of the PKK's (Kurdish Workers Party) to instability in the region, are briefly examined. It is emphasized in the chapter that there are several reasons related with cultural, social, economic, and strategic conditions of the region that create instability.

Meliha Benli Altunışık's chapter *Turkey's Middle East Challenges Towards a new Beginning* focuses on Turkey's policy towards the Middle East in general in the post Cold War era. Regarding the problems that Turkey faces in her policy towards the era, she, for instance, underlines that "On the one hand, Turkey is sometimes criticized for its 'disinterest in the Middle East' and 'severing its ties with the region'. On the other hand, when Turkey is active in the region there are apprehensions about its role. It is either considered as a 'Western stooge' or 'trying to impose a hegemony', political, military and economic".

The third chapter about the Middle East belongs to H. Bülent Olcay, *Politics of the Euphrates and Tigris Waters*. He focuses on the water issue between Turkey, Syria and Iraq. He examines the purpose of Turkey's water management projects and its influence on relations with her neighbors, the effect of water on Turkey's position in the Middle East and other important foreign policy matters related with the Euphrates and Tigris rivers.

Deniz Ülke Arıboğan's chapter *Opening the Closed Window to the East; Turkey's Relations with East Asian Countries* examines Turkey's relations with Far East Asian countries. She concludes, "by building moderate relations and maintaining a trustworthy profile, Turkey can build a perfect bridge between East and West, between Turks and Asians and between Muslims and non-Muslims creating an accord rather than a clash of civilizations."

The last chapter of the book belongs to Hüseyin Bagci and Saban Kardas; *Post-September 11 Impact: The Strategic Importance of Turkey Revisited*. This chapter analyzes the debate surrounding Turkey's increasing strategic importance in the wake of the September 11 terror attacks on Washington and New York. The chapter analyses from different perspectives that following the September 11 attacks, the importance of Turkey increased in world politics. They, for instance, argue that "The conventional importance attributed to Turkey's strategic value became more visible following the events of September 11, and consequently Turkey has come under the spotlight. As a result, Turkey and Turkish foreign policy started to receive great interest, and the mood in the discussions about Turkey and Turkey's strategic importance was usually optimistic."

1 Turkish Foreign Policy: Principles-Rules-Trends, 1814-2003

Cengiz Okman

From a methodological point of view, foreign policy is a very particular field of study of overlapping perspectives, and in general terms it can be conceived as a never-ending phenomenon of a specific unit, namely the state. It is through such a process that the state constantly tries to adjust itself to its ever-changing environment[1] in a manner to coincide with its internal process of differentiation.[2] Outcomes of these processes are of vital importance to any state providing it with the chance of survival in a desirable way and direction. For this reason, both processes are supposed to be underlined by consciously designed purposeful systematic activities. These activities are defined in accordance with certain rules and principles–whether or not they are officially declared.[3] By the very nature of the concerned organisms -- here the states -- these internal and external orientations can be evaluated in accordance with specific rules and evolve along with certain principles. However, in clarifying foreign policy principles, the determination of the essential characteristics of the system prevailing during each, period under analysis deserves particular attention since related principles are usually constructed with reference to structural imperatives.

On the Conceptual Framework

Turkish foreign policy can be visualized in its historical depth since its systemic regularities have been functionalised in the course of a long differentiation process in periodic cycles, also marked by occasional transformation periods. In this sense the 19th century is the remarkable period providing us with the basic facts in drawing some conclusions consistent with the

---

[1] One way or the other, either -- for instance, in Grotian terms--by diplomatically tracing a path by abiding with the rules of "material-physical" and "moral" conditions or in Machiavellian terms, by taking such norms as flux or change, fear and greed, negotiating from strength and techniques of bargaining into consideration, or sometimes tracing completely the Kantian path, the "state" undergoes a process of adjustment. The main objective for the "state" – in trying to trace such styles and ways of diplomacy (in the sense of foreign policy) – is to adapt itself to the requirements of the environment imposed upon itself. On these terms see, Gabriele Wight and Brian Porter, "Theory of Diplomacy", Gabriele Wight and Brian Porter, (Eds.), *Diplomacy*, London: Leicester University press, 1990, pp.180-205.

[2] Such a differentiation is not limited to specific sections; on the contrary, it extends over entire segments of the socio-political order. On the concept of differentiation in this sense see, D.D. Katz and R.L. Kahn, "Common Characteristics of Open Systems," F.Emery (Ed.), *Systems Thinking*, London: Penguin Books, 1970, pp.81-105.

[3] The activities of the states in specific -- especially earlier-- periods of history might not have been determined and declared in accordance with certain rules and principles openly. Yet, with the advance of theory in our times, we have the full opportunity to analyze the orientations of the states and deductively explain their activities in accordance with some theoretical rules retrospectively; and, affiliate their actions with certain principles. In this way, it may be possible to assign certain principles to their political orientations whether or not they are officially and consciously adopted and announced in the past.

developments in the 20th century. Indeed, a close analysis indicates that the Ottoman initiatives have -- though in varying scope and forms -- always been underlined by the basic principles dictated by the prevailing systemic structure (namely balance of power -- BOP) and its related rules in this period. The final structural design that began to shape up in the form of a kind of "balance of terror"[4] towards the end of the century began to impose new sets of strains upon the Empire with serious implications leading towards the greatest transformation in its history starting right after the First World War. It was upon such a background that the foreign policy orientations of a modern state began to be organized into a new structural framework under quite different environmental conditions soon leading to another particular global order after WWII. Through such a historical process the evolution of the foreign policy has been marked by two distinct structural periods, each followed by transitionary terms, the one still in progress at present.

Consequently, "responsiveness to structural attributes" can be assigned to Turkish foreign policy as a general theoretical framework in its historical depth. It is such a general framework that the selected principles turn out to be the styles and ways adopted as the underlying basics for the policy moves in each period.

The 19th Century; The Longest Structure Relevant Period

The 19th century can be labelled as the period of relative consistency in the sense that the Empire persistently tried to adjust its policy attributes to the continuously changing requirements of the BOP politics for over one hundred years. Shifts in the 19th century dynamics naturally caused some fluctuations in the Ottoman orientations; yet, the general trend remained the same.

In this century, the Ottoman Empire faced both external and internal problems. It had a very large territory yet did not possess the technical, economic and institutional resources to integrate its diverse populations into a single political community capable enough to meet external demands. The Empire was in a critical state subjected to the potential threat of gradual territorial dismemberment and ethnic cleansing. Thus the fundamental problem was to establish a stable and positive link between internal and external conditions. The survival of the Empire was at stake and a careful diplomacy was thus key to Ottoman survival. The ultimate solution rested on exploiting the balance of power (BOP) among the main European states and the prevailing fear among them that if either one power or a coalition of powers dominated the Ottoman Empire, this would lead to a major show down with their rivals. This was the conceptual framework chosen by the Empire; and, foreign policy and diplomatic styles were to be adjusted to the systemic/structural imperatives.[5]

One of the traditional weaknesses that have affected the ottoman foreign policy has

---

[4] In reality, starting from the third quarter of the century, the essential characteristics of the classical BOP order began to change and the states no longer seemed to be abiding by the established rules of the system. The new trend was towards a pre-transitive period to be labeled as the "balance of terror", as stated by many writers, to denote a rapidly evolving arms race and building rival camps.

[5] The findings on what the Ottoman governments thought or planned in the foreign policy field and their conceptualization of then existing structural realities for the most part are not based on official documents, especially until the third quarter of the century. Most of the findings on this subject thus rest upon the later analyses and partially inferred from their actions, or from what other sources and findings of European diplomats believed and reported at the time.

been the insufficient institutional resource available for it.[6] However, in the course of the continuous initiatives that were launched throughout the 19th century, the Ottoman Empire has been able to build up a reasonably effective foreign policy structure, similar to those of other autocratic monarchies at the time.[7] This was one of the positive aspects of the differentiation that could be attributed to the Ottoman state apparatus in its efforts to try to adjust itself to environmental imperatives at the time. Though academically it might not have been properly and sufficiently worked out and presented clearly, in reality the Ottoman state always acted in accordance with a "fundamental goal" and "policy line" relevant to the circumstances and position at the time.

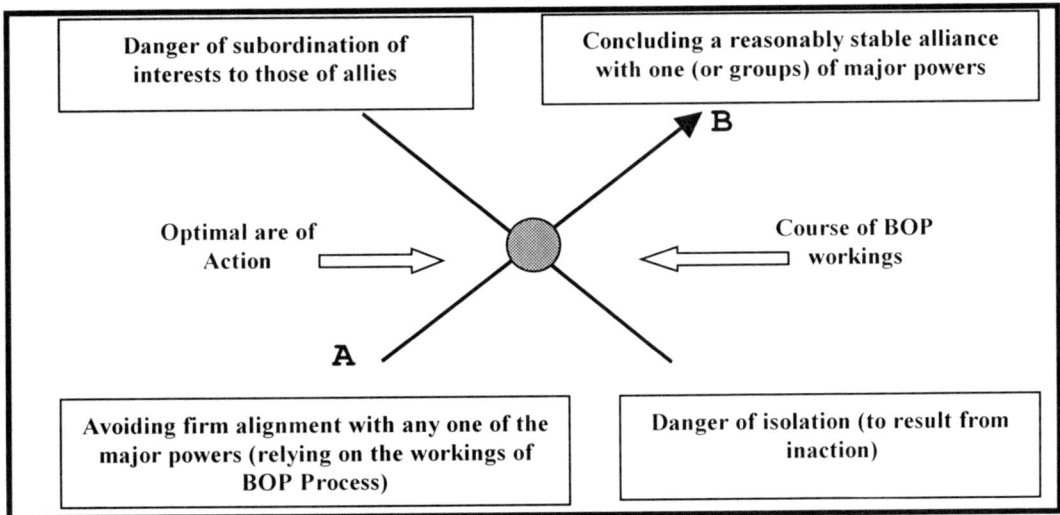

Alignment-realignment optimisation axes for the Ottoman Empire

Indeed, to handle the problem of survival in meeting the principal threats in three main zones of conflict (in the Balkans, the Straits and Egypt and to some extent the Middle East) was to be handled by assessing and exploiting the international situation to their advantage. The preferred policy line, then, was to be marked by the broad range of "flexible alignments" design based upon fully pragmatic approaches depending on the circumstances at the time. It is in such a general framework that the Ottoman foreign policy was constantly aimed at the optimization of its "zones of action", the term denoting the time–and direction of the engagements as possibly the most rational choices.

---

[6] J.C. Hurewitz, "Ottoman Diplomacy and the European State System," *Middle East Journal,* Vol.15, 1961, pp.141-52.

[7] It was not in this long lasting process that, starting from the establishment of the permanent embassies in various European capitalist (1793-96) and continuing during the Tanzimat reforms of 1839-1856 and changes after late 1870s, a series of incremental adjustments were simultaneously introduced and diplomatic methods were revised. See, İlber Ortaylı, "Osmanlı Diplomasisi ve Dış İşleri Örgütü." *Tanzimattan Cumhuriyete Türkiye Ansiklopedisi,* Vol.1, pp.278-81; Roderic H. Davidson, *Reform in the Ottoman Empire, 1856-76.* New Jersey: Princeton University Press, 1963, a scholarly study of Turkish political reform and diplomacy.

In the century–long process of alignment re-alignments, Great Britain and Russia have mutually taken part in two extremes, one as the frequent ally and the other as the constant enemy, and the other powers have also taken part in between periodically.[8] However, towards the end of the century with the BOP order beginning to shake to its foundations, Germany emerged as the most likely and enduring candidate for the alliance. In this way, two traditional land powers, both with central positions in their respective regions, began to proceed towards a common but undesirable destiny for both.

However, such an undesirable end does not mean that adaptation of the supreme strategy of exploiting BOP was a wrong path to trace. On the contrary, the Ottoman Empire had been quite successful in at least slowing down the decline, but they had never been able to prepare essential capabilities to provide themselves with the opportunity to adapt to a different structural order once the 19th century order began to crack.[9]

In the 19th century one very important development to be noted is the gradual evolution of the European–Ottoman systemic exchanges into a new functional framework. Accordingly, socio-cultural and socio-political dynamics of the internal structures from the both sides have mutually begun to function as driving forces in the formation and direction of their foreign policies respectively.[10] Taking internal domains as the centers of interests was a new phenomenon. On these premises a new process that was gradually facilitated by the European demands in socio-political and cultural terms and the systemic Ottoman responses on the same directions began to evolve. It is in this process that the Ottoman Empire, in a way, constantly sought recognition by the European powers on multi-dimensional bases. The Treaty of Paris signed in 1856, is a fine example in this respect.[11] This treaty had a great deal of significance, since it was treated as recognition of the Empire's status as a European power.[12] Here, the important point is that "the continuation of this recognition has since remained one of the Turkish State's main

---

[8] In the essence of the British Ottoman combinations lies a theoretically proven fact that a maritime power – a circumferiential actor—always needs a land power, particularly with a central position over the landmasses. This positional link in global politics is not an ephemeral phenomenon, rather it repeats in different periods in different forms (e.g., today US –Turkey). This has been the case with Ottoman foreign policy that has continued up until the present age, yet in the final period the British were replaced by another maritime actor; that is, the USA. On the rising and declining cycles see, J. Peter Taylor, *The political Geography of the Twentieth Century: A Global Analysis*, New York; Wiley& Sons Inc., 1993, pp.31-62.

[9] In fact one of the systemic deficiencies inherent to Turkish Foreign policy has been its ineffectiveness in coping with adaptation problems during each transition period. Periods covering the post Napoleonic wars era, the late 19th and early 20th centuries and the 1990s exhibit identical experiences in this respect.

[10] On this mutually evolving process see, C. Okman, "Avrupa Birliği", *Karizma*. Ocak-Şubat-Mart 2001, No.5, pp.147-161.

[11] In the first decade of the 19th century Sened-i İttifak (Covenant of Union) set the initial signs of the new process and was followed by the Tanzimat reforms of 1839 (and the Statute of 1855) and 1876, 1908 constitutional movements are the substantial precedents for the contemporary movements starting in 1923. From an analytical point of view, all of these turning points can be, conceived as the integral parts of a unique evolutionary process still in progress at present.

[12] Bernard Lewis, *The Emergence of Modern Turkey*, London; Oxford University Pres, 1961. Roderic H. Davison, *Reform in the Ottoman Empire*, 1856-1876, New Jersey: Princeton University Press, 1963.

foreign policy goals.[13]

Initial Decades of the 20th Century

The period dated back to the late 19th century and extending all the way up to the second World War was the age of declining hegemonic powers that were gradually being replaced by others; for instance, Great Britain was to refer to appeasement policies as the only rational way of consolidating its global status, and sought permanent alignments as the means of providing security in Europe.[14] Rising inter-bloc rivalries accompanied by an intense arms race, and new tendencies in handling crises gradually invalidated the remaining traces of the rules and dominant principles of the classical BOP period. The classical order began to disintegrate.[15]

After the first showdown (between 1914-1919), the point of intersection of the rising and declining powers was discernable in definitive terms; the British in decline (partially accompanied by France) and the USA-Germany on the rise. Never settled inter-state rivalry, in scope and character, evolved into a stage opening the ways to yet another great show down, the greatest that has never been witnessed. Prevailing global conditions in overall terms did not represent any particular type of structural order.[16] Rather, in terms of the general outlook of the interstate exchanges and the way essential systemic attributes were conceived, this period exhibited the characteristics of a "transition" epoc, the longest one in history, lasting for almost 40 years.[17]

---

[13] Remarkable parallels can be drawn between the terms of the Treaty of Paris then and the Copenhagen Criteria at present; indeed, after the Crimean war of 1855-56 in Paris, the signatories agreed to respect the independence and integrity of the Ottoman Empire in return, the Ottoman government agreed to give guarantees of good treatment of its Christian subjects. One of the remarkable points was that the Europeans could provide the Ottoman Empire with the chance of Joining the European Concert if suggested reforms could ever be put into effect. Çoşkun Üçok, *Siyasal Tarih 1789-1960*, Ankara: Sevinç Matbaası, 1975, pp.123-125.

[14] On the British appeasement policies at the turn of the century see, D.C. Watt & John Bull, *America in Britain"s place, 1900-1975*, Cambridge: Cambridge University Press, 1984. This period is labeled as the world order of the British succession (1904-WWII) George Modelski, "The long Cycle of global politics and the Nation State", *Comparative Studies in Society and History*, April 1978, pp.214-35; J. Peter Taylor, pp.39-49.

[15] In this period, it seems that the conceptualization of the rules—and the principles—relating to such attributes as the "stability-instability", "differentiation etc., at both intra and interstate levels," coincided neither with ones that existed in the classical BOP nor with those of the Cold War Period. On the conceptual part see, Sten Sparic Nilson, "Measurement and Models in the Study of stability," *General Systems Year Book*, V. XIV, pp. 121-35; Charles W. Kegley, Jr. And Eugene R. Wittkopf, *World Politics; Trend and Transformation*, 5th ed., New York: St Martin's Press, 1995, pp.73-82.

[16] Taking 10 different world orders (3 have already been lived up, and the rest with only hypothetical value) into consideration, the period comprising 4 initial decades (especially the last two) can hardly be fitted in any one of these groups. On the structural explanations see, Morton Kaplan, *System and Process in International Politics*, New York: John Wiley& sons-Inc., 1967, pp.21-54.

[17] Within the time framework chosen for this study, three such periods can be identified; the first one, starting right after the Napoleonic Wars, the second in the process of the collapse of the classical BOP starting from the early 20th century and maturing after the Firs world War and the last one after the end of the Cold War which is still in progress. On the conceptual premises see, Rein Taagepera, "The Growth Curves of Empires," *General Systems Year Book of the Society for General Systems Research*, Washington

In meeting the radically altering external as well as internal requirements in the course of this transitionary period, nature and the scope of the general guideliness of action–directly and indirectly–adopted by Turkish Foreign policy makers were exhibited in three different periods consequently.

The first period included the initial decades of the 20th century starting from the last years of the 19th century. In this period the foreign policy was to be adjusted to the dominant principles of a new type of power balance. Contrary to the classical BOP period, the Ottoman Empire was gradually to be re-orientec towards a permanent alliance process and to choose a suitable power and to be party to a multidimensional harsh intra-continental rivalry. Such a methodological shift was justified on pragmatic grounds since by the late nineteenth and early twentieth centuries the freedom of movement for Turkish diplomacy was to go through heavy constraints due to the fact that it was becoming more difficult to play off one European power against another in the wake of the wide spread division among main European states in two camps. This situation created a hard dilemma for Turkish foreign policy in that old avenues of alignments soon were to be blocked. Britain, for instance, was working for an entente with France and Russia and major powers were very anxious not to provide each other by establishing close ties with the Ottoman government.[18] Soon, it was to become clear that ever lasting neutrality would not be a positive –or even possible—choice either. Alliance with Germany found its course under very the particular developments in 1914 leading to the long expected outcome, namely the First World War.[19] The war gave rise to some developments; however, with powerful effects on the post-war Turkish state's foreign policy, one of these was the tragic epoch concerned with the so-called Armenian case with ramifications lasting until the present time; the other concerns the relations with Arabs under the negative psychological impact of treachery; and, finally, implications of the changing regime in Russia. Another interesting development in its historical setting was related to the fundamental reversal of the positions adopted by the British and Soviet policies on the straits as the British began to seek to have the straits opened to warships while the Soviets armed to keep them closed. The war appears to have marked the end of the another ground rule of earlier Ottoman diplomacy in the sense that the empire joined a war among the major powers for the first time taking its own initiative—after the battle curisers

---

D.C.: Menthol Health Research Ins., 1968. Vol. XIII, pp.171-177. Kurt Finsterbusch, "World Systems and the Theory of National Actors", *General Systems; Yearbook of the Society for the General Systems Research*, V.XIX, pp.147-153.

[18] Such a shift would not take place spontaneously with the early signs of division among the European Powers. The Ottoman Empire would try to maintain the minimum conditions of survival through a semi-neutral position; and especially after the Young Turk Revolution they would switch to the policy of trying to establish friendship with all of the main powers. Yet, by the end of the first decade of the 20th century, this policy would leave the Ottoman State without an alliance with any of the European Powers. This became evident when it faced its final trial of strength in the Balkans in 1912-13 see; Hasan Ünal, "Young Turks" Assessments of International Politics, 1900-9." *Middle Eastern Studies*, Vol.32, 1996, pp.30-44.

[19] Initiatives launched consecutively Nov. 1908 through 1913 for a defensive alliance with British or for some form of alignment with the triple entente have been the final attempts in this respect. Even the offers to Russia were to be turned down Just before the outbreak of the war. Frank Weber, *Eagles on the Crescent: Germany, Austria and the Diplomacy of the Turkish Alliance, 1914-1918*, Ithaca, NY.: Cornel University Press, 1970, pp.135-6 and 142-156.

Goeben and Breslau incident—without any immediate and direct threat to its own territories; this was an orientation that had never been the case until then.

The second phase, from structural point of view, is the period of 1920-31, which can be conceptualized as a kind of power vacuum interlude. This stage of geopolitical order could–through analogy—be visualized like the "rivalry and concert" order after 1871 with two powers in favor of status quo, one in Europe and one in the rest of the world.[20] The problem was not just to build a peace, but rather to construct a peaceful international order that would successfully manage all international conflicts in the future.[21] The years, following the World War I, witnessed the high points of political idealism known as the period of institutionalization in this respect.[22] The state sovereignty was to be brought under the jurisdiction of international norms and rules.

The greatest episode for Turkey in this period was marked by the collapse of the Ottoman Empire in 1918, almost immediately leading to the process of the "national struggle with the supreme objective of achieving independence and founding a new nation-state to be underlined by a new set of fundamental principles referring to the conception of the "national unity" and "nation".[23] These principles were to be accepted as the bases of the broad guidelines of action shaping Turkish foreign policy in the following decades. In overall terms, this period of struggle exhibited a remarkable example of a political orientation of a general strategy of the "indirect approach".[24] The principles inherent in such a strategic thought were successfully put into effect in the implementation of foreign

---

[20] Yet according to Taylor, this is where the similarities end. After Versailles, France see med to be the leading power though its position was quite artificial and short term soon to be replaced by Germany. In the rest of the world Britain remained the status quo power, but on the line of the decline since 1871. J.P Taylor, pp.45-48.

[21] Kalevi J. Holsti, Pearce and War; *Armed Conflicts and International Order, 1648-1989*, Cambridge: Cambridge University Pres, 1991, pp.175-176 and 208-209.

[22] On the process see, William R. Keylor, *The Twentieth Century World: An International History*, New York: Oxford University Press, 1984, pp.95-133.

[23] The New Concept of Unity was officially to be announced by the voting of the National Pact (Misak-ı Milli) in January 1920, and the Contextual and qualitative aspects of the concept of nation and citizen were to be explained by Mustafa Kemal Atatürk in his series of statements defining the nation of the Turkish people in reference to an inclusive understanding of the human element as affiliated with a political authority regardless of differences in ethnic, religious and language terms. A. Afet İnan, *Medeni Bilgiler ve Mustafa Kemal Atatürk'ün El Yazıları*, Ankara: T.T.K. Basımevi, 1969, pp.351-491 and 21-47 Also the idea of "peace at home peace in the World," is a fine example of the understanding on the organic relationship between the Underlying mentalities of the internal and external policy orientations; Tuncay Mete, *T.C.nde Tek Parti Yönetiminin Kurulması: 1923-31*, İstanbul: Cem Yayınevi, 1985, p.453; Nimet Arsan, *Atatürkün Tamim Telgraf ve Beyannameleri* 1917-35 Ankara: Ankara Üniversitesi Basımevi, 1964, p.351. On the essentials of the Turkish Politics; Enver Ziya Karal, *Atatürk: Düşünceler*, İstanbul: Milli Eğitim Basımevi, 1986. It is also worth noting that the Treaty of Laussane (Section II) on the concept of the Turkish citizen, shares the similar views with Atatürk and above stated authors.

[24] Departing from the actual experineces of the past, a broad analysis of the concept of the "indirect approach" is submitted by liddel Hart see. B.H. Liddel Hart, *Strateji: Dolaylı Tutum*, translated by Cemal Enginsoy, Ankara: Gen. Kur. Harp Tarihi Başkanlığı, 1973. However, to have a sound vision of the Turkish experience, the findings of this study have to be reinterpreted by applying the related norms of the "control" and "maneuver" notions in a broder framework. See, Cengiz Okman, *On the Theory of Strategy*, İstanbul: D.H.O. Basımı, 1998.

as well as internal policies by the forces identified as the "national movement" without even official recognition as a state and under the actual conditions of the post-war occupation.

It was in such a framework that the "national action" was effectively divided into two stages: the first covering the months between May 1919 and early 1920, and the second until October 1923. In the first stages of the policy of indirect approach was facilitated through congressional actions (July through September in Erzurum and Sivas) leading to the declarations of the National Pact (Misak-ı Milli) on 28 January 1920. These declarations can be assessed as the basic documents fully coinciding with the future imperatives of Turkish foreign policy.[25]

During the second stage the style of the indirect approach changed its general outlook by placing relatively heavier emphasis on coercive policy manoeuvres including the selective use of military assets by carefully analyzing external and internal conditions and trying to exploit the balance of power and rivalries among the main European states.[26] In fact, this was the basis on which their Ottoman predecessors had relied throughout the 19th century. In this sense, the founders of the new state also proved their distinct conceptual ability in perceiving and exploiting the situations in their historical depth in political as well as social and psychological terms. This ability was of vital importance in conveying and applying the basic principles of the above stated type of political approach. Signing the Treaty of Friendship in Moscow (16 march 1921), concluding a treaty with French (October 1921), then, can all be conceived as the basic stages of a policy that would lead to the armistice agreement in Mudanya (10 October 1922); and, through the same perspective, was the political environment whose further and successful exploitation in this manner marked the final stage in Lausanne in the summer of 1922.

The second stage of the global transition period, covering the years 1920 through early thirties, can be defined as a kind of "Power vacuum interlude" during which the geopolitical order was superficially like the rivalry and concert order after 1871.[27] In Europe, France, one of the status quo powers, seemed to be a leading actor in the continent, and Britain in the wider world but in a constant process of decline. Under the light of the realities of the time, the respective positions of both powers were quite artificial and therefore would not continue to fulfil the requirements of maintaining stability on the continent. In reality both of them were insecure, Britain beyond Europe and France within Europe. It was becoming clear that a new co-sponsor of any world order would inevitably be needed. The US., on the other hand, with selective policies in its interventions was tracing a gradually rising trend well beyond isolationism.[28] By this time

---

[25] Basic lines on the type, scope and qualitative aspects of the foreign policy were formulated in these sessions organized consecutively in a short period of time. On the summary of documents see. M. Gönlübol, (Ed.), *Olaylarla Türk Dış Politikası*, Ankara: Akım Kitabevi, 1989.

[26] The use of force has been carried out on selective grounds as the "rules of the force application" -- starting from İnönü I continuing through İnönü II, Sakarya and ending up in Afyon--have carefully been determined and applied in accordance with established modes of indirect approach.

[27] Peter Taylor, p.43.

[28] French efforts in seeking security guaranties from other powers (following the US"s failure to Join the League) through Rapallo (1922) and Lacarno (1924) initiatives; and outside Europe, on the part of Britain, naval agreements with Japan and the US as the second round of appeasement policies were prerequisites

the world situation was rapidly changing. The process of deteriorations in the global economic order reached a very critical stage following the financial collapse of the New York Stock Market in 1929, withdrawal of the British currency off the gold standard (two events that severely effected the popularity of the governments throughout the world); and, the Manchuria crisis in China putting Japan into political rivalry were the main events marking the end of the phase of the power vacuum.

For the new Turkish state this phase signifies a historically remarkable episode during which, a) the structural and functional transformations in the internal order were to be harmonious and carried on further in a manner to meet the requirements of survival as a modern state at the time, and b) the essential systemic conditions for an effective and efficient adaptation to the rapidly evolving political environment were to be assured. This was a formidable challenge to face that required a prudent approach in the selection and timing of the priorities and consolidating the principles of the new state at home and abroad. However, the geopolitical conditions in the second phase of the transition period offered a unique security environment without any immediate threat -- perhaps for the first time since the last quarter of the 18th century--that provided the Turkish state with the chance to achieve a degree of security and international recognition.

Such a contextual framework enabled Turkish decision makers to design a comprehensive unified political vision coinciding with the realities of the foreign and internal domains under a general defensive posture. Accordingly, foreign policy would take second place to internal reconstruction where the Turkish state determined to proceed on quite untraditional lines through an ambitious modernization process.[29] Western ideas and institutions, concepts and models have effectively and efficiently adjusted to the socio-political realities of the internal domain of the time.[30] In the end, these western attributes came to serve not as the channel of transmission for foreign influences but as the self-reliant political leadership and philosophers of a changing nation state.[31]

In its overall design the foreign policy -- in terms of the conversion of principles into the process of strategic action—was designated to a) prepare the proper environmental conditions suitable to the domestic processes, and in this respect b) eliminating the problems left over from the prewar phase of the transitionary period, and to this end c) preparing the essential grounds to see the country recognized as a respected European power and safeguarding its security coinciding with internal and external realities at the time. Thus, a policy of neutrality with a general conservative outlook and antirevisionist stand -- in an environment where alliances were simply unavailable and practically

---

for a new balancer within the system. See, W.R. Keylor, pp.3-40.

[29] A Comprehensive account of the Turkish modernization process -- in its historical context-- is submitted in; Robert E. Ward and Dank Wart A. Rustow, (Eds.), *Political Modernization in Japan and Turkey*, New Jersey: Princeton University Press, 1968.

[30] As it is defended by R. Davison, "much of the foreign contribution to Turkish political modernization came in the form of ideas and institutions, concepts and models, which the Turks could make their own by adoption or adaptation," Roderic H. Davison, "environmental and Foreign Contributions", *Political Modernization in Japan and Turkey*, pp. 64-117.

[31] As stated by Schorger, "The impetus for modernization of the society derives from modernized indigenous elements as much as, or more than, from external sources. Turkish experience bears this out." Ibid., p.115 (in reference to a paper submitted by William Schorger, in 1961).

meaningless at the time --was assumed to be a dominant policy posture. It was within such a general framework that the series of issues starting form the population settlements and related disagreements on property procedures and on the status of patriarch mainly with Greece, to the critical Mousul dispute of 1923-1926 with Britain had been stabilized. At the same time, such timely policy initiatives as the Treaty of Neutrality and Friendship with the Soviet Union (in Dec. 1925) and reapproachement manoeuvres to wards Greece and partially towards Britain by the late 1920s played an important role in the preparation of an environment suitable to the rapid systemic differentiation at home.

In fact, such an overall orientation was soon to be proven as rationally very effective when -- starting from the early 1930s -- the freedom of action attained that far would enable Turkey to design and pursue policy moves abroad even under the light of the rapidly deteriorating global conditions in the last phase of the transitionary period. In global terms the last phase marked by the gradual reconstruction of the division, giving rise to formulation of the pan-region theories precipitating the collapse of the free trade order and finally leading to the formation of the antagonistic world blocks.[32] Instability mounted to a peak level; and taken in its overall context, "the period from 1914 to 1945 has often been designated as the Thirty Year's war of the twentieth century".[33]

In the last phase of this episode Turkey abandons its initial introverted stand and gained an extraverted position to its fullest extent. Tracing an essentially anti revisionist line, the main determinants of the foreign policy were selected in a manner to meet the challenges through two interrelated time perspectives; a) as a long term perspective, preparing the normative premises and taking political initiatives accordingly, and b) as the short term perspective, preparing reliable and credible ways and means of countering rapidly evolving critical situations. In its general outlook an active stand was dominant; and, the "indirect approach" was still a preferred framework for strategic action.[34] In this respect, affiliation with the League of Nations and adoption of its principles as the basis of the international reality (July 1932), and the establishment of a sound future vision for the historically contested status of the straits through the Agreement of Montreux (July 1936) were fine examples of the achievements realized through the manoeuvres on the first line.[35] Such a policy frame could be worked out without breaking the links with

---

[32] On the evolution of the pan region theories, J. O Loughlin and H. Vander Wusten, "The Political Geography of Panregions," *Geographical Review*, No.80, 1990, pp.1-20 and further on the process of division, J.P. Taylor, pp.46-49; and S. Dalby, *The Coming of the Second World War*, London; Pinter, 1990); and on the economic processes, I. Walterstein, "Long Waves as Capitalist Process", *Politics of the World Economy*, Cambridge; Cambridge Un. Press, 1984, pp.559-75.

[33] William R. Keylor, p.43.

[34] In this period in the practice of "indirect approach" as a political guide to action --in contrast to the previous decade--the relative weight of the military domain increases. Military assets are often, yet very carefully, referred to as the partial means of political maneuvers (at least lurking in the background) in the related processes of coalition formations (e.g.) British, French and Balkan processes) as well as handling issues and solving problems (e.g. Hatay case in 1938-39). Stanford j. Shaw and Ezel Kural Shaw, *History of the Ottoman Empire and Modern Turkey*, Vol. II, Cambridge: Cambridge University Press, 1977, pp.373-388.

[35] As it was stated by Tevfik Rüştü Aras, the integral maintenance of the convenant of the League was to be conceived as the foundation of Turkish foreign policy. See, Brock Milman, "Turkish Foreign and

Moscow and even without irritating Italy and Germany. In addition, limits of neutrality were skilfully manipulated without radical shifts from the established lines of political direction.

In conclusive terms, the last two phases of the long transitionary period can be conceived as having a very special meaning in the Turkish foreign policy tradition. Indeed, Turkey was able to transform the entire order into a different "systemic whole" in the 1920s and, departing from these newly established premises was able to launch initiatives (in 1930s) and realized remarkable achievements with strong future ramifications. In quantitative terms of "time and number of achievements ratio", there has not been any comparable period until the present.

The Cold War: The Exceptional Period

It was not possible to continue on the evolving line of the global power division to the extent of giving rise to the pan-region schemes, especially when the geopolitical codes of the great powers began to overlap. Thus, by the end of the 1930s, the division of the world rapidly evolved into a power struggle between two alliances to last for over fourty years.

Turkish policy stand was essentially underlined by the simple principle of not assuming any involvement in power struggle unless all the alternative options were exhausted and legal requirements for such involvement were met.[36] Thus, a "balanced neutrality" was selected as a national guidance of policy. It was balanced in the sense that relations with both sides—through summit meetings and ambassadorial processes—could efficiently be carried on almost until the last stages of the war.[37] However, such uneasy neutrality inflicted serious implications upon Turkey's economy causing severe shortages of goods and wild inflation, forcing the government to take a series of legal and financial measures.

In the decades following the war, the power configuration basically evolved into a relatively "tight bipolar" order.[38] In this period the USSR replaced Germany as a new source of threat for the western order, yet the emerged structure proved to be more permanent than any other that had gone before. However, as the result of the inability of the major powers in their efforts to create a desired new world order (starting from where they had left off in the 19th century) the bipolarity introduced itself as an exceptional period, rather than as an order produced by a rationally designed--and agreed upon--scheme. In that sense, it was not submitted, especially in the form of a "Cold War" within such an unexpectedly evolved framework, it was possible to think about the British

---

Strategic Policy, 1934-42", *Middle Eastern Studies*, 1995, Vol.31, p.491.

[36] Legal requirements for such involvement were determined by the agreements concluded with France and England in 1939 consecutively and have continiously been subjected to a series of reviews held among Turkey, England and France in the course of the war. (e.g.) Adana meetings).

[37] The treaty of nonaggression (July 18. 1941) and a trade agreement (oct. 9. 1941) could be designed without damaging the ties with allies.

[38] In a "relatively tight" bipolar order –which prevailed in this period—the system is stable when both bloc actors are (at least relative to the loose type) hierarchically organized, and the rules of the system are to a much greater extent dominated by the bloc actors than would be the case in a looser type. The Cold War bipolarity also presents a "relative" type as compared to the "tight" type in its absolute terms where other actors cease to exist on the theoretical ground. Morton Kaplan, pp.36-45.

imperialist Mackinder's world as finally coming into being in the form of the Cold War geopolitical order.

Coinciding with its unexpected emergence and unique character, the Cold War has never been conceived of in a framework of a uniform design--and even in structure. On the contrary, the Cold War represents a very particular period that has evolved through different stages exposing various forms of inter-bloc (and also inter state in a broder frame work) exchanges providing different forms of stability depending on the conditions in each specific stage. It is exactly in these terms that the Cold War, as a general process, can be divided into phases covering three to four different exchange periods.[39]

Taking these phases into consideration within a single comprehensive framework, the essential features of the period can be expressed in terms of, a) deepest division and lack of communication in the process of setting the antagonistic positions mutually (1947-53), b) initiating a series of conflict and concert as well as contest or conspiracy types of action parallel to the evolving processes of the Third World and non-aligned movements, and rising issues of international economy (search for a new economic order) and proliferation of new non-governmental actors (1953-69), c) creation of conditions of the co-existence leading to along process of detente and establishment of talks at a strategic level (e.g., SALT-START), meanwhile increasing the number and scope of coercive actions and periodic tensions in different parts of the world without loosing prudent sight of the supremacy of deterrence among main power and other actors (1969-79), and finally d) re-constructing the process of harsh confrontation opening a new phase in the arms race (particularly during the Reagan and Brezhnev administrations) leading to a final rapprochement.[40]

In terms of systems thinking, perhaps one of the most remarkable structural alternations can be traced within two different –yet closely interrelated—domains; namely, a) the complex functional and structural differentiation in the domain of economics, and b) the differentiation in the form of multi dimensional institutional proliferation within the overall framework of the global organizational domain. These interrelated processes have introduced new elements into global politics resulting in the evolution of the systemic attributes of globalization.[41] Together with these developments international politics was provicted with different qualitative dimensions that gradually to change the technical and organizational structure of the world, eventually preparing the grounds for the end of the Cold War.

For Turkey, the end of the war marked the beginning of the drastic shifts both in

---

[39] These phases are specified in three main groups by Kegley and Witt Kopf, but in four groups by Peter Taylor. However, the Classification and explanatory style chosen by Taylor seems to be better organized in applying theory in general and geopolitical concepts in particular to international political process. Kegley &Wit Kopf, pp. 91-99. P. Taylor, pp.48-59.

[40] This period – as it marked the end of the bipolar order—is identified as a "Process of freeze-thaw with deadly side effects by Taylor." P. Taylor, p.57.

[41] Starting from the Bretton Woods system, the rise of the IBRD, IFC, IDA, and the evolution of the GATT rounds (from Geneva 1947 to Uruguay 1986-1994) and OECD, 67 movements, and soon, are the few examples gradually leading to a different world order in this respect. See, Convey W. Henderson, *International Relations; Conflict and Cooperation* at the Turn of the 21st Century, New York: Mac Graw Hill, 1998, pp.237-309.

foreign policy orientations abroad and in the general policy processes at home. In this sense, the Cold War period can be assessed as the combination of a series of systemic-reactions with the supreme aim of becoming adjusted to the newly rising (external-internal) environmental conditions. However, this was a kind of structural order in which the internal stabilities and cooperative capabilities of the actors (especially in the Western bloc) would play an important regulatory role in the maintenance of the block stability.[42] This was especially true for Turkey. Indeed, in this period the impact of the internal parameters began to play a heavier role on the foreign policy choices than had ever been the case. Consequently, a new task for Turkey was to bridge the realities of the two-way challenges; a) continuing a differentiation at home, and b) being able to adapt to multilateral intra-bloc political processes gradually.

In this respect, the most remarkable alteration in the overall outlook of Turkish foreign policy was its orientation to an alliance on the permanent basis. This was an important episode in its historical framework in the sense that this process marked the end of Turkey's traditional view of regulating power politics through the pragmatic manipulation of the realities of the BOP order. On the other hand such a decisive shift also signifies Turkey's continuous sensitivity towards systemic-structural alternations.[43] It is in this general framework that--following the substantial Soviet threat--the developments following the Truman Doctrine (March 1947). The Marshall Plan (June 1947), and outbreak of the Korean War (1950) resulted in the admission of Turkey (together with Greece) into NATO in 1952.[44] With the Truman Doctrine and the Marshall Plan Turkey was gradually taking part in the limited containment which came into being at the time, and with the outbreak of the Korean War, the scope of the containment was to be replaced by global dimensions.[45]

The Turkish assessments on the overall course of the alliance were exhibited positively during the initial stages of the Cold War, though this contented attitude had long carried the signs of relative passivity in policy initiatives that would eventually lead to some adjustment problems in later stages. One of the complications in this respect was noticed in the lack of proper initiatives (in time and scope) towards the non-aligned movement that, in fact, was the major challenge to the assumption of a bipolar order. Indeed, Turkey had not been successful enough in balancing bipolar systemic attributes with those of the excentric trends properly. This situation was directly reflected in Turkey's occasional dissatisfaction in the international forums and gradually led to a kind of intimidation towards multilateral processes and growing preference to intra-alliance exchanges.[46] As

---

[42] In such an order, even the insistence of the leading national actor upon policy objectives "may produce deviant reactions among non-leading members of the bloc, thus inducing the capabilities and possibly the membership of the bloc" (e.g.) Kaplan, pp.41-42.

[43] There may be fluctuations with ups and downs and with successes and failures in this orientation; however, the ultimate purpose has—as an imperative—remained the same; that is" try to adjust to the extent that is possible."

[44] Peter Calvocoressi, *World Politics Since 1945*, 5th ed.

[45] Essentially limited European policy was complicated by the outbreak of war in Korea which "converted containment from a European to a more nearly global policy". Ibid. p.15.

[46] This attitude was especially evident towards the UN General Assembly initiatives concerning the

time went on, such a stand imposed a kind of limiting effect on Turkey's political freedom of movement, decreasing its capability to respond to certain events effectively; the Cyprus episode became the most remarkable on in this respect.[47]

As a general trend, Turkey's alliance with the West (with a defensive military doctrine) was fairly unproblematic until the Cyprus crisis.[48] The Cyprus episode marked the beginning of the serious clash of perceived interests between Turkey and United States, which --in later stages-- amounted to a level that initiated some calls even for a reconsideration of the alliance and for a more independent line.[49] Certain events such as the Cuban Missile Cisis (October 1962), ophium dichotomy in the seventies led to the developments contributing to such diversion in the political stand.[50] In fact, in an overall framework, these developments marked the beginning of a new trend in Turkish-American relations that evolved--with fluctuations--until the end of the Cold War, preparing the bases of the strategic partnership at present.[51] In the same framework Turkey tried to increase its initiatives towards the Middle East, the Third World and --starting from the early 1980s-- towards Israel.[52] It is in this context that—towards the end of the 1970s— three particular developments (coming to power of a theocratic regime in Iran, Soviet invasion of Afghanistan, war between Iraq and Iran) raised new threat perceptions on the grounds of the secular nature of Turkish politics at home and created a cooling effect on the lately warming psychological environment that reinforced Turkey's determination to remain committed to NATO and also gave rise to a balanced policy towards Iraq and Iran.

In this period, another remarkable trend has been traced, following the formation of the EEC and Turkey's associate membership in it beginning in 1963. This trend represents a particular section of a historical process--starting from the mid 19th century-- and continues to form one of the lasting pillars of Turkish foreign policy. However, internal developments starting from the early eighties created the formidable drawbacks

---

Cyprus issue starting from the mid fifties. However, it is interesting to note that the similar attitudes— though in a different context—was also discernable to the bloc leaders (USA-USSR) at the time, as they often refrained from involving themselves in polemics on general in the presence of the Third World representatives. See, Peter Taylor, pp.50-53.

[47] These were the symptomatic signs resulting from Turkey's efforts to adjust its overall system to an entirely new organizational ordering under the newly emerging conditions. These efforts were not confined only to external domain but also to internal order. Indeed, this was the period during which a rapid systemic differentiation was also operational in the internal domain.

[48] President Johnson's letter of 1964 marks a turning point. For the complete texts exchanged between İnönü and Johnson. See, *Middle East Journal*, Vol. 20, 1966 Summer, pp.386-93.

[49] In 1978-79 the signs of such a line was clearly discernable. For the detailed explanations see. Nasuh Uslu, *Türk Amerikan İlişkileri*, Ankara: 21 Yüzyıl Yayınları, 2000, pp.138-208.

[50] Ibid., pp.144-160 and pp.223-258.

[51] In systemic terms this is the expression of a structural – functional differentiation moving away from passive exchange state towards active Exchange state. In this period all systemic attributes are in the process of rearrangement.

[52] Nasuh Uslu, "1947'den Günümüze Türk Amerikan İlişkilerinin Genel Portresi", *Avrasya Dosyası*, Summer 2000, V.6, No.2, pp. 92-116. M.H. Yavuz and M.R. Kahn, "Turkish Foreign Policy Toward the Arab-Israeli Conflict: Duality and the Development, 1950-91", *Arab Studies quarterly*, V.14/4, 1992, pp.81-82. Since 1964 the Muslim members of CENTO Joined the Regional Cooperation for Development (RCD) in the hope of improving political freedom of movement.

leading to loss of political freedom of action in Turkey's moves towards the EU in the future. Thus the EU process, under the never diminishing economic--as well as political-- necessities continued to remain as an ideal.

One of the systemic changes in Turkey's foreign policy can be diagnosed as dictated by the economic and financial imperatives. Accordingly, trying to compromise the requirements of evolving inter national economic order with the rising domestic demands was a formidable challenge to face, throughout different stages of the Cold War. Turkey's internal economic situation had deteriorated rapidly as a result of the war; entry into the Western world following the war was paralleled by new and more liberal political, economic, and social attitudes and policies in the country. In this respect, the Bretton Woods Agreements (July 1944) signalled the rise of a new order and also began to constitute the institutional framework for Turkey's economic orientations abroad. It has never been easy to adjust its system to newly evolving order; indeed, periodic economic crises at home meant that Turkey had to pay growing attention to the prescriptions of the IMF and other international institutions in determining macro-economic policy.

As the trends indicate the relative weight of domestic pluralism on foreign policy increased starting from the mid sixties parallel to the rise of the leftist factions and increasing ideological and economic frictions. Nevertheless, it can be stated that--in spite of the constant adjustment problems--Turkey's leaders have always seen their democratic-secular system as an ideal choice for themselves and as a desirable model for other states in their region. They have regarded their country as a bridge-builder between Europe and Asia on all kinds of levels.

From the 1990s: The Transitionary Period

The end of the Cold War marked the beginning of the third and last structural transition period since the end of the Napoleonic Wars. The demise of the USSR might have created a vacuum in classical terms; however, it is not yet possible to identify the new outlook with a specific power--like the USA--in definitive terms but in relative parameters. In this respect, though the US still remains the largest political power and economic force in the world, it is theoretically too early envisage a world order of US domination.[53]

The structural framework is dominated by general trends of globalization not only in classical economic, financial and socio-cultural terms but also in political and security (in extended form) dimentions.[54] In the classical direction the multi-dimentional institutional process has reached its most complex stage to cover entire aspects of the technological social reality; however, the second part relating to the political and security domains is still in a state of formation, thus still exposing serious structural problems. In this general

---

[53] In reality this power vacuum has taken place not as US economic strength was at its peak level, but after two decades of relative decline. In this respect the US is in the position of employing strategies similar to those of Britain (during the second transition period) to maintain its power. Appeasement policies of some sort will be expected to continue. S. Strange, "The persistent myth of lost hegemony," *International Organization*, Vol.41, pp.551-74. Rather than the "mono-polarity", a particular type "multi-centrism"— with an actor exhibiting relatively dominant regulatory functions in an environment of institutional polarization – can better define the present reality.
[54] On the concept of the "extended Security" and its relevance to today's Europe see, Ole Weaver, *Journal of Common Market Studies*, March 1996, Vol. 34, No.1, pp.103-132.

framework the geopolitics retain their relevance yet need to be redefined not on deterministic grounds but on new political, socio-cultural, economic-financial and technological shifts and the converging and/or diverging trends in this sense.[55] In this respect the relative significance of certain regions like central Asia and the Caucasus is rising and the stability conditions in some others--like the Balkans and the Middle East-- are radically changing. Increasingly, global policies are taking shape as most states identify many of the same problems and recognize they must work together in a world of growing "interdependence". In a world of growing interdependence, the process of "concert and rivalry" takes its fifth historical turn since the Congress of Vienna (of 1815) three of these processes denote transitionary periods. Today there is a crucial mismatch between political and economic trends at global level and the concert and rivalry processes take place in this context.

However, it is interesting to note that there have been shifts between the relative positions of the areas of the concert and rivalry process since the end of the Cold War. During the initial years of the 1990s, the relative weight of the UN General Assembly (as in the 1970s) was taken over by the Security Council with the five permanent members acting in concert as status quo powers. It was in this period that the Gulf Crisis of 1990 and the initial stages of the Balkan crises were handled on the basis of multilateral actions. On the other hand, it was in the economic arena that the rivalry continued as witnessed in the meetings of the General Agreement on Tarrifs and Trade (GATT), the bilateral disagreements between Japan and the US and Europe (particularly with France) and the US. Yet, the developments leading to the Kosova crisis (in 1998) and finally to the invasion of Iraq (Spring 2003) marked the beginning of a new debate on the future credibility of the UN Security Council design and on the future relevance of the five-power concert. Signs of such diversion were noticeable even during the Bosnian and Somalia crises. It was not the changing character of the UN initiatives within the context of the "second generation interventions" system that caused such diversion, but the diminishing credibility of the Security council (the systemic regulatory mechanism) as a result of growing lack concensus among the great powers and the rise of the unilateral tendencies as exhibited especially by the USA and England starting from the Kosova process. Such developments should never be assessed as the signs of growing tendency towards the refusal of legality as the integral part of the international reality; however, as the systemic symptoms resulting from the growing mismatch between the organic realities of the world structure and existing legal rules and mechanisms. In this respect, the general norms, principles and concepts of law and order are not the focus of debate, but the need for re-definition of the new global order (organism) and reorganization of the mechanism and methodologies. Closely related to this point, perhaps the most remarkable aspect of the present stage of the globalization process (as distinguished from the previous ones) can be traced in the growing apprehension towards new threats.[56] However, the biggest

---

[55] In Gray's terms, today "the argument... is neither geographical setting determines policy and strategy in some all-but-mystical way, nor that the implications of that setting remain constant as technology evolves, but rather that geographical factors are pervasive in world politics." See, Colin S. Gray, "A Debate on Geopolitics: The Continued Primacy of Geography," *Orbis*, spring 1996, pp.247-259.

[56] Today the world is faced with complex phenomena of new processes, starting from the ecological and

dichotomy in this respect is traced in the rapidly growing methodological as well as policy differences among the big powers in aiming at this new phenomenon. What is threatening in this context is the immediate and the most disturbing effects of the delays and lack of consensus--though only with a hypothethical value of consideration at present—that would be traced a) through the inevitable destructive efforts in the economic-financial institutional order which has been in progress since the time of Bretton Woods agreements, and b) through the rise of an undesirable world order.[57] It is in such an intellectually debated environment that the US and Europe are trying to define their future responsibilities outside Europe, and it is to this end that the US and NATO backed European Security and Defence Identity (ESDI) initiatives parallel to European initiatives towards Common European Security and Defence Policy (CESDP) are taking their parts respectively. It is also in this period that the Balkans, the Caucasus and Central Asia, and the Middle East form the respective corners of the hypothetical "triangle of instability", Turkey being placed in its center.

In the light of the historical experiences and in the course of developments after the fall of the Berlin Wall, some constant and variable elements of Turkish foreign policy once more became discernable. Among the constant features were:

a) Decisiveness in defining foreign policy objectives on the fundamental basis of a pluralistic and democratic Society coinciding with the permanent principles of the Republic as declared in the 1920s;[58] b) closely related to this is the dominance of the Western Orientation as the strategic guidance;[59] c) tendency towards gradual differentiation and positive adaptation to changing structural environmental conditions;[60]

---

environmental problems, rising population and diminishing resources, psychological impacts of technology, and extending all the way up to include ethnical and border disputes, and worst of all, fanatic-terrorism accompanied by the possibility of mass immigration and mafia degeneration. These are the full expression of negative regulatory elements that would cause "entopic tendencies" in the world order. They may resemble snowflakes today and thus not drown timely attention; yet, they are regarded as having the capacity to evolve into an avalanche in the future if not handled in proper times and ways. Then, "wars of some sorts could be justified. Wallace J. These "Rethinking the New World Order," *Orbis*, fall 1994. pp.621-634.

[57] Any type of polarization can be regarded in this respect. Wallerstein, for instance, discusses the possibility of two global zones under certain circumstances, though this still sounds like another type of bipolar order in terms of who sickles with whom. I. Wallerstein, *Geopolitics and Geoculture*, Cambridge: Cambridge University press, 1991.

[58] This feature has evolved in two consecutive stages, a) the first, and evolutionary stage covering the period until the end of the First World War, and b) the second and maturing stage opening with the rise of the Republic.

[59] Shifting centers of the periodic attachments and the changing weights of the western actors in policy preferences dues not form any exception to this principle; Essentials of the overall policy frame remained the same.

[60] Adjustment to newly rising conditions has always been problematic during the transition periods and this has also been reflected into initial stages of each new structural period in the various forms of adaptation difficulties. However, as historical experience proved, the Turkish socio-political system possessed positive homeostatic tendencies particular to its own that provides the system with a certain degree of flexibility even in the "turbulent environments." On the related conceptual explanations see, F.E. Emery and E.L. Trist, "The Causal Texture of Environments," F.E. Emery. (Ed.), *Systems Thinking*, London: Penguin Books, 1970, pp.241-59.

and finally d) an anti-expansionist general policy orientation with passive active defensive periodic tendencies has firmly been entrenched in the system as one of the historically accepted guiding principle.[61]

The end of the Cold War and the opening of a new transition period also underwent some changes in Turkish foreign policy behavior. Multi-dimensional global trends, shifting relevance of the importance of geographic centers, changing domestic and global demands, newly rising threats and related problems all contributed to the formation of new trends that played important roles in this change. In this overall framework, the most important change has been noticed in the relatively rapid shift from passive defensive foreign policy posture to active defensive type; a clearly assertive-- a more capable-- policy stand was assumed.[62] Turkey has been in full realization of its changing security environment--both in regional and global terms--and its growing "Positional" capabilities and rising responsibilities.[63]

Through the realization of an overall strategy of active defense, Turkey has been seeking to anticipate trends and attempts either to redirect them or to turn them to advantage. However, it was the proper assessment and timing of the global trends as the environmental essentials that provided Turkey with a relative chance of success in the tactical applications of such a national strategic vision.[64]

For Turkey, assertiveness is conceived in its relative sense meaning a gradual movement away from the classical intra-alliance framework of the Cold War towards the forefront of international politics.[65]

A careful assessment of Turkey's overall approaches to international issues and crisis management processes points out a growing understanding of the definitions of such policy essentials as the "framework-strategy- tactics"–and on the choices related to each.

It is in such a conceptual design that Turkish foreign policy has been in search of a stable order by trying to contribute to various processes in terms of the organizational developments in Europe, economic interdependence in its wider context, relations with Russia and the as region, and humanitarian assistance programs and multilateral

---

[61] This view was finely phrased by Atatürk in his well-known dictum "peace at home peace in the world", Mete Tunçay, p.453.

[62] On the related concepts of passive and active defensive and assertive foreign policy see, Chas W. Freeman, Jr. *Arts of Power: Statecraft and Diplomacy,* Washington: US. Institute of Peace Press, 1992, pp.71-75.

[63] The positional values of the attributes form the "whole", here the global structure as it is today. In this sense, whether or not it may prove functionally less effective relative to others, "positional value" —of any unit—is the politically important issue which is always in awareness of the other—especially the dominant—powers in any giver period. On the concept of "whole", A. Angyal, pp.11-30.

[64] In this respect some discrepancies with relative disappointments might have been witnessed regarding initiatives towards Central Asia and the Caucasus, Cyprus and the Middle East. However, more than a search for success with higher/highest benefit at lowest cost, what counts is the fact that the conception of an active stand on a wider range of issues for beyond the limited geographical framework – as defined in the course of the Cold War—became relevant. Indeed, conceiving the global trends under the light of the new generation of threats, and regions as the bases of the calculations at the "strategic appraisal" stage of the national strategy formulation is one proof of this fact.

[65] An assertive diplomatic strategy –beyond the active defensive type—refers to a state orientation actively seeking broad change in the existing international order; therefore, Turkey's position should be assessed carefully. See, Chas W. Freeman, pp.74-75.

initiatives in general.[66]

Framework	Strategic Posture	Tactical orientations
General: international complexity	general: indirect approach	-Trying to utilize international norms and rules (human rights-human decency- no use of force-legality, etc.)
Choice: understanding the realities of globalization	Styles: - trying to mobilize attention - trying to activate	- Trying to emphasize various forms of multilateralism.
	International forums and institutional processes	-Trying to increase the mass, relevance, impact, sustainability of capabilities in relation to other states.

One of the remarkable aspects of change has been the rising role of public opinion on evolving concerns and attitudes of security elites in exhibiting their assertiveness. The signs of change in this respect have been clearly discernable in Turkey's approaches towards, a) Central Asia and the Caucasus regions, b) the Turkish residents in Germany, c) the Balkans on ethnical premises, d) Cyprus on many grounds (e.g., ss-300 missiles case, skirmishes on the green line and the rest of the intercommunal dialogues in general), e) Syria in regard to Abdullah Öcalan's case and Iraq as affiliated with the PKK process and soon. However, the Kurdish issue has been one of the most controversial and undesirable developments that imposed negative implications upon Turkey's assertive tendencies, hampering the improvement of a proper influence mainly over Europe by giving rise to a never-ending dichotomy.[67] Yet, the misunderstanding on this issue as expressed by Europeans has never been shared by the Turkish public so far. The last intervention in Iraq (Spring 2003) signaled the opening of a new phase in this never-ending episode. Nevertheless, the final crisis in Iraq seems to have activated some regional potentialities, timely exploitation of which could provide Turkey with opportunities to increase its strategic initiative in the long run. It is in this context that a) Turkey's chance to contribute to regional stability has potentially increased. A rationally designed big brother image over the ethnic groups in Iraq could be worked out and utilized with constructive results; b) at the same time, under the prevailing conditions of systemic disturbances and rapidly evolving complex authority configurations, the relative possibility of influencing Iran and Syria in the desired direction in a manner to coincide with extra-regional trends has increased, and closely related to this point, c) parallel to the likely external efforts in preparation at the moment, new initiatives for mediation between Arabs and Israel can be assumed in a different context.[68] These possibilities indicate an

---

[66] On the further explanations in this respect see, Kemal Kirişçi, "The End of the Cold War and Changes in Turkish Foreign Policy Behavior," *Foreign Policy*, 1993, Vol.XVIII, No.3-4, pp.1-43.

[67] According to Lesser, for instance, the Turkish claims regarding "the establishment of a Kurdistan carved, in part, from Turkish territory" is considered as an incredible perception in Western circles. Yet, for Turkey this issue has broader implications exceeding the arguments of "incredibility" in this respect. Ian Lasser, "Turkey in Changing Security Environment" *Journal of International Affairs*, Fall 2000, Vol.54, No.1, pp.183-199.

[68] Arab memories of past Ottoman domination and Turkey's friendliness towards Israel, especially under the conditions that have prevailed until the present, have somehow inflicted limiting effects on Turkey's

increase in Turkey's regulatory capacity. Thus, one of the main responsibilities for Turkey will be searching and eliminating excentric forces that would prevent effective utilization of such potentiality. The American position in this respect deserves special attention.

In the post Cold War era, it is methodologically advisable to conserve Turkish American relations on two closely interrelated frameworks. The first one relates to the traditional framework that represents a kind of historically formed nucleus, and the other denotes the framework consisting of the periodic circles building around this center. In this respect the nucleus that had already been formed in the course of the British-Ottoman relations since the 19th century was inherited by the US on the same premises, starting mainly from the end of the Second World War.[69] And, the Turkish American relations with fluctuations (sometimes in excessive limits)--caused by the periodic partial conflict of interests-- continued within a kind of conflict and harmony model. It is in such a process that, in the 1990s, the general character of the second framework evolved into a strategic partnership design (from the stage of dominance by the US), thereby exposing the signs of deeper fluctuations, relative to previous stages. In this sense, the Iraq crisis (of spring 2003) can be assessed as one of the peak points marking the conflictual exchanges. Consequently, trying to draw some definitive conclusions, only by departing from the outer framework of the relations can be misleading; in the essence of the Turkish-American relational domain (the nucleus area) essential long-term interests in their broader terms somehow remain to be identical. Indeed, there is a shared vision in defining their overall interests in their broader context, involving the essential features of multilateralism and consensus building, understanding and collaborating against new threats and in agreeing to build a new world order with properties of stability quite different from those that had ever existed. Thus, diverging and converging elements will continue to characterize the relations; therefore, periodic differences in policy priorities will naturally exist, especially in times when differences between Turkish American tendencies in defining and expressing their threat perceptions increase. Such a conceptual stand is of vital importance at a time when "the alliance between the two countries is moving in new directions filled with unprecedented challenges".[70]

In the elimination of the periodical problems, the possibility of conceptualization of the issues in their broader contexts and historical depth plays an important role in the

---

capabilities in mediating in the area. Iran, too, has not favored any settlement of the conflict through Turkish agency. Consequently, the Turkish role in general has been regarded cautiously. Jonathan Farley, "Turkey's Foreign Policy," *Round Table*, Jan. 1995, No 333, pp.81-89 (p.81).
[69] Basic elements of such a nucleus were introduced by the British state whose fundamental policy principles have denoted a maritime oriented state's strategy. As a rule of survival such an orientation has always been identified, partially in reference to its links established with some powers exposing central (land-locked or land-power oriented) positions. Relative importance of the land-locked positions has always changed depending on the political landscape. In this respect, in the decades following the Napoleonic wars for the British this central position was contributed to the Ottoman Empire.
[70] Mahmut Bali Aykan, "Turkish Perspectives on Turkish-US Relations concerning Persian Golf Security in the Post Cold War Era: 1989-1995," *Middle East Journal*, Vol. 50, No:3, Summer 1996, pp.344-358. As it is stated by the author, "a relationship that has grown over fifty years of shared experiences must be capable of meeting these new challenges." (p. 358)

determination of policy choices and ways of practical solutions. It is ironical that the lack of availability of such a possibility,[71] for instance in approaching the Caucasus and Central Asia regions, has been one of the main reasons in limiting the capabilities of Turkey in designing required policies with desired effect in these areas than a future vision designed on historical premises, an "incremental policy" approach has been the preferred course of policy.[72]

Another systemic orientation has taken place towards Europe, yet in this case, on precisely confirmed historical premises. As stated previously, tracing a historically determined line starting from the late 1830's --Turkish Western European relations--as a continuous exchange process--has passed through several evolutionary stages.[73] In this respect, the period after the Cold War marks the last part of the episode during which the relations have entered the most comprehensive and extensive stage. Within the last two decades some substantial qualitative changes within the environmental context of Europe created new disturbances for European order itself, giving rise to changes in its internal ordering.[74] As a natural consequence, this situation--in one form of another--has directly reflected upon the relations with Turkey in the form of rising demands both in contextual and qualitative terms. Thus, Turkey itself being in a process of change of its own under the same globally framed environmental conditions, has naturally began to face some problems in adjusting itself to this accelareted stage of exchanges. Since the level and conditions of the mutually set adjustment processes has once more undergone a considerable alteration, new demands from European circles impose new strains upon Turkey.[75] However, as the attitudes, styles, and general policy lines of the parties reveal, both sides are in full awareness of the historical essentials of the European Turkish exchange process in its overall terms. They also realize the fact that today there is a growing interdependency between the two sides. This interdependence, from European side, can be traced in the "Idea of Europe"[76] and "Europeanization", from the Turkish

---

[71] In spite of the fact that the necessity of such a vision was once expressed in explicit terms in 1933, and repeated indirectly on several occasions by M. Kemal Atatürk, proper attention in this respect was never given until suddenly emerging conditions in the region after the Cold War. On the related statements of M.Kemal Atatürk to a doctor (Md) named Zeki, during a reception (on 28 October 1993) illustrating this subject. See, İsmet Bozdağ, *Sovyet Marxizmi Çin Marxizmi ve Türkiye Gerçekleri*, Ankara: Kültür ve Tanıtma Bakanlığı, 1987, No.800, pp.451-54.

[72] On incremental policy making see, Malcolm Rowan, "A Conceptual Framework For Government Policy Making," *Canadian Public Administration*, 1968, No.197, pp.277-296.

[73] See footnotes 10 and 11.

[74] Such changes as the changing security environment in its broader terms in an age of an entirely new type of globalization, following the Maastricht Treaty, the European Security and Defense identity and Common European Security and Defense Policy processes, passing to common currency ordering, Copenhagen and Helsinki processes and so on, all are signs adding up to a new "qualitative leap" for Europe. In this respect, the end of the Cold War signaled an accelerated stage of differentiation for the European system itself in its historical context.

[75] The most pronounced demands within last decade, seem to revolve around, a) the likely impact of the influx of semi-skilled workers, b) the Cyprus issue, c) in broader terms the issue of human rights, and partially affiliated with this, the Kurdish issue. See, Jonathan Farley, p. 83.

[76] Edward Mortimer, "European Security after the Cold War", Adelphi Paper, No.271, London: 115 Brassey's, Summer 1992, section I, pp.5-19; Ole Weaver, pp.103-104.

side, in their defining the global stability conditions in the future and their understanding of the basics of human values. At a time when European ideals are expressed so as to conceive even the Middle East as a "back yard"[77] within a particular framework of integration, Turkey's regulatory position in such a hyphothetical domain can easily be discernible. On the other hand, from Turkey's side, as the persistent efforts to remain on the broad quideliness of the principles defined by Kemal Atatürk (though they too are continiously elaborated and re-defined under the evolving world conditions with the purpose of securing the fundamentals of national strategy) the differences between Europe and Turkey are to be regarded as respective matters of timing, methodology, and definition of priorities, not as the need to redefine historical premises. An identity crisis within each and between two systems may continue; however, as well stated by Andrew Mango, "the question of whether the Turks are European or not does not admit a clear answer, since the concept of the European itself is vague."[78]

In conclusion, it is not a matter of hypothetical prediction to assume that to gain a dominant stand on the Turkish foreign policy phenomenon would definitely require a prudent judgment in understanding its nature and the essentials of the constant elements on the one hand, and its variables on the other, and the respective positions of these two with reference to time, space and international reality.

---

[77] Gerd Nonneman. (Ed.). The *Middle East and Europe: an Integrated Communities Approach,* Brusel: Federal Trust for Education and Research, 1993. In the "conclusions" section of the comprehensive Report it is explicitly stated that, "...mean that Europe has no alternative to maintaining the keenest interest in its Middle Eastern Backyard," p.253.
[78] Andrew Mango, "European Dimensions," *Middle East Studies,* Vol.28, 1992, p.398.

2 Turkish Foreign Policy in Turbulence of the Post Cold War Era: Impact of External and Domestic Constraints

Ramazan Gözen

Analyzing Foreign Policy in Turbulance

Foreign policy is formulated in a political process in which there are three essential dimensions: the decision maker(s), decision-making unit of the state, and domestic and external environments. Any country's foreign policy is actually made by its official decision-makers who act under the constant influence of prevailing conditions, developments, demands and pressures emanating from domestic and international environments. In the process decision-makers not only insert their own thoughts, ideas, visions, views -- called as psychological environment --, but also take into consideration external and domestic factors -- called as operational environment.[1]

Moreover, external and domestic environments are not 'isolated from', or 'irrelevant to' each other, but closely interconnected and interactive. All developments in the external environment may have direct or indirect influence on developments in the domestic environment, and vice versa. Both enter into the decision-making process directly or indirectly through formal or informal channels.

The question 'of which of these two environments is more important in the foreign policy making' is not very easy to answer. There are two contending theories for answering this question. Realist theory argues that external factors are the main element to play a leading role in foreign policy making. Since they view the state as 'a billiard ball' whose domestic environment is not considered as an important factor but taken as given, they concentrate on the influence of the external environment over the states. On the other hand, Liberal theory focuses on the influence on the governments of domestic political, economic, social environments that actually make foreign policy. State rulers make their foreign policy in the view of demands, pressures, conflicts and competition

---

[1] This is a rather classical theoretical approach to foreign policy making analysis. For instance, Richard Snyder *et.al.*, "Decision-Making as an Approach to the Study of International Politics", R.C.Snyder *et.al.* (Eds.) *Foreign Policy Decision-Making*, New York: The Free Press, 1962; Harold Sprout and Margaret Sprout, "Environmental Factors in the Study of International Politics", J.Rosenau (Ed.) *International Politics and Foreign Policy*, New York: The Free Press, 1969; M.G. Hermann and C.F.Hermann, "Who makes foreign policy decisions and how: An Empirical Inquiry", *International Studies Quarterly*, Vol.33, 1989, pp.361-387.

generated by the domestic groups.[2]

Indeed, both theories look at foreign policy making from different angles and consider only one face of the process. Thus each negates one face: while the Realists negate the importance of domestic factors/environment, the Liberals negate that of external factors/environment. But the one-faced-analysis does not reflect a full picture about foreign policy-making especially because of globalization process where borders between domestic and external environments were blurred, and became closely interlinked and interactive. Because of these two reasons, one must examine the impact of both environments together.

However, it is also important to argue that their weight on foreign policy making may not be same for all countries and every time. Depending on time and conditions, one of them can be more important and decisive than another. It is for the researcher to find out how these two environments interact, and which of them is more considerable.

In the case of Turkey's foreign policy-making process in the post Cold War period, during the 1990s, although there was an interactive process between the two, the external environment was the main determining factor. Due to turbulent changes and ubiquitous challenges in the global and regional level systems, Turkey faced a number of problems and difficulties at political, economic, social and geopolitical levels. Turkish foreign policy makers at the state level had to cope with a number of external developments in the Middle East, the Balkans, and Central Asia and the Caucasus. While these surprising challenges loomed large on Turkey's domestic and foreign policy agendas in the post Cold War era, Turkish politics has been more vibrant and volatile at all levels for adapting to the new conditions. Thus, this work argues that the external environment influenced Turkish foreign policy making process not only directly by influencing Turkish decision-makers, but also indirectly through its influence on Turkish domestic politics, which in turn influenced Turkey's foreign policy-making process.

In this regard, this work composes of three parts: Firstly, the new characteristics of the external environment will be analyzed as far as its implications for Turkey are concerned. Secondly, responses of the domestic environment will be analyzed in so far as their implications for foreign policy. Finally, patterns in Turkish foreign policy during the 1990s will be analyzed.

The Challenge of External Changes

The end of the Cold War was a historic turning point for international political system and process. In retrospect, it can be seen as one of the landmark developments in world history, quite similar to the end of the Napoleonic, the First and the Second World Wars. The common characteristic of all these big wars is their wide-ranging effects on world politics such as: collapse of a great power, changing structure of international political system, emergence of a power vacuum, and a number of uncertainties in the new

---

[2] For basic assumptions and views about Realist and Liberal theories see, Paul R. Viotti and Mark V. Kauppi, *International Relations Theory: Realism, Pluralism, Globalism*. New York: Macmillan Publishing Company, Second Edition, 1993.

international system, and so on.[3]

The history taught us that when empires collapse there inevitably come out a power vacuum in that part of the international system leading to new kinds of developments and problems due to competition and conflict among great powers to create a 'new international order'. As an empire's political system, ideology, influence and control, geographical-political borders and prestige start to decline, constituent members of the empire look for a new position and future, try to build up new and better conditions in the new era, and adapt themselves into the emerging new order. This was the case when the Arabs and others looked for their independence towards the end of the Ottoman Empire in the beginning of 20th century and during the First World War in particular.

Afterwards there emerges a kind of power competition among rival global and regional powers over the ex-imperial territories to fill in the vacuum. In other words, global and regional powers try to have a sphere of influence over the ex-empire territories, while the ex-empire countries seek to establish ties with those regional and global powers in order to integrate to the new world order for a better future. Consequently the collapse of the empire creates a set of political, economic, socio-cultural and military complexities in world politics.

This was the fate of the post-European empires and the post-Ottoman empire in the early Twentieth Century, and indeed of the post-Soviet empire since the beginning of the 1990s. The collapse of the empires at the beginning of both twentieth and twenty-first centuries was generally taken as an opportunity to start a 'new world order'. The concept became very popular for politicians, academics and even for the men-in-the-street in each period. After the collapse of the Ottoman empire, Woodrow Wilson of the United States believed that there could emerge a new world order where his idealist project based on his '14 points' would lead to a peaceful world. International problems would be resolved by using mechanisms of the international organization, i.e. the League of Nations, and international law. The ex-Ottoman countries could get their self-determination and democratic systems.[4]

However, it shortly became clear that Wilson's idealism was dashed by power-seeking policies of France and the United Kingdom. It was clearly seen that the latter countries were only aiming to have a greater influence over the ex-Ottoman territories under the Mandate system. Consequently, what emerged was nothing more than a new world 'disorder', which culminated in the Second World War.

The end of the Soviet empire was not dissimilar to the previous ones in this respect. The end of the Cold War was caused by the collapse of the Soviet empire which was controlling a large area in Eastern Europe and Asia, and influencing many other regions and countries in other parts of the world. With the end of Soviet empire, not only did its 'colonial territories' in the Caucasus and Central Asia get their independence, but also Central and Easter European countries, as the members of the Warsaw pact, ended their

---

[3] For example, Trevor Taylor (Ed.), *The Collapse of the Soviet Empire: Managing the Regional Fall-out*. London: RIIA, 1992.
[4] On Wilsonian Idealism, Lloyd E.Ambrosius, *Wilsonian Statecraft: Theory and Practice of Liberal Internationalism during World War I*. Wilmington DE: Scholarly Resources Inc., 1991.

fifty-year-old ties with the Soviets. In addition, it must be noted that pro-Soviet states in different parts of the world also needed to look for new political identities and foreign policy directions in the absence of the Soviet Union. In short, theoretically speaking, the collapse of the Soviets meant the withdrawal of the Soviet forces firstly from the Union territories at the local level, secondly from the European territories at the regional level, and thirdly from the Eastern bloc countries at the global level. Thus, it caused a large geopolitical/power vacuum in those regions.

As the Soviet Union withdrew its forces from the ex-territories, there emerged a new kind of international power politics. Three of them can be particularly mentioned. Firstly, although the Soviet empire collapsed, its influence and 'ghost' over the ex-territories has not vanished yet. Although it formally ended its 'empire' over those territories and peoples, the successor state, Russia, has maintained its influence and control over there. The so-called near-abroad policy of Russia aims to do that. Thus, Russia is still present in the Caucasus and Central Asia thanks to its continuing ethnic, economic and military connections with these regions.

Secondly, the newly independent states have tried to improve their level of independence, and play a role in the new world order. They struggled hard to adapt themselves to new world order by establishing close economic, commercial, political and security-based relations with other countries in the international system. They aimed to socialize themselves within regional and global arenas alone or with the help of other states.

Soviet withdrawal from these countries and regions was in doubt good for them as it provided opportunities to gain their independence and freedom from foreign rule. They could now act more effectively to develop their economies, improve their living conditions, upgrade their political, social, military systems to the level of the modern world. Accordingly, they could have a better position in world politics, and choose their destiny in accordance with their own interests. As the Cold War between the West and the East ended, they could integrate themselves into the world system, and have close relations with the developed-Western countries for improving their position in the world.

However, due to their long-term dependence on the Soviet system, they encountered a number of problems in the process of integration into the world system. Because their political, economic, social and military systems had long been designed in line with the socialist ideology under the Soviet power, the end of the Soviet control was only half of the salvation. The other half could be achieved only building up new, modern and efficient systems instead. In the replacement of the old with the new, they needed a suitable international environment and such international support that would improve their security, welfare and prestige.

However, thirdly, neither Russian attempts nor newly independent states' efforts were easily achievable. There has been a high level of competition and conflict in this process at three levels. At the local level, there has been a balance of power game between Russia and the ex-Soviet territories, mainly in the form of settling border disputes, controlling economic resources and relations, manipulating ethnic-social-political minorities, and maintaining military forces, etc. At the regional level, there has been a new balance of power game between the newly independent countries and the states in the neighboring regions, Iran and Turkey in particular. At the global level, global powers involved in those regions in order to establish 'their sphere of influence' directly or indirectly. They tired to make a new pecking order in the region.

Many people hoped that the new world order would bring better conditions for the world community. International peace and order would prevail, and countries in the East and the West would co-operate with each other rather than engaging in military conflicts and confrontations. International law, institutions, and regimes would be more efficient and effective in the resolution of international problems and so on. After the collapse of the Soviet empire, the world was to enter a new historical period in which such liberal values as democracy, market economy, human rights and freedoms, pluralist civil society could now spread to the rest of the world in general and to the post-Soviet regions in particular.

In retrospect, however, the developments during the 1990s falsified the above expectations. Most of the prophecies were not materialized. On the contrary, the post-Soviet era could be described not as a 'new world order', but more objectively as 'a new world *disorder*'. The evidences for this are many: the post-Soviet regions -- the Caucasus, the Central Asia, the Balkans, the Middle East, and the surrounding countries--did not witness any development of liberal values, but a number of instabilities, crises, wars, etc. More surprisingly, there emerged a number of new, unexpected and uncontrollable problems, which fully destroyed the hopes of creating the so-called new world order. Instead of a peaceful and stabile order, there happened several wars in these regions, most of them were caused by new types of problems such as ethnic-micro nationalism, religious fundamentalism, and terrorism.

The end of the Cold War was an end not only of the Soviet empire, but also of the world system structure. As a result of the vanishing power of the East, the bipolar world structure has come to an end. But it was replaced with a chaotic one. The type of the new system has yet to be defined unquestionably. According to some, it can be defined as a unipolar structure, the USA being the hegemony. According to this line of thinking, the US plays a dominant role in the process of international developments. This argument seems true as fas as military issues are concerned, which were clearly seen in US operations in ex-Yugoslavia, Afghanistan, and Iraq. In all of these cases, US military has shown its preponderance over other states. Indeed, Iraq's invasion of Kuwait was ended only with the overwhelming military power of the US. Serbia's invasion of Bosnian territories was ended by US's decisive military intervention. The Taliban regime in Afghanistan was also toppled by US's military power. Finally, Saddam Hussein and his Ba'athist regime in Iraq was defeated by US's military power. Hence there is no doubt that the US is a hegemonic power in military issues.

However, that does not necessarily mean a unipolar system because US's military hegemony was not matched by other power elements. In economic issues, it is challenged by other economic powers (e.g. EU and Japan), while its political power is challenged by other great powers inside and outside the UN. As a result, the post Cold War system structure can better be defined as a multi-layered system structure. Namely, there are several power centers of international system including military, political, economic and socio-cultural dimensions. And it can be argued that unlike the unipolar military structure, there is multi-polarity in political and economic structures. This can be clearly seen in the global level developments as well as in the regional level developments.

At the global level, there is a great competition/rivalry among three economic blocs, the North American Free Trade Area (NAFTA) led by the USA, the Asia-Pacific Economic Co-operation (APEC) led by Japanese and Chinese economic powers, and the European Union (EU) led by Germany and French. Although these trading blocs may have common economic, financial and commercial policies through the G-8 mechanisms and rules, they have created the so-called fortified regional camps to improve intra-group solidarity against the influence of other regions-countries.

At the regional level while the above regions have had great improvement and progress, some other regions are unable to achieve them. The area extending from the Balkans to Central Asia, the so-called Eurasia region, is divided, weak and unstable, facing a lot of difficulties in adaptation to the new world conditions.

As a result of these developments, the end of the Cold War era became more volatile and unpredictable than the previous order during the Cold War years. Although the end of the Cold War between the USA and the Soviet Union, and the independence from the Soviet Union of some countries were positive developments, there emerged new kinds of instabilities and uncertainties. These developments have had negative impact on some countries, if not on all countries in the world. In particular they brought challenges to Turkey and Turkish foreign policy, which is located at the center of all these changes.

Parameters of New World Disorder for Turkey

As far as Turkey and Turkish foreign policy is concerned, there were four dimensions of the new world disorder in the 1990s: The collapse of the Soviet Union, the Second Gulf War of 1990-1991, the US domination in the regions around Turkey, and the globalization process. Each of these dimensions individually or collectively had a number of political, ideological, economic, social and cultural effects on Turkey's domestic politics and foreign policy. Both Turkish domestic politics and foreign policy faced challenges and opportunities arising from these changes.

The collapse of the Soviet empire unleashed various problems, which can be grouped as follows: the forces of fragmentation such as ethnicity, religious fanaticism; anti-democratic state regimes, governments, rulers; historical and political bilateral disputes; pressure of change, reform and adaptation to the modern world conditions. More specifically, these outcomes had serious implications on Turkish decision-makers, society and state, and on Turkish foreign policy *per se*. Before analyzing the type and degree of their impact on Turkey, there will be an analysis of the nature of the volatile environment around Turkey.

Ideological/Political Vacuum

After the collapse of the Soviet Union and communist ideology, there emerged a large ideological and political vacuum in the world. According to Davutoğlu, there were two grand theories to fill in the ideological/political vacuum in the post Cold War. While 'The End of History' theory made by Francis Fukuyama 'glorifies the universalization of the political values and structures of western civilisation', 'The Clash of Civilisations' theory made by Samuel Huntington 'attempts to explain alternative civilisation processes which mobilise the masses into political action and confrontation'.[5] They look contradictory, but are actually parts of the same picture: 'providing the hegemonic powers with a theoretical justification for the overall political and military strategies required to control and reshape the international system'.[6]

Barry Buzan called it as 'Civilisation Cold War' between the center (the West) and the periphery (the Islamic East), which was a result of migration and the ensuing clash of cultures. According to him, 'the deeper reality is that the center is now more dominant, and the periphery more subordinate than at any time since decolonialization began'.[7] These positions generate multiple security problems for world politics in such a way that they cannot meet each other's expectations.

The Western intellectuals and writers expected that the Western values would spread to other parts of the world, and adopted by the so-called periphery countries. According to this line of thinking, in order to achieve development, security and peace in the world, all other countries were supposed to adjust themselves according to the Western values as described above.

However, this expectation did not come through because the periphery (Islamic) countries did not adapt to the Western ideology, but, quite contrary, returned to their own original values and resisted against the Western world. In other words, most of the regional countries and groups did not embrace the 'End of History' theory and its prophecies.

There can be shown three reasons for this failure. Firstly, these countries were not persuaded that the Western liberal ideology was a solution to their practical problems. Indeed, foreign policy practices in the region of the US and other European countries were not based on the Liberal philosophy, but on the Realist power-seeking philosophy. Secondly, thus, the USA and EU countries failed to bring respectable solutions to the life-and-death problems of Bosnians, Iraqis, Azeri Turks, and so on. Their passivity and interest-based approach towards these crises and wars caused loss of trust in liberal politics and Western polity. Why have not the liberal US, and the liberal EU countries to a certain extent, cared about the plight, and human rights problems of Palestinians, Bosnians, Iraqis, Azeris, and other victims? Thirdly, in the same years, the Clash of Civilizations theory of Samuel Huntington argued that there would emerge new types of conflicts and wars between different civilizations, in particular between the Western civilization on the one hand and the Islamic civilization on the other. He was implying that there would be 'a fighting' between the Western countries and the Islamic countries.

---

[5] Ahmet Davutoğlu, "The Clash of Interests: An Explanation of the World (Dis)Order", *Perceptions*, Vol.II, No.4, December 1997-February 1998, ss.93-94. Davutoğlu's referred works are: Francis Fukuyama, *The End of History and the Last Man*, New York: The Free Press, 1992; and Samuel Huntington, "The Clash of Civilisations", *Foreign Affairs* 72, Summer 1993.

[6] Davutoğlu, *The Clash of Interests: An Explanation of the World (Dis)Order*, p.95.

[7] Barry Buzan, "New Patterns of Global Security in the Twenty-First Century", Steven L.Spiegel and David J.Pervin (Eds.), *At Issue: Politics in the World Arena*, New York: St.Martin's Press, seventh edition, 1994.

Given such an outcome, and in response to that possibility, some Islamic countries/groups took their guard, and preferred to return back to their fundamental values, i.e. Islamic way of life, rather than subjugating to the pressures from the Western civilization. The difficulties and problems faced by the people of Islamic countries in the Balkans, Middle East and the Central Asia played a critical role in their soul-searching--an endeavor for a new ideology to survive in the turbulent era.

Turkey was one of such countries. The Turkish people, above ninety percent of its population being Muslim, were shocked to have seen that the Western countries did not help save the Bosnian people from the Serbian aggressions, the Azeris from the Armenian aggression, the Palestinians from the Israeli occupation, and so on. The UN was not so successful in solving these problems as it was in the Gulf war. Nor did the Western countries stop Serbia, Armenia, Israel, as they stooped Saddam Hussein's regime.

This negative image made such a negative impact on some Turkish people that some thought that 'The Turks do not have any friend in the world other than themselves-*Türkün Türkten başka dostu yoktur*', which became very popular in the 1990s. The Western countries' contradicting policies towards the problems were one of the main reasons for the growth of Islamic and nationalist parties in the 1990s.

Micro/ethnic nationalism

Partly as an extension of the ideological vacuum and soul-searching zeal and partly as an outcome of the collapse of the Soviet system, there was a formation of new identities in the Caucasus, Central Asia, the Balkans, and in the Middle East. Ethnic groups sought to redefine their political-cultural identity, which led to a change of status quo and instability in the regional countries. Serbs in the Balkans, Kurds in Iraq and Turkey, Chechens in Russia, and Armenians in Azerbiajan threatened the political structure of the regional system. These movements challenged existing political and territorial borders of the regional countries as they spilled over into the neighboring countries.[8]

Turkey faced the same problem in the Kurdish issue. After the Gulf war, the Kurdish groups living in Iraq tried to increase their 'national' identity by having political autonomy in the north of Iraq. This development had a direct influence on the Kurds of Turkey. Thus, Turkey's Kurds demanded a kind of political autonomy as well as cultural rights in the form of language, traditional rituals (e.g. nevruz celebrations), education, etc. In reaction to it, Turkish nationalism improved its ideological and political gravity in the society and political system in the 1990s.

The Great Game

There developed an increasing 'power politics' and 'balance of power politics' as an overarching characteristic of the new world disorder. The 'Great Game', the name of a different power politics, was played by the USA, Russia, and some big EU countries over the so-called Eurasia extending from the Balkans in the west to the borders of China in the East, and to the Arabian Sea in the south.[9] These big powers penetrated into the

[8] Myron Weiner, "Peoples and States in a New Ethnic Order?", Steven L.Spiegel and David J.Pervin (Eds.), *At Issue: Politics in the World Arena*, New York: St.Martin's Press, seventh edition, 1994.
[9] Stanley Kober, "The Growing Divide in Eurasia", speech made in International Conference titled

region to have a sphere of influence over the new power vacuum in the region. This was a power struggle not only for the control of regional political developments, but also for the control of the economic resources of the region. The politics of new economic relations focused on oil, markets and globalization.

In the Great Game, the great powers had regional 'allies' to achieve their objectives: There was an informal alliance (in addition to the NATO context) among the USA, Turkey, Israel, Azerbaijan, and Georgia, among Russia, Iran, Armenia, Syria, and among France, Iran, and Armenia.

Although the US has been accepted as the only superpower in the new world disorder, its leadership is challenged by the regional and global coalitions, which were seen in the US war in Iraq and Afghanistan. If not a declared one, there can be seen a number of differences and sources of rivalry between the USA and the French-German wing of the EU, and between the USA and Russian-led Asian block. This can be described as power struggle in the Caucasus and Central Asia.

Turkeyís New Position

In that struggle, Turkey has got a unique position.[10] As a member of NATO and many Western organizations, and a member of Turkish and Islamic world, Turkey's position was described in different terms, sometimes as a 'middle power',[11] and sometimes 'insulator'.[12] Whatever the description, it has played a key, if not fully successful, role in the developments in the region. Turkey's position endowed her with a number of opportunities in the new Turkish republics and the Middle Eastern politics, but also a number of constraints and burdens to act in this new world. These constraints and burdens were partly due to the challenges from the outside, and partly to the clash of ideas in the domestic politics.[13]

The end of the Cold War unleashed a set of uncertainties for Turkey at three levels. At the global level, Turkey's position in the Western Alliance has been changed from being the southeastern bastion of the Alliance to being epicenter of Eurasian security order. In this respect, while Turkey's relations with the USA and Russia were redefined in geopolitical and geostrategic terms, the globalization process had great influence for Turkey's politics. At the regional level, Turkey found completely novel geopolitical conditions around. At the local level, Turkey had an unsettling development in its

---

"Building a Secure Eurasia for the 21ˢᵗ Century", organised by Arı Movement, Friedrich Naumann Stiftung and East-West Institute, İstanbul, 8-9 June 2000.

[10] For a comprehensive analysis of Turkey's position in the Cold War era, see Graham E. Fuller and Ian O. Lesser, with Paul B.Henze and J.F.Brown, *Turkey's New Geopolitics: From the Balkans to Western China*, Boulder: Westview Press, 1993.

[11] Meltem Müftüler and Müberra Yüksel, "Turkey: A Middle Power in the New Order", Andrew F. Cooper (Ed.), *Niche Diplomacy: Middle Power after the Cold War*, London: Macmillan Press Ltd., 1997.

[12] Buzan, *New Patterns of Global Security in the Twenty-First Century*, pp.254-5.

[13] Stephen J.Blank, Stephen C.Pelletiere and William T.Johnsen, *Turkey's Strategic Position at the Crossroads of World Affairs*, Carlisle, PA: Strategic Studies Insitute, US Army War College, 1993; and Ziya Öniş, "Turkey in the Post Cold War Era: In Search of Identity", *Middle East Journal*, Vol.49, No.1, Winter 1995.

neighborhood in Iraq, Yugoslavia, Azerbaijan in particular. In this change of geopolitical conditions, Turkey faced a number of completely new political, economic, military and cultural conditions.[14]

We can see that there emerged a four-dimensional regional picture for Turkey in the post Cold War era, each having a completely different process and characteristic: The Central Asia, the Middle East, the Balkans, and the Central and Eastern Europe. Broadly speaking, there is an important difference between the first three regions and the last one: Whereas the first three regions faced aspects of instability, chaos, disorder and fragmentation, the last one had a stable, gradual and harmonious transition to the developed world though its integration into the EU. Thus while the first three had a direct impact on Turkey's politics, the fourth one can only be seen as a model for Turkey's relations with the EU.

In the Middle East, the Gulf war of 1990-1991 and the ensuing power vacuum in Iraq had a very negative impact not only on the Middle East in general but also on Turkish domestic politics and foreign policy. The decimation and weakening of the Ba'athist regime led by Saddam Hussein unleashed a dangerous power vacuum in Iraq, which was de facto divided into three parts by the US-led military coalition including Turkey. During the 1990s, Iraq continued to be a source of concern for Turkey for three reasons: Firstly, terror organization PKK established camps in northern Iraq from where launched attacks to Turkish people in Anatolia. Thus, the PKK terror sharply intensified in the post-Iraq war. This was not a coincidence because PKK terrorists were using the advantage of the power vacuum in Iraq. Although Turkey, having deployed Poised Hammer forces in İncirlik in south of Turkey, launched a number of military operations in northern Iraq to strike PKK camps, it could not stop their terror activities in Turkey. Indeed, there was a growing influence of PKK-orchestrated Kurdish separatism based on the Kurdish ethnic identity. Despite PKK's wide-ranging efforts for drawing ordinary Kurdish people into its side, Kurdish people did not give enough support and assistance to PKK propaganda. Yet the terror activities continued unabated until the end of the decade, causing about 40,000 people killed and hundreds of thousand injured, and billions of dollars spent for fighting against the PKK terror.

Secondly, de facto fragmentation of Iraq into parts concerned Turkey due to possibility of establishment of a Kurdish state in the region. There are two big Kurdish groups in northern Iraq trying to get Kurdish independence from Iraq: The KDP led by Mesut Barzani and the PUK led by Jalal Talabani. These groups mainly fought against the Ba'atihst regime in order to have a better position in Iraq since the 1950s. During the 1990s after the Iraqi war, having got military, political and economic protection from the Western countries including Turkey, they intensified their activities to form an ethnically-divided federal Iraq. Turkey opposed to such a development due to its potential threat to Turkey's territorial, social and political integration. Thus Turkey established close ties and relations with those groups so as to pre-empt the establishment of such a state in the

---

[14] For example: Fuller and Lesser. *Turkey's New Geopolitics: From the Balkans to Western China*; and F. Stephen Larrabee and Ian O. Lesser. *Turkish Foreign Policy in the Age of Uncertainty*. Santa Monica, CA: Rand, 2003.

south of Turkey.

Thirdly, after the Iraqi occupation of Kuwait, in the view of the UN Security Council resolution 661, Turkey imposed wide-ranging sanctions upon Iraq, suspending its lucrative economic, commercial, financial and social relations with this country, which was one of Turkey's best foreign economic partners in the 1980s. In particular, Turkey suspended the operation of twin oil pipelines; stopped activities of Turkish firms in Iraq; and ended export and import relations with Iraq. All these actions cost Turkey around 50 billion dollar in the 1990s.[15] All those problems had great influence on Turkish domestic politics as well as on Turkish foreign policy developments during the 1990s.

In Central Asia and Caucasus, after the collapse of the Soviet Union, there emerged a new geopolitical environment in which new actors and factors have come to play a critical role for Turkey. Theoretically speaking, the independence of the Central Asian and Caucasus countries generated new opportunities and hopes for Turkey. Turkey's historical, ethnic, cultural and socio-psychological ties with five Turkish republics in Central Asia and Azerbaijan in the Caucasus created euphoria in Turkey. Turkish leaders, such Turgut Özal until his death in 1993 and Süleyman Demirel during his presidency and the government, paid close interest to the region. As Özal argued, the Turks believed that 'The Twenty-First Century will belong to the Turks living in the area from the Adriatic Sea to the Wall of China'.

However, it soon became clear that the region has faced a number of difficulties and crises that led not to a viable regional order but to a disorder due mainly to the problems of transition from old Soviet system to a new and modern one. They can be grouped as follows: increasing ethnic nationalism and fighting, Islamic radicalism, nationalist ideological rivalry, lack of democratization, social polarization, economic failures, and failures to adapt to globalization process.[16]

All these were part of the 'Great Game' in the region. During the 1990s, there was a high competition between the actors of the Great Game on what kind of an order to prevail in the region. Although the key players were the USA, Europeans, Russia, China, other middle-range regional and non-regional countries such as Turkey, Iran, Israel, Saudi Arabia heavily involved in the making of the regional order. The competition and rivalries were based on such economic, political, strategic and religious/sectarian issues as: the exploration and transfer of region's oil resources, the type of political system, the extent of the impact and role of religion and radical religious states, and the violation of territorial integrity of Azerbaijan.[17]

---

[15] See Ramazan Gözen, *Amerikan Kıskacında Dış Politika: Körfez Savaşı, Turgut Özal ve Sonrası*, Ankara: Liberte Yayınları, 2000.

[16] For details of these problems see Graham E. Fuller, "A New World Order in Eurasia? Ideology and Geopolitics", Hafeez Malik (Ed.), *The Role of United States, Russia, and China in the New World Order*, London: Macmillan Press, 1997; Alexander Rondeli, "The Forces of Fragmentation in the Caucasus", speech made in International Conference titled *"Building a Secure Eurasia for the 21st Century"*, organised by Arı Movement, Friedrich Naumann Stiftung and East-West Institute, İstanbul, 8-9 June 2000.

[17] Kober, *The Growing Divide in Eurasia*. Also Hafeez Malik, "Roles of the United States, Russia, and China in the New World Order: An Introduction", Hafeez Malik (Ed.), *The Role of United States, Russia, and China in the New World Order*, London: Macmillan Press, 1997.

Turkey was the most important regional power due not only its historical, cultural, geopolitical, and political connections with the region, but also to its alliance relations with the USA. The US Administrations supported Turkey's involvement in the region. As Mark Parris, US Ambassador to Turkey, stated, Turkey could play several roles in the region: as a leader in the process of helping the nations emerging from the Soviet empire, as pioneer of Western values, as model for a stable, secure, secular, dynamic, and economically strong country in the region.[18] Thus, the vision of Turkish leaders and public overlapped that of the USA that was also aiming to boost the establishment of a regional order endowed with democracy, market economy, cooperation among the regional actors, security, stability and peace.[19] To the consensus between US and Turkey was joined by Israel in the 1990s.[20] However, The US-Turkish-Israeli cooperation for bringing a new world order in the region was challenged by a counterbalancing cooperation among Russia, Iran, Syria, Armenia, and Greece in retaliation.[21]

Indeed, Turkey has had close cooperation with Israel on its fight against PKK terror. The cooperation was intensified especially from the mid-1990s after Turkish Deputy Chief of Staff visited Israel to sign a strategic agreement in 1996. From then on, both countries exchanged information about terror organizations and activities, culminating in the capture of Abdullah Öcalan, PKK leader, in 1999. Thus, Turkey's policy towards the Middle East, Central Asia, and the Caucasus were made and implemented in cooperation with Israel and the USA–called as 'Strategic Alliance'.

In the Balkans, the most important development was the collapse of Yugoslavia and the ensuing invasion of the Bosnian territory by the Serbian army. This was more than a territorial conflict, but a war between the cultures and traditions. Thus, its impact was wider, including not only the Christian Serbs and the Muslim Bosnians per se, but also other Muslim countries and Christian countries in other parts of world. But at the top of these countries were Turkey and Greece due their geopolitical and geo-cultural connections with the region. Yet, it must be underlined that the war was caused mainly by the ethnic policy of the Serbian government that aimed to maintain its long-standing control over the Bosnians, Croats, Kosovans, and other groups.

The war had religious, cultural, political outcomes for Turkish politics. Given that there is a large number of Balkan-origin Turkish citizens, plus the Ottoman past, Turkey was bound to pay interest to the Bosnians' conditions. Not only these people but also majority of the Turks felt close sympathy towards the Bosnians. They expressed their

---

[18] Mark Parris, "Keynote Address to Building a Secure Eurasia for the 21ˢᵗ Century", speech made in International Conference titled *"Building a Secure Eurasia for the 21ˢᵗ Century"*, organised by Arı Movement, Friedrich Naumann Stiftung and East-West Institute, İstanbul, 8-9 June 2000.

[19] Parris, *Keynote Address to Building a Secure Eurasia for the 21ˢᵗ Century*.

[20] Richard Perle, "Main strategic Concerns for the USA, Israel and Turkey", speech made in International Conference titled *Security and Cooperation in Eastern Mediterranean* organised by Friedrich Naumann Foundadion in cooperation with Arı Movement, and Begin-Sedat Center for Strategic Studies, İstanbul, 9-10 June 1999.

[21] For example, see Svante E. Cornell, "Regional Politics in the Caucasus and Central Asia: The Position of the US, Turkey ans Israel", speech made in International Conference titled *Security and Cooperation in Eastern Mediterranean* organised by Friedrich Naumann Foundadion in cooperation with Arı Movement, and Begin-Sedat Center for Strategic Studies, İstanbul, 9-10 June 1999.

sympathy in various ways such as making public protests and demonstrations, extending economic and financial support, and even going to Bosnia for fighting, etc. All these activities and pressures had influence on Turkish foreign policy making towards the region.

Whereas the aforementioned regions have faced deteriorating conditions in the post Cold War era in the 1990s, there was a very positive and admirable development in Central and Eastern Europe. They took great steps to reform themselves in line with the Copenhagen Criteria to become full members of the European Union. They not only developed their economic, political and social conditions, but also increased peace and stability in the region. Their efforts were contributed by the EU and NATO. Turkey's connection with this region was mainly through these organizations.

The final external development for Turkey was the development of globalization process in the world during the 1990s. The globalization can be defined as the shrinking and deepening of world as a result of growing economic, commercial, social, and even political relations by the help of advanced transportation, communication, information technologies in the world.[22] The globalization process opened up new channels for societies and individuals to know the world developments faster and easier, and learn new ideas, methods, and alternatives for their problems. Thus individuals and societies at large gained new identities and engagements with other parts of the world. As a result of these transactions and relationships, cultural, social, economic and political borders between different societies were blurred, leading to an identity crisis and soul-searching in the public level. For example, the man-in-the-street in Turkey could learn developments and problems in the four regions fast, and show its reaction strongly.

When comparing situations in the above regions around Turkey, it can be concluded as follows: while developments in the Middle East (mainly Iraq), the Balkans (mainly Bosnia), Central Asia, and the Caucasus generated political, security, and economic problems for Turkish society and politics, developments in Eastern and Central Europe could be seen as a model for Turkey's full membership into the EU.

The following section will look at their implications on the Turkish domestic politics in the 1990s.

The New Domestic Disorder

Negative affects of the external developments in the post Cold War period were seen both at domestic politics and foreign policy behavior. At the domestic realm, Turkey was polarized at social, cultural and political levels leading to a political instability and uncertainty during the 1990s. The main reason of this polarization was the differing positions and reactions to the developments around Turkey. Turkish people have been greatly sensitive about the problems in the post Cold War era for several reasons.

Firstly, the miserable conditions and suffering of Turks and/or Muslims in Iraq, Bosnian, Azerbaijan, Palestine and elsewhere was perceived as the result of unjust and brutal policies conducted by the USA, Serbia, Armenia, Israel respectively. Majority of

---

[22] See Anthony G.McGrew and Paul G.Lewis, *et.al. Global Politics: Globalisation and the Nation-State.* Cambridge: Polity Press, 1992.

Turkish public opinion, having strong sympathy and empathy towards these people were keen on extending help to them.

Secondly, Turkish people expected both Turkish governments and international community to stop their sufferings by taking collective actions. May be paradoxically, but strongly, they expected UN-led actions against these aggressions just like the one conducted against Iraq's invasion of Kuwait in 1990-1991. Having seen no effective action to find a solution to the above problems and end the sufferings of the Muslims and the Turks, they lost confidence to Western countries and international organizations such as the UN, NATO, and the EU. The West's failure created a negative perception of the West leading to anti-West, anti-Christianity, and anti-world order feelings.

Thirdly, Turkish public opinion was also disappointed with the failure of the Turkish governments to have, when necessary, unilateral actions to end these sufferings and wars. Although Turkish coalition governments formed by Süleyman Demirel and Erdal İnönü, later by Tansu Çiller and Murat Karayalçın, and the then President Turgut Özal tried to orchestrate multilateral campaign in order to end the Serbian invasion of Bosnians and the Armenian invasion of Azeris under the auspices of the United Nations and NATO, none of their attempts produced an effective action to end the aggressions and to save these people.

All these perceptions and feelings motivated some of the Turkish people towards soul-searching, looking for an alternative identity for a greater and stronger Turkey. In this respect, three traditional socio-cultural and political groupings were redefined: Political Islam, Nationalism, and Westernization. While the first two were in rise, the last one in decline. Turkish political system moved towards the right and even extreme right especially after the 1994 elections.[23]

The history of political Islamic sentiments goes back to the 1950s, but it gained new dynamism and power in the 1990s.[24] The failure of Communist ideology and the Soviet Union as well as the disappointment with the Capitalist-Western countries in solving the regional problems motivated some Turkish people to turn to religious and nationalist roots. There has been growing sympathy and adherence to the Islamic way of life and nationalist ideology, and search for new political models in the wake of an ideological vacuum in the new world disorder.

Although both Islamism and nationalism grew out as a reaction to these developments in the external environments, their political outcomes in domestic and foreign policy were different due their ideological differences. Islamism is based on a religious way of life shaped by Koran and Prophet Muhammed's sayings and practices (hadith). This way of life could be seen not only in their daily practices (dressings, religious rituals, socio-cultural connections, activities, etc.) but also in their political (and voting) behavior

---

[23] Cengiz Çandar, "Redefining Turkey's Political Center", *Journal of Democracy*, Vol.10, No.4, October 1999; and Andrew J.A.Mango, "Testing Time in Turkey", *The Washington Quarterly*, Vol.20, No.1, Winter 1997.

[24] On history of Islamic political development see, Mustafa Erdoğan, "Islam in Turkish Politics: Turkey's Quest for Democracy without Islam", *Liberal Düşünce*, Bahar 1999; Jeremy Salt, "Nationalism and the Rise of Muslim Sentiment in Turkey", *Middle Eastern Studies*, Vol.31, No.1, January 1995.

regarding domestic and foreign policy. In other words, pro-Islamist social groups voted for political Islamic parties to institute an Islamic system in Turkey, and also believed in the unity of the Islamic communities, i.e. the 'unity of ummah'.

However, the nationalism, though having sympathy and adherence to the Islamic teachings, is based on a secular way of life shaped by Turkish traditions and rituals, which are generally similar to those adopted by the Islamists. The nationalists are not so keen about religious teachings and orders as about the roots of the Turkish traditions. Indeed, the main difference between these two groups could be seen in their political/ideological belief systems. Unlike the Islamists, the nationalists supported nationalist parties and secular political system in Turkey, and believed in the unity of the Turkish communities wherever they are, ranging from the Balkans to China, i.e. the 'unity of Turan'.

Another part of growing nationalism in Turkey in the 1990s was the rise of Kurdish nationalism, which manifested itself in the form of terrorism perpetrated by the PKK. PKK's terror activities caused not only atrocities and killings, but also social schism, though at low level, between the Kurdish and Turkish nationalists. As a result of that, there was a kind of civil war between the PKK and the Turkish Military, causing tens of thousands of losses and injuries of life in both sides. However, we can safely argue that Kurdish nationalism did not take a considerable reception by the Kurdish people in general because most of the Kurds living in the southeast and other parts of Turkey did not give ideological and material support to PKK.

However, the Kurdish people did give support to the Kurdish parties, which appeared in the arena under different names such as HEP (People's Labour Party), DEP (Democratic Labour Party), HADEP (People's Democracy Party), DEHAP (Democratic People's Party) after each was closured by the Turkish Constitutional Court. These parties never get a vote big enough to pass the electoral limit of 10% for a seat in the Turkish Grand National Assembly (TGNA). Because of this, they entered into the TGNA only once through a coalition with the SHP (Social Democrat People's Party) in the 1991 elections. During its performance in the TGNA, HEP deputies, although minority group in the Parliament, advocated a pro-Kurdish policy, culminating in their overthrow from the Parliament and the closure of the Party in 1992. Moreover, its members were put into jail. After that occasion there was no other Kurdish party in the Parliament in the rest of the 1990s.[25]

Thus the 'End of History' theory did not have a strong reception by the Turkish people. Yet it must be pointed out that there was a developing liberal movement in Turkey in the 1990s. There were some civil society groups and foundations in spreading liberalism in Turkey. For instance, the Association for Liberal Thinking was founded in

---

[25] For a brief history of the growth of Kurdish problem in Turkey: Philip Robins, "The overlord state: Turkish policy and the Kurdish issue", *International Affairs*, Vol.69, No.4, October 1993; Nilüfer Narlı, "Political Instability in Turkey: The Rise of Islamist Movement and Ultra-Nationalism", speech made in International Conference titled *Security and Cooperation in Eastern Mediterranean* organised by Friedrich Naumann Foundadion in cooperation with Arı Movement, and Begin-Sedat Center for Strategic Studies, İstanbul, 9-10 June 1999.

1992. It published books and a quarterly journal, organized conferences, and performed social and political activities for promoting liberalism in Turkey. As a result, they seem to have had a great impact on political parties and governments.

These groups had influence on political system and on the governments' foreign policies during the 1990s. Especially, the Islamists and the nationalists had social, economic and political activities to demonstrate their reactions against Serbia, Armenia, Russia due to their attacks to the Bosnians, the Azeris, and the Chechens respectively, against the Western countries for their silence to stop these attacks, and against the Turkish governments for not having enough and effective action to help them.

In that, the ethnic composition of the Turkish nation was an important factor. There is a large number of Bosnian, Chechenian, Turkish citizens of Azeri origin in Turkey. As Windrow argued, between four to ten million of the population of Turkey are estimated to be of the Balkan origin.[26] These groups played a leading role in motivating not only the Turkish society in terms of civil society activities, but also Turkish governments in terms of influencing their foreign policy making.

As result, Turkish political system was dominated by these socio-political power groups: In the years from 1991 to 1994, center right and center left parties (DYP- True Path Party- and SHP respectively) formed a coalition government. In this period, while President Turgut Özal, as a liberal-conservative leader having sympathy to the West and the East, advocated an active, even unilateral, involvement in the developments around Turkey, the coalition government showed more hesitant position and pursued a multilateral approach. The Turkish public did not like the government's approach. Meanwhile, the Islamic party, RP (Welfare Party) led by Necmettin Erbakan, used this as an advantage to propagate against the government.

Consequently, in the 1995 elections, the RP won the majority of the votes by increasing its votes from only 5 percent in 1985 to 21.4 percent, which made it the biggest party in the Parliament for the first time in Turkish history. And the main, if not the only, reason behind this growth was the new developments in the post Cold War era.[27] However, the RP could form only a coalition government after some difficulties with the center right party DYP led by Tansu Çiller. During the RP-DYP coalition government lasting only one year from June 1996 to June 1997, there was a split in the management of the government policies: While the RP emphasized Islamic policies in domestic and foreign policy, the DYP tried to maintain secular and pro-Western ideas.

During this period while Prime Minister Erbakan led the formation of a new coalition of states called D-8 (i.e. Developing Eight countries: Turkey, Nigeria, Libya, Egypt, Iran, Pakistan, Malaysia, Indonesia); Deputy Prime Minister and Foreign Minister Çiller of DYP led the completion of the customs agreement with the European Union. Whether these were conflicting processes is debated by scholars. Some argued that although Erbakan during its office had some openings towards the Islamic world on bilateral and

[26] Wareth Windrow, *Where East Meets West: Turkey and the Balkans*, London: Insitute for European Defence and Strategic Studies, 1993.
[27] İhsan Dağı, *Kimlik, Söylem ve Siyaset: Doğu-Batı Ayırımında Refah Partisi Geleneği*, Ankara: İmge Kitabevi., 1998, esp.37-41; And Jenny B. White, "Pragmatists or Ideologues?: Turkey's Welfare Party in Power", *Current History*, Vol.96, No.606, January 1997.

multilateral ways, he did not attempt to make any considerable change, but preferred 'continuity and complementarity' in Turkish foreign policy.[28] However, some expressed criticism about Erbakan's view of democracy, secularism and economy policy.[29]

In particular, the US feared that Erbakan's ideas would pose threat to Turkish foreign policy, leading to a change of direction from the Western world towards the Islamic world.[30] This line of interpretation was also strong particularly among the Turkish army and bureaucracy. Thus the RP-DYP government was ousted by a coalition of groups including the Military, some social groups, bureaucrats, and intellectuals in the so-called 28 February Process. The 28 February Process aimed not only to oust Erbakan's coalition government, but also to suppress the growth of the Islamic social movements by closing down religious schools, foundations, organizations, sects, and by banning religious dressings in the street, and scarf in public and private schools and public places.[31]

In the following elections held in 1999 after transition government of ANAP (Motherland Party) led by Mesut Yılmaz from 1997 to 1999 after the overthrow of the RP-DYP government, the nationalist party MHP (Nationalist Action Party) led by Devlet Bahçeli won a historical 18 percent, being the second party in the Parliament following DSP (Democratic Left Part) led by Bülent Ecevit. Now, it was turn for the nationalist ideology and party to come to the government in coalition with the previous government parties, the DSP and ANAP. The MHP, being the second biggest party, preferred to have coalition with DSP of Ecevit and ANAP of Yilmaz, not with closer VP (VirtueParty) led by Recai Kutan as the successor of the RP. This choice was important because it showed the level of marginalization and isolation of the Islamists in the 28 February Process.

The 28 February Process led to a deep social crisis and schism as Turkish society came in the brink of divisions such as 'Islamist against secularist', 'sunni against alavi(shia)', 'Turks against Kurds'. These divisions widened especially in the 28 February Process because of some orchestrated campaigns against pro-Islamic groups, individuals, and organizations. With the help of media, some civil society groups, and political actors, these divisions were fomented to such an extent that Turkish social, political and security system was paralyzed, and that the economic corruptions and abnormalities increased. Social divisions negatively affected political and economic order, culminating in a big economic crisis of 2000-2002.

An important point about Turkish political system in the 1990s is the high number of governments formed during the decade: There were ten coalition governments in ten years, each of which was formed by opposite parties. For the first time in Turkish history, the left and the right parties formed coalition governments. Amid these there were even ultra-right parties such as the RP and MHP. In other words, the political electorate system was so fragmented that different ideologies had to coalesce to form a coalition.

[28] Philip Robins, "Turkish Foreign Policy under Erbakan", *Survival*, Vol.39, No.2, Summer 1997.
[29] For example, Atilla Yayla, "Turkey's Leaders: Erbakan's Goals", *Middle East Quarterly*, Vol.IV, No.3, September 1997.
[30] Carol Migdalovitz, "Turkey: Political and Economic Change and Implications for the United States", CRS Report for Congress, The Library of Congress, 20 September 1994.
[31] On the developments in the 28 February Process, Mustafa Erdoğan, *28 Şubat Süreci*, Ankara: Yeni Türkiye Yayınları, 1999.

Moreover, there was greater number of foreign ministers shifting throughout these government changes.[32]

In addition, due to their clashing ideologies, they were unable to pursue strong and unitary policies. In the wake of lack of a strong political consensus and unity in the governments, other state institutions come forward. In that, the National Security Council became a dominant decision-making institution in foreign and security policy making in particular. The NSC usurped the rights of the governments and the TGNA, while the governments were unable to show a strong unity. Thus the Military increased its influence in foreign policy making. The military bureaucracy involved in Turkish politics by various ways: By fighting against PKK terror and Kurdish nationalism they had influence on the social structure; by overthrowing the RP-DYP government and suppressing the political Islam in a post-modern *coup d'etat*, they manipulated the political system; and by dispatching troops to northern Iraq to fight against the PKK and influencing governments' policy towards Iraq and other regions the Middle East, the Balkans, and Caucasus and Central Asia, they involved in foreign and domestic policy making as part of the NSC.[33]

The cost of the fight against the PKK and abnormalities and corruptions during the 1990s was big. While Turkey's security-oriented domestic and foreign policies widened, it faced greater economic costs. The cost of Turkey's security policies is estimated roughly around $100 billion divided as follows: spending above $50 billion for fighting against PKK terror, and losing about $50 billion due to suspension of economic and commercial relations with Iraq. All these losses culminated in two big economic crises in 2000 and 2001, along with a big financial crisis, closure of several banks and firms, and high number of unemployed in two years.

According to World Bank's World Development Report, Turkish economy was placed into the Middle Income Country Group. With its $2780 per capita income in 1997 Turkey was in the 85th place out of 133 countries. In terms of inflation, with 65 percent inflation Turkey was in the third place. The growth of Turkey's GNP declined from %5.3 in 1980-1990 to %3.2 in 1990-1995. While Turkey's foreign debt increased from $19.131 billion in 1980 to $73.592 billion in 1995, the ratio of foreign debt/per capita income increased from 27.4 to 44.1 respectively. This means that Turkish citizens' indebtedness was increasing drastically in the 1990s. Here military spending must be also noted: In the same period, in the budget, the rate of the military spending increased from %15.2 in 1980 to %15.8 in 1995, whereas that of social spending declined from %33 to %21.6 respectively.[34]

The cost of the economic crises and of social, political and security divisions were paid not only by the Turkish people, but also by the political parties which came to power in the 28 February Process. They all lost, and their leaders were put outside the TGNA on

[32] William Hale. *Turkish Foreign Policy, 1774-2000*, London: Frank Cass, 2002.
[33] See Erhan Canikoğlu, 1990'larda Türk Dış Politikasını Oluşumu: Güvenlik Kaygıları ve Milli Güvenlik Kurulu'nun Rolü, Yayımlanmamış Yüksek Lisans Tezi, Sosyal Bilimler Enstitüsü, Atılım Üniversitesi, Ankara, 2003.
[34] *Ekonomik Forum*, Year 4, No.11, 15 November 1997.

3 December 2002 elections. After that a new era seems to have started in Turkish politics, which is now dominated by a single party government of AKP (Justice and Development Party) ten years later. Interesting enough, the leader of the AKP, Recep Tayyip Erdoğan, was one of the victims of the 28 February Process!

Finally, it is important to note that during the 1990s Turkish society experienced the formation of several non-govermental organizations (NGOs) in several fields areas and issues such economy, politics, religion, environment, etc.[35]

Foreign Policy in Turmoil

In the vortex of turbulent changes in both external and domestic environments during the 1990s, Turkish foreign policy has been dominated by security-oriented understanding due to high security-loaded challenges and pressures from inside and outside. Thus Turkey involved actively in all fronts in the south regarding Iraq, in the west regarding the Bosnia and other tensions in the Balkans and Europe, and in the east and north regarding the Caucasus and Central Asia. This much changes and challenges made Turkey and Turkish foreign policy active in all directions.

At the early stages of the post-Cold War era, there was great debate on where Turkey should orient. While some argued that Turkey is now left outside the Western world, the others believed that Turkey would maintain its place in NATO, playing important role for the Western world.[36] Huntington described Turkey and its foreign policy as a 'torn country' being in dilemma in choosing either 'Mecca' or 'Tashkent' or 'Brussels',[37] i.e. Islamic world, Turkish world, or the EU respectively as its own direction in foreign politics. In a 'Survey on Turkish people's foreign policy orientation' conducted by TESEV, Turkish people were divided in similar ways: 47.9 percent preferred the EU (Brussels); 21.7 percent preferred the Islamic world (Mecca); and 20.5 percent preferred the Turkish world (Tashkent).[38]

It was not very easy for Turkey to choose only one of these because of two reasons. First, although all the developments around Turkey were pregnant to fundamental changes, the outcomes of which would concern Turkey very much. Indeed, each of these regions had conflicting implications for Turkish foreign policy. Secondly, the Turkish state and society could not have a solidified approach towards foreign policy, but were divided into the different camps with negative implications on Turkey's foreign policy performance. As a result of these conflicting pressures and demands from inside and outside, Turkey's foreign policy behavior reflected three kinds of patterns in the 1990s as follows. Firstly, playing a 'mediator role' to help the reformation and transformation of the Eurasia. Secondly, struggling to preserve status quo and stability in the borders. Thirdly, keeping up with the long-term objective of Westernization.

---

[35] Heinz Kremer, *A Changing Turkey- The Challenge to Europe and the United States*, Washington D.C.: Brooking Institute, 2000.
[36] William Hale, *Turkish Foreign Policy 1174-2000*, London: Frank Cass, 2000, pp.192-195.
[37] Huntington, *The Clash of Civilisations*, p.43.
[38] Cited from Y.Esmer, "Turkish Public Opinion and Europe", *Cambridge Review of International Affairs*, Vol.10, No.1, 1996, p.80 cited by İhsan D. Dağı, *Kimlik, Söylem ve Siyaset: Doğu-Batı Ayırımında Refah Partisi Geleneği*, p.77.

The Struggle for Transforming the Eurasia

Turkish foreign policy towards the Eurasia was based on the objective that the region should be integrated into international system by transforming its politics, economy, and society into a western style. As such, they could get rid of the Soviet/Communist past, promote their development, and act in international system independently. On the other hand, the western countries led by the USA wished to involve in their transformation not only for improving stability, peace and security in the region, but also for increasing their national interests. In particular, the Western countries aimed to explore rich oil resources of the region and pump it into the Western markets. Thus these countries started a multidimensional process so as to change their domestic systems and foreign policy orientations towards the Western world.

Turkey was seen as a model for the transformation of these countries by the Western countries as well as by the Turkish leadership. Turkey could serve as a model for these countries because of its strong connections with both sides. Turkey was part of the Western world due to its western, secular, democratic, market-economy and socio-cultural characteristics, and also could be seen as part of the newly emerging states in Eurasia due to its historical, ethnic/national, socio-cultural characteristics.[39] In addition, Turkey's geo-political position as part of the NATO and other western organizations gave it a role to play in these regions.

Turkish leadership worked hard to play such a role in the 1990s. Firstly, Turgut Özal as Turkish President dedicated himself to this role. Until his death in 1993, he had an active involvement in the international politics of Balkans, the Caucasus, Central Asia, and the Middle East. His aim and policy was based on the idea of Neo-Ottomanism, meaning that Turkey must play multiple roles in the area formerly ruled by the Ottoman State.[40] He tried to end the Serbian invasion of Bosnian territory, just like ending the Iraqi invasion of Kuwait in 1990-1, and to defend the Azerbaijan against the Armenian attacks by use of force if necessary. In addition, he tried to improve Turkey's relations with these regions at all levels, be it military, social, economic, social, educational and cultural.[41]

Indeed, starting with Özal, Turkish governments improved relations with these countries at bilateral and multilateral levels. At bilateral level, Turkey enhanced its diplomatic, political, social, cultural, economic, commercial, and educational relations with Central Asian and Balkan countries. At the multilateral level, Turkey played a decisive role in their full membership into the Economic Cooperation Organization, the Black Sea Economic Cooperation Organization, and the Islamic Conference Organization. As such, Turkey has been a mediator between them and the world community.

Özal's Neo-Ottomanizm aimed to get the transformation not only of the Central Asian,

---

[39] İdris Bal, *Turkey's Relations with the West and the Turkic Republics: The rise and fall of the "Turkish Model"*. Aldershot: Ashgate, 2000.

[40] Şaban Çalış, *Hayaletbilimi ve Hayali Kimlikler: Neo-Osmanlılık, Özal ve Balkanlar*. Konya: Çizgi Kitabevi, 2001.

[41] For a comprehensive analysis of Özal's ideas see İhsan Sezal and İhsan Dağı (Eds.), *Kim Bu Özal? Siyaset, İktisat, Zihniyet*. İstanbul: Boyut Yayınları, 2001.

Caucasian and Balkan countries, but also of the neighboring countries, Iraq in particular. In this context, he was planning to increase Turkey's influence over the Kurds of Iraq. To this end he used not only 'hard politics' instruments such as the deployment in Incirlik of the multinational military force called as 'Poised Hammer forces', to give protection to Iraqi Kurds against Saddam's attacks, but also 'soft politics' instruments such as improving diplomatic dialogue with the Kurdish groups in Iraq. Furthermore, for this to be successful, he was prepared to make bold reforms about the Kurdish problem in Turkey. He clearly suggested that the Turkish Republic should give the Kurds the right to express, and to participate in Turkish politics with their cultural identity.

After Özal's death, the Neo-Ottomanism project was put out of political agenda, if not of intellectual agenda. Özal's 'soft power approach' was replaced by 'hard politics approach', which was based on a Nationalist Policy. The nationalists dismissed Özal's approach towards the solution of the Kurdish problem, and preferred a high level of military fighting. Regarding the Turkish world, the nationalists tried to achieve the unity of the Turks in the Turkistan, or Turan. Although having a number of similarities with the Neo-Ottomanism, the nationalist project had a different look at the Turkish world. Unlike Neo-Ottomanism, it focused on the unity of the Turks in Eurasia excluding the non-Turkic areas. And it was in favor of military struggle for the solution to PKK terror. The difference between the two projects was clearly seen in Turkey's changing approach to the Kurdish problem after Özal's death in the second half of the 1990s. In the implementation of the national projects, there was a number of actors at various levels such as: a political party named MHP, some think-tank institutions such as ASAM, and some bureaucrats and even military officials.

Erbakan's D-8 project was an attempt to improve Turkey's connection with Africa, East and Far Asia. This was the first such attempt in Turkish foreign policy. It was based on the idea of forming an 'Islamic community/ummah' to unite the Islamic countries under Turkey's leadership in the long run, if successful. However, because Erbakan's coalition government could not stay in power more than a year, that idea did not make any progress. Although the D-8 remained as an organization intact, its spirit does not persist so long as Erbakan thought of.

Despite some important achievements in adapting these countries into the Western world, Turkey's efforts to reform and transform the regional countries did not produce expected results.[42] For instance, the Armenian invasion of Azerbaijan's lands was not ended; the Serbian aggression directed towards the Bosnian territory was ended only after three years of fighting, with the help of US-led NATO operation in 1995; nor has Turkey's energy policy in the region achieved a concrete success yet.

There can be shown three main obstacles and problems for Turkey's failure: Firstly, Turkey's involvement in regional politics was challenged by regional and global actors, in particular by Russian. Secondly, Turkish governments could not show their trustworthiness to the regional countries because of lack of enough effort to solve their

---

[42] Bal, *Turkey's Relations with the West and the Turkic Republics: The rise and fall of the "Turkish Model"*.

problems. Thirdly, Turkey-US cooperation did not have enough steps in the transformation of the region.

The Struggle for Preserving the Status Quo

Turkey was satisfied with the end of the Cold War and the collapse of the Soviet Union for two reasons mainly. Firstly, due to the end of the Soviet/Communist threat to Turkey, and secondly due to new opportunities in the new era regarding the Turkish world in particular. But at the same time it was unhappy with the emergence of new forces and problems likely to threaten Turkey's territorial and political integrity. Turkish state was worried by the negative impact of the ideological/power vacuum and the separatist movements and groups inside and outside Turkey's borders, which would break up the status quo in Turkey and around. That was contrary to Turkey's traditional understanding of 'misak-ı milli philosophy (sanctity of national pact)'.

Such a threat came from one source only: The post-Gulf war developments in Iraq. Iraq's defeat by the Gulf coalition resulted not only in the collapse of Iraq's power, but also in a large power vacuum in the north of Iraq where the Kurdish separatist groups led by Barzani and Talabani were planning to establish a Kurdish state by carving lands from Iraq, Turkey and Iran. Moreover, after the Gulf war, Iraqi territory was de facto divided into three parts by US's air power: the northern Iraq above the 36th parallel, the central Iraq around Baghdad, and the southern Iraq below the 32th parallel. Thus Iraq's military forces were unable to enter the northern and southern parts of the country. This brought Iraq to the brink of disintegration and fragmentation.

Added to this was growing terrorist activities of the PKK in Turkey. The PKK militants based in the border between southeast Turkey and northern Iraq launched brutal terror attacks against Turkish military forces as well as to Turkish and Kurdish civilians in Turkey. In order to retaliate the Turkish armed forces fought against the PKK terrorists in Turkey and northern Iraq for almost ten years. This fighting once came so far as to the point that Turkish government was having difficulties in keeping law and order in the southeast region bordering the northern Iraq. Indeed, there was a potential civil war in the region.

In response to this threat, Turkey implemented a number of domestic and foreign policy actions. Domestically, Turkey waged military campaign against the separatists, banned pro-PKK radical Kurdish parties, vacated pro-PKK villages, spent a high budget, and cooperated with pro-State Kurdish groups called 'village Guards', and so on. Externally, Turkish foreign policy was formulated almost in view of the struggle against PKK at various levels. At the military level, Turkish army combated PKK terrorists not only inside Turkey, but also in northern Iraq. Thus, during the 1990s Turkish armed forces launched operations in the northern Iraq up to 40 kilometers, and took control of an area in the region to stop infiltration of PKK terrorists into Turkey. These kinds of operations were repeated several times in the 1990s despite the strong protests from the Western countries.[43]

---

[43] Mahmut Bali Aykan, "Turkey's Policy in Northern Iraq, 1991-1995", *Middle Eastern Studies*, Vol.32, No.4, October 1996.

At the policy level, Turkey maintained good and friendly relations with those countries that supported Turkey's struggle against the PKK, while having tension and unfriendly relations with those countries that gave any kind of support to the PKK. The Kurdish problem and the PKK terror influenced Turkish foreign policy not only towards its neighbors, but also towards other countries in the West and the East. In this respect, Turkey experienced a number of crises with many Western European countries such as Holland, Belgium, Germany, the United Kingdom, Greece, an so on, as well as with others such as Russia, Syria, and Iran that had some kind of intimacy with the PKK. In the wake of these developments, Turkey needed to develop an anti-PKK foreign policy in order to stop their criticism of Turkey's military operations in the northern Iraq and/or to change their attitude against the PKK activities in their homes.

On the other hand, a close military and political cooperation was developed with the USA over Iraq in particular and over other developments in the post Cold War era. At the top of that cooperation was the deployment of Poised Hammer forces in İncirlik in the south of Turkey, which can be seen as a manifestation of military cooperation between the two countries over Iraq. Turkey used the advantage of this cooperation not only by having military and political scrutiny over the developments in Iraq, but also by checking the US policy towards Iraq. By these means, Turkey sought to maintain status quo in the region. Later in the 1990s Turkey's cooperation with the USA was joined by Israel, with which Turkey exchanged intelligence information about PKK and other terror organizations in the region.

The Struggle for Maintaining Western Connection

Turkey's Western connection did not show a stable progress in the 1990s because of some problems and uncertainties with the Western countries. First of all it is essential to point out that there are two wings of the Western world: Europe represented by the European Union, and the United States. Although Turkey has had close relations with both sides as NATO allies, there have been some discrepancies in Turkey's approach towards both sides. It must be pointed out at the outset that there were a number of crises in Turkey's relations with the EU, but a strategic cooperation with the USA on many issues.

Turkey's relations with the EU fluctuated between good and bad. Turkey's application in 1987 for full membership into EU was refused in December 1989 because of Turkey's economic and political problems and of EU's own concerns in changing world conditions. As an alternative to full membership, the EU proposed the completion of the customs union that had started in 1973. Thus, the customs union agreement was made in 1995 and came into affect from 1 January 1996. That was a good and promising step in Turkey's integration into the EU. But it was only half of the picture because there was further deterioration in the political dimension.

After the Gulf Crisis and ensuing new developments in Turkey, Turkey's 'hard power approach' drew criticism from the EU countries. They found Turkey's anti-terror policy as against EU standards. They criticized Turkey for failing to have enough democracy, human rights, civil rule, and for its military-dominated policies in the fight against terror. In particular, torture, closure of political parties, position of the Kurds were main points of the EU criticism.

The relations went from bad to worse in the 28 February Process as the military bureaucracy and the National Security Council played role, albeit indirect, in the overthrow of Erbakan-Çiller coalition government. The tide went down to the lowest point when EU Luxemburg Council of 1997 put Turkey out of the list of potential EU members. Turkey was placed behind 12 Eastern and Central European countries including Malta and Cyprus standing in the queue for full EU membership by 2004. In retaliation, Turkish coalition government led by Mesut Yılmaz decided to suspend all political-diplomatic contacts with the EU institutions, excepting bilateral relations with EU countries.

Indeed, this was basically a by-product of domestic and external developments in the sort of interaction Turkey was engaged in. For Turkey's fight against the PKK terror emanating from the northern Iraq negatively affected Turkey's foreign policy toward the EU. In turn, the EU's criticism towards Turkey negatively affected Turkey's domestic environment as some Turkish groups and organizations adopted anti-EU and anti-Western positions. As a result of these positions, Turkey's connection with the Western world weakened with negative counter-effects for both Turkey and the EU.

Turkey's estrangement from the Western world could lead to a growing instability and disorder in and around Turkey. Such fears motivated EU Helsinki Summit in 1999 to restore Turkey's position as one of the candidates for membership into the EU. Since then, there has been a good progress in the relations.[44] The level of rapprochement increased particularly after the US war in Iraq in 2003. Now, if the current trend continues positively, Turkey is ever closer to get a 'date' to start negotiations for full membership.

The other part of Turkey's Western connection has been its alliance with NATO and the US. Compared with the relations with the EU, Turkey's relations with the USA continued at a better level as the two had close strategic cooperation over most issues in the region such as the Iraqi problem, the transformation of the Caucasus and Central Asia, and the promotion of peace and order in the Balkans.

The extent to which US Administrations gave importance to Turkey was clearly expressed by Secretary of Commerce Ron Brown in the words: 'The United States has never lost sight of the great importance of Turkey, both strategically and economically. Turkey is a key NATO partner, and its future as a democratic, secular, Muslim state in a volatile region has never been more important'.[45] With these characteristics, Turkey, accepted as one of the 'Big Emerging Markets', was seen as a 'Gateway to Central Asia and the Middle East'.[46]

The elements of Turkish-US cooperation can be summarized in the following headlines: preserving stability, peace, and order in the post Cold War era; political

---

[44] İhsan Dağı, "Avrupa Birliği ve Türkiye: Batılılaşmanın Neresindeyiz?", Şaban Çalış, İhsan Dağı, Ramazan Gözen (Eds.), *Türkiye'nin Dış Politika Gündemi: Kimlik, Demokrasi, Güvenlik*, Ankara: Liberte Yayınları, 2001.
[45] "Turkey: The Emerging Market Bridging East and West", *Foreign Affairs*, May-June 1996.
[46] *Turkey: The Emerging Market Bridging East and West.*

support to each other's policies towards the Balkans, the Middle East, Central Asia and the Caucasus; co-operation in the transformation of the Caucausia and Central Asian countries, and in the production and transfer of regional energy sources through Turkey by the Baku-Ceyhan pipeline project; having a 'NATO First' perspective on the construction of new European security architecture; last but not least, IMF-World Bank connection due to Turkey's economic crisis in 2000 and 2001.

However, there were some differences of opinion and disagreement between Turkey and the USA on some issues: the US's criticism to Turkey's human rights records and handling of the Kurdish problem, US's belated reaction to end the Serbian invasion of Bosnian territories; and lack of confidence in US policy towards Iraq on the issue of a Kurdish state in the region due to its ambiguous relations with the Iraqi Kurds; and finally, the lack of mutual perception about the future of Iraq since the US's war in Iraq in 2003.

Conclusion

Like any country in the world, politics of the Turkish state is greatly determined by the prevailing conditions in the world. Like any organism, Turkey tries to adapt itself to the changes in the external environment in the post Cold War era. But the challenges and constraints were so big and multi-faceted that Turkish society and the state could not produce a unified and solidified response good enough to promote Turkey's domestic and foreign policy conditions. Due this failure, Turkey has experienced a number of weaknesses and problems since the early stages of the post Cold War era.

During the 1990s, Turkey passed through three serious crises: The first crisis was 'political-security crisis' due to PKK terror, which divided the country into ethnic and political lines. The second crisis was 'socio-political-cultural crisis' due to the 28 February Process, which divided the society into social and cultural lines with effects on political system and process. And the third crisis was 'socio-economic crises' due to corruptions, lavish spending, mismanagement, and the fighting against terror during the 1990s, which put Turkish people into a dire condition. Indeed, each of all the crises, singly and combined, made Turkish politics disable to work for adapting to the new world conditions, and to manage the regional politics.

However, in the beginning of the 21st Century, after new developments in and out of Turkey, a new period started in Turkish politics. The results of which are not known yet.

3 Impacts of International Capital Flows to Turkish Economy During the 90's

Saziye Gazioglu
Erol Bulut

Introduction

The literature on financial crisis has grown since the end of Bretton woods system. Masses of papers have been written to explain the causes of volatility of the exchange rate.[1] International capital flows have been increasingly affecting developing countries during the post Cold War era. The second half of the 1990s, several countries experienced financial crises in an environment of increased international capital flows, casting doubts on the ability of such flows to stimulate long-run growth in developing economies. This goes hand in hand with emerging stock market in developing countries. Although the volatility of capital flows does inhibit growth, there is some evidence that countries are learning to manage volatility better, but with high cost.[2]

Development of stock exchange in newly industrial countries created emerging markets. Attraction of short-term foreign capital inflows leads to financial vulnerability of these markets. Financial crises in these countries often affect most people in various ways. Since foreign capital is attracted to some countries in various regions in different periods, the history shows examples of contagion, which induces the spread of a crisis from one market to other markets and propagation of a domestic crisis to other regions, often leading to an international contagion, common factors affecting all countries. Financial crises strike a country or a region when they are least expected. There is no distinct pattern in the occurrences of financial crises in a particular country or worldwide. However, it is imperative to understand an anatomy of a generic financial crisis in order not to be caught off guard when the disaster hits.

The 1990s witnessed several acute currency crises among developing countries that invariably spread to other nearby countries at risk. Speculative foreign investments and high-volume movements of capital in and out led to financial crises in the emerging markets such as Mexico, Thailand, South Korea, Russia, Brazil, Argentina and Turkey. Insufficient domestic controls further undermined these economies.

Recent financial crises, beginning in Mexico in 1994–95, the Asian crisis of 1997–1998, and the crises in Russia, Brazil, and other Latin American countries in 1998–99,

---

[1] These include Dornbusch type of models and models of currency substitutions.
[2] T. Komuainen, "Currency Crises in Emerging Markets: Capital Flows and Herding Behaviour", *BOFIT Discussion Papers*, No:10, 2001, pp.15-20.

Argentina crises in 2002 and lastly November 2000 and February 2001 crises in Turkey illustrate the risks of financial volatility and macroeconomic instability during the process of economic growth and development.

These crises also raise issues regarding the management of risks associated with liberalization and global integration, particularly in financial markets. Concerns about the implications of international capital flows for developing countries have grown with the sharply increased volume of these flows since the late 1980s. It is said that emerging markets have been the innocent victims of mercurial global investors.[3]

The size, composition and geographical distribution of international capital flows to developing countries have undergone fundamental shifts during the past three decades. Until the early 70s, the most important sources of external financing for developing countries were official loans and aids, the provision of which was based on the recognition that developing countries suffered from resource gaps resulting from their low levels of income and savings and that their ability to fill these gaps through commercial borrowing at market terms was severely limited. Official development assistance continued to expand rapidly in the 1970s thanks, in part, to Cold War politics. At the same time, however, there was also a rapid expansion of private financial flows, primarily in the form of syndicated credits from banks in industrial countries, which served to recycle the surpluses of major oil exporters. This expansion was greatly facilitated by the liberalization of capital markets following the demise of the Breton Woods system.[4]

The expansion came to an end with the debt crisis of the 1980s, when total net capital inflows of developing countries fell sharply due to a cutback in commercial bank lending, and stagnated at this level during the rest of the decade. Official financing also stagnated, while its terms and conditions became more stringent, reflecting the policy of the major creditor countries and the multilateral financial institutions of emphasizing private financing for development.[5]

The 1990s have indeed witnessed a rapid expansion of private capital inflows, whilst official financing, remarkably official development assistance, declined. The surge in private inflows was greatly influenced by rapid liberalization of markets and privatisation of economic activity in most developing countries. In contrast to earlier decades, private sector has become the principal borrower in international markets as most developing countries relaxed control over such borrowing. An important proportion of private inflows, however, have taken the form of so-called non-debt creating inflows and as a result, the outstanding stock of debt of emerging-market economies roughly doubled between 1988 and 1997, from \$1 trillion to \$2[6] trillion.[7]

---

[3] R.J. Barro and J.W. Lee, "IMF Programs: Who Is Chosen And What Are The Effects?", *NBER Working Paper*, No: 8951, May, 2002, pp.10-13.
[4] H.P., Lankes, and N. Stern, "Capital Flows to Eastern Europe and the Former Soviet Union", *EBRD Working Paper*, No: 27, February, 1998, pp.25-32.
[5] Lankes, and Stern, Capital Flows to Eastern Europe and the Former Soviet Union, pp.29-33.
[6] D. Rodrik and A. Velasco, "Short-Term Capital Flows", *ABCDE Conference at the World Bank, 1999*, pp.2-7.
[7] The group covers 10 countries in Latin America, 8 in Asia, 8 in Europe, and 11 in the Middle East and North Africa.

As mentioned above, the financial crises started to surge after the collapsing of Bretton Woods System and boomed during the 1990s. To parallel these developments, the literature of financial crises grew rapidly and economists began to deal with the causes, impacts and results of the crises. Additionally, the literature on financial crises has a long history and extends well beyond the scope of this article[8]; even so, the models that try to explain causes of the crises are explained briefly. The theoretical models on financial crises can be classified into three generations.[9]

The first generation of models attempted to explain the crises as a result of unsustainable fiscal deficits financed by seignorage from central banks. In a seminal paper, "A Model of Balance of payment Crises", Krugman (1979) stressed the role of the weak fundamentals as a triggering factor of the currency and financial crises. He assumed that the government budget deficits were at the root of speculative attacks on pegged exchange rates. These models argue that the currency crises are preceded by the macroeconomic imbalances in the economy that are inconsistent with the maintenance of fixed exchange rates. According to the model, under a fixed exchange rate regime, monetization of fiscal deficits, which creates domestic inflation, leads to an appreciation in the real exchange rate. The deteriorating effect of increasing domestic prices on the current account balance causes a gradual loss of reserves and ultimately, leads to a speculative attack against the currency. When the authorities are no longer able to defend the fixed exchange rate, they are forced to abandon the parity.[10] This is the most common view of financial crisis of February 2001 in Turkey. This is the view that present government takes.

A second category of the models is called second-generation models that focus on (following Obsfeld, 1986) self-fulfilling speculative attacks. These models are not opposed to the role of the fundamentals in the economy. Nevertheless, financial crises are not always necessarily determined by the weak fundamentals. The term "self-fulfilling" mentioned in these models reflects an indeterminacy of equilibrium when a speculative attack is simply expected. An important critique to the first generation models, according to second-generation models, is that it assumes perfect price flexibility, which makes monetary policy ineffective.[11]

The second-generation models[12] consider non-linear behaviour rules by one or more agents. Hence, these nonlinearities can lead to multiple solutions. For instance, a multiple

---

[8] For more detail see the survey in Berg et al (1999)

[9] J. Berg and et. al., "Anticipating balance of payments crises: the role of Early Warning systems", *IMF Occasional Paper* no: 186, Washington DC, 1999, pp.20-23.

[10] G. Kibritcioglu and et al., "A Leading Indicators Approach to the Predictability of Currency Crises: the Case of Turkey", *Hazine Dergisi*, V.12, July, 1998, pp.33-37.

[11] G. Bird and R.S. Rajan, "Financial Crises and the Composition of International capital Flows: Does FDI Guarantee Stability?", *Institute of Southeast Asian Studies*, Visiting Researchers Series No.6, 2001, pp.12-17.

[12] A brief explanation of the first generation model is one in which a budget deficit is financed by the government printing money, resulting in the eventual collapse of a fixed exchange rate. In second generation models, the crises results from a conflict between a fixed exchange rate regime and the desire to maintain a more expansionary monetary policy; investors bet that the authorities will abandon the peg rather than compromise, on perhaps employment, and this bet is self-fulfilling.

equilibrium exists in the foreign exchange market because of the contingent nature of the policy makers' and governments' objective function. To these models, maintenance of the fixed exchange rates depends on government' decision. The authorities might abandon a peg; if it were concerned that economic policies necessary to maintain the exchange rate might have adverse effect on other macroeconomic variables. In this context, these models stress the trade-offs between the benefits of a credible exchange rate peg and the costs in terms of higher interest rates, higher unemployment or lower growth of defending peg.[13]

As far as the crises occurred during the 90s are concerned, they are more suitable to the explanation of second-generation models than first-generation models. Especially, the recent Asian crisis seemed to settle the consensus toward the second –generation models as more representative of more recent crises.

The recent studies of Krugman (1999) and others in the aftermath of the structural financial crisis in Asia can be viewed as "third generation" of financial crises models. These new models consider some disputed issues such as (1) moral hazard and asymmetric information problem that lead to an under pricing of the risks associated with investing in emerging markets, (2) herding behaviour of bankers and portfolio managers and (3) international contagion effects appearing by some transmission channels such as trade and financial linkages between countries.[14]

The Mexican crisis of 1994, and the 1997 Asian crisis with its effect on Russia and Brazil, showed that the phenomenon of currency crises was getting more frequent, and required a deeper investigation. Taking this point into account, it is seen that the power of explanation of macro-based models are not sufficient to show the reasons of the crises. However, if microeconomic and institutional approaches are considered we will be able to put forward a new approach using firm level data to investigate corporate performance in the crises. The microeconomic approach provides new evidence that suggests that the causes of the Asian crises may lie in firm based decisions.[15] An alternative view is that short-term foreign capital inflows increase the stock market index that can be a strong indication of forthcoming currency crisis when foreign currency outflow creates currency crisis, leading to high foreign debt.[16]

The rest of the article is organised as follows: In section 2, we give an account of Turkish economy after 1980, in section 3, we discuss the 1994 crisis and in section 4, we have the anatomy of November 2000 and February 2001 crisis in Turkey.

---

[13] Kibritcioglu and et al., "A Leading Indicators Approach to the Predictability of Currency Crises: the Case of Turkey", pp.38-40.

[14] Kibritcioglu and et al., "A Leading Indicators Approach to the Predictability of Currency Crises: the Case of Turkey", pp.39-41.

[15] J. Furman and J. Stiglitz, *Economic Crises: Evidence and Insights from East Asia*, Brookings Papers on Economic Activity, 1998, p.25-36.

[16] S. Gazioglu "An Emerging Market, Volatility of Real Exchange Rate: The Turkish Case" *Middle East and North African Economies, the online journal of MEEA*, 2001, American Economic Association, AEA, Conference proceedings. And S. Gazioglu, "Capital Flows to an Emerging Market: Turkish Case study", *International Advances in Economic Research*, Vol. 9, No. 3, August, 2003, St. Louis, USA.

A Brief Account of Turkish Economy after 1980

Turkish economy has long been experiencing high inflation for nearly the last three decades despite of some fruitless disinflation programs. Among them the 24 January 1980 program, which, actually, was a medium-term "structural adjustment program" aimed at changing the development strategy of Turkey from "import substituting industrialization" to "export-led growth". Before 1980, Turkish economy had typical characteristics of textbook definition of "financially repressed economy" such as "negative real interest rates"; segmented capital markets; high tax burden on financial earnings; high liquidity and reserve requirement ratios. The banking system was inefficient and there were hardly a capital market and stock exchange, which forced firms to either use internal resources or bank credits to finance their investments. Fiscal deficits were mostly financed by the central bank through monetization.

Turkey confronted a severe foreign debt crisis in 1979 due to the fiscal policy effects of oil shock of 1974 and the destabilizing foreign borrowing strategy of the governments.[17] In 1979 Turkey signed a stand-by program with IMF and started negotiations with foreign banks in order to get a new schedule for the debt payments. In 1980, in line with the IMF program, an economic package that is clearly distinct from others that had been implemented until that time put into practice. In line with this program, Turkey started to liberalize its external accounts starting from its trade accounts. Besides this, removal of exchange rate controls, adoption of special policies with generous incentives to attract foreign direct investment, liberalization of market interest rates to encourage private savings, privatisation of state-owned entrepreneurs (SEEs), and shifting to income transfers through public spending (mostly in the form of interest payments) instead of price mechanisms via subsidized pricing of SEEs (which were used as one of the main policy instruments in the previous era to provide cheap industrial inputs for the private sector) were some of the components of the new economic program implemented under the guidance of IMF and World Bank. The program started with a huge devaluation (TLR/USD 47.1 to TLR/USD 70, which was about a 50% devaluation rate), increase in interest rates and export subsidies.[18]

A couple years after the liberalization of trade, quotas were substantially eliminated, the exchange rate was depreciated and foreign exchange regime was completely liberalized. At the beginning, the program seemed to succeed in stabilization: it reduced inflation rate from 107% in 1980 to 25% in 1982. Because of the positive real interest rates after financial liberalization, demand for broad money has increased and this interest rate policy is one important factor that helped inflation rate went down since the increase in money demand helped the government to get rid of monetary restraint.[19] However, this

---

[17] Major part of the foreign inflows went to convertible Turkish Lira deposits scheme and this scheme provided a public exchange rate guarantee to private borrowers regardless of Turkish inflation and devaluation. When foreign banks refused to rollover credits this game ended with empty reserves.

[18] İrfan Civcir, "An Econometric Approach to the Analysis of the Monetary Sector and Balance of Payments in Turkey", Ankara, *Turkey: Capital Market Board, 1996, pp.58-60.*

[19] Dani Rodrik, "Premature Liberalization, Incomplete Stabilization: The Ozal Decade in Turkey", *NBER*

success was not continuous, after 1982, inflation which had risen up to 20 percent levels started to increase again and in 1983 it reached 50-60 percent plateau. After this year, inflation stayed at a level around 60-70 percent during the 1980s. In the exchange rate side, Turkey faced a massive currency substitution pressure after liberalizing the foreign exchange market in 1984 by allowing foreign currency denominated bank accounts, and allowing commercial banks to engage in foreign currency transactions. In the credit market, via the measures such as changes liquidity and reserve requirement systems, Central Bank's control over banking system was simplified. Finally, most notable changes were the re-establishment of Istanbul Stock Exchange (ISE) in 1986, the establishment of interbank money market (1986), Open Market Operations within Central Bank (1987) and the bond market for Treasury bonds and so on. In 1986 interbank money market was established to support banks in their short-term liquidity requirements. At the same time, to regulate capital markets, "The Capital Market Board" was established and reopening of ISE was introduced. To encourage share holding, some tax incentives were initiated. In 1987, Open Market operations was started in order to give Central Bank more tools in conducting monetary policy. In 1989, the selective credit policy was abandoned. And 1990, Central Bank announced its first monetary program aiming at limiting public sector's borrowing opportunities from Central Bank and monetization of fiscal deficits.[20]

After the first turning point in the economy in 1980, starting in 1988 and by the end of 1989, the process of capital account liberalization was completed; capital flows were fully liberalized in the external accounts and as a result, in February 1990, Turkey applied to the IMF for the full convertibility of Turkish Lira. The 1989 benchmark was, indeed, the second turning point in economic policies of the post-1980 period in terms of both its distributional implications and macro-economic consequences. The fiscal and financial dimensions concerning the cause and effect relation between the 1989 shift towards populism and capital account liberalization contained the seeds of further crises in Turkish economy. The macro-economic consequences can be analysed in four directions: optimistic expectations on financial deepening within the domestic financial markets did not materialize. Capital account liberalization increasingly forged the economy to become dependent on the newly emerging financial cycles. Substantial leakages from net inflows, i.e. through capital outflows and reserve accumulation transmuted the conventional linkages between growth, current account balance and capital flows. And, finally, arbitrage-seeking ("hot money") inflows and outflows started to constitute a rising share within capital movements, and contributed to rising external and domestic instability.[21]

1994 Crisis in Turkey

In the beginning of 1994, the Turkish economy found itself in a very severe financial

---

Working Paper Series, N.3300, 1996, pp.7-9.

[20] Erinç Yeldan, "Financial Liberalisation and Fiscal Repression in Turkey: Policy Analysis in a CGE Model with Financial Markets", *Journal of Policy modelling*, Vol. 19, No.1, 1997, pp.85-90.

[21] K. Boratav and E. Yeldan, "Turkey, 1980-2000: Financial Liberalization, macroeconomic (In)-Stability, and Patterns of Distribution", 2001, *http://www.bilkent.edu.tr/~economics/*, pp.12-16.

crisis, which, in turn, hit the real economy. The Turkish Lira depreciated by almost 70 percent against the US dollar in the first quarter of 1994. The central bank heavily intervened in the foreign exchange market, and as a result, lost more than half of its international reserves. Overnight interest rates jumped to unexpected levels, such as 700 percent, from stable pre-crises, from a stable pre-crisis level around 70 percent. Economic growth declined by 6 percent. The natural questions that arise are: What are the causes of the 1994 crisis? What are the roles of fundamentals versus self-fulfilling expectations? Strictly speaking, the reasons of the crises were based on the two important turning points in Turkish economy (24 January 1980 decisions and the decisions in 1989).

In the first half of the 1990s, there were imbalances in the macro economic variables such as increasing and high public sector deficits, inadequate private savings to finance these deficits and as a result of these two deficits growing external deficits. After the financial liberalisation in 1989, Turkey attracted capital inflows due to high real interest rates. This led to an overvaluation of the Turkish Lira. The appreciation of the currency and also the tariff reductions in 1989 caused current account deficits. The pressures on the exchange rate and the interest rates, and the open position of the banking system increased the demand for dollars.[22]

Towards the end of 1993, Turkish government was trying to reduce the very high level of domestic public debt stock by cutting interest rates on the Treasury bills. The Treasury started to rely on the central bank's resources instead of domestic borrowing.[23] At the same time, public debt stock and deficits as a percentage of GDP reached record high levels and the burden of interest payments increased. Cancellation of several Treasury auctions and limited domestic borrowing through treasury auctions as a result of this policy, led to an excess liquidity in the market and to pressure on the exchange rates in the last months of 1993, which continued in early 1994.[24] This excess liquidity caused a run on foreign currency and loss of international reserves. The Central Bank intervened in the foreign exchange market to defend the exchange rate. The decrease in the international reserves started in November 1993 and continued until April 1994.

The 1994 crisis was not an unexpected event because many economic indicators were giving warning signals. The fundamental fiscal variables were deteriorated, public sector deficit was financed by domestic credit expansion and the demand for foreign currency was increased. Besides these developments, there was a great loss of international reserves. With these characteristics, it can be said that the Turkish currency crisis was an example of first-generation models. Nevertheless, the 1994 crisis had some features of the second-generation models. Due to the forthcoming local elections, the government was reluctant to increase the interest rates to avoid the devaluation of the TL. In that respect, the 1994 currency crisis of Turkey might be explained by the second-generation models because of the government's objective function.[25]

---

[22] Kibritcioglu and et al., "A Leading Indicators Approach to the Predictability of Currency Crises: the Case of Turkey", pp.39-45.
[23] O. Celasun, "The 1994 Currency Crisis in Turkey", *World Bank Working Paper*, No:1913, 1998, pp.10-17.
[24] F. Ozatay, "The Lessons from the 1994 Crisis in Turkey: Public Debt (Mis) Management and Confidence Crisis", *Yapi Kredi Economic Review*, 1996, 7/1, pp.21-25.
[25] Kibritcioglu and et al., "A Leading Indicators Approach to the Predictability of Currency Crises: the

The Anatomy of November 2000 and February 2001 Crises[26]

The timing and the process of liberalization and opening up of foreign trade and capital markets started after Turkey fell into foreign debt payment problems in the late 1970s. The stabilization program began to be implemented under the International Monetary Fund conditionality. Foreign trade was liberalized basically in the early 1980s, and further in the process of joining the customs union with the European Union in 1996. Financial deregulation began in 1981 when controls on interest rates were removed. In 1984 foreign exchange trade was liberalized. In 1986 Istanbul Stock Exchange was reopened. In 1987 the central bank began open market operations. The benchmark date for financial liberalisation is 1989 when controls over capital movements were removed and Turkish currency became convertible. After this date Turkey became a financially open economy.

Below is the analysis of the extension of foreign capital flows to Turkey. Besides this we will concentrate on the reasons, results and the process of the 2000 and the 2001 crises by considering capital flows.

The 1990s witnessed a surge in capital flows to the developing countries. As measured by the surplus on the capital account, the developing countries of Latin America and Asia alone have received a sum of $670 billion of foreign capital from 1990 to 1994. Net flows decreased significantly in 1995 in the aftermath of the Mexican crisis. Furthermore, a structural shift was observed in the composition of the private flows, with portfolio and other short-term capital flows gaining importance. Parallel to these developments, the crises confronted in the 90s revealed that the expected beneficial effects of capital inflows have been overshadowed by the adverse effects of excessive stock market volatility and the persistence of exchange risk against unforeseen fluctuations in the exchange rates. What is more, in such a world of volatile exchange rates, the traditional dictum regarding the global equalization of interest rates failed to take place. In such a world, it is clearly observed that the free capital movements do not suffice to equalize real interest rates that are denominated in different currencies.[27]

It is also to be noted that while the post-financial liberalisation are characterized by very large gross capital flows, they have generated rather small net transfers. Net capital flows from the developed to the developing economies had been only on the order of $150 billions per annum during the 90s. This figure remains very low comparing to daily volume of speculative foreign exchange transactions, which are nearly $1.5 trillions. It can be said that the gross volume of international capital flows across the national boundaries is far in excess of the financing needs of commodity trade flows or investments on physical capital, and is mostly driven by speculative considerations of risk hedging and currency speculation. Thus, under these features of the post-financial liberalisation episodes, large capital inflows as witnessed in recent years have posed serious dilemmas and created significant policy challenges. Indeed, the recent history of

---

Case of Turkey", pp.39-45.
[26] From now on, the graphs mentioned in the paper can be seen in the appendix.
[27] E. Balkan, and et. al., "Patterns of Financial Capital Flows and Accumulation in the Post-1990 Turkish Economy", *www.networkideas.org*, 2002, pp.11-14.

the financial crises in the "successful emerging markets" has clearly disclosed the undesirable macroeconomic effects of the large, uncontrolled capital inflows, such as persistence of high real interest rates, inflationary pressures, limitation of the power of the central banks to contain the pressures of monetary expansion and of the threat of currency substitution, real exchange rate appreciation, and widening current account deficits. Nevertheless, the type of capital inflows is important to determine severity of the results. While short-term capital flows (hot money) are more volatile than long-term capital flows due to their high sensitivity to macroeconomic disturbances, short-term capital flows result in severer shocks and necessitate deeper adjustments.[28]

Likewise the developments mentioned above, after a decade of volatile and erratic growth, persistent high rates of inflation, a deteriorated fiscal performance and rapidly increasing debt burden, Turkey initiated an extensive stabilization program to restore its macroeconomic balances in December 1999.

At the end of 1999, the state of the Turkish economy looked rather miserable. That year growth, or rather economic contraction, had been -6.1%, annual wholesale price inflation had reached 70%, the budget deficit had risen to unsustainable levels, whilst average weighted cost of borrowing to the Treasury was 106% per annum. An economic structure which had endured double digit inflation, interrupted by short periods of triple digit inflation, for the past thirty years appeared to be fast reaching an unsustainable point. The next step looked likely to be a transition into a hyperinflationary period.[29]

Turkey welcomed the year 2000 with the introduction of a new economic stabilization program supported by the IMF. The program had three basements:
(1) fiscal discipline encompassing both the central government budget and the rest of the public sector,
(2) determination of exchange rates under a pre-announced crawling peg arrangement,
(3) implementation of structural reforms and, especially, an acceleration in privatisation. The fundamental aims of this framework were the reduction of inflation and attainment of sustainable economic growth. The budgetary leg of the program principally involved an increase in tax revenues to achieve a higher primary surplus with the goal of reducing Treasury's domestic debt burden, and thus interest rates. This approach would be supported through the partial substitution of external debt for domestic debt, and in this manner, the financing gap would be plugged by both higher tax revenues and additional external borrowing.[30]

The highlight of monetary policy was the ceiling of the net domestic assets of the Central Bank. This was set at -1,200 trillion TL (roughly US$ 2 billion) and was a performance criterion under the IMF stand-by arrangement. The Central Bank would create Turkish Liras, and thus provide additional liquidity only via foreign exchange

---

[28] E. Balkan, and et. al., "Patterns of Financial Capital Flows and Accumulation in the Post-1990 Turkish Economy", pp.15-20.
[29] E. Yeldan,, "Behind the 2000/2001 Turkish Crisis: Stability, Credibility, and Governance, for Whom", *http://www.bilkent.edu.tr/~economics/*, 2002, pp.3-6.
[30] E. Yeldan,, "On the IMF-Directed Disinflation Program in Turkey: A Program For Stabilization and Austerity or A Recipe for Impoverishment and Financial Chaos?", *http://www.bilkent.edu.tr/~economics/*, 2001, pp.12-18.

inflows. In other words, the main monetary policy tool was the adoption of the exchange rate as a nominal anchor. This anchor arrangement is generally accepted to be a delicate and unsustainable policy. The Turkish authorities, in collaboration with the IMF, had designed the program with the foreknowledge of the dangers involved, and had thus planned at the onset to impose a widening band-crawling band -exchange rate regime following a year and a half of a crawling peg policy. The substitution of greater taxation, in conjunction with fresh external loans, in place of domestic borrowing would lower Treasury's domestic borrowing requirement, and thus permit greater funds to be channelled to other agents in the economy, whilst foreign exchange inflows would preclude a liquidity squeeze in the markets.[31]

The positive market sentiment greeting the announcement of the new economic program led to a reduction in the cost of borrowing to the Treasury, from an average of 106% per annum at the end of 1999 to 37% per annum by January 2000. Average overnight interest rates in the interbank market fell from 66.6% in December 1999 to 34.1% in January. The dramatic decline in interest rates, irrespective of the causes, heralded a dangerous development in the anti-inflation struggle. An old dilemma had resurfaced. A decline in interest rates led to a lower debt service burden, but the Central Bank's anti-inflation policy would be damaged. The Central Bank should not have permitted this under normal circumstances. The Central Bank simply followed this trend. The transition from an annual average yield of 106% to 36.4% in the very first month of the program brought to fore important problems in the fight against inflation. Pent-up consumption demand finally spilled into the economy with alacrity. Savings were channelled towards consumption with the support of low interest rates offered to retail customers by banks.[32] The result was a slower than expected convergence of inflation to targeted levels because of vigorous aggregate demand.[33]

The Seeds of the Crises

The first seeds of the crises were the rising trade and current account deficits due to the use of the exchange rate as a nominal anchor. The external imbalance had risen beyond expectations, and the authorities' response had been too little too late.

Banks moved to close their open foreign exchange positions towards the end of October for regulatory and balance sheet purposes. This move created a liquidity squeeze and caused interest rates to rise somewhat. This development was expected and widely acknowledged because banks engaged in this ritual every year.

The general state of the Turkish economy at the end of October was as follows:[34]

---

[31] E. Yeldan, "On the IMF-Directed Disinflation Program in Turkey: A Program for Stabilization and Austerity or A Recipe For Impoverishment and Financial Chaos?", pp.18-21.

[32] The substitution of savings to consumption refers to the flow of savings. In other words, the reference is to the proportion of savings from the income flow, which is channeled towards consumption as a result of lower interest rates.

[33] Y. Akyuz, and K. Boratav, "The Making of the Turkish Financial Crisis", http://*www.bilkent.edu.tr/~economics/*, 2001, pp.28-34.

[34] Y. Akyuz, and K. Boratav, "The Making of the Turkish Financial Crisis", pp.30-35 and E. Voyvoda and E. Yeldan, "Managing Turkish Debt: An OLG Investigation of the IMF's Fiscal Programming Model for Turkey", http://*www.bilkent.edu.tr/~economics/*, 2003, pp.12-18.

- Annual economic growth was along at 6.5-7%. In this manner the -6.1% growth rate of 1999, or more correctly the economic contraction of 1999, was cured through renewed positive growth.
- National income growth, and therefore aggregate demand growth, focused on both domestic goods and services and imports.
- Annual inflation did fall from 69% to sub-40% despite vigorous aggregate demand. The reason for the slowness in the reduction of inflation was vigorous aggregate demand, fuelled by retail loans from banks. The shortfall of actual inflation from targeted inflation was thus the result of a faster than expected decline in interest rates, share of consumption rising at the cost of reduced savings in income flows, and, consequently, higher aggregate demand growth as mentioned previously.
- On the budgetary side, the primary surplus was heading towards an all time record high. The inflationary pressure of budget deficits was thus slowly disappearing.
- In spite of delays in structural reforms, they aimed at the agricultural sector had moved ahead with small, but significant steps. Restructuring of the banking sector was also on track.
- Privatisation revenues in 2000 had exceeded the sum of privatisation revenues for the past fifteen years in spite of various delays.
- The biggest problem had emerged to be a current account deficit far in excess of initial expectations, heading to the US$ 8-10 billion range. Nevertheless, this deficit was not believed to be an imminent threat.
- Banks were thus slowly closing their open foreign exchange positions, whilst foreigners were rushing to balance their accounts by year-end; all creating greater foreign exchange demand, and thus putting pressure on Turkish Lira interest rates.
- New regulations aimed at the banking sector suddenly picked up pace in the same period. This new development pushed banks to close their foreign exchange positions in a speedy and abrupt manner. Banks raised their liquid positions in order to be able to purchase foreign exchange.
- Higher liquidity demand naturally led interest rates to rise much faster than before.

The Main Economic Developments During the Crises

Turkey experienced two severe crises in November 2000 and in February 2001 just eleven months after launching the disinflation program. More than $6 billion dollars of short-term capital fled to the country, creating a severe liquidity shortage in the domestic commodity and asset markets. After the first crisis, the public disclosure of a political dispute between the prime president and the president of the Republic on February 19, 2001 badly hit the uneasy markets. The Central Bank was forced to sell a great part of its foreign reserves in an attempt to support the TL as the short-term interest rates (overnight) rocketed to above 5.000 percent. In what follows, the government could not endure the pressures of the markets any further, and declared the surrender of the pegged exchange rate system (crawling peg) on February 22, thereby letting the exchange rates to free float.[35] Following the collapse of the exchange rate based disinflation program, the newly appointed minister, Kemal Dervis (Former Vice President of the World Bank), submitted a new letter of intend to the IMF. The new economic program aimed at minimizing the short-term adverse macroeconomic aspects of these crises whilst making structural adjustments for the resumption of disinflation and growth. The Turkish government adopted a 3-step strategy in order to achieve its targets:

(1) structural policies to correct the distortions in the banking sector and to improve the sector's role in the process of economic restructuring

(2) fiscal and monetary policies to restore financial stability and facilitate disinflation and

(3) a strengthened social dialogue to promote wage moderation and social security.

At the beginning of 2000, the first program (disinflation) was launched and observed to be materialized especially in the second half of its implementation. Despite the fact that the annual rate of change in the price level has exceeded the program's end-of-year targets by a significant margin, it, nevertheless, displayed a break in its 30-year trend towards a lower plateau. The monthly rate of change of both the CPI and WPI was nearly a desired level. At the end of the year, the annualised rate of inflation reached to 33% in WPI and 39% in CPI. Concerning the exchange rates, these inflation rates meant an appreciation of 10.8 % and 15.8 % against the WPI and CPI, respectively.[36]

At the end of the 1999, Turkish economy experienced another contraction just 5 years after the 1994 crisis. GNP contracted by 6.1%, in 1999 and 9.4% in 2001. The financial crises of November 2000 and February 2001 had a severe impact on the real economy. Thus, Turkish economy had big losses in its production power during the crises. As it can be seen in Graphs-1 and Graphs-2, after the crises, the number of newly established firms drops and the number of liquidated firms increases. These developments led to a loss of confidence. As it can be seen Graph-3, despite the fact that the real sector confidence index fluctuated during the 90s, one can say that the worst periods of it are seen just after the crises.

Graph-4 and Graph-5 provide information on how consolidated budget deficits were financed in the post Cold War era. With cutting the Central Bank resources, the Central Bank lending was nil since 1997. Hence, the budget deficits were not financed by the Central Bank resources in the period preceding the crisis. That is, the central element of the first generation models was not on the stage. Instead of using the Central Bank resources, the governments tend to use the commercial bank resources by selling treasury bonds. These developments, of course, caused the fragility of the banking sector.[37]

Given the fragility of the banking sector, this condition made life very difficult for those banks that had desperately chosen to borrow in short-term maturity and lend to the

[35] E. Yeldan, "On the IMF-Directed Disinflation Program in Turkey: A Program for Stabilization and Austerity or A Recipe For Impoverishment and Financial Chaos?", pp.21-30.
[36] Ibid., pp.18-25.
[37] F. Ozatay and G. Sak, "The 2000-2001 Financial Crises in Turkey", *Brookings Trade Forum 2002: Currency Crises*, May, 2002, Washington, pp.10-12.

government in relatively longer terms along with state banks suffering from duty losses. This relation constantly increased the interest payments of the Treasury to the commercial banks in particular after 1995 (see Graph-6). Moreover, this structure of the economy led to November crisis in 2000. The immediate origin of the November financial turmoil in Turkey was the cutting of credit lines[38] by other banks to Demirbank (ninth largest bank at the time in terms of asset size). There were persistent rumours that this was a concerted effort. By cutting credit lines to this institution, the other banks would have effectively forced it to raise funds by selling a portion of its securities holdings, which the others could then buy at bargain prices. Creditor institutions defended themselves by pointing to the large short-term funding structure of Demirbank. It had a serious maturity mismatch, depending too heavily on overnight repo financing, while its assets were dominantly government bonds bought at relatively high prices (low yields). Demirbank's illiquid state caused upward pressure on interest rates. Foreign banks, which had been lending on the overnight market, withdrew funds as well after sensing these problems, causing further upward pressure on interest rates. Eventually, what had started as a lack of confidence amongst the banks grew into a lack of confidence in the whole economic program.[39]

During the November crisis, Central Bank allowed foreigners to buy foreign exchange by removing its net domestic asset (NDA) ceiling and providing liquidity to the markets. The idea was that if all foreign exchange demand by non-residents were satisfied, then demand for foreign exchange should cease.[40] Central Bank reimposed a new NDA ceiling on December 1st to avoid a complete meltdown in international reserves. Financial turmoil did not abate. Only an emergency loan from the IMF on December 6th, an informal blanket guarantee on interbank lending and guarantee to all creditors (including to international parties), and takeover of Demirbank by the government finally halted the crisis on December 6.th

According to calculations in Akyuz and Boratav (2001) and Boratav and Yeldan (2001), the economy enjoyed a positive net capital flow of $15.2 billion during the first 10 months of 2000 on account of a large net inflow by non-residents which financed not only mounting current account deficits, but net outflows by residents and increases in reserves. In his paper, Yeldan (2002) argues that the amount of $9.8 billions of the net capital flows was used in financing of the current account deficits of 2000. It is understood that the net inflows of non-residents were instrumental in covering the net capital flight of the residents, which reached to a cumulative net sum of $5.2 billions over the same period. Additionally, the banking sector had succeeded in increasing the net inflows of foreign credit by $4.7 billions to reach a total of $11.1 billions. During this process total short-term debt stock of the banking sector had increased to $16.9 billions from its level of $13.2 billions. Thus, during the period, much of this accumulated short-

---

[38] Central Bank governor noted that banks" free deposits at CB had risen on November 22nd to TL 1.1 quadrillion despite overnight interbank rates of up to 250% simple.

[39] F. Ozatay and G. Sak. "The 2000-2001 Financial Crises in Turkey", pp.15-18.

[40] A distinction between residents and non-residents was of little use ultimately because lack of confidence in the local currency and the financial system is exacerbated by foreign capital flight. Rumours were indeed rife that deposits could be frozen, for instance. Restoration of confidence in the economy thus requires measures, which halt capital flight whatever, its origin.

term debt had financed residents' capital flight.[41]

The entice of the uncontrolled flows of speculative gains clearly unleashed all its might throughout 2000, during when the currency risk was eliminated and the whole liquidity generation mechanism was based on the short term, hot money inflows. Yet, with the loss of markets' trust on the programme, the foreigners would start to pull their financial capital out of Turkey. In the last week of November 2000 alone, Turkish financial markets had lost $5.3 billions via non-residents' short-term speculative operations. In fact, with this rapid change of direction, net flows of non-residents' foreign capital would turn to $8.7 billions after November. This means that following November 2000, Turkish asset markets' loss of foreign exchange reached $23.9 billions (15.2 + 8.7) during the course of the crisis. Besides this, over %90 of net inflows by non-residents was debt creating.[42]

It is evident that, faced with these numbers, not only a financially shallow emerging market economy such as Turkey, but also no economy in the world could endure the disruptive results of such financial shocks. Yet, the 2000 disinflation programme has completely ignored the fragile conditions of the Turkish financial markets, and exclusively disabled both the monetary (the Central Bank) and the fiscal (the Treasury) authorities from utilization of their traditional tools of austerity by way of rendering them powerless against the speculative forces of the markets, all in the name of good governance. In addition, the crisis was in fact the end result of the culminating pressures of this fragile environment.

It is worth at this juncture to note that reversals of capital flows are often associated with deterioration of the macroeconomic fundamentals in the recipient country. However, as the Turkish episode documents, such deterioration often results from the effects of capital inflows themselves as well as from external developments, rather than from shifts in domestic macroeconomic policies. On the other side, if we look at the Graph-7, we can see the bubble in Istanbul Stock Exchange just before the November crises. It can be seen as the impacts of capital flows from the non-residents. After liberalizing its capital account in 1989, Turkey started to attract capital flows. Net portfolio investments fluctuated abruptly through the 1990s between $3.9 billion (1993) and $ -6.7 billions (1998) and $ -4.5 billions (2001). Such inflows enabled, on the one hand, financing of the accelerated public expenditures, and also provided temporary relief of the increased pressures of aggregate demand on the domestic markets through cheapening costs of imports. By contrast long-term foreign direct investment performance was meagre, never crossing the $1 billion, save for the exceptional period of 2001 (see Graph-8). It is interesting to note that net flows of securities by residents yield a negative figure almost all over the 1990s, with the exception of 1994 (see Graph-9). On the liability side, net flows of security purchases of non-residents in Turkey yield positive-yet modest-

---

[41] The data relating to capital movements and the IMF"s facilities can be seen in the Graphs-7, 8, 9 and 10. As can be seen in the graphs, there are huge volatilities comparing the period preceding the crises and the post crises term, in particular, during the crises, the economy uses the fund"s resources instead of capital inflows.
[42] E. Yeldan,, "Behind the 2000/2001 Turkish Crisis: Stability, Credibility, and Governance, for Whom", pp.17-20.

magnitudes until 1997. During 1997 and end of 1999 the portfolio Investment Liabilities turns severely negative (see Graph-10). We also observe an increase in the usage of Fund Credits and Loans during 1999, an increase in 2001 followed by a fall in 2002 (Graph 11). Hence, summing over 1992 to end of 2001 one can find that cumulative net flows of securities by residents and non-residents combined reach to $-15.9 billons. The extension of the net transfer of liquid funds from Turkey to global financial centres has indeed been substantial.[43]

As for short-term foreign credits received by the banking sector, it can be noted that the particular importance of gross flows, rather than the net acquisitions. Net flows are dwarfed by the massive turnover of banking credits in the short-term. Gross inflows of foreign credits obtained by banks reached to $122 billions in 1993 and to $209 billion in 2000. Both of these years were followed by the severe crisis episodes of 1994 and February 2001.[44]

As a result of capital flows, especially short-term (hot money), Turkish Lira has been observed to be mostly on an appreciation trend since 1989. Looking at the Graph-12, it can be said that TL[45], especially the second half of the 1990s, is becoming overvalued. Admittedly, this is a result of "hot-money policies". Increases in consumption and investment are associated with appreciation of the real exchange rates. If the capital flows mostly leak to financing of consumption rather than investment expenditures, it makes real exchange rate appreciation more likely. On the other hand, excessive increase of aggregate demand generates inflationary pressures with real exchange rate appreciation and a widening current account deficit. Nevertheless, the resulting effects on inflationary pressures and exchange rates will be largely determined with the exchange rate regime and amount of the reserve accumulation. It is interesting to mention that the Central Bank's gross foreign exchange reserves have increased constantly reaching to its high levels just before the crises. As can be followed from the Graph-13, after November and February crises, Central Bank started to lose a substantial amount of its reserves.[46]

Real interest rate is another factor to attract capital flows. Especially, high short-term interest rates prepare an attractive environment for speculative arbitrage seeking short-term capital flows. Regardless of the initial level of interest rates and exchange rates, capital inflows to the developing countries apt to create an arbitrage margin by increasing domestic interest rates and appreciating real exchange rates later. In the post Cold War era, current account deficit has been mostly negative; however, its size is rather modest as a ratio to GNP. Except for the pre-crises years of 1993 and 2000, the size of the current account deficits has been less than 1.5% of the GNP. In the pre-crises periods, huge capital inflows of these periods were separated on current account accumulation took place to keep the real exchange rate constant that was a post-crisis policy. Yet, the high sensitivity of the financial investors to the deficit is clearly visible in that both surges of

[43] E. Balkan, and et. al., "Patterns of Financial Capital Flows and Accumulation in the Post-1990 Turkish Economy", pp.20-25.
[44] E. Balkan, and et. al., "Patterns of Financial Capital Flows and Accumulation in the Post-1990 Turkish Economy", pp.25-27.
[45] According to CPI based real effective exchange rate index, (1995=100).
[46] E. Balkan, and et. al., "Patterns of Financial Capital Flows and Accumulation in the Post-1990 Turkish Economy", pp.27-32.

the current account deficits in 1993 (3.6%) and in 2000 (4.8%) were associated with the sudden reversals of the hot money flows and concomitant financial crises of 1994 and 2001.[47]

Another indicator of the crises was high domestic debt and interest payments in the consolidated budget. As it can be seen in the Graph-14 and the Graph-15, total public borrowing requirement (PSBR) and PSBR / GNP ratio was very important indicators in terms of the crises. Although the targeted values of the 2000 and 2001 public expenditure programme were achieved, burden of interest payments on the domestic financial markets continued to increase. Interest expenditures as a ratio of tax revenue increased to 77.1% in 2000, and rose to 103.3% in 2001. It can be seen from the Graphs-16, 17 and 18 that, since 1995 Turkish Economy has been in a big debt trap. In the literature, this borrowing is called as "ponzi-finance". Besides this, total foreign debt of Turkey has increased to roughly $130 billions by the end of 2002, especially; since IMF came to Turkey to implement the programme in 1998 the total outstanding debt has increased constantly (see Graph-16). It is observed that Turkey's short-term liabilities of foreign debt have reduced over the course of the same period: the stock of short-term foreign debt which stood at $22.9 billions at the end of 1999, and increased to as much as $28.3 billions at the end of 2000, was reduced to $15.2 billions in 2002.[48]

As far as the February crisis is concerned, the excess liquidity needs of public sector banks played a very important role. This diagnosis confuses cause and effect, however. We believe that the origin of the February financial turmoil was the desire by local private sector banks to close their foreign currency open positions in anticipation of a crisis (devaluation) (see Graphs-17, 18).[49] The local banks had lost trust/confidence in the economic program especially after the November crisis, and believed (despite additional IMF loans amounting to US$ 7.5 billions in November 2000, bringing the total IMF package to US$ 10.4 billions) that they needed to close their open positions gradually, but surely. The local banks precipitated the February crisis themselves by rushing to buy foreign exchange from Central bank.

Turkish authorities finally relented on the maintenance of the crawling peg regime, and permitted the Lira to float,[50] on the morning of February 22nd. IMF immediately voiced its continued support of Turkey's anti-inflation drive despite the setback.[51]

Conclusion

Since the 90's, financial crises have erupted in half a dozen developing and emerging market countries in Asia, Latin America and Russia as well as in Turkey. The costs for the countries affected have been heavy, with the crises leading to bank failures, corporate

---

[47] E. Balkan, and et. al., "Patterns of Financial Capital Flows and Accumulation in the Post-1990 Turkish Economy", pp.30-35.

[48] E. Yeldan., "Behind the 2000/2001 Turkish Crisis: Stability, Credibility, and Governance, for Whom", pp.22-29.

[49] As can be followed from Graph-13, foreign exchange transactions reach at its highest peak just before the February crises, of course, the reason why the transactions surge is the November crisis. Actually, it can be said that the November crisis triggered the following February crisis.

[50] Defending a new peg at a lower parity could have been difficult anyway, hence the decision to float the currency rather than devaluing.

[51] E. Yeldan, "Behind the 2000/2001 Turkish Crisis: Stability, Credibility, and Governance, for Whom", pp.25-29 and F. Ozatay and G. Sak, "The 2000-2001 Financial Crises in Turkey", pp.27-36.

bankruptcies, job losses, increased fiscal burdens, depletion of foreign exchange reserves, depressed economy activity, and even, in a few cases, political and social turbulence.

Initial research on the causes of the crises highlighted weakness in the afflicted countries' economic fundamentals, excessive short-term foreign borrowing by governments and private sector entities, and volatile short-term capital flows. Recent studies, however, increasingly point to the important role of weakness in national financial systems in triggering or exacerbating crises. For this reason, the international community has been stepping up its assistance in strengthening banks and other financial institutions.

After liberalizing its capital account in 1989, Turkey started to attract capital flows. This decision led to the Turkish economy three big financial crises in 1994, November 2000 and February 2001. Irregularities and the loop-holes in the legal system relating to Banking and financial sector in Turkey caused the hot money to take advantage and lead to the financial crisis. The choice was either to increase the borrowing from the IMF or adopt limited restrictions on the hot capital outflows, following Malaysian example. Application of Tobin Tax is also possibility to present such crisis.

APPENDIX
GRAPH-1

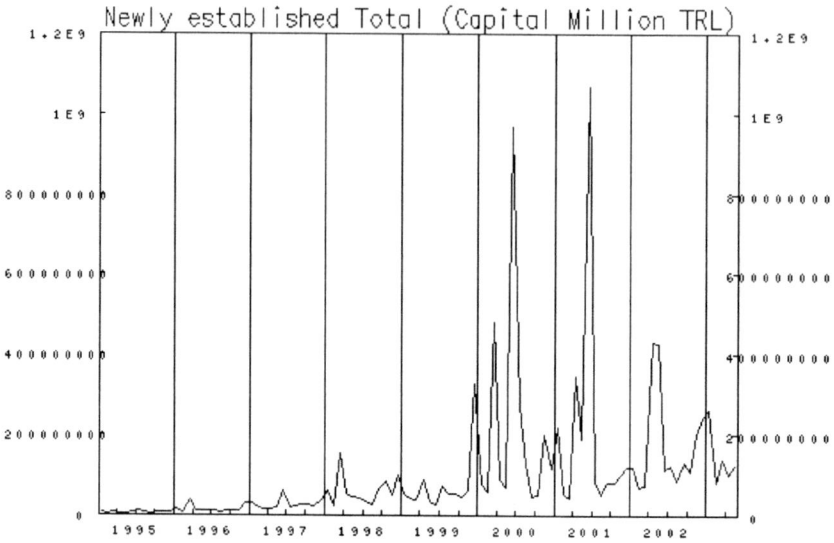

Newly established firms

GRAPH-2

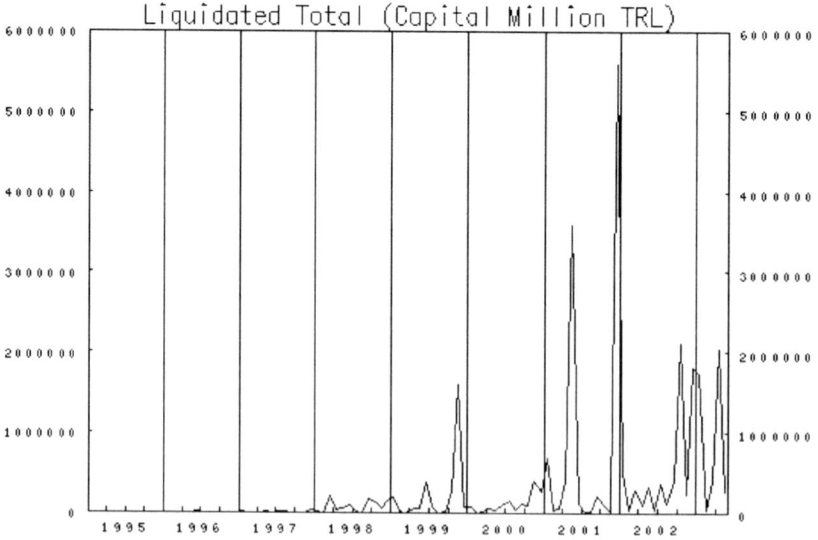

* Liquidated firms

GRAPH-3

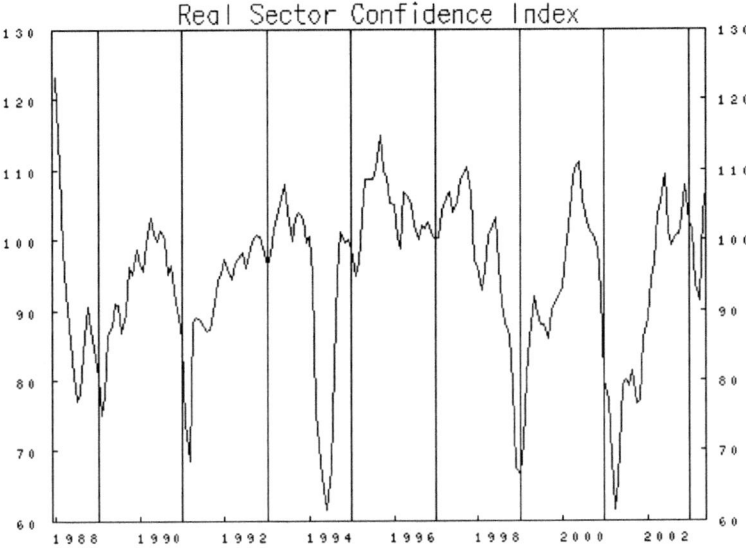

* *(1987=100)*

GRAPH-4

* *Billions TL, Central Bank to Central Government*

GRAPH-5

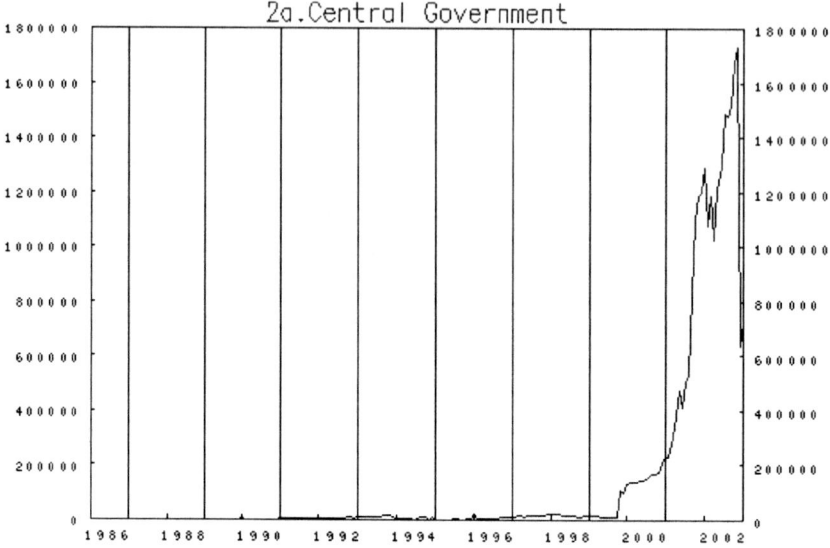

* *Billions TL, Commercial banks credit to Central Government*

GRAPH-6

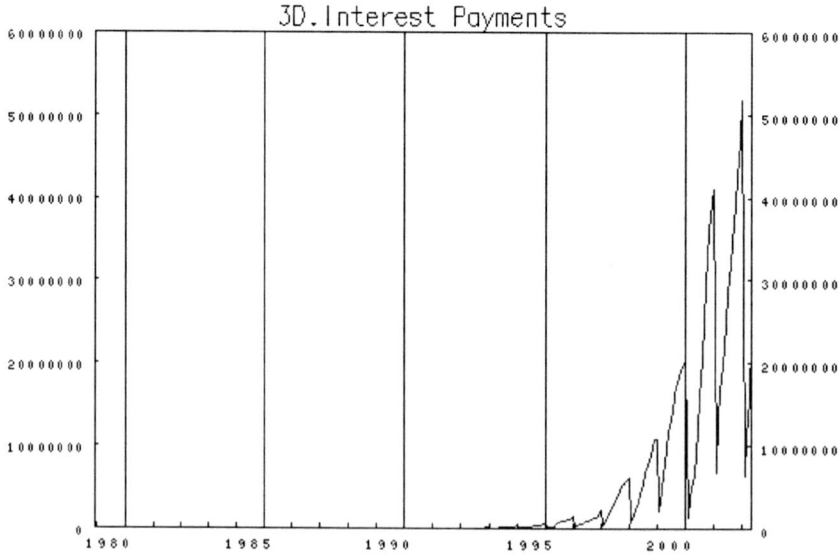

* *Billions TL, Consolidated Budget (Treasury)*

GRAPH-7

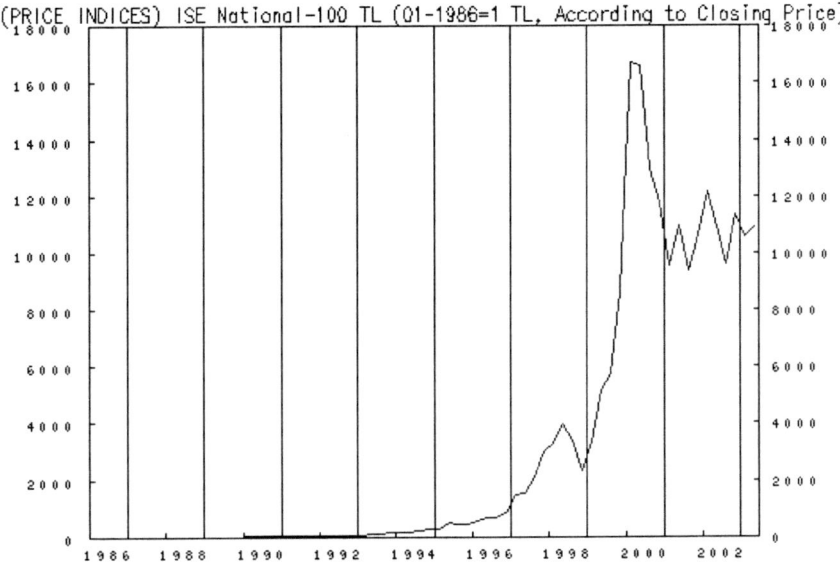

GRAPH-8

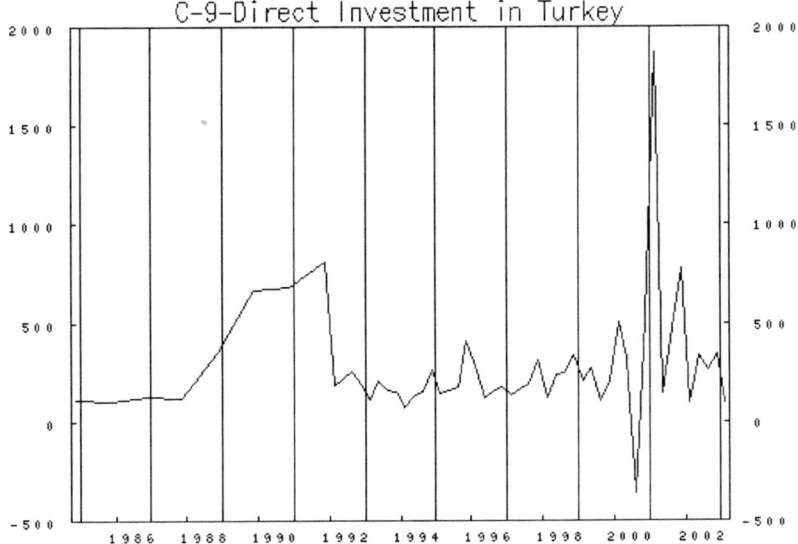

*Million dollars

GRAPH-9

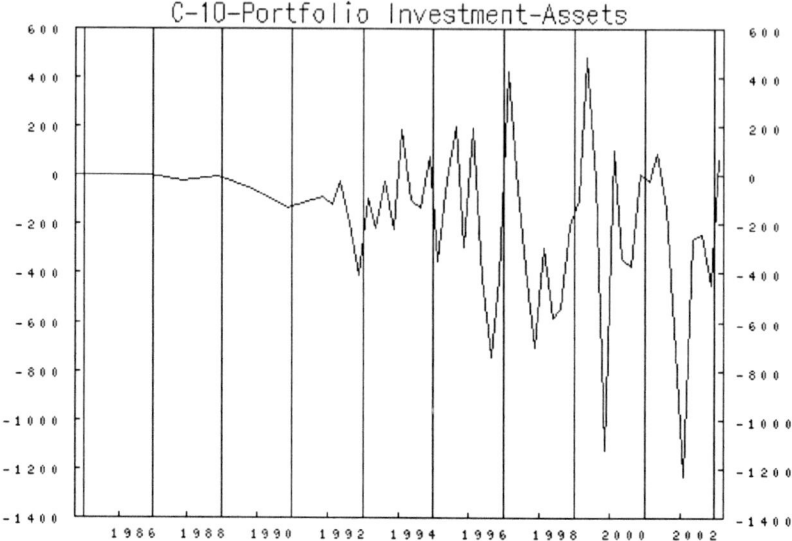

*Million dollars

GRAPH-10

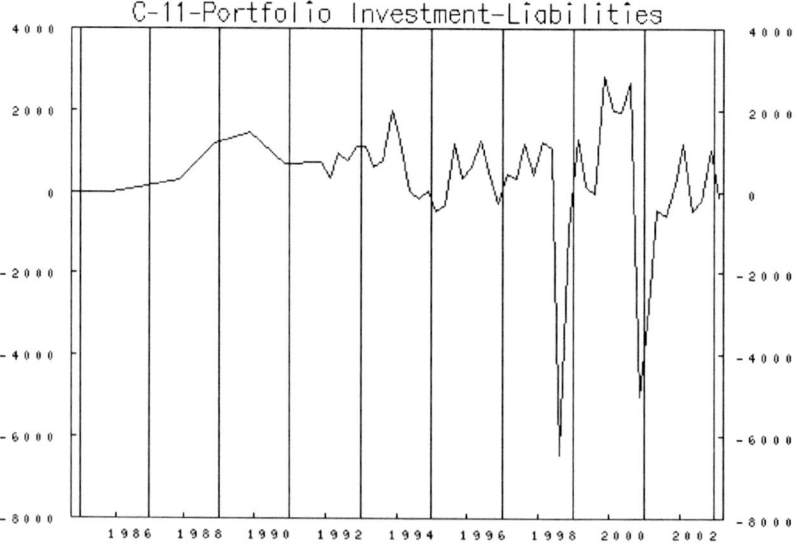

*Million dollars

GRAPH-11

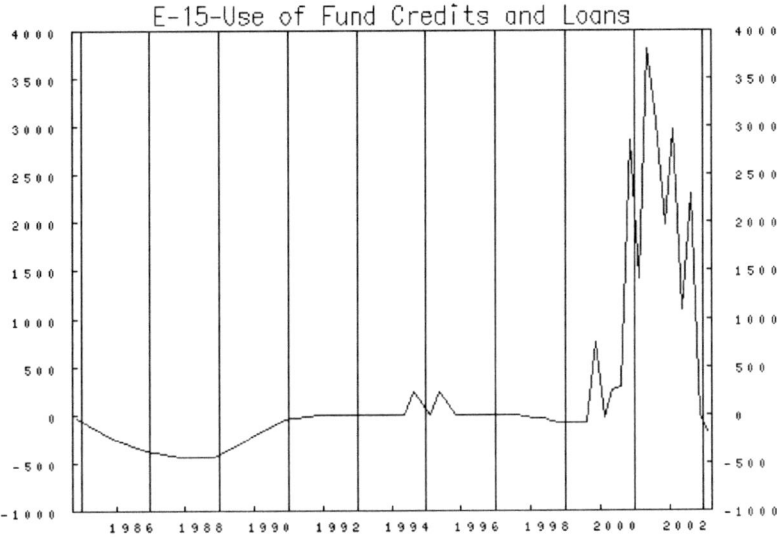

*Million dollars
* Istanbul Stock Exchange (ISE) Daily Trading Volume (Business)

GRAPH-12

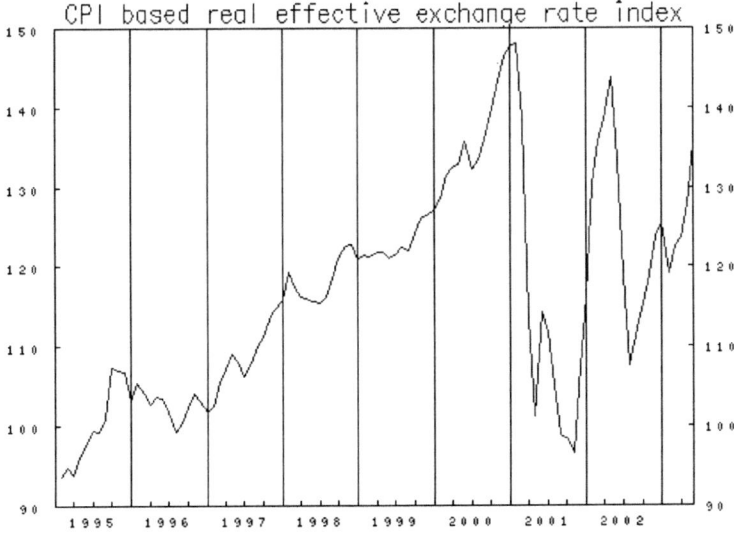

* (1995=100)

GRAPH-13

*Million dollars

GRAPH-14

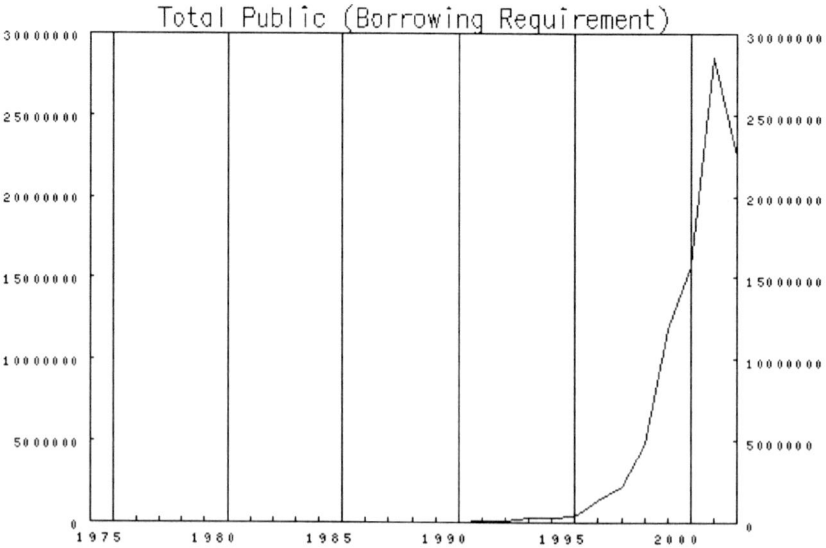

* Billions TL (Public Sector Borrowing Requirement (Annual)

GRAPH-15

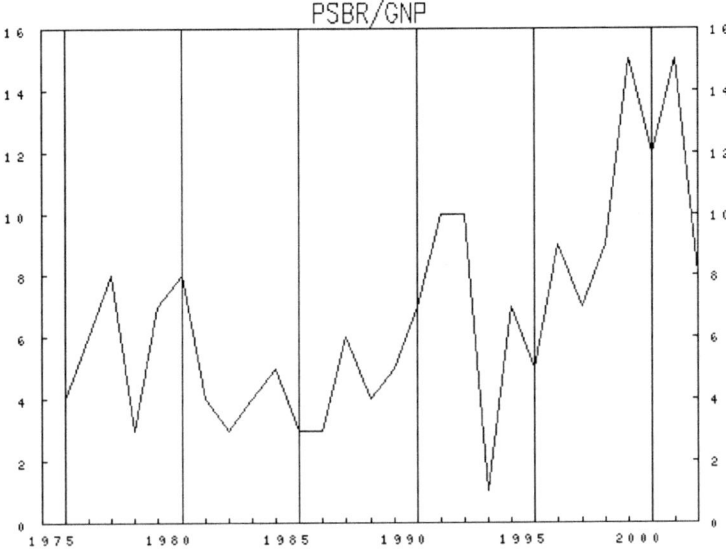

*

%PSBR/GNP

GRAPH-16

Million dollars Outstanding External Debt (New Desc.) (Treasury)

GRAPH-17

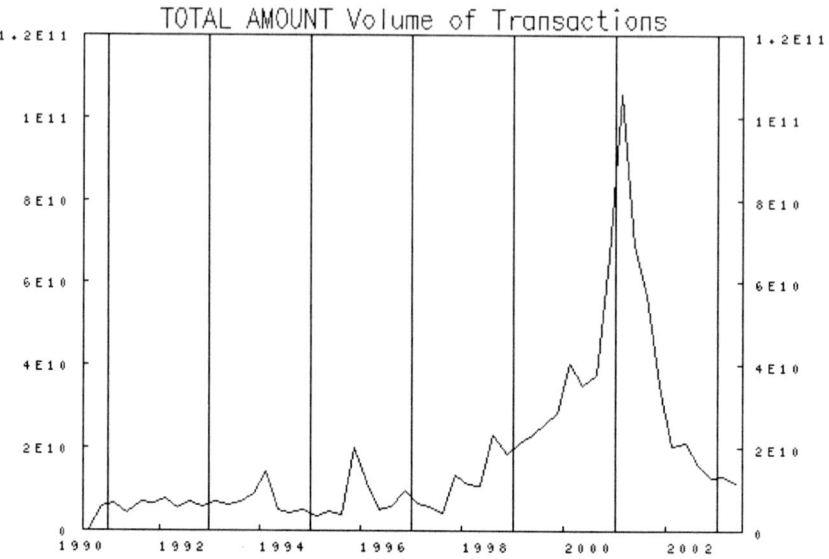

* Foreign Exchange and Banknotes Transactions (Business, US $)

GRAPH-18

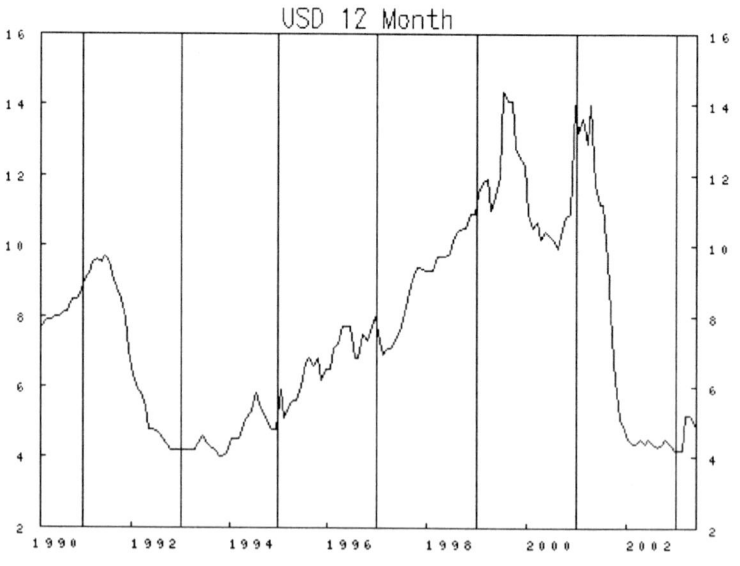

* (Interest Rates on FX Deposits-Weighted (Monthly)

4 Turkey and the World in the 21st Century

Faruk Sönmezoğlu

The Basic Characteristics of International Politics in the 21st Century

The Heritage of the Past

The 21st century's world has been shaped (and continues to be shaped) by various developments that took place at the end of the previous century. Two of these developments may deserve more attention: the demise of the bipolar international system, and the intensification of discussions on the role of nation-states in international politics.

The Demise of the Bipolar International System

The disintegration of the Warsaw Pact and the Soviet Union, and the simultaneous disappearance of the Soviet-type administrative model in Eastern Europe and ex-Soviet geography have led to a radical transformation of the international system. This process has produced two basic outcomes: *The breakdown of the Soviet-type socialist model, and the disintegration process or the crises that the federations founded upon an ethnic/religious base have gone through.*

Firstly, due to a process that began in Eastern Europe and then spread to the Soviet Union, a social organization model that had gained momentum in the 1917 Russian Revolution and, with various modifications, had survived and ruled for about seven decades as the "Soviet Model" has come to an end. Perhaps more correctly, the model in question has lost its capability to serve as a beacon, although there are currently several nations with a similar social organization model, such as The People's Republic of China, The Republic of Cuba, and The Democratic People's Republic of Korea. It is important to note that none of these countries tends to serve as a model for others anymore. Rather, they seem to be living in very different societal conditions, and engrossed in their own practical problems related to their daily lives–although, the unique position of The People's Republic of China in this context has to be pointed out.

Secondly, the ethnically based federations such as the Soviet Union and Yugoslavia have disintegrated when the ideologies, which glued each of these heterogeneous bodies together, have lost their power and/or when the strong and unifying leadership in each country has come to end. These developments occurred in the Soviet geography under relatively peaceful conditions in comparison to the widespread cruelty and bloodshed in Yugoslavia. As for Czechoslovakia's "velvet divorce" into a Czech Republic and Slovakia, it was an exceptionally peaceful example of such a process in action.

Discussions About the Role of Nation-States in International Politics

One of the most important recent developments in the international system is the emergence of interdependence and globalization in response to the tremendous advancements in technology, particularly in communications. The future of nation-statehood is a most popular ground to discuss the effects of these developments on international politics. There are two polar approaches to this issue.

According to the *first* approach, the nation-state has lost its primary and dominant position in world politics mainly due to the advancements in the communication technology, which has facilitated the fast and free flow of information between countries. States today are not in full control of the flow of information, or the flow of goods, services, and capital across their borders. This is especially true in democratic societies due to the stronger and ever-growing presence of non-state channels of communication in such societies.

The developments in the technology of war and international terrorism have also made the state frontiers and the absolute sovereignty of state authorities within these borders more porous. Due to today's non-conventional war technology in nuclear, chemical and biological weapons, all countries today, including the USA and the Russian Federation, are more vulnerable, as the 11 September assault on the USA has shown. Along the same lines, the international relations literature today also tends to argue that the state has lost its absolute sovereignty over its territory as well as its primary position as the unit of analysis in world politics. The supporting developments are observable in the European geography where *supra-nationalism* and *infra-nationalism* have recently become prominent.

According to the *second* approach, the primary and dominant position of the nation-state in world politics is still intact. In the 1990's, after the developments in Eastern Europe, or in the old Soviet geography and Yugoslavia, a type of micro-nationalism based on ethnic/religious differences has surfaced. At first glance, this may seem to contradict the position of the nation-state as a social organization model. Upon investigation, however, one can see that the main goal of these separatist nationalist movements tends to be the formation of a new nation-state in a foreseeable future, supporting the evidence on the continuing importance of the nation-state as a social organization.

The claim that impressive developments in the communications technology have caused nation-states to lose their control over classical sovereignty areas is not necessarily true, either, mainly because the same technology may also be utilized by nation states to increase their control over their respective sovereignty areas, even as tools to extend their territorial control.

Although both of these perspectives point out important facets of actual world politics, the reality is probably somewhere in the middle. On the one hand, it is not easy to argue that the nation-state is still an unchallenged focus-unit in international politics as it was some decades ago. On the other hand, it is also true that the nation-state has been able to keep her primary and dominant position until now and is likely to do so for the foreseeable future.

The Structure and Characteristics of the New International System and the Expected Future Developments

The Structural Characteristics of the Balance of Power in the International System

- *Most of the authors on world politics are in agreement that the basic characteristic of the current international system is its multi-centeredness.* The concern, however, is that the system may be unstable. The history of international relations is, indeed, full of examples of instability and conflict in such systems.
- *It is not feasible to do a thorough analysis of the political/military and economic aspects of the international system at a single structural level.* This infeasibility becomes apparent when one tries to classify and to grade various state pairs (e.g., the USA and Japan, Germany and Russia, Hong Kong and Sudan) according to their influence capabilities. Although the USA is the only remaining "super power", even she no longer has the capacity to form a hierarchic order at every level (political, economic, etc.) of the international system.
- *If one presumes a soft pyramidal political/military hierarchy in today's international system, the USA is the natural candidate for the top position.* My criterion for this evaluation is based upon a state's capability to conduct military operations in distant and different territories. From this point of view, it was only the USA who could carry out the Gulf War in 1991 and the Afghanistan War in 2001-2002. Similarly in the Bosnian War, the armed conflict could not be stopped until the USA, in the main, intervened militarily.
- *The above hierarchy would be quite different if it were based upon a country's economic and technological capacity and mobilization capability. From this new perspective, one could consider a multi-centered structure in today's international system.* Indeed, during the 1991 Gulf War, the same USA that is at the top of the political/military pyramid wanted financial support from the Gulf states, Saudi Arabia, Germany and Japan as the economic burden of the operation would probably be too heavy for the US economy to carry out alone. This seems to indicate that the USA, although a great economic power, is not without competition in this field. In terms of economic data, the USA produces approximately 25% of the total world Gross National Product, whereas the EU countries produce 32%, the People's Republic of China 13%, and Japan 9%.
- *Therefore, today's international system has a structure in which the hierarchic and the multi-centered relation format function together. When one superimposes this theoretical framework upon the real world, it can be argued that under the "guided leadership" of the USA, an oligarchy of great powers has been managing, at least exerting significant control on the current international system.* Although the power parity and/or the composition of these states or institutions are not the same, they all belong to the same oligarchy. In today's world, the members of this oligarchy, aside from the USA, are the European Union, the People's Republic of China, the Russian Federation and Japan. The global and the regional balance of power in the current international system have

been determined (and, most likely, will continue to be determined in the near future) mainly by these principal actors.

- *The emerging international system is also "sub-system dominant" in character.* It is not easy anymore to explain most of the regional facts and figures only with reference to the rivalry between the USA and Russia. In analyzing a problem in the Middle East, for example, we have to take into consideration the ethno-religious structures, local rivalries and the balance of power in the region at least as much as the global systemic determinants. We cannot analyze Lebanon's state of affairs, for example, without taking into account these local factors. The situation is not totally different in other regional sub-systems such as those in the Balkans, Caucasus, and South Asia.

- It is possible to see some the basic characteristics of the classical balance of power in today's regional sub-systems in terms of the degree of autonomy of regional sub-system from the current structure of the global international system. Following the dissolution of the ideological glue in the aftermath of the ideology-based bipolar system, the balance of power approach, which tends to be based on geopolitical considerations and state interests, has gained great importance, particularly at some regional levels.

The Dominant Tendencies in the International System

Determining the dominant tendencies is also important to understand how the international system works. These tendencies are not the structural characteristics of the system. Rather, they simply point out some of the important promoting or demoting values in the system.

- *The great powers are gradually losing their monopoly on non-conventional (nuclear, chemical and biological) mass destruction weapons.* There are treaties, currently in effect, which ban or limit the production, use and transfer of non-conventional technology and weapons. The most important of these treaties is the Non-Proliferation Treaty (NPT), which the USA, USSR and Great Britain agreed upon in 1967, signed in 1968, put into effect in 1970, and renewed in 1995. Although many states have carried out clandestine programs to possess a nuclear bomb, it is not easy to have a complete nuclear weapon along with its delivery system. Producing or supplying a sophisticated delivery system requires a highly complicated technology (probably requiring a serious amount of successful intelligence activity), and a great amount of money. This means that there are certain barriers, other than the NPT, preventing the ownership of nuclear weaponry. The situation is different for other non-conventional mass destruction weapons, namely chemical and biological. Chemical weapons were banned for the first time by the Geneva Protocol of 1925, and more recently, by the Chemical Weapons Convention of 1993. Similarly, the Biological Weapons Convention of 1971 banned the production and the use of biological weapons. It is, however, more difficult to control such weapons as they tend to require much less money to purchase and much less sophisticated technology to produce. It is for this reason that these weapons are sometimes called the "poor countries' atomic bomb".

Obviously, some non-nuclear countries having problems with the great powers or with their otherwise unbeatable neighbors have a great motivation for acquiring these weapons. Since it is very difficult to stop these countries from doing so, the best preventive option may be to increase the political and the economic cost of owning such weapons.

- *International terrorist tactics have gained a considerable place in world politics.* Various personal characteristics and group dynamics have supported this trend. Another culprit is the direct use and/or support of such methods by various states to further their agenda. The continuing and even widening gap between the have's and have not's within the international system has also contributed to this trend. Moreover, the newly acquired ease for the have not's to be aware of and to exploit this gap (as it has become more difficult to control the international flow of information, goods and services, capital, and even humans) is a main factor contributing to the rise of international terrorism to its current worldwide level. Therefore, it seems quite impossible to solve the problem by one dimensional methods and limited support from the world public opinion.

- *We have to examine with some precaution the proposition that ethno/religious factors have played and will continue to play a primary role in the foreign policy formation of countries.* The origins of this controversy are mainly derived from Samuel P. Huntington's "Clash of Civilizations" thesis. Probably the explanatory power of this thesis is much greater for the *long-term* rivalry between civilizations. Perhaps the same thesis can even explain the causes of a recent conflict like the one in Bosnia. But when we analyze the relationship between states and state groups or the formation of state foreign policy on a certain problem, the same thesis appears to be insufficient. In my opinion, ethno/religious factors may often be the main attributes in the formation of a policy as long as those factors are not in direct contradiction to the interests and the aims of the state. If a contradiction exists, the ethno/religious factors tend to be easily thrown away for the sake of *raison d'etat*.

- *For the Western democratic-pluralist socio-political system and liberalism, a significant alternative is not obvious for the short -and the medium- term.* The most important rival, namely the socialist socio-political system, has eroded in its significance as an alternative. In the current political environment, authoritative rules trying to isolate a country from the outside world are becoming more difficult, if not impossible, to maintain. However, it is also unavoidable that some reaction against the globalization of the Western democratic-pluralist socio-political system and political thought will eventually emerge. In particular, the sharp division between the "have's" and "have not's" and the absence of any significant attempt to diffuse the situation constitutes (and probably will continue to constitute in the near future) the main motivation for this reaction. Currently, although radical Islam represents only a fraction of the "have not's", it can manage to channel the general anger of the masses to support its own anti-Western agenda. Only then could it be a threat for the Western system and its values as an alternative socio-political system and political thought, and only within some parts of the Islamic geography. Therefore, radical Islam will probably represent opposition and rebellion, but not a dominant tendency for the near future.

- *One of the main tendencies of today's international system is disintegration.* This disintegration process that became evident with the collapse of the Soviet and the Yugoslav federations, seems to cause serious side effects on unitary states as well as on federations, particularly those that are based on ethnicity. The new states, which have emerged after the collapse of the Soviet and the Yugoslav federations, are the main victims of this process. Indeed, the Karabakh Question and the conflict between Azerbaijan and Armenia, the Abkhaz uprising against Georgia, and the Chechen uprising against the Russian Federation are examples from the Soviet geography. The situation in former Yugoslavia is not any different, either. It will be overly optimistic to hope that these problems or their newer versions are about to be solved. The basic question, in this regard, is making the concept of self-determination operational, by determining who has the right to utilize this principle and who does not. I do not expect the international community to reach an agreement on this matter in the foreseeable future. However, it can also be argued that the current disintegration process in the international system will not proceed, at least at its current rate. The states which have emerged in the aftermath of the Soviet and the Yugoslav federations, for example, are known to have been developing solutions and measures against this "disintegration shock".

- *It seems that the integration hopes and initiatives at various levels will also increase during the next decades. This may be a consequence of the attractiveness of the European Union process or of the reflection upon the inter-dependence relationships.* The EU has become a twentyfive-member union after its most recent enlargement, and the admission of three additional candidates is on the agenda. It is important to note that the EU's aims of integration and enlargement are mutually competitive elements, and the fate of the Union is likely to depend on the outcome of this dilemma. Problems among Germany, France and the United Kingdom, or the racist and extreme rightist developments in Europe are among the factors against integration. The general trend, however, is towards integration. A similar trend is also observed in various other economically and politically attractive centers of the world. A less ambitious example in this regard is the 1992 North American Free Trade Agreement (NAFTA) between the USA, Canada and Mexico.

Developments in the United Nations and the International Law

United Nations

At the beginning of the new era, many people were probably thinking that the UN would keep the peace and security more easily than before. Since the Soviet Union was no more and the Cold War had ended, "the mutual Soviet and USA vetoes in the Security Council" blocking the UN capability to intervene in a serious crisis had also come to an end, as we were able to witness during the Gulf Crisis of 1990-1991.

Then, various public opinion centers and many statesmen began to argue that the UN performance to keep peace and security was not satisfactory. The main criticism was that the influence of the USA and other great powers on the UN was even greater than before, and that the UN did not have the capability to intervene successfully unless the intervention was supported by the great powers, or, at least, unless the intervention was not contrary to the interests of the great powers. In fact, the UN system was not (and is not) working any differently than before. The likely reason for today's intense reactions to the situation may be related to the highly unrealistic expectations for the UN peacekeeping functions after the end of the Cold War. The critical question in this regard should be whether it is possible for the UN to behave any differently than it actually does.

We can answer this question at two different levels:

- Firstly, if we believe the UN should behave like the armed forces of a state on a larger scale, and if we expect the UN forces to implement the decisions of the International Court of Justice or the orders of the Secretary General against states or entities who are perceived to be threatening or destroying peace and security, then the reasonable answer is a "no". The UN's legitimate use of force, which is possible only with a Security Council resolution, is not comparable to a state's legitimate and monopolized use of force on state territory.

- Secondly, the UN's performance in establishing or keeping the peace and security may not be satisfactory when we take into consideration the UN's structural and functional shortcomings. The demise of the bipolar international system had, indeed, produced great hopes for the role of the UN. A short time later, however, a totally different atmosphere began to dominate the world public opinion along with the realization that there was a great increase in the number of local conflicts and civil wars concurrent with a considerable decrease in the probability of a large scale nuclear war. It is important to note that the UN is not properly designed to intervene in domestic conflicts and civil wars, which are conventionally confined within a state's internal sovereignty and jurisprudence.

The International Law

As a result of the developments in the international system after 1991, new perspectives have emerged with respect to the current practices of international law:

- First of all, the classical point of view positing "states and their relations with each other are the basic and, often, the only topic of international law" has disappeared or, at least, has lost its dominant position. Instead, new regulations for organizations and individuals have become an integral part of the international law.

- Although the classical *consent* doctrine positing, "states are bound only by the agreements which they have accepted" is still the basic principle in international law, the popularity of the *consensus* doctrine positing that "agreements accepted by an overwhelming majority of states are also binding on the states that are not signatories to the agreement" is increasing.

- In classical international law, sovereignty is the most essential part of a state. Yet, state sovereignty does not have an absolute meaning in today's international law or international politics. There are many examples of imposing limits on state sovereignty either through agreements in which the states have participated deliberately or through regulations that have been accepted without the state's consent, but with the overwhelming majority of other states. Certain human rights topics, in particular, have gained an international dimension although they are considered to be internal problems of a sovereign state in the classical international law. As is well known, treaties and customs are the basic sources of international law, and we can also talk about "soft" rules and norms, which do not bind but have a "limiting" or "directing" effect. The rules and norms on human rights regulations are examples of the "soft law". There is a complex definition and application problem related to human rights practices. The major problem in this regard is to decide whether the current human rights concerns are universal or not. The same concerns were defined in relation to the East-West axis during the Cold War, and have reappeared in relation to the North-South dividing line after 1991.

• Among the non-classical subjects of international law, the environmental law has an important place. Due to various developments especially during the last century, the natural environment has been gradually deteriorating. However, as the "Common Territory of Global Village" concept becomes more popular, new judicial regulations about the environmental concerns and the related mechanisms for exercising these judicial regulations are being introduced, albeit very slowly. Overall, judicial regulations on environmental issues are in the process of gaining greater importance.

• Also, the laws of outer space and electronic communications, and judicial regulations on biological and genetic research seem to be the next candidates in which international law will show more interest.

The Main Characteristics of the Turkish Foreign Policy in the 21ˢᵗ Century

The above-mentioned recent developments have had an enormous impact on various countries and their foreign policies. The foreign policy of Turkey is one of those that have been affected the most. The disintegration of the Warsaw Pact and the collapse of the Soviet Union have brought about a debate on the position and the importance of NATO. These developments deeply affect the Turkish foreign policy, often based upon and in alignment with NATO's basic preferences, as Ankara has tried to adapt to the new environment. In this context, before discussing the Turkish foreign policy exercises at the global and the regional levels, it may be useful to go over the factors that tend to determine (and which ought to determine) the Turkish foreign policy formation process.

How Should a Countryís Foreign Policy Be Formed in Todayís International Environment? The Case of Turkey.

• In this context, effectiveness, or the ability to guide others in one's preferred direction, is related to a country's capability to influence. Although effectiveness can be increased through alliances, a country's role at the international and regional levels is mainly determined by her own capability to influence. There are military, economic, and political aspects of this capability. It is important that each of these different aspects is at a sufficient level in its own right, but it is even more important that these different aspects support each other. Economic structure and national resources, for example, should support the military power and mechanism. Also, the political system behind the economic structure producing this capability is important. An economic structure supported by a participatory political system, for example, could be more conducive to a strong national defense than a non-participatory system would.

- Although military capacity may still be the more important and conclusive determinant of a country's capability to influence, the economic and financial factors have been gaining ground, and this trend is likely to continue in the near future. This shows that the meaning of being a "big country" is gradually becoming related more to gross national product than to total population or land mass. Although Turkey's geographic location makes it almost impossible to consider military capacity as a secondary capability factor, it seems that the term "big country" in Turkish political rhetoric, even in reference to Turkey, has come to refer to economic capacity rather than population or land. Thus, as a country that is a legal and legitimate candidate for membership to the EU, Turkey will have to give priority to developing the economic elements of influence capability over the other elements.

- If the principal preference is minimum conflict and maximum stability in Turkey and in the region, the priorities in the foreign policy process have to gain precedence over some of the necessities of domestic politics. The degree of progress in a democracy can be measured by its citizens' active participation rate in national problems through various channels over and above the regular general elections. The foreign policy formation process, however, is somewhat different. As in most developed and democratic states, ordinary Turkish people are not as well informed about foreign policy matters as about domestic politics, although the separation between domestic and foreign policies is gradually becoming more difficult to recognize. Therefore, the lower rate of democratic participation of ordinary people in foreign policy matters, relative to that in domestic politics, does not necessarily reflect a negative tendency for reaching the minimum conflict and maximum stability equilibrium in foreign policy. Quite naturally, this conclusion is true in relation to ordinary people, rather than well-informed public opinion centers with expertise. At first glance, this may seem to be an extremely "elitist" perspective, but ordinary people with their emotional baggage, interest groups with their group interests, or media members with news and sensation as their likely priorities may not be the proper source to turn to for foreign policy processes. In other words, "participatory democracy" may not be the proper way for determining the preferences and the initiatives related to a successful foreign policy process aiming to minimize conflict and maximize stability. Although success is not guaranteed when foreign policy is conducted by professionals and experts who tend to know much more about the issues and the global background, in the probabilistic sense, at least, the chances for an irrational choice is not going to be nearly as high.

- Some factors like ideological affinity, ethnic/religious proximity etc., should be taken into consideration only when those factors are in accordance with a country's overall foreign policy premises. Foreign policies that are based solely on ideology, ethnicity, and religion are not likely to produce positive results, although the activities for preserving humanitarian values should be taken as an exception. Recently, and particularly in Turkey's geography, ethnic and religious factors have, indeed, been the main cause of international problems. However this does not change the basic fact that Turkey and the great majority of her neighbors tend to form their foreign policies according to their "national interest". If an ethnicity or religion-based policy happens to be in alignment with foreign policy interests, foreign policy makers generally explain their policies by this ethnic/religious factor. The real test, however, is when a country's national interest-based foreign policy contradicts her ethnicity and religion-based foreign policy. In almost all cases and in all countries, then, decision-makers tend to ignore ethnic/religious factors in favor of national interest.

- In the last decades, Turkey may not have been seen as supporting the role of international organizations and international law in international conflict resolution. In relation to the Cyprus Question, for example, Ankara does not accept some of the United Nations resolutions as a basis for solution, in relation to the Aegean Question Ankara does not accept to refer the problem to the International Court of Justice, and in relation to the Water Problem among Ankara, Damascus and Baghdad, Ankara does not accept to bring the conflict before international organizations and international law. The correct inference, however, may not be as obvious as it may seem, and Turkey is not a country far behind in law and order in international relations. For one thing, Turkey does not really trust international conflict resolution mechanisms, sometimes on justifiable grounds and sometimes out of prejudice. Nevertheless, I personally believe that in the 21st century, a Turkey that desires to live in peace within the international community has to pay much more attention to conflict resolution mechanisms at the international level.

The Foreign Policy Environment and the Practice of Turkey

Turkey and Global Politics

a) The Strategic Importance Theme

After the Cold War, Turkish foreign policy did not face the initially expected lack of support from the Western powers, specifically from the USA, mainly due to the 1990-1991 Gulf crisis. During the Cold War, Turkey was important for Western/USA strategy for having the longest frontier in NATO with the Soviet Union. In the aftermath of the Cold War, Turkey's strategic importance for the USA began to be defined in terms of her presence in the Middle East. Due to oil concerns and Israel, the USA pays more attention to the region and, therefore, to Turkey, with her unique location in the region, with her Western-style democracy, and with her predominantly Moslem population. Particularly after "September 11, 2001", within the context of the new "struggle with terror" campaign of the Bush administration, Turkey's position appears to have strengthened.

Some of the recent developments indicate that the USA has also begun to take an active interest in the Caucasian and Central Asian energy politics. This means that USA does not want to let Russia play alone in this region. The USA is currently supporting the delivery of some Caucasian Azerbaijani oil and Central Asian oil and natural gas to Europe via Turkey (not Iran) instead of completely via Russia. This preference of USA is due to strategic calculations rather than economic. By adopting such a policy, the USA is putting a dependable partner forward to have a vicarious control over the oil flow against Russia, and particularly Iran. These facts make Turkey an important ally in the eyes of the United States just as during the Cold War.

b) The "Turkish Model" Argument

Although, Turkey's strategic importance may be a major factor in the Turkish-Western relationship, it may not be sufficient to induce the West to give unconditional support to Turkey. A similar example may be found in the relationship between the anti-Western regimes of Iran and Iraq versus the Soviet Union. The indispensable characteristic of Turkey for the USA and other Western countries is not her strategic importance alone, but also her being a "Western-style democratic and Islamic country model" for the Middle East, and particularly for the Central Asian Turkish republics. Although the current political regimes of these republics are far different from the "Turkish model", the West may utilize this model as an important reference point in the future. The September 11 terrorist attack on the United States has also delineated for Washington and other Western capitals the importance of Turkey for Western interests.

c) The Balance Between the USA and the EU

It is easier to assert what ought to be done at the international level than at the regional in Turkish foreign policy. Turkey has to be cautious not to confront the USA and the EU at the same time. Turkey must try to maintain the close relationship with both parties, at least with one of them. In the political and military spheres, however, the importance of the USA is unrivalled and her support indispensable. Due to the capability of the USA to adapt to different situations, Washington is the primary and the most dependable ally for Ankara. In return, Turkey is an important ally for the USA, whose interests as a world state extend to regions outside of Europe, as well. At the economic level, however, Turkey has the closer relationship with the EU, due to a preference arising from the requirements of the international system. Indeed, in the current international economic relationships, states have been joining together to form economic groups such as the EU and the NAFTA. The formation of such groups has been a main tendency in the international economic system, and Turkey, who wishes to live within the world economy, must not remain outside of these developments. From this point of view, the EU is the single most important social and economic project for Ankara, although this does not mean that there is no alternative for Turkey other than the EU.

There is no doubt that membership in the EU is the best option for Turkey, who is already in a customs union with the EU. However, if full membership in the EU cannot be realized in the foreseeable future Ankara may have to reconsider her customs union membership, as well. Although not a real alternative, a special trade agreement with the USA, similar to the one that Israel has, is likely to be the best solution for Turkey if the EU decides to deny full membership.

Turkey and Regional Politics

Recent developments, new structures, and new behavioral forms influence Turkey's relationship with her neighbors. It is significant for Turkey that certain characteristics of various geographical regions have gained greater importance to understand and to explain the international relations with these regions.

a) General Policies

If rationality-based maximum stability and maximum influence with minimum conflict and minimum cost are considered as the main goals, it is important to be well-informed with the basic facts, rules and the needs of the international system and the regional sub-systems. During the bipolar international system, a country belonging in one of the poles could not perform regional policies different from those of the bloc. It was very hard for Turkey, for example, to form a different Middle East policy from that of NATO in the 1950's without taking into account the rivalry between the USA and the Soviet Union. Since 1991, the situation has changed considerably. The most important change has been the emergence of regional sub-systems, not independent but autonomous from the international system. Turkey is a neighbor to three or four different regional sub-systems and has to measure correctly the domestic dynamics and the degree of autonomy these regional sub-systems have within the structural and behavioral characteristics of the international system. The new environment has given rise to a new potential for further initiative and flexibility for the Turkish foreign policy. Along with this new potential, however, capacity constraints in the conduct of foreign policy as well as the incompatibility issues among different goals have also arisen.

- In this context, it can be said that the logic of classical balance of power is beginning to prevail over Turkey's neighboring regional sub-systems. It is natural that this factor has affected and will continue to affect Turkey's relationships with her neighbors.

- Turkey ought to base her foreign policy neither on ideological premises, as was the case during the Cold War, or some ethno-religious criteria, but on the requirements of the balance of power at the international and/or regional system levels. This is not a new or unexplored fact. All along the frontiers of Turkey, from Greece to Iran, from Armenia to Syria, such strategy and tactics are already being exercised against Ankara. This is not an obstacle for Turkey to develop a special and long-term relationship with Europe, with whom she shares a similar economic, social and political experiment, with the Central Asian Turkish Republics, with whom she shares ethno-cultural affinity, and with the Moslem countries, with whom she shares the same religion. It is important, however, to note that none of these factors should legitimize a policy that is incompatible with the Turkish national interests. Having a close relationship with the West is not likely to bring Turks to accede to the Greek desires in relation to the Cyprus question. Sharing the same religion with Iran, Syria, Iraq cannot change the fact that some of these countries are practicing hostile, at least unfriendly, policies against Turkey. Likewise, the "brotherhood and kinship" themes are not sufficient in their own right to develop brotherly relationships with the Central Asian Turkish Republics.

- Turkey has to formulate her foreign policy within the limits of these international and regional criteria. Turkey needs some bargaining chips to play her hand well, a necessity arising from the policies of some of Turkey's neighbors. Indeed, bargaining chips are necessary if Turkey wants to solve the problems through negotiation rather than conflict, as no country is likely to give up anything without receiving something else in return. Until now, Turkey has not used (and has not wanted to use) such bargaining chips. Either the traditional seriousness and caution of the Turkish foreign policy, or the bloc-solution methods employed during the Cold War era had made such "give and take" methods underutilized. However, the situation is different today. Most of Turkey's neighbors have their bargaining chips to use against Turkey in a negotiation. Turkey, in contrast, does not seem to have a comparable advantage, beyond a few unimportant exceptions.

- Another important point for Turkey is to prevent the rival neighboring countries from forming trans-regional alliances. It is a geopolitical necessity for Turkey that the rival countries not form a trans-regional encirclement. If this proves impossible to prevent, Turkey should counteract with alliances of her own. An alliance formed by Greece + Syria + Armenia, for example, would put Turkey under pressure on three different fronts. In fact, Greece did begin to have close contacts with Iran in 1991, signed military agreements with Russia and Syria in 1995, and a similar agreement with Armenia in 1996, presumably in an effort to encircle and isolate Turkey.

b) The Military Front

After 1991, interesting developments have taken place in relation to armaments in Turkey's geopolitical environment. In the bipolar world, the international balance of power depended on nuclear weapons. This type of strategic logic was also relevant for a country like Turkey, whose entire defense policy relied on USA/NATO, even though she did not have any nuclear arms of her own. After the collapse of the bipolar world and its related logic, the situation has changed. The new strategic logic mainly depends on the balance of power over conventional arms, although nuclear power continues to retain its relevance indirectly.

In this context, the most interesting developments have occurred in the Middle East. In the aftermath of the Cold War, the Middle East has become the most popular region for various attempt of possession and control of mass destruction weapons. After the collapse of the Soviet Union, socio-economic conditions in the Russian Federation gradually turned for the worse and many experts on military technology become unemployed, and began to seek for well-paying jobs in the wealthier Middle Eastern countries. The same region has also been a good market for military equipment sales by the Russian government. In fact, Turkey's Eastern and Southern neighbors Iran, Iraq and Syria have been trying to develop their military capability by such purchases of arms and military equipment.

The quality and the quantity of military equipment and arms are among the most important indicators to predict the expected outcome of a conflict. However, a comparison based only on these categories may not be sufficient. It is hardly possible to accurately evaluate the variables in a conflict, such as the power mobilization capacity (influence capacity) of the parties and the realization of alliances among the parties. Besides, various characteristics of the human nature and social capacity such as education, courage, strategic thinking, leadership quality etc., play an important role in warfare, and such variables cannot be easily evaluated in advance. Moreover, a balance between the military capacity of rivals is not a guarantee for regional stability, either. Expecting every decision-maker to be rational, to have full information about the other party, and to incorporate all this information in the decision making process is too much to ask, especially during periods of crisis and conflict.

When we consider Turkey and her neighbors in relation to their weapons capacity, the most differentiating characteristic is whether these countries have offensive missiles. Turkey does not have such weapons, whereas her Southern and Eastern neighbors not only have them, but they are also working hard to develop them into more sophisticated versions. In the Caucasus, the Russian army has offensive missile capability. On the Western side, only Bulgaria has some semi-offensive Russian missiles. With a range in excess of 200 km and the capability to reach a target quickly, these missiles are suitable for a surprise attack.. Also, the capability of these missiles to deliver conventional, nuclear, chemical as well as biological heads makes them more potent [On the positive side, most of these missiles are Soviet-made, and they have a low strike capability].

Syria's Soviet made *Forg* missiles are very short range and are not suitable for using with different warheads. However, the Soviet-made *Scud B/C*'s with 280-575 km range, and the Soviet-made *SS-21*'s with their 120 km range are a considerable threat for some regions of Turkey. It is also well known that Syria has just obtained warheads containing chemical weapons for these missiles.

Iraq has Soviet-made *Frog* and *Scud* missiles. The Iraqi government was not satisfied with the performance of these weapons in the war with Iran, and has worked to improve the range of these missiles since then. At the end of the 1980's, the Baghdad administration developed the 600-km-range *El Hussein* and 900-km-range *El Abbas* missiles.[1] Turkey felt the pressure from these developments in the Iraqi weapons system during the 1991 Gulf Crisis. In this conflict, Turkey acted in complete alignment with the USA-lead United Nations, adhered to the sanctions against Iraq immediately and accurately, and also stationed its army along the Iraqi border to support the allied forces in the South. For her part, the USA deployed her *Patriot* missiles and *F-16* aircraft in Turkey to prevent retaliation from Iraq. After the United Nations Security Council decision to destroy or to take under control all of the offensive weapons of Iraq, and Iraq's acceptance of this decision, Turkish concerns in this regard have lost their urgency.

Turkey can take various measures against this threat from the South[2]. First of all, Turkey must continue to support the treaties on non-proliferation of mass destruction weapons, although the unstable political environment in the Middle East makes it difficult for such treaties to succeed. Against this threat, Turkey may also use the NATO support, as she did during the 1991 Gulf Crisis. Or, Turkey may try to have some ATBM's (*Anti-*

---

[1] Thomas G. Mahnken ve Timothy D. Hoyt, "The Spread of Missile Technology in the Third World," *Comparative Strategy*, Vol. 9, No.3, 1990, p.25.
[2] See. Gülden Nurşin Ateşoğlu Ayman- Güney, "Değişen Uluslararası Koşullarda Strateji, Türkiye ve Komşuları", Faruk Sönmezoğlu, (Der.), *Türk Dış Politikasının Analizi*, 2. baskı., İstanbul: Der Yayınevi, 1998, pp.151-152.

Tactical Ballistic Missile), although they are very costly and are not a complete guarantee against offensive missiles. Another option is to have offensive missiles systems the way her neighbors do. Such missile systems, however, tend to be very expensive, and they also violate certain treaties to which Turkey is a signatory. Still another option is to have more military aircraft to balance out the lack of missile systems.

The Caucasus is another neighbor-region with great strategic importance in relation to the political and military balance between Turkey, Russia and Iran. After the collapse of the Soviet Union, Turkey and Russian Federation ended up having no common borders anymore. However, when the Caucasian states within the Russian-dominated CIS (*Commonwealth of Independent States*) accepted the stationing of Russian soldiers on their soil, Turkey, once again, began to feel the pressure from the " Big Neighbor in the North".

Conventional Forces in Europe Treaty (CFET), between 22 member countries of NATO and the Warsaw Pact, was signed on 19 November 1990 in Paris. This treaty is the most important document for determining the military balance in the region. CFET required important military reductions for the ex-Soviet geography in the East. CFET also introduced military limitations[3] for all parties, and a separate arrangement for Turkey, Norway, Iceland and Greece from the Western Bloc and the Soviet Union, Romania, and Bulgaria from the Eastern Bloc. According to this arrangement, on the flank territories Leningrad, Odessa, North and Trans-Caucasian, every state-group had the right to have a maximum of 4.700 tanks, 5.900 armored vehicles and 6.000 artillery units.[4] Due to their "common frontiers with some non-members of CSCE (*Conference on Security and Cooperation in Europe*)", territories to the East and South of a line drawn from South Eastern Anatolia to Mersin-Gözne, constituting about a quarter of Turkey's total territory, were excluded from this maximum limit. Greece intensively resisted this exclusion, particularly for the region around Mersin. Although Athens could not succeed in excluding the Mersin harbor from this special treatment, she was able to prevent the line of exclusion from reaching Mersin-Erdemli.

This treaty has produced a considerable benefit for Turkey. The resulting surplus in the arms and equipment of some NATO members, particularly of Germany, were transferred to Turkey. Among these were armored vehicles, tanks, assault helicopters, and ground-to-air missiles, leading to a comprehensive modernization, particularly of the Turkish land forces. Due to this treaty, Turkey received 1050 tanks from NATO, while discarding 1078 of her older tanks.

However, after the collapse of the Soviet Union, problems began to emerge for Turkey. The most important of these for Turkey are the demands by the Russian Federation to increase the limits on Russian tanks and armored vehicles in the Caucasus. Turkey responded by rejecting the proposal at once, but did not get enough support from the USA or from other NATO members. In the end, Russia was able to exceed her CFET limits in Georgia and Armenia, effectively invalidating the treaty in the aftermath of the bipolar international system.

---

[3] See for a detailed knowledge: Gülden Ayman, *Konvansiyonel Kuvvetlerin Denetimi*, İstanbul: Alfa, 1994.
[4] Ayman-Güney, *Değişen Uluslararası Koşullarda Strateji*, p.153.

After George W. Bush came to power in 2001, the *National Missile Defense System* project of the Clinton era became popular again. There are certain technical and judicial problems in the way of realizing this project,[5] which is important for Turkey. As mentioned above, some of Turkey's neighbors have mass destruction weapons and the missiles to deliver them. Those who do not have these systems are trying to have them, and those who already have them are trying to improve them. In contrast, there is no serious evidence that Turkey is involved in similar activities. Therefore, if the USA develops the *National Missile Defense System* and shares it with Turkey, it is going to have positive consequences for Ankara's defense strategy. Furthermore, the new *National Missile Defense System* endorsed by George W. Bush is more favorable for Turkey than the version endorsed by Clinton. In Clinton's version, the missile deployment bases were to be located on USA territory, whereas in the new project some of the bases are planned to be located in allied countries close to target states. In addition, although the former missile defense system was for offensive missiles targeted only against the USA, the new system is designed against missiles, against the allies of the USA as well as the USA herself. For an ally country like Turkey, surrounded by neighbors with missile systems, the new defense system provides at least as much security as the former.

Naturally, the new system has its own problems, as well.[6] Currently, there are no clear signs as to when this technology will be ready for deployment and, also, it is not known whether the USA will be willing to share this technology with her allies. Therefore, Turkey may have to be cautious in giving full support to this system because of the possible negative reactions from some of her neighbors. Russia and China are also known to be against this project, and especially the Russian reaction is important for Turkey. It is quite probable that Russia is going to consider the states participating in the new missile defense system as potential targets. Moreover, Turkey needs a missile defense system, such as *Patriot, Arrow* or *S-300*, which is effective against short-range ballistic missiles, although the system to be deployed in Turkey is likely to be against the ICBM's. It is important that the new missile defense system be in harmony with the interests of Turkey as well as the USA.

Concluding Remarks

The world in the 21st century is different in terms of its system structure, its actors and their roles, and its dominant values. In this new environment, the Turkish foreign policy ought to be somewhat different, with more initiative than before. Many new actors and variables have emerged, and Ankara does not have enough control over these developments. Although the diversification of foreign policy elements has brought about new opportunities for the Turkish foreign policy, it has also introduced new variables that are difficult to harmonize. Therefore, the foreign policy process for Ankara has become more complex and more difficult.

What are the means for a successful foreign policy in such a complicated

---

[5] For the reason and problems of this project see. Mustafa Kibaroğlu. "Amerikan Ulusal Füze Savunma Sistemi (*American National Missile Defense*)", *Avrasya Dosyası*, Cilt.6. No.2. Yaz 2000. pp.90-105.
[6] Ibid.. pp.100-102.

environment? Political stability, harmonious relations between the state and society, economic support, and military deterrence are the *sine qua non* factors. In addition, the foreign policy process requires longer and more diversified formative elements. Today, there is no justification for defining the problems as simple zero-sum games. The non-zero-sum game mentality has been gaining validity and will probably continue to do so in the future.

The Turkish foreign policy needs to base its analyses on regional characteristics and factors as much as their global counterparts. Some of the problems should also be considered from the standpoint of humanitarian values and their related applications. Finally, the Turkish foreign policy in the 21st century must not be simply reactive, but rather more proactive and more carefully planned. Within the goals of maximum interest and minimum conflict, these are the fundamental elements of a successful foreign policy aiming to reach targets with minimum cost.

5 Turkish Foreign Policy in Post Cold War Era: New Problems and Opportunities[*]

Hüseyin Bağcı
İdris Bal

Introduction

That Turkey did not enter the Second World War is seen as İnönü's most important achievement after Atatürk's death. Turkey was neither economically nor militarily ready for a war in 1939, but there were additional reasons behind the Turkish decision not to enter the war. Because of the traumatic experience of the War of Liberation (1919-1923), Turkey was very sensitive about its freedom and independence, and Turkish decision-makers who had experienced the First World War and the War of Liberation played a vital role in the decision not to enter another war. Atatürk's statement `Peace at home, peace in the world' was used, as the principle motto of Turkish foreign policy and neutrality became the best way of securing Turkish interests. Despite the provocations, both domestic and external, Turkey managed to stay out of the war. Following the emergence of two superpowers, the United States and the Soviet Union at the end of the war, Turkey was to choose the side of the United States and the West in the new bi-polar system. There were good reasons for this choice.

Although Turkey did not enter the Second World War, Turkey's fear of war did cease when the war ended in 1945. This was mainly because of the Soviet Union who did not want to renew the Treaty of Neutrality and Non-Aggression of 1925 unless its demands were answered positively. The Soviet Union demanded four concessions from Turkey in any new treaty. First, Kars and Ardahan, Turkish areas near the Soviet-Turkish border in the northeast of Turkey, which had been occupied by Russia during the First World War, had to be returned. Turks had liberated these areas after the Russian Revolution in 1917, and an agreement had been signed between the Soviet Union and Turkey. The second Soviet demand was for military bases on the Bosphorus and the Dardanelles; the third was for a revision of the Montreux Strait Convention; and the fourth, for a revision of the Thracian border in favor of the communist-dominated Bulgaria. The Soviets were serious in their demands; Soviet troops were massed on the Turkish-Bulgarian border in the frontier region of Thrace, and in Moscow and Sofia a hostile propaganda campaign against Turkey had begun. Furthermore, these developments indicated "Moscow's final objective was not simply revision of the Montreux Convention and territorial adjustment, but that the Soviet Union wanted to reduce Turkey to the position of a

[*] This chapter is an English version of the following article; Hüseyin Bağcı & İdris Bal, "Turkish Foreign Policy in Post Cold War era: New Opportunities and Handicaps", Dirk Rochtus, Gerrit De Vyder and Veli Yuksel, (Ed.), *Turkije: Springstof voor de Europese Unie?"*, Grant, Leuver/Apaldom 2002.

satellite."[1] Obviously this was a major threat to Turkey's sovereignty, and Turkey refused to make any concession to the Soviet demands. Because of the expansionist policies of the Soviet Union, Turkey's political agenda was entirely dominated by this issue, and this is seen as the main reason, which led to Turkish application for membership of NATO.[2] Naturally there were other reasons that encouraged Turkey to make this application. Firstly, Turkey was eager to enter a prestigious club. Secondly, the desire to become a westernized society was another factor, which had an important impact on Turkey's willingness to integrate with NATO. Westernization and modernization formed an implicit link between strategy and other aims held in common with her new Western identity. But at the same time the ideological aspiration to become an integral part - at least in terms of military alliance - of the Western world without any doubt played a decisive role in Turkey's decision.

Thus, Westernization, indicating co-operation with the West, became the leading philosophical principle of Turkey's foreign policy in the real sense, and developments since the Second World War indicate that Turkey has been following the principle of Westernization in foreign policy. For example, in the early post-war period Turkey demanded assistance from the West against the Soviet threat, and was supported by the West through the Truman Doctrine and the Marshall Plan. Turkey became a founder member of the Council of Europe and joined the North Atlantic Pact. It applied to the European Community for membership in 1959 and the Ankara agreement was signed in 1963 with the objective to make Turkey a full member. In 1987 Turkey applied for full membership, and to fulfill the conditions which would ease its acceptance, in January 1988, it gave its citizens the right to make individual applications to the European Human Rights Commission, and signed the Council of Europe Convention against Torture and Inhuman and Degrading Treatment, becoming the first country to ratify this.

Some right-wing politicians regarded the Turkish foreign policy style before the 1980's as being passive and reactionary. For example: Kamran İnan argues that after the rule of Atatürk, Turkey adopted a passive foreign policy style, and did not want to be active in international relations. The accusation is that also during this period, Turkey also turned its back on the Turkic world, and that this passive policy worsened Turkey's image in international relations.[3] The exception to this passive policy was the 1950's, during the rule of the Democrat Party[4] and its celebrated Foreign Minister Fatin Rüştü Zorlu.[5] However, analysts such as Deringil label the same period as 'non-adventurist'. Deringil

---

[1] Ferenc A. Vali, *The Turkish Straits and NATO*, California: Hoover Institution Press, 1972, p.76.

[2] Vali, A Bridge Across the Bosporus The Foreign Policy of Turkey, London: The Johns Hopkins Press, 1971, p.34; Mete Tuncay, and others, *Çağdaş Türkiye 1908-1980*, Istanbul: Cem Yayınları, 1992, pp.138-139; David Barchard, *Turkey and the West*, London: Routledge & Kegan Paul, 1985, p.44; O. Sander, "Turkish Foreign Policy : Forces of Continuity and of Change", Turkish Review, Winter 1993, p.45.

[3] Kamran İnan, *Dış Politika*, İstanbul: Ötüken Yayınları, 1993, pp.44-45; Kamran İnan, "Dış Politika", *Yeni Türkiye*, Vol.1, No.3, 1995, p.95; Also see his book: Kamran İnan, *Hayır Diyebilen Türkiye*, Istanbul: Timaş Yayınları, 1995.

[4] For Turkish Foreign Policy in 1950's see, Hüseyin Bağcı, *1950'lerde Türk Dış Politikası*, Ankara: METU Yayınları, 2001.

[5] F.R. Zorlu was Foreign Minister in the Democrat Party government until the 1960 military coup, following which he was hanged.

claims that "It is only since the mid-1980's and early 1990's that foreign policy has moved away from the basic premises guiding it since 1923, and that occurred despite the best efforts of the professional diplomats of the Foreign Ministry, and was due to the direct intervention in foreign affairs by non-experts in various Motherland Party governments. Since 1983 Turgut Özal and the Motherland party increasingly diverted from the traditional non-adventurist line of Turkish foreign policy".[6] In the 1990's, Turkish decision-makers started to be more active, searching for possibilities of co-operation in the region. There was considerable change in Turkish foreign policy style; especially the traditional Turkish policy of non-interference with the Turks living outside of Turkey changed.

Özal who advocated an active, if not aggressive, Turkish image initiated this change. For example: during the Gulf War, he actively supported the international coalition against Saddam Hussein, a policy which dismayed the Foreign Ministry and the chief of staff, who later resigned. Another example was Özal's declaration to a Greek newspaper in May 1991 that "the Dodecanese Islands were never Greek, they belonged to the Ottoman Empire. If I had been in İsmet İnönü's place [in 1944] I would have gone in and taken them. Turkey committed a historic error in this case".[7] He also proposed the Black Sea Economic Co-operation; advocated active support for Azerbaijan, and even mentioned military intervention against Armenia.

Although Özal's active foreign policy understanding and his charismatic leadership was important in this changing style of Turkish foreign policy, there were other factors which forced Turkey to be active and look for possible alternative co-operations. Firstly, with the end of Cold War parameters in international relations have changed and regions around Turkey have destabilized and several conflicts took place. Because of her strategic position Turkey has been affected by these conflicts and had to act accordingly. Because of new parameters of new era, Turkey had to reformulate and re-identify herself and her foreign policy. Secondly, with the end of Cold war the importance of Turkey for the West declined in terms of East-West confrontation. In the new era Turkey began to struggle to find new arguments to prove that she was still important in global politics and for Europe. Thirdly, cool relations between the European Community and Turkey played a role in Turkey's search for alternative areas of co-operation and relations with new partners. Lastly, lack of support for Turkish position in international circles on crucial issues such as the Cyprus issue, Separatism in South East Anatolia and the water conflict with Syria and Iraq, encouraged Turkey to look for new allies in the international community. All these factors forced Turkey to be more active in international relations and reformulate her policy according to new parameters.

The aim of this article is to analyze Turkish foreign policy in terms of new problems and opportunities in post Cold War era. To this end, firstly changing parameters and problems for Turkey will be underlined. Secondly new opportunities for Turkey and Turkey's strategic importance will be analyzed.

---

[6] S. Deringil, "Turkish Foreign Policy Since Atatürk", C. H. Dodd (ed.), *Turkish Foreign Policy*, London: The Eothen Press, 1992, p.5.
[7] Ibid., p.6.

End of Cold War and Changing Parameters: Problems for Turkey

Since Turkey has established in 1923, Turkish foreign policy has entered the most important and changing period with the end of Cold War. During the Cold War, Soviet threat, problems with Greece and Cyprus issue, how relations could be developed and strengthened with NATO, US and EC, were main agenda of Turkish foreign policy. In 1980's Turkey began to feel terrorist threat (PKK) supported by her neighbors like Syria, Iraq and Iran.[8] Later the support to PKK began to come from other regions of the World including Turkey's some allies like some of Western European countries in one way or another. During the Cold War era, Turkey's environment was more stable as Cold War had frozen the map to large extent in the region as well as in the globe. USSR was controlling Central Asia and Caucasus. There were socialist countries in the Balkans. Mainly because of Tito's hard rule and Cold War discipline Balkans were stable as well. Middle East was not stable place as Iran - Iraq war and Arab - Israeli wars took place. However because of the effects of Cold war other problems were frozen in Middle East as well. End of Cold War was like an end of control mechanism that prepared a suitable base for new conflicts to flourish.[9] With the end of the Cold War all the regions around Turkey have been destabilized. Religious and ethnic irredentism have found a suitable ground to flourish and problems began to emerge in Balkans, Caucasus and Middles East causing new tensions for Turkey.

With the end of Cold War all regions around Turkey have destabilized. Former Yugoslavia was disunited and wars break out between the ethnic and religious groups in Balkans. Although Serb-Bosnian and Serb-Croat wars ended with the intervention of international community, Balkans is still today an unstable region. One third of Macedonian population is consists of ethnic Albanians and UÇK guerillas from Kosova attacked Macedonia demanding some portion of Macedonian territory. Although clashes between Albanian UÇK guerilla groups and Macedonian army was ended by the intervention of international community, ethnic and religious structure of Balkans are suitable to feed new conflicts.

Middle East is also another unstable place in the region. Since the end of Ottoman Empire number of powers has tried but failed to establish stability in Middle East. Middle East is one of the unstable regions of the world. There are several reasons that create instability in the region. First group of factors are related with the economic, cultural, social and ethnic structure of the region. Creation of artificial maps and nations, richness in religious variety and sects and uncompleted nationalization process, importance of tribes, rich petrol reserves, scarcity of water and problems related with the division of waters of some rivers, deficiency of democratic regimes in the region are some important factors that create instability in the region. For example, the region is important for Islam, Christianity and Judaism. There are several sects in the region and people established separate and sometimes confronting groups as well.[10] Second group of reasons that

---

[8] Alan Makovsky and Sabri Sayarı (ed.), *Türkiye'nin Yeni Dünyası*, İstanbul: Alfa Yayınları, 2002, pp.1-2.
[9] See İdris Bal, "Turkish Foreign Policy (1960-1980)", *Ansycholopedy of Turkish History*, Ankara: Yeni Türkiye Publications, 2002.
[10] See Mehmet Atay, "Ortadoğuda Terör Savaşı ve Barış Arayışları", Ümit Özdağ and Osman Metin Öztürk, *Terörizm İncelemeleri*, Ankara: Avrasya Stratejik Araştırmalar Merekezi Yayınları, 2000, pp.203-204.

created instability in the region is related with Arab-Israeli conflict. This is the central problem in the Middle East and because of this conflict several wars took place and terrorist and guerilla groups were created and in turn these helped the instability of the region. Third group of reasons are related with Gulf war, Iran and ideological issues. The emergence of Iran as a anti-west and anti- US state in the region and de facto division of Iraq after the Gulf war, and presence of Lebanon state in name but has no authority over her land, USSR connection with some states like Iraq, Syria and Libya and the emergence of the tradition of using of terrorism as a foreign policy instrument are other factors that helped the rise of instability in the Middle east. Fourth group of reasons are potential reasons that can cause further instability in the region. The end of Cold War discipline affected Middle East as well. For instance, Iraqi occupied of Kuwait in August 1990. In post Cold War era new problems between Arab states can emerge and even these problems might lead to new wars. Especially when Arab Israeli dispute is over and when foreign interventions and influences in the region is declined, it is highly likely that new disputes and may be new wars will take place in the region over the artificial boundaries and sharing of the natural resources of the region.

After the end of USSR Caucasus destabilized as well. Chechens revolted against Russia. Abhazians revolted Georgia and Abhazia established a de facto state. On the other hand Armenia and Azerbaijan fought over Karabagh and Armenians occupied one fifth of Azeri land and one million Azeri people had to migrate other regions. Although a cease-fire was declared in 1994 and it is still valid, it is possible to argue that Azeri public opinion in these days encouraging Azeri government to take active steps in order to liberate Armenian occupied territory. Further more Azeris are psychologically preparing themselves for a new war against Armenia to liberate the occupied territory and they accuse Russia for backing Armenia. Turkey is trying to help efforts to find a peaceful solution. However because of cultural and ethnic connections Turkish public opinion is very sensitive on this issue and encourages Turkish government for a more active policy and help to Azeries for cultural and humanitarian reasons. Problems and conflicts in the regions around Turkey caused new headaches for Turkey and Turkish foreign policy.

During the Cold War era Turkey was an important country for the West as Turkey shared a common border with the USSR and as a member of NATO it defended thirty-seven percent of the common borders with the Communist block (Warsaw Pact) and had the second-largest army in NATO. In the case of an actual war, it would have been the first country to confront the Soviets. Following the collapse of the USSR, Turkey's importance for the West seemed to decline. The possibility of a confrontation between the Western and Eastern blocks no longer exists, former socialist countries started to reform their old systems by adopting market economies and multi-party systems with the assistance of the West and old hostilities motivated by ideological and military competition were replaced by new friendships. This new situation meant that Turkey was no longer an important partner for the West (including the US) as a buffer against the Soviet Union. However, for Turkey the threat from the 'East' did not disappear; and Turkey felt its position becoming more vulnerable as the support of the West declined. Historically Russia had claims on the Straits and the eastern provinces of Turkey, and had wanted to penetrate the South and reach the Mediterranean Sea. Therefore, Turkish politicians felt (and still feel) that in spite of the death of communism, no one could be sure that Russia had given up their expansionist ideas. Later, the rise of Zhirinovsky confirmed Turkish worries which are best expressed by President Süleyman Demirel's words in 1994: "Will Russia re-create the Russian empire? There is the phenomenon of Zhirinovsky, which brings this doubt to mind. ...If it is true that one in every two people in Russia thinks like Zhirinovsky, it becomes clear that this problem is more serious than the Zhirinovsky phenomenon...".[11] After Yeltsin, Vladimir Putin became president of Russia and he is following an active foreign policy. He has given an end to de facto state of Chechnya and trying to improve Russia's relations with Iran and China. Especially relations are being developed with China and Central Asian republics (except Turkmenistan) under the umbrella of Shanghai Cooperation Organization.[12] Following 11 September terrorist attacks on US, Russian US rapprochement has been seen as well. In fact, Russia is trying to balance China in the region by US and vice versa. Rise of Putin can ratify Turkish worries as well as possibility of close relations between Chine, Iran and Russia.[13] However, as will be dealt below Russia at the same time constituted a new era of cooperation for Turkey. If Turkey can develop her economic relations with Russia in that case possibility of confrontation between Turkey and Russia could be eradicated.

Turkish politicians felt that the West would be reluctant to help Turkey in the case of any dispute with Russia (or Syria and Iraq) because the West did not presently regard Russia as the enemy. Therefore, Turkey's political leadership wanted to convince the Western powers that although the Cold War had finished Turkey still occupied an important strategic position in global politics and was still important to the West. Turkey needed to find some arguments with which it could approach the Western powers.

In post Cold War era, to maintain international peace, US and Western powers aimed to undermine regional power centers, prevent spreading of nuclear technology, limit development of regional threat factors.[14] Iran-Iraq war lasted eight years and then Iraq occupied Kuwait in August 1990. After the occupation, Turkey became one of the most active and enthusiastic supporters of the American–led United Nations coalition which first imposed sanctions on Iraq and then in January 1991 waged war on that country. Turkey's active support of the Western coalition against Saddam Hussein during the Gulf War was an attempt to convince the West that Turkey was still important in global politics, and also to persuade the European Union to admit it as a member. Turkey's effective closure of the Iraqi pipeline to the Mediterranean (through which Iraq exported fifty four per cent of its oil, or approximately 1.5 million barrels a day); extension until December 1991 of the Defense and Economic Co-operation Agreement which gave the US access to military bases in Turkey,

---

[11] *Cumhurbaşkanı Sayın Süleyman Demirel'in Türk İşbirliği ve Kalkınma Ajansı'nın Üçüncü Çalışma Yılının Başlangıcında 'Günümüzde Avrasya' Konulu Toplantıda Yaptıkları Konuşma,* 14 September 1994, Ankara: TIKA, 1994, p.10.

[12] See, İdris Bal "The Rise of Shanghai Cooperation Organization in Eurasia: Is it an Effective Tool in a New Big Game", Ertan Efegil (ed.), *Geo-Politics of Central Asia in the Post Cold War Era: A Systemic Analysis,* Holland: Sota, 2002.

[13] İdris Bal, "ABD'nin Orta Asya Politikasine Etki eden İç ve Dış Faktörler, *Startejik Araştırmalar Dergisi,* Sayı.12, Nisan 2001, pp.59-65.

[14] Cemil Oktay, "Soğuk Savaş Sonrasında Ortadoğu'yu Okumak", Sabahattin Şen, (ed.), *Su Sorunu Türkiye ve Ortadoğu,* İstanbul: Bağlam Yayınları, 1993, p.96.

deployment of over 100,000 troops along the Iraqi border, and its allowing the use of NATO air bases such as İncirlik, played a vital role in the success of the anti-Iraqi coalition. At the expense of its economy, Turkey abided by UN sanctions on Iraq and this helps the rise of inflation and economic crisis in Turkey. US President George Bush appreciated Turkey's effective role in the Gulf War. In his speech at Ankara Esenboğa Airport, said:

When Saddam Hussein invaded Kuwait, Turkey acted courageously to ensure that aggression would not stand. And as the whole world knows, the international coalition could not have achieved the liberation of Kuwait without Turkey's pivotal contributions.[15]

Turkey's Middle East policy, and the dispute over water should be considered as additional factors that encouraged Turkey to support the Western coalition against Saddam. Iraq and Syria were (and are) opposed to the South East Anatolian Project (SEAP-GAP), and tried to stop the building of dams for GAP. For example, former President Özal pointed out at a meeting of regional directors of the Turkish State Water Administration that the construction of the Atatürk Dam on the Fırat (Euphrates) would not have been possible if the Iran-Iraq war had not diverted attention away from the issue. He added that "They [Iraq and Syria] would now be doing their utmost to prevent us from building this dam had we not started its construction during this period [the war]". As Özal's statement suggests, Turkey considered Syria and Iraq as potential enemies and Gulf war was a good instrument for Turkey to undermine Iraq as a possible threat.[16] Yet, in contrast to Turkey's expectations, Turkish support for the anti-Iraq coalition did not bring enough backing from the West for Turkey's position in terms of its relations with the EU and its problem with Kurdish separatist terrorists in South East Anatolia.

In contrast to Turkey's positive expectations, liberation of Kuwait was not the end of the problem and one may argue that the problem then has began for Turkey. Iraq was divided in three parts: North of the 36th Parallel, South of the 32nd Parallel and Iraq between 36th and 32nd Parallels. Iraq cannot implement its authority in the North and South. In the South, Shia opposition close to Iran is dominant while in the North, Kurdish groups: KDP (Kurdish Democrat Part headed by Mesud Barzani) and KPU (Kurdish Patriotic Union headed by Celal Talabani) controlled the region, which constitutes a de facto state. There is an embargo on Iraq imposed by Security Council of United Nations. This embargo undermined Iraq's economy as well as neighboring countries' economies that used to have economic relations with the Iraq. Therefore not only Iraq, but also other countries like Turkey was also punished, and international community has not so far repaid Turkey's losses incurred because of the embargo. This is a problem that causes instability in the region. Also the threat of Kurdish state and its attraction for the Kurdish people in the region as it encourage Kurdish nationalism in the region, is a factor which can further instability in the region. In general, unstable Iraq may cause new problems in the region[17]

---

[15] See "President George Bush's Speech at Ankara Esenboğa Airport, 20 July 1991", *Turkish Review*, Vol.5, No.25, Autumn 1991, p.104.

[16] See Süha Bölükbaşı, "Turkey Challenges Iraq and Syria: The Euphrates Dispute", *Journal of South Asian Middle Eastern Studies*, Vol.16. No.4, Summer 1993, pp.9-32.

[17] For the details of this isuue see, Ramazan Gözen, "Kuzey Irak Sorunu", İdris Bal (ed.), *21. Yüzyılın Eşiğinde Türk Dış Politikası*, İstanbul: Alfa, 2001; Ümit Özdağ, *Türkiye Kuzey Irak ve PKK*, Ankara:

and Turkey is affected by these developments in negative ways. Especially Turkey has been disturbed by the fact that Gulf War has created a de facto Kurdish State in Northern Iraq. Therefore Turkey advocates territorial integrity of Iraq and apposes a new war against Saddam.

In the case of Turkey's relations with the EU, it is obvious that they were (and are) far from being perfect. Especially after the Turkish application for full membership of the EC in April 1987, it was realized to a significant extent that Turkish attempts to integrate with Europe would end in despair (at least in the short term) because this application was rejected and there was no indication that Turkey would be accepted as a full member in the near future. Luxembourg summit (in December 1997) had demonstrated that Turkish membership to EU was not possible in the near feature. Kamran İnan, a former Ambassador and a Minister of State, argues that the possibility of joining the EU in the future is diminishing because of developments in Eastern Europe, and argues that Europe is giving priority to Eastern European states rather than Turkey for cultural reasons.[18] Developments in post Cold War era ratified these claims and Turkey, which has been waiting for full membership since 1963, was put behind ex-Communist Eastern European states. Turkey entered the Customs Union with the EU without becoming a full member in 1996. Turkey's courageous move can be interpreted as Turkey's reliance to her economy to compete in European markets. However after the Customs Union with EU trade between Turkey and EU has developed in the favor of EU not for Turkey. There is no other country in similar position. In contrast, some of the full members of EU like Greece first gained memberships, then they made preparations for customs union getting economic help from the Union and finally they entered Customs Union. Although Turkey wants to see the Customs Union as a first step of the full membership, there is no such automatic established procedure. Although Turkey has been recognized as an official candidate for the full membership of the EU in Helsinki summit in December 1999, it is obvious that Turkey will probably be able to gain a full membership after Eastern European countries become full members. There is also no timetable for Turkish membership and no one knows when Turkey will be a full member.[19]

EU is trying to form its own armed forces. On the other hand, the US wants to maintain regional and global balances to safeguard her position as a single superpower in the globe. Therefore, US does not want to see an independent European army and wants to manipulate developments via NATO. Turkey is located in a sensitive place and there are several conflicts around Turkey. Turkey is a member of NATO but not a member of EU. Turkey wants to have a veto right in the cases that EU uses facilities of NATO. On the other hand, EU wants to use NATO facilities without Turkish veto that can undermine Turkish position in NATO. If Turkey insists, in that case there is possibility that EU can form her independent army without needing NATO that is not welcomed by USA. This is

Center for Eurasian Strategic Studies Publications, 1999.
[18] Kamran İnan, *Dış Politika*, Istanbul: Ötüken, 1993, p.70; Veysel Bozkurt, *Türkiye ve Avrupa Topluluğu*, Istanbul: Ağaç Yayıncılık Ltd. Şti., 1992, p.104.
[19] İdris Bal, *Turkey's Relations with the West and the Turkic Republics*, Aldershot: Ashgate, 2000, p.48. For Turkish EU relations see Veysel Bozkurt, *Avrupa ve Türkiye*, Bursa: Vipaş, 2001.

mainly because independent European power can refuse American hegemony in Europe as well as in the globe. In that case, this will mean end of US hegemony in the World. This situation puts Turkey in a very critical position between EU and USA.[20]

Although Turks and Greeks lived side by side around three hundred years under the banner of Ottoman Empire and there are some cultural similarities between two nations, Turkish Greek relations are taking place in the form of confrontation rather than cooperation. There are several problems to be solves or to put on the table such as problems related with Aegean Sea, Turkish minority in Greece, and Cyprus. However, Greece is member of EU and these problems are becoming problems between EU and Turkey. This is very dangerous for Turkey. The dispute over Cyprus with Greece has been one of the most serious problems for Turkish foreign policy because it has become a dispute between Turkey and the European Union. It is highly likely that other Turco-Greek disputes, such as those over the islands in the Aegean Sea, will become disputes between Turkey and the EU, and it is clear that Turkey will be under more pressure in the future.[21] Thus, it will be too difficult for Turkey to balance EU in the future. Therefore in mid-term if Turkey cannot be a full member of EU, EU itself will be biggest threat for Turkey and Turkish interest because of Turkish Greek disputes unless Turkey can establish alternative relations with other parties that can balance EU. This dangerous process is being realized by different degrees by different parts of Turkish society and Turkish institutions. For instance Secretary General of National Security Council, General Kılıç, recently criticized Turkish foreign policy and her relations with EU and he advocates improving relations with Russia and Iran. These reactions can be regarded as initial steps of Turkish side in search of alternative relations to balance EU in the future. The importance of the cool relations between Turkey and the EU is that negative developments have been pushing Turkish public opinion away from the West and urging Turkish decision-makers to search for more creative foreign relations policies.

The belief in Turkey that Turkey is without support and is "lonely" in international relations as having problems with her neighbors and have not good relations with neither with Western World nor with Islamic World. This may be worth emphasizing here as a potentially important factor affecting its reactions and decisions in post Cold War era. In the 1990's, in spite of Turkey's close relations with the EU, the EU did not give enough support her on crucial issues such as fighting cross border terrorism and Kurdish separatism, the disputes with Greece, Cyprus problem and the water dispute in the Middle East.

The outstanding problem of Turkey in the late 1980's and through 1990's was the Kurdish terrorist activities mainly in South East Turkey carried out by the Kurdish Workers Party, PKK. With the end of Cold War some of the former Communists of Turkey canalized their activities towards Kurdish separatism that made this movement more effective. Abdullah Öcalan founded PKK (Kurdish Workers Party) in November 1978. PKK has begun its terrorist activity in the southeast Turkey in 1984. Gradually, the scale of PKK activities increased. In 1989, the PKK concluded an alliance with a number

---

[20] See Hüseyin Bağcı, "Türkiye ve AGSK: Beklentiler, Endişeler", İdris Bal (ed.), *21. Yüzyılın Eşiğinde Türk Dış Politikası.*
[21] İdris Bal, "European Union, Turkic Republics and Turkish Dilemma", *Pakistan Horizon*, Vol.49, No.1, January 1996, p.77.

of extreme left wing urban guerrilla groups (Dev Sol, TİKKO, DHKP-C and others) which increased its ability to strike in Turkey's big cities[22] and the cost of stopping PKK activities grew more expensive through 1990's for the Turkish republic. To sustain security in the region and to fight against the PKK, the Turkish government has been spending a significant part of its income to finance around 120.000 soldiers in South East Anatolia. Some researchers claim that the cost of PKK to Turkey is more than 100 billion $.[23] If indirect effects of the problem are taken in to account cost of the problem is obviously much greater than this amount. In the clashes between PKK and Turkish security forces about 40.000 civilian as well as offical people lost their lives. Moreover, on the international arena Kurdish separatist activities have formed a barrier before Turkish foreign relations in general, relations with EU in particular. PKK badly undermined Turkey in every aspect. In general Turkish image and Turkish foreign policy were weakened in international arena. Thus, attraction of Turkey in the region declined, this made negative effects on other countries' policies towards Turkey too. It gave an appearance that Turkey cannot pursue a stable policy as it is even in difficulty to keep together its own territory and it is on the food steps of the separation. Turkish foreign policy was undermined and it became a barrier before Turkey's relations with all regions. The West as the US does not support Turkey's position on Kurdish separatism in South East Anatolia and Western states have been supporting a political solution to the dispute and pressing Turkey towards this.[24] However, it is necessary to make a distinction between US and Western countries. Because US played an important role in getting Abdullah Öcalan captured and is more empathetic towards Turkey. But US and EU tend to approach the issue from the human rights perspective, Central Asian states regarded the issue as an indicator of weakness of Turkish power and Turkish model. By forcing Turkey to spend its limited resources in fighting with terrorism, PKK and its supporters handicapped Turkish foreign policy and destabilized Turkey in general. As a result of it, economic problems in the region, military coups, and some mistakes that Turkey has done such as banning Kurdish language made negative affects on Kurdish problem and gave good instruments to PKK to justify itself and its propaganda. Although Abdullah Öcalan was captured in Kenia in 1999 and this affected PKK in negative way, it is the fact that PKK is still an important organization and trying to canalize its struggle to the political ground.[25] The PKK pulled out of Turkey to its bases in the breakaway enclave of northern Iraq and Iran after Öcalan was sentenced to death by Turkish court in 1999 for having responsibility for the killings of more than 40,000 people. "The PKK now says it has abandon the fight for Kurdish self-rule and wants cultural rights for the country's some 12 million Kurds. But Turkish authorities refuses the PKK overtures as a bid to save Öcalan from execution and warns

---

[22] Erik J. Zürcher, *Turkey, A modern History*, London: I.B. Tauris & Co. Ltd. Publishers, 1994, p.314.

[23] For detailed explanations about PKK see Nihat Ali Özcan, *PKK (Kürdistan İşçi Partisi)*, Ankara: ASAM, 1999.

[24] İdris Bal, *Turkey's Relations with the West and the Turkic Republics*, Aldershot: Ashgate, 2000, pp.46-48.

[25] Ibid., pp.24-29.

that the group was still a terrorist one having the capability to strike".[26]

Although Turkey has been trying to follow parallel policies with the West especially since the establishment of modern Turkey, Turkey has been disappointed by the European attitudes towards herself. For instance the EU angered Ankara by excluding Turkish terrorist groups such as the Kurdistan Workers Party (PKK) and the Revolutionary People's Liberation Party-Front (DHKP-C) from its December list of terrorist organizations. Most of these groups are active in the European countries under different banners. Ecevit attended two-days of European Union summit meeting in Barcelona in March 2002, urged the bloc to give efficient support for Turkey's fight against terrorism. "I hope entire members of the European Union will give us effective support in our fight against terrorism," said Turkish primeminister Bülent Ecevit addressing to the participants in the summit. Turkey is also disappointed with no change of track by the EU in the wake of the September 11 attacks that killed thousands in the United States. Turkey was the first country that declared full backing for U.S. anti-terrorism campaign after the September 11 and hoped that the European countries would be empathetic towards its 15 years of struggle against the PKK.[27] However, EU has not until now changed its attitues towards terrorism in Turkey and that constitutes an important problem between Turkey and EU.

Similarly Turkey's position on the water dispute in the Middle East is not supported. Turkey, Iraq and Syria are involved in the water dispute, with Iraq and Syria opposing Turkey's South East Anatolian Project (SEAP-GAP), claiming that Iraq's share of the Euphrates would decline from 30 billion cubic meters to below its minimum need, and that 50% of Syria's 31.8 billion cubic meters annual Euphrates supply would be cut off. Hence, it is argued that after the end of the Cold War the major threat to Turkey now comes from the South East, namely from Iraq and Syria and that this shift would be reflected in Turkey's new defense strategy. Especially, Syria has been an important source of anxiety on the part of Turkey, because "Syria was for a long time perceived as a source of threat due to its military association with the Soviet Union. A treaty of assistance between the two and the flow of sophisticated Soviet weaponry to Syria, together with the presence of the Soviet navy in the eastern Mediterranean, gave rise to a feeling of having been encircled by Soviet power to the north and the south". After the collapse of the Soviet Union, although the Soviet-Syrian connection was broken, there was a proliferation of sophisticated weaponry - ballistic missiles, chemical weapons - "and of nuclear weapons capability in the immediate neighborhood of Turkey".[28] In general, since the First World War, Turkey's relations with the Middle Eastern Arab countries have been cool. Recognition of the Turkish Republic of Northern Cyprus (1983) internationally was a test case for Turkey and when it was not able to draw enough support from the Arab states, this was understood as a clear sign that they were not 'friends' of Turkey.

---

[26] *Turkish Daily News*, 16 March 2002.
[27] *Turkish Daily News*, 16 March 2002.
[28] Duygu Bazoğlu Sezer, "Threat Perceptions in Southern Europe: The Case of Turkey", Laszlo Valki (ed.), *Changing Threat Perceptions and Military Doctrines*, Basingstoke: Macmillan Press, 1992, pp.234-235.

Cyprus was a former Ottoman territory populated by ethnic Greeks and Turks. Later British Empire began to rule the island in 1870s and in 1960 an independent Cyprus republic was established. Since that time Cyprus to a large extent overshadowed Turkish foreign policy and Turkish policy towards almost all regions is affected by Cyprus problem. After consultations with Britain, which did not want to take joint action under the Treaty of Guarantee, Turkey intervened as a guarantor power on 20 July 1974 in conformity with its treaty rights and obligations. The Turkish intervention blocked the way to the annexation of the island by Greece, stopped the persecution of the Turkish Cypriots and brought peace to Cyprus. However, the Turkey's Western allies as well as rest of the world criticized Turkish intervention and Turkey was punished with embargo by the US, Turkey's closest ally. From 1974 onwards, Greek Cypriot side continued with its sovereignty claims over the entire island. This prompted the Turkish Cypriot side to assert its rights by proclaiming the Turkish Republic of Northern Cyprus (TRNC) in 1983. An important development is that Greek Cypriot side unilaterally applied for membership in the EU on behalf of Cyprus as a whole in 1990. The Greek Cypriot side perceived EU membership as a way of achieving dominance on the whole of the island and ensuring a more favorable position for Greece (a member of the EU) than Turkey (a non-member) over Cyprus. Mr. Clerides, the leader of the Greek Cypriots, told his people that once "Cyprus" was accepted as a member of the EU, the national cause of Hellenism would triumph, as the Treaty of Guarantee would be inapplicable against a member state. Therefore, the period as of 1990 has been overshadowed by this application. Though fully undermining the UN negotiating process, the Greek Cypriot administration insisted on proceeding with EU membership. Finally, at the Luxembourg Summit of December 1997, the EU decided to open membership negotiations with the Greek Cypriots.[29] This situation constitutes an important problem for Turkey and Turkish Republic of Northern Cyprus. TRNC is not recognized either by Western counties or by Islamic or any other countries (except Turkey). Cyprus case can be regarded as test case for Turkish prestige and Turkish foreign policy and it proves Turkey loneness in international relations.[30]

In the post Cold War era, in the search for new allies Turkey established strategic alliance with Israel. This move helped Turkey to balance Syria and Iraq regarding sharing of Waters of Euphrates and Tigris rivers. Also it helped Turkey to get sophisticated US weapons through Israel. However, Turkey has been trying to establish close relations with Middle East Arab countries since 1960's. One can argue that Turkish Israeli alliance can further alienate rest of the Middle East countries from Turkey. Therefore, cost and benefit calculations should be made again regarding Turkish Israeli strategic alliance. Alternatively, some of the Arab countries should be attracted and hopefully some of the Arab countries should be persuaded to join this alliance. Arabs are disturbed by Turkish Israeli alliance. For example on 17 March, Arab League foreign ministers ended their two-day meeting with a communique that expressed concern over Turkey's military relationship with Israel. The statement called on Turkey to end

[29]   Foreign   Ministry   Publications,   Cyprus   7   Questions   &   Answers,
http://www.mfa.gov.tr/grupe/eh/default.htm
[30] For a brief discussion of Cyprus Problem see Nasuh Uslu, "Kıbrıs Sorunu", İdris Bal (ed.), *21. Yüzyılın Eşiğinde Türk Dış Politikası*, İstanbul: Alfa, 2001, pp.263-301.

its military ties with the Jewish state. The communique expressed Arab League concern over "Turkish-Israeli military cooperation and its serious repercussions on security and stability in the area. We want to stress once again that Arab countries are keen to continue their traditional relations with Turkey and to develop these relations. We express increasing anxiety over growing military cooperation between Turkey and Israel and ask Turkey to reconsider this cooperation which poses a danger to Arab security and stability in the area." However, The Arab League has also called on Turkey to negotiate water rights with neighboring Iraq and Syria that justifies Turkish Israeli rapprochement in order to balance Syria and Iraq. If Turkey should reconsider her policy towards Israel, Arab countries should reconsider their support to Syria and Iraq against Turkey as well.

New Opportunities for Turkey: Why is Turkey Strategically an Important Country?

One of the obvious implications of the Cold War was that it had frozen maps in the World and there was some sort of stability even under the shadow of weapons. When the Cold War ended it was believed that a New World Order would be established, liberalism and human rights risen and a peaceful world order established. In contrast to these optimistic expectations, regional problems have emerged immediately after the end of Cold War. Ethnic and religious aspirations have found suitable conditions to flourish and be materialized. Therefore, new conflicts and wars took place in the world, especially, in the Middle East, Balkans and Caucasus. End of the Cold War led to the emergence of new power vacuums in different parts of the World as well as an increase importance of regional powers.

Apart from causing new problems, end of Cold War has created new opportunities for Turkey as well. While relations between Turkey and the EU were reaching a crisis point, end of Cold War and the USSR opened a window of opportunity for Turkey from the Balkans to China and the strategic position of Turkey became more important then before. Turkish intellectuals and higher bureaucrats stressed the political and economic advantages of the new developments for Turkey. For instance, for Seyfi Taşhan (Head of the Foreign Policy Institute); and Bilal Şimşir (Ambassador and Foreign Ministry Director-General of Relations with the CIS), Turkey was transformed from being marginal to Western security interests to being a central power in the region.[31] Although the collapse of the USSR radically improved the strategic position of Turkey, and provided new opportunities, this did not alter Turkey's pro-Western policy. Therefore, Turkey set out to fulfill its ambitions with regards to the West while making use of the opportunities that the New World order presented.

In the early 1990s Turkey began to consider several potential structures: the Black Sea Economic Co-operation (BSEC), a free trade agreement with the United States, and the Balkan Co-operation Council.[32] In addition to these, new opportunities appeared, such as the Economic Co-operation Organization (ECO) and more importantly co-operation with the Turkic Republics.

However, because of Iranian Turkish completion and ideological problems ECO as an

---

[31] *Jane's Defence Weekly*, 18 April 1992.

[32] Daniel A. Connelly, "Black Sea Economic Cooperation", *RFE/RL Research Report*, Vol.31, No.26, 1 July 1994, p.32. Also see; Faruk Şen, "Black Sea Economic Cooperation: A Supplement to the EC?", *Aussen Politik*, Vol.44, No.3, 1993.

organization cannot function properly in the region. On the other hand, Turkey did not consider BSEC seriously rather Turkey wanted to use this organization in order to show her importance in the region to the West. Turkey invited Greece for membership of BSEC to make concession with Greece regarding Turkish membership to EU. Greece became a member of BSEC but Greece attitude towards Turkish membership to EU has not changed and presence of Greece and Armenia is main handicap for cooperation in BSEC. Therefore success of BSEC is open to the discussion as well.

In the post Cold War era, Turkey needed allies, and in this respect reformation of Central Asia, Caucasus, Balkans and Middle East presented new opportunities for Turkey. For cultural, ethnic, economic and security reasons, regions around Turkey can be regarded as "near abroad" for Turkey similar to Russian claims for former USSR's territory. Especially the emergence of the Turkic Republics as independent states was important; it was hoped that because of their common culture, ethnicity and history, these Republics who were regarded as natural allies, would support Turkey in the international arena. At the same time, promotion of the Turkish Model to newly independent Central Asian republics by the West became an instrument through which Turkey could show its continuing importance for the world politics in general. Therefore, Turkey's main objective was to see these new Turkic Republics gain and keep their independence. This tendency was later illustrated by the fact that the Turkish Republic of Northern Cyprus was also invited to some of the meetings that took place among the Turkic Republics. With the end of Socialist domination in Balkans, apart from new conflicts, a new area of cooperation was opened for Turkey. Especially growing relations between Albania and Turkey is an example of this cooperation. At the same time a competition between Turkey and Greece can be observed in Balkans. Since 1995 Greece has been trying to pursue an active policy towards Balkan nations including Macedonia and Albania. Greece's position as a member of EU help her in her cause.[33] The end of Soviet connections with the Middle East was also a positive development for Turkey. For instance, if Soviet-Syrian connection did not end, it would be too difficult for Turkey to threat Syria with war, unless Syria deported Öcalan from her territory.

There are several factors that make Turkey a strategically important country in the region in post Cold War era. Turkey is located at the center of Balkans, Middle East and Caucasus. Turkey has borders with Nakhichevan and Georgia. There is a land road connecting Turkey to Central Asia over Georgia. After the end of Cold War, all three regions around the Turkey destabilized. International community needed and still needs Turkish help to find solutions for conflicts in Balkans, Caucasus and Middle East. This is the ratification of Turkish importance in the region as well as in the globe.

An important factor that underlines Turkish importance in the region is that Turkey has ethnic, cultural and historic ties with the region as Ottomans governed the area around four centuries. This historical background and geographic closeness and cultural and ethnic ties enable Turkey to play an active role in all three regions and plus in Central Asia and makes Turkey a strategically important country. From all regions from Balkans to Middle East and from Caucasus to Central Asia public have relatively warm attitudes towards Turkey in

---

[33] See Hüseyin Bağcı, *Turkey and Balkans (1992-1994)*, Ankara: Foreign Policy Institute, 1994.

general and most of the peoples of the region regard Turkey as a second homeland. Therefore it is possible to find people who migrated to Turkey from all the regions around Turkey. After the end of Ottoman Empire hundreds of thousands of people migrated from all other regions to Turkey as Turkey is regarded as a second homeland by especially Muslim peoples of the region. The last wave of migration took place during the Bosnian war and Kosova conflict. There are even some districts in Istanbul called as Arnavut köy (Albanian Village), Yeni Bosna (New Bosnia), Çerkez Köy (Cirches Village, migrants from Caucasus) and so on, which proves the importance of Turkey for the peoples of the region. Because of these ties public opinion towards Turkey are relatively positive. For instance, if democratic regimes have been established in Middle East, because of relatively positive public opinions towards Turkey, Turkish Middle East relations can be developed more easily.[34]

Central Asia was not under Ottoman rule but there is kinship, common culture, and language history that unify Anatolian Turks and Central Asian Turks. As Pipes pointed out it is difficult to distinguish politics from ethnicity.[35] Turkey has strong cultural historic and ethnic ties with the peoples of the region. Because of the presence of these ties there are positive public opinion in the region towards Turkey and this is an advantage for the Turkish government and Turkish firms. This advantage puts Turkey before other actors in the region. For a Turkish citizen, it is relatively easy to understand behaviors, the way of thinking, tradition, reaction, in brief psychology of the peoples of the region. Languages of the same family are spoken in the region except Tajikistan. Languages of Azerbaijan and Turkmenistan are closer to Turkish language spoken in Turkey in comparison with Kazakh and Kyrgyz languages. Peoples of the region and people of Turkey celebrate same religious days. All these are plus for Turkey and helps Turkey and Turkish people. The President of Kyrgyz tan, Askar Akayev, in his speech, said that "Turkey is a morning star which shows the true path to other Turks".[36] Leaders of other republics have similar remarks as well. Their attitudes did no change drastically but they become more realists and they understand the limits of Turkey and they want to develop relations with Turkey. Ten years of relations showed that because of weak economy and terrorism Turkish success in her Central Asian policy is limited. At the begging of 1990s it was thought that Turkey would be main actor in the region. However, Turkey was not successful enough. Because of her problem Turkey has lost her attraction and central Asian republics began to develop their relations with the West as well as Pacific countries and neighboring China and Russia. The assumption that they would be Turkey's natural allies are open to discussion as some of the presidents of Turkic republics visited Erevan and declared their support to Armenia regarding Armenian claims of genocide (regarding 1915 events during Ottoman Empire).

In the post Cold War era, Turkey became an important country for global politics as well. In the post Cold War era, the US strengthened her position in the world politics and became single superpower as former superpower USSR, leader of the Socialist block, left

---

[34] See more details, Tayyar Arı, "2000'li Yıllarda Türkiye'nin Ortadoğu Politikası", İdris Bal (Der.), *21. Yüzyılın Eşiğinde Türk Dış Politikası*, İstanbul: Alfa Yayınları, 2001.

[35] *International Herald Tribune*, 14 February 1990; Andre Gunder Frank, *The Centrality of Central Asia*, Amsterdam: VU University Press, 1992, pp.22-23.

[36] *Kirgizistan*, Turki Cumhuriyetler Dizisi, Sabah, 1992.

the competition and disunited. Therefore even some circles called the US as "police of the world". The United States attempted to establish New World Order and promoted liberalism, market economy and human rights. However, there were some challenges ahead. It was too difficult to fill the power vacuums created by the end of USSR in the world and the US was not alone to fill them. Regional and global powers were in a competition to take advantage in the new situation. The world history and natural rules suggest that one power cannot be dominant over other powers for a long time. Therefore, those who are disturbed by the present system and jealous will like to be rival to US and try to follow opposite policies. In fact, there are developments in this direction. It is possible to observe that Russia, China, India, EU, and Germany and Japan are rising in international scene economically, politically and militarily. At present, some of these countries have good relations with US and some others, for example China and Russia, have some reactions to US policies and have ambiguous relations with it. Some analysts have begun to describe new era as tri-polar international system: USA, EU and Russia-China-India strategic triangle.[37] However, although it is the fact that China, Russia, India and EU are becoming important power centers in the present world, to call or describe post Cold War international system as tri-polar is an exaggeration as it is too early to call the international system in this way. Further more calling present international system as multi polar or three polar at this stage will be miscalculation of US power economically and politically. The US is still overshadowing other emerging power centers in the world in all aspects. The relations also among China, Russia and India are not enough deep and comprehensive to be labeled as strategic triangle. On the other hand, US has been checking and balancing all these three powers, developing her relations with each power separately and undermining the possibility of emerging strategic triangle. However, in the long term, this can change depending on US and other powers' performances.

Russia and China are not happy with the present international system as well as growing US hegemony. They have shown their reactions to the US in some occasions, for example in Gulf War in 1991, following US-Iraq conflicts, Bosnian War and Kosova Conflict. By criticizing US, Russia and China meant that they were also important powers in the globe and they should have been consulted and cooperated in terms of international affairs. They are trying to put forward themselves as alternative powers and they are attempting to open a path for a new multi polar international system. These indicators have shown that US hegemony can be challenged globally as well as regionally therefore, while formulating her foreign policy, US should take these and possible other challenges in to account. EU is also in a way of being separate power center and trying to limit the US influence over Europe. European currency has replaced national currencies in 2002; EU is trying to follow common foreign policy and trying to establish European army. If this trend continues in this direction successfully, this process ultimately will end up with the emergence of a new power center and EU will no longer obey to the wishes of US in the future.

With the end of Cold War, a power vacuum has been created in Eurasia. Eurasia,

---

[37] Çevik Bir, "Güvenli Bir Avrasya İçin", *Ulusal Strateji*, Vol. 2, No.14, September – November 2000, p.19.

especially central Asia is still important for regional as well as global politics. Central Asia is not an ordinary region in the world. According to Halford Mackinder, region has vital geo-strategic importance to control the world politics. According to Mackinder's theory of "heartland", with the development of railways, the importance of land domination increased in comparison with sea domination. According to the theory, the power that controls Eurasian land mass and especially center of this land, Central Asia, will control the whole World. In other words, the power that governs and develops center of Eurasia will dominate the whole world politics.[38] In brief, Sir Halford Mackinder in his theory of Heartland portrayed the Central Asia as heart of the World and in order to control the world, this piece of the world has vital importance and must be controlled. Because of developments in technology, communication and transportation and son the validity of this theory of course open to discussion. However Eurasia is still important for other reasons. Firstly, Central Asia is located in the heart of Eurasia, among important countries, such as China, India, Iran, Pakistan and Russia. Especially China, Russia and India are outstanding powers and important for regional as well as global politics mainly because of their nuclear capabilities, military powers, natural resources and economic potentials. Secondly, Central Asia can also be regarded as a source of possible threats towards regional and global powers. Outstanding examples are drug smuggling, terrorism and fundamentalism that frighten Russia, China as well as most of the other regional and global powers. Recent terrorist attacks on USA and following this, US led operation in Afghanistan, underline importance of region for security reasons. Thirdly, Central Asia is extremely rich in energy resources as well. Apart from strategic importance of the region, newly discovered carbohydrate resources in Central Asia and Caspian Sea are enough to make the region still important for the regional and global politics. Because in the most part of the 21st century the carbohydrates will still be main source of energy. For this reason, new oil and gas resources in the region attract attention of regional and global powers towards the area. Apart from political and security reasons, natural resources have encouraging regional and global players for competition in the region in post Cold War era. Therefore, although arguments have changed to some significant extent, the region has still vital importance for the world politics. If a New World Order is going to be created, developments in Central Asia has to play a vital role in the process of forming the New World Order. There are several candidates who wish to fill the gap in the Eurasia and they have different bargaining tools. However, growing cooperation between China and Russia and rise of the SCO (Shanghai Cooperation Organization) disturbed US; therefore, the terrorist attacks gave a good opportunity to the US to deal with Eurasia issue directly. Although US are overshadowing other powers in all aspects at present, in the long term, US hegemony is bound to her performance in Eurasia. US have to stop emergence of independent powers in Europe and Eurasia that will refuse US hegemony.[39]

---

[38] Bilgin Erdoğan, "ABD'nin Orta Asya Siyaseti", Mim Kemal Öke (ed.), *Orta Asya Türk Cumhuriyetleri*, İstanbul: Alfa Yayınları, 1999, p.230. And also see Sami Karamısır, *Türkiye'nin Siyasi Meseleleri*, İstanbul: Osmanlı Araştırmaları Vakfı, 1994, pp.187-194; Gerald Robbins, "Post-Sovyet Anayurdu", *Avrasya Etüdleri*, Vol.1, No.3, Winter 1994.

[39] See Anıl Çeçen, "ABD Süper Güç Olarak Kalabilir mi?", *Avrasya Dosyası*, Vol. 6, No. 2, Summer

Therefore, US have to follow developments in Eurasia as well as in Europe (EU) with care. US cooperation with Russia and Uzbekistan are important steps however, they should not be exaggerated. In the long-term, Russian and Chinese potentials, such as large territories, rich natural resources, population (especially important for China) and psychological factors, will encourage these powers to play more determining role in the world politics and be rival to US hegemony. Expectations of other Slavs and Slav countries from Russia can be a factor that encourages Russia to be superpower as well. For this reason, US cooperation with Russia at present should be regarded as tactical step.

In the post Cold War period, US have been trying to manipulate changes and preserve regional and global balances that can be regarded as foundations of American hegemony. This was a duty for US as otherwise she could (and can) loose her position as a superpower. Therefore, US followed the developments in Eurasia with patient. It cooperated with Turkey in Eurasia and attempted to limit Iran and Russia. Therefore Turkey has emerged as unique country for US for cooperation and US Turkish relations reached to the level of strategic partnership. This can be regarded as ratification of Turkish importance for not only regional politics but also for global politics. In the future, in order to balance regional and global developments, US need to take more steps forward. US-Turkish cooperation should continue and concrete projects should be put forward. US can support Turkish Speaking Nations' Summits and this process can be institutionalized similar to the EU and new members can be adopted (including US). In other words, Turkish-American strategic alliance should be further developed and expanded under the umbrella of an institution similar to the SCO or EU. Azerbaijan, Central Asian republics, Pakistan and Afghanistan should be attracted and be member of this Organization. There are some developments that indicate US decision to give more roles to Turkey in the region. For instance, it is highly likely that as an ally of US, Turkey will take leadership of international peace force in Afghanistan from UK. In the case of EU, US must monitor developments in EU, for instance, may be by means of Turkey's membership. Apart from UK, Turkish membership can provide US with new instrument for her European policy. Otherwise, strong EU will not take order from US in the future. Loosing its control in Europe means for the United States loosing the game in Eurasia. Ultimately, it will lead to the end of US leadership in the world.

Although with the Afghan operation, US settled in the region, if USA cannot manipulate developments, Russia-China-India strategic triangle alliance can be established and other powers, such as Iran, can join this in 21st century. In that case, Japan and South Korea can side with the US in this competition. If potentials of Russia, China and India are taken into account, it can easily be argued that it will be too difficult for US to compete with this potential new alliance. Iran and China are cooperating on nuclear weapons. Iran and Russian relations are developing as well. Hatemi visited Russia 12th March 2001 and they agreed on several issues. For example, Iran decided to buy weapons from Russia worth of 7 Billion dollars. In order to check and balance new developments,

2000, pp.233-251.

especially Russian, Iranian and Chinese rapprochement in the region, and help to protect independence of Central Asian republics, Turkey is important as well. US put economic interests before other goals such as security and human rights. With the 11 September attacks this changed and US began to regard Eurasia very important for security reasons as well. However, unless Russia and her allies are checked and balanced in the region, even independence of the new republics are at stake. These developments make Turkey as an ally of the US more important to balance and manipulate developments.

Furthermore, president Bush pointed out Iran, Iraq and North Korea as satanic triangle. Two of these countries are neighbors of Turkey. Syria is also accused for supporting international terrorism. These developments make Turkey more important after 11 September attacks on US. As mentioned above, Turkey played an important role in 1991 Gulf war. However, US still regards Saddam regime as dangers and therefore regards Turkish help important in a next campaign against Iraq. Turkey took part in Gulf War in 1991, as Dick Cheny's visit in March 2002 suggests US still needs Turkish help to give an end to Saddam regime in Iraq. Turkey is playing an important role in the region as well as in globe to balance Middle East countries such as Iraq, Syria and Iran. Turkey is also import for the big game replayed in Eurasia. In this regard Turkey is important to balance Russia.

Russians and Turks grew in the history at the expense of other side in general. Russia was a city under the control of Golden Horde a Turkish Empire in 13.century. Then by the 20.th century Russia controlled all the Turkic regions in Caucasus and Central Asia except Anatolia. Russians have a traditional goal of reaching Mediterranean Sea but they have failed to reach Mediterranean Sea as Anatolian Turks stopped them in the history. During the Cold War again Anatolian Turks, Turkey stood in front of Russians and defended southeast flak of NATO. The collapse of USSR was a minus for Russians while the same thing was a plus for Turks as most of the Turks under the control of Russians established their own independent republics. Although USSR has disunited, with its huge territory, natural resource, population and military capacity and nuclear weapons Russia is still an important power and Russia still has the capability of hitting USA. After the collapse of the USSR, Russia initially gave priority to domestic affairs, and it was assumed that Russia did not want to regain control over the former Soviet territory. Most people therefore talked about a power vacuum created in the region by the end of the USSR. However, especially after 1993, Russia clearly announced its intention of regaining control over the former Soviet territory known as the 'near abroad' policy, Russia justified her policy in three ways. There were economic reasons, as the Russian economy depended on the other Republics (and vice versa); security reasons, as Russia wanted to control nuclear power and did not want to see a rival power settled in the former Soviet territory. Around 25 million ethnic Russians living outside Russian territory also encouraged Russia to control the former Soviet territory in order to guarantee their civil rights. In 1994, Russia signed several agreements with the Turkic Republics and Russian bases reopened in the region. This was not a terrible development for the West, who preferred to deal with one nuclear power in the region rather than four, and was seeking the stability in the region, which Russia could provide. Therefore, in contrast to Turkish expectations, the West allowed Russia to implement the 'near abroad' policy as if it was Russia's legitimate right to control former Soviet territory. Russia has been using ethnic conflicts to penetrate to the region and to interfere the domestic politics of the regional states.

For example instability in Tajikistan serves Russia to turn back to the region and open Russian bases. Russia is justifying her presence in the region with terrorism and ethnic problems. Turkey is important to balance Russia statically and geographically. There is no guaranty that democratization; market economy will make Russia a peaceful state and a friend of the US and West in the region. In fact Russia tends to play a rival role against USA.

Turkey is close to the Caspian energy resources. In the 21 Century it is believed that petrol and gas still will be main sources of energy. Countries of Caucasus and Central Asia are rich in oil and gas and they want to transport their oil and gas to the World markets. For instance, Turkish proposal of Baku-Ceyhan pipeline project was backed by US and an accord setting out terms for seeking commercial investment in the proposed 1,600-kilometer pipeline from Baku, the capital of Azerbaijan, to the Turkish Mediterranean port of Ceyhan has been signed in the summit of the Organization for Security and Co-operation in Europe (OSCE) in Istanbul on 18th November 1999.[40] However, Russia has monopoly of access to Caspian oil and gas at present. A new pipeline project call Caspian Pipeline Consortium has completed. It begins in Kazak territory and ends in Russian Black Sea port, Novorossisk. US support to Turkish project (Baku Ceyhan) is also open to discussion.[41]

Russia is at the same time a new area for cooperation. Trade is developing as seen in the case of suitcase trade. Russia is selling gas to Turkey and there are new project such as Blue Stream project. Trade (import plus export) between Turkey and Russia was more than four billion dollars (4.230.800.000$) in 1997.[42] This number declined later on because of economic crises. It is the fact that if economic relations are developed between Turkey and Russia, this will force politicians for cooperation.

Turkey is also important to balance Iran in the region. Iranian revolution has not only changed political structure but it is defined as third path apart from Capitalism and Socialism. Once a close ally of USA, after the Islamic revolution became an enemy of West and US. In order to export Islamic revolution Iran has targeted regional states. This was true especially during the Humeyni regime. Therefore, Iran supported radical groups in these countries and carried out propaganda in this direction. This in turn helped the isolation of Iran in international arena economically and politically as well as instability in the Middle East. Then Iran's policy has changed and Iran began to put national interest before the ideological interest.[43] After Islamic revolution, although neither Turkey nor Iran has admitted it, these two countries become rival powers in the region. Although Iran has some geo-strategic advantages in the region, it has significant handicaps as well. Primarily, although Iran is an Islamic state, the effect of Iran in the Muslim Republics in Central Asia and

---

[40] *TRT Avrasya TV.* News at 6.00 p.m., 18.11.1999.

[41] See for details, A. Nejdet Pamir, *Turkey: The Key to Caspian Oil and Gas,* Jerulamam and Washington: Institute for Advanced Strategic and Political Studies, IASP Research Papers in Strategy, September 2001, No.13.

[42] Web page of Turkish Embassy in Moscow: http://www.turkishline.ru/embassy/rus_tek.html, pp.1-4.

[43] İdris Bal, *Turkey's Relations with the West and the Turkic Republics, The rise and fall of the Turkish Model,* Aldershot (UK): Ashgate Publishing Limited, 2000, p.118-120; For details see Edmund Herzig, *Iran and the Former Soviet South,* London: Royal Institute of International Affairs, 1995.

Caucasus and in fact over the Islamic World is very limited. This is mainly because there is a divide between Shiite and Sunni Muslims, and a hostile attitude between these two sects. Iran is a Shiite state; on the other hand the majority of the population of the region around Turkey is Sunni, except for the Azeris. Iran's influence even over the Azeri population is very limited, as Azeris are Turkic and their nationalistic feelings are strong. Also, Iran has an ethnic Azeri population of some twenty million living in the north of the country, and is worried about the possible unification of these peoples. Over the years Iran has changed her radical policy as realized her limits in the region as well as in globe. Iran did not become involved in a struggle to export its regime to the Muslim Republics in Eurasia. In fact it has been looking for possible cooperation in economic fields, after being isolated by the West. Therefore Iran's policy was pragmatic and realistic rather than adventurist. Instead of supporting Azerbaijan, Iran sided with Armenia in the Azeri-Armenian war and since then Iran's relations with Armenia is developing. Although a race between Turkey and Iran was constantly mentioned, neither Turkey nor Iran openly admitted to this race and in contrast they stated that they were not competing with any country in the region. Although there are ideological differences and there were elements of competition between Iran and Turkey, there are common interests as well. Both of them are members of ECO, they have common borders and Iran strategically occupies an important place between Turkey and the Turkic Republics. These factors encouraged Turkey and Iran for co-operation. However, the West, USA and Turkey as well as all the democratic countries in the World continue to regard Iran as a potential danger and Turkeys position as a neighbor of Iran is important to check and balance this power.

Turkish model is a factor that makes Turkey an important country in the region as well as in the globe. The common desirable achievements of the model as defined by various sources were: a secular state (in a country where the majority of the population is Muslim), a multi-party system, co-operation with and closeness to the West, and a market economy.[44] Turkey is the only Muslim state, which featured all these principles in its system. With the end of Cold War East West confrontation has ended. However, some circles such as Samuel Huntington argued that new confrontations would take place between civilizations, especially between the West and Islam.[45] 11 September attacks on USA were an important event that reminded us clash of civilizations. Under these conditions Turkey is a very important country and a model as Turkey is Muslim populated country with secular state and close to the West. Therefore, Turkey is regarded as a model for all Muslim states, not only for the Turkic republics.[46] Turgut Özal, ex-president of Turkey, used to underline Turkey as a model for all the Muslim World. Similarly, before and during in his trip to Turkey in November 1999, US president Bill Clinton ratified Özal's claim by indicating that Turkey had a significant role to play in the shaping of the next century. He drew attention to the need to bridge the gulf between Europe and the Islamic World and implied that Turkey would have an important role in that task. He emphasized that Turkey was a bridge between the Muslim and Christian cultures. At the same time he underlined some duties that Turkey should

---

[44] See, İdris Bal, *Turkey's Relatins with the West and Turkic Republics: The Rise and Fall of the Turkish Model*, Aldershot (UK): Ashgate, 2000.

[45] See Samuel Huntington, "The Clash of Civilizations", *Foreign Affairs*, Summer 1993.

[46] Daniel Pipes, "Islam's Intramural Struggle", *The National Interest*, Spring 1994, p.85.

fulfill in order to be able to play its role in the region and World politics such as minority issues, human rights and democracy issues and problems with the neighboring countries.[47] By making emphasis on Turkey, Clinton has shown his desire to see a world of co-operation and peace in the next century. He defended co-operation between civilizations rather confrontation and in this sense, he challenges Samuel Huntington.[48] By pointing out the role model of Turkey in Islamic World, at the same time, he has sent a message to the rest of the Islamic World that to live in peace and integrate with the rest of the World in the next century, they should adopt Turkish way of development, democracy, secularism and co-operation with the West rather than confrontation. In other words, by pointing out Turkey he wanted to mobilize Islamic world in this direction. US want Turkey to play its role as an attractive force in Islamic World. These remarks became more meaningful after 11 September attacks. Because of her model, strategic, geographic position and strong cultural historic ties with the region and rest of Islamic World Turkey can be an important actor for regional and global peace. Turkey can be a locomotive for Islamic World adopt multiparty system, market economy, secularism and closeness and cooperation with the West. Therefore Turkey could be regarded as an example for the rest of the Islamic world in establishing peaceful relations with the West and integrating to the World in general.

Conclusion

After the end opf the Cold War, Turkey found herself in a new security environment and had to adap herself to the new condition. In particular since the September 11 attack on the twin towers in New York and in Pentagon in Washington has increased Turkey's geostrategic importance. Turkey is now an important country for the global fight of international terrorism and is expected to play a much more active role in regional as well as in global politics. The differences between Turkey and the EU in terrorism definition will further last but the relations will improve gradually with the EU in particular in the year 2002. Most probably, Turkey will get official dates for the full membership negotiations within this year.

Turkey is having a multidimensional foreign policy and most probably it will play a stronger regional power role, as it was the case before. Whether Turkey will be able to meet the emerging challenges, which have been mentioned above, is to be seen. However, Turkey from today seems much more prepared for facing the challenges as it was not the case after the end the Cold War.

---

[47] *Turkish Daily News*, November 10, 1999; *Turkish Daily News*, November 17, 1999.
[48] See Samuel Huntington, "The Clash of Civilizations", *Foreign Affairs*, Summer 1993.

6 Turkey-USA Relations and Impacts of 2003 Iraq War[*]

İdris Bal

Introduction

The fact that Turkey sent troops to Korea in 1950 helped Turkey to be admitted to NATO. Hence, under the circumstances, Turkey turned completely to the West in that time. US supported Turkey within the framework of the Truman Doctrine and the Marshall Plan. Between 1945 and 1960 Turkey experienced very close and amicable relations with the West and especially with the USA In the same period, Turkish relations with the USSR and the Middle East were cool.

In the period 1960-1980, Turkey had experienced problematic relations with the USA. In the 1960s, especially with the emergence of the Cyprus crises, some problems began to shadow US-Turkish relations and Turkish Greek relations were badly undermined. Between 1960 and 1980 the Cyprus issue was the main agenda in Turkish foreign policy and shaped Turkish policy towards all regions.[1] In this period, the 1962 Cuban Missile Crises and removal of Jupiter missiles from Turkey following an agreement between the USA and the Soviets, the Johnson letter in June 1964, conflict over the production of opium poppy, and the 1975-78 US embargo on Turkey and Turkish closure of US bases in Turkey were severe crises in Turkish US relations. Thus, Turkey revised her relations with the USSR and the Middle East and drew closer to them. The impact of the Cyprus issue on Turkish foreign policy declined and US Turkish relations began to improve in the 1980s. Additionally, the Islamic revolution in Iran had an important effect on Turkish-US relations. With the end of the Shah's regime in Iran, the USA lost an ally in the region and furthermore, emergence of an anti-American and Islamic regime in Iran irritated the USA As a result, the importance of Turkey for US in the region as an ally naturally increased. Additionally, the Soviet invasion of Afghanistan in 1979 caused an escalation of the Cold War, which made Turkey more important and encouraged USA to again improve her relations with Turkey.

On the other hand, the military coup on 12 September 1980 in Turkey, provided an opportunity for the USA to repair relations with Turkey. The military regime in Turkey was anxious to legitimize itself in the international arena. Because of this anxiety, Turkey

---

[*] I would like to express my thanks to Prof. Dr. Cemal Kafadar (Director of Center for Middle Eastern Studies, Harvard University) for reading and commenting on the Turkish version of this manuscript. The article by İdris Bal; "War in the Middle East and USA and Turkey", *Stardigma.com E-Journal*, April 2003" (it has been written before the war) has been used in the preparation of this chapter.

[1] For an article analysing the 1960-1980 period see, Idris Bal, "Turkish Foreign Policy (1960-1980)", *The Turks*, Vol.5, Hasan Celal Guzel, Kemal Cicek, Salim Koca, Ankara: Yeni Turkiye Publications, 2002, pp.263-280.

accepted the Rogers plan that enabled Greece to return to the military section of NATO. By doing so Turkey had lost its bargaining card against Greece. The military regime in Turkey lasted three years. The Anavatan (Motherland) Party won the first general elections and the first Özal government was established. Özal was a liberal politician advocating close cooperation with USA The Anavatan Party government ruled Turkey until 1991. Most of the damage in the relations with USA was repaired during the Özal period. Close cooperation had been seen between the USA and Turkey during Saddam's invasion of Kuwait in 1990 and following the second Gulf War in 1991. In this, Özal played a key role in Turkey. The Turkish contribution to US policies toward Iraq in 1990s was valuable. Without Turkish cooperation it would have been too difficult to prevent Saddam controlling northern Iraq. Even in this period, when damaged relations were repaired, especially the Armenian question,[2] the gradual emergence of the Kurdish question, problems regarding Turkish-Greek relations and the Cyprus question, economic assistance, military and economic issues continued to form obstacles in US-Turkish relations.[3] However, neither side allowed these problems to overshadow relations.[4]

Post Cold War Era: Strategic Partnership

Turkey was an important country in the Cold War era for the West and the USA Turkey was feeding the second largest army in NATO after the US and was a neighbor of former USSR and Bulgaria. Therefore, Turkey acted as a barrier before Soviet power and the Communist threat in general. However, with the demise of the Soviet Union and the end of the Cold War, the importance of Turkey in this sense declined. Mainly because of this reason Turkey was looking for a new agenda and new arguments to prove that she was still important for the West, especially for the USA. However, Turkish relations with the USA did not decline, but increased in the post Cold War era. Although Turkish relations with the USA were not as advanced as the US's relations with Israel and the UK, Turkey's relations with the USA were begning to be called a strategic partnership. In this outcome, on the one hand, the USA's expectations from Turkey and on the other hand, expectations of Turkey from the US played determining roles. There were several reasons that led to this conclusion.

In the post Cold War era, the USA became a single super power. To safeguard her position, the USA needs to maintain global as well as regional balances and needs to monitor and direct developments. On the other hand, the USA faced some problems in the regional and global politics and needed to take some measures.

---

[2] See for the beginning of US interest in the Armenian question. H. Tahsin Fendoglu. "Turk (Osmanli) ABD İlişkileri Bağlaminda Ermeni Sorunu". Idris Bal & Mustafa Çufalı (Der.). *Dünden Bugüne Türk Ermeni İliskileri*, Ankara: Nobel. 2003. pp.223-230.

[3] Ilhan Uzgel. "ABD ve NATO ile Iliskiler". Baskin Oran, *Turk Dis Politikasi, II. Cilt*, Istanbul: Iletisim. 2001. pp.34-81.

[4] For Turkish Foreign policy from the Ottoman State up to the end of the 20th Century see, William Hale. *Türk Dış Politikası 1974-2000*, Istanbul: Mozaik. 2000; Philip Robins. *Suits and Uniforms, Turkish Foreign Policy Since the Cold War*, Washington: University of Washington Press. 2003. F. Stephen Larrabee & Ian O. Lesser. *Turkish Foreign Policy in an Age of Uncertainty*, Santa Monica: Rand. 2003.

Global Developments and Problems

At the global level China and Russia are still important powers in terms of population, natural resources, nuclear power, economic capacity and strategic position. China and Russia have been trying to institutionalize their relations under the umbrella of the Shanghai Cooperation Organization since 1996.[5] All Central Asian countries except permanently neutral Turkmenistan joined this cooperation. Under the umbrella of this organization, China and Russia began to criticize US global policies.

In order to be able to deal developments in Eurasia, the USA approached India. With its population of nearly 1.1 billion (1,049,700,118),[6] a developing economy, nuclear power and democracy, India is a key country in the region.[7] India is in competition with China as it used to be during the Cold War era. India and Pakistan are in conflict. Pakistan was an ally of the US during the Cold War era. On the other hand, India was close to and supported by the USSR, and China supported Pakistan against India. China-Pakistan relations are still strong. Israel is also developing her relations with India and it is possible to talk about the USA-India and Israel rapprochement. Japan and South Korea are allies of US in the region. However, the USA-India rapprochement does not mean that India had entered US orbit. India aims to follow an independent global and autonomous policy in the world is also in close cooperation with Russia, heir to USSR. For instance, Indian and Russian troops carried out maneuvers in Arabian Sea in April 2003 and France also took part as an observer.[8] Apart from the EU, China and Russia, if India continues to develop her economy successfully, it is highly likely that she will be one of the power centers of a possible future multi-polar system. Therefore, for the US, India is a partner as well as a power that needs to be checked and balanced.[9]

On the one hand, the US is trying to deal with global competitors in Asia, on the other hand, she needs to monitor and direct developments in Europe and deal with the EU in order to be able to safeguard her position in the world. The US supported Europe during the Cold War era and helped her economic and social development to be able to prevent Soviet invasion or possible communist revolutions. For this reason, the US encouraged cooperation movements in Europe. However, the USA never wants to see a rival united Europe in the future. During 2003 the Iraq war revealed some of the problems between Europe and the USA. Members of NATO and the EU were divided as pro-Americans and anti-Americans. Critiques of some NATO and the EU members against the USA were important indicators for future developments and opposition against the US in Europe.

---

[5] See, İdris Bal, "Rise of Shanghai Cooperation Organization (SCO) in Eurasia: Is it an Effective Toll in a New Big Game", Ertan Efegil, (Ed.), *Geopolitics of Central Asia in the Post Cold War Era: A Systemic Analyses*, Harlem: The Research Center for Azerbaijan and Turkestan, SOTA, the Netherlands, 2002.

[6] http://www.cia.gov/publications/factbook/geos/in.html

[7] See, George Perkovich, "Is India a Major Power?", *The Washington Quarterly*, Vol.27, No.1, Winter 2003-2004, pp.129-146.

[8] Erdem Yüksel, "ABD'nin Türk Ordusu Düşmanlığı: Tehditten Silah Çekmeye", *Teori Aylık Dergi*, Eylül 2003, Sayı.164, p.6.

[9] Colin L. Powel underlines India along with China and Russia as a big power. See, Colin L. Powel, "Strategy of Partnership", *Foreign Affairs*, February 2004.

Especially criticism of Germany and France, which can be regarded as the engine of the EU, and their cooperation with Russia during the Iraq war (2003) against the US, was important for the US and indicator of emergence of EU in global politics. Therefore, the USA wants to (and should) monitor and guide developments in Europe.

Apart from the Russian-Chinese rapprochement, it is possible to talk about the Russian–Chinese and Iranian rapprochement. There are claims that Iran is cooperating with Russia and China on nuclear weapons. Iran is an important customer of Russian weapons. For instance, during Hatemi's visit to Russia in 2001, Iran and Russia agreed to the purchase of Russian weapons by Iran worth of seven billion dollars. Iran's main feature is not only the fact that with the 1979 revolution it changed regional balances. Furthermore, with the end of the Cold War capitalism won the race against Communism. However, it is believed that with the Iranian Islamic revolution, Islam has risen as an alternative ideology against capitalism. Therefore, Iran's position is vital not only for regional balances but for global balances as well. Following Iran's revolution, it was feared in general that Iran would export her ideology to the rest of the Islamic world. Especially in the post Cold War era, the possibility that Iran might export her ideology to Central Asia and Caucasus and help the establishment of an anti-American and anti-Western block against the US and the West, caused some anxiety in the US.[10] As a parallel to this approach, Huntington argues that competition will be among civilizations in the future. The fact that importance of ethnic, cultural and religious values increased in the post Cold War period and that they became more influential over foreign policy making, ratifies and supports Huntington's approach.[11]

Another threat that has risen with the end of Cold War is international terrorism. International terrorism is strengthened by ethnic and religious irredentism, which used power vacuums and instabilities created by the end of the Cold War and all opportunities created by globalization. As a result, with the 9/11 attacks against the US, it became obvious to everyone that even the single super power of the world is not immune against terrorism. Then, the US began to regard terrorism as a primary threat and enemy.[12] Furthermore, radical Islam began to be regarded as a dangerous enemy because of some reasons such as the Islamic names of people who carried out 9/11 attacks, their Islamic motifs, their ties with Al-Qaide terror organization, etc. Therefore, US declared a global war against terrorism and overthrew the Taliban regime in Afghanistan in December 2001. In the 1990s, the US had supported the Taliban regime and had expected that the Taliban could bring stability to Afghanistan,[13] which was needed by US companies in the region. The US justified occupation of Afghanistan with some arguments such as connections with Al-Qaide, being a training field for terrorist groups and so on. In the

---

[10] İdris Bal, *Turkey's Relations with the West and Turkic Republics: The Rise and Fall of the Turkish Model*, see third chapter.

[11] See, Samuel P. Huntington, **Clash of Civilizations and the Remaking of World Order**, Touchstone Books, 1998.

[12] See, Colin L. Powel, "A Strategy of Partnership", *Foreign Affairs*, February 2004.

[13] See, Saule Baycan & İdris Bal, "Orta Asya Ülkeleri Taliban"a Yaklaşıyor mu?", *Stratejik Analiz*, Cilt.2. No.1, January 2001, pp.48-54.

second stage, as analyzed below, with similar justifications, the US brought to an end the Saddam regime in April 2003.[14] However, these steps were not enough to bring to an end international terrorism, in contrast some arguments started to be put forward that these steps nourished international terrorism. Following the 2003 Iraq war (the third Gulf War), terrorist attacks spread out of Iraq including Turkey and Saudi Arabia. For instance, in Turkey, synagogues, a bank belonging to a British citizen but of the Jewish religion, and the British consulate were attacked. By these attacks, terrorists tried to give messages to Turkey, the US, the UK and Israel. On the other hand, president Pervez Muserref of Pakistan survived after two-assassination attempts against himself in December 2003. On 21st December 2003, the US increased security units to orange alarm level against terrorist attacks. That was the fifth time that alarm level was advanced to the level of orange since the alarm system was set as a precaution against terrorism in March 2002.[15] These developments are indicators of the increased threat of terrorism not the decline of it. The US is searching for possible solutions to the terrorist threat. Which kind of measures should be taken against terrorism? What is the scope of global war against terrorism? Which method is more reliable? ...similar questions have emerged. The opposition in the US is accusing the Bush administration, criticizing the invasion of Iraq and they argue that the US had lost internal credibility because of the Iraq war.[16] The capture of Saddam in December 2003, Libya's abandonment of her plans regarding weapons of mass destruction and her acceptance to cooperate with the US and the UK, some positive steps taken by Iran in the way of cooperation and recovery of the US economy, are some developments that can help the Bush administration against opposition and preparing a suitable base for Bush's second success in the coming November 2004 elections. However, the question of terrorism still preserves its importance and encourages the US to search for new solutions. The Greater Middle East Initiative can be regarded as a new method of dealing with international terrorism in general.

Regional Developments and Problems

Apart from the damage it caused, one of the positive aspects of the Cold War was that it had to a significant extent frozen maps of the world. In the post Cold War era new instabilities took place in several regions. Ethnic and religious irredentism that was not able to find a suitable base during the Cold War era, have risen. Yugoslavia had dissolved, first Croat-Serbian then Serbian-Muslim conflicts took place. Then, Macedonia and Kosova conflicts have been seen in the Balkans. The Middle East was already an unstable place.[17] Even during the Cold War era, on one hand, the Arab-Israel wars and conflicts took place, on the other hand, the Iran-Iraq war (1980-1988) cost the lives of more than one million people in the region.[18] With the end of the Cold War, Saddam

---

[14] For Bush Doctrine see, Robert Jervis, "Understanding Bush Doctrin", *Political Science Quarterly*, Vol.118, No.3., 2003, pp.365-388.

[15] http://cfrterrorism.org/home/

[16] See, Wesley K. Clark, *Winning Modern Wars: Iraq, Terrorism, and the American Empire*, Public Affairs, October 2003.

[17] See chapter.16 in this book.

[18] http://www.fap.org/man/dod-101/ops/war/iran-iraq.htm

occupied Kuwait and assisted instability in the region. This was followed by the Second Gulf War in 1991, the March 2003 invasion of Iraq (Third Gulf War) and the capture of Saddam in December 2003. The US wants to maintain and direct balances in the region. US wants the continuation of the peace process and to strengthen the position of Israel in the region. Iran is as mentioned above, regarded by the US as a threat to regional and global peace and therefore, the USA tries to control and isolate Iran.

Caucasus destabilized in the post Cold War era as well. On one hand, Chechens attempted to separate from the Russian Federation, on the other hand, Armenia having the support of Russia, was involved in a conflict with Azerbaijan concerning the Nagorno Karabakh region. Armenians occupied 20% of the territory of Azerbaijan. Although the two sides reached a ceasefire agreement that gave an end to the war after Haydar Aliyev became president in Azerbaijan in 1994, the problem still continues and a new war can begin unless Armenia returns the lands she captured from Azerbaijan. Georgia on the other hand, was not able to unite her country after she gained her independence. There are de facto autonomous regions within Georgia. Abkhazia and South Ossethia separatisms significantly undermined Georgia. Russia still has military bases in Georgia. It was claimed by Georgian opposition that the November 2003 elections were distorted by the administration, and therefore, Eduardo Shevardnadnze, former president of Georgia, was forced to resign because of public uprising that emerged following the November elections.[19] Although the US supported Georgia, it criticized Russia about Chechen conflict especially before the 9/11 attacks, this policy was weak in order not to provoke Russia and therefore, US policy did not create concrete results. On the one hand, the USA was looking for stability and to undermine the influence of Russia in the region, on the other hand, under the influence of the Armenian lobby, the US supported Armenia against Azerbaijan. However, this policy was contradicting with the US policy of isolating Iran and undermining the influence of Russia in the region. Therefore, in December 2001, "the Bush administration succeeded in getting Section 907 of the Freedom Support Act-which barred direct U.S. government support to Azerbaijan-repealed. The section, introduced under pressure from the American-Armenian lobby, significantly constrained US freedom of action and policy options. Vis-à-vis Azerbaijan."[20]

The US, as a single superpower that is sometimes called the gendarme of the world, was supposed to deal with the regional as well as global problems that have been outlined above.[21] In this regard, the US has tried to use the UN and NATO efficiently to deal with new problems in the new era. Apart from these institutions, as was seen in the 2003 Iraq war, the USA sometimes pursued an independent policy relying on her own power and military strength. However, in order to be able to produce polices and take measures regarding global and regional developments and problems, the US needed regional as well as global partners. Therefore, in the post Cold War era, Turkey has began to be regarded

---

[19] http://www.cia.gov/cia/publications/factbook/geos/gg.html
[20] F. Stephen Larrabee & Ian O. Leser, *Turkish Foreign Policy in an Age of Uncertainty*, Santa Monica: RAND, 2003, p.116.
[21] See about American hegemony, Burcu Bostanoğlu, *Türkiye-ABD İlişkilerinin Politikası*, Ankara: İmge Kitabevi, 1999, pp.222-237.

as a more important partner by the US for strategical, psychological, cultural and ideological reasons.

Meaning of Turkey for the USA in the Post Cold War Era

The US believed that Turkey could play an important role in the struggle against regional as well as global problems in the post Cold War era for a variety of reasons. Especially to deal with developments in Eurasia, the US put Turkey in an important position. The fact that Turkey was a determining power in the region from the past up to present, straightened Turkey's position. Turks had acted as a barrier before the Crusades and defended the whole Islamic World. Arabs who presently criticize Turkey in other issues admit this reality, and during the Crusades era, they regarded Turks as champions, protectors and fighters of Islam.[22] Then, the Ottoman State dominated the Balkans, Eastern Europe, North Africa, an important portion of the Mediterranean, the Middle East, the Black Sea, some territory above the Black Sea and some portions of Caucasus. Later on, although Russia grew in the region and became an important power, the Ottoman State had managed to stop the Russian Empire's penetration to the south and acted as a barrier. After the 1917 revolution in Russia, Communism was regarded as a threat. During the Cold War era, Turkey as a member of NATO became a barrier before the USSR and Communist expansion. After the end of the Cold War, all regions around Turkey destabilized. These conditions made Turkey a center rather than periphery in world politics. This situation encouraged the USA to cooperate with Turkey and therefore, Turkish-USA relations didn't decline but increased to the level of a strategic partnership. They started to cooperate in regional as well as global politics.

The USA and Turkey have cooperated in Central Asia regarding a power vacuum created by the end of the USSR. For instance, the Turkish Model was proposed to Turkic Muslim populated states in Central Asia and Caucasus. By the term 'Turkish Model', it is referred to some principles rather than the present form of administration in Turkey. The Turkish Model was used as a symbol to refer to multiparty democracy, secularism in a Muslim population, market economy, closeness to and cooperation with the West. The aim was to attract the attention of the republics towards the West rather than the Islamic Middle East, especially Iran and Saudi Arabia. This policy was eventually successful.[23]

While the USA was trying to balance Russia and China, on the other hand the US wants the independent republics created by the end of the USSR, to safeguard and strengthen their independences. Turkey is also important to assist the independence of republics in Central Asia and Caucasus. Apart from geographic closeness to the region, Turkey's ethnic, linguistic, cultural and religious ties with the region encouraged the US to cooperate with Turkey in its Eurasia politics. Turkey has regarded new republics in Central Asia and Caucasus (except Armenia) as natural allies for cultural and historical reasons and supported their independence and wants their independence strengthened.

---

[22] Professor of Beirut American University, Abdulrahim Abu-Husayn put forward a similar argument in his speech; Abdulrahim Abu-Husayn, Professor, Department of History and Archaeology, American University of Beirut, and Visiting Professor, Harvard University, "Perceiving Turkey in the Arab World", *Study Group on Modern Turkey*, Center For Middle Eastern Studies, Harvard University, 26 November 2003.

[23] For details of this policy see, Idris Bal, *Turkey's Relations with the West and Turkic Republics: The Rise and Fall of the Turkish Model*, Aldershot: Ashgate, 2000.

Turkey helped the new republics in their state building and tried to strengthen ties with them. It was assumed that the influence of Russia would be undermined and limited in this way. Unless Russia is checked and balanced in the region the independence of these republics will be at risk.

The US has also been trying to break the Russian monopoly on transportation of oil and gas issues. As summarized above, the US is trying to limit Iran and undermine her influence in the region and isolate her. Turkey represents Western and US influence in the region. Turkey is neighbor of Iran and has proximity to Russia via sea. For these two objectives, Turkey is important and for this reason the US is supporting the Baku-Ceyhan project that bypasses Russia as well as Iran. In fact, with the backing of the USA, an agreement was signed in 1999 and this project is now being realized. It was expected that this project would be completed in 2006.

The USA needs to monitor and influence the EU as a power emerging at the global level. Therefore, if Turkey can be a full member of the EU, apart from England, Turkey can be another tool that the USA can use to monitor and influence developments within the EU. In another words, Turkey might be regarded as a second brake mechanism like that of the UK within the union. Therefore, US support of Turkish full membership to the EU should be interpreted in this way, apart from Turkish demand of US help and US encouragement of cultural dialogue at the global level.

Since the establishment of Turkish republic, there were some claims that Turkey could be a model for the rest of the Islamic world. However, with the 1979 Iran revolution, Islam had risen as an alternative ideology at the global level and the claim that Turkey could be model for the rest of the Islamic world became more meaningful. Furthermore, with the end of the USSR, the Turkish model was put forward as a right path to be followed by Muslim republics created by the end of the USSR. President Clinton had underlined Turkey as a model for the Islamic world before the September 11 attacks and he claimed that in the formation of the next century, the role that Turkey can play would be vital.[24] Especially the September 11 attacks made Turkey more valuable because of her model. Turkey is regarded as a bridge between the Islamic world and the West and the role of Turkey is getting more important for the dialogue and peace.[25] This is a factor that encouraged the USA to cooperate with Turkey in the post Cold War era and it will continue to encourage in the future as well. However, in order to be able to play her role in global politics, Turkey initially needs to solve her problems at home and reach peace and consensus among her population. If Turkey successfully manages to solve her problems at home and create a successful model, then it will be possible to talk about the possible impact of this model over rest of the Islamic world and be a bridge between the West and the Islamic World.

Terrorism as a mounting global threat in the post Cold War era, necessitate international cooperation. Turkey has long experience in struggling against terrorism. ASALA and rightist-leftist terrors were replaced by the PKK in the 1980s and Turkey has

---

[24] *Turkish Daily News*, November 10, 1999, *Turkish Daily News*, November 17, 1999.

[25] For Turkish Model see, Idris Bal, *Turkey's Relations With the West and Turkic Republics: The Rise and Fall of the Turkish Model*, Aldershot: Ashagate, 2000.

been struggling against this organization. This experience makes Turkey an important country in the global war against terrorism.

Regional problems encouraged the US to cooperate with Turkey. Hopes for world order in the post Cold War era were replaced by world disorder. East-West competition was replaced by rise of ethnic and radical demands and conflicts especially around Turkey in the Balkans, Caucasus and the Middle East. Above all, these regions can be regarded as potential ground that may grow threats to the USA The 9/11 attacks underline the importance of this factor. Because of her ethnic cultural historic ties, Turkey can be regarded as key player in the region. Turkey has cultural and ethnic links with Central Asia that made Turkey an ideal partner for the USA. Turkey as a strategically important country, located at the center of the Middle East, Caucasus and the Balkans, was important for the USA to deal regional development as well as global developments. Apart from Turkey's geographic location, Turkey has psychological closeness to all these regions as the Ottoman state governed these regions (except Central Asia) for around four hundred years, which created ethnic, cultural and psychological closeness. For instance, names of some districts in Istanbul are indicators of this closeness such as Arnavutköy (Albanian Village), Yeni Bosna (New Bosnia), Eyüp and so on. These regions can be regarded as Turkey's "near abroad" or back garden. Security, historical, cultural factors underline the position of Turkey that cannot be ignored in any scenario related with the region. Apart from the second Gulf War (1991), developments in the Balkans and Caucasus proved the importance of Turkey in the region.

If Turkey can solve her problems, be a center of attraction in terms of economy democracy, human rights, she can play a role of locomotive in bringing peace and stability to the region. There is a suitable psychological base for such role for Turkey. For instance, Turkey has esteem and impact in the Middle East not just over Muslims but Jewish people as well. This puts Turkey in an important position in search of possible solutions to the region's problems.

For instance, Israel wants Turkey to be a mediator in her problems with Syria. Turkey maintains her dialog with both sides in the Palestine-Israel conflict and because of trust of both sides to Turkey; she became an important third party in the possible resolution of the problem.

Beside the regional as well as global roles that Turkey can play, Turkey represents US and Western axis and influence. Turkish Republic have been established on Western values and the West has been regarded as a target to be reached by Turkey. This is important for regional as well as global politics, which has an additional role that encouraged the US to regard Turkey as import and to cooperate.

Basically under the impact of these factors, the US regarded Turkey as an important country to tackle regional as well as global developments and problems in the post Cold War era and thus relations increased to the level of strategic partnership. However, in this result, apart from US expectations, anxiety and perceptions, Turkey's expectations, anxiety and perceptions were influential as well.

The meaning of the USA for Turkey in the Post Cold War Era

As mentioned above, Turkey was a significant country for the West and the USA during the Cold War. However, after the collapse of the Eastern Block and the USSR, and the end of ideological threat of communism, Turkey's importance for the USA and the West disappeared within this context. For this reason, Turkey began searching for new arguments to prove that Turkey was still important. Within this context, Turkey put forward the Black sea Economic Cooperation Project. Turkey started developing its relations with Pakistan and Iran within the frame of the Economic Cooperation Organization (ECO). Then, Afghanistan, Azerbaijan and five other Central Asian Republics joined this organization and the number of member countries increased to ten. Turkey has started developing close relations with the Turk Republics by using ethnic and cultural links. Turkey began searching for new cooperation in the Balkans. After that, the D-8 project was put forward during Erbakan's Government. All these developments can be explained by the anxiety of Turkey to discover new arguments after the end of the Cold War. In the same period, the USA attached importance to Turkey and cooperated with Turkey in the region and Eurasia, which was a pleasing development for Turkey as she was looking for new arguments.

On the other hand, although Turkey is a member of the Western Block, it has never been thought of by its Western allies as an equal country sharing common values with them. They only appreciated the role of Turkey in the region due to their security anxieties. Turkey has been mainly left alone in the Cyprus problem, problems with Greece, Armenia problem, terrorism, and water problems.

After the end of the Cold War Turkey began to feel more alone. Although the Western Block continued to exist, and the Eastern block collapsed, due to the loose inter-block relations, NATO's search for new roles in this environment caused some anxiety for Turkey. Because Turkey didn't have the support of its Western allies, neither Islamic nor the other countries gave their support to Turkey. That is why Turkey began searching for a friend, which can support her in the international area.

On one hand, the independence of the Turkic Republics was a hope for Turkey, on the other hand, generally the weakness of these republics, not having influence in the international field, being busy to construct their own countries, miscarried Turkey's hope. After the Turkic republics realized the limitations of Turkey, they became reluctant to pay attention to issues crucial for Turkey. Naturally, instead of integrated approaches, each republic must be considered on its own and there are big differences among them. Especially, Azerbaijan must be considered different from the rest of the Central Asian republics and due to the overlapping of the interests of Azerbaijan and Turkey; this country is more sensitive to the interests of Turkey. However, this situation deepens the loneliness of Turkey in the international field. There are other open examples of this loneliness except for the Armenian problem.[26] The Turkish Republic of Northern Cyprus (KKTC) was established in 1983 but nobody recognized it except Turkey. These

---

[26] Switzerland recognized the so-called day of Armenian genocide in December 2003, *The New York Times*, December 17, 2003.

examples are the indicator of Turkey's respect and that she could not get support of any kind. Turkey needed powerful and effective foreign support. For this reason, after the end of the Cold War, Turkey started to see the USA as a strong ally, which supported Turkey in important fields. Although Turkey was not able to get support from the USA on the Cyprus problem and Turkey-Greek relations, the USA supported Turkey in the field of terror and had cooperated while Greece and Italy tried to hide Öcalan. Nevertheless, there are differences in the field of the Kurdish problem.

On the one hand, although the collapse of the USSR pleased Turkey and Russia was now a new field of cooperation for Turkey, on the other hand, the existence of Russia in the region as a strong country with nuclear strength still continues to discomfort Turkey and encourage Turkey to find a power that can balance Russia. Even though, Turkey is a member of NATO, the role of NATO has changed dramatically and getting closer to the USA directly become priority and preferable within this context.

Similarly, although relations between the EU (EC) and Turkey had a historical background of 44 years, it is far from being without problem. Even these relations become more problematic as Turkey lost her bargaining card (security argument) against the West. In the post Cold War era, the impact of psychological and cultural factors on foreign policy increased and this has also affected Turkey's relations with the EU in a negative way as some circles do not recognize Turkey as European. The Turkish application for full membership in 1987 was refused. Therefore, close relations with the USA were important for Turkey. Because if Turkey cannot be a full member of the EU, the EU will be an important country that threatens Turkey and Turkish interests because of problems with the Greeks. That means that all problems with Greece will be problems between the EU and Turkey. Turkey will need an important country to balance the EU in that case. Although the present government is doing its best to open the gate of the EU, Turkey needed the USA in post Cold War era and might be in need of the USA regarding the EU as well.

In the post Cold War era, Turkey did not want to deal with conflicts emerging around herself, and refrained from interfering on her own. Although the pro-Turkish president of Azerbaijan, Elchibey, insisted in signing a common defense agreement with Turkey, Turkey refused to do so and did not want to oppose Russia and Armenia on her own. Demirel pointed out that he worried that there was possibility of an emergence of a Christian-Muslim conflict similar to the Palestine Conflict in Caucasus and he claimed that Turkish intervention to the problem could lead to intervention of other powers as well.[27] Turkey had followed a similar policy regarding the Bosnia conflict. Although there are pro Azerbaijani, and pro-Bosnian public opinion, instead of taking unilateral action regarding the issue, Turkey preferred to act with the international community and tried to bring the issue to the attention of international institutions such as the UN, NATO and the Organization of Islamic Conference. In the post Cold War era, the US became a best partner for Turkey to deal with the conflict around Turkey as the US was a single super

---

[27] See, İdris Bal & Cengiz Başak, "Rise and Fall of the Elchibey's Administration and Turkey's Central Asian Policy", *Foreign Policy*, Vol.22, No.3-4/1998, pp.42-56.

power and influential over international institutions especially the UN and NATO. In fact, the Bosnia conflict proved the insufficiency of Europe and conflict had been stopped by the intervention of the USA. However, the problems in both the Balkans and Caucasus were not solved but they were frozen.[28] Conflicts can erupt again. This indicates that the US and Turkey will need to cooperate to deal with conflicts in the region.

Another factor that encouraged Turkey to cooperate with the USA has been related with economic and technological issues. Economic crises that Turkey faced showed the weakness of the Turkish economy. In order to recover, Turkey needs financial as well as technical help. The USA is the best country to give such help. Turkey also needs international support to realize her projects such as Baku Ceyhan, Peace Pipeline Project. Therefore, Turkey needs some international support for these projects. Because of this factors Turkey needs cooperation with the USA

Following the Second World War very close relations between Turkey and the USA were established and these relations were institutionalized under the umbrella of NATO. These relations psychologically caused a strategic habit and resulted in interdependences (especially for Turkey as Turkey become dependent on US weapons). This factor also encouraged the USA to establish close relations with Turkey.

In the post Cold War era, in most issues, Turkish interests were overlapping with US interests. Both countries have similar world-views and they also share common worries. Both countries required peace and stability in the Balkans, the Middle East, Caucasus and Central Asia. Both countries wanted to undermine the Russian influence in Eurasia. Both countries wanted to undermine Iranian influence in the region and feared possible Iranian export of her regime to the Central Asian Muslim populated states. The USA aimed to strengthen Israel and break the isolation of this country in the region. Since 1996 Turkey on the other hand approached Israel with her security anxieties. The USA was pleased with Turkish-Israeli cooperation. Both the USA and Turkey support the peace process in the Middle East and regard international terrorism and radicalism as a common enemy. This situation encouraged cooperation between Turkey and the USA.

Mainly because of these reasons, Turkey needed the USA in the post Cold War era. Therefore, the end of the Cold War did not undermine US Turkish relations but strengthen them and relations advanced to the level of strategic partnership.[29]

On the other hand, although relations are labeled as a strategic partnership, some problems continued to be present within the relations such as the Northern Iraq and Kurdish issue, the Armenian question, relations with Greece, Cyprus and human rights.[30] Because of these problems Turkish-US relations and strategic partnership were open to discussion. However, both sides, Turkey and the USA, emphasized those issues on which the two countries have similar views and they did not allow problems to shadow relations.

---

[28] For discussion of these subjects, see Ahmet Davutoğlu, *Stratejik Derinlik*, İstanbul: Küre Yayınları, 2001.

[29] İdris Bal, "Jeoplitik Güç Merkezleri Arasında Güç Mücadelesi ve ABD-Türkiye Ortaklığı", *2023 Dergisi*, 15 Agustos 2003, Sayı.28, pp.42-43.

[30] See for details, Alan Makovsky, "U.S Policy Towards Turkey", Morton Abramowitz (Ed.), *Turkey's Transformation and American Policy*, New York: The Century Foundation Press, 2000, pp.219-266.

However, the Turkish failure to meet America's demands in the US war against Iraq in 2003 again shook the alliance.[31]

Iraq war 2003: Is it the end of the Strategic Partnership?

As emphasized in other chapters on the Middle East in this book, the Middle East is very instable region of the world and there are several factors that prepare and feed instability in the region.[32] Instability began in the Middle East with the end of Ottoman control and then several powers attempted to provide stability but they all failed. Because of several reasons such as strategic position, natural resource, social, cultural and political structure and so on, the region witnessed and is witnessing several competitions and power games. During the Cold War era, the region was instable mainly because of the Arab-Israel conflict, intervention of outside-global powers and war between Iraq and Iran. With the end of the Cold War, new problems emerged as well. The Occupation of Kuwait by Saddam and subsequent developments are obvious examples. Furthermore, an instable Middle East became a safe haven for terrorist groups in the world. Efforts of some countries within the region as well as outside the region to use terrorist groups as an instrument of their foreign policy feed instability in the region. The Middle East has become a safe refuge and almost an asylum for the global terrorist groups due to its instability. Consideration of these terrorist groups by both countries inside and outside the region as a means of foreign policy has contributed to the instability of the region. Following the 1991 intervention (Second Gulf War), Iraq has actually been split into three, leading to the imprisonment of the Saddam regime between the 36th and the 32nd (then 33rd) parallels. Yet, insistence of Saddam on government has only continued the US disturbance and in the aftermath of the attacks on the USA on September 11, has led to the 2003 Iraq war to end Saddam's regime and to demilitarize and disarm Iraq.

The War on Iraq in 2003, on the one hand led to the emergence of difference of opinions between global powers and mistrust between Europe and Atlantic, on the other hand, caused serious crises between Turkey and the USA. In fact, up to the 2003 Iraq war (third Gulf War), Turkey was in cooperation with the USA. Turkey collaborated with the USA in the second Gulf War, and then in order to be able to protect the Kurds in the North from the Saddam Regime, Turkey cooperated with the US in the context of 'Poised Hammer' (Çekiç Güç) and 'Operation Northern Watch' (Kuzeyden Keşif Gücü). Furthermore, although it undermined the Turkish economy, Turkey obeyed sanctions from the beginning. Unless Turkey cooperated with the USA, it would be too difficult to protect Kurds from Saddam in the Northern Iraq. However, in the third Gulf War Turkey did not positively answer US demands, which caused problems in the relations.

2003 Iraq War and Understanding the USA

Although Iraq had been divided into three parts following the end of the the second Gulf War, Saddam Hussein remained and was left to remain in power between the 36th and

---

[31] Mehmet Kocak, "Turkish-US friendship is a guarantee for democratic values", *Turkish Daily News*, October 14, 2003.

[32] See the chapter by Idris Bal in this book; "İdris Bal - Instability in the Middle East and Relavant role of PKK".

32nd (then 33rd) parallels. As such securing of Saddam led to much speculation and further commentaries concerning post-Saddam scenarios by some, others claimed that the USA has spared Saddam intentionally in order to legitimize her further presence in the region.[33] Yet, as the embargo following the 1991 war proved, not as expected, Saddam only gained further prestige in the eye of his public, claiming he had weapons of mass destruction that he also wished to multiply, the international powers and the USA led to the UN inspectors enter Iraq for further research on the issue. Following the 9/11 attacks, the USA strongly decided to disarm Saddam this or that way considering the UN inspectors and international pressure on Iraq being ineffective. Thus, the USA wanted to intervene in Iraq, considered a new UN decision unnecessary for her planned attack as she regarded decision no. 1441 of the UN Security Council as sufficient. The USA was not able to get a new decision that would justify the occupation of Iraq from the UN Security Council mainly because of the opposition by France, Germany, Russia and China.

The USA basically regarded this war as part of a war on global terrorism. The first step was the overthrowing of the Taliban regime in Afghanistan and give an end to the support to terrorism of this regime. The Second step took place in the form of the occupation of Iraq and bringing to an end the Saddam regime. Bush and Blair emphasized that by occupying Iraq, they would control weapons of mass destruction; chemical and biological weapons and make Iraq a safe place. Apart from armament of Iraq, possible ties with terrorism and the personality of Saddam and similar claims, there are other factors that need to be examined in order to understand the third Gulf War (2003).

First of all, the USA had become, by the end of the Cold War, the sole superpower in the world. In order to preserve her status, the USA naturally took a course to retain both global and regional equilibrium as present. To this end, as the USA on the one hand has to monitor and supervise the Shanghai Cooperation Organization[34] together with the Russo-Chinese proximity, on the other hand, she has to keep Europe whom she had protected under her very wings during the Cold War years from full autonomy. On the regional level, the USA has chosen to control leaders who may attempt to change the present established balance. Within this context, Saddam has drawn the profile of a leader who needs to be stopped due to his eight-year war with Iran, his armament efforts, his invasion of Kuwait and his expansionist policies in the region. This situation encouraged the USA for a war to dethrone and demilitarize Saddam.

Secondly, the Middle East is the region in the world, which enjoys the richest resources of oil. Although many new reserves are also being discovered in the Caspian Sea and in Central Asia, the Middle East still retains her strategical vitality. As the Middle East holds almost two thirds of the global petrol reserves (65.3%) which it can process cheaply and more than one third of the global natural gas reserves (36.1%), she turns into a point of attraction for foreign powers and forces the latter to intervene in

---

[33] Ahmet Davutoğlu, *Stratejik Derinlik*, İstanbul: Küre Yayınları, 2001, p.443.
[34] See, İdris Bal, "Rise of Shanghai Cooperation Organization (SCO) in Eurasia: Is It an Effective Toll in a New Big Game", Ertan Efegil (Ed.), *Geopolitics of Central Asia in the Post-Cold War Era: A Systemic Analysis*, Harlem, the Netherlands: Research Center for Azerbaijan and Turkestan, SOTA, 2002.

regional policies.[35] 685.6 billion barrels, which is 65.32% of the total petroleum reserves of the world (estimated to be some 1 trillion 50 billion barrels) is in the Middle East. And 36.1% (55.91 trillion m³) of the global natural gas reserves, (estimated to be 155 trillion m³), are again found in the Middle East.[36] Iraq is especially important in terms of oil reserves as 11% of the total global oil reserves are located in Iraq.[37] On the other hand, with her 3,149 trillion meter cubic natural gas reserves, Iraq owns a little bit more than 2% of the total global natural gas reserves.[38]

The leaders of the two blocks, the Soviet Union and the USA have adjoined themselves to the Middle Eastern policies during the Cold War era. Especially the USA and other Western powers in the post Cold War period showed interest in Middle Eastern policies. Yet, other powers such as Russia and China have not entirely lost their interest as they still wish to have influence over the oil and natural gas reserves, over their production and pricing. The USA naturally wants to be the sole controller over all this as she is also the global leader. Thus, the USA has no choice of ignoring fait-accompli such as the invasion of Kuwait by Iraq, which may effect the distribution of these resources. US lobbies which also have interest in these resources also encourage the full and active US control in the region and support an American war on Iraq.

For the third, no matter to what extent Saddam has been left to keep his power after the Gulf Crisis, the Saddam regime and the Iraq Conflict has remained the axis of American domestic and foreign policies. US leaders had many daring claims about Iraq, especially the Bush Government following the September 11 attacks. It has been strongly emphasized both in the USA and globally that Saddam posed a threat for the regional as well as global peace as Iraq had weapons of mass destruction. As the situation on the one hand prepared for the legitimization of the action that the US government was to take against Saddam, on the other hand, it has led the USA, perhaps unintentionally, to undertake the task of disarming Saddam alone. In other words, an inescapable sort of "psychological drive" has been created. If the USA ever changed her mind on the war on Iraq, she would lose immediately all global and domestic credibility. Thus, except for surprises such as Saddam's escape from Iraq or alike, there was no possibility for the USA such as taking a step back. Thus, this psychological factor as well motivated the USA in her decision.

For the fourth, decisions taken by the American foreign policies are products of multilateral deal mechanisms. Many lobbies are included in this deal mechanism.[39] There are, in the US system more than six-thousand registered and an equal amount of

---

[35] Distribution of the Global Petrol Reserves see, Table 1: Distribution of Oil Reserves in the World, within the Chapter 16: "Instability in the Middle East and the Relevant Role of the PKK" by Idris Bal.

[36] Distribution of the global natural gas reserves see, Table 2: Distribution of the global natural gas reserves, within the Chapter 16: "Instability in the Middle East and the Relevant Role of the PKK", by Idris Bal.

[37] Burak Ulman, "Savaş ve Petrol Bağlamında Dünya Düzenini Anlamak", *Foreign Policy Türkiye Baskısı*, Mart-Nisan/Mayıs-Haziran 2003, p.56.

[38] http://www.indexmundi.com/iraq/natural_gas_proved_reservep.html

[39] İdris Bal, "External and Internal Dynamics that Shape US Central Asian Policy", *Stratejik Analiz*, No.12, April 2001, pp.60-61.

unregistered lobbies and organizations and individuals or functions alike. The individuals and organizations represent the voters of the senators, big and small companies, and trade groups, assurance companies that are indispensable in the American system, unions and foreign countries' political interests. That is to say that these individuals and organizations are involved in activities of imposing their interests on the parliamentarians. The American system does not present the President with total power but envisages the sharing of power with Congress. The President suggests and Congress moulds the idea. Legislation of one Presidential decision is only possible by the consent of the majority of Congress that has 535 congressmen. This is where lobbies gets involved. Thus, lobbyism has almost become a sector in the U.S. Parliament and government.[40] In the American tripartite political chain of legislation, execution and jurisdiction, Think Tanks are the fourth ring. Presently, there are in the USA more than 300 think tanks, some of which gradually lose interest in remaining at a distance from ideologies.[41] Lobbies, at this point, are the fifth link in the chain.[42] Shaping to a great extent the U.S. internal policies, lobbyism also plays a great part in international relations with the USA.[43] Thus; other countries also lead lobbyist activities in the USA. The known number of lobbyist individuals and organizations that lobby for other countries in the USA is more than 900.[44] As, for example, the Greek lobby may influence America's policies on Turkey; the Jewish Lobby may influence the pro-Israel and the Middle Eastern policies. The Jewish Lobby in the USA is of extreme importance. Iraq has been one important obstacle that Israel, aiming at power in the region since 1948, is faced with. Thus, it is all so natural that both the USA and the Jewish Lobby support an intervention in the region, which will destroy an enemy straining Israel. This is as well another factor that encouraged the USA to fight in the region.

Lastly, the personality of president Bush, his beliefs, the composition of his administration, his worldview and ideas as well as his bureaucrats played an important role in US policy and in the decision for a war against Iraq. Bureaucrats within the Bush administration who are called Neo-Conservativeists, advocate that the US should play a more active role in world politics and they advocate that leadership of the US needs to be fortified by using power. Their approach was naturally influential over president Bush and US foreign policy.[45]

Basically, under the influence of these factors, and due to many internal, foreign and global policies, the USA seemed well decided on a war on Iraq. However, this time the USA did not find the international support she had enjoyed in the 1991 Gulf Crisis and in

[40] Aydan Kodaloğlu, "Lobbies and Lobbyism in the U.P.A." *Avrasya Dosyası*, Vol.1, Issue.4, Winter 1994, p.31.
[41] Andrew Rich, "US Think Thanks and the Intersection of Ideology, Advocacy, and Influence", *NIRA Review*, Winter 2001, p.55.
[42] Kodaloğlu, *Lobbies and Lobbyism in the U.P.A.*, p.30.
[43] For pressure groups in USA see, Tayyar Arı, *Amerika'da Siyasal Yapı Lobiler ve Dış Politika*, İstanbul: Alfa Yayınları, 2000.
[44] Kodaloğlu, *Lobbies and Lobbyism in the U.P.A.*, p.32.
[45] Süleyman Bulut, "Amerikan Dehşetinin Mimarları: Neoconlar", *2023 Aylık Dergi*, Ağustos 2003, pp.22-27.

her Taliban operations. On the contrary, the UN, NATO as well as the EU grappled with internal disputes. France and Germany openly object to the USA, Canada, a neighbor of the USA, did not support her as well. Although Russia and China had supported the toppling of Taliban as they had shared interests, they did not support the toppling of Saddam and the occupation of Iraq. 146-membered Independents Movement was also against the war.

The US had some demands from Turkey, which was a neighbor of Iraq and a strategic partner of the US in post Cold War era. The US wanted to use Turkish territory to attack Iraq from the north and wanted Turkey to take an active role in the crises. The US was planning to place 62,000 US soldiers, 255 warplanes and 65 helicopters in Turkey.[46] On the other hand, Turkey's situation was even more fragile and Turkey was undecided and hesitant. Moreover, being Middle Eastern herself, Turkey is the successor of the Ottoman Empire, which had ruled over the region for more than 400 years. Turkey defended a peaceful resolution of the problem, demanded that Iraq obey the decision of the UN. If an operation was necessary, Turkey argued that a decision by the UN Security Council was necessary. Regarding a peaceful resolution, in January 2003, Prime Minister Abdullah Gül (now foreign minister) visited Egypt, Saudi Arabia, Jordan, Syria and Iran. Then, on 23rd January 2003, foreign minister of the aforementioned countries gathered in Istanbul. However, they were not able to reach any concrete conclusion. Eventually, Turkey did not send her troops to Iraq did not take an active part in the war and further more she did not allow American troops to use Turkish territory. Later on, in order not to further undermine relations with the USA, after the war began, Turkey opened her airfield to US planes. A third motion that gave permission to send Turkish Troops to Northern Iraq and allowed Foreign Troops to use a Turkish airfield was accepted by Turkish Parliament on 20th March 2003.

2003 Iraq War and Understanding Turkey

There are, in Turkey, some who believe that Turkey should have been kept out of the crisis, saying "no" to the USA and that such approach would be an indicator of Turkey's national dignity and independence as well as others (weaker than first group) who claim that this war would engulf Turkey out of her will and lead to her sitting at the table to protect her national interests. There were several factors that needed to be taken in to account by Turkey in order to assess US demands and possible War in Iraq. In fact these factors were encouraging Turkey to cooperate with the US.

Geography is some very crucial data that countries should never omit in the creation of their policies. Turkey, above all, is a Middle Eastern country and a neighbor to Iraq. Thus, Turkey being drastically effected by and even taking a part in the war was highly possible.

Considering Turkey's situation from a more comprehensive perspective, Turkey definitely did not have enough power to keep the USA out of the war considering the regional and global balances. The USA was strong enough to lead this war without

---

[46] Tayyar Arı, "Türkiye, Irak ve ABD: Soğuk Savaş Sonrası Dönemde Basra Körfezinde Yeni Parametreler", İdris Bal, *21. Yüzyılda Türk Dış Politikası*, Ankara: Nobel Yayınları, 2004, pp.701-724.

Turkey's hand. Thus, saying "no" to the USA never meant that the risk of war was done with. However, although the author of this chapter expressed this view in several occasions before the war, it was usually expressed in media as well as in intellectual gatherings in Turkey that the USA would not occupy Iraq without a Northern front and Turkish help. This affected public opinion and decision makers. Yet, dissolution of the alliance with the USA would lead to political and economical costs including the security in Turkey. And in the case of Turkey's inclusion in the US op on Iraq, she would partially have a right of expression on such an issue concerning people that she is culturally bound, and have a right to take initiatives for the Iraqi people. A limit of such chance would only depend on the degree that Turkey chooses to undertake her activities. For instance, following the war, news such as cultural heritage was undermined, registrations of title deeds belonging to Turkmens were destroyed, etc. have been released from Iraq. For instance, because of common Ottoman heritage, the cultural heritage of Iraq can be regarded cultural heritage of Turkey and regarding this, if Turkey followed an active policy, she could play a positive role to protect libraries, museums, mosques and so on.

For the second, Turkey's close relations with the USA in NATO that have taken the form of a strategical partnership following the end of the Cold War root back in time until the end of WW II. As well as helping Turkey who has been left over on the international arena, this situation is also profitable for the USA in the pursuit of her regional and global policies. These tightening relations and strategical habits encourage Turkey to cooperate with the USA. On the contrary, Turkey, who was already a loner on the international arena would be forced into an even darker solitude. Whereas, for example, there are great differences between the Turkish and the European perspectives on terrorism, where Turkey has been constrained by both the European attitudes and support of the PKK, the USA had, to some extent, been the ally to Turkey and the two even cooperated in arresting the terrorist leader of the PKK, Abdullah Öcalan.

For the third, Turkey currently experiences a drastic economical crisis. The US support has so prevented Turkey from shouldering the entire burden. As Turkey will evidently need further debts, crossing with the USA would lead her to further financial problems. Also, after the war in Iraq, in case of no unexpected surprises, trade is expected to boom unlike the embargo of the 1991 Gulf Crisis. Thus, keeping out of the actuality, Turkey would lose her chance to profit from such trade boom. Therefore this situation was encouraging Turkey to cooperate with USA.

For the fourth, although the demands of the USA can be ignored, it is very hard for Turkey to exclude herself from all this regarding her national interests. Turkey had some expectation as well as anxiety regarding developments in Iraq. As on the one hand, Turkey tried to defend the rights of the Turkmens of Northern Iraq and claim that the Turkmens should not be ignored in the post war formations, on the other hand, Turkey did not want to see a Kurdish state in Northern Iraq. Turkey wanted to get rid of the remnants of the PKK completely in the region. Besides this, as mentioned above Turkey wanted to have a share in the market that would be created after the end of Iraq war and Turkey also wanted to play a role in the reformation of Iraq. This situation rendered Turkey's neutrality almost impossible. Thus, getting involved in the crisis is, for Turkey, an unintentional, unwanted requisite in order to claim her authority on issues of the post war era. Otherwise, there was a possibility of emergence of an independent Kurdish state in Northern Iraq that could be exploited by the regional and global powers against Turkey. In fact this was a de facto state in Northern Iraq before the war controlled by Talabani and Barzani forces. What they needed was international recognition. Ironically, Turkey had fed emergence of a de facto Kurdish state in Northern Iraq; in order to prevent the control of Saddam, 'Poised Hammer' (Çekiç Güç) and 'Operation Northern Watch' (Kuzeyden Keşif Gücü) were organized. However, Turkey was trying to prevent this trend from reaching its final goal; an independent Kurdish state. Otherwise, this formation had to either be Turkey's friend or be forever impeded. On the other hand, the Turkmen could neither afford their own self-defense nor could organize themselves and have any military deterrence. Their future depends on Turkey's very active defense of the Turkmens in the region.

As a conclusion, in spite of the facts that urged Turkey to actively play a role in the looming war and to accept the requirements of the USA, members of the Turkish Parliament rejected permission for Turkish soldiers to be sent abroad and Turkish land to be used by the US forces. This was a shocking surprise for the USA. Thus, the USA cut hope of opening the Northern Front. This was a result of a few facts, which are discussed below.

Before considering the diverse factors that were effective in Turkey at the time, we should consider the American approach to the matter. For the American government to assume that they will definitely gain the support of Turkey, caused them to take the matter related to Turkey very loosely and not to undertake active efforts with the Turkish Military Forces, members of parliament, the President, the Chairman of the Parliament or pressure groups. Since the American government has unquestionably relied upon the close (or strategical) relationship between the two countries and has easily obtained an extension for first the Poised Hammer (Çekiç Güç) and then the Northern Watch or Northern Reconnaissance Force of the USA from the Turkish Parliament, they have exhibited such an attitude. Moreover, the US government was encouraged more with a permit that was given to the American military force to bring their personnel to Turkey for the purpose of modernizing their military base and ports in Turkey by a decision taken on 6th February 2003. They also did not carry out any activities that would adequately convince the Turkish people of the necessity of the war; hence war and USA opponents diversely affected the public. The habit of seeing Turkey as a sure thing has actually caused America to neglect Turkey. For example, although Özal was known as a leader with liberal and American advocative ideas, the USA was only represented by the assistant Foreign Minister, Clifford Wharton, during the funeral of Turgut Özal who was the President of Turkey when he died in April 1993, whereas the same USA was represented by the Foreign Minister, Adelein Allbright during the funeral of Hafiz Al-Asad, the president of Syria, in June 2000.[47] When the King of Jordan died, both the

---

[47] Alan Makovsky, "U.S Policy Towards Turkey", Morton Abramowitz (Ed.), *Turkey's Transformation and American Policy*, New York: The Century Foundation Press, 2000, p.239.

President William J. Clinton and the ex-president Jimmy Carter were present at the funeral. While USA was defining the Turkish-American relations as strategical and showing neglectful or even despising attitudes towards Turkey, the argument of strategical partnership has started to loose meaning.

Secondly, the Turkish media was heavily opposing any war and constituted a considerable pressure towards saying "No" to the USA and to stay away from the war. There appeared in the Turkish media many articles and thoughts such as; Turkey's damages in the second Gulf War in 1991 not being compensated, hence America's promises are not trustworthy; taking an active role in the war will load heavy economical burdens onto Turkey; for Turkey to take part on the side of America during the war would cause a serious opposition to Turkey from the Arabs, hence the relationships between Turkey and Arab countries would deteriorate, then Turkey will be isolated, moreover, if Turkey participates in the war, the new government that will be formed in Iraq after the war will not be neighborly towards Turkey and future relations of the two countries will be negatively affected by this, Turkey should take its own independent decisions, benefits of Turkey and the USA are conflicting in Iraq, there is no legitimate ground for this war. The Turkish media at the time was filled with comments like Americans would not be able to attack Iraq without the support of Turkey in the Northern Front, if they do Iraq would be a second Vietnam, Saddam would strongly resist against the USA, by saying "No" to USA we could stop the approaching war and actually to say "No" is a must for national pride. Both the public and the parliament members were to a certain extent affected by these arguments. What is more, some foreign newspapers publishing some articles and cartoons depicting Turkish soldiers as mercenaries diversely affected the Turkish decision makers and the public opinion.

Thirdly, the Turkish government was lacking sufficient experience and Recep Tayyip Erdoğan, the leader of the AK (Justice and Development) Party was neither a parliament member nor was he the prime minister. Instead Abdullah Gül, present time Foreign Minister, was performing the duty of prime minister, which was causing some discipline problems within the party. Claiming to be the protector of the human rights and democratical values, the AK party can be counted as a partner to the USA as America is always in the forefront of such values. We can actually claim that the USA supports the AK Party in that matter. On the contrary to expectations, the party failed in gaining the support of parliament about participating actively in the war. However, because there were hesitations even in the party itself about entering the war and trusting the USA in every action, all these factors ensued the negative answer to the motion (tezkere).

Fourthly, the President of Turkey openly stated his own views, which were completely against the demands of the USA and any kind of war. The president assigned that the occupation will never be legalized unless it is supported by a decision taken by the Security Council. However, the US government was claiming that Assignment no.1441 would be sufficient. Since the President is himself a jurist and was selected president while he was the Head of the Turkish Constitutional Court, he has thus been very sensitive towards the principles of law and reacted to the matter as known. It is certain that, when President Sezer adopted a manner against war, this affected TBMM (Turkish

Grand National Assembly) and at least caused some reluctance.

Fifthly, like the president, the Chairman of TBMM also expressed his opposition to the demands of the US government. His worries were mainly originated from a legitimate and humanistic view. We can guess that the manner adopted by the Chairman may also have affected the other members of the Assembly both from the AK party and from the opposition.

Sixthly, the Turkish Military Force was also not very fond of entering the oncoming war in Iraq and was implicitly rejecting the demands of the US Government. In some cases officials of the army had openly expressed their opposition. For example, on the 26th of March 2003, Mr. Özkök, the Chief of General Staff, expressing how the Turkish Military Staff approached the matter, said in a press conference in Diyarbakır "this war is not our war, this duty is not our duty".[48] Therefore, the TSK (Turkish Military Force) did not take any steps to encourage TBMM (Turkish Parliament) and what is more, some events occurred which caused TBMM's reluctance. In its meeting held in February 2003, contrary to expectations, the National Security Council (MGK) made no decision about the matter. However, this was the most important issue related Turkey's security and the Council was supposed to take a decision related to the matter and deliver a recommendation to the Government. For the Council not to issue any opinion about the matter, drove members of parliament who were already in a great dilemma into even more faltering. This silence of the Council was assumed as an implicit opposition.[49] These events might even have caused fear among parliament members from being responsible in the future for a misjudgment that they will have adopted.

Some factors might have affected the manner of the TSK. First of all, traditionally, the Turkish army is not very willing to send its soldiers to foreign lands. TSK was against Turkey's active involvement in the second Gulf War in 1991 and a conflict occurred between Özal and Necip Toruntay, the Chief of General Staff at the time, and as a result of this conflict, Toruntay had to resign. Secondly, the TSK might have sincerely considered that the USA will not take any risk without Turkish support from the Northern Front and tried to prevent a possible war, carrying humanistic concerns. Thirdly, from the opinions of the present Chief of General Staff, we can see that according to the TSK, the interests of Turkey and the USA in Iraq are not congenial. Especially concerning the Kurdish issue, there is a wide gap between the Turkish and American sides. This might naturally have affected the manner adopted by the TSK.[50] Otherwise, if TSK officials had expressed their support, the possibility of the motion (tezkere) passing through TBMM would be higher and the CHP, the opposition party, would not adopt a group opposition.

---

[48] Gencer Özcan, "Dört Köşeli Üçgen Olmaz: Irak Savaşı, Kürt Sorunu ve Bir Stratejik Perspektifin Kırılması", *Foreign Policy Türkiye Baskısı*, Mart-Nisan/Mayıs-Haziran 2003, p.48.

[49] Gencer Özcan, "Dört Köşeli Üçgen Olmaz: Irak Savaşı, Kürt Sorunu ve Bir Stratejik Perspektifin Kırılması", *Foreign Policy Türkiye Baskısı*, Mart-Nisan/Mayıs-Haziran 2003, p.47.

[50] Professor Lenore Martin claimed that TSK might have tried to isolate and weken AK Parti during the Iraq War. She expressed this view in the discussion part of the speech by İdris Bal, Fulbright Visiting Scholar, CMES, Harvard University, Assistan Professor, Faculty of Security Sciences, Ankara, "Test Case of U.S-Turkish Relations: Iraq 2003", *Center For Middle Eastern Studies, Harvard University, Study Group on Modern Turkey*, 19 November 2003.

Due to the army's silence and implicit opposition, some members of parliament might have fallen into hesitation.

Seventhly, the CHP, the opposition party, was also openly against the permission. They alleged that this war is not legitimate, Turkey should say "no" to America to protect its own interests and should stay away from this war. It is nearly a tradition anymore for opposition parties in Turkey to oppose nearly everything that the leader party carries out domestically and to act together with the leader party when national interests are under concern in foreign policies. However, about the Iraq crisis, the CHP adopted a completely opposite mode of behaviour to the government and has never been supportive. The reason that the CHP followed such an offensive manner was probably something to do with the approaches of the TSK and the public towards the issue. As the CHP might have intended to subvert the AK party by leaving it alone, but also it is already in the CHP's tradition in Turkish foreign policy since it was first formed, not to take any risk, to be much too prudent, to be reluctant to take active steps and to be undesirous in taking a side with any country concerning the conflicts in the Middle East. Furthermore, since the CHP agreed on a group decision, even Kemal Derviş who was seen as an envoy of the USA in Turkey could not vote for the permission. Hence, the attitude of CHP determined the end of the voting process. If they would not take a group decision, in most probably there would even have been members from the CHP who would liked to have voted for the motion. This result put the AK party in a difficult situation, however on the other side, this has revealed that the AK party is not that "anti-American" and the CHP is not that "Western" and "receptive for cooperation with the USA" as expected.

Eighthly, there are some groups in Turkey who consider the USA as a power that will completely change the status quo in the country. These groups carry worries that the USA will finally destroy Kemalism in Turkey and because of this they acted against the USA. Since Atatürk, the commander of the Turkish armies during the independence war, the founder of the modern Turkish Republic and the first Turkish president, generally has a very renowned position in Turkey, this kind of drawback might have diversely affected the public and the decision makers.

Another factor is related to the ongoing efforts of Turkey to enter the European Union, which have continued for 44 years. As the Iraq war caused a conflict within NATO, it also caused divisions within the EU as England and Spain supported the USA, while France and Germany opposed the USA and cooperated with Russia. On the other hand, in Turkey, opinions favor acting together with Germany and France, since these two countries are the major players in the EU and acting with them means emphasizing the European side of Turkey, this will help in the EU membership process of Turkey. This is another argument, which depicted the opposition to the USA more elaborately.[51] However, although Turkey determined its side by saying "No" to the USA, she still could not achieve any concrete, positive progress in the EU.

Many sectors that are summarized above, were mainly concerned about the legitimacy

---

[51] For the influence of Europe over Turkey see. Ian O. Lesser. "Turkey, the U.S and Europe-A Troubled Triangle", http://www.aicgp.org/c/lesser.shtml

of the war. At first glance, this was a correct approach. Because the USA could not release a decision out of the Security Council for the war. However, this way of approach has many other dilemmas in it. For example, if the UN Security Council decides to expel Turkish forces from Cyprus in the future, what sort of reaction will be given to that? On the other hand, there are already decisions taken by the UN completely against Turkey's interests. How are these decisions considered? The problem with this approach is perceiving the UN Security Council as a very just high court. The UN is a political institution. It is an arena where international powers impact with another and the interests of mainly five permanent members are reflected. That's why, it is always debatable for this institution to obtain a position of legalization. The UN Security Council's decisions are determined according to the national interests of members, especially those who bear the right of veto. Even so, it certainly plays a positive role in providing peaceful international order. Because, it at least serves greatly to achieve a correspondence between the world powers and prevents conflict occurring between these powers. However, it is questionable for every country, especially a country like Turkey that has no effect in the UN and moves alone in the international arena, to arrange their actions according to the UN. Moreover, even the USA, the most effective member of the UN, did not take any notice of the UN when they realized that they will not be able to obtain what they wanted during the third Gulf War (Iraq 2003) and alleged that Assignment no.1441 was still valid. When the structure of the UN and the events until today are examined, we can see that this attitude of the USA is not necessarily counted as strange. Anyhow, the UN was formed after the Second World War to protect the present status quo, in another words to maintain the interests of winner states and only thus to protect the peaceful situation. Otherwise, no one can explain why the veto right is given to England and France, but not to Japan and Germany. There are many interesting examples about the legitimacy of a war. Before the 1950 Korean War, the USSR protested the meetings of the Security Council and did not participate in the meetings. In the absence of the USSR, the UN Security Council has been able to take a decision and the war was legalized under the UN. If the USSR, instead of protesting, would participate in the meetings and use its veto right, that war would not be legitimate. Similarly, if Iraq would invade Kuwait not in 1990, but in 1979, most probably the USSR would prevent any interference in the UN Security Council against Iraq and use its veto right. Then any war against Iraq would be considered as illegitimate. Likewise, there was no UN Security Council decision for the NATO intervention in the conflict in Kosovo, but Turkey rightfully participated in the intervention.

The same structure was also valid for the League of Nations. The Mosul region (now in Iraq) where Britain could not occupy during the First World War, after the Montreux Truce, Britain invaded Mosul for their strategical plans and never gave the region back to Turkey in the Lousanne Act, since the region is very rich in petrol reserves which would ameliorate the status of Turkey in the international era. After the Lousanne Act, Turkey offered to have a plebiscite in the region, but England rejected the offer and took the matter to the League of Nations where itself obtained a great impact upon the decisions and as expected, the region has been detracted from Turkey. This is a very important strategical success for England. As can be seen from the examples given above, although the UN serves international peace and order, the legalizing side of the UN is arguable and usually decisions are taken according to the national interests of some countries and it is an arena for a power show. Hence, for Turkey to demand the condition of legitimacy for the war is a subject of debate. Furthermore, other than not having a decision of Security Council, the terrorism and Weapons of Mass Destruction grounds that were put forward by the USA to legalize the Iraq war, are still not satisfactorily proved.

Under the conditions summarized above, the motion for participating in the war was not accepted in Turkey. After the war started, Turkey opened its airfields to America on 20th March 2003. This was an indication from Turkey of an intention of continuing peaceful relations with the USA without straining them too much. Although this was a favorable step to take, it was still not enough to compensate the losses between the USA and Turkey caused by the permission crisis.

On the other hand, for the relationship between Turkey and the USA to be constrained due to the rejection of the motion, elimination of Turkey's effect upon the USA, for Turkey to stay away from the war and not to take an active role in process has rightfully made the Kurdish groups in Northern Iraq very happy. Because, they were scared to loose position if Turkey would be active in the war. When this possibility was voided, for Kurdish groups, a suitable ground was formed to play important roles in reconstructuring Iraq after the war.

War and Post War Developments

As expected the USA occupied Iraq from the South without Turkish help and without a northern front and brought the Saddam regime to an end in April 2003. This showed the weakness of the argument that the US would not occupy Iraq without Turkish backing and opening a northern front. US and British forces attacked from the south and as expected Kurds allied with US forces in the north as well. The Saddam regime was not able to resist the occupying forces as expected and Saddam himself was captured in December 2003. The US began to establish foundations of new state in Iraq. The Iraqi Governing Council consisting of 25 members was formed on 3rd July 2003. The Presidential Council, consisting of nine members, was formed out of the members of the Iraqi Governing Council. 5 Shia, 2 Sünni and 2 Kurdish members were selected for the presidential Council. Members of Presidential Council chair Iraqi Governing Council in alphabetic order. The US appointed Paul Bremer as a civilian governor to Iraq. At the end of August 2003, the Iraqi Governing Council selected ministers of New Iraq as well. Each member of the Iraqi Governing Council became a minister; 13 Shia, 5 Sunni, 5 Kurdish, 1 Turkmen and 1 Asuri. Following the war, looting was widespread and especially title deeds belonged to Turkmens were destroyed and some attacks took place to intimidate Turkmens. While the Turkmens were not able to play a significant role in the reformation of Iraq, Kurds started to play vital roles. For instance, the speaker of the Iraqi Kurdistan Democratic Party, Hoşyar Zebari, was appointed as a foreign minister.

While on one hand the USA is trying to form new state, on the other hand, guerilla attacks and uprisings against US forces in Iraq continue. On 1st May 2003, the US announced the end of the Iraq War (2003). However, US losses after the war are greater than their losses during the actual war. In US domestic politics, Democrats are criticizing the Bush administration regarding the war and accuse Bush of starting an unnecessary war. They criticize the Bush administration in terms of the method they pursued during the war. These claims aim to undermine the position of the Republican Party in the next general election (November 2004). However, the recovery of the US economy, the fact that Hillary Clinton did not become a Republican candidate (she probably assumed that Bush's chance was so high in the election), attacks of international terrorism in various countries including Turkey, the capture of Saddam, declaration by Libya that she will cooperate with the international community over her weapons of mass destruction, and similar developments help George W. Bush for the next election. However, quick transformation of authority to the Iraqis will help US interests and it will at the same time satisfy Iraqis and undermine illegal activities. If the Bush administration can manage to transfer power successfully it will also help Bush in the next elections.

Although opponents of Saddam regime had welcomed the US occupation of Iraq, some unfortunate events such as looting of public building, museums, libraries, torture of Iraqi prisoners, and widespread instability in Iraq undermined image of the US in Iraq. In Iraqi eyes, the decision of US –led forces not to put Baghdad under curfew immediately after the city fell was the first and, in the immediate postwar period, most grievous error. "The ensuing orgy of looting and destruction by people who had been repressed and impoverished for decades was foreseeable and preventable, they (the Iraqi people) say. Many believe the rampage did more damage to the public infrastructure than the war did."[52] According to Mohsen Abdul Hameed, secretary general of the Iraqi Islamic Party and a Sunni Muslim leader of the Governing council, "Iraqi people now think that the coalition forces led the way to the destruction of the infrastructure."[53]

Another important development for Turkish US relations took place in post Iraq War era was the US decision to give economic aid (1 billion dollar donation or 8.5 billion dollar credit) to Turkey on 13th April 2003.[54] This step can be interpreted as although the US was unhappy because of Turkey's refusal to cooperate over the Iraq War (2003), the US did not want to alienate Turkey and wants to keep Turkey as an ally.

The most important development that took place following the Iraq War in 2003 was the detention of Turkish soldiers by American forces in Suleymaniye on 4 July 2003. This incident was the indication of lack of cooperation as well as lack of confidence between the US and Turkey, which had undermined increasing US-Turkish cooperation following the end of the Cold War. Some people in Turkey argued that this incident was psychological warfare.[55] Above all, this incident was the indicator of the fact that Iraq was under the control of the US, and other actors could act in Iraq with the consent of the USA.

---

[52] Charles A. Radin, "Baghdad residence point to failures by US after Iraq's fall", *The Boston Globe*, November 8, 2003, p.A10.

[53] Charles A. Radin, "Baghdad residence point to failures by US after Iraq's fall", *The Boston Globe*, November 8, 2003, p.A10.

[54] See, Tayyar Arı, "Türkiye, Irak ve ABD: Soğuk Savaş sonrası Dönemde Basra Körfezinde Yeni Parametreler," İdris Bal, (Ed.), *21. Yüzyılda Türk Dış Politikası*, Ankara: Nobel Yayınları, 2004.

[55] See, Ümit Özdağ, "Türk Amerikan İlişkilerinde Irak Krizi", *Stratejik Analiz*, Cilt.4, Sayı.40, Ağustos 2003.

Another post war development that was important for US-Turkish relations was the US demand of Turkish troops for Iraq. In order to be able to struggle against guerilla attacks, the US decided to get the help of Turkish troops. Under the influence of preceding developments and in order to help repairing problems of US-Turkish relations, the Turkish Parliament had adopted a motion that gave the permission to send Turkish troops abroad, on 7th October 2003. As general Myers pointed out, the US demand of Turkish troops was a test case for US-Turkish relations.[56] On the other hand, by saying "yes", Turkey indicated that she needed to cooperate with the USA, the USA was still important for Turkey, and the two countries were still allies. These developments were positive steps to repair the wounded US-Turkish relationship.

Although the US demanded Turkish troops in Iraq and Turkey was ready to send her troops, the US then changed its mind and did not want to see Turkish troops in Iraq. The argument used by the US to explain the shift of opinion regarding Turkish troops in Iraq was so weak. The fact that the Ottoman state had governed the region for a long time was regarded as a negative factor and it was argued that Iraqi people did not want to see Turkish troops in Iraq. Naturally, no people of any country want to see another country's troops in their country. However, on the other hand, do the Iraqi people prefer troops of for instance, Britain who ruled the country after the end of Ottoman rule, to Turkish troops? It is difficult to say, "yes" to this question. In fact, the Iraqi people do not want to see any troops in Iraq.[57] The assessment of Ottoman rule of the region is another aspect of the issue. In fact, as almost everyone admits, tolerance was basic feature of Ottoman rule and gave freedom to all ethnic and religious groups. The presence of Millet rule (Nation system), extensive freedoms, the fact that people of Iraq were a part of the Islamic nation, and similar factors indicate that the Iraqi people were not discriminated against during the Ottoman rule. Especially regarding Northern Iraq, it is the fact that Britain occupied the area after the end of World War I, but not during the actual war. The Mondreux armistice allowed the Britain to occupy Northern Iraq. There was a dispute regarding the future of the region and Turkey had proposed to carry on a plebiscite. However, Britain had rejected this proposition mainly because of the fact that people of the region were supporting reunification with Turkey. These factors indicate that the Ottoman state left heritage of friendship rather than hostility in the region. Furthermore, in recent times, because of the pressure posed by Saddam following the second Gulf War (1991), Kurdish people living in the region escaped to Turkey and Iran as a safe haven. If they regarded Turkey as an enemy state in the region, they would not escape to Turkey as a saviour. Therefore this argument was just a pretext to refuse Turkish troops. The main understandable reason on the other hand was that the USA did not want to see Turkey in

---

[56] ihlas@attglobal.net, Washington Mektubu/Hasan Mesut Hazar/Haber Vitrini için yazıyor./2, Ekim 2003, "Washington haber" <washingtonhaber-owner@yahoogroupp.com>; Some people have regarded Iraq war as a test case for US Turkish relations see, for instance, Nuri Gürgür, "Türkiye ABD İlişkileri Test Sürecinde", *Türk Yurdu*, Ağustos 2003, Cilt.23, Sayı.192, p.2.
[57] This approach has been ratified by Abdulrahim Abu-Husayn; Abdulrahim Abu-Husayn, Professor, Department of History and Archaeology, American University of Beirut, and Visiting Professor, Harvard University, "Perceiving Turkey in the Arab World", *Study Group on Modern Turkey*, Center For Middle Eastern Studies, Harvard University, 26 November 2003.

Iraq in this stage for the sake of her scenarios regarding Iraq. This is manly because, Turkey was a neighbor of Iraq, and a big country that has her own expectations as well as anxieties or in another words scenarios. If Turkey sent her troops to Iraq, she would try to influence reformation of Iraq, demand some amendments in the plans of the USA regarding Iraq, and undermine the position of Kurds who allied with the USA during the war. Therefore, bearing in mind all these, the USA decided to withdraw her proposal that required Turkish troops for Iraq. Because, the USA assessed that the situation was not so deteriorated and Turkish troops would bring more headaches then benefits for the USA On the other hand, the government in Turkey declared that they would not use the permission given by Turkish Parliament to send troops to Iraq on 7th November 2003.

In the decision of the USA regarding Turkish troops, Kurdish groups whom position would be undermined in the case of presence of Turkish Troops in Iraq, played vital roles. It was a big relief for them when they learned that Turkish troops were not coming to Iraq. However, the attitudes of Kurdish leaders should be regarded as a political one. Otherwise, the belief that Kurdish people of the region regarded Turkey and Turkish people as an enemy does not reflect the reality. Furthermore, from a cultural and historical perspective, the people of the Northern Iraq can be regarded as a fragment of people that established the Turkish republic.

In brief, the argument that the USA put forward to abandon her proposal regarding Turkish troops was a pretext. If the problem deteriorates surprisingly, as some claim it becomes similar to Vietnam,[58] in that case, the US may ask for Turkish troops again. Another aspect of the issue is that Ottoman State had governed the Balkans as well. However, Turkey played vital roles regarding the Bosnia and Kosovan problems and sent her troops. Friendship and cooperation have been seen between Turkish troops and people of the region rather than antagonism. Furthermore, as Halberstam pointed out because of very worm attitudes between the Muslims of Bosnia and people of Turkey, Mladic, a commander of Milosovic, regarded the Muslims of Bosnia as Turks.[59] In fact, in some Serbian nationalist marches, the Muslims of Bosnia are referred to as Turks. Because of this closeness Greece and Serbia had opposed the idea of sending Turkish troops to the Balkans. In fact, whenever a conflict took place around Turkey in the former Ottoman lands, Turkey became a target of migration. Especially Muslims of the region regard Turkey as a second homeland and a safe haven. The composition of the Turkish people is evidence of this. In the process of dissolution of the Ottoman Empire, according to axis of culture, some of the Muslim people retreated to Anatolia, which was regarded as a last shelter. This migration also continued after the establishment of the Turkish republic. Atatürk, the founder of Turkey, was himself born in Saloniko, now in Greece, and several high ranking generals in the Turkish army, civil politicians and elit were and are of Balkan, Caucasus, Central Asian and Middle Eastern origin. For instance, the family of Kenan Evren, former coup leader and former president of Turkey migrated to Turkey from the Balkans. These developments formed the present Turkish nation. There are

---

[58] Analogy with Vietnam can be misleading. Because in the case of Vietnem, in fact two block were clashing to a digree.
[59] David Halberstam, *War in a Time of Peace*, New York: Scribner, 2001, p.296.

several groups and peoples who live outside the Turkish borders that have strong ties with the Turkish people. Following the Ottoman rule, although new regimes made propaganda against the Ottoman State and Turkey, especially for the Muslim peoples of the region, Turkey is still a friendly state, Turkish people are a sister people and further more during crises, Turkey is regarded as a second homeland. Therefore, Ottoman heritage did not leave a burden for Turkey, but left an area suitable for cooperation. In fact, if former Soviet territory was a 'back yard' for the Russian Federation, in a similar way and for similar reasons, the former Ottoman lands and in fact Central Asia might be regarded as a 'back yard' of Turkey. In fact, as summarized above, the influence of Turkey in the region is not a negative factor for US-Turkish relations, in contrast, this is a factor that encouraged the USA and Turkey to cooperate in the region. In brief, the US request of troops from Turkey gave an opportunity to Turkey to show her attitudes towards the USA. Although USA changed her mind and did not want Turkish troops, while this was an unpleasant development for Turkey and the Turkish public, the Turkish parliament on the other hand gave permission to government to send troops and this was a corner stone in the way of repairing Turkish-US relations.

In brief, especially the capture of Saddam in December 2003 cheered up the US soldiers in Iraq and the position of the Bush administration at home and around the globe strengthened. However, the capture of Saddam didn't mean the end of guerilla attacks against the occupying forces in Iraq. Furthermore, news of torture coming from Iraq in April and May 2004 is not a positive development for the Bush administration as well as the future of Iraq. Such incidents can undermine the image of the USA who occupied Iraq to bring democracy and human rights. Recent developments may help terrorist groups and uprising within Iraq. On the other hand, it is extremely difficult for a liberal state to struggle against terrorists and guerillas. There are several problems that liberal states face in their fight against terrorism such as selection of suitable methods, intelligence, defense, deterrence, and retaliation.[60] Besides, there is a risk that continuing disorder in post war era in Iraq, guerilla attacks, increasing losses of Iraqi civilians, news of torture and similar developments, can create a negative public opinion or may be hatred towards the USA and US forces in Iraq. The Iraqi people believe that maintaining security is a duty of occupying forces in Iraq.[61] Therefore, it seems that to transfer authority to Iraqis in the shortest time is the best solution. Otherwise, it is highly likely that the cost of war for the USA will increase in every aspect every passing day.

Conclusion: Result of the War and Future of US-Turkish Relations

As expected the USA occupied Iraq, ended the Saddam regime and furthermore, managed to capture Saddam Hussein. Although guerilla attacks against occupying forces and

[60] For details see, İdris Bal, "Liberal Devlet Terörizm ve Uluslararası İşbirliğinin Önemi", İdris Bal, (Ed.), 21. Yüzyılda Türk Dış Politikası, Ankara: Nobel Yayınları, 2004; for English version see, Idris Bal, "Terrorism, Liberal State and International Co-operation", *Turkish Yearbook of Human Rights,* Vol.21-25, 1999-2003, pp.117-132; See also, George Friedman, The Iraq Dilemma: Frying Pan or Fire?", *The Staratfor Weekly,* 12 November 2003, www.stratfor.com

[61] Ian Fisher, "As Iraqis Become the Targets of Terrorists, Some Now Blame the American Mission", *The New York Times,* December 17, 2003.

uprisings continue in Iraq, the USA is taking concrete steps regarding repairing infrastructure, reformation of the state, works for transferring authority to Iraqis and establishing a new friendly regime.

It seems that the US has to a significant extent achieved her political, economical and security objectives. Control of Iraqi economy and natural resources, full occupation of Iraq (although there are some uprising and attacks) and permanent military bases in the long term, establishment of a friendly government and a strategic partner of the USA are some indications of this success.

An import development that took place following Iraq War 2003, because of the deterrence of the USA, Libya and Iran started to compromise regarding weapons of mass destruction. Therefore, these developments can be regarded as a success for US policy. Furthermore, unless a surprise development such as deterioration of torture cases takes place, these developments can help Bush in the general elections and it seems that his chance is still high.

Developments in Iraq and US policies can open the gate for democracy in the Middle East in the long term. This situation can prepare a suitable base for cooperation and even for regional integration. For instance, president Bush reminded Syria and Iran as well as the USA's allies in the region, Saudi Arabia and Egypt that the toppling of Saddam was an important step of the global democratic revolution and he warned them to adopt democratic traditions and implement reforms.[62] Besides this, because of determined US policies, as mentioned above, Libya has begun to cooperate over weapons of mass destruction and Iran also took some positive steps. The toppling of Saddam in Iraq and his capture by US forces, and similar developments may undermine, as a beside, the public prestige and authority of previous dictators and despotic regimes in the region. It is obvious that the democratic Middle East will form a new area of cooperation for Turkey and it will open the gates for dialogue and cooperation between peoples. However, it will be too early to expect rapid changes in the short term.

On the other hand, developments following the third Gulf War (Iraq War 2003), created some doubts and problems regarding the US understanding of democracy and Human rights and US prestige in international arena. Some critics began to appear from within the US as well as all over the world regarding human rights and democracy. Especially, the detention of over six hundred people without bringing them before any court in US naval base in Guantanomo, was regarded as a violation of human rights.[63] This situation can undermine US interests in the future by leading to the loss of US prestige as well as weakening the US rhetoric of human rights and democracy. Therefore, as Wilkinson pointed out, the primary objectives of a counter-terrorist strategy must be the protection and maintenance of the liberal democracy, rule of law and upholding the state's constitutional authority. It cannot be sufficiently stressed that achieving these primary objectives over-rides in importance even the objective of eliminating terrorism

---

[62] David E. Sanger. "Bush Asks Lands in Mideast to Try Democratic Ways", *The New York Times*, November 7 2003.

[63] David G. Savage. "Justices Take Guantanomo Detainees' Case", *Los Angeles Times*, November 12, 2003.

and political violence as such. Even in the most severe crises, therefore, a liberal democracy must seek to remain true to itself, avoiding on the one hand the danger of sliding in to repressive dictatorship, and on the other, the evil consequence of inertia, inaction and weakness in upholding its constitutional authority and preserving law and order.[64]

Another question created by the third Gulf War is that if the occupation of Iraq was a part of the Global War on terrorism, has the occupation undermined international terrorism or has it accelerated it? Although it is difficult to answer this question at this stage, current developments do not allow us to draw an optimistic picture.

Another question widely discussed in the international arena is related with the justification of the war. As discussed above (especially in the context of Turkey), several circles in the US as well as all over the world claim that there was no justification for this war. Although the main argument about this is the fact that there was no decision by the UN Security Council regarding the war, however, there are other questions about the justification of the war. Especially, it is usually claimed that Iraq had no ties with international terrorism, there were no Weapons of Mass Destruction in Iraq and in fact, these arguments were used as pretexts to justify the war. Unless the US takes some concrete steps to put forward evidences that justify the war and her activities, this war can be an example for the rest of the world that in turn, might threaten international peace and order. For instance, some states may occupy some countries or regions by claiming that they were supporting terrorism and so on. In this regard, Russian accusation of Georgia, and the activities of Israel in the region can be meaningful. Therefore, it will be beneficial for the US to bring up evidences that justify US actions and the war and also to give a more important role to NATO and the UN.

Another dimension of the developments in Iraq that can affect the region as well as the world is that there is possibility of the disintegration of Iraq. Unless the new administration creates economic, democratic attraction at the center, there will still be a risk of disintegration. The nationalization process has not been completed successfully in Iraq. While Arabs are divided as Shias and Sunnis, Sunnis on the other hand are divided as Arabs, Kurds and Turkmens.[65] Following the end of the Ottoman rule, the region was culturally perished and nationalization struggles were not successful. During the propaganda to undermine the Saddam regime backed by the US, the US supported various groups to be organized on the bases of their separate identities, which in turn strengthened group consciousness. However, such division and separate organizations and different identities can undermine the unity of Iraq in the post Saddam era. Especially the fact that Kurds allied with the USA during the war, might undermine solidarity among people, especially between Kurds and Arabs. Similar to the attitudes of Turks who accuse Arabs (in fact some of them) as people who allied with the enemy during the World War I, Iraqi Arabs may accuse Kurds in a similar way. In the long term this attitude will serve not for unity but for division. This situation may help separatist trends. However, if new

---

[64] P. Wilkinson, *Terrorism and Liberal State*, London: Macmillan Press Ltd., 1977, pp.121-123.
[65] There are Shia Turkmens as well.

Iraq becomes a center of attraction this division can be prevented.

In the case of a division, there will certainly be a Kurdish state in the North. This possibility will not be a pleasant development for Turkey, Iran or Syria. Also an Arab state possibly established at the center of Iraq will not be happy with the Kurdish sate as well. Under these circumstances, any newly established Kurdish state will be surrounded by hostile states and land locked. Therefore, this new sate will have to depend on the USA and Israel. If this possibility comes true, beyond it creates problems in Turkish domestic politics; it will affect Turkish-US relations to a significant degree. A new Kurdish state, dependent on the US and Israel and disputed with her neighbours, will be ready to play any role given by the US. In this case, the US's need for Turkey due to her strategic position will decline. Because a lonely Kurdish state will be eagerly ready and will be more competitive and easygoing. On the other hand, the US may prefer small and more obedient Kurdish state to a more powerful Turkish Republic, which has an ability to follow more autonomous polices (as seen during the third Gulf War in 2003).

Turkey's exclusion from the war, on the other hand, the alliance of Kurdish groups with the USA during the war, prepared a suitable political as well as psychological base for the Kurds to be able to play an active role in Iraq. Therefore, the fact that Turkey did not play an active role in the war and post war era pleased Iraqi Kurds very much. Although Turkish parliament had given permission to the government on 7th October 2003 to send Turkish troops to Iraq, the US had changed her mind and did not want Turkish troops in Iraq anymore. This policy of the USA may be interpreted as indicator of US willingness of giving Kurds vital roles in the formation of new Iraq if not her approval of a possible independent Kurdish state in Northern Iraq. That is the reason why; the US did not want Turkish interference in Iraq in that stage. As a result, Turkey had to abandon all her plans and scenarios regarding Iraq and her influence over Iraq minimized. The Suleymaniye incident was a clear message and warning that was given to Turkey by the US that Turkey could do nothing in Iraq without US consent. Then Turkey abandoned her red lines, possibility of intervention to Northern Iraq, and similar issues. Therefore, if one argues that the policy that Turkey pursued before and during the war was a "mistake", under the light of these developments in Iraq, their side effects and possible outcomes and future risks, this claim will not be an exaggeration. In the case of establishment of the Kurdish state, unless Turkey takes positive steps regarding economy, democracy, human rights, become a united whole with her people and create a center of attraction, this new formation will arbitrarily influence Turkey; accelerate separatist movements in Turkey. Even if such a Kurdish state does not come to be, Turkey has lost initiative regarding her expectations and anxieties such as developments in Northern Iraq, PKK, position of the Turkmens, economic issues, formation of the new state and so on, and Turkey has been excluded from the bargaining table regarding Iraq. The main important feature of this policy was that Turkey showed to the world that if Turkey wanted she could follow autonomous policies in the region even if the issue was related with the most powerful country of the world.

Israel's policies are indicators of the possibility of establishment of an independent Kurdish state in the region, as well as Israel's preparations for such a possibility. For instance, it is claimed that Kurds were Jewish in origin. The fact that an independent Kurdish state in the region is not welcomed by Turkey, Iran and Syria, on the other hand, US-Kurdish and Israel–Kurdish rapprochements were crated by the developments in the region. These developments prepared a suitable ground for the propagandas to be successful and influential over the Kurdish public as well as elite. Such propagandas aims to create a suitable psychological base for possible future Kurdish-Israeli cooperation. Therefore, the activities of Israel can be regarded as a successful psychological warfare.

Moreover, the USA may favor establishment of an independent Kurdish state. However, in the case of dissolution of Iraq, although there will be a friendly Kurdish state in the North, it is not clear yet how other sates (two or three) that might be established will react to the USA. Will the state that might possibly be established by the Iraqi Shias people, be close to Iran? Is not there any possibility that states that might be established by Shia and Sunni Arabs be anti-American in the long term (if not in the short term)? Bearing all these in mind, it might be argued that the US will try to maintain the unity of Iraq under the umbrella of a friendly regime in Iraq in the short term. Because, in the case of the dissolution of Iraq, no one will be sure about the consequences of the developments and furthermore this option will alienate Turkey and further undermine Turkish-US relations as well. However, there is a possibility that developments can go out of control in the long term.

Either if a Kurdish state is established or Iraq maintains her unity, in both cases, Kurds will play vital roles in Iraq and new state will be a friend of the USA. The importance of this for Turkey is that the existence of a friendly Iraq will most probably undermine the importance of Turkey for the USA in the region. Because, the USA will have military bases in Iraq as well and the new regime will be closer and more dependent on the USA. Under this condition, the US's need of Turkey will decline if not end.[66]

Implication of these developments for Turkey is that as outlined above, while Turkey had regarded the US as an ally that will help Turkey and remove her loneliness in the international arena, cooperate on several issues, and be a balancing power against possible threats against Turkey, Turkey will need to search for alternatives because of the erosion of the Turkish position for the USA. These developments can deepen Turkish loneliness in the international arena in the short term unless relations are repaired. At present both the Turkish government and the US administration are taking positive steps to straighten relations.

In spite of all these, both Turkey and the USA will need each other. Therefore, it is possible to argue that problems will be solved and relations will again advance. Because, neither new Iraq nor a possible Kurdish state (if Iraq disintegrates), will be able to play the role that Turkey can. Because Turkey is a big country and heir to the Ottoman state, that has great potentials and influence over the region. Therefore, Turkey will be important in the region under all circumstances. Turkey's need of the USA can change in

---

[66] In his answer to my question, David Philips ratified this opinion; David Philips, "Post-War Failings in Iraq", Deputy Director, Center for Preventive Action, Council on Foreign Relations and Visiting Scholar, CMES, *Middle Esat Seminer*, Jointly Supponsered by the Weatherhead Center for International Affairs and the Center for Middle Eastern Studies, Harvard Univbersity, October 30, 2003.

the long term according to regional as well as global developments.

In the new era, created by the end of the Third Gulf War factors that caused the relations between Turkey and the USA to advance to the level of strategic partnership have not completely disappeared. Although Turkish-US relations have been undermined because of the 2003 Iraq war, the USA and Turkey still have similar and overlapping approaches, expectations and worries regarding several regional as well as global issues. Some example of these issues is that the two countries have a similar view are as follows; balancing Russia, developments in Eurasia, control of Iran, international terrorism, issues regarding Hydrocarbon resources in the Caspian Sea and Central Asia, instability in the regions around Turkey, radical movements, etc. Especially on the one hand Turkey's need for a strong friendly country in international relations, on the other hand, apart from the global war on terrorism, the US emphasis on the "Turkish model" and moderate Islam for the cooperation between the Islamic World and the West, will urge both sides to closer cooperation.

Additionally, after the control of Iraq by the USA, the two countries became neighbors from one point of view. Even if the USA transfers authority to the Iraqis, this situation will not change as long as a friendly (with the USA) regime is established in Iraq. This new situation encourages US-Turkish cooperation as well.

On the other hand, while it can be expected that close relations between Turkey and the USA will continue, some problems will keep shadowing those relations. Perhaps these problems will be more important, for instance the Armenian question can again come to the US political agenda more strongly. Furthermore, the USA might recognize the Armenian genocide claims. Apart from different approaches of the two sides regarding the Kurdish Question, unless Turkey takes the necessary steps regarding human rights and democracy, this subject will be another problem between the two countries as it used to be in the past. There are different approaches about developments in the Middle East as seen during the Third Gulf War (2003).[67] Because of the relative erosion of the position of Turkey for the USA, the pressure of these problems over Turkey might be heavier unless Turkey takes necessary steps.

After the collapse of the Ottoman Empire, the Middle East has been turned into a symbol of instability. Turkey, being the Ottoman successor, can undertake the mediatorship that the Jews, the Christians and the Muslims can at once trust in bringing peace and stability to the region due to her cultural and historical heritage, her experiences of Westernization and her time-honored understanding of tolerance. Alongside with being one "bridge state" Turkey should as well be the "center" of the region and manage the job well. Yet, above all, she first has to be able to stand couragously on her own and direct her power to her backyard, to somewhere else than home. If Turkey manages to be a country of attraction (democracy, human rights,

---

[67] For differant perspectives see, Heinz Kramer, *A Changing Turkey*, Washington, D.C.: Brookings Institution Press, 2000, pp.228-231.

economic wealth, etc.), Turkey would be the guarantee for peace in the Middle East in the long term.

7 The European Union and Turkey

İbrahim S. Canbolat

Introduction

Without being comprehended truly within the sui generis structure and within the historical development of the union, it will be a lacking and misleading attempt to evaluate the European Union (EU) especially within the context of relationships with Turkey. It is not so logical to compare the European Union with any international institution as it may seem to be; above all, to think of the relations of Turkey with the EU member states on the basis of assumptions and the arrangements of politics and the follow-up actions developed accordingly may very possibly result in detrimental effects on the overall national policy in the short and long run.

In fact the EU is a kind of value sharing system and therefore it requires the sharing of sovereignty in related fields as it focuses on the participation in all the related fields in mind. The most concrete example of this is to substitute Euro with national money of the member states. Withdrawn of the national money, which is printed and put into circulation within the national authority and the most important sovereignty right, and acceptance of a money which will be used commonly with others is a job of mind and management before everything.[1] The economic aspect of the money that is thought to be the first function of it comes after this. So we need to see the European Union as a political, social, cultural and economic integration process. Firstly, this fact should be understood adequately, both of the governors, officers in bureaucracy and the people of each part of the society should make a fresh start considering this reality.

In this article, first, the formation and the systematic feature of the European Union will be examined, and then the relations of Turkey with this foundation will be considered.

A New Model Search in Europe

After the Second World War various plans evolved to make Europe become a united whole. All of them have focused on the point of developing a European Union to maintain peace and prosperity in Europe continuously.

There are three separate opinions as to what helps all these countries to unite regardless of all the existing differences.[2] Firstly, a "universal" European Union opinion including East and Western Europe; secondly, the opinion of proposing a form of United States within Europe, which depends on constitutional arrangements; and thirdly the opinion of defending a European against all the possible economic and political conditions that may develop all of a sudden. Regarding this third proposition foregrounding functional feature, favorable the conditions for a well-grounded European Constitution

---

[1] See about this theme for detailed knowledge and analyse, Ibrahim S. Canbolat, *Avrupa Birliği* , 3. baskı, İstanbul: Alfa Yayınları, 2002.
[2] See, Frank Pfetsch, *Die Aussenpolitik der Bundesrepublik*, München, 1981, p.138.

did not seem to exist at that time. Before starting constitutional proceedings, it is believed that functional and economic integration will be more influential.

The foundation and the development of the European Union have been this way. After Europe loses the characteristic of being the center where politics of world are shaped, the only chance for Europe to be "the third power" between the two super powers is to unite the countries on the Continent by actualizing economic and political union in the first place. Therefore, especially Germany and France which have developed an eternal rivalry due to wars that lasted for years should get closer to each other. In this way peace and tranquility on the Continent could be maintained.

In retrospect, we see that thoughtful propositions have been made public from time to time in order for the union of Europe to come into existence since the Middle Age.[3] When we look deeply into the idea of unifying the countries concerned, we find Saint Pierre and Victor Hugo speaking of building a union made up of European states. Immanuel Kant projected his own thoughts on "the Provision of Eternal Peace". Likewise, Montesquieu, Voltaire, Proudhon and Saint Simon explained their own views favoring the integration of the states to reach a union for the sake of establishing peace and political liberalism among the member countries. In the 17th century Emeric Cruce proposed the development of international trade by means of abolishing the customs in order to unite all the European States, if possible.[4] In this union, where the decisions can only be taken unanimously, there should be an authority to decide when, where and how to use military power to launch operations against external threats. In order to encourage trade among the European States, it also requires functional economic integration that this will probably lead to the practical applications in line with the terms reached unanimously.

In the 18th century, J.J.Rousseau also explained his own view that a supranational qualified federal union would very possibly propose a resolution to any possible disputes among prospective member countries. As the "Federal Union" would be authorized by the member states to make use of the power of sanction, when necessary, in order for them to fulfill their responsibilities.

In the first half of the twentieth century among the philosophers and practitioners of such well-grounded thoughts highlighting the significance of European values to form a central government around were Edward Herriot and Jean Monnet. The economic union made up of Belgium, Netherlands and Luxemburg was the subsequent stage of the steps taken led by Edward Herriot. Later on, this union, also known as the Benelux Union, appears to be an important step for the European Union to come into being.

In 1948 the idea of founding a European Parliament by the help of France came true only by founding the European Council in 1949 as a consequence of the rejection of England. In fact it is not very different from a sort of cooperation, which has the capacity to develop into an organization bearing the distinctive features of any stereotype union based on European values rather than universal ones. The European reality made it compulsory to make it Europe-oriented union within the borders of the Continent.

Common economic, political and even military facilities were needed under the control

---

[3] See, especially for Saint Pierre's proposal regarding the common decisions amongs the European countries, A. Daltrop, *Politics and the European Community*, London: Longman, 1986, p.1.
[4] See, K. Perry, *Britain and The European Cummunity*, London, 1984, pp.1-2.

of supranational "High Authority". For the provision of peace and union in Europe, primarily the reciprocal rivalry and insecurity between France and German should be wiped out. The solution to the uncertainty that the union may encounter in the future could only be reached if both countries agree on transferring their sovereignty rights for their national benefits. In 1951, the thought behind Schman's plan, which was also backed up by Jean Monnet, paved the way for trade union known as European Coal and Steel corporation that served as a basis to build an international body of administration including all the arrears of cooperation within the scope of the European Community. According to Monnet, Schuman's Plan could only come true if the governments of the other countries that did not, at first, intend to take active roles in the formation of the European Community would give consent to the integration of the European governments to start cooperation in all the areas ranging from economy to education.

The European Union System as a Model of Value Allocation and Sharing

The European Union was born with three separate groups around a possible model, which appeared to be very tentative at first. This model formed around the idea of sharing sovereignty and balance of power on the basis of sharing benefits. And it developed as a consequence of the combined efforts of six West European countries headed by Germany and France in the aftermath of the World War II. In fact, as it was mentioned above, the initial steps towards the formation of the union of Europe were taken years ago; nevertheless, the act of creating a well-formed thought centered around European Union happened was actualized after the World War II came to an end. In this period, the "European Thought" was put forward clearly, comprehended truly and introduced as a reasonable choice as it focused on the necessity of reshaping European politics. Undoubtedly, as a consequence of this development, the political and economic conditions of the period following the World War II were very effective and set the pace accordingly.

The logic that the European Community followed, as the president of the European Community Comission (Delors) in 1988 mentioned, was that the strategies necessary for a "united Europe" would be based on the fierce competition between Europe and the rest of the world.[5] If the conditions for a "political and institutional cooperation" are not appropriate, then the process of economic union should be started. Having developed the Common Market, the project of "creating a real economic, political and educational cooperation through a well-developed union" was the first step taken in 1985 to achieve this objective set long before.

Nevertheless, it was needed to improve the decision-making mechanism of the community, and the parliament should have actively involved in this process to be more effective. By "Single European Act", which came into force in 1987, new arrangements accelerated the process of building the European Union to meet the demand the way it was defined.

The idea of making Single-European Act is seen as an instrument aimed at forming a political union in line with the Treaty of Rome to make institutional improvement by means of single community. Among the renewals brought out in accordance with the Single Act are: increasing the effect of the parliament, accelerating the decision-making process following the rules of qualified majority system in voting, and developing

---

[5] See, *EC News*, 22th April, 1988, p.1.

cooperation in security, foreign policy, domestic market and common market economy.

The fourth paragraph of the thirteenth item of the Single European Act emphasizes the significance of active participation of European Parliament in the foreign policy of the EU.

In addition, discussions on creating "Domestic Market" or "Single European Market" have also made a political fact come to the fore all along the process. In such a "Single Community"[6] based on the ethical and moral values of "European Citizens", the rights of using power is well-proportioned among all the citizens of the community so that every individual could benefit from such a wide range of cooperation regardless of their nationality.

The capacity of the political system drawn on the authoritarian value distribution has shown a development depending on various factors. The most important facts involved in the dynamics of integration process have common areas towards a specific aim between the national systems and the community system. The first one has to do with the capacity of the community pertaining to the power of influence that affects the decisions of member countries. Therefore, integration appears to be a fact shared commonly between the community and the national systems. As a result of this integration, some factors play the role of common problem solving strategies.

Political foundation at supranational level doesn't mean a threat for national politics. All the possible attempts made to increase the effect of political competence both at national and supranational level require activities designed to develop cooperation in the fields of economy and politics.

In the context of the developmental activities of the European Community have not made any destructive effects in national systems. The expectation is that the act of acquiring a common identity will help support the system in solving common problems through the institutions of the community. There is a utilitarian identity acquisition. So, the European Community (even formal) has been developing on the economic basis. Speaking of Haas's model,[7] it refers to any possible cooperation here will be more influential in the act of integration in the future.

The required support for the project towards carrying out the economic program of European Union simplifies strengthening the supranational institution by turning over of some of the national sovereignty rights to these institutions.[8] Conducting authoritarian decision-making procedure for the benefit of the community depends totally on the systematic support and institutional capacity, too.

The community aiming at enhancing individual efficiency is considered to be politics-oriented. It is a community united around benefits arising from cooperation in line with the acts of law regulating all aspects of cooperation.[9] In this respect, European Union has been operating at full speed to prove functional within the context of political system.

In West Europe, this has been undertaken by the member countries of the European

---

[6] See, Commission of the European Cummunities, *Commission Opinion of 21 October 1990: Political Union*, p.11.
[7] Ernst Haas, *The Uniting of Europe*, Stanford: Stanford University Press, 1958, p.14.
[8] Lindberg-Scheingold, *The Uniting of Europe*, p.62.
[9] See, Marcel Prelot, *Politika Bilimi*, Çev.: Nihal Önal, İstanbul, 1972, p.26.

Community. The European Community founded to facilitate all sorts of operations and/or proceedings in the related fields has acquired new institutions in the process of time, stressed the political importance of the union and started the decision-making process through a participatory model of governing system, allowing every single individual equal opportunity to vote. In other words, it has been talked about the European Community, which appears to be firm in the in the act of value distribution as part of political system, putting premium on "single community" in effect.

The Enlargement and the Relations with Turkey

The European Union summit took place in Luxemburg in December 1997. They decided to enlarge the European Union by adding new members. They decided as to which candidate countries would participate in the enlargement period, and determined membership requirements for the process to start and complete in due time. The two important requirements the EU and candidate countries have to complete are as follows: the provision of the EU institutions functioning effectively in accordance with the Amsterdam Treaty and the intentions of the candidate countries to exhibit the values of the EU, to share the objectives and to prove this with concrete political proceedings and precautions.

There is totally related to the technical side of the procedures besides the structural conditions related to the preference style. This has been arranged in accordance with the 49th item of the European Union Treaty:

Every European country can apply to be a member of the EU. The application is done to the Council. The Council decides unanimously after taking both the proposal of the Commission and the approval of the Parliament. The parliament has to approve with majority.

The changes required as a consequence of being a member state are made by the new member, right after the approval, in complete agreement with the member countries. This agreement will be valid, whenever approved by the council, in order for the new member to make decisions related to the necessary constitutional changes in line with the criteria defined clearly in the contract signed by the governments of the member countries.

With the acceptance of "the Communication Strategy for Enlargement" developed by the European Commission in May 2000, by the EU Council in the summit in Nice in 2000, the process of enlargement of the community started at a considerable pace. As preparation for the process of enlargement, the procedure at first was conducted on two basis known as" Pre-accession Strategy" and "Participation Negotiations" by adding "The Communication Strategy" as the third one to complete whole picture of the process. In this way, the tasks and the responsibilities of both candidate countries and member countries, in the enlargement period of the EU, will be undertaken and performed with due care and caution. In relation to this strategy, the following objectives are set prior to application for the membership:[10]

Three main aims for the member countries:

-To proclaim the necessity of the enlargement in a way of decreasing the negative

---

[10] http://europa.eu.int/comm/enlargement/communication/pdf/explaining_enlargement.pdf

factors and facilitating the common understanding in the period of enlargement.

-To establish a dialogue in every part of the society with the aim of providing development in the negotiations related to enlargement.

-To inform the candidate countries to prepare a favorable atmosphere for the general mutual understanding.

Three main aims for candidate countries:

-To provide the general knowledge and understanding about EU to become widespread.

-To proclaim what the participation contains for each country.

-To tell about societal connection between the preparations for membership and process of negotiations.

This provides the EU with the laws regulating membership requirements for those planning to enter the union by making necessary changes in the system of domestic law and also in the administrative structure of the whole system. This will help understand why the negotiations in different countries are held at a fairly different pace.

These following three main principles have been determined for the success of communication strategy:[11]

   a) Subsidiary: This strategy has considered a subsidiary method of taking specific requirements and conditions into consideration in both candidate and member countries in the process of membership.

   b) Flexibility: It is necessary for struggling against communication ruining factors that stem from main dynamic processes.

   c) Common Effect: It is for the studies of Commission, European Parliament, member countries, and the groups in the society to result in the way of completing and strengthening.

In order to realize the objectives of communication strategy in the direction of the principals above, there are funds given by the council of the EU. For example, just after the Cold War a ''Phare Program'' was developed for Middle and East European countries to facilitate required economic and political structure. Before participation in the content of strategy Phare Program was developed as time passed. Moreover, there is a fund called SAPARD towards developing agriculture and rural areas and there is another fund called İSPA for transportation and environment substructure. For the term of 2000-2006 11 billion euro financial support has been provided for the sole purpose of institutional development of the candidate countries within the framework of the Phare Program.

The above-mentioned support is provided for the following fields and objectives:[12]

-To make the public administration and institutional structure of candidate countries suitable to the domestic structure of EU.

-To shorten the transition term by making legislation in line with the internal order of the EU.

---

[11] http://europa.eu.int/comm/enlargement/pas/phare/intro.htm#1. Introduction
[12] http://europa.eu.int/comm/enlargement/pas/phare/intro.htm#1. Introduction

-To accelerate the process of economic and social changes to adjust well to the system.

Now, let's analyze the relations between Turkey and the European Union. Turkey made its first application for European Economic Community as one of the founding fathers of the European Community in 1959 and started the membership proceedings in line with the Association Agreement signed in 1963. After a long preparation period, transition process started to be a member of the Customs Union first, and then a member state of the Union. For full membership, the application was submitted in 1987. Community explained its decision in 1989 stating that country did not fulfill the requirements for full membership.

The candidate membership of Turkey to the European Union was admitted at Helsinki Summit in December 1999. At the same summit, it was stated that Turkey was to act in accordance with the same criteria as the other candidate countries did, and also encouraged to make necessary reforms to fit right in with the rest of the Community by following pre-accession strategies for a full membership.

To achieve full membership, it appeared s prerequisite for Turkey to carry on its close relations with the EU, like other countries, a process known as 'Accession Partnership'. As it has been pointed out recently that accession negotiations for membership of Turkey will start at the end of 2004 provided Turkey fulfills the requirements for a full membership.

Accession partnership of Turkey was admitted officially by the EU on 8th March 2001 in the aftermath of the European Council summit held in Helsinki in December 1999. The pre- accession strategy is required of Turkey to follow to become a member endowed with all the rights and privileges thereto. According to the authorities of European Union, Turkey has already been a road map, an itinerary, so to speak, to follow through in order to know whether she complies with the strategies to meet the criteria in order to start the process of accession as a member state of the EU.

The economic and political reforms proposed for Turkey to carry out in addition to the other follow-up adaptation activities are current issues of utmost importance to handle accordingly. The accession partnership is the legal process imposed upon Turkey to go through as she has already admitted all the requirements and standards drawn on the laws developed on a political, economic and social basis.

The reforms have been proposed in line with the criteria of Copenhagen made in the field of politics. For instance, some issues regarding the rights of expressing thoughts openly and meeting when and where appropriate, abolishment of death penalty, and some new legal regulations have been defined and described clearly.

Turkey felt the need to design a National Program with all the necessary steps to implement it in stages to meet the acquirements of European Union. The National Program, which was approved on March 19 2001 by the Turkish National Assembly, required some constitutional regulations in the political, economic, cultural and social issues to respond to the acquirements of European Union positively. Legal arrangements have been made regarding the issues of the release of the prisoners of conscience regardless of their ideology, freedom of speech, religious belief, death penalty and torture of the prisoners without reservation, human rights violations, corruption of officials and civil servants, functioning and efficiency of adjudication including State Security Courts, decreasing the regional imbalances for increasing the social and cultural opportunities and the like.

In the introduction of the program, the principles which constitute the basis of Turkish Republic have been explained as determination in peace-keeping efforts made decisively in external politics, laicism, the rule of law, devotion to participatory and pluralistic democratic system, basic freedoms and human rights. Having mentioned that Turkey has been looking for, security, stability, and peace in international relations, it has been expressed that Turkey has been improving relations with its neighbors. On Cyprus dispute, in particular, it is stressed that sides have wanted a solution based on the equal sovereignty on the island.

On the other hand, in case of obtaining full membership, it is claimed that Turkey would set a model for the emerging Turkish Republics, and even for the Moslem countries as a secular and democratic state. Moreover, it is put forward that Turkey can play as a key role in Balkan, Caucasians, the Middle Asia and Middle East.

In fact, all these matters can be seen as a potential alternative richness and capability of Turkey. But this does not mean that Turkey cannot play the key role in these regions. What is needed for Turkey is to develop in accordance with its historical, demographic and cultural background. Turkey will have economic, political, strategic advantages when the project of Bakü-Ceyhan pipeline is built. At the same time, it will diminish dangers of the transition of freighters through the Bosphorus. This will be beneficial for the security of the environment.

It would be out of question that Turkey could never take on an active role in the process of imposing new order in the region concerned. Being a member of the EU means that Turkey would be able to participate actively in the decision-making process regarding any policy that can be put into effect in the following years. Accession to the EU is not the sole aim, but just one of the many as Turkey is determined to be actively involved in what is going on in the neighboring countries, in Europe and in the whole world. However, if Turkish people develop objective point of views in favor of both the EU considering the historical, cultural and religious background of the member countries shaped around their national identities, the good things are just around the corner following the process of full membership.

There are two different approaches about the relations between Turkey and EU:
a) It is necessary to think EU in it's own context of formation, development and existing conditions considering already-existing conditions in Turkey.
b) It is necessary to think of Turkey and the EU as a whole employing a central governing system without forgetting all about the obligations likely to be imposed in the process of time.

Research, Approaches and Different Agenda on Turkey's Application to the European Union

There are different views in Turkey and Europe to Turkey's application to the European Union for full membership. Now, let's analyze these in short.

In Turkey we have three groups opposing to the membership of Turkey to the EU. First, those in opposition are socialists and Marxists who consider the European Union to be a capitalist integration form; second, people approach the EU with their own views developed around nationalist movements based on historical, psychological and cultural values that foreground hyper sensitivity. And third, those who think they cannot preserve their political, economic and bureaucratic independence coated with national identity within the EU system.

Nevertheless, not all the socialists and nationalists argue that they develop counter arguments as to the prospective membership; however, they intend to emphasize that due to its colonial past the EU is seen as an international organization where capitals gain superiority over labor degrading the value of human effort by paying attention to the colonial experience of the EU member countries in the past. Therefore, socialists are in doubt because capitalist approach never hesitates to exercise its domination over labor, human rights and equality even though democracy is said to be in place sooner or later to secure peace and tranquility within the Union. Moreover, parliamentarian democracy is thought to be the most stable and secure type of governing system based on capitalist ideology, as they believe that this will result in social inequality in every aspect of life underlying class differences.[13] According to this view based on the absolute equality among the members of the same community, the reason why Turkey submitted a petition to start the proceedings to be a member of the European Union in 1999 is that the role assigned to the Turkish governments is to protect private interests of the capitalist bloc to set up and strengthen its own domination over the whole world once again. Due to its geopolitical potential, the EU and the USA appear to be so enthusiastic to integrate Turkey into the union.

Amongst socialists some have been tended to consider the EU different, not firstly in the meaning described above. According to this approach, the European Countries have adopted not only imperialist willpower and suitable administration but also historical monopoly of the labor. Now, anti-imperialism is seen as a problem when it make impossible to find alternative solutions within the system, so that it should weaken imperialist domination to what exetent it can.[14] The European Union would be of use in this respect if it could help develop democracy experience in Turkey.

Those who evaluate Turkey and its adaptation process to become a member state of the EU from historical and cultural perspective and the application criteria find that Turkey does not seem to be very close to the European Union. Historical, cultural, religious and psychological factors play significant roles as they are considered essentials forming the cornerstones of the union. Due to the fact that the union has already developed a different perpective after going through a procees of alienation by calling the

---

[13] See, Merdan Yanardağ, "Türk Solunda Yeni Islahatçılık", V-Özgürlük, 11 Aralık 1999, kt.Temel Demirer v.d., AB mi? Hayır!, Sibel Özbudun -Temel Demirer, (Der.), *Avrupa Birliği ve Sosyalistler Akıntıya Karşı*, Ankara: Ütopya Yay., 2000, p.353.
[14] See, Erdoğan Aydın Tatlav, "Emeğin Avrupa'sına Evet", V-Özgürlük, 11 Aralık 1999, p.6, akt. Temel Demirer v.d., AB mi? Hayır!, Sibel Özbudun - Temel Demirer, (Der.), *Avrupa Birliği ve Sosyalistler Akıntıya Karşı*, pp.358-359.

rest of the world the "other", it has already caused people to develop some negative connotations associated with their blatant unfavorable approaches and attitudes displayed towards the would-be member states, i.e, Turkey, and also non-European countries. The EU member states seem to have someting in common, a shared assumption so to speak, as they suppose that their national identities is very much associated with their long history in Anatolia. They have already developed a negative attitude based on the shared assumption that Turks invaded their lands putting an end to their civilizations deeply rooted in harmony with their religion inTurkey.

What do those all mean? Honestly, it is obvious that Europe has modified itself to exist as a national state governing itself by a well-established system that staterted to develop in the 17th century, and then in the 19th century. They have displayed very firm attitudes in their combined efforts to impose the central governing system requiring national changes on a large scale. It is interesting to state that the procees of change manifests itself in two completely different ways: first empires disintegrated giving birth to smaller states formed around national identities of the people, and second, a sort of European state built up around shared values or rather myths.

However, because of long-term conflicts realized in the efforts to hold the absolute power to manipulate international benefits, interests, disputes, and also the bipolar balance of power in the aftermath of World War II, a supranational European governing system became decidedly necessary to impose an order upon chaos and disorder that marked that long period. The philisophy behind European Integration suggests that member states find it crucial to transfer some sovereignty rights over to one another to develop a union by means of one constitution.

Now, the European Union has been founded after a long meticulous study through a process of change realized in the historical and political domain as well. If Turkey wants to join the union, she must take a closer look at the unifying principles that have created the union. It is a prerequisite on the part of Turkey to admit all the sanctions based on strict rules or rather obligations to fulfill. Some national licenses will partly have to be handed over to supranational EU institutions to make them effective in the proceedings they conduct on behalf of the EU. It seems that over 70% of people in Turkey are for idea of becoming a member of the EU without knowing much about the EU and possible sanctions that may appear to be against national benefits.

Several groups in the country will be regarded as "minorities" by the EU and some issue will be discussed and negotiated in the period of the candidacy of Turkey for membership. Knowing that the EU provides not only an economic benefits but also allocate social, political and cultural values, the above-mentioned agenda may be seen as a normalcy in EU system. All these will be be a part of daily life to protect the savings of the society by signing agreements designed in detail not to cause any misunderstanding on the part of the general public. For example the European Council summit in Tampera, Finland, in 1999, the member states agreed on the development of a common law policy regulating emigration, political asylum, criminal investigation and bureaucracy to put an end to the diversity in official proceedings among the EU countries.[15]

In this context, "Euro just" is to be consistent with law court procedures, prosecutions and police investigations the same way as conducted in the EU countries. As a result, there shall never be contradictory verdicts on national judgments for the sake of maintaining one single law court procedure. The member states are expected to agree on assigning intergovernmental body of legislature that will supply coordination and consensus amoong the member states to back up the legislative system to meet the needs of the member states in the field concerned.

What does Turkey think about such developments as it hopes to be in such a system? The policy makers, executives, academicians, judges, prosecutors and people do not seem to reach a common agreement as to how put the resolutions into effect regarding social, cultural, political, economic and institutional procedures. Those who are keen on joining the union and those who reject point-blank thinking that this governing system will cause a lot of trouble for it seems to have a devestating effect on the already existing system that cannot supply early and fair trial in line with the principle of "equal justice under law". For example, Norway has high standards of living and so its many people think joining the EU is not necessary for them whereas Greece insisted on joining the EU for political and economic reasons and national interest in the region. Turkey can do the same by developing a coherent plan as to what to do in logical steps from now on by concentrating more on how to put the plan into practice and by taking into consideration she has had a long experience in this process as she first applied in 1959 for the membership and renewed it in 1987.

However, what is unacceptable on the part of Turkey is that the EU makes use of different strategies in its relations with the countries in line for membership. For instance, application and membership process Norway went through seems quite different from those of Turkey as the process still goes on no matter when she submitted first application for the membership. Indeed, the demands that Turkey have made so far are not specific to Turkey as the same demands have been made by all the other countries wishing to join. Domination licenses must be planned to give to the EU institutions, partially in some certain subjects. From this point of view, there must be some amendments made to the Turkish constitution.

This will be of importance for Turkey to be a member of the European Union. People should neither hate the EU nor daydream about it. This hope for the membership or the worry should never be used for political reasons. People should have easy access to the correct information in orderto be certain so that they could make own decision regarding the membership to the European Union. This informative approach in favour of interaction and proper communication between the goverment and the general public will be needed prior to the referendum following the negotiation period. Every EU country has experienced whatever happens in the usual process of membership. Moreover, the European Parliament should approve of the membership of candidate country to the EU.

Although Turkey is on the way for becoming a member of the EU in accordance with

---

[15] See, http://ue.eu.int/de/Info/eurocouncil/index.htm

the project mentioned above, she still seems to lag behind the schedule as she has not undestood the process and met the requirements in time with due care and caution, especially those related to the necessary changes in all the areas to fit in with the union. Turkey sets a good example for those countries still waiting in the queue for becoming a member since she is still a "square peg in a round hole". Therefore, the criteria that the candidates should meet in order to complete the process of integration may seem to be demands to these countries, posing a threat to the national unity. Nevertheless, the European Union is a common playground or living area that must utterly be homogeneous. Turkey has developed more sensitivity because of its historical, geopolitical and national situation, but it is not meaningful to stay isolated while the process of globalization still goes on at full speed ahead. Turkey may have develop such a fear that the area that Turkey is located in is also surounded by the countries in turmoil and in the interest of the powers due to its geopolitic importance. Membership to the union gains significanve as he European Union has the sort of balance of power to bring stability and peace to the region when Turkey's asymmetric relationships with super powers are taken into consideration like USA in a bipolar world.

8 "Turkestroika" as Precondition for Turkey's European Dream

Dirk Rochtus

Introduction

'Fear of Encirclement', that is how one could define the attitude of mind which characterizes big parts of the political and military establishment of Turkey. Behind the domestic problems and challenges many politicians, and especially the generals as the guardians of Atatürks heritage, tend to perceive the machinations of foreign enemies willing to dismantle the Turkish state. Syria's former support of the PKK, the armed arm of Kurdish separatism, or Iran's sympathy towards the political Islam in Turkey seemed to confirm the politicians and generals in their beliefs that there would be a link between internal and external threats. The Sèvres Trauma still haunts the Turks. It was against the partitions plans drawn up at the French town of Sèvres (1920) after World War One that Mustafa Kemal took up arms as the leader of the National Liberation Movement. This would lead to the foundation of the "one and indivisible" Republic of Turkey in 1923. It is against every real or pretended threat of the integrity of the republic that those politicians and generals that see themselves as heirs to Atatürk's ideas or 'Kemalism' are opposed.. Internal dangers like Kurdish nationalism or Islamist fundamentalism are seen in the light of attempts to destroy the pillars of the Kemalist system, namely republicanism and secularism. It is significant to see how much the governing AKP is trying to enfeeble the suspicions as if it were led by fundamentalist ideas.

The resurgence in the eighties of those ideas, namely Kurdish nationalism and political Islam, which already threatened the young republic, proves that not much has changed since the days of Atatürk. The problems remained the same for Turkey, and the way in which they were dealt with, does not differ very much from the beginning period. This is because Kemalism as the state doctrine is still dominating the minds of the leading groups in the Turkish society. The struggle which the Kemalist establishment was conducting against Kurdish nationalism and political Islam, was a struggle with arms or with political and jurisdictional means against the forms in which they appeared, against DEHAP, PKK or KADEK, or against Islamist parties under whatever name the latter participated to elections. Even when at the present day a so-called moderate Islamist party, the AKP with Prime Minister Tayyip Erdogan and foreign minister Abdullah Gül, has come to power, Kemalists remain suspicious, fearing that party might have a "hidden agenda". Although the armed arm of Kurdish nationalism has been shattered since the capture of their leader Öcalan in February 1999, the Kemalist state still worries about the impact that some form of Kurdish autonomy in Northern Iraq could have on the Kurdish population in South East Anatolia.

Being anxious about the security and the integrity of the Turkish territory the Kemalist establishment never has had any empathy for the internal reasons which lie at the base of the challenges that both Kurdish nationalism and political Islam pose to the Kemalist state. Both phenomena might have counted on sympathy or even support from abroad, even from external enemies of Turkey, this however does not alter the fact that they are a reaction to Kemalism itself, i.e. they first originate from inside. Only from the moment on that the Kemalist establishment will understand this, it will be able to see why many people and circles in the European Union look so "prejudiced" against an eventual membership of Turkey. Lack of empathy not only towards the critics of the Kemalist doctrine but also towards the fears and worries of the EU is the biggest stumbling block of Turkey on its path towards Europe. So it is of the greatest importance to Turkey, especially the Kemalist establishment, to understand the nature of the challenges which are posed by the groups striving for more cultural autonomy (by Kurdish nationalists) and religious freedom not only by Islamist forces, but also by the prospect of membership of the EU as a supranational construct sui generis and the consequences of this for a state like Turkey which is still so fixed on homogeneity and national self-complacency. These are the three challenges to the Kemalist state and the way it is conducting its domestic and foreign policy on which now a light will be shed.

Foundations of the State

A homogeneous nation-state

When Mustafa Kemal, the later Atatürk, founded the Republic of Turkey in 1923, he did this by distinguishing it from its predecessor, the Ottoman Empire, in territorial as well as in moral regard. He knew that the republic could not be an empire anymore. That was the past. The Allied Powers, who had won World War I, would not have allowed it. The Turks had to be content with the fact that at least they got an own state after having brought heavy sacrifices during the War of Liberation. Therefore, they had to give up all big dreams like those that the Pan-Turks had dreamt of. Turkey had to accept the borders that the Lausanne Treaty had drawn. As compensation for the territorial reduction of what once used to be the Ottoman Empire, the territory of the new republic itself would be inviolable and most of all indivisible. Mustafa Kemal had declared at the opening of the Congress of Erzurum on 23 July 1919 that the country would be "free, independent and Turkish". Herewith the foundations were laid for Kemalism as an ideology and a state doctrine, legitimizing the struggle against everything that is seen or depicted as separatism. The inviolable and indivisible territory became the platform for the construction of a homogeneous nation-state. Ethnic and cultural differences should not derogate the "civic nationalism", the citizenship which was promoted by the new republic and in which every one could participate who confessed, as in an "acte de volonté", to be proud to be Turk, or in the words of Atatürk: "Ne Mutlu Türküm Diyene". The problem however is the lack of self-criticism that is implied in this jacobine concept of the state. Citizenship namely is never ethnically neutral. The Turkish state, which pretended and pretends to be a state in which all individuals have the same rights and duties whatever their ethnical background or whatever their culture may be, is the state of the ethnic majority of the Turks. The best proof of this is the fact that the sole official language is the mother tongue of this ethnic majority. A state may pretend to be neutral, a language never is. The choice for one language that is not spoken by all citizens puts forward the question how one has to deal with the languages that are spoken by other groups in the same society. Kemalism did not find an answer to this question-the Kemalist establishment thought the same way as the French revolutionaries did in 1789, who despised other languages than the French as "dialects", and did not even consider the matter until Kurdish nationalism as a reaction to that jacobine cultural and language policy started to develop itself.

As Mustafa Kemal, who in 1934 was named "Atatürk", wanted, the Turkish state was also a project of modernization. Europe was the aim to be achieved. In a modern, Western- oriented state there was no place either for obscurantism or religious fundamentalism. Atatürk carried through several reforms in order to change Turkey into a secularist society. In 1931 his Republican People's Party, the only admitted party, moulded Kemalism into Six Principles on which the Republic as a counter-model to the Ottoman Empire was resting: republicanism; secularism; nationalism; populism; statism; and revolutionism.[1] But even although Turkey distanced itself from the Ottoman Empire, many continuities between both states could still be discerned. Ordering principles like a strong state power, the role of army and bureaucracy, the predominance of the collective had survived the collapse of the Ottoman Empire. The difference now was that a strong elite had been formed which saw itself not longer as a coordinator/mediator between the several groups in the society, but as the creating and steering force of a secularist Turkey. Moreover, the state was legitimized not by Islam, which had been functioning as cement during the times of the multi-ethnic Ottoman Empire, but by secularism and Turkish nationalism.[2] Also the importance of strong personalities in state and party system was reminiscence to the Ottoman period. It is no coincidence that a personality cult grew up around Atatürk in order to fill the "ideological void" of Kemalism which "lacked coherence, and even more importantly, emotional appeal."[3] The result was a Turkey, which was "conceived of as a modern state uniquely defined by its own position and people".[4]

Turkey lays for the most part in Asia, but bents its thoughts towards Europe, considers itself not to be a Muslim country, but a country of Muslims. In order to get the modernization project accepted and to protect its achievements against a hostile world the Kemalist establishment has created a whole range of bureaucratic and military instruments. Army, justice and education were and are put into service of a concept that made their defenders act even more jacobine than the French revolutionaries ever did. Ethnic-cultural differences were swept away as if they did not matter at all, whereas even in the centralistic France they are still tolerated; the European understanding of laicism and separation of Church from State had to yield to the removal of religious utterances

---

[1] Erik-Jan Zürcher, *Turkey. A Modern History*, London/New York, 2001, p.189.
[2] Udo Steinbach, *Geschichte der Türkei*, München 2000, pp. 36-37.
[3] Cit. Zürcher, p. 190.
[4] Malcolm Cooper, "The Legacy of Atatürk: Turkish political structures and policy-making", *International Affairs*, Vol.78, No.1, 2002, p.116.

and symbols from the public sphere and a strict control of this process by the state. The "Kulturkampf" of the Kemalist state against the society of which this ethnic-linguistic diversity and the religious experience are an undeniable part, has been conducted in such a dogmatic way that some consider this to be proof of the inability of the state to make the crossing to a democracy of Western-liberal signature.[5] In this regard, the denial of the cultural diversity by not granting group rights to minorities on the one hand and keeping the society in tutelage on the other hand would explain the crisis to which Turkey is exposed. The economic problems also could be understood as a result of the dominating role that the state bureaucracy upholds in the economic sphere. Any criticism of the immobility and rigorism of Kemalism as the doctrine of the state is immediately seen as a sign of conspiracy against Turkey. Even the urging by the European Union for more democracy and human rights and for more respect of the cultural freedom for Kurds is perceived by Turkish decision-makers "through the lens of Sèvres" and "as part of a devious agenda aimed at undermining the integrity and sovereignty of the Turkish state."[6] The words which former vice prime minister and leader of the MHP Devlet Bahçeli spoke in January 2002 illustrate this attitude very clear. According to him his party was not against democratic reforms that should make Turkey ready for accession to the EU, as long as they did not endanger the national unity and were not a pretext to make concessions to the Kurdish separatists.[7]

Therefore, Kemalism means an engagement of the state bearing powers to secularism, territorial integrity and cultural homogeneity, all values that are anchored in the Constitution. They influence the spectre through which the decision-makers look at foreign policy, especially how they have to act in consideration of the eventual accession of Turkey to the European Union. Those forces within Turkey who put this codex of values into question have been confronted with the repression by the state. Kurdish nationalism and religious fundamentalism have been until now the biggest challenges to the Kemalist state. The military as the praetorian guard of the Kemalist state has been fighting over the last decades against both movements that, in the eyes of Kemalists, impede as reactionary phenomena to the modernization process of the state. However, what if Kemalism itself is not consistent with the whole idea of European integration? It is hard to imagine that a state that sticks so much to a dogmatic secularism or to cultural homogeneity at the expense of its own minorities complies with a European Union, which is characterized by values like respect for minority languages and religious or philosophical self-expression. Assessing Kemalism means also assessing the framework in Turkey in which foreign policy can develop itself.

The Role of the Army

Historical experiences account for the high esteem that falls into the Turkish army's share

---

[5] M. Hakan Yavuz, "Turkey's Fault Lines and the Crisis of Kemalism", *Current History*, January 2000, p.34.
[6] Dietrich Jung and Wolfango Piccolo, *Turkey at the Crossroads. Ottoman Legacies and a Greater Middle East*, London/New York, 2001, p.117.
[7] *Turkish Daily News*, 26 January 2002.

in state and society. The public confidence has been socio-culturally determined and goes back to Ottoman times when "for long periods, the army (...) virtually took over the state".[8] Therefore, as long as state and politics remained and remain weak in Turkey, the position of the army was and is strong. Kemalism strengthens the self-esteem of the army, or as Bal remarks:

> (...) the Turkish army strongly believes that it represents enlightenment, secularism and modernism (...) that their mission is to defend the state (which they set up) not only from external threats but also from what they would regard as internal threats.[9]

In the West however, especially in the European Union, one is very suspicious towards the role the army is playing in Turkey. Its power and authority seem not to be consistent with the democratization, which is required for Turkey's accession to the EU. The interventions by the military already raised questions in the past, and so does the role of the National Security Council (Milli Güvenlik Kurulu, MGK), which radiates too much influence on the government. Gareth Jenkins points to the fact that the public's mandate for the Turkish military applies to "intervention rather than rule".[10] Indeed, the people used to expect that the army took action when the government failed to put an end to chaotic or state menacing situations. This is a big difference from the situation in Western-styled parliamentary democracies where the army gets its instructions from parliament and surely may not act solely when chaos is caused by an inefficient government. Problematic anyway was that the public by putting its trust into the army in restoring order gave up its own responsibility. Yet this confidence got badly damaged when in the aftermath of the earthquake of august 1999 the army reacted too slowly to offer assistance to the distressed population. The shocked confidence was coupled with a strengthening of the "civil society", the feeling that the common citizen had to stand up much more for his own rights and responsibilities, a phenomenon which should make Turkey look more European like. Turkish history has seen several direct and indirect interventions of the army in political life. Its role had never been put into question until the perspective of joining the EU prompted Turkish policy-makers to think it over again. Since the summer of 2003 attempts have been made by the AKP government in order to curtail the influence of the army within the National Security Council.

The Kurdish Question

The kernel of the Kurdish problem is the assimilation policy that the Turkish Republic since its foundation in 1923 has tried in vain to impose on the Kurdish population. According to the Treaty of Lausanne the Kurdish people are not considered as a minority because they are Muslims. But since the end of World War II new criteria like culture or language have become more important in Western political thinking to define whether a group of persons makes up a minority or not. As the Kurdish people living in Turkey

---

[8] Idris Bal, *Turkey's Relations with the West and the Turkic Republics. The Rise and Fall of the "Turkish Model"*, Aldershot, 2000, p.21.
[9] Ibid.
[10] Gareth Jenkins, *Context and Circumstances: The Turkish Military and Politics. Adelphi Paper 337*, New York, 2001, p.20.

speak a language other than the majority of the Turkish citizens, the ethnic Turks in fact, they are regarded by the West as a cultural and ethnic minority and are entitled to the right to conserve their culture and language not only in the private atmosphere. Sociologically seen Ankara wanted to make up for that kind of process that a jacobine and over centralized state like France has adopted towards its own minorities. One should not forget that at the time of the French revolution only 50% of the people spoke French. The French Jacobins tried to extinguish the other languages, like German, Dutch, and Breton, which they depicted as "dialects or relics of feudalism". In the Twentieth Century it is not possible and even not wishful anymore to deny the right of people to use their own language in education and broadcasting, even when it has not yet been recognized as an official language. The peoples have discovered the value of their own cultures and are trying to translate this into a policy of self-determination as it has been dangled before their eyes by the US president Woodrow Wilson in his famous "Fourteen Points" (1918).

Turkey that managed to thwart the breaking-up plans of the Sèvres Treaty, would not hear of some kind of cultural autonomy for the Kurds. The struggle that took place in South East Anatolia between 1984 and 1999 between the PKK and the Turkish army, mirrored the clash between two concepts: the state nationalism of the Turks and the ethnic nationalism of the Kurdish movement. The latter was a reaction to the état-nation that had been called into life by Mustafa Kemal. The état-nation pretends to be ethnically neutral, but in reality imposes the culture and language of a (mostly also demographically) dominating group of the population on all the inhabitants of a certain territory, setting aside the fact that some of these might have been recognized as a minority. The dichotomy "civic nation/ethnic nation" is artificial, or as Dominque Schnapper remarks: "Historically nations have emerged from one or more pre-existing ethnic groups."[11] The cultural problem is attended with the socio-economic one: the Kurdish regions belong to the less developed ones.

Where does the will for Kurdish self-government come from? The weakening of the Ottoman Empire together with the awakening of nationalism in the Nineteenth Century led Greeks and Serbs to strive for more autonomy or even independence. The role that the Christian minorities in the Empire played lessened and the distrust of the ethnic Turks towards non-Turks started to grow. The more the clerical element in the last decades of Ottoman rule declined and Islam lost his position as the cement of all the groups, the more ethnic nationalism started to inflame the hearts of the people. The Kurds rebelled for the first time in the years 1879-81 under Sheik Ubaydallah. After 1918 they fought as allies along side of the Turkish National Movement, but after the Turkish victory autonomy was not granted to them. In the new Turkish Republic there was no room for dividing-lines on the base of language or ethnic feelings. The notion of "minority" only applied to non-Muslims. The Muslim Kurds had to give up own nationalistic aspirations.

Compared to other nationalistic movements elsewhere in Europe, Kemalism was progressive because it exceeded the thinking in categories of "blood and soil", yet it was not modern as far as the state structure is concerned. It was the time, just after World

---

[11] Dominique Schnapper, "Beyond the Opposition: Civic Nation versus Ethnic Nation", Jocelyne Couture/Kai Nielsen/Michel Seymour (ed.), *Rethinking Nationalism*, Calgary, 1996, p.230.

War I, where several peoples in the name of self-determination demanded autonomy or even independence, although self-determination not necessarily has to lead to separatism. All the peoples that had lived on the territory of the Austrian-Hungarian Monarchy got self-government, be it in the form of an own state (Hungarians) be it in a federal structure (Czechs and Slovaks). Of all the peoples that had belonged to the Ottoman Empire the Kurds came off badliest. For seven decades to come they would even been regarded not as Kurds, but as "mountain Turks", and their indo-European language would even wrongly be depicted as a dialect of Turkish, which belongs to the Altaic language family. Kurdish rebels would soon rear their heads as a reaction to these attempts to deny the own identity of the Kurds. Especially in the periods 1925-37 and 1984-99 Kurdish nationalism would press Turkey and its reputation in the world very hard.

What the Kurdish rebels, before and after World War II, have in common is that their nationalism leant against another ideology. In the twenties of last century Kurdish nationalism was not yet fully developed in order to mobilize many followers. Therefore, the rebels approached Sheik Said, who was in sympathy with the Kurdish cause and who could not accept the abolishment of the Caliphate in 1924. Stimulated by Kurdish nationalists he called upon his followers to fight against the "godless" republic. So the Kurdish rebels might rest assured of a bigger support in their struggle against the centralistic authority. Several motives merged in the rebellion: Kurdish nationalism, Islamism, tribalism. In the sixties Kurdish nationalism revived after having needed several decades to recover from the heavy blows that the Turkish state had struck it. In a climate of polarization between left and right Marxism-Leninism cast a spell on the young Öcalan, who was studying political science in Ankara. His personal ambitions could not be satisfied by the Turkish Left, which he blamed for having not enough attention for the specific needs and demands of the Kurds. Öcalan, therefore, founded a leftist Kurdish movement in 1974, the Ulusal Kurtulus Ordusu (National Liberation Army), and in 1978 the Partiya Karkeren Kurdistan (PKK) (the Workers Party of Kurdistan). In both periods Kurdish nationalism was linked to another ideology that gave a broader support to the movement. The Kurdish question so was put in a broader framework exceeding narrow nationalism. The Kemalist state on the other hand was able to seize this coupling of Kurdish nationalism to Islamism and later on Marxism-Leninism to legitimize its struggle against separatism also as a struggle against respectively reactionary forces and "the red danger."

Affinities however also exist between Kemalism and Kurdish nationalism.[12] Leftist Kurdish nationalists used to express their admiration not only for Sheik Said or Lenin, but also for Atatürk as a man symbolizing the anti-imperialist struggle. A more profound affinity was to be found in the task for the internally divided Kurds to do that what Atatürk had done for the Turks in 1920: to have forged them to a unity by the creation of a common identity. The Kemalists had shaped a Turkish nation, and a similar task was to be fulfilled by the Kurdish people whose members are divided over several tribes and languages. But where the Kemalists had liberated Anatolia from foreign rule and had then

---

[12] See Jung/Piccolo, p.124.

made coincide nation and state in a Turkish "état-nation", the latter had been realized at the expense of the second largest ethnic group, the one of the Kurds. Only in the Diaspora the Kurdish nationalists had the disposal of the space and the means in the form of cultural institutes or broadcasting to let a Kurdish community thrive as a cultural nation. Another affinity between both ideologies was the readiness to find a way out for problems by using violence. The Kemalists had conducted their "reconquista" by arms and still use the army as a means to protect the state against real or pretended enemies. The Kurdish nationalists took up arms in order to lend force to their aims. The Turkish army tried all possible means in the fight against the "separatist danger", whereas the PKK let nothing unimpeded to create a situation of chaos and instability. The result was a circulus vitiosus of blood and despair that ruined the international fame of Turkey and hindered its own democratization process.[13]

Fundamentalism

At the municipal elections of March 1994 the Welfare Party (Refah), the party of the pretended "fundamentalists", made a successful bid for the majority in more than two hundred cities and municipalities, among them also Istanbul and Ankara. This was only a foretaste of the landslip that occurred at the parliamentary elections in December 1995 when Refah pinched 21.4 % of the cast votes. To keep it remote from power the Motherland Party (ANAP) and the "Party of the Righteous Path" (DYP) forged a centre right coalition, but it was not granted to live long as their respective leaders Mesut Yilmaz and Tansu Ciller were flying at each other all the time. In June 1996 Ciller made terms with Erbakan, Refah's leader, who became Turkey's first Islamist prime minister. But the military brought it off that "sensitive" posts–everything concerning security in the broad sense of the word–were assigned to the DYP, the Ministry of Defense and also the post of Foreign Affairs which was entrusted to vice prime minister Çiller.

The success of the "fundamentalists" did not appear out of the blue. Their advance had started earlier, in fact already shortly after World War II. During his reign Atatürk had frozen the public religious life, but his Western-styled reforms had not managed to drive out the Islam as a cultural factor from society. The Democratic Party (DP), which came to power in 1950, lent its ears to the religious sighs of the population by building new mosques, reopening of pilgrimage places and constructing religious schools. Politicizing of Islam would soon come. The fundamentalists were able to live on the alienation which secularism brought about between state and society and on the material problems that were caused by several economic crises. The latter became still clearer after the coup of 12 September 1980. Where President Kenan Evren, the former staff chief of the army who had organized the coup, was engaged in foreign affairs and security matters, Turgut Özal, who had become prime minister after the tremendous election victory of ANAP in 1983, applied himself to the reorientation of the Turkish economy towards the export. The productivity rose, the growth rates climbed, but all this had a heavy social price as it decreased spending-power, inflation and austerity policy augmented the cleavage between rich and poor. Thanks to the "labour division" between

[13] Henri J. Barkey, "Kurdish Geopolitics", *Current History*, January 1997, p.4.

Evren and Özal, the latter was able to go his own way and to distribute public means at his discretion. Corruption and clientelism were reinforced by all this. The economic slump and the disfunctioning of the democratic system paved the way for those who wanted to break out from the Kemalist state or its ideological shackles like respectively Kurdish nationalists and Islamist fundamentalists.

There is a link between neo-liberalism and globalization, which do not stop at the gates of Istanbul, and the Islamist revival in daily life and in the party system. Refah played the game very clever. Whereas the traditional parties perpetrated clientelistic practices, the fundamentalists stepped up to the people. They did not only preach social justice and making an end to corruption and favouritism, but they also did something. Refah jumped into the social gap that had been created by the deregulatory policy of the neo-liberals and offered an anchorage to the victims of modernization, especially where welfare facilities were failing in the big cities in which the masses from Anatolia were fleeing into. The modernization was not reflected by the cities into the countryside, but vice versa the traditional values entered from the village into urban life.

The election results of December 1995 shook the Kemalist establishment. In fact it could have armed itself better if it had made a more thorough analysis of what had happened in the previous fifteen years. Moreover in the seventies conservative politicians had rediscovered Islam as a weapon in the battle against leftist ideas and after the 1980 coup the military even broke a lance with a "Turkish-Islamic Synthesis" as a means to strengthen the moral power of the country and as an antidote against Kurdish nationalism. Where the military strengthened the role of religion in the educational system, president Özal patronized in the bureaucratic system those people who originated from the lower social classes. For those people however it was not so much Kemalism but Islam that reflected "Turkey's true identity."[14]

Once Refah got to power, the fundamentalists followed out certain reforms in daily life that should make the position of religion stronger. What however struck most, especially abroad, were the visits that Prime Minister Erbakan paid to Islamic states like Iran, Libya, and Pakistan. In the West many leading people wrinkled their eyebrows because these actions of Erbakan were seen as an attempt to call a kind of Islamic trade bloc into existence. Maybe Erbakan was inspired by tactical and economic considerations. Due to the fact that he had concluded an agreement about the use of Turkish air force bases by the United States of America, he had to soothe his rank and file with an Islamic initiative. His visits to Singapore and Malaysia also pointed to the direction of economic diversification.

The Turkish military was not happy with Erbakan as prime minister. The more his self-consciousness was growing, the more he started to take measures that irritated the Kemalists. Symbolically significant was the Ramadan dinner, which Erbakan offered on 11 January 1997 to the leaders of a number of religious brotherhoods who formally are forbidden. Now the army did not want to sit on the fence anymore. During its meeting on

---

[14] Jenny White, "Pragmatists or Ideologues? Turkey's Welfare Party in Power", *Current History*, January 1997, p.28.

28 February the National Security Council (MGK) issued the so-called "Eighteen Recommendations" (tedbir) in an attempt to hold up fundamentalism.[15] In the months to follow the pressure on Erbakan was mounting so high that finally on 18 June 1997 he resigned. After being expelled from power Refah Partisi was accused of having violated the secular character of the state. In January 1998, the party was forbidden, but this was not yet the end of fundamentalism. A new party, Fazilet (Virtue Party), was soon founded by former parliamentarians of Refah, but at the elections of April 1999 it got only 15.5% of the votes. Once again the military had outspoken a warning, some weeks before the elections, that it would not tolerate a victory of Fazilet. In June 2001 also Fazilet was forbidden by the Constitutional Court. In August 2001 however Tayyip Erdogan, the former mayor of Istanbul, founded the AKP (Adalet ve Kalkinma Partisi), which finally, due to the charisma of its founder and its presenting itself as the alternative to the corrupt and non-efficient policy of the Ecevit-government, would come to power in November 2002. Since then the one-party-government of Prime Minister Tayyip Erdogan and foreign minister Abdullah Gül in its pro-EU-stance has carried through several reform packages that are welcomed by the EU and reinforce Turkey's chances to become a member of the EU. The military establishment however remains suspicious of the AKP-government, fearing the Islamists have a "hidden agenda."

Membership of a Supranational EU?

In Kemalist circles certain uneasiness prevails with regard to the consequences of an eventual membership of Turkey to the EU. The question whether the national integrity is guaranteed, gives birth to most concerns. Kurdish nationalists however and the so-called "fundamentalists"–some call them "Light Muslims",[16] are much in favour of the accession of Turkey to the EU. Whether this stems from a deep conviction or from a belief in the values that the EU postulates still has to be proved. A EU-membership of Turkey offers protection to both movements and their leaders. Erbakan knocked at the door of the European Court of Justice, Öcalan set his hopes on the European Court of Human Rights in Strasbourg in order to shun the execution of the death penalty. Tayyip Erdogan and his AKP-government expect more religious freedoms to come with the EU-membership. The Turkish citizens of Kurdish origin can only benefit from the perspective of Turkey becoming a EU-member state. The EU compels the political class to carry through reforms of which all Turkish citizens, whatever their religious or ethnic background may be, will reap the fruits. It moreover introduces concepts that Turkey cannot neglect: concepts that are involved in subsidiary, cultural autonomy, linguistic diversity, exactly those things that the Kemalists still fear as threats to the national integrity and sovereignty.

The Kurdish nationalists, in the first place those of the PKK, have conducted a hard and bloodstained fight against the central authority in Ankara. The question remains whether this has yielded results or whether it has been counter-productive. The human

---

[15]   Niyazi Güney, "Implementing the "February 28" Recommendations: A Scorecard", http://www.washingtoninstitute.org/junior/note 10.htm.

[16] Sean Michael Cox, "Turkey's "Light Muslim"s and the West", *Turkish Policy Quarterly*, Spring 2003, pp.47-56.

suffering and the material damage are tremendous whereas the Kurdish nationalists did not attain their original aim, an independent "Kurdistan". During more than 14 years the democratization process in Turkey itself stood still.[17] Liberalization was enacted in the economic, not in the political field. Yet the Kurdish separatists, who now may not consider themselves like that but rather like "autonomists", anyway attained two things: in the first place that the international reputation of Turkey was very much injured, although this is more due to the awkward way Turkey reacted to the Kurdish struggle, and in the second place that a process of consciousness awakening took place in Ankara. The establishment cannot surpass the problem anymore. The time that Kurdish people were called "mountain Turks" is over. There is a debate ongoing on the place of the Kurdish language and culture within the Turkish state system. The violence made Ankara aware that there was a "Kurdish problem". It is a deplorable but at the same time global phenomenon: in order to draw the attention of the national and international media to their demands certain groups revert to deeds of violence and even terror. The solution does not lie in semantic adjurations that these are just "terrorist actions" and nothing more, but in looking for the causes and thinking about the own mistakes in dealing with those who have become hostile to oneself. The Kurds namely can be regarded as the victims of history. Atatürk paid a high territorial price for the fulfillment of his dream, the creation of a Turkish republic resting on cultural and linguistic homogeneity. Those who did not fit into the picture like the Kurdish nationalists wanting in the first place more language rights for their own people so would become a problem. But the victims of the future could become the Turks, if they are no able to fall in with the cultural aspirations of their Kurdish co-citizens.

It is all about Turkey being acceptable for the EU and about its esteem in the world. A European Union, of which several member-states are organized on a federal base, or have large minorities with their own rights, like, for instance, Slovakia, an applicant member state which grants cultural rights to its own Hungarians, - such a EU is not willing to understand why Turkey would be reluctant to be more generous towards its own Kurdish population. One of the reasons why Turkey threatened to invade the Northern Part of Iraq during the last war against Saddam was out of the fear that the rising of an independent Kurdish state centered around Mosul and Kirkuk would inspire separatist revendications among the Kurds of South East Anatolia. The best way of keeping upright or even strengthening the loyalty of the Kurdish-speaking citizens is to further democracy in Turkey, which also implies the possibility to express oneself in his own mother language, be it not at all levels of society. The behaviors of the Turkish generals during the war between the "coalition" and Saddam's regime show how much Turkey in its foreign policy is led by domestic considerations. The Sèvres syndrome is still vivid and influences the way Turkey's establishment sees the world. The political Islam is an integral part of Turkish society. It voices among other motives the protest of those people who feel frustrated. Many "Modernisierungsverlierer", victims of modernization, are looking for security within the value system that the fundamentalists disseminate. In Europe the use

---

[17] Ahmet Erdogan, "De Europese Unie en Turkije: pro's en contra's" , *Internationale Spectator*, December 1999, p.668.

of the word "fundamentalist" is commonplace for the followers of political Islam. In Turkey the word "irtica" (reactionary) as it is used by the Kemalists to denounce political Islam and to describe the way its adherents think, suggests that it has more to do with a sociological than with a religious background. Nevertheless secularists have to bear in mind that a handful of extremists suffice to land the political Islam in fundamentalism. The followers of political Islam do not even have to be extremists themselves for turning society into a place where religion is dominating. The measures with which Erbakan tried to impose the will of the fundamentalists on daily life, demonstrates how vulnerable "Open Society" is. It was still possible to chase way Erbakan off power, but that does not mean that secularism cannot be endangered anymore.

The Turkish government managed to have several reform packages been approved by parliament since the spring of 2003, for instance, reforms aiming at reducing the role of the army within the National Security Council. Since long the European Union is insisting on bringing the army under civilian control, as it is appropriate to a full democracy. Yet the attitude towards the army often still lacks consistency as the debate about sending troops to Iraq in the summer of 2003 indicated. The Republican People's Party parliamentary group deputy chairman Mustafa Ozyurek hinted to the contradiction in the government's endeavor to get a strong endorsement of the MGK for dispatching troops to Iraq: "Those who demand the military take an active political position regarding sending troops to Iraq cannot complain of the army's interference in other political issues."[18] The question is whether Turkey might come from the frying pan into the fire. Until now the army is fulfilling the role of watchdog of the jacobine and secularist state Turkey pretends to be. As far as the former qualification of the Turkish state is concerned, this has not always been a boon, as for instance, the Kurdish people can testify. Religious and linguistic minorities had to comply in the Turkish "bed of Procrustes" with the assimilation policy of the state. Concerning the secularist task of the army things look different. If the military were driven back, the way would maybe free for those forces that do not mean so well by the secularist character of the state. This danger exists as long as politics are weak. Due to the electoral threshold of 10% only 55% of the voters are represented in parliament. Moreover, since the Siirt by-elections in March and the joining of some independent deputies the AKP since 14 August 2003 has with 368 deputies 2/3 of the total seats of Parliament. By exceeding the required minimum of 367 the AKP acquired the power of legislating through Parliament constitutional amendments without risking a referendum.[19]

No one knows exactly what the AKP, the party of so-called moderate Islamists, is after. The Kemalists are afraid of a "hidden agenda" of the AKP, who wants to restrict the powers of the president and to change the educational system. Because Erdogan is justifying the reforms with the demands of the European Union, there is not much choice left to the president and the army than to approve them. One of the explanations why Erdogan is taking such a pro-EU stance could be that Turkey's membership to the EU might bring much more religious freedom, for instance, the right for pious women to wear

---

[18] *Turkish Daily News,* 22 August 2003.
[19] *Turkish Daily News,* 17 August 2003.

the headscarf even in official functions. Islam however remains the most important stumbling-bloc for Turkey's accession to the EU. That does not mean that other shortcomings of Turkey could be neglected. The Oostlander-report of the European Parliament lists the wash of all the demands which Turkey still has to fulfill before it may even dream of an accession to the EU. For rapporteur Arie Oostlander, the concept of the nation-state with its cultural and religious homogeneity lies at the core of the problem.

Whereas the underlying philosophy of the Turkish State compromises elements such as nationalism, an important role for the army, and a rigid attitude to religion, which are hard to reconcile with the founding values of the European Union, and has to be adapted in order to enable a less rigid and more open-minded cultural and religious diversity as well as a modern and tolerant concept of the nation State, (...).[20]

For most EU-citizens, however, the Islamic character of Turkey itself is the problem, so it is almost an "ontologic" problem. The question they ask themselves is whether the accession of Turkey with its large Muslim population will reinforce the moment of Islam in Europe or not. The problem lies not with Turkey but with the EU itself, as it is apparent from the words of the German bishop Heinz Josef Algermissen in an interview with an influential German daily newspaper: "Unsere Schwäche macht den Islam stark" (= Our weakness makes Islam strong).[21] In face of the indifference of many EU-citizens towards the Judeo-Christian roots of Europe stays the self-consciousness of most Muslims, their feeling to have an own identity and to belong to a specific culture to which they are attached, and as the vast majority among them, without being radical. Having this scene in his mind a man like bishop Algermissen–and with him many other spiritual authorities in Europe-might fear that the accession of Turkey could further oppress the Christian value system in Europe. His words anyway make clear why especially German Christian-Democratic politicians feel uneasy about and even oppose Turkey's EU-membership. Their repugnance stems from the insight that at the moment the EU has not yet an own identity that is strong enough to cope with the accession of a country like Turkey whose self-consciousness is very well developed. It has not much to do with the EU being a "Christian club" as Turkey used to grumble over, when it felt offended by remarks of Valéry Giscard-d'Estaing in his function of president of the EU-Convention in December 2002. On the contrary, exactly because the EU is not a "Christian club", but is based on a secularist view of politics and society, leading Christian politicians and intellectuals fear that Turkey's accession would act as a catalyst on Islam which is already represented in Europe by millions of people. Among common EU-citizens the prejudice is widespread since 09/11 that Islam and fundamentalism are one.

To take away this fear and prejudice from the public opinion in the EU one could refer to Lebanon where there are almost as many Christians as Muslims and where the balance of power between both communities is regulated by a system of assigning posts to their representatives. The difference with Europe is that the Lebanese Christians are more

---

[20] Report on Turkey's application for membership of the European Union (COM (2002) 700 – C5-0104/2003-2000/2014(COS)). Committee on Foreign Affairs, Human Rights, Common Security and Defence Policy. European Parliament, 20 May 2003, p.7/19.

[21] *Die Welt*, 4 August 2003.

aware of their own religious identity, so there is no vacuum in any community in which extremists of another community could penetrate. If Europe's Christians and Freethinkers, the latter being well-organized in countries like Belgium and France, would stand up for their respective values, the integrity of the human being within a religious norm system and the freedom of thought within a secular state, there would be no reason to fear the accession of a Muslim country to the European Union. This assumes that Turkey remains a secular state that also, on the base of reciprocity, will grant the same rights to Christians and Freethinkers as Muslims already enjoy within the EU itself.[22] The outlook of becoming member of the EU is changing Turkey, or as the American political scientist Ricard Falk says, "The pressures associated with preparing Turkey for the EU are complementary to recovering the multi-ethnic spirit of diversity associated with the Ottoman past."[23]

Even when the Kurdish problem and the religious issue would be solved one day, Turkey would still face another problem that will gain importance and will affect its foreign policy the more it is advancing on its path to the EU, namely the Armenian issue. The EU does not like to import problems between states, as it is for the moment the case with the borders between Turkey and Armenia being closed and enmity between both states still pending because of the painful past. The eventual membership of Turkey would namely strengthen the existing European ambitions of Georgia and then, logically, also of the other Southern Caucasian states, so that the problem could not be disregarded.

Although it is the Ottoman Empire that bears the responsibility for the alleged crimes, which were committed on the Armenian people in 1915, the Turkish Republic refuses to recognize them as "genocide". The fear exists that the Armenians might put forward territorial and financial demands. A step forward towards a better relationship between both states would be the recognition of the existing borders and the refraining from any kind of revisionism on both sides. This requires a wise foreign policy in both countries, which does not fall victim to domestic pressures.

Conclusion

Turkey is an up to date example of a state walking on the slack-rope between ethnic demands (by the Kurdish people) on the one hand and the build-up and protection of democracy (against fundamentalists) on the other hand. The fixation on just one aspect, the ethnic one, as European critics of Turkey used to do in regard to the Kurdish question, is dangerous. It shuts one's eyes to what matters in the first place: the rights and freedoms of a human being as an individual and a citizen. The freedom to express oneself in one's own language, culture or religion surely is one of these basic rights. Kemalism had laid the foundation for a state in which people without regard to race or gender are able to live and work as free citizens. Yet it also has deployed sometimes a rigid attitude towards those who do not fit in the schemes of laicism and cultural homogeneity. Secularism in Turkey has fed the need for another kind of "religion" (the Latin word "religion" literally meaning something which is binding), namely nationalism. In a society where civic rights

---

[22] Ludger Kühnhardt, "Die Türkei und Europa", in *Mut*, Nr. 431, July 2003, p.46.
[23] *Turkish Daily News*, 12 August 2003.

and freedoms are stressed like in Turkey, even when this is not yet perfect, where a person in the first place is being defined as a citizen, the togetherness of the religious community (as it was existing among Muslims in the Ottoman Empire, be they Turks or Kurds) is shifting to the concept of the nation-state in which nationalistic thoughts and symbols are becoming more important. When the republic was founded in 1923, it followed the path of other Western democracies. The Western European states however changed their character after World War II (the result of excessive nationalism) in becoming member of a European Community, which transcended the narrow scope of nationalism. The European project of the EC (later to be named EU) was meant to surpass the chauvinism of the homogeneous nation-state. EU-member states are transferring sovereignty to the higher level of the EU on the one hand and are subject to several kinds of regionalism on the other hand. Subsidiarity, cultural autonomy and linguistic diversity belong to the political vocabulary of EU-member states. Turkey, on the contrary, lags behind with its nationalistic and homogeneous state concept. It has a "European dream", but as long as it does not have empathy for other cultural and religious "expressions", it does not understand the EU. Maybe Turkey can learn from its own "pre-republic" history. Becoming to look more like the Ottoman Empire in this sense that it acknowledges its own cultural and religious richness not only in words, but also in deeds, implicates at the same time to look more like a member-state of the European Union. What Turkey needs and what the perspective of EU-membership brings about, is: a Turkish "Perestroika" or, to use a neologism, "Turkestroika".

9 The Role of Turkish Migration and Migrants in Turkey's Relations With the EC/EU

Fulya Kip Barnard

It has been the paradox of European migrations that millions of migrants have been living in European countries but are not classified as immigrants. Large scale migration from Southern European countries, and especially Turkey, to Europe took place in the context of the manpower migration process of the 1960s. This migration was mainly due to the labour needs of the booming European economies and was expected to be a temporary phenomenon. European countries did not see themselves as countries of immigration. Migrant workers were expected to return to their country of origin after a period of work, however the majority preferred to remain in their host countries. Family unification and later, family formation, increased the numbers of migrants in the European countries. Despite the wishes of the host countries, made clear by the cessation of recruitment of foreign workers during the early 1970s, a permanent and settled population of ethnic minorities began to form. Migration was a low politics issue in the 1960s as the migration was desirable, and neither the EEC or the migrant countries developed any concrete global migration policy. In this sense Turkish migration to the EEC countries in the early sixties, and in particular to Germany, proves this statement. Since large scale Turkish migration to the EC/EU countries started in the 1960s, both Turkey and the Member States of the EC/EU did not consider themselves as either emigration or immigration countries. This resulted in no well defined immigration or emigration policies being developed by both sides.

A dilemma appeared in Turkey's relations with the EEC due to the provisions of the Turkey-EEC Association Agreement and the Additional Protocol concerning free movement of workers and further social provisions. One of the basic targets of European integration put forward by the EEC was the development of arrangements aimed to initiate and encourage intra-European movement of labour. This pillar of the Rome Treaty was similarly set out in the Association Agreement that Turkey signed with the EEC in 1963. Although contractually granting the right of free movement of workers, it has yet to be implemented by the decisions of the Council of Association consisting of Turkey and the EEC, and set up to facilitate the provisions of the Association Agreement and the Additional Protocol.

Basic Characteristics of Turkish Migration to the EC/EU

Turkish migration to the EEC started as an initiative under the competence of the Member States of the EEC through bilateral treaties signed between the Member States and

Turkey.[1] As the Member States' economies were expanding and in need of labour Turkish migration was desirable although it was perceived by the Member States as a temporary phenomenon. This was amenable to Turkey who wanted a steady stream of trained return migrants and a continuous flow of remittances, whilst reducing its employment problems.[2]

Turkish migration quickly became large-scale and by 1973 the number of Turks within the EEC was 1,350,000 of which 900,000 were workers and 450,000 were dependants.[3] Turkey's policy of encouraging the emigration of labour was seen as a short-term measure at a particular stage in the development of Turkey's economy.[4] For this reason the Turkish government did not direct or control the migration effectively and did not look after the interests of the migrant workers within the EEC or educate them about conditions there. Furthermore Turkey did not research the long- term benefits of the migration or consider the developmental needs of Turkey from 1963 to 1972. Policy formation was *ad hoc* and under the competence of various ministries and bodies. No central body co-ordinating the labour migration was set up. Turkey did give priority to a quota of migrant workers from the underdeveloped regions however this was abused by potential migrants who registered in these regions for priority access.[5] In 1972, Turkey began co-ordinating the migration policy more and set up bodies including the Department of Problems of Workers Abroad and the Inter-ministerial Committee.[6] Unfortunately recruitment stopped in 1973 and since 1973 problems have related to the migrants already legally resident in the EC/EU.

The main benefit to Turkey of Turkish labour migration to the EC/EU was the flow of

---

[1] *The Bilateral Agreements on the Supply of Turkish Migrants with the FGR, Austria, Belgium, Holland, France, Switzerland, Australia,* Ankara: İş ve İşçi Bulma Kurumu Yayınları, 1970; Nermin Abadan-Unat, "Turkish Migration to Europe and the Middle East: Its Impact on the Social Structure and Social Legislation", Laurence Michalak and Jeswald Salacuse, (Eds.), *Social Legislation in the Contemporary Middle East,* Berkeley: University of California Institute of International Studies, 1986, p.331; Philip L. Martin, *Unfinished Story: Turkish Emigration to Western Europe,* Ankara: International Labor Organization Office, 1991, p.35.

[2] Charles Kindleberger, *Kindleberger Report, OECD,* 1979; Samuel S. Lieberman, & Ali S. Gitmez, "Turkey in International Labor Migration in Europe", Ronald E. Krane (Ed.), *International Labour Migration in Europe,* New York: Praeger, 1979, pp.201-220; Bülent Ecevit, "Labor in Turkey as a New Social and Political Force", Kemal H. Karpat (Ed.), *Social Change and Politics in Turkey,* Leiden: Brill, 1973, pp.171-172; Barbara Schmitter Heisler, "Sending Countries and the Policies of Emigration and Destination", *International Migration Review (Special Issue: Civil Rights and Socio Political Participation of Migrants),* Vol.19, No.3, 1985, pp.469-484.

[3] Erol Kutlu, *Uluslararası İşgücü Hareketi Teorisi Çerçevesinde Türkiye'den AT'ye İşgücü Göçünün Türkiye Ekonomisi Üzerindeki Etkilerinin Analizi,* (An Analysis of the effects of Turkish Emigration to the EEC on Turkish Economy in the Framework of the International Labour Movement Theory), p.36.

[4] Hüseyin Ramazanoglu, "Labour Migration in the Development of Turkish Capitalism", Hüseyin Ramazanoglu (Ed.), *Turkey in the World Capitalist System,,* Vermont: Gower Publications, 1985.

[5] State Planning Organization, *Dış Ülkelere İşgücü Göndermede Kooperatif Kurumu Köylere Öncelik Tanınması Projesinin Uygulanması Üzerine Bir İnceleme (An Analysis Report on Village Development Cooperatives Project),* Ankara: State Planning Organization, 1960.

[6] *The Official Government Journal of Republic of Turkey,* published the first functional description of the duties, personal make up, domestic and foreign activities and general goals of the General Directorate for Workers Abroad on 13 April 1972, (Law No.1579, Acceptance date: 6 April 1972).

remittances that reached $1.2 billion by 1973.[7] These helped the Turkish economy particularly through reducing the balance of payments deficits from the mid 1960s onwards.[8] However the remittances were used for consumption and not invested in capital projects, and cannot be relied upon to remain at any level.[9] A second point is that Turkey expected a continuous flow of trained workers returning to Turkey. Turkey did not suffer from skill drain during the 1960s and 1970s but it did not benefit from a return flow of skilled workers.[10] Many Turkish workers preferred to remain in the host countries in the EEC and furthermore many workers had less skilled jobs in the EEC than they had held in Turkey.

Turkish migration took a new dimension following the signing of the Association Agreement between the EEC and Turkey in 1963.[11] Turkey expected that the agreement and later, the Protocol of 1970,[12] would replace the bilateral agreements with the Member States and would benefit from Turkish migration through the provisions for free movement for workers and social security provisions. However this depended on several factors including the EC/EU's immigration policies and attitudes of the Member States towards immigration.

Factors Affecting Turkish Migration to the EC/EU

The Agreement of 12 September 1963 and the Protocol of 23 November 1970 signed between Turkey and the EEC foresaw a possible further integration including accession between Turkey and the EC/EU rather than just the Customs Union, which was introduced in 1996. Because of this, the Agreement and the Protocol which were modelled from the Treaty of Rome contained provisions not only on the free movement of goods, capital and services but provisions on the free movement of persons as well.

However several factors affected the implementation of the provision relating to the free movement of workers between Turkey and the EC/EU. These include direct effects such as the EC/EU's immigration policies and indirect effects including Turkey's domestic economic and political situation, Turkey's relations with the EC/EU and Turkey's emigration policies.

During the period from 1963, the Turkish economy and Turkish politics suffered from several setbacks. Economically the Turkish economy experienced instability until the 1980s. This was reflected in volatile economic growth, high inflation and balance of

---

[7] İsmet Ergün, *The Problem of Freedom of Movement of Turkish Workers in the EC*, p.185; Rinus Penninx, "A Critical Review of Theory and practice", *International Migration Review*, Vol.16, 1982, p.797.

[8] William Hale, *International Migration Project Country Case Study: Turkey*, Durham University, Department of Economics, 1978, pp.66-67.

[9] Nermin Abadan Unat, "Turkish Migration to Europe (1960-1975)", Nermin Abadan Unat (Ed.), *Turkish Workers in Europe 1960-1975: A Socio Economic Reappraisal*, Leiden: E. J. Brill, 1976, p.24-25.

[10] Suzanne Paine, *Exporting Workers: the Turkish Case*, Cambridge: Cambridge University Press, 1974, p.129.

[11] The Agreement was published in the *Official Journal of the European Community*, L 217 of 29 December 1964.

[12] *Official Journal of the EEC*, L 293 of 29 December 1972.

payments deficits.[13] The political situation was also unstable.[14] This was due to frequent changes of government and polarisation at different levels of the Turkish bureaucracy. This polarisation was caused by the emergence of extreme political groupings from the late 1960s until 1980.[15] Starting from 1960 Turkey experienced three military interventions that stopped the proper functioning of democracy within the country. These interventions were precipitated by either power vacuums within the political establishment as in 1960[16] and 1971,[17] or the need to restore public order due to civilian unrest, as in 1980. However these developments affected Turkey's relations with the EC/EU. During the 1960s and early 1970s relations between Europe and Turkey were focused more on economic aspects and were considered low politics by the EC/EU. For example the 1971 military intervention in Turkey did not attract much criticism from the EEC as relations were smooth and mostly based on economic issues. However, after the 1973 oil crisis, which adversely affected the economies of the Member States of the EEC and Turkey, relations entered a new phase.[18] The EEC Member States, experiencing rising unemployment, ceased recruitment of Turkish labour in 1973/4.[19] On the other hand, whereas the EEC had already abolished its customs duties according to the Association Agreement, Turkey, in 1977, could not carry on its obligations relating to customs reductions and requested a freeze on its reductions in 1978 for five years.[20] This resulted in the EEC's demand to freeze the functioning of the whole agreement, including free movement of persons, which Turkey did not want. In 1980 Turkey wanted to revitalise relations with the EEC, but following the military coup in September 1980, relations deteriorated further, and were interrupted for six years.[21] The EEC's reaction to the 1980

---

[13] See Zvi Yehuda Hershlag, *The Contemporary Turkish Economy*, London and New York: Routledge, 1988; Ziya Öniş, "The State and Economic Development in Contemporary Turkey: Etatism to Neo-liberalism and Beyond", Vojtech Mastny & Robert Craig Nation (Eds.), *Turkey Between East and West: New Challenges for a Rising Regional Power*, Boulder Colorado: Westview Press, 1996, pp.155-179; Atila Eralp, Muharrem Tünay & Birol Yeşilada (Eds.), *The Political and Socioeconomic Transformation of Turkey*, London: Praeger, 1993.

[14] See Ahmad Feroz, *The Making of Modern Turkey*, London: Routledge, 1993; Jacob M. Landau, *Radical Politics in Modern Turkey*, Leiden: E. J. Brill, 1974; Clement H. Dodd, *The Crisis of Turkish Democracy*, Beverley: Eothen, 1990; Feroz Ahmad, *The Turkish Experiment in Democracy:1950-75*, Boulder Colorado: Westview Press, 1977; Andrew Finkel & Nükhet Sirman (Eds.), *Turkish State, Turkish Society* London: Routledge, 1990.

[15] Şerif Mardin, "Youth and Violence in Turkey", *Archives Europeens de Sociologie*, Vol.19, No.1, 1978, p.243.

[16] Clement H. Dodd, *The Crisis of Turkish Democracy*, Ahmad, *The Turkish Experiment in Democracy:1950-75*.

[17] Mehmet Ali Birand, *The General's Coup in Turkey*, London: Brasseys Defence Publishers, 1987, pp.12-16.

[18] Stephen Castles, Heather Booth & Tina Wallace, *Here For Good: Western Europe's new Ethnic Minorities*, London: Pluto Press, 1987, p.29; Faruk Şen, "Turkish Communities in Western Europe", Vojtech Mastny and Robert Craig Nation (Eds.), *Turkey Between East and West: new Challenges For a Rising Regional Power*, Boulder Colorado: Westview Press, 1986, p.237.

[19] Stephen Castles, Heather Booth & Tina Wallace, *Here For Good: Western Europe's new Ethnic Minorities*, p.29.

[20] Meltem Müftüler, *Turkey's Relations with a Changing Europe*, Manchester UK: Manchester University Press, 1997, p.36.

[21] Roswitha Bourguignon, "A History of the Association Agreement between Turkey and the EC", Ahmet Evin. & Geoffrey Denton (Eds.), *Turkey and the European Community*, Opladen: Leske and Budrich,

coup in Turkey was much more critical compared to the 1971 military intervention. This was mainly due to the increasing importance attached to political factors, compared with economic ones, when assessing candidature to the EEC.

The first general elections in Turkey after the 1980 coup took place in 1983. However these were not accepted as a return to proper democracy by the EEC due to the ban applying to several political parties in Turkey. The 1984 local elections within Turkey were seen as the first steps towards a normalisation in Turkey's politics by the EEC.[22]

From 1984 to 1986 attempts were made by the EEC and Turkey to restore relations and the EEC-Turkey Association Council met for the first time after six years in 1986.[23] From 1986 onwards Turkey's policy towards Europe was to apply for full membership to the EC/EU rather than separately discussing different aspects of the Association Agreement or Additional Protocol. Although the Turkish government declared Turkey's intention for full membership as early as 1981, because of the political situation in Turkey the formal application was made in April 1987.[24]

Following the decisions of the Turkish government in January 1980, in which Turkey would adopt a more market based system of resource allocation and an outward oriented trade strategy, Turkey's economy grew rapidly for the rest of the decade. This compared with Turkey's economic underperformance in earlier years in which it applied a strategy of protection and import substitution. Thus in 1987 Turkey believed that it was ready for full membership to the EC/EU both politically and economically. However this was not a good timing for the EC/EU. The EC/EU rejected Turkey's application on the grounds that the EC/EU had just completed its second and third enlargement including Greece, Spain and Portugal and was preparing for the single market in 1992.[25] Furthermore, the reply by the EEC stated that Turkey's political situation, economy and Turkey's relations with Greece, particularly the Cyprus issue were considered obstacles in the way of Turkey's accession.[26] Turkey's eligibility for membership was mentioned but no future date was given for a possible accession.

The EC/EU and Turkey attempted to improve relations further from 1989 to 1995,

---

1990, p.57-58.

[22] Atila Eralp, "Turkey and the European Community: Prospects for a New Relationship", Atila Eralp, Muharrem Tünay & Birol Yeşilada (Eds.), *The Political and Socioeconomic Transformation of Turkey*, Westport Connecticut: Praeger, 1993, p.201

[23] See Turkish and the European Press for the developments before and after the Association Council Meeting on 16.9.1986, "Halefoğlu"nun Brüksel Dosyası Kabarık", *Cumhuriyet*, 13.9.86; Mehmet Ali Birand "Yunanistan Yalnız kaldı", *Milliyet*, 17.9.86; "AET'den Tedbirli Yeşil Işık", *Tercüman*, 17.9.86; Quantil Peel, "EEC fails to break Athens Veto over Turkey", *Financial Times*, 17.9.86; "Howe signals return to Community political relations with Turkey", *The Times*, 17.9.86; "The Reviving Man of Europe", *The Times*, 18.9.86.

[24] *Bulletin EC*, 4-1987, p.11.

[25] *Agence Europe*, No.4698, 13 January 1988, p.12.

[26] For an analysis of Commission"s Opinion on Turkey's Application see "Turkey and the European Community, Report on the Relations Between the Republic of Turkey and the European Community arising from the Ankara Agreement and the Application For Membership", *Marmara Journal of European Studies Special Issue*, Vol.2, No.1/2, 1992; "IKV Araştırmalarına Göre Avrupa Topluluğu Karşısında Türkiye'nin Durumu" (Turkey's Position in the Face of the European Community According to the IKV Studies), *IKV Yayınları*, No.121, October 1992, pp.83-85.

including measures to prepare for the customs union due to start in January 1996[27] and the full functioning of bodies established by the Association Agreement, including the Association Council and Committee and the EEC-Turkey Joint Parliamentary Group. However the main concern of the EC/EU was still the political situation in Turkey, including human rights and Kurdish issues. Furthermore relations with Greece continued to impede relations between the EC/EU and Turkey. Several proposals including the fourth financial protocol were vetoed by Greece, referring mainly to the Cyprus issue.[28]

This period ended with a customs union between Turkey and the EC/EU[29] without any future agenda for Turkey's possible accession and without any reference to the free movement of Turkish workers within the EC/EU. The achievement of the customs union was in line with the interests of most of the member states and Turkey and the member states were willing to pass the competence in this issue to the EC/EU. However the issue of Turkey's full membership including the full practice of rights given to the Member States, such as a role in decision making with in the EC/EU or in the sphere of free movement of people, was against the national interests of some member states. These issues are considered high politics by some member states such as Germany in the case of free movement or Greece in its foreign policy.

Evaluation of Turkish Migration to the EC/EU From 1963 to 1995

Turkish migration from 1963 to 1973 can be considered smooth and promising. During this period Turkey signed the Association Agreement in 1963 and the Additional Protocol in 1970, which included provisions related to the free movement of workers between Turkey and the EEC and social security provisions.

The initial design of the Agreement and the Protocol regarding migration issues was aimed at the gradual realisation of the free movement of workers between Turkey and the EEC.[30] The outcome expected of Article 12 of the Agreement and Articles 36-39 of the Protocol, which was binding on the national political units, was the implementation of the principle of free movement of workers and social security provisions in the period between 1976 and 1986. These provisions were concluded as plans for the future realisation through the decisions of the Association Council, which was established as the highest decision making body in respect of the implementation of the mentioned plans.[31] The first stage of negotiations in respect of migration issues included supranational

---

[27] The European Parliament, Committee on Foreign Affairs and Security, "Draft Report on Turkey-EC Relations", Rapporteur: Mrs Raymonde Dury, 28 January 1992, p.6; *Agence Europe*, No.5189, 8 February 1990, p.7.

[28] *Agence Europe*, No.5491, 15 May 1991, p.8.

[29] "Gümrük Birliğinin Türk Ekonomisine Etkileri: Önlemler, Öneriler", (The Effects of the Customs Union on Turkish Economy: Precautions and Proposals), IKV Yayınları, No.125; Hans Von den Broek, *Turkey and the EU: The Challenge of the Customs Union, Brussels: Forum Europe*, 24.4.1995; Ambassador Ali Tigrel Ph.D, Chief Advisor to the Prime Minister and EC Co-ordinator, *Effects of the Customs Union on Turkish Economy*, Ankara Industry Council: unpublished document, 15-16 June 1995.

[30] For the Agreement Establishing an Association between EEC and Turkey see "Collection of the Agreements concluded by the European Communities", *Bilateral Agreements EEC-Europe 1958-1975*, Vol.3, pp.539-555.

[31] *Collection of the Agreements concluded by the European Communities*, p.551

tendencies in the decision-making. As a low politics issue of the time, the issue of migration was less debated by the Community side in respect to other issues such as customs or agricultural issues. Turkey insisted on the realisation of the freedom of movement due to its economic needs rather than considering other long-run aspects of the issue.

Even though the issue of freedom of movement is a right for both parties, neither Turkey nor the Community discussed possible migration from the EEC Member States to Turkey. If the freedom of movement was realised, Turkey may face difficulties due to its regulation on social security and other aspects. However, taking into consideration the low possibility of such a kind of migration, this side of the issue never came to the agenda of the negotiations. As a consequence, the issues discussed in the later stages have been the free movement of Turkish workers in the EEC rather than free movement of workers both in Turkey and the EEC.

The Association Agreements, except the Athens Treaty, do not include provisions related to free movement of workers. Article 12 of the Agreement and Article 36 of the Protocol derives its explicit nature from the supranational tendencies of the Contracting Parties to find a solution for the migrant Turkish workers within the platform of EC-Turkey Association, rather than by way of bilateral treaties as have been referred to before. Being a low politics issue in the early years of Turkey's relations with the EEC, migration issues under the competence of the EEC were not challenged by the Member States.

The stage of Turkish migration from 1974-1980 included the cessation of labour recruitment by the EEC countries in 1973-4,[32] but included a continuing process towards the realisation of free movement of workers and a social security regime. Starting from the second stage, the issues of migration become more sensitive and took a definite place in the agenda of the Member States of the Community itself, and this trend was followed by the Community institutions. The originally smooth negotiations started to get tougher and the platform for negotiations started to take place more and more at intergovernmental level.

During this period decisions for the initiation of a social security regime had to be taken before 1974, and decisions for the initiation of free movement of workers before December 1976. However there were delays by both parties, but mainly from the Member States opposition. In 1975 Germany requested from the EEC the removal of Article 12, free movement of workers, from the Association Agreement, but this request was not supported by the EEC at that time.[33] However the favourable proposals from the Commission for the improvement of social security and the initiation of the first stage of free movement, including a second priority for Turkish workers within the EEC was

---

[32] Nusret Ekin, "Migration and Reintegration Problems of Turkish Workers", paper (unpublished) presented to the European-American Workshop on *The Security of Turkey and Its Allies: Self Development and Interdependence*, Istanbul, 10-12 September 1979, p.11.
[33] Rıdvan S. Karluk, *Turkey and the EC*, Ankara: Yapı ve Kredi Yayınları, 1994, p.461; Hüseyin Pazarcı, "Türk İşçilerinin Ortak Pazarda Dolaşımı Engellenirse", *Milliyet*, 23 April 1975; İlhan Tekeli & Selim İlkin, *Turkey and the EC*, Vol.II, Ankara: Ümit Yayıncılık, 1993, p.153.

rejected by the Association Council due to opposition from Member States. The Decision 2/76 taken by the Association Council to regulate the first stage of the realisation of free movement only included the improvement of working conditions of Turkish immigrant workers already legally resident in the EEC Member States.[34] This decision did not mention free movement for Turkish workers within the EEC. Although Turkey insisted for a second priority for its workers, the Association Council refused citing difficulties within the Member States' labour markets. Even Turkey's request for a second priority once the labour market difficulties within the Member States had passed was rejected by the Association Council.

The decision for the second stage of the realisation of free movement of workers had to be taken before December 1980. Furthermore there were delays in respect of a decision for the improvement of the social security situation of the Turkish workers in the EEC. The negotiations for both of the decisions took longer than expected and the meetings were postponed several times. The final decisions taken, Decisions 1/80 and 3/80, did not satisfy Turkish demands. Decision 1/80 superseded Decision 2/76 but still did not include the free movement of Turkish workers in the EEC and the only improvements made concerned the working conditions of Turkish immigrant workers in the EEC.[35] Free movement was only granted to Turkish workers in the EEC countries in which they settled and depended on the time they had worked there. The Decision 3/80 on social security aspects was modelled from the regulation that applied to the nationals of the EEC with some differences. In that respect it was promising but needed a further regulation for the implementation.[36]

A third period of Turkish migration, from 1981-1987, was a difficult one not only in respect of Turkey's overall relations with the EC/EU but in particular in respect of migration issues. The period started with the introduction of visa applications by the EEC Member States in the 1980s, precipitated by Germany's introduction of visas for Turkish nationals in 1980,[37] and the opposition to the realisation of the free movement of workers by the EC, initiated particularly by Germany and followed by other Member States. During this period the EC-Turkey Association Council had to take a decision for the final stage of the realisation of free movement of Turkish workers in the EEC before December 1983. However due to the deterioration in overall relations, mainly due to Turkey's political situation, this meeting was never held.[38]

Problems in the implementation of the provisions of the Agreement and the Protocol

---

[34] *Collected Acts, EEC-Turkey Association Institutions,* 1 24; EC-Turkey Council of Association, *Twelfth Report,* p.37; Trevor Wornham under the supervision of Elspeth Guild, *The Immigration Lawyer's Guide to the Turkey-EC Association Agreement,* London: ILPA, 1994, pp.41-48.

[35] Wornham, *The Immigration Lawyer's Guide to the Turkey-EC Association Agreement,* pp.41-48.

[36] *Official Journal of the EC,* C110 of 25 April 1983. For the full text of the Decision 3/80 see Annex.

[37] The dates of visa applications to the Turkish nationals by the Member States of the EC/EU as follows: Germany and France 5 October 1980, Benelux countries 1 November 1980, Denmark 1 May 1981, the United Kingdom 23 June 1989, Ireland 19 November 1989, Italy 3 September 1990, Portugal 24 June 1991, Spain 1 October 1991. Greece has applied visas for Turkish nationals before its membership to EC, since 24 April 1965. See Karluk, *Turkey and the EC,* p.466.

[38] Karluk, *Turkey and the EC,* p.461.

concerning migration issues increased in the 1980s. The supranational bodies of the EC such as the Commission, the European Parliament and the European Court of Justice (ECJ) were more sympathetic and positive in their attitudes towards the problems of Turkey arising from the implementation of the Agreement. The Member States and the Council have constantly refused the implementation of the proposals in favour of Turkish migration by these bodies and adopted a more negative stance.

Analysis of Decisions 2/76 and 1/80 reveals that the regime applying to the Turkish workers already settled in the EC/EU would not be restricted further. The EC Member States would not try to reduce the number of already settled Turkish immigrants by introducing new restrictive legislation or repatriation laws. However the decisions analysed here did not grant free movement of Turkish workers in the EC/EU. It only granted free movement within individual Member States. A second priority for Turkish workers in the EC after the EC nationals was adopted with those decisions, despite the opposition by some Member States including Germany and the UK.[39]

Regarding free movement of Turkish workers in the EEC, the Community was in a difficult position. It had a contractual relationship with Turkey based on Article 12 of the Agreement and Article 36 of the Protocol. However starting from 1973/4 the Member States of the EC/EC were experiencing difficulties in their employment markets and increasing opposition towards further migration from their public, including increasing attacks towards immigrant populations. Considering the non-application of free movement of Turkish workers in the EC, as mentioned by Emile Noel, General Secretary of the European Commission as early as in 1976, Turkey could accuse the EEC of breaking its contractual promises.[40]

In the late 1970s and early 1980s the Member States of the EC hoped that stopping labour migration and the restrictive environment towards migrants would cause a large-scale return of workers including Turks. However, the majority of Turkish workers preferred to stay in the EEC and brought their dependants, so the total migrant population grew.[41] The family reunification, and later family formation, contradicted the aims of the migrant receiving countries and was initially rejected leading to increasing restrictions being brought by the Member States. The unplanned nature of these processes ended with the marginalisation of the Turkish migrant populations and increasing problems of integration.[42]

In theory, the free movement of workers between Turkey and the EC should have started from 1 December 1986 at the latest. The concern in the EC was that the implementation of the principle of free movement of Turkish workers in the EC could lead to large inflows of migrant workers from Turkey.[43] Finally the Articles were not implemented.

Turkish migration from 1987-1995 started with deadlock due to the non- application

---

[39] Tekeli & İlkin, *Turkey and the EC*, p.208.
[40] *Milliyet*, 14 November 1976.
[41] Ahmet Akgündüz, "Labour Migration From Turkey to Western Europe (1960-74)", *Capital and Class*, No.51, Autumn 1993, p.153.
[42] Klaus Bade & Myron Wiener, *Migration Past, Migration Future*, Oxford: Berghahn Books, 1997, pp.26-27.
[43] Martin, *Unfinished Story*.

of the free movement principle and the impasse regarding the social security regime. This period ended up with the customs union without mentioning free movement of workers and the social security rights of third country Turkish nationals. The significance of this period concerned important decisions taken by the European Court of Justice[44] in respect of the rights of Turkish nationals legally residing in the EC countries and the non-application of the provisions of the Agreement, Protocol and decisions of the Association Council by the Member States. The decisions of the ECJ, a supranational body, were binding on the Member States although they were challenged by some Member States.

The final decisions of the ECJ and the opinions of the Member States show the very different approaches taken by the national Governments and the Commission as a supranational institution of the EC/EU, in the context of the cases related to the provisions of the Decisions taken by the Association Council for the realisation of the free movement of Turkish workers in the EC.

Through these consecutive stages it was not only the nature of the migration, but also the attitude of the European countries towards migrants that changed. In the early stages, Turkish migrants were mostly accepted as temporary guest workers. However, in the following stages they became minorities. The tolerance initially shown by the host countries become more hostile.[45] The political, social and cultural aspects of migrants gained importance compared to the role that economics played in the early stages. During the early stages, employment problems were the main concern to the Member States but in the later stages a wider range of issues such as housing, education of children and the social integration of families became more important. As Commission of the European Communities stated in its expert report on policies regarding "Immigration and Social Integration of Immigrants in the EC" in 1990, integration is an inescapable policy in order to defuse the tensions inherent in the immigrant populations including Turkish immigrants in the Member States of the EU.[46]

A Theoretical Analysis of the Changing Role of Migration in Turkey's Relations With the EC/EU

The central argument concerning the negotiations on migration between Turkey and the EC/EU is that the issue of migration has become a high politics issue. In addition, the method of action in respect of migration issues in Turkey's relations with the EC/EU has taken an intergovernmental form as against the supranationalist basis of the Association

[44] Case 12/86, Demirel, *Reports of Cases before the Court of Justice*, Luxembourg, 1987; Case 192/89, Sevince, *Reports of Cases before the Court of Justice*, Luxembourg, 1990; Case 237/91, Kuş, *Reports of Cases before the Court of Justice*, Luxembourg, 1992; Case 355/93, Eroğlu, *Reports of Cases before the Court of Justice*, Luxembourg, 1994.

[45] Jan Laurens Hazekamp & Keith Popple, *Racism In Europe*, London: UCL Press Limited, 1997. William Hale, "Turkey: A Crucial but Problematic Applicant", John Redmond (Ed.), *Prospective Europeans*, London: Harvester Wheatsheaf, 1994, p.120; Faruk Şen, "Working Group Report DG1 Migrants and Their Homelands: Opinions about Migrants in their Host Countries", *Human Dimension Seminar On Migrant Workers*, Warsaw: CSCE, 25 March 1994.

[46] Experts Report drawn up on Behalf of the Commission of the EC, *Policies on Immigration and the Social Integration of Migrants in the EC*, Brussels: Commission of the European Communities, 1990, p.14.

Agreement signed between Turkey and the EEC in 1963, and the Protocol in 1973.

The Shift in Turkish Migration to The EEC From Low Politics to High Politics

European integration was initially thought to be a gradual process starting in the fields of lower politics and ending up in the sphere of high politics.[47] In this respect, for instance, an exercise in the integration of foreign policy of the Community members from the early establishment of the EEC has been regarded as the last step towards integration.

During the early years of European integration immigration issues were not under the competence of the EEC but were left to the competence of the Member States. There were no such moves to crystallise the policy framework for immigration at a supranational level at that time. Furthermore migration to the Member States of the EEC was desirable due to their expanding economies and need for labour. This was also true in the case of Turkish migration to the Member States. Turkey signed bilateral agreements with Germany, the Netherlands, France and Belgium between 1961 and 1963 to facilitate the migration of Turkish workers to these countries. The EEC-Turkey Association Agreement was signed on 12 September 1963 under these conditions and contained provisions for the realisation of the free movement of Turkish workers within the EEC. Turkish migration to the EEC was considered a low politics issue at this time and the EEC signed the Association Agreement, which meant that the Member States transferred competence in this field to the EEC. The Additional Protocol of 23 November 1970 went further and included social security arrangements for Turkish Workers, which were again transferred to the competence of the EEC.

Turkish migration to the EEC became a high politics issue after the 1973/4-oil crisis, which caused the European economies to slow, leading to increased unemployment. The Member States of the EEC ceased recruitment of workers from third countries except through intra-EEC migration. However, although labour migration to the EEC virtually ceased in 1973/4, Turkish migration to the EEC continued through family reunification, and later family formation and through asylum seekers. The social costs of the Turkish immigrants to the host societies, which include education, housing, health and social security benefits thus increased during the 1970s and 1980s.

Furthermore Turkey suffered increasing political and economic instability during the 1970s and early 1980s. This manifested itself in two military interventions in Turkish politics by the Turkish army, one in 1971 and the other one in 1980. This affected the economic and political relations between Turkey and the EEC overall and seriously concerned the Member States. The Member States, particularly Germany with the majority of the Turkish immigrants, feared that the realisation of free movement for Turkish workers in the EEC would result in a large influx of Turkish migrants.

Whilst these developments were occurring the EEC was preparing for the single market which would include the abolition of borders to the free movement of persons within the EEC, which was stated in Article 8 of the 1986 Single European Act (Article 7

---

[47] Stanley Hoffman, "The European Process at Atlantic Cross Purposes", *Journal of Common Market Studies,* Vol.3, No.2, February 1965, pp.85-101.

of the Maastricht Treaty).[48] This was important because for the abolition of their borders the Member States had to transfer their competence in the field of immigration to the EC. Due to the high politics aspects of this issue progress has been slow.

This was reflected in the EC/EU's attitudes towards third country nationals including Turkish nationals. Although Turkey had a contractual basis for the implementation of the decisions of the Association Council in respect of Turkish immigrant workers' employment and social security rights due to the sensitivity of the issues to the Member States, they were reluctant to implement these decisions. Thus Turkish migration to the EC/EU and the rights of Turkish immigrants already legally residing in the EU has remained a high politics issue for the Member States of the EC/EU since 1973/4.

The Shift in the Balance of Power Between the Supranational and Intergovernmental Organs of the EC/EU Concerning Turkish Migration Issues

The method of decision making of the EC/EU has followed a pattern including both supranational and intergovernmental aspects since its establishment.

The supranational character of the Community was secured through the role of the High Commission and the Commission in the Establishing treaties that built a balance between the organs of the Community in decision making.[49] The major body which represented the supranational interest of the Community as a whole was the Commission in the EEC and Euratom, and the High Authority in the ECSC. These were merged in 1965 into a single Commission under the Merger Treaty.[50] The Merger Treaty states that: "...they shall neither seek nor take instructions from any government or from any other body..." (Article 10, para.2 of the Merger Treaty). Given the independence of the Commission, the treaty entrusted the Commission with the task of initiating Community policy through making proposals for EC action or legislation. It was laid down in article 149 of the EEC Treaty that: "where in pursuance of this Treaty, the Council acts on a proposal from the Commission, unanimity shall be required for an act constituting an amendment to that proposal."[51]

The decision-making in the Community is built upon the dialogue between its organs. Through its different stages the Commission represented the supranational character of the Community and the Council of Ministers the intergovernmental. Stanley Hoffman was one of the first scholars to emphasise the unwillingness of the European Governments to transfer their sovereign powers to functional agencies, particularly in the field of high politics. Although Hoffman did not use the term intergovernmentalism, his article

---

[48] *Single European Act*, Brussels: Council of the European Communities, 1986, p.18

[49] See Clive Archer and Fiona Butler, *The European Community, Structure and Process*, London: Pinter Publishers, 1992; Simon Bulmer and Wolfgang Wessels, *The European Council*, Basingstoke: MacMillan, 1987; Richard D.Keohane and Stanley Hoffman (Eds.), *The New European Community: Decision Making and Institutional Change*, Oxford: Westview Press, 1991; Juliet Lodge (Ed.), *The EC and the Challenge of the Future*, London: Pinter, 1989.

[50] *Merger Treaty, Treaties Establishing the European Communities*, Luxembourg: Office for Official Publications of the European Communities, 1987, Article 10, para.2.

[51] *European Economic Community Treaty, Treaties Establishing the European Communities*, Luxembourg: Office For Official Publications of the European Communities, 1987.

"Obstinate or Obsolete? The fate of Nation State and the case of Western Europe" can be regarded as an early statement of intergovernmentalism.

According to another scholar, Bulmer, the main postulate of intergovernmentalism was that "national governments retained power despite neo-functional assumptions".[52] Intergovernmentalism was basically used to describe the relations among governments in the European Community. Paul Taylor defined intergovernmentalism in the Communities as a "style of decision making which came to focus upon building a consensus among governments rather than upon building an adequate majority in the Council".[53] Another scholar, Carole Webb, viewed organisations as "intergovernmental in which Member States refused to accept any formal limitations on their sovereignty, insisting on the maintenance of a national veto".[54]

Although the EC/EU succeeded supranational decision making in the low politics issues decisions related to high politics such as foreign policy or immigration issues are made at the intergovernmental level.

The shift towards a common immigration policy by the EC/EU was discussed during the 1980s and 1990s due to the realisation of the single market. The first attempts towards a migration policy came through intergovernmental initiatives such as Schengen[55] and TREVI.[56] Until the Single European Act immigration issues were not within the competence of the EC/EU apart for a few exceptions. One of these exceptions was the Turkish case including the EEC-Turkey Association Agreement, the Additional Protocol and the decisions of the Association Council. As stated by the ECJ in the Demirel case and others, according to Article 177 of the Treaty of Rome the above mentioned agreements are a part of EC/EU law and under the competence of the EC/EU.

In Turkey's case there was a shift from supranational tendencies towards intergovernmental methods after the 1973/4 oil crisis. Free movement for Turkish workers within the EEC was stated in the Agreement as a framework. The Protocol stated that free movement was to be realised between 1976 and 1986 at the latest by stages that were to be decided by the Association council. Furthermore the Protocol included social security provisions, again to be implemented through the decisions of the Association Council. However the Association Council was composed of the Commission, the

---

[52] Simon Bulmer, "Domestic Politics and European Community Policy Making", *Journal of Common Market Studies,* Vol.21, No.4, June 1983, p.355.

[53] Paul Taylor, *The Limits of European Integration,* London: Groom Helm, 1983, p.20.

[54] Carole Webb, "Theoretical Perspective and Problems", Helen Wallace, William Wallace & Carole Webb (Eds.), *Policy Making in the European Community,* New York: John Wiley and Sons, 1983, p.22

[55] Julian J.E.Schutte, "Schengen Its Meaning for the Free Movement of Persons in Europe", *Common Market Law Review,* No.28; ILPA, *The Movement of Aliens in the European Area,* London: Simmons & Simmons, May 1995, pp.11-12; Annex "Schengen Acquis" in Andrew Duff (Ed.), *The Treaty of Amsterdam, Text and Commentary,* London: Federal Trust, Sweet and Maxwell, 1997, p.50.

[56] Since 1956 Interpol has been an important organization for international police co-operation. For more detailed analysis see Cyrille Fijnaut, "Policing Western Europe: Interpol, Trevi and Europol", *Police Studies,* Vol.15, No.3, Fall, 1992; Johannes Peek, "International Police Co-operation within the Justified Political and Judicial Framework: Five Theses on Trevi", Jorg Monar and Roger Morgan (Eds.), *The Third Pillar,* Brussels: European University Press, 1994, pp.201-9.

Member States and Turkey. Due to the high politics nature for some Member States of the provisions relating to Turkish migration the decisions of the Association Council were either postponed, prolonged or inadequate for their implementation. This was because of the unanimity required for decision-making within the Association Council, which meant that decisions were determined relative to the lowest common denominator within the Association Council.

These tendencies towards intergovernmentalism were observed in the continual rejection by the Member States of Commission proposals for the improvement of the situation of the Turkish workers legally residing in the Member States of the community. An example of this involved a proposal for a regulation for the implementation of Decision 3/80 of the Association Council concerning social security rights for Turkish workers. This was not implemented due to the opposition of Member States, mainly Greece.

A further example is Turkey's relations with Germany, one of the leading figures in the formation of the EC/EU policies. Germany was one of the countries supporting Turkey's application towards full membership of the EEC starting in 1959 and continuing until the time the issue of the free movement of Turkish workers in the EC came to the agenda of the EC/EU as a high politics issue. Having the largest Turkish immigration population, the realisation of the free movement of Turkish workers clashed with its national interest. In order to prevent the implementation of this principle, Germany adopted a negative attitude towards Turkey and attempted to affect the shaping of common policies by the EC regarding Turkey's relations with The Community. Being aware of the provisions of the Agreement and Protocol, Germany tried to bring other issues such as Turkey's political and economic situation to the agenda and leave aside the realisation of the free movement. Even during the period 1980 to 1986, the negotiations relating to free movement of Turkish workers in the EEC took place between Germany and Turkey rather than Turkey and the Community, which was against the spirit of the Association Agreement.[57] Although Turkey insisted on using the institutions and mechanisms of the Community, Germany insisted on bilateral talks.

Finally, after substantiating the argument that the intergovernmental mechanism adversely affected the direction of the issues relating to different aspects of Turkish migration, the role and importance of the European Court of Justice must be mentioned. In Turkey's case, improvements were brought by the Decisions of the ECJ, particularly regarding the implementation of the Agreement, the Protocol, and the related Decisions of the Association Council, via the cases of Demirel, Sevince, Kuş, Eroğlu and others.

To summarise, in Turkey's case the shift from supranational tendencies to intergovernmental methods took place at the same time as the shift in Turkish migration issues from low politics to high politics in the view of the Member States. On one hand the Agreement and the Protocol lay down the legal basis for the realisation of the free movement of Turkish workers in the EEC as being a gradually evolving process.

---

[57] Dietrich Schlegel, "Turkish-European Pragmatism", *Aussen Politik*, Vol.37, No.3, pp.283-303; *Dünya, Ekonomi-Politika*, 6.11.1982; Castles, *Here For Good*, p.207.

However when it came to implementation, analysis of the decision-making machinery shows that the process was totally an exercise in intergovernmental co-operation.

However, the jurisprudence of the ECJ established that in respect of the EC-Turkey Association Agreement Turkish workers have directly enforceable rights in respect of employment and/or social security benefits. It is important because where a right is found to be directly enforceable by the ECJ it is a part of the acquis- communutaire and must be applied by the Member States of the EU.

Most recently the EU is in the process of forming of a common immigration policy that started with Tampere summit in 1999. This is a current challenge to the previously analysed intergovernmentalist tendencies in this field. A further challenge comes from Turkey's candidate status since Helsinki, December 1999, which necessitates further co-operation between Turkey and the EU in respect of Turkish migration.[58] All these new factors should be evaluated in the light of future developments that would be interesting to analyse their impact on Turkish migration to the EU, and its effect of future Turkey-EU relations.

---

[58] Kemal Kirişçi, *Justice and Home Affairs İssues in Turkish –EU Relations,* İstanbul: TESEV Publications, 2002.

10 Turkish Foreign Policy towards the Balkans: Quest for Enduring Stability and Security

Mustafa Türkeş

Introduction

Many analysts of Turkey's Balkan policy tend to base their accounts on an exaggerated image of Turkey as if she has an objective of regaining supremacy in the Balkans.[1] Conversely, some critic of Turkey's foreign policy tend to argue that active foreign policy is one of Turkey's hegemonial requirements in the region and that the Turkish policy makers were so inactive to respond to the crises and the appeals of the Turkish and Muslim minority in the region.[2]

These two accounts are, expectedly, feeding each other. Both are looking for somehow a uniform Turkish master plan to be implemented in the Balkans, in order, while the former, to show potential, hidden neo-Ottomanist strategy of Turkey, and the latter, to promote an assumed neo-Ottomanist master plan.

I have so far come across no uniform Turkish plan to be implemented in the Balkans as to reinstate Turkish supremacy in the region. Here, it is argued that there is no clear-cut blueprint that directs the Turkish foreign policy towards the Balkans in line with regaining of Turkish supremacy, let alone Turkey's policy is not uniform towards all the Balkan states. Turkey's Balkan policy is formed by complex interactions between quest for enduring stability and security, and the swift, complex systemic as well as circumstantial Eurasian-wide changes as well as inter and intra-state possessive and relational power changes in the Balkans. It should also be noted that characteristic to Turkey's Balkan policy since the end of the Cold War is that Turkey refrained from taking any unilateral action in the Balkans, even when it, in the eyes of many, seemed necessary to do so in the closing years of the 1980s and at the very beginning of the 1990s, and managed to take a legal-realist stance within an institutional framework.

This paper attempts, first, to sketch out underlying factors which played significant roles in the process of the formation of Turkey's Balkan policy, and second to identify

---

[1] Stephen F. Larrabee, (Ed.), *The Volatile Powder Keg, Balkan Security After the Cold War,* Washington: The American University Press, 1994; J. F. Brown, "Turkey: Back to the Balkans", Ian O. Lesser and Graham Fuller, (Ed.), *Turkey's New Geopolitics: From the Balkans to Western China,* Boulder: Westview Press, 1993, p.150; Vojtech Mastny, *Turkey between West and East: New Challenges for a Rising Regional Power,* Boulder: Westview Press, 1998.

[2] Cengiz Çandar, "21. Yüzyıla Doğru Türkiye: Tarih ve Jeopolitiğin İntikamı", *Türkiye Günlüğü,* 19 yaz 1992, pp.33-34; Nur Vergin, "Türkiye"nin Kendinden Korkmaması ve Aslına Rücu Etmesi Lazım", *Türkiye Günlüğü,* 19, Yaz 1992, pp.43-46; Cengiz Çandar, "Türkiye, Bosna ve Tarihle Barışmak", *Türkiye Günlüğü,* 1/3 Mart-Nisan 1995, pp.280-285.

and analyze foreign policy strategy taken up by the Turkish governments, and finally to discern continuity and change in Turkey's Balkan policy from 1990 to 2003.

The underlying factors which played significant roles in the process of the formation of the Turkish foreign policy towards the Balkans in the post Cold War years may well be encapsulated as follows:

a) historical legacy and the complex minority problems in the Balkans,
b) the wars, long lasting instabilities and the existence of potential hot spots in the Balkans,
c) the geo-strategic significance of the Balkans; three meeting point,
d) cycles of interventions and the failure of the EU as well as the USA in analyzing sociological realities in the region,
e) a clear, though, provocative appeal of regional and larger powers that Turkey should play larger role in the Balkans and
f) the dual images of Turkey in the Balkans,
g) In the second half of the 1990s, new factors would be added to the above-noted ones, which would have impacts on the formation of overall Turkish foreign policy towards the Balkans: Incorporation of the East European states into Euro-Atlantic structures dominated the agenda and perhaps, the most single determining factor was the decision of the EU to incorporate in the first place East-Central Europe, then South Eastern Europe and finally the Western Balkans, and finally, in the early 2003, a new phenomenon arose as the US/UK, Anglo-American axis, decided to launch an attack on Iraq.

In the closing year of the Cold War, Turkey faced a huge influx of the Turkish minority from Bulgaria to Turkey. In June 1989 some 350 000 people emigrated to Turkey as a result of severe harassment by the Bulgarian officials who had forced the Turkish minority to adopt Bulgarian names instead of their own names as well as illegally confiscating their properties.[3] In view of this tragedy, it appears that the Turkish government under Turgut Özal was shocked. Whether the Özal government contemplated to take unilateral action against these atrocities is not clear for it is not yet revealed the content of initial reaction of the government.[4] What is clear is that the Özal government did not go beyond putting political pressure, trying to get international organizations involved in the problem, thereby gaining time to see how the Gorbachev's reform attempts affect the ruling Zhivkov regime in Bulgaria. Unofficial human right groups, largely led by Muslim Turkish activists, who later would form the Movement for Rights and Freedom (MRF),[5] had already embarked on anti-Zhivkov street demonstrations, which later culminated into a huge demonstration in October 1989, involving large Bulgarian

---

[3] Ali Eminov, *Turkish and Other Muslim Minorities in Bulgaria*, London: Hurst 1997; Ali Dayıoğlu, *Bulgaristan"daki Müslüman-Türk Azınlığı (1878-2000)*, Unpublished PhD Thesis, Ankara: Siyasal Bilgiler Fakültesi, 2002; Hugh Poulton, *The Balkans, Minorities and States in Conflict*, London: Minority Rights Publications, 1993; Hugh Poulton and Suha Taji Farouki, (Ed.), *Muslim Identity and The Balkan State*, London: Hurst,1997.
[4] For an interview with Özal see *Türkiye Günlüğü*, 19, Yaz 1992, pp.14-15.
[5] Nurcan Özgür, *Etnik Sorunların Çözümünde Hak ve Özgürlükler Hareketi*, İstanbul: Der Yayınları, 1999.

citizens. Although such demonstrations did not deliver down fall of the Zhivkov regime, it, nevertheless, put the necessary pressure on the politburo to carry out an intra-party coup in November 1989, opening up a series of changes in the Bulgarian Communist Party leadership, of which the first was replacement of Zhivhov with Mladenov, and finally forcing it to agree on round-table negotiations[6] with the spontaneously emerging opposition, largely led by newly formed United Democratic Forces (UDF) under Zhelyu Zhelev. Zhelev would then be elected as the first non-Communist Party president in August 1990. Zhelev's presidency did not only avert the deepening of the crisis between Turkey and Bulgaria, but it was also a real watershed in the process of normalization of the relations between Turkey and Bulgaria. To show readiness to normalize her relations with Bulgaria, the Turkish government would withdraw a symbolic number of its military forces from the northwestern front.[7]

A number of comments may well be done to see the strategy taken up by the Turkish governments. First and foremost, Turkey did not seek to make use of this crisis to destabilize Bulgaria, though she could have done so, perhaps leading even to further chaos and civil war in Bulgaria as well as regional destabilization. Instead, Turkey tried to single out Bulgaria, taking the issue to every possible, from Western to Islamic, international organizations. In addition, Turkish officials made it clear that Turkey was not interested in territorial revision; thus, once more reinstating her acceptance of the Lausanne Treaty of 1923 and its territorial status quo. This is a clear reference to Turkey's refusal to indulging in neo-Ottomanist policy in the Balkans, though during the Gulf War of 1990-91 some advisors of Özal considered to get indulged in the self-defeating project of making Turkey as a sub-super power-meant sub imperialism. The Turkish officials, particularly bureaucrats of the ministry of foreign affairs and the chief of general staff of the army, were extremely cautious not to upset the balance established during and after the Lausanne Treaty of 1923. Within this framework, the Turkish officials, however, were extremely careful not to see similar harassment of the Turkish and Muslim minorities in the Balkans, who were officially recognized by the treaties but repeatedly mistreated, particularly in Greece. Turkey was also concerned with the possibility of spill over and domino effect of the treatment of the Turkish and Muslim minorities in the region.

By and large, the Turkish policy towards the minority question in the Balkans aimed at preserving the minorities as where they were living and encouraging them to integrate to political and economic structure of the country they were in. It appears that the Turkish policy makers were not interested in, nor is there any convincing evidence, showing Turkey indulging in making use of the minorities as a fifth column. Instead, the Turkish policy makers adopted a strategy to encourage the Turkish minority to get integrated into the country where they were living, however, keeping their cultural, linguistic and religious specifities as distinct from the majority within the existing treaties and in line

---

[6] Joseph Rothschild, *Return to Diversity A Political History of East Central Europe Since World War II*, Second Edition, Oxford: Oxford University Press 1993, pp. 250-253; Ömer E. Lütem and Birgül Demirtaş Coşkun, (Ed.), *Balkan Diplomasisi*, Ankara: Avrasya Stratejik Araştırmalar Merkezi Yayınları, 2001.
[7] Private interview with Doğan Güreş, who was Chief of the Staff of Turkish Military Forces.

with legal institutional frameworks.

There has been a clear systematic coercive policy to remove remnants of Turkish and Muslim minorities since the 1878 in the Balkans, largely at times backed by the Western powers, or largely, ignored by the Western powers even though the world media highlighted that some local powers put pressures on the Turkish minorities in the Balkans. In the first half of the 1990s, the major problem for the Turkish policy makers was how to slow down the rapid immigration of the remnants of Turkish, Muslim and even non-Turkish Muslim minorities, all saw Turkey as a safe heaven in times of crises. In times of stability, Istanbul, İzmir and Bursa are cultural attraction centers for Balkan people. This is partly because Istanbul is the largest metropolitan accommodating different cultures as well as providing legal and illegal jobs and partly, above all, almost every minority group in the Balkans has a relative living in somewhere in Turkey. In a similar fashion, the immigrated Turks have family connections with their relatives living in the Balkans. Memories of the turbulent years from the 1878 War and particularly the Balkan Wars of 1912/13, during which clear ethnic cleansing occurred that the Turks were forcibly removed from the Balkans, are still passed over from generation to generation. The proportion of the sons/daughters of immigrated Turks in bureaucracy, industry, trade, military, intelligentsia and notably musician are not less, who have nostalgias passed over from earlier generation, though let it be clear that they seek no irredentism.[8] The Kemalist version of territorial status quo and citizenship of Turkey seems to be well accepted by them.

In the first half of the 1990s slowing down of rapid immigration from the Balkans was primary concern of the Turkish governments, in the second half of the 1990s the reintegration of the remnants of the Turkish and Muslim minorities to the political, economic and administrative systems, through the newly established multi-party representative democracy, gradually became a significant concern for Turkey. It may well be discerned that the Turkish governments have been encouraging both the sovereign states and minorities in the Balkans to work out a social contract based on civic understanding of citizenship, rather than indulging in provocative support for any kind of harassment and thus separatism. Being one of the essential social forces of democratization, the establishment and survival of civic minority political parties seem to be a promising element for Turkey's quest for the reintegration of Turkish and Muslim minorities to the country they are living in. While many of the sovereign Balkan states saw significance of the establishment and survival of civic minority political parties, all of which contributed to smooth transition from ethnic polarization to political reintegration, the Greek governments have not yet permitted for the materialization of the establishment of such parties, though she is the member of the EU. Legally the Turkish minority is not prevented to set up a minority party, but the 3 percent nationwide threshold by law, de facto, prevents them to set up a Turkish minority party.

Equally pressing problems would come into the agenda as the regime change took

---

[8] A novel of Necati Cumalı, *Viran Dağlar Makedonya 1900*, (Macedonia 1900) is a fantastic expression of such nostalgia as well as reflection of the turbulent years.

place from 1989 onwards in Eastern Europe. The existing dictatorships were fallen down in Poland, Hungary, Czechoslovakia and Bulgaria without bloodshed, while in Romania the regime change took place by a swift bloody clash, assassinating Ceausescu. Even more challenging, more dramatic, multi-dimensional and long lasting series of changes would take place in Yugoslavia. The economic decentralization policies of 1963/64 and the 1974 constitutional reforms surely were steps towards democratic decentralization, but when debts crisis made itself felt from late 1970s onwards, coupled with the death of charismatic leader Tito in 1980, cohesion between the republics rapidly undermined.[9] Tito had offered at least two interwoven ideology and political-administrative system; socialism and equality of different nations under federal political-administrative system. Process of undermining of the both started as early as the debt crisis made itself felt by the end of 1970s during the Tito years and the nationalist leaderships of all of the republics further worked for the weakening of economic and political cohesion between the republics. What Tito had offered to different nations in Yugoslavia was either removed altogether or was reversed by the nationalist leaderships of the republics. By the end of 1980s the decentralized federal administrative system would give way for a discussion of three conflicting proposals; restructuring of Yugoslavia on a confederation, creation of a loose federation and recentralization. While the most developed republics of Yugoslavia; Slovenia and Croatia, advocated the first proposal, the second was proposed by Bosnia-Herzegovina and Macedonia and the third by the Republic of Serbia. In a similar fashion, rhetoric of friendship of people of Yugoslavia would soon be replaced by diversity and nationalism of each republic. By 1991, it seemed to be impossible to keep territorial integrity of Yugoslavia intact. Even worse, Milosevic's idea of establishment of greater Serbia necessarily consolidated counter-nationalism of other republics in Yugoslavia. The competing miscalculations of each republic's leadership and selfish inaction of Western policy makers transformed the crisis into an actual long lasting wars and disintegration, and thus providing an opportunity for local powers to execute the fourth cycles of ethnic-cultural cleansing; the Balkan Wars of 1912/13, the WW I, WWII and the post Cold War. Yugoslavia would then be presented as a 'failed state', "representing a collapse of sovereign capacity",[10] and implying that it had to be reconstructed and reshaped in line with the current hegemonic neo-liberal projection of creating a minimal state. This may well be interpreted as a continuation of the Wilsonian principle of fragmented small independent state, this time under hegemonic discourse of neo-liberalism. Regardless of what the Bush administration in 1991 seemingly put forward to keep territorial integrity of Yugoslavia, the Bush administration remained inactive, except for encouraging Mr. Panic, a Serb origin US businessman, to compete against Milosevic in an election. This, indeed, meant working in the hands of Milosevic because Mr. Panic was regarded by Serbs as an outsider to be transplanted into the politics in Yugoslavia. Such poor sociological analysis would not only help consolidating

---

[9] Selver Buldanlıoğlu, *Dismemberment of Yugoslavia and the Emergence of New Interventionism*, Unpublished MSc Thesis, Ankara: Middle East Technical University, 2003, pp.10-31.
[10] Susan L. Woodword, "Failed States, Warlordism and "Tribal" Warfare", http//www.nwc.navy.mil/press/default.htm, accessed 15 December 2003.

nationalism and counter-nationalism in Yugoslavia, as did so, but it also would mean helping in the hands of Milosevic. Mr. Panic lost the competition against Milosevic and soon after he was swept away from the politics. Equally poor argument was proposed by the EC; a commission would assess whether aspirant republics were eligible to be recognized as independent state or not.[11] In times of actual conflicts, such an assessment would not only be impossible, but it would also be unwise for a reason that those who might fail meeting the EC's criteria for recognition might well become a target of aggression. Germany's unilateralist strategy of early recognition of Slovenia and Croatia was not the cause of dismemberment, but it precipitated the dismemberment, a month later EC followed suit, and in fact it was an early signal of how the EC and then the EU would treat the whole region; a 'perfect laboratory'. Equally worse practice of the Western powers was the treatment of Milosevic and the warlords. Suffice it to give two examples; Milosevic was for a long time treated as a recognized actor to negotiate, to agree and even to secure his signature in order to have the Dayton Accord concluded, though there had been sufficient evidence to blame him for atrocities and war crimes. Similarly, Milosevic met with Holbrook of the USA and signed agreement with him to solve the Kosovo problem in October 1998. Milosevic would, two years later, be arrested one day before the Serbian constitutional court took a decision about whether to hand him over to the War Crime Tribunal in The Hague, and was taken by the US Special Forces in consultation with Zoran Djndic, Prime Minister of Serbia, in return for 1.2 billion US $, to The Hague for a trial of being War Criminal. Similarly, Karadzic of Serbs of Bosnia had not been invited to the London Conference of 1992 as an official actor, but he was then invited to the conference by Hurd, British minister of foreign affairs and Eagleburger, acting secretary of state of the USA, thereby recognizing him as an official actor to be negotiated.[12] Even worse is; while he was wanted as suspect of War Criminal, Karadzic met several times with the NATO commander during the War in Bosnia-Herzegovina.

The geo-strategic location of the Balkans is a significant factor for the Turkish foreign policy in a larger context.[13] The dismemberment of Yugoslavia and the follow up developments posed a few problems on the Turkish foreign policy towards the Balkans. First, Turkey had to take a position whether and when she would recognize the aspirant republics as independent states. The Turkish government decided to recognize all the republics as independent states in consultation and coordination together with the regional governments.[14] Unlike Germany, Turkey did not want to take a unilateral decision to

---

[11] Marc Weller, "The International Response to the Dissolution of the Socialist Federal Republic of Yugoslavia", *The American Journal of International Law*, 86/3, July 1992, pp.569-607

[12] Mustafa Türkeş, "Bosna-Hersek Problemi: Londra Konferansı (1992) ve Siyasi Sonuçları", *Prof. Abdurrahman Çaycıya Armağan*, Ankara: Hacettepe Üniversitesi, 1995 pp.469-482.

[13] Duygu Bazoğlu Sezer, "Implications for Turkey's Relations with Western Europe", *The Implications of the Yugoslav Crisis for Western Europe's Foreign Relations*, WEU Chaillot Papers, 17, October 1994; see also Ali Hikmet Alp and Mustafa Türkeş, "The Balkans in Turkey's Security Environment", *Turkish Review of Balkan Studies*, 6, Annual 2001, pp.123-144.

[14] Şule Kut, "Turkish Diplomatic Initiatives for Bosnia-Hercegovina", Günay Göksu-Özdoğan and Kemali Sayıbaşılı (Ed.), *Balkans A Mirror of the New International Order*, Istanbul: Eren Yayıncılık, 1995,

recognize independence of the republics because Turkey's dual image might be exploited by larger as well as regional powers. In a similar fashion, in view of the aggression carried out by the Serbs against Bosnians, Hikmet Çetin, Turkish minister of foreign affairs, argued that there was a need to take a multilateral action under umbrella of the UN. Turkey did not wish to take a unilateral action, though some provocatively asked Turkey to take a unilateral action against the aggressor as part of her historical responsibility. What is more is that Turkey played a significant role in channeling financial aid of the Islamic countries within an international framework.[15] All these indicate the fact that Turkey committed herself to multilateralism and legality within the framework of international organizations. Of course, this process was not easy because there were large numbers of Balkan immigrants in Turkey, putting pressure on the Turkish government to be more active as well as, if possible, a unilateral action against the aggressors and that the critics of the government's foreign policy followed suit pushing the government to make use of the crises to turn towards neo-Ottomanist policies, perhaps not in the form of actual irredentism, but as part of Turkey's hegemonial requirements. Erbakan of the prominent Islamists expressed it saying, "Süleyman Demirel, Prime Minister, is a fake Süleyman, if he had been Süleyman the Magnificent, he would have forcibly gone to Bosnia-Herzegovina up until now." Interestingly, Jeremy Paxman of news speaker of the BBC 2, would ask in the same manner to Hikmet Çetin, minister of foreign affairs of Turkey, "When do you think Turkey will take action unilaterally? Is it not your historical responsibility to act as protector of the Muslims in Bosnia?" Such questions, indeed, show dual images of Turkey in the Balkans. If the Turkish governments acted within the framework of legality and international organizations, Turkey was questioned as not doing enough, if Turkey advocated any proposal, then Turkey was suspected of working for regaining of her supremacy in the Balkans. Regional actors, particularly Greece, presented the case as if Turkey working for the establishment of creating a new networks of alliances of Muslim countries and minorities, as known the 'Muslim belt'. Involvement of Greek irregulars to support Milosevic's atrocities against the victims is presented as if they were working against the establishment of Turkish hegemony, however, the Greek policy, in fact, contributed to the atrocities as well as instabilities in the region. Even more, whole discussion was translated into as if a war between Greek-led Orthodox World and Turkish-led Muslim World might have erupted.[16] Some tended to argue that this was a third Balkan War. The Western media went beyond this and was quick to propose that there would soon be two axes in the region; Orthodox axis, composed of Greece, Serbia and Russia, and the Turkish-led axis, composed of Turkey, Bulgaria, Macedonia, Bosnia-Herzegovina and Albania. All of

---

pp.295-315.
[15] Kut, "Turkish Diplomatic Initiatives for Bosnia-Hercegovina", p.298.
[16] See, Misha Glenny, "Heading off War in the Southern Balkans", *Foreign Affairs*, May-June 1995, pp. 99-108; Duncan Perry, "Macedonia: A Balkan Problem and a European Diemma", *RFERL Report*, 1/25, June 1992, pp.35-36; Michael W. Weithmann, "Macedonia: The Land between Four Fires", *Aussen Politik*, 44/3, 1993, pp.270-271; Stefan Troebst, "Macedonia: Powder Keg Defused", *RFERL Report*, 3/4, January 1994, pp.33-34.

these lacked deep analyses of the sociological realities in the region. It is true that neither Turkey wished to see Greece, or any other power, making use of the crisis, to become a hegemonic power in the Balkans, nor did Greece wish to see Turkey gaining ground in the region, but these foreign policy considerations did not mean either that she was ready or capable to take advantage of the crisis so as to establish her own supremacy in the region. This does not mean that they had no intention of consolidating their positions. Of course, both Greece and Turkey worked to consolidate their advantageous positions in the regional politics; while Greece energetically made use of her EU membership to consolidate her position, even sometimes contributing to prevent solution, and in the case of Macedonia problem, went to blockade the EU aids, as well as imposing economic and political embargo to Macedonia, thereby strangulating them in order to make Macedonians to change their name from the Republic of Macedonia to somewhat absurd and pejorative connotation as Former Yugoslav Republic of Macedonian (Yugoslavia legally disappeared now!). As for Turkey, she supported any formula contributing to the rapid stabilization of the region, for otherwise, all the Turkish minorities as well as Muslim and non-Turkish minorities turned their face to Turkey seeing her as a safe heaven. In order to contribute to stabilization of the Balkans, Turkey made her military forces to contribute IFOR, SFOR and supported regional security initiative of Balkan Multinational Peace Force. At this point, it should be underlined that enduring stability and security in the Balkans is in the interest of Turkey. One of the reasons is already noted above. Equally important is the fact that actual conflicts and long lasting instabilities are undermining Turkey's existing advantageous position in the region. Conflicts and crises are not offering Turkey to consolidate her position regardless of the unsubstantiated rhetoric of neo-Ottomanism. To show this categorically, suffice it to say that the dismemberment of Yugoslavia resulted in Turkey's loss of one of stable ally, who had no ambition of undermining Turkey's Balkan policy.[17] When it became reality that Yugoslavia dismembered, then Turkey had to reestablish her bilateral relations with each of the independent small-sized states, whose relations with immediate neighboring countries were troublesome. Turkey had to play a role of honest mediator to achieve regional stability.[18] Since Turkey had dual images and since Greece as well as many poor intellectuals approached any initiative proposed by Turkey as suspected to hidden agenda, Turkey had to be too cautious in her endeavors to achieve enduring stability in the Balkans. This is why Turkey consciously supported institutional and multilateral initiatives. While the West, particularly European powers, interpreted the conflict in Bosnia-Herzegovina as not big enough to threaten the existing Western security

---

[17] Mustafa Türkeş, "Türkiye Avrupa İlişkilerinde Balkanlar Faktörü ve Yeni Eğilimler", Atila Eralp (Ed.), *Türkiye ve Avrupa*, Ankara: İmge Yayınları, 1997, pp.305-349.
[18] Şule Kut, "Turkish Policy toward the Balkans", Alan Makovsky and Sabri Sayarı (Ed.) *Turkey's New World Changing Dynamics in Turkish Foreign Policy*, Washington: The Washington Institute for Near East Policy, 2000, pp. 74-91. İlhan Uzgel, "The Balkans: Turkey's Stabilizing Role", Barry M Rubin (Ed.), *Turkey in World Politics: An Emerging Multiregional Power*, Boulder: Lynn Rienner Publishers, 2001, p.59.

structure,[19] thus was satisfied with a strategy based on containment of the conflict, Turkey considered it a cause for long term instability in the region, therefore she urged particularly the international organizations to seriously consider about stopping the violence. The strategy taken by the Turkish governments may well be defined as in the first place Turkey tried to normalize her relations with newly independent states, second, opted for multilateral initiatives, and third, priority is given to regional cooperation whether it be three laterals or quadruple. The best example to illustrate this is the fact that Turkey supported the three lateral cooperation scheme composed of Turkey, Bulgaria and Romania, and gave her consent to cooperation between Greece, Bulgaria and Romania.[20] In similar line, Turkey repeatedly argued that the Kosovo problem could be settled by a regional cooperation, trying to persuade Yugoslavia to extend autonomy for Kosovo, and even went some way to substantiate it in the 1997 Antalya meeting of Heads of State and Governments of South East European Cooperation Process, which is truly composed of regional actors. It is clear that Turkey pursued a similar strategy with regard to the Kosovo problem: In the first place, Turkey sought to see a diplomatic solution, giving her consent to various proposals, ranging from the nineteen seventy four plus formula to Kosovo's accession into the Yugoslav federation as the third republic, but the Milosevic regime refused it before hand in an irrational way. When it became impossible to stop atrocities in Kosovo, Turkey gave her reluctant support to illegal NATO attack on Yugoslavia in March 1999. The NATO intervention might well be considered as not the best way to address the problem; nevertheless, it did stop the violence, but by no means solved the Kosovo problem. Its status still remains unclear: "The deliberate ambiguity". This NATO intervention did not solve the problem; however, it transformed the problem from one form to another one. Moreover, it is likely to be one of the sources for long-term instability in the region. Evidently recognition of an independent Kosovo is as difficult as keeping it under the protectorateship of international organizations.

As to the recent cycle of crisis in Macedonia, it appears that the Turkish policy is based on keeping territorial integrity of Macedonia and ensuring that the pressures applied by both Macedonians and Albanians should not squeeze the Turkish minority. Therefore, the Turkish government seems to have urged both Albanian and Macedonian opinion makers to form dialogue mechanisms to settle the problem. It is obvious that the Macedonia problem may have a domino effect in the Balkans since Macedonia is surrounded by the hostile four wolves: Greece, Bulgaria, Serbia and Albania.

Another significant problematic would be on the agenda of the Turkish governments on the morrow of the Cold War. As Soviet Union was dismantled, Warsaw Pact and COMECON abolished, the East European states began to incorporate into the Euro-Atlantic structures. The Western organizations, likewise, launched reforms to accommodate Eastern Europe into the Euro-Atlantic structures. As early as 1991 NATO

---

[19] For a discussion see John R. Lampe and Daniel N. Nelson (Ed.) *East European Security Reconsidered*, Washington: The Woodrow Wilson Center Press, 1993.
[20] Mustafa Türkeş, "Geçiş Sürecinde Dış Politika Öncelikleri: Bulgaristan Örneği", Mustafa Türkeş ve İlhan Uzgel (Ed.) *Türkiye'nin Komşuları*, Ankara: İmge Yayınları, 2002, pp.171-210.

made it clear its enlargement towards the East Europeans.[21] In 1993 the EU also set its Copenhagen criteria for new membership. In view of such a given framework and a clear message, East European states took their positions. As early as 1991 the Visegrad states, composed of Czechoslovakia, Hungary and Poland, formed an initiative to distinguish themselves from the rest of Eastern Europe. In the same year the CEI (Central European Initiative) was formed with the same objective. The War in Yugoslavia and the regional initiatives such as Visegrad and CEI marked the beginning of reconfiguration of the Former Eastern Europe. The Former Eastern Europe would then be divided into as East Central Europe, South Eastern Europe and the Western Balkans. From now onwards, they would compete against each other to meet the Copenhagen criteria, though it would become clear that application of the criteria would differ from East Central European states to South East European states, depending on the attitudes and strategic contemplation of influential major powers. South East European countries were to wait until Helsinki summit, while East Central European countries had been given a clear message long before. In the Madrid summit of NATO, Czech Republic, Hungary and Poland were named to be member of the NATO, while MAP (Membership Action Plan) was worked out for South East European countries. They were to be named as member of NATO as late as Prague summit of November 2002.[22] As to the Western Balkans, the wars and a decade long instabilities did not only put them off entering among the list of potential aspirant countries, but provided perhaps the best opportunity for the other East European countries to distinguish themselves. The Western Balkans was to be offered only an empty and disfunctioning Stability Pact. It is true that all of the former East European countries were given a clear green message to be incorporated into the Euro-Atlantic structures as early as 1991; however, the way in which the former East European countries are being taken into the process of accession deepened and widened the already existing gaps between them, thus leading to reconfiguration of the Former Eastern Europe into three sub-categories: East-Central Europe, South Eastern Europe and the Western Balkans.[23]

In view of the quest for incorporation into Euro-Atlantic structures, it may well be said that in the first half of the 1990s Turkey pursued a policy of wait and see, and then as being a member of NATO Turkey would give her support to all and particularly Bulgaria and Romania to be incorporated into the NATO. The Balkan states' quest for NATO and EU memberships was interwoven. The political elite of the Balkan states argue that the

---

[21] Michael Mihalka, "Creeping Toward the East", *Transition*, 1/1, 1995, pp.80-85; Douglas L. Clarke, "Uncomfortable Partners", *Transition*, 15 February 1995, pp.27-31; Robert B. McCalla, "NATO's Persistence After the Cold War", *International Organization*, 50/3, 1996, pp.445-475; Lawrence S. Kaplan, *The Long Entanglement-NATO's Fifty Years*, USA: 1999; Robert E. Hunter, "Maximizing NATO: A Relevant Alliance Knows How to Reach", *Foreign Affairs*, May/June 1999, pp.190-203; Michael E. Brown, "Minimalist NATO: A Wise Alliance Knows When to Retrench", *Foreign Affairs* May/June 1999, pp.205-218.

[22] Mustafa Türkeş, "NATO Bağlamında ABD-Türkiye İlişkilerinde Devamlılık ve Değişim", Faruk Sönmezoğlu (Ed.), *Türk Dış Politikasının Analizi*, 3. Baskı, İstanbul: Der Yayınları 2004.

[23] Mustafa Türkeş, "The Double Process: Transition and Integration and Its Impact on the Balkans", Petar Emil-Mitev (Ed.), *Towards Non-violence and Dialogue Culture in Southeast Europe*, Sofia: Ivan Hadjysky The Institute for Social Values and Structures Publications, 2004, pp.13-28.

NATO and the EU membership are not only of a political issue, but it may also contribute to economic stability and overall security in the region,[24] which overlapped the objective of Turkey. Being a member of NATO, Turkey can play a significant role in the EU, like the others. Turkey is subject to political decision of the EU as well as meeting normative criteria formulated and imposed by the EU at the Copenhagen EU Council meeting of 1993. Hence, the most problematic issue is the fact that the EU appears to be a moving object for the aspirant countries, while for the already member states Europeanization is yet to be started off.

In the early 2003, a new phenomena arose as the US/UK, Anglo-American axis, decided to launch an attack on Iraq on the basis of unsubstantiated claims that Saddam Hussein had biological and chemical weapons to be used against neighboring countries; therefore, Eastern and Central European countries were forced to make a choice between the two axes;[25] while the US/UK wanted to attack on Iraq without necessary UN Security Council decision on the one hand, and the staunch anti-war advocate of the German government under Schroder, together with half-hearted French anti-war opposition, though it should be kept in mind that the latter was against early war, thus tried to postpone it, while the former went as far as basing his 2002 election strategy on the anti-war campaign. In view of such a clear-cut stance of the US, the East European governments were forced to show their color. The decision of the Eastern and Central European countries were made known on 30 January 2003, supporting the US/UK axis,[26] while the Turkish parliament, on 1 March 2003, would refuse to allow some 62 000 strong US troops to be stationed in Turkey, though Turkey had earlier permitted the US to use Turkey's air corridor to attack on Iraq. In view of this new factor, the newly formed Turkish government under Prime Minister, Erdogan, has not yet touched upon this significant phenomenon. Nor is there any tangible sign that the Erdogan government establishes a linkage between Turkey's overall policy towards Eastern Europe, EU and the emerging situation of East European states' search for a dual guarantee policy; ensuring soft security from the EU and seeking defense guarantee from the US/NATO. It is unlikely that the Erdogan government of Turkey may change the overall Turkish foreign policy strategy towards the Balkans.

Conclusion

The unquestionable historical legacy left by the Ottoman Imperial period, with which Turkey is often too easily and superficially identified, is felt even today. The removal of the Ottoman Empire from the Balkans was not only so bloody and tragic, but also threatening for the future because while retreating from the Balkans, she had to leave substantial minority, who were apparently mistreated and systematically forced to leave for Turkey. Even so, ethno-cultural connections between Turkey and the remnants of the

---

[24] Türkeş, "Geçiş Sürecinde Dış Politika Öncelikleri: Bulgaristan Örneği", p.199.
[25] Peter Ford, "New Europe's Iraq squeeze Frantic jockeying at the UN over possible war with Iraq puts Poland and other Eastern European nations in a tough spot", *The Christian Science Monitor*, 11 March 2003; Ian Traynor, "Poland Snubs EU by buying US jets" *The Guardian*, 19 April 2003; Ian Traynor, "New Europe gets shock lesson in realpolitik", *The Guardian*, 28 April 2003; Elaine Sciolino, "4-Nation Plan for Defense of Europe", *The New York Times*, 30 April 2003.
[26] Declaration of the 8 Countries, see *London Times*, 30 January 2003.

Turkish and Muslim minorities did not disappear; the social interaction is still evident on both sides. The strong solidarity between Turkey and the Muslim populations in the Balkans, who are victimized by all accounts during the recent long lasting wars and crisis, has been often misinterpreted by some of both the Western and Turkish analysts as being an instrumental to reinstate Turkey's supremacy in the Balkans. The actual foreign policy pursued by the Turkish governments falsified them. The Kemalist foreign policy, not inclined to irredentism and based on sovereign equality in the Balkan states, was constantly reproduced and applied by the Turkish governments of the 1990s in an institutional framework.

Turkey's close interest in the Balkans is not only resulted from the historical legacy, but the geo-strategic location of the Balkans as well as the latter is a significant factor for the Turkish foreign policy in a larger context. The Balkans occupies a pivotal position between Western Europe and Eurasia, making it important for the USA, Europe, Russia and Ukraine, as well as for Turkey, which is a regional and Eurasian actor at the same time. While the region's conventional military importance faded away as the Cold War ended, it is by no means its geo-strategic significance disappeared at all. The Balkans offers complimentary energy routes, and it is the three meeting point between the presence of the US, the EU and the Russian Federation in the long term. Thus, Turkey's security interests in the region cannot be limited to conventional military analysis but have to be conceived in a larger political and economic context. This requires support for the political and economic stability of the region, prevention of any hostile hegemonic, countering of hostile rivals, protection of the Turkish minorities and of the cultural heritage. Ensuring unhindered access towards Western Europe is of vital importance. Obviously, these objectives require a positive and active involvement of the regional states and a great deal of institutional support of international organizations.

Turkey has been a major party to and a significant player in the Balkans. Turkey's overall policy towards the Balkans, it may well be stated, was shaped in accordance with the following analysis and objectives; a) the establishment of enduring security and stability, b) ensuring prevention of any single regional power to become hegemonic in the region, c) slowing down of the migration from the Balkans to Turkey and if possible preserving the ethno-political status quo in the region, d) trying not to be dragged into Muslim versus Orthodox collusion as well as playing a constructive role between the West and the Islamic countries, e) supporting the quest of the Balkan states' incorporation into Euro-Atlantic structures.

Turkey's Balkan policy is continually formed by complex interactions between quest for achieving enduring stability and security, and the swift, complex systemic as well as circumstantial larger changes as well as inter and intra-state possessive and relational power changes in the Balkans. Characteristic to Turkish foreign policy towards the Balkans is the fact that Turkey consciously refrained from taking any unilateral action in the Balkans, even when it, in the eyes of many, seemed necessary to do so in the closing years of the Cold War and in the 1990s. Turkey openly opted for taking a realist-stance within an institutional framework and worked for not to permit any single power becoming a hegemonic power in the region. It may well be commented that Turkey is in favor of keeping the reproduced status quo of the post Cold War sovereign equality in the

Balkans.

It may well be stated that there is a clear continuity in the Turkish foreign policy in the 1990s and 2000s. It is clear that Turkey contributed to political stability in the post Cold War years, particularly not playing on ethno-politics and advocating civic character of national integration and regional cooperation. Even more is the fact that Turkey is one of the significant security and stability providers in the Balkans.

11 The Cyprus Question Between 1974 and 2004 and Its Relation to Turkish Foreign Policy*

Nasuh Uslu

Introduction

The future of Cyprus has always been determined by the outside powers. After being ruled by the Ottomans and the British for centuries, the powers of the Western camps set out the structure of Republic of Cyprus and became its guarantors. Turkey, Greece, the United States, NATO and the European Union are the powers, which will have some kind of impact on a future Cyprus solution. The views and interests of these powers on the Cyprus question also inevitably affect the developments in this important matter. On the other hand, the Cyprus issue is an important factor that will be able to shape the mutual relations among the United States, Greece and Turkey. The interactions between these three powers have importance to the extent that they will take part in the establishment of the new world order. It is, therefore, necessary to analyse the Cyprus question in the context of conflicting and varying interests of the concerned powers. Especially the vital importance of the Cyprus issue for Turkey and the American involvement in the matter has the potential to affect the future of Cyprus. The Turkish side's reaction to the Greek and Cypriot-Greek side's co-operation with the European Union in shaping the future Cyprus state representing the whole island and the American intervention in this development might create repercussions not only for Cyprus, but also for the region and the whole world. In this article, the recent events related to the Cyprus issue will be studied with constant references to views, interests and interventions of the concerned powers. Especially the Turkish and American actions and approaches will be the main focus of the study.

The Background

During the Ottoman Empire period the Turks had lost Cyprus to Britain in a tricky way. The founders of the Republic of Turkey, too, surrendered the island with the Treaty of Lausanne to Britain officially as a part of their policies aiming at completing internal reforms and ending their problems with the European countries. With some help from the British and the Americans, Turkish rulers managed in a sense to regain Cyprus through the London and Zurich Agreements in 1960; this is still considered one of the major

---

* Nasuh Uslu is author of *"The Cyprus Question as an Issue of Turkish Foreign Policy and Turkish-American Relations 1959-2003"*, New York: Nova Science Publishers, Inc., 2003. This article has been prepared in the light of some parts of this book. For a detailed discussion of the subject please see this comprehensive book by Nova Science Publishers.

achievements of Turkish foreign policy-makers in the history of the Turkish Republic. The fact that Turkish Cypriots, whose rate within the total population of Cyprus dropped to 18 percent because of the policies of the Ottoman Empire and the British administration and under the effect of other factors, became co-founders of the Republic of Cyprus and were allowed to share the rule with the Greek Cypriots was really a big success for the Turkish side.

However, after the Greek Cypriots ousted the Turks from the state mechanism by resorting to force in 1963, the Cyprus issue became one of the most important problems of Turkish foreign policy and Turkey's relations with big powers as well as its main foreign policy tendencies stayed under the influence of this matter. In 1964 Turkey could not intervene in Cyprus to protect the lives of Turkish Cypriots by using its rights given by the international treaties because of the pressures of the United States and the other Western countries. But there were also other facts showing that accusing the others was not a right attitude. In 1964, Turkey did not have the ability to launch a military intervention in Cyprus and Prime Minister İsmet İnönü tried to ensure the American opposition to such a Turkish intervention in order to be able to explain the non-intervention to his people. Turkey itself recognised the resolution of the UN Security Council in March 1964 on Cyprus, which brought about the international recognition of Greek Cypriots' administration as the official representative of Cyprus. Turkey also did not spend serious efforts in the 1964-1974 period to reverse this resolution and it did not bring up the issue in international meetings to express its own views seriously. It was also Turkey, which took into consideration the American-sponsored proposals, called double enosis and suggesting the unification of Cyprus with Greece in return for some kind of concession to Turkey. But Turkey insisted that a territory which will be large enough to meet Turkish security needs should be put under Turkish sovereignty. Given these negative points, the coup carried out by the Greek Cypriots on 15 July 1974 was a golden opportunity for Turkey. If the coup had not occurred, Turkey would not have been able to intervene in the island militarily and Greek Cypriots would not have agreed to accept a solution of the Cyprus problem based on federation. It was highly likely that inter-communal talks would have continued without bringing any concrete results and the situation of Turkish Cypriots, who did not attract any sympathy of the international public opinion in spite of all their sufferings and miseries, would have been forgotten totally.

The Turkish intervention in 1974 assured the security of Turkish Cypriots and made it possible for them to establish their own autonomous administration. The failure of the Americans to show an enforcing reaction to the Turkish action played to the hands of the Turkish rulers. But it should not be forgotten that the Americans did not show a severe reaction to the Cypriot coup, too. Moreover, the American administration was about to collapse because of the Watergate scandal, and therefore, it was not in the position to launch a serious initiative in foreign policy. The general American policy in this period was to avoid taking actions which would bring about losing Turkey and Greece and to accept the de facto situation, the separation of Cypriot Turks and Greeks from each other. The American embargo, which was implemented against Turkey from the early 1975, was mostly a product of a struggle between the American administration and the Congress. For the American Congress, the embargo was a golden opportunity to teach a lesson to the administration, which abused and went beyond its original authorities since 1969. With the implementation of the embargo, a troublesome period began for Turkey, in which the Cyprus issue became the main problem and menace of Turkish foreign policy. The embargo also made the Cyprus issue a constant trouble point in Turkish-American relations, and Turkey was put under pressure by the American authorities in this matter.

The 1974-1990 Period

In the aftermath of the 1974 events, the American administration continued to recognise the Greek government as the sole representative of Cyprus, and the USA and the other members of the UN Security Council accepted the constitutional demands of the Turkish Cypriots to join the Cypriot administration in a partnership project.[1] Although the United States did not favour the Cypriot Greek side openly in the Cyprus issue, Turkey came under the heavy American pressure. When Turkish rulers were demanded to initiate some positive developments in the Cyprus issue in return for the removal of the embargo, they felt the pressure of the Turkish public not to act in this direction. Even if they wanted to fulfil demands of the Americans, they could not have done so because in this case they would have given the impression that they were retreating under pressure.

In the American elections in 1976, the Cyprus issue became an important matter attracting the attention of the whole American nation. After the Nixon and Ford administrations failed to reverse the partition of Cyprus, the candidate of the Democrat Party for the presidency, Jimmy Carter, stated that a positive approach should be adopted toward the Cyprus issue. The unexpected demonstration of interest by the American people in the matter led President Carter to send former defence minister Clark Clifford to Ankara, Athens and Cyprus to find out the realities on the Cyprus question and to make contribution to a peaceful solution. In this way, Carter tried to prevent weakening NATO's southern flank and to reduce the tensions between Turkey and Greece.[2] The proposal of Clifford was that the disagreements in the Aegean, Cyprus and making a defence agreement with Turkey should be dealt with collectively. In 1977, the representatives of the Greek Cypriots and the Turkish Cypriots, Denktash and Clerides, signed a document, which demonstrated that they agreed on important basic points. But the severe Greek Cypriot reaction to the American initiative in 1978 led the American authorities to take a relatively passive attitude on the matter in the following years. Meanwhile, the meeting of American State Secretary Cyrus Vance in 1978 with the leader of the Turkish Cypriots, Rauf Denktash, as the successor of Dr. Fazil Kutchuk, who had been elected as the vice-president of the Republic of Cyprus, showed that the Americans

---

[1] James H. Wolfe, "United States and the Cyprus Conflict", Kjell Skjelsbaek (ed.), *The Cyprus Conflict and the Role of the United Nations*, Norwegian Institute of International Affairs, Kasım 1988, p.51.
[2] Brian Mandell, "The Cyprus Conflict: Explaining Resistance to Resolution", Norma Salem (ed.), *Cyprus: A Regional Conflict and its Resolution*, New York: St. Martin's Press, 1992, p.213.

might extend some kind of recognition to the Turkish Cypriot side.[3]

In the following period, the Cyprus question lost its position as a matter having the potential to affect the American elections for the presidency. Beginning with the Reagan administration, it was no longer an issue, which the American president would consider worthwhile to attract his attention and to affect its development. The Cyprus issue was handled and policies were produced about it not by high-level policy makers, but by experts and special envoys. The Reagan administration evaluated in a narrow regional context and never saw it a first-class problem that would concern the American interests seriously. As a parallel to this American approach, the American and Soviet representatives did not consider the Cyprus issue when they met to deal with regional problems.[4] Reagan did not choose to resort to personal diplomacy by assigning the task of mediating for the Cyprus issue to a special envoy. But State Secretary Alexander Haig created a permanent desk within the State Department, which would deal with the Cyprus issue: the special co-ordinator for Cyprus. Among the remarkable American diplomats who served as the special co-ordinator were Reginald Bartholomew, Christian Chapman, Richard Haass, James Wilkinson and Thomas Weston. At the beginning, the special co-ordinators were interested only in the Cyprus question, but as the matter receded to secondary importance these diplomats began to undertake other tasks.[5]

American Special Co-ordinator for Cyprus Richard Haass was opposed to launching dramatic initiatives on the Cyprus issue. In his opinion, the United States should take modest actions to normalise the relations between the two communities in Cyprus and should focus on the confidence building measures. The Turkish side's proclamation of its own independent republic on 15 November 1983 constituted a radical development contradicting the American attitude of recognising the Greek Cypriot government as the official representative of Cyprus. The White House expressed its displeasure over the Turkish action and the State Department prevented the recognition of the new state by the Muslim countries by warning them one by one. However, the American reaction did not amount to taking forceful measures and American authorities continued to give support to holding negotiations between the two communities to find a solution.[6] In the period following 1985, the apparent war between the American administration and the Congress on the Cyprus issue began to be replaced by the opinion that the two organs of the state should launch joint actions to persuade the parties to the Cyprus problem.[7]

The proximity talks in 1984-1986 were considered especially by American Secretary of State George Shultz as the best and last chance for the sides to reach a solution.[8] As a result of this thinking American President Reagan sent a special letter on 22 November 1984 to Turkish President Kenan Evren, calling for serious efforts to reach a speedy

---

[3] Wolfe, "United States and the Cyprus Conflict", pp.52, 53, 55.
[4] Ellen Laipson, "The United States and Cyprus: Past Policies, Current Concerns", Salem (ed.), *Cyprus*, pp.96, 97.
[5] Wolfe, "United States and the Cyprus Conflict", p.56.
[6] Mandell, "The Cyprus Conflict...", p.215.
[7] Laipson, "The United States and Cyprus...", p. 96.
[8] Mandell, "The Cyprus Conflict...", p.216.

solution in Cyprus. In Reagan's opinion, the ultimate aim should be to establish a federal republic, which would end the partition of the island. It was reported that the apparent American pressures led the Turkish rulers to persuade the Turkish Cypriots in moderating their attitude toward the Greek Cypriots.[9] In this conjunction, the American administration promised the Turkish rulers that it would end its pressures if they accepted the UN written proposals on 17 January 1985 and 29 March 1986, the Turkish side gave its approval to the documents, but the Americans directed their pressures toward the Turks again instead of criticising the Greek Cypriots, who rejected the proposals.[10] The Turkish side was further alienated in September 1986 because of the treatment of their leader by the Americans. In contrast to their attitude in the aftermath of the 1974 events, which considered the Turkish Cypriots as the co-partners of the Cypriot states, the Americans now avoided giving the slightest impression that they recognised the Turkish Cypriot administration. However, the Turkish Cypriot bureau in New York, which was opened in spite of intensive Greek opposition, was able to become one of the players of the diplomatic game. While the Turkish Cypriot representative established contact with American authorities and foreign missions in New York, Harold Rhode, an official of Pentagon did not hesitate in visiting this bureau.[11]

In the 1988 American presidential elections, an American having Greek origin won the candidacy for the presidency for the first time, but the Cyprus issue never became an important matter for discussion between the candidates. The organisers of the Dukakis campaign issued a statement on 11 May 1988, calling for implementing principles of law in Cyprus and withdrawal of the foreign troops from the island, but Dukakis did not see it necessary to make another statement on the Cyprus issue.[12] This apparent American indifference to Cyprus would begin to change with the successes achieved in the solution of regional problems in 1988.

The Strategic Factor

Before passing to the analysis of events in the 1990s, it will be useful to study the relationship of the Cyprus issue with the Cold War. The Americans always approached to the Cyprus question from the perspective of their global leadership in the context of their global interests and security. Their main concern was to prevent the outbreak of a war between the two NATO allies, namely Greece and Turkey, and thus to hinder the weakening of NATO's southern flank. The Americans had to intervene in the Cyprus crises not to allow them to bring strategic losses for the United States and the Western bloc.[13] The non-aligned policies pursued by Greek Cypriot leader Makarios and the

---

[9] Glen D. Camp, "Island Impasse: Peacemaking on Cyprus 1980-1994", Vangelis Calotychos (ed.), *Cyprus and Its People: Nation, Identity and Experience in an Unimaginable Community 1955-1997*, Boulder: Westview Press, 1998, p.143.

[10] Sabahattin İsmail, *Kıbrıs Üzerine Bildiriler*, Lefkoşa: CYREP, 1998, p.287.

[11] Wolfe, "United States and the Cyprus Conflict", p. 52, Yılmaz Polat, *Washington Entrikaları*, İstanbul: Milliyet, 1999, pp.150-152.

[12] Wolfe, "United States and the Cyprus Conflict", p.58, Laipson, "The United States and Cyprus...", p.96.

[13] John Roper, "The West and Turkey: Varying Roles, Common Interests", *The International Spectator*, vol. 34, No. 1, January-March 1999, pp.93, 101.

strength of the Cypriot communist party, AKEL, concerned the Americans greatly. The Cold War mentality of the Americans required that the Cyprus question should be resolved in accordance with interests of the USA, NATO, Greece and Turkey. Makarios could not be allowed to make Russian influential on the Cyprus issue. He should be irritated or removed from power by the Greek junta. The most suitable solution could be the unification of the island with Greece in return for some concessions to Turkey. In this way, Cyprus could be opened to the unrestricted use of NATO and the United States. When the Greek Cypriot opposition and the Turkish insistence on the size of the territory that would be given to Turkey prevented the success of this scheme, the Americans tried to keep the issue under control with its present situation not to allow an outbreak of Greek-Turkish war on the matter.[14] If the Cold War conditions did not exist, the enmity of the non-aligned bloc toward the West did not help Makarios and the hands of the Americans were not bound with the Cold War restrictions, a solution could have been reached in Cyprus on the basis of granting limited autonomy to the Turkish Cypriots.[15]

The strategic importance of Cyprus still affects the approach of the Americans toward the Cyprus issue and their approach, in turn, has the potential to affect the future of the problem. Cyprus is located at the crossroads of the routes reaching the Middle East, which is the most important and the most troublesome region of the world. It has the potential to serve as a suitable base to intervene in serious developments in the region. The Gulf War demonstrated that the military bases which will be established on Cyprus, the ports, which will provide great help to the American navy and weapon systems and reconnaissance facilities, which will be installed on the island, will have great importance for the United States. The Americans use at the moment the sophisticated military support and intelligence gathering stations in the south of the island, which serves security interests of the Western world in the eastern Mediterranean, the Middle East and the northern Africa. There is also antenna of the US Federal Broadcast Information Service on Cyprus. These installations, which are the property of the British, had no task related to NATO, but they serve the American and Western interests with their capacity of gathering electronic intelligence.[16] In the past, Makarios, who pursued non-aligned policies, permitted the use of these bases by the US forces for such purposes as minesweeping operations or high-altitude intelligence gathering flights.[17] The Americans naturally do not want to endanger these facilities by pursuing harmful policies. Even it can be said that since it is the Greek Cypriot side, which provides various services to the USA, the Americans do not act completely in accordance with the principle of equality by favouring the Greek Cypriots.[18] However, in the last analysis, the American authorities attribute more importance to their relations with Greece and Turkey and do not want to alienate these two countries from their Cyprus policies. In this context, the USA is criticised on the ground that it prevents the emergence of more practical and realist

---

[14] Mehmet Hasgüler, *Kıbrıs'ta Enosis ve Taksim Politikalarının Sonu*, İstanbul: İletişim, 2000, p.147.

[15] Monteagle Stearns, *Entangled Allies: US Policy Toward Greece, Turkey and Cyprus*, New York: Council on Foreign Relations Press, 1992, p.17.

[16] Stearns, *Entangled Allies*, pp. 107, 125.

[17] Wolfe, "United States and the Cyprus Conflict", p.48.

[18] Clemenet H. Dodd, *The Cyprus Imbroglio*, Huntingdon: The Eothen Press, 1998, p.116.

choices with its policies based on strategic thinking.[19]

The strategic concerns are also apparent in the American attitude of not pursuing completely anti-Turkish policies and not exercise excessive pressures over Turkey regarding the Cyprus issue.[20] Even in the periods when the Congress applied pressures on Turkey, the American state and defence departments and the National Security Council emphasised that Turkey should not be alienated from the USA by underlying the strategic importance of this country. The end of the Cold War did not reduce this importance, but, on the contrary, Turkey became a strategic partner of the United States in a period in which new threats emerged in the surrounding region of Turkey, concerning the Americans closely. In the opinion of American Deputy Secretary of State Strobe Talbott, US-Turkish relations have even more of a hard-headed geopolitical, strategic rationale in the post Cold War period than during the Cold War.[21] Since the Americans considered Turkey as a base and antidote against radical religious movements and as a democratic, secular model for the regional states and as an ally for Israel, they prevent the total condemnation of Turkey and the enactment of forceful measure against Turkey in the UN Security Council on the Cyprus issue.[22]

Intensive Initiatives and Increasing Tensions on the Cyprus Issue (the early 1990s)

The Background of the Initiatives

In spite of the apparent American inclination toward Turkey in the early post Cold War period, it was not guarantee that the United States would consent to the non-solution of the Cyprus problem eternally and that it would not force Turkey for a solution when it considered the situation suitable. The American pressures on its closest ally, Israel, in the aftermath of the Gulf War to persuade it to make peace with Palestinians showed that the United States might resort to pressure tactics to force its allies to act in a certain way.[23] The Cyprus issue could not be an exception in this regard. While the détente became the dominant phenomenon in the world politics and local problems were solved one by one, the United States would not allow that the Cyprus problem, which was closely related to the Western alliance, would continue to exist and thus to harm the American prestige in the eyes of world public opinion. NATO did not want to see any longer the Cyprus question as a source of discord among the allies, but it preferred to see it as an area of co-operation with its solution as soon as possible. The Greek-Turkish confrontation was one of the most important obstacles to the efforts of increasing NATO's effectiveness and reliability and of consolidating the new world order. It was, therefore, necessary not allow the Cyprus issue to take Turkish-Greek relations as a hostage and to solve this problem in

---

[19] Laipson, "The United States and Cyprus...", p.93, Ronald J. Fisher, "Conclusion: Path Towards a Peaceful Cyprus", Salem, (Ed.), *Cyprus*, p.245.

[20] SİSAV Dış Politika ve Savunma Grubu, *1997 Yılı Sonu İtibariyle Kıbrıs Sorunu*, İstanbul: SİSAV, March 1998, p.31.

[21] Alan Makovsky, "New Activism in Turkish Foreign Policy", *SAIS Review*, Winter-Spring 1999.

[22] Mustafa Aydın, "Cacophony in the Aegean: Contemporary Turkish-Greek Relations", *The Turkish Yearbook of International elations*, No. 27, 1997, p. 124, Mandell, "The Cyprus Conflict...", p.222.

[23] Nasuh Uslu, "Körfez Savaşı ve Amerika"nın Politikaları", *Ankara Üniversitesi SBF Dergisi*, Vol.54, No. 3, July-September 1999, pp.165-199.

order to strengthen the solidarity of the Western alliance.[24]

In a period in which the Middle East gained more importance as a centre of crisis, allowing the weakening of the south-eastern flank of NATO in the field of military effectiveness because of the Cyprus question could bring about much more serious consequences than it could have brought during the Cold War period. It was reported that the American ambassador in Nicosia, Robert Lamb, said the following things on 18 February 1993: the UN Secretary-General and the Security Council were so busy with other international problems that it was not right to trouble them with the Cyprus issue. If the Cypriots wanted a solution, they should know that the solution would come out as a result of the negotiations held between the two sides.[25] In this period, the United States was pressurising the sides continuously, was trying to keep the inter-communal talks activated and was putting more pressure on the side which seemed to avoid negotiations. Since Turkey and the Turkish Republic of Northern Cyprus were perceived as the sides causing difficulties in negotiations in the early 1990s, they were subjected to more American pressures.[26] Meanwhile, with the active participation of the European Union into the process of trying to find a solution to the Cyprus problem, it was inevitable that Turkey would come under more pressures because Turkey was not a member of the EU and was considered the absolute criminal side in the matter. The EU would appoint a permanent envoy on the Cyprus issue and would be one of the most important parties of the problem by accepting the application of the Greek Cypriot side for the EU membership. The Turkish side only could hope that the tendency in the early 1990s of giving consent to the secession of ethnic groups from their state to maintain the regional balances might help the position of the Turkish Cypriots.[27]

The Ledsky Initiative

At the end of the 1980s, the Americans were continuing their efforts not to allow the interruption of the dialogue between the Cypriot communities. They were more eager to support the UN initiatives since they considered Greek Cypriot leader Vasiliou as a more modest politician. They appointed Nelson Ledsky as the special co-ordinator for Cyprus. The American president met with the Greek Cypriot leader in the White House in June 1989. The president called the Cypriot communities to hold new negotiations. As a part of the new American attitude, the American administration gave full support to the Resolution 649 of the UN Security Council.[28]

In the eyes of Turkish Cypriots, the real motive behind the new American initiative was to promote the candidacy of Cyprus for the European Union. The EU members and

[24] Hasgüler, *Kıbrıs'ta Enosis ve Taksim...*, pp.148, 297, 307.
[25] Mehmet Arif Demirer, *Türkün Onur Sorunu: Kuzey Kıbrıs Türk Cumhuriyeti*, Ankara: Turhan Kitabevi, 1993.
[26] SİSAV Dış İlişkiler ve Savunma Araştırma Grubu, *Kıbrıs Sorunu: Gelişmeler ve Görüşmeler*, İstanbul: SİSAV, September 1990, pp.74-75.
[27] Aydın, "Cacophony in the Aegean...", pp.123-124, Ecmel Barutçu, *Hariciye Koridoru*, Ankara: 21. Yüzyıl Yay., 1999, p.274.
[28] Van Coufoudakis, "Domestic Politics and the Search for a Solution of the Cyprus Problem", Salem (ed.), *Cyprus*, pp.31, 33, 34-35.

the United States were hastening to solve the problems relating to Cyprus and thus to remove the obstacles to the membership of Cyprus into the EU. According to Turkish Cypriots, Ledsky had come to Cyprus to save Vasiliou, who faced a difficult situation when Turkish leader Denktash proposed on 11 October 1989 declaring an "announcement of joint good will". In fact, Ledsky's statements during his visit contributed the stubbornness of Greek Cypriots in solving the problem by seeming to support their views. He voiced the following views: The Cyprus wall should fall down as the Berlin wall fell down. The Americans did not accept a Turkish state in Cyprus and we would not do so in the future. The Turkish Cypriot community had one alternative: negotiating with the Greek Cypriot community with a new understanding. The Turkish Cypriots should not spend their time and money in vain for legal arguments to prove the legitimacy of the Turkish Republic. The American administration would never recognise their state.[29]

In the eyes of the Americans Turkish Cypriot leader seemed the most important obstacle in finding a solution for Cyprus. Since they were not able to control him through direct pressures, they only could ask the Turkish authorities to persuade Denktash in holding more moderate attitude. But, in a meeting held in the American State Department, the drawbacks of pressurising Turkey in this regard were mentioned. Since the situation of the Turkish-American relationship at that time was not in a desired level, the Americans only could only support the initiatives of the UN Secretary-General and could hope that the EU would be influential on the Turkish side in moderating their approach. Meanwhile, Turkish President Turgut Özal seemed to come under the influence of the Americans and to apply pressures on Denktash in accordance with the request of American authorities. Turkish Foreign Minister Mesut Yılmaz, who did not join Özal's visit to the United States, must have been disturbed from the talks in Washington; he made a non-scheduled speech in the Turkish Parliament, criticising the United States and emphasising that "no Turkish government can make concessions which the nation cannot accept."[30]

The Cyprus question was also discussed in the summit meeting between American President George Bush and Soviet leader Gorbachev on 2 June 1990. Commenting on the summit, American Secretary of State James Baker gave the following information: Bush and Gorbachev discussed all the aspects of the Cyprus issue. The two world leaders, who shared the opinion that the two countries should do their best to help the solution of the problem, stated that they would continue to support the efforts of the UN Secretary-General on finding a solution.[31] In the same month (June), the Cyprus question came to the forefront again, this time because of the Defence Co-operation Agreement signed between the United States and Greece. The Greek governments, as a traditional policy, had perceived a threat from Turkey on the integrity of their territory; and in order to

---

[29] Sabahattin İsmail, *Self-Determinasyon ve Kıbrıs Türk Halkı*, İstanbul: Kastaş Yay., June 1990, pp.28, 53, 86, 185, 186-187, 199, 232, 286, 290, 292, 293; Mustafa Evran, "Türkiye-Avrupa Birliği İlişkileri Çerçevesinde Kıbrıs'ın Avrupa Birliği Üyeliğine Başvurusu", Çiler Eminer and Gülden İlkman (ed.), *Avrupa Birliği ve Kıbrıs*, Lefkoşa: KKTC Dışişleri ve Savunma Bakanlığı, pp. 19-20, Demirer, *Türkün Onur Sorunu*, pp. 48-49, Orbay Deliceırmak (ed.), *Haklılık ve Kararlılık*, Lefkoşa, February 1993, p.40.
[30] Polat, *Washington Entrikaları*, p.97.
[31] SİSAV, *Kıbrıs Sorunu*, p.55.

overcome their insecurity in this regard, they had sought guarantees from the United States in various forms, ensuring that no attempt would be made to solve Greek-Turkish differences through other than peaceful means. As an extension of this policy, some sentences requiring the protection of the military balance of power in the region and expressing that the United States gave some assurances in this direction were included in the preamble to the US-Greek Mutual Defence Co-operation Agreement (DCA). This worried Turkish authorities. Ankara had interpreted those sentences to the meaning that they would encourage Greece to initiate fait accomplices in the Aegean and in Cyprus with the help of Greek Cypriots. Turkish authorities voiced their displeasure in their highest level contacts with the American officials. The fact that the Turkish attendance at the US ambassador's reception on 4 July 1990 stayed in a very limited level was nothing more than expressing this pleasure in an open way. At the end, Turkish officials managed to get assurances from the Americans that the preamble was not directed against Turkey.[32]

The Set of Ideas

After the inter-communal talks failed in March 1990, the American administration considered that in the positive atmosphere created by the success in the Gulf War, the Turkish-Greek dialogue on Cyprus could be given a new push. It was believed that American President Bush was in favour of holding an international conference on Cyprus, but he could not apply pressures in this matter not to alienate Turkey, which provided great help to the USA during the Gulf War.[33] Nevertheless, the American insistence on solving the Cyprus problem brought about serious negotiations under the auspices of the UN. In the American eyes, the most important obstacles in this regard were the Turkish Cypriot stubbornness and the Turkish failure to establish a stable government.[34] They could trust in their close friend Turkish President Özal in overcoming the first obstacle.

The proposal of holding a four-partite meeting between the representatives of Turkey, Greece, and the communities in Cyprus, which was put forward by Turkish President Özal on 30 May 1991, represented a diversion from Turkey's traditional policy of not involving in Cyprus negotiations. In Özal's view, if the four leaders came together in the style of the Camp David negotiations and discussed the problem, a serious progress could be achieved in the solution of the Cyprus question. But Greek and Greek Cypriot authorities rejected the proposal. Their counter-proposal was that an international conference should be held with the participation of the nine states including the five permanent members of the UN Security Council apart from the sides of the problem. This time the Turkish side objected to the conference proposal, believing that the real intention of the Greek side was to put Turkey under the pressure of the great powers.[35]

The next event, the meeting between Turkish Prime Minister Yıldırım Akbulut and

[32] Ibid., p. 56. Stearns, *Entangled Allies*, pp.99-100.

[33] Süha Bölükbaşı, "The Turco-Greek Dispute: Issues, Policies and Prospects", Clement H. Dodd (ed.), *Turkish Foreign Policy: New Prospects*, Huntingdon: The Eothen Press, 1992, p.51.

[34] Ian O. Lesser, "Bridge or Barrier? Turkey and the West After the Cold War", Graham Fuller et al., *Turkey's New Geopolitics: From the Balkans to Western China*, Boulder, 1993, p.112.

[35] Dodd, *The Cyprus Imbroglio*, p. 43, Bölükbaşı, "The Turco-Greek Dispute...", pp.32-33.

Greek Prime Minister Mitsotakis on 6 July 1990, demonstrated that the attitude of Turgut Özal did not change. Mitsotakis suggested that the Greco-Turkish dialogue should be focused on the Cyprus issue. If a sufficient progress was achieved in the solution of the Cyprus problem, then the other problems could be negotiated by the two states. Akbulut gave his consent to the proposal. However, the meeting between Turkey's new Prime Minister Süleyman Demirel and Mitsotakis at the end of 1991 showed that the attitude of the Turkish side changed. Mitsotakis asked Demirel to put pressure on Denktash to persuade him in making more concessions. But Demirel refused to intervene in Denktash's handling the inter-communal talks. It seemed that the Turkish government readopted its previous attitude that only the Cypriot leaders could find a solution to the Cyprus problem through bilateral talks.[36]

In 1992, intensive initiatives were launched on the Cyprus issue. The inter-communal talks under the auspices of UN Secretary-General Butrous Ghali reached a serious point with the proclamation of the Set of Ideas put forward by the Secretary-General. The UN Security Council ratified that the Set of Ideas constituted a suitable framework for finding a solution to the Cyprus problem. At the beginning, Turkish Cypriots were pleased with the UN's speaking of a sovereignty that would be established with the joint participation of the two sides. On the other hand, the Greek Cypriot side emphasised the idea of "a state of Cyprus with a single sovereignty and a single citizenship", which was formulated in the Set of Ideas. Later the UN Security Council combined the opinions of the two sides and proposed a federal republic that would have "one sovereignty which is indivisible and which emanates equally from the Greek Cypriot and Turkish Cypriot communities", but the Greek side objected this formulation.[37] As we return to the Set of Ideas, Turkish Cypriots found it acceptable the 91 articles of the package. They definitely rejected the remaining 9 articles since they proposed a federal system in which the Turkish Cypriots would not have their own sovereignty and the right of self-determination. This amounted to the refusal of the package of the UN Secretary-General.[38]

Some criticisms voiced by Turkish Cypriots on the Set of Ideas should be mentioned here since they reflected the attitude of the Turkish Cypriot leadership to a great extent and showed their distrust toward the United States and the United Nations. According those Turkish critics, by accepting the resolutions 649, 716, 750, 774 and 789, the UN Security Council tried to impose a solution, which would destroy the sovereignty of the Turkish community and which aimed at dissolving the TRNC and putting Turkish Cypriots under the authority of the Greek Cypriot state. The members of the UN Security Council not only recognised the Greek Cypriot government as the official representative of the island, but they also tried to impose their own choice of solution by joining the negotiation table on behalf of the Greeks in a sense and thus they violated the principle that the sides should continue the talks with their free will. The diplomats of the UN and the United States lobbied intensively among journalists, businessmen, industrial and

---

[36] Bölükbaşı, "The Tuco-Greek Dispute...", p.48.
[37] Clement H. Dodd, "Confederation, Federation and Sovereignty", *Perceptions*, Vol.4, No.3, September-November 1999.
[38] İsmail, *Kıbrıs Üzerine Bildiriler*, p.227.

commercial unions, political parties and people in TRNC. They aimed to give damage to
the prestige of President Denktash, the Turkish Cypriot Parliament and the government
and to impose their own proposal of solution on the Turkish side by intervening in internal
affairs of Turkish Cypriots. The American officials and UN Secretary-General Ghali,
who was under the great influence of the Americans, tried to reduce the size of TRNC as
a condition of establishing a federation and focused only on the situation of the Greek
Cypriot refugees as if they were the only refugees on the island. Their efforts of imposing
on the Turkish side an agreement which would lead to the establishment of the Greek
Cypriot authority on the island and which would bring back the dark days of the period
before 1974 would cause nothing more than turning the island to a battle field. The thing
that upset Turkish Cypriots the most was that Turkish President Özal accused them of
not continuing the talks after the UN Security Council Resolution 649, preventing the
four-partite summit and causing the enactment of the UN Security Council Resolution
716. However, this was not the truth. The United States tried to impose an agreement by
bringing the sides to New York before the preparations were not completed. When it was
failed to do so, the anger it felt led it to agree with the Greek side on passing an anti-
Turkish resolution in the Security Council.[39] It was unfortunate that the enmity the
Americans felt against Denktash spread to the Turkish leadership as well. Denktash
himself stated that he was sure on the existence of an organised effort directed to
humiliate him and to replace him with another person.[40]

The speech made by Denktash in the Turkish Grand National Assembly during his
return journey from the New York talks, in which he felt suffocated under duress, was
rather interesting. He made the following points. The Security Council member had
focused on the Varosha issue. If Turkish Cypriots acted in the way they wanted by
yielding to their pressures, it was inevitable that further concessions would be demanded.
By hurling threats such as "if you do not accept our proposal, we will impose an embargo
on you and Turkey will be held responsible for your attitude", they would take up other
issues. Since they knew that Turkish Cypriots were sensitive on not causing any harm to
Turkey, the representatives of the five great powers considered this situation a weakness
of the Turkish side and continued their threats basing on this fact. The representative of
each power made speeches in front of the negotiators, supporting the report read by the
Secretary-General and gave the sides a certain time to sell the proposals to their people.
Denktash himself witnessed for the first time that such a treatment was applied to the
representative of a people under threats and restrictions. The members of the Security
Council did not let Turkish Cypriots mention their sovereignty, diluted their equality,
opposed taking executive decisions in a harmony existed in federations, and tried to
recreate the dreadful situation before 1964 by snapping territory from the Turkish side
and allowing settlement of Greek Cypriots on other parts of the Turkish territory. The
declaration issued on the same day in the Turkish Parliament with the participation of all
the political parties was intended to show that Turkey would not yield to pressures of the

[39] Ibid., pp.226-227, 228, 229, 238, 244, 246, 273, 275, 287, Sabahattin İsmail, *Egemenlik, Konfederasyon ve Kıbrıs Türk Halkı*, November 1993, pp. 168, 177-178, 179.
[40] Deliceırmak (ed.), *Haklılık ve Kararlılık*, p. 34.

great powers. The declaration stated: TGNA appreciated the peace efforts spent by Denktash. The Turkish nation would not accept a solution that was not accepted by the Turkish Cypriot nation. TGNA considered holding negotiations in an atmosphere distant from every kind of pressure as a dispensable condition of a lasting compromise.[41]

With the failure of the Set of Ideas, the Cyprus question continued to be an irritating point in Turkish-American relations. Ankara avoided taking actions that were seen by the Americans as the confidence building measures such as reducing the number of Turkish troops on the island. But the Turkish authorities had to persuade the Turkish Cypriot leadership in continuing the process of seeking a solution not to cause a crisis in relations with the United States. On the other hand, the American leaders were extremely displeased with the determination of Denktash in not accepting the plans put forward by the UN. In the opinion of the Turkish side, the Set of Ideas was based on giving territory in return for constitutional rights. This was normal for the Americans, who had the understanding of horse trade. But the Turkish Cypriots attributed more importance to basic principles such as the recognition of the equal status.

Following the failure of the Set of Ideas, the Americans began to focus on the confidence building measures again. With their initiative, the UN Secretary-General met with the representatives of the Turkish Cypriots to find a solution to the problems related to Varosha.[42] On 20 January 1995 Denktash issued a fourteen-point peace plan, explaining the views of the Turkish side on finding a solution to the Cyprus problem. The UN and the United Nations admitted that there were positive elements in the document, but Greek Cypriots rejected it.[43] On 23 January 1995, the American president's special emissary for Cyprus, Richard Beattle, conveyed a special message of President Clinton's to Denktash. In his message, Clinton mentioned the American support for the establishment of a bizonal and bicommunal federation in which the two political communities would live as a one state. He also emphasised that the only way of making progress in the Cyprus question was the implementation of the confidence building measures.[44] As it was understood from the message, the United States was still not pleased with the attitude of Turkish Cypriots. When the Turkish side put more emphasis on their sovereignty and right of self-determination from the end of 1995, the Americans' fears increased further.

The European Union Connection

With the application of Greek Cypriots for the membership of the European Union at the early 1990s, the Cyprus question gained importance for the EU and its enlargement as well. Thus the Cyprus question acquired a new aspect that could facilitate or bring new difficulties for the solution of the problem. The intervention of the EU in the problem, which was not a considerable factor up to that time, was also a development that could

[41] Demirer, *Türkün Onur Sorunu*, pp.54, 57, 58, 61-63.
[42] Dodd, *The Cyprus Imbroglio*, pp.53, 58-59.
[43] Ibid., pp.70, 91.
[44] The statements of the American authorities and the American government, which will be mentioned in the following section are taken from the web site of the American embassy in Cyprus if no footnote is used.

bring serious consequences for the Turkish-EU and Turkish-American relations. It was also inevitable that the approach of Turkey to the Cyprus question would change considerably.

On 17 September 1990, the Ministerial Council of the EU decided to transfer the application of the Greek Cypriot administration to the EU Commission. At that time, the American administration was opposed to such a development since it considered that it would complicate the problem. Some circles in the USA were of the opinion that the Cyprus question should be solved in accordance with the political and geopolitical interests of NATO and they were opposed to the intervention of the EU in the matter since Turkey was opposed to it.[45] Even Nelson Ledsky claimed that the membership of Cyprus in the EU would deteriorate the disagreements between the two communities rather than bringing them together.[46] But there were also Americans, who hoped that the EU aspect would lead Turkey to reconsider its standing in the Cyprus issue since it needed the American support for its membership in the EU.[47] Later the Americans would encourage the Turkish side to see the EU aspect as an opportunity in finding a solution to the Cyprus problem.

For the Turkish and Turkish Cypriot leaders, the application of the Greek Cypriots for the EU membership was nothing more than a Greek game launched to put the whole island under their rule. In their opinion, if the EU accepted the Greek Cypriot application, this would amount to the indirect enosis and the TRNC would not be able to continue its existence as it was. In this way, many principles, which the Turkish side defended insistently, such as sovereignty, the Turkish guarantee for Cyprus and bizonal state, would become non-functional and meaningless. After such a development, it would be impossible to prevent the likelihood of the Greek Cypriot domination over the Turkish community. Moreover, the Helenism would gain a great victory because the Treaty of Guarantee would not be used against a member of the EU. With the implementation of the EU laws, all the parameters, which emerged up to that time for the establishment of a bizonal and bicommunal state, would lose their meaning.[48] There was also a common view of the Turkish side that the European leaders would use the Cyprus issue and the Greek Cypriot application as a tool to keep Turkey outside the EU. In the following period, Turkey tried to prevent or soften the EU decisions in promoting the candidacy of the Greek Cypriots by approaching the EU countries and the USA. It also initiated some joint arrangements with the TRNC and declared from December 1995 that these arrangements would be expanded if the process of Cypriot application continued. In addition, Turkish authorities frequently stated that the continuation of the process

---

[45] Coufoudakis, "Domestic Politics...", p.35, Nicholas Emiliou, "Knocking on the Door of the European Union: Cyprus' Strategy of Accession" in Heinz-Jürgen Axt and Hansjörg Brey (ed.) *Cyprus and the European Union: New Chances for Solving an Old Conflict?* Münih: Südosterapa-Gesellschaft, 1997, p.28.

[46] Sabahattin İsmail, *150 Soruda Kıbrıs Sorunu*, İstanbul: Kaştaş Yay., August 1998.

[47] Laipson, "The United States and Cyprus...", p.98.

[48] Barutçu, *Hariciye Koridoru*, p. 267, Mümtaz Soysal, *Aklımı Kıbrıs'la Bozmak*, Ankara: Bilgi Yay., August 1995, p. 170, Denktash's letter to British Foreign Secretary Robin Cook, dated as 25 March 1998 (the official statements of the Turkish side in the following section is taken from the web site of the Turkish Foreign Ministry if no footnote is used).

torpedoed the Cypriot negotiations, which were held under the auspices of the UN Secretary-General.[49]

In spite of this apparent Turkish attitude, it was rather surprising that Turkey gave the green light to the continuation of the membership negotiations of the Greek Cypriots in return for signing the Customs Union agreement with the EU in March 1995. On 6 March 1995, the EU Council announced that the membership negotiations with the Greek Cypriots would start six months after the completion of the inter-governmental conference in 1996. In fact, behind this announcement lied a bargaining, which was carried out with the encouragement of the Americans. Greece withdrew its threat of vetoing the Customs Union agreement between the EU and Turkey, and in return, Turkey kept quiet about the EU decision to schedule the membership negotiations with Cyprus.[50] In the eyes of the Americans, the new moderate attitude of the Greek government was positive and valuable. Greece itself would benefit from supporting the Turkish bid to become a part of Europe. Keeping Turkey outside Europe might result in the establishment of a military or radical government in Turkey,[51] and such a development would create new problems for Turkish-Greek disagreements including the Cyprus issue. The American administration also encouraged the EU to include the Turkish Cypriots in the membership negotiations without staying under the fact that it recognised only the Greek Cypriot side as the official representative of Cyprus. Especially American Presidential Envoy for Cyprus Richard Holbrooke tried to persuade Turkish authorities on that Turkey had vital interests in the participation of the Turkish Cypriots to the membership negotiations. In his opinion, the most important obstacle in this regard could be overcome in the following way: Neither the Greek Cypriots should give up their claim of becoming the only representative of the island nor the Turkish Cypriots should withdraw their demand of the recognition of the TRNC. But the two sides should come together and should sit on the EU table together in spite of their conflicting attitudes.[52]

However, in the opinion of the Turkish side, their participation to the membership negotiations before their equal status was recognised would mean giving up their opinions, which they defended up to that time, and would result in the loss of their basic rights and powers. As their objections were not taken into consideration, Turkey and the TRNC signed an economic co-operation protocol and a financial support agreement on 3 January 1997. The two states also concluded a Partnership Council agreement on 20 July 1997, aiming at partially integrating the TRNC with Turkey. The new approach of the Turkish side was to carry out among themselves all the structural co-operation and adaptation arrangements, which were done between the EU and the Greek Cypriots. The Americans, who did not show any serious objection to the EU-Greek Cypriot

---

[49] SİSAV, *1997 Yılı Sonu İtibariyle Kıbrıs Sorunu*, p.23.

[50] Andreas Theophanous, "Cyprus, the European Union and the Search for a New Constitution", *Journal of Southern Europe and the Balkans*, Vol. 2, No. 2, 2000, p. 223, Soysal, *Aklını Kıbrıs'la Bozmak*, p.169.

[51] Monteagle Stearns, "Yunan Güvenlik Meseleleri", Graham T. Allison and Kalipso Nikolaydis (ed.), *Yunan Paradoksu*, (translated to Turkish by Bülent Tanatar), İstanbul: Doğan Kitap, October 1999, pp.89, 90.

[52] Tözün Bahçeli, "Cyprus in the Post-Cold War Environment: Moving Toward a Settlement", Calotychos (ed.), *Cyprus and Its People*, p.109, Dodd, *The Cyprus Imbroglio*, pp.111-112.

negotiations, stated that the Turkish-TRNC agreement would not help the solution of the Cyprus problem and warned that they did not want to see initiatives which would undermined the negotiation process held under the auspices of the UN.[53] On the other hand, Turkish authorities were adamant in extending to the Turkish Cypriots the suggestion that the integration with Turkey would always be available for them as an alternative.[54]

In spite of the initial EU and American unwillingness, it was the Greek and Greek Cypriot side, which managed to make the matter of membership to the EU an inseparable part of the Cyprus question with their insistent policies.[55] The plan of the Greek side was the following:

> *If the Greek Cypriots entered the EU as equal members even before a solution to the political division of Cyprus has been found, then–in Athens's view–there would be a more active and favourable European involvement. This would force Turkey, which is interested in close relations to the community, to accept a solution of the Cyprus problem in favour of Greek positions.[56]*

Regardless of the motives of the parties were, some circles began to question whether the EU membership could play a catalyst role in bringing the two communities in Cyprus together. The UN Security Council and the EU Council had some hopes in this direction. They held the view that this new aspect could help the solution of the problem by putting pressures on both sides. But it was also asserted that the EU should work on the basis of what had been achieved by the UN Secretary-General and should remain in close touch with the American side. The European leaders also should "avoid a situation where facilitators competed with each other or are played off against one another."[57] Some argued that the prospect of negotiations for Cyprus admission to the EU challenged the relatively stable division of the island and was complicating rather than helping the resolution of the problems between the Greek and Turkish Cypriots.[58] Turkish Prime Minister Ecevit claimed that American special envoy Holbrooke stressed that the EU was largely responsible for the stalemate on the island.[59]

The Holbrooke Initiative

In early 1996, the Americans intensified their efforts to solve the Cyprus problem again. After ensuring the signing of the Dayton Agreement in Bosnia-Herzegovina, American President Clinton appointed the architect of this agreement, Richard Holbrooke, as his special envoy for Cyprus to benefit from the positive atmosphere in solving the Cyprus question. But Holbrooke, who spoke of

---

[53] SİSAV, *1997 Yılı Sonu İtibariyle Kıbrıs Sorunu*, pp.13, 14.
[54] The statements of Foreign Minister İsmail Cem in his press conference during his visit to the TRNC.
[55] Emiliou, "Knocking on the Door...", pp.127, 128.
[56] Peter Zervakis, "The Accession of Cyprus to the EU: The Greek Viewpoint", Axt and Brey (ed.) *Cyprus and the European Union*, p.139.
[57] Franz Eichinger, "Cyprus and the EU from the German Point of View", Axt & Hansjörg Brey (ed.) *Cyprus and the European Union*, p.201.
[58] Roper, "The West and Turkey...", p.93.
[59] Ahmet C. Gazioğlu (ed.), *Cyprus, EU and Turkey: Selected Extracts from the World Press*, Nicosia: CYREP, 1998, p. 101.

applying the Dayton model to Cyprus, had to postpone his scheduled visit to Cyprus at the end of January 1996 because of the Kardak crisis between Turkey and Greece. Thus it was apparent in very start that the Cyprus question was not only an ethnic conflict, but it was included in rather complicated problems and relations of the two important states of the region. In spite of apparent negative points of this problem, the Americans still believed that new initiatives would bring positive developments because of some factors. Firstly, the Greeks had started to pursue more pragmatic policies as it was proved by their attitude toward the EU-Turkish Customs Union agreement. Secondly, the European decision of starting the membership negotiations with Cyprus could lead the Turkish Cypriots to hold a more conciliatory attitude. Finally, the USA was in a better position compared with its previous standing in playing the role of mediator between the sides.[60]

In the aftermath of the Kardak crisis, Turkish Foreign Minister Mesut Yılmaz offered "to the Greek government a package of solutions and proposals concerning all problems in the Aegean and set no precondition in order to create an atmosphere of confidence." The American administration expressed its pleasure with the Turkish proposal and announced that it was ready to participate into the negotiations as the third party.[61] However, the Greek indifference to the matter prevented the likelihood of a serious progress that might also help the Cyprus issue. The events of July 1996 in the Turkish-Greek frontier in Cyprus further aggravated the situation. When a Greek Cypriot was killed because he tried to lower the Turkish flag, the American administration showed a severe reaction to the incident. The spokesman of the American State Department, Nicholas Burns, stated that the flag was not important than human life, whereas the coalition partner in the Turkish government, Tansu Ciller threatened "to break the hands which stretch to the Turkish flag". The effort of American Secretary of State Madelaine Albright to arrange a meeting between the military commanders of the two sides in order to reduce the tensions and prevent the events in the frontier, too, failed.[62]

In the following period, the American authorities were worried about the outbreak of a Turkish-Greek war and therefore they avoided taking the Greek side as the EU did in the disagreements between the two states.[63] The Cyprus question was one of the most important issues that the Americans handled sensitively in this regard. In May 1997, with the encouragement of the Americans, the Greek Cypriots announced that Greek warplanes would not fly over Cyprus during the Greek-Greek Cypriot joint military exercises. Turkey responded favourably to this action by declaring that it would not fly its warplanes over Cyprus. However, in October 1997 the Greeks and the Greek Cypriots carried out the joint military exercise of Nikiforos and Turkey and the TRNC retaliated by organising the exercise of Toros.[64]

Meanwhile, American special envoy for Cyprus Holbrooke intensified his initiatives in

---

[60] F. Stephen Larrabee, "Yunanistan ve Balkanlar: Politika Önerileri", Allison and Nikolaydis (ed.), *Yunan Paradoksu*, pp.138-139.

[61] Hüseyin Bağcı, "Cyprus: Accession to the European Union- A Turkish View", Axt and Brey (ed.) *Cyprus and the European Union*, p.165.

[62] Dodd, *The Cyprus Imbroglio*, p.95; Polat, *Washington Entrikaları*, pp.163-164.

[63] Fotios Moustakis and Micheal Sheehan, "Greek Security Policy After the Cold-War", *Contemporary Security Politics*, Vol.21, No.3, December 2000, p.109.

[64] Roper, "The West and Turkey...", p.93.

the second half of 1997. At first, he waited for the end of Denktash-Clerides meeting in Troutbeck on 9-13 July, which was their first face to face meeting after a three-year interval. In the meantime, the visit of Turkish Prime Minister to Cyprus to join the celebrations for the anniversary of the Turkish military intervention in 1974 agitated the Americans. In their eyes, it was important not to harm the atmosphere of good relations between Turkey and Greece, which was brought about by the Madrid summit of NATO on 8-9 July,[65] through these kinds of actions.[66] During the Denktash-Clerides negotiations in Switzerland on 11-16 August, UN Special envoy Diego Cordovez presented two documents, one of which was a draft of joint statement, including the points the sides agreed. The other was about the negotiation process and principles. While Denktash declared he would not accept any document in the negotiations, Clerides stated that their attitude toward the document was positive though they had some reservations. This development led the UN Security Council members to hold the Turkish side responsible for the failure of the negotiations. On 26 September 1997, Denktash and Clerides met again, this time in Nicosia, to talk about the security matters, but nothing came out from the meeting.[67] In November, Holbrooke told Denktash during his visit to the United States that the participation of the Turkish Cypriots in the EU membership negotiations would be in the interest of Turkey. On 11 November, Holbrooke held a meeting in Ledra Palace on the Green Line with the leaders of the Cypriot communities. Apart from some progress on missing persons, nothing was achieved. Holbrooke was not upset because he did not expect serious outcomes from that kind of unofficial meeting.[68]

The end of 1997 witnessed serious developments on the Cyprus issue. In its Luxembourg summit, the European Union decided to start full membership negotiations with the Greek Cypriot administration, whereas Turkey's name was not mentioned among the countries with which the EU would start membership negotiations in the future. The decision had been taken in spite of the opposition of the Americans, who believed that starting negotiations with the Greek Cypriots would be balanced with the acceptance of Turkey's candidacy for full membership. The Turkish side concluded that seeking for a bizonal federal state solution and continuing the inter-communal negotiations lost their meaning. The Turkish Cypriots would then try to acquire the recognition of the TRNC as having the status of equal and independent state before sitting the negotiation table. Turkey declared that it would not talk to and consult the European Union any political matter including the Cyprus issue in the future. As it was stated by Turkish Foreign Minister İsmail Cem in his press conference on 30 March 1998, Turkey was in favour of the continuation of the TRNC's separate independent entity. If a federal state would be established in the future, this could be possible only with the continuation of the independent and equal status of the Turkish Cypriot side.[69]

In early 1998, Holbrooke launched a new peace initiative by talking to the authorities

---

[65] Suat Bilge, *Büyük Düş: Türk-Yunan İlişkileri*, Ankara: 21. Yüzyıl Yay., October 2000, p.269.
[66] Dodd, *The Cyprus Imbroglio*, pp.101, 103.
[67] SİSAV, *1997 Yılı Sonu İtibariyle Kıbrıs Sorunu*, p.15.
[68] *The Turkish Yearbook of International Relations*, No.27, 1997, pp.157-158, 160.
[69] Theophanous, "Cyprus, the European Union...", p.223.

in Nicosia, Athens and Ankara. But his proposals were not satisfactory for both sides. When he accused the Turkish side of not taking the negotiations seriously, the Greek Cypriots felt pleasure. When he mentioned the existence of the two communities, whose ethnic origins, languages and beliefs were different, the Turkish Cypriots considered it the approval of their viewpoints. Holbrooke's stated in his press conference on 4 May 1998: "I think it is very clear... that Glafcos Clerides does not represent or have control of the people of northern Cyprus." According to Holbrooke, the issues that were involved were all solvable, but the sides had to have a negotiation. If one of the sides did not wish to negotiate, that would not be a catastrophe. Holbrooke did not consider his trip a failure. He was of the opinion that the problems he countered were part of the process.[70]

Turkish authorities did not feel any special resentment toward Holbrooke. The spokesman of the Turkish government, Şükrü Sina Gürel claimed that the failure of Holbrooke's initiative was due to the completely erroneous approach of the EU, which decided to start unilateral membership negotiations with the Greek Cypriots. According to Prime Minister Ecevit, there were some positive points in the attitude of Holbrooke. The American envoy had openly said that the southern Cyprus had no authority at all on the other part of the island and he, for the first time, referred to the north with its proper name (TRNC). Holbrooke also seemed to have realised that the Dayton model or the Irish model could not be applied to Cyprus. In the opinion of Turkish Cypriot leader Denktash, the Greek lobby in the USA started attacking Holbrooke after he referred to Denktash as the elected leader of the Turkish Cypriots. If there were not the Greek lobby, Holbrooke would have spoken more openly.[71]

An important development that occurred during Holbrooke's term as special envoy for Cyprus was the initiative of the Greek Cypriots to purchase S-300 missiles from Russia. Turkish Foreign Minister Tansu Çiller responded severely to this development by declaring that Turkey would not hesitate in removing these missiles by force, if necessary. The spokesman of the American State Department, Nicholas Burns, did not approve of this reaction and he emphasised that Turkey did not have the right to threaten Greece. But the Americans were also not happy about the Greek Cypriot initiative. Carey Cavanagh, the director of the Office of South European Affairs, toured the capitals of the sides to obtain the assurance that the missiles would not be deployed for the following sixteen months. The threat to the stability to the eastern Mediterranean caused by the rapid armament of the Greek Cypriots and the severe Turkish response led the Americans to intervene in the matter.[72] On 6 January 1997, the American administration criticised the Greek Cypriots severely for their initiative of purchasing S-300 missiles. According to Yalçın Doğan, during his visit to Washington in the second half of 1998, Turkish Prime Minister Mesut Yılmaz obtained assurances from American President Bill Clinton that Russia would not sell those missiles. Clinton wanted to prevent the Turkish side, which was felt free itself in taking any action because of the EU's attitude on the candidacies of Turkey

---

[70] From the web site of the Turkish Foreign Ministry.
[71] Interviews with Denktash and Ecevit, *Turkish Daily News*, 12 and 17 May 1998.
[72] Dodd, *The Cyprus Imbroglio*, pp.99, 101.

and the Greek Cypriots for full membership, from launching a radical action in Cyprus.[73]

In February 1998, the following development was mentioned in the press: the S-300 missiles was supposed to reach Cyprus in April, but the American pressures led the sides to promise that the delivery of the missiles would not be materialised at least until August.[74] In the eyes of the Americans, the initiative was a needlessly provocative effort complicating their diplomatic efforts on Cyprus. Russia, whose primary aim was to prop up their ailing military industry, might have other motivations such as extending their influence to the regions and creating problems for NATO. American authorities also believed that the deployment of the S-300 missiles would undermine the security of Cyprus. These weapons were effective enough to worry the Turks, but not effective enough to alter the basic military equation or prevent a Turkish invasion.[75] Meanwhile, some newspapers accused US officials of spreading rumours about the possibility of a serious incident in Cyprus. Their main aim was to raise local opposition to the deployment of the missiles and to undermine the morale of the Greek Cypriots in order to force them to accept any solution.[76]

In the end, the American pressures played a role in the Greek decision of installing the missiles in the island of Crete instead of Cyprus. Although they did not admit their role publicly, the only reason for this attitude was not to annoy the Greek Cypriots for the sake of reaching a solution. The American spokesman stated in the Pentagon regular briefing on 4 February 1999 that the USA had long opposed the deployment of the S-300 missiles to Cyprus because it held the view that anything which increased the tensions between Turkey and Greece did not serve any interests of these two countries, the USA or NATO. When he was asked whether American officials asked the Greeks to do got the missiles instead of Cyprus to the island of Crete, the spokesman answered: "I cannot tell you whether we played that active role in this issue or not." American Secretary of State Albright told Greek Cypriot Foreign Minister Kosoulides on 17 February 1999 that their courageous decision not to deploy the S-300 missiles to Cyprus opened up new opportunities to find a resolution for the Cyprus problem.

The 1999-2001 Period

The Events

The mutual sincere offers of help during the devastating earthquakes in Turkey and Greece in 1999 brought about a new period of détente in relations between the two countries. The mutual visits of the foreign ministers of Greece and Turkey, George Papandreou and İsmail Cem, to each other's country and their positive approach caused new hopes for the solution of the Cyprus problem as well. The problem had reached a point of deadlock because the EU membership process of the Greek Cypriots continued

---

[73] SİSAV, *1997 Yılı Sonu İtibariyle Kıbrıs Sorunu*, p.19.
[74] Steve Rodan, "Russia Asks Israel to Keep Out of S-300 Deal", *Defense News*, 23 February- 1 March 1998.
[75] Micheal R. Gordon, "Russia Planning to Ship Anti-Aircraft Missiles to Greek Cypriots", *The New York Times*, 29 April 1998.
[76] "Stop Playing Poker with the Missiles" (The Editorial), *The Cyprus Mail*, 14 May 1998.

while Turkey was not granted even the candidacy status. The Turkish side was adamant that it would not negotiate with the Greek Cypriots unless its equal status was recognised. But the new positive atmosphere could not be missed. It was inevitable that the outside powers, especially the USA, would intervene and the sides would start proximity talks to meet the reservations of the Turkish side. In fact, American President Clinton informed the press members aboard Airforce One en route to Ankara for the OSCE meeting that Clerides and Denktash accepted an invitation to start proximity talks in New York on 3 December. The goals of the talks would be to prepare the ground for the meaningful negotiations leading to a comprehensive settlement of the Cyprus problem.

It appeared that the suitable conditions for a progress on Cyprus were present. Turkey and Greece were living through an extraordinary détente period. Turkey had the opportunity to demonstrate its strategic importance by hosting the meeting of the OSCE. American President Clinton, who considered Turkey as the centre of the world politics of the 21st century, was visiting Turkey. The high-level representatives of Turkey, the USA and the other concerned countries signed a document expressing their support for the realisation of the Baku-Ceyhan pipeline. At this important turning point, Turkey could bring about some progress in Cyprus to strengthen its increasing strategic importance in world politics. If the Cyprus issue were solved, Greece and Turkey would save their foreign policies from the restrictions of this problem and would be able to use their resources for their economic development. Moreover, President Clinton would increase his prestige greatly by solving an ages-old problem before the end of his presidency.

It seemed that with the encouragement of the Americans, Turkish authorities persuaded the Greek Turkish Cypriot leadership in joining the proximity talks in New York. The dialogue on Cyprus reached high points. American diplomats put forward proposals through their colleagues in the UN.[77] As an interesting coincidence, the proximity had started one week before the Helsinki summit of the EU. The EU's granting Turkey the status of candidacy for full membership with the removal of the Greek veto was a development that boosted the Cyprus negotiations. One reason for Turkey's adamant attitude on Cyprus had been abolished. It appeared that a different version of the Turkish-Greek bargaining on 6 March 1995 was put into practice again with the help of the Americans. This time, in return for gaining the candidate status, Turkey seemed to give implicit approval to the EU decision that a political settlement of the Cyprus problem would not be a precondition for Cyprus' accession to the EU.[78] Nevertheless, Turkish authorities seemed to feel more pleasure rather than enmity toward the EU decisions. President Clinton, too, was happy about the development; he thanked Greek Prime Minister Simitis for Greece's strong support for Turkey.[79]

The mutual visits of the Greek and Turkish foreign ministers to each other's capital in January and February 2000 (these visits were the first in their kinds, which were made after 37 and 40-year intervals respectively) were encouraging for the Cyprus issue as well. According to President Clinton's letter to the Speaker of the House of

---

[77] *The Economist*, "Talks About Talks", 4 December 1999, Vol.353, No.8148, p.49.
[78] Theophanous, "Cyprus, the European Union...", p.223.
[79] Moustakis and Sheehan, "Greek Security Policy...", p.111.

Representatives and the Chairman of the Senate Committee on Foreign Relations, dated as 7 March 2000, UN Secretary-General Annan reported that the Greek and Turkish Cypriots were engaged seriously in the whole range of issues that divided them. American President's Special Envoy for Cyprus, Alfred H. Moses and his team provided critical diplomatic support for the UN efforts. Moses, too, emphasised in his arrival statement at Larnaca Airport on 7 March 2000 that what constructive was that Denktash and his party were engaged in a negotiating process. In that point, the Americans did not comment on whether the position of one side or the other was constructive. They were not the party that had to decide on the agreement. Both sides encouraged them to come with fresh ideas. The sides had positions that were different, but there was recognition that what was ultimately in the interest of both sides was a comprehensive settlement on the island. Security was critical in the negotiations. The parties had to feel secure. Moses also stated on 10 March that he was encouraged by the commitment on both sides that this process was one that should be pursued to reach a comprehensive settlement. In his opinion, they were moving in the right direction. Both sides were serious and both sides expressed to him that there was no alternative to a united Cyprus.

The fourth round of the negotiations were held between 12 and 16 September 2000 in New York. In the opening of the talks, Kofi Annan made a speech emphasising that the communities on the island were politically independent parties not representing each other. He underlined the necessity that the parties should reach a comprehensive solution requiring a new partnership through negotiations, to which they would participate with their equal status. In his opinion, the equal status of the parties should be transformed to clear political provisions and should be included in the comprehensive solution clearly.[80] These statements were pleasing for the Turkish side while they attracted the reaction of the Greek Cypriots. In spite of the long-held negotiations, the failure in making any progress in solving the problem brought the worry again that it might have been returned to the fruitless efforts of the past. The Nikiforos-Toksotis military exercise of the Greeks and the Greek Cypriots between on 17 and 21 October 2000 strengthened this fear. According to the statement of the Turkish foreign ministry, the exercise was carried out on the basis of the scenarios of attacks against the Turkish side and Greek warplanes landed on the airbase in Paphos.[81] The statement of the UN Secretary-General on 8 November included points that attracted the reaction of the Turkish side. Annan emphasised that his statement constituted a basis for further negotiations and he called the sides to give a response to its content, but the Turkish side had already been alienated from the negotiation process. The negotiations were interrupted and it was not clear when they would resume.

On 11 January 2001, during his visit to Ankara, American President's Special Envoy for Cyprus Moses gave information on the negotiation process: In their discussions with the representatives of Turkey, Greece and the Turkish communities, he and his team emphasised the importance of continuation of the UN-led negotiations. All of the leaders with whom they met were of the opinion that a comprehensive settlement was preferable

---

[80] *Dışişleri Güncesi: September 2000*, Ankara: TC Dışişleri Bakanlığı, p.135.
[81] *Dışişleri Güncesi: October 2000*, Ankara: TC Dışişleri Bakanlığı, p.197.

to the continuation of the status quo. Denktash and Turkish Prime Minister Ecevit had some objections to the current process. The American team discussed the issue of the Turkish side's coming back to the negotiating table with Denktash intensively. Although Denktash gave the assurances that he would carefully consider the views of the Americans, the Turkish Cypriot side did not finally agree upon the ideas of the American, and there were also no commitments from the Turks to resume talks at that time. In the opinion of the Americans, the oral remarks of the UN Secretary-General on 8 November 2000 were not intended to be a framework agreement or something comparable to the Set of Ideas. They were not something definite that either party had to accept or that was intended to favour one side or the other. In short, from the American point of view, the Turkish side indicated their displeasure with the continuation of the proximity talks, proving that they were the side that did not want to dance.

According to Turkish Foreign Minister İsmail Cem, there was no interruption in the negotiation process, but it was entered into a period of waiting. The change of the American administration and the scheduled elections in the Greek Cypriot part of Cyprus on 27 May 2001 played a significant role in this development. First of all, the new American administration would determine its Cyprus policy if the Americans insisted on the resumption of the negotiations after the Greek Cypriot elections, the parties would have to meet again. In his first Cyprus report, which he sent to the Chairman of the Senate Committee on Foreign Relations, Jesse Helms, and the Speaker of the House of Representatives, Dennis Hastert, new American President George Bush mentioned the contacts of Clinton's Special Envoy for Cyprus Moses, Special Co-ordinator for Cyprus Tom Weston and American Ambassador in Nicosia Donald Bandler with the concerned parties. One important development in that conjunction was the abolishment of the office of President's Special Envoy for Cyprus by the Americans. This development might be interpreted as that the new American administration was not willing to put pressures on the parties to the Cyprus problem. Since the Turkish side felt more outside pressures, they could be pleased with this incident. But the eruption of heavy economic crises in Turkey and the TRNC underlined the possibility that the Turkish side might be open to more pressures on Cyprus because of their need for foreign economic help. Moreover, one possibility was that Cyprus would become a serious problem in Turkish-American relations. According to one scenario, Turkey would try to obtain the American opposition to the completion of the Greek Cypriot membership negotiations with the EU. Since they would know certainly that their efforts would not be successful, the Americans would only watch the Greek Cypriot side's becoming a full member of the EU. When the Turkish side, which was alienated totally, chose to integrate the TRNC into Turkey, their relations with the USA and the EU countries would deteriorate seriously and they would be isolated in the international arena. It can be derived from this scenario that the USA would not feel necessity to pressurise the sides of the Cyprus problem and to take the issue to the international agenda.

The Third Sides

One party that expressed its opinions on Cyprus to the disadvantage of the Turkish side is the Group-8. Especially the Americans are able to convey their opinions, which they cannot express openly because of the fear of alienating the Turks, and letting them unit with the international public opinion through the G-8 joint declarations. The G-8 generally asserts that the two sides should sit around the negotiation table without any precondition. Since the Greek Cypriots are the side, which are recognised officially, they would be allowed to benefit a great deal rather than the Turks. The Turkish Grand National Assembly, which believes that the G-8 considers the Cyprus issue along with the initiative of Greece, has stated that the G-8 gives orders to the UN in the Cyprus issue and has condemned the intervention of the G-8 in the matter. In one of his interviews with a Turkish newspaper, Foreign Minister Cem stated the pressures of the external powers such as the G-8 escalated the situation in Cyprus and rendered a settlement more difficult.[82] The Turkish foreign ministry responded to the joint declaration of the G-8 on 23 July 2000 by emphasising that the G-8's proposals of solution did not have any opportunity to be accepted since they were not based on the consent of the sides.[83]

The decisions, actions and attitude of the UN Security Council, too, are generally in contradiction with the opinions of the Turkish side on the Cyprus issue. Recently, a serious disagreement has emerged between the two sides on the extension of the term of the UN Force in Cyprus. The Council's resolution on 14 June 2000 stated that the term of the force was extended with the consent of the government of Cyprus without mentioning the consent of the Turkish Cypriot side. On the contrary to the past practices, the Council did not issue this time an addendum which required that the UN Force sign an agreement with the TRNC regulating its activities on the north of the island. The reaction of the Turkish Foreign Ministry to the UN resolution was harsh: There was no government in Cyprus, representing the whole island as it was stated by the resolution. The UN Force was able to continue its activities with the co-operation of the TRNC government. The resolution was contrary to the principle of the equality of the sides in Cyprus. Turkey would not recognise this resolution and would reconsider the future of its relations with the UN Force. Turkish President Ahmet Necdet Sezer reacted to the resolution by stressing that the northern Cyprus was neither the territory or land of 'no man' under the authority of the Greek Cypriots. If the UN Force wanted to continue its activities in Northern Cyprus, it had to obtain the consent and co-operation of the Turkish authorities.[84]

The resolution of the UN Security Council on 13 December 2000, too, mentioned only the consent of the Cypriot government. Thus, the UN established the practice of not taking the consent of the both sides. According to the Turkish side, this situation undermined the basis of the activities of the UN Force in Northern Cyprus. This was a dangerous development. The Turkish Foreign Ministry issued a statement asserting that the UN resolution was contrary to the text and spirit of the statement of the UN Secretary-General on 12 September 2000, which emphasised the political equality of the two communities. Turkey announced once more that it would not recognise such kind of resolutions. The American authorities did not share the views of the Turkish side on this

---

[82] Interview with İsmail Cem, *Turkish Daily News*, 28-29 July 1999.
[83] *Dışişleri Güncesi: July 2000*, pp.86-87.
[84] *Dışişleri Güncesi: June 2000*, pp.71, 105-106.

matter. In the State Department's noon briefing on 14 December 2000, Spokesman Boucher clarified that the renewal resolution urged the Turkish side to rescind the restrictions that it had imposed on peacekeepers. He also added that the American administration would strongly oppose any additional measured to restrict the operations by the UN forces in Cyprus.

Another party whose opinions and actions on Cyprus are not approved by the Turkish side is the EU. In the opinion of the Turkish side, the EU has exhibited an unjust act violating principles of law and complicated the Cyprus question further by starting membership negotiations with the Greek Cypriot side. Statements, decisions and practices of different organs of the EU on the Cyprus issue as well as their attitude of considering this matter as a precondition of Turkey's becoming a member of the EU annoy the Turkish authorities considerably. While responding to the acceptance of the report of Reporter Poos on the situation of Cyprus's membership negotiations by the General Assembly of the European Parliament on 4 October 2000, the Turkish Foreign Ministry stated that the members of the European Parliament approached the Cyprus issue by holding a biased view and leaving the realities aside. The EU's general attitude of considering the Turkish forces in Cyprus as the occupying forces, too, cannot be acceptable form the Turkish point of view.[85]

In the latter period of 1997-1999, the EU concerned that leaving Turkey outside the candidacy status for the EU membership might end the Cyprus diplomacy completely and might bring about serious crises between Greece and Turkey.[86] Ultimately, the EU ratified the candidacy status of Turkey in the Helsinki summit and thus the hopes for a progress in Cyprus were renewed. However, the EU made no substantial change in its attitude toward the Cyprus issue, did not undertake any commitment on the membership of the Greek Cypriot and did not start membership negotiations with Turkey. The possibility that the Greek Cypriots could be a member of the EU before Turkey was still high.[87] The new approach of the EU was that it would take into consideration all the relevant factors to decide on the membership of Cyprus, but it would take its decision without being bound with the opinions of the sides. It was clear that the EU did not agree with the Turkish side's view that the international agreements and regulations of 1960 on Cyprus prohibited Cyprus's becoming member of the EU. The EU's announcement that the political solution of the Cyprus problem would not be a condition of the membership of Cyprus in the EU was also not in the interest of Turkey.

Some strategists still argue that through the policies that it pursues on the Cyprus issue, the EU will prove that it is an able power. In their opinion, the EU will also disprove in this way the claims that it cannot handle serious international problems such as Cyprus and cannot solve them without the help of the USA. If the EU pursues a

---

[85] *Dışişleri Güncesi: October 2000,* pp.39, 248.
[86] Alan Makovsky, "Turkey and the European Union: One More Try"; Makovsky, "New Activism in Turkish Foreign Policy". (The articles of Makovsky are taken from the web site of The Washington Institute).
[87] Ishtiaq Ahmad, "Prospects of Cyprus Settlement After the Helsinki Summit", *Marmara Journal of European Studies,* c. 8, No.1-2, 2000, p.60.

coherent and strong foreign security policy, it would be able to contribute to the solution of the Cyprus problem substantially. And if the EU solves this problem and completes the accession of Cyprus to its structure, this would symbolise its commitment to the security of the Mediterranean and the West decisively and would demonstrate its weight in world politics. On the contrary, if the EU fails to take such a determined attitude, its ability to influence developments in Cyprus would be reduced and it would appear that the EU is not a major power that is able to compete with other world powers. That kind of attitude would also have a negative impact on the interests of the EU itself in the eastern Mediterranean and beyond.[88] Such provocative opinions imply serious repercussions such as being isolated in the Cyprus issue for Turkey. It is assumed that in such likelihood, Turkey will expect that the Americans will resist the EU action to maintain its world leadership, but the Americans will not act in this way not to alienate from the newly emerging European power.

Turkeyís Approach

Turkey supported the inter-communal talks on Cyprus, which were held in the context of the UN Secretary-General's good will, beginning in December 1999. However, determining the real character of these talks was very important for the Turkish authorities. In their opinion, since no suitable basis had been created yet to bring the sides together, the main purpose of those talks was to lay the groundwork for negotiations directed to finding a comprehensive solution. Turkish rulers considered the proximity talks as an important step that was taken in this direction and therefore they supported the continuation of the talks. However, as the two sides passed from one round to another, it became clear that the common ground could not be established and the Greek Cypriots did not give consent to recognising the equal status of the Turkish side. In that point, the Turkish authorities declared that the decision of moving to the phase of face-to-face negotiations would be taken by the president of the TRNC and the Turkish Cypriot government. They also asserted that the proposal of the Turkish Cypriots, projecting the establishment of a confederation and taking into consideration the EU aspect, was the most realist and viable alternative. Now it was up to the Greek Cypriots to take advantage of the talks to prepare the convenient ground. The Turkish government supported the views of the Turkish Cypriots completely and appreciated the leadership of Denktash.[89]

In his various statements, Turkish Foreign Minister İsmail Cem emphasised that it was the Turkish side, which was more active, more consistent with its opinions and which maintained the control over the development of the Cyprus issue. In his opinion, only the Turkish side brought proposals to the negotiating table, established dialogue with the

---

[88] Theophanous. "Cyprus, the European Union...", p.224.

[89] The statements of Vice Spokesman of Turkish Foreign Ministry Sermet Atacanlı on 17 February and 23 February 2000, *Dışişleri Güncesi: February 2000*, pp.62. 123, the statement of the Turkish Foreign Ministry on 3 August 2000, *Dışişleri Güncesi: August 2000*, Ankara: TC Dışişleri Bakanlığı, p.18, the statement of Turkish Prime Minister Ecevit on 8 September 2000, *Dışişleri Güncesi: September 2000*, Ankara: TC Dışişleri Bakanlığı. p.43, the interview with Foreign Minister İsmail Cem on the Turkish television channel NTV, *Dışişleri Güncesi: May 2000*, Ankara: TC Dışişleri Bakanlığı, p.17, the statement of the Turkish Foreign Ministry on 31 January 2000, *Dışişleri Güncesi: January 2000*, p.144.

USA, Britain and the EU on its own project, the confederation, and answered various opinions of these states in the matter. As a result, only the projects of the Turkish side were discussed and the other side did nothing other than rejecting the suggestions. Cem himself talked to the officials of the Western countries by feeling the comfort of being on the side that put the proposal of confederation and asked their opinion on the deficiencies of this project, but they could not find any deficiency. The only objection was raised against the term 'confederation'. According to Cem, the Turkish side was going on in the right direction, its project was the strongest project and it should continue to follow this road. In this way, the insincerity of the Greek Cypriots would become apparent and the other powers would take more conciliatory attitude toward the Turkish side's position by understanding it more clearly.[90]

One position of the Turkish side, which was insistently proclaimed by Cem, was that Turkey would not raise the Cyprus issue with the Greek authorities in bilateral relations in the détente period between the two sides. Cem's statement in this matter was very clear:

> *Cyprus is not a matter of our bilateral relations... The Cyprus issue concerns only the two communities in Cyprus. Therefore we will not discuss this question in the context of the Greek-Turkish relations.*[91]

However, this attitude contradicted with the opinion of the Americans that the issue should be solved with the joint efforts of Turkey and Greece. Turkish authorities frequently complain about the actions of the Greek Cypriots, for not communicating 'goodwill' across. When the Greek Cypriots tried to prevent the international activities of the Turkish Cypriot universities, Turkish Foreign Ministry Spokesman Sermet Atacanlı considered it as an intervention in the right of education, demonstrating the hostile intentions of the Greek Cypriots toward the Turkish side.[92] The Turkish authorities also accuse the Greek Cypriot side of using the EU membership prospect as a tool to steal the rights of the Turkish Cypriots, granted by international agreements, and to tilt the balance in favour of Greece. Therefore, the Turkish side strongly opposes to the intervention of the EU in the Cyprus question and to the establishment a connection between the Cyprus issue and Turkey's future membership in the EU. Turkish authorities also are not pleased with the intervention of other third sides in the matter to force the Turkish side to a compromise by leaving aside its rights and interests. In their opinion, only the Cypriot communities can solve the problem.

Sporadic statements made by the UN and US representatives in order to arouse the effect that the Turkish and Greek Cypriot communities are equal peoples having separate and independent entities are considered by Turkish authorities as positive steps taken in

---

[90] The interview with Foreign Minister Cem on 2 April 2000 on the Turkish television Star *Dışişleri Güncesi: April 2000*, p.32, the interview with Foreign Minister Cem on 28 May 2000 on the Turkish television TRT1, *Dışişleri Güncesi: May 2000*, p.144, the press conference of Foreign Minister İsmail Cem on 1 September 2000, *Dışişleri Güncesi: September 2000*, p.20, the interview with Foreign Minister İsmail Cem on 13 April 2000 on the Turkish television NTV, *Dışişleri Güncesi: April 2000*, pp.135-136.
[91] The press conference of Foreign Minister İsmail Cem on 1 September 2000, *Dışişleri Güncesi: September 2000*, p.19.
[92] The briefing of the Turkish Foreign Ministry on 27 March 2000, *Dışişleri Güncesi: March 2000*, p.123.

the right direction. But they also face great difficulties in their foreign relations because of the restrictions imposed by the other powers on the basis of the Cyprus question. The American tendency of tying economic and military aid and sales to Turkey to the Cyprus issue is one matter displeasing Turkish rulers. The possibility of the Americans' pressurising the Turkish administration in finding a solution to the Cyprus problem by complying with EU demands is also a source of worry for Turkish officials. It might be speculated that Turkey would resist the American and EU pressures on Cyprus in order to prove that it is an important regional power having a say on international issues as well. In spite of experiencing serious economic and political problems, Turkish rulers' holding an adamant attitude towards Cyprus is one possibility. Apart from openly protesting against the EU, some Turkish statesmen such as Foreign Minister Cem and Defence Minister openly state that they do not share and approve of the views of the Americans on the Cyprus issue. They frequently declare that no power can put pressures on the Turkish side to accept a solution harming their interests.[93]

Cyprus has such an importance for Turkey that Turkish rulers feel compelled to continue their stance on the issue in spite of all outside pressures and negative developments. According to Turkish diplomatic circles, the gains, obtained in the Cyprus issue over the years, constitute the most important diplomatic victories of the Turkish Republic since its establishment.[94] Giving in the pressures on this matter will mean a total failure of the Republic's diplomacy. There are internal dynamics in Turkey, which should be taken into consideration by outside power trying to push Turkish authorities for a solution. The Turkish Cypriots are considered as an integral part of the Turkish people and their struggle is seen as the struggle of the Turkish people. Therefore, Turkey is ready to make every sacrifice to maintain the sovereignty of the Turkish Cypriots.[95] No Turkish government can put aside the interests of the Turkish Cypriots without risking a serious, hostile and even calamity-bringing reaction at home. On the other hand, Turkey's close relations with the USA and the generally West and its need for the Western economic, political and military assistance restrict its capability of action and make the Cyprus issue an important problem of Turkish foreign policy.

One claim on Turkey's internal dynamics related to Cyprus is that Turkish authorities have the tendency to use the Cyprus issue as a tool in Turkey's accession to the EU.[96] Two possibilities are mentioned in this regard. One possibility is that if the Turkish elite do not want to join the EU for the time being, it will take an adamant stance on the Cyprus issue to please the Turkish people and to provoke the EU authorities not permit Turkey to join their organisation. Turning the Turkish people completely against the EU in this way will provide them the opportunity to pursue policies of their own choice without any public hostility. The second possibility is that if Turkish authorities decide definitely to join the EU, they will change their Cyprus policies to please the Europeans

---

[93] The joint press conference of Çakmakoğlu and Cohen on 15 July 1999.
[94] Barutçu, *Hariciye Koridoru*, p.266.
[95] The speech of Turkish President Ahmet Necdet Sezer in Cyprus on 22 June 2000, *Dışişleri Güncesi: June 2000*, Ankara: TC Dışişleri Bakanlığı, p.110.
[96] Hasgüler, *Kıbrıs"ta Enosis ve Taksim...*, p.274.

and they will make Turkey's EU membership a condition of the solution of the Cyprus problem. Even if there are such tendencies among Turkish rulers, it is clear that reaching a vital objective of foreign policy by trusting in only one tool is not a rational act. Moreover, the special characteristics of the Cyprus question, as mentioned above, do not allow its use for a flexible tool. Nevertheless, the claim that Turkey might use the Cyprus issue as a tool against Greece seems to have some validity. According to this claim, the presence of Turkish military forces in Cyprus leads to be cautious in the Aegean. "The Greeks are cognizant of the fact that in the event that they escalate the crisis in the Aegean to a hot conflict, this will force Turkey to take military measures in Cyprus."[97]

Given the fact that the Greek Cypriots are recognised as the only official representative of Cyprus, the Turkish side insists on the recognition of their administration as an independent and equal entity existing on the island before progressing on substantial talks.[98] In the opinion of the Turkish side, the basic parameter of the Cyprus question is the protection of balance between the Turkish and Greek communities, which is based on the principle of equality, as well as the balance between the positions of Turkey and Greece in the Aegean and Cyprus.[99] In this context, only a con-federal solution, which will be based on the equality and sovereignty of the Turkish and Greek Cypriot communities, will be a viable solution protecting the security of the two sides.[100] Some Turkish circles hope that the requirements and pressures of globalism as well as the recognition of the TRNC by some Central Asian or Muslim countries will end the isolation of the Turkish Cypriot administration in the international arena.[101]

The USA's Approach

The United States established positions such as the special co-ordinator for Cyprus to facilitate negotiations between the Greek and Turkish Cypriots, to promote a comprehensive peace settlement on Cyprus and to ensure policy-level co-ordination of efforts related to Cyprus. American special envoys and co-ordinators work closely with the Cypriot parties as well as the interested governments, maintain an active dialogue with the Congress and have regular contacts with the Secretary General of the UN and his representatives.[102] The American authorities consider the Cyprus issue as the most important problem, on which the approaches of Turkey and the USA clashed with each other.[103] The Americans state that the status quo in Cyprus, which is based on the

---

[97] Barutçu, *Hariciye Koridoru*, p. 253, Moustakis and Sheehan, "Greek Security Policy...", pp.96-97.

[98] The press conference of Vice Spokesman of the Foreign Ministry Sermet Atacanlı on 19 January 2000, *Dışişleri Güncesi: January 2000*, p. 100, the statement of Vice Spokesman of the Foreign Ministry Sermet Atacanlı on 17 February 2000, *Dışişleri Güncesi: February 2000*, Ankara: TC Dışişleri Bakanlığı, p.62. The press conference of Vice Spokesman of the Foreign Ministry Sermet Atacanlı on 23 February 2000, *Dışişleri Güncesi: February 2000*, p.124.

[99] The speech of Turkish President Ahmet Necdet Sezer in Cyprus on 22 June 2000, *Dışişleri Güncesi: June 2000*, p.109.

[100] The statement of the Turkish Foreign Ministry on 3 August 2000, *Dışişleri Güncesi: August 2000*, Ankara: TC Dışişleri Bakanlığı, p.18.

[101] Ahmad, "Prospects of Cyprus Settlement After the Helsinki Summit", p.68.

[102] The statement of the press secretary of the White House on 3 September 1999.

[103] Alan Makovsky, "Special Policy Forum Report: Ecevit's Turkey", Alan Makovsky, "Good Vibes, Little

partition, cannot be acceptable and insist that inter-communal negotiations should be continued without any precondition.[104] American rulers also are firm in that a bizonal and bicommunal federation is the only way of solving the Cyprus problem.[105] Moreover, Washington criticises the Turkish Cypriots because of their insistence on the recognition of their state and the interruption of the EU membership process of the Greek Cypriots before reaching a comprehensive solution. The American pressures on the Turkish side aimed at leading them to resume substantial negotiations, to take positive steps for a rapid solution and to make considerable concessions cause tensions between the Americans and the Turkish side.[106]

The American rulers emphasise that the status of the Turkish Cypriots cannot be a precondition of starting substantial negotiations for a solution, but they suggest that it will be better if this issue is left to other phases to be solved as a part of the final solution.[107] As they recognise the leader of the Greek Cypriots as the president of Cyprus, the Americans avoid making any comment on the status of the leaders participating in the negotiations. In their opinion, the leaders represent their communities in some way. The authority in the north speaks on behalf of the Turkish Cypriots and the government in the south is the one the Americans recognise.[108] The American view that the Turkish side should cede some amount of territory for making it possible to reach a final solution displeases the Turks. In fact, the American intervention in the matter within its own scope is considered by the Turks as a factor supporting the Greek Cypriots because the Greek Cypriot side are able to obtain the American support in many incidents, thanks to the mighty Greek lobbies in the USA. They act in the comfort of the belief that the Americans will prevent a radical change that will ruin their interests. The American authorities seek ways to prevent the eruption of crises because of the Cyprus problem since they know that they will have to intervene in such an event that will bring about more dangerous situations. Their main effort concentrates on pushing the Turkish side for a rapid solution. The American failure to fulfil Turkish demands in other areas weakens their ability to affect the Turkish side on Cyprus. On the other hand, President Clinton's statement in Athens on 20 November 1999 ("Turkey cannot be fully integrated successfully into Europe without solving its difficulties with Greece") gives the signal of cornering Turkey in its weakest point. In other words, Turkey's need to have partnership relations with the USA and the EU weakens its hand on Cyprus. President Clinton's statements cited in the White House report on 27 October 2000 demonstrates the American seriousness in this matter.

To see entrenched and immoveable positions in Cyprus in what really ought to be a fairly straight-forward problem to solve, keep them apart and keep Turkey more at

---

Cash in Store for Ecevit".
[104] The joint press conference of Çakmakoğlu and Cohen on 15 July 1999, the speech of American Secretary of State Madeleine K. Albright on 12 May 2000, the speech of President Clinton in Athens on 20 November 1999.
[105] The joint press conference of Çakmakoğlu and Cohen on 15 July 1999.
[106] Makovsky, "New Activism in Turkish Foreign Policy".
[107] The press conference of Moses in Larnaca Airport on 9 January 2001.
[108] Ibid.

arm's length from Europe, I think it's price not worth paying... It just makes no sense in the larger context of the future of Greece..., Turkey... and the Cypriots themselves, to maintain this present impasse with all the bad feelings and conflicts and estrangements that it has brought us.

It is also possible to hear from the Americans statements that please the Turkish side. American Defence Secretary Cohen stated on 14 July 1999 that they preferred to live up to the Greek and Turkish governments to resolve their differences including the Cyprus issue and he emphasised that the US did not seek in any way to become an arbiter or any way to pressure either government.[109] According to the Americans, the structure and terms of a settlement are matters for Cypriots to decide and a negotiated settlement has to obtain the positive support of Greece and Turkey.[110] In the past, when rumours erupted that the US applied pressure tactics against the sides on a solution, the American authorities denied it. American Defence Secretary Cohen stated in his press conference in Ankara on 15 July 1999 that they did not seek to put pressure on either Greece or Turkey on the Cyprus question and that they did not intend to try and impose their own view. He also emphasised their belief that the solution must be brought about through direct dialogue between the parties concerned.[111] American Special Co-ordinator for Cyprus Thomas Weston exhibited the same attitude with his statement on 8 September 1999:

I very firmly believe that addressing the issues on the island must come from the people and from the leaders on the island. It is not for the US or anyone else to seek to impose a plan from the outside.

Other views and attitudes of the Americans on the Cyprus issue can be summarised as follows: If the problem can be solved there will be no embargo imposed on the Turkish side and it will be possible move towards the two sides being more equal in their economic well-being. The Americans, who do not want to make any comment on the legality or illegality of the settlers in Cyprus,[112] would like to see a united Cyprus enter the EU, to be followed closely by the accession of Turkey to the EU. They do not come up with ideas and suggest the sides accept their thoughts. On the contrary, American officials prefer to work in the framework of a dialogue out of which emerged certain ideas that are being considered.[113] They spend efforts for the continuation of negotiations, but they are not involved in the substance of the negotiations, which are held under the auspices of the UN, not the USA. If one of the sides does not want to continue with the process, their response to that side will be the same regardless of their ethnic origin: 'try to find a basis'.[114] American officials, who believe that a Turkey rejected by the EU would be a strategic loss for the West, warned the Europeans in the past that if Turkey were granted the EU candidacy, one of the negative consequences would be the end of the Cyprus diplomacy.[115] Clinton's speech in Athens on 20 November 1999 is important in

---

[109] The statement of Cohen on 14 July 1999.
[110] "US-Cyprus Relations" (From the web site of the American embassy in Cyprus).
[111] The joint press conference of Çakmakoğlu and Cohen on 15 July 1999.
[112] The statement of Moses in Nicosia on 10 March 2000.
[113] The press conference of Moses in the American embassy in Ankara on 11 January 2001.
[114] The press conference of Moses in Larnaca Airport on 9 January 2001.
[115] Makovsky, "Turkey and the European Union: One More Try".

pointing that Turkey will be persuaded to solve the Cyprus issue if it is accepted to the EU:

> *It is very much in your [Greek] interest to see Turkey become a candidate for membership in the EU, for that will enforce Turkish secular, democratic, modernising path, showing Turkey how much it has to gain by making progress on issues like Cyprus and the Aegean matters... For many of these same reasons, we...have also strongly supported the EU's decision to start accession talk with Cyprus.*

The 2001-2002 Period

On the Cyprus question, five rounds of proximity talks were held between 3 December 1999 and 10 November 2000 "with a view to preparing the ground for meaningful negotiations which would lead to a comprehensive settlement". The opening statement made by the UN Secretary-General Annan at the fourth round on 12 September 2000 reaffirmed that the two peoples on the Island are politically equal parties who do not represent each other and underlined the need for the two parties to reach a comprehensive settlement through talks in which they would participate as equals. The Greek Cypriot side rejected it in a decision of its "House of Representatives" on 11 October 2000. On the other hand, as a response to a paper entitled "Oral Remarks", which was presented by the UN Secretary-General to the two sides on 8 November 2000, Turkey and the Turkish Republic of Northern Cyprus stressed that it was not possible to take the views expressed in this paper, which, let alone "confederation", fell behind even "federation", seriously. The Turkish side considered it useless to continue with the proximity talks due to the negative way in which the talks progressed and until the reasonable and realistic parameters put forward by the Turkish Cypriot side were accepted.

One important recent development on the Cyprus question was the abolishment of the office of President's Special Envoy for Cyprus by the Americans. This development might be interpreted as that the new American administration was not willing to put pressures on the parties with regard to the Cyprus problem. Since the Turkish side felt more outside pressures, they could be pleased with this incident. But the eruption of heavy economic crises in Turkey and the Turkish Republic of Northern Cyprus underlined the possibility that the Turkish side might be subjected to more pressures on Cyprus because of its for being in need of foreign economic help. Moreover, one possibility was that Cyprus would become a serious problem in Turkish-American relations. According to one scenario, Turkey would try to obtain the American opposition to the completion of the Greek Cypriot membership negotiations with the EU. Since they would know certainly that their efforts would not be successful, the Americans would only watch the Greek Cypriot side's become a full member of the EU. When the Turkish side, which was alienated totally, chose to integrate the TRNC with Turkey, their relations with the USA and the EU countries would deteriorate seriously and they would be isolated in the international arena. It can be derived from this scenario that the USA would not feel any necessity to pressurise the sides of the Cyprus problem.

After unsuccessful attempts of the UN representative to bring sides together again, on 4 December 2001 the leaders of the two Cypriot communities, Clerides and Denktash held an unexpected face-to-face meeting in the buffer zone in Cyprus. UN representative De

Soto was also present for the purpose of note taking. De Soto read a statement after the meeting, announcing that the two leaders agreed to enter into direct talks in mid-January 2002. According to the statement, the negotiations would start without preconditions, as all issues on the table and continue under the auspices of the UN until a comprehensive settlement was achieved and nothing would be agreed until everything was agreed.[116]

The new development could be seen as the result of different factors. The EU would decide on the accession of Cyprus at the end of 2003 and it was possible that Cyprus could be among the first line countries whose accession process would be completed in 2004. For the Turkish Cypriots, it was important to launch one more initiative to find a political solution to the Cyprus problem with the Greek Cypriots before this process was completed. If their initiative brought success, they could join the EU with the Greek Cypriots in conjunction with the high possibility that Turkey would be granted an opportunity for becoming a member of the EU in a near future after this development. If Cyprus became full member of the EU before a political solution was found to the Cyprus problem, the Turkish Cypriots might have to take radical steps as a reaction. In this case, they would not want to be accused of not holding serious negotiations with the Greek Cypriot side before the process was completed. By initiating the new round of negotiations, they would be able to defend their radical acts in the future.

On the other hand, the Greek Cypriot side definitely expected that Cyprus would be a full member of the EU in a near future, a likelihood which would force the Turkish Cypriot side to recognise the authority of the Cypriot government and which would rob them of every kind of opportunity to take steps harming the Greek Cypriot interests. Holding inter-communal negotiations with the Turkish side for the time being would not bring any problem for them, and on the contrary, it would increase their prestige in the eyes of the international community. They had nothing to lose except the possible failure in the negotiations. In addition, the ongoing negotiations would decrease the likelihood that the world powers such as the United States would oppose to Cyprus's becoming member of the EU for strategic reasons.

In the new development, outside intervention was also possible. The Western world under the leadership of the USA now faced a new international situation after the terrorist attacks in the USA on 11 September 2001. In the new period, it was very important for the United States to maintain the unity of the Western world and to solve the problems constituting source of trouble for the West in order to struggle against new threats more powerfully. The Cyprus problem had always the potential to cause a major conflict within the West and to harm the US interests in critical regions such as the eastern Mediterranean, the Middle East and the Central Asia. Turkey and Greece were important partners of the USA, which had vital place in American policies directed to these regions. The American authorities believed that it was now high time to remove the Cyprus issue from the agenda of Turkey, Greece, the USA and the EU as an irritating point. It was possible that the Americans might have persuaded the Greek and Turkish authorities in bringing their respective allies in Cyprus to negotiating table again.

---

[116] http://www.mfa.gov.tr/grupb/bf/developmentsCyprus.htm.

However, the atmosphere was not suitable altogether. The position of Turkey and the Turkish Cypriots was particularly sensitive. Although Turkey definitely chose the West as the only direction, in which its march would continue, there were some fears and doubts felt by the Turkish people, politicians and rulers including the military ones about the American and European attitude toward the issues of Turkey. The statement of one high-level military official that Turkey should consider co-operating with Iran and Russia in case it had problems with the Western countries and the suggestion of some leading politicians and statesmen that Turkey should not consider the EU membership as the only alternative could be sited as examples in this respect. The Cyprus issue was the most important matter on which Turkish rulers and people might challenge the West at all costs and which might be turned to a tool of anti-Western stance. It was at least clear that Turkish people would not sacrifice Cyprus, which was one of their most important causes, for short-term gains. Such an action would devastate the Turkish perception that their state was an important regional country, which had the potential to affect world policies. On the other hand, Turkish authorities were aware that they could not stay outside the EU and the Western world. Co-operation with the EU and the USA was a necessity for Turkish interests. Finding a political solution to the Cyprus problem would be a great help in this regard.

One possibility at this point was the initiation of a new bargaining in the context of the EU while maintaining the status quo on the island. In 1995, Turkey did not protest strongly against the EU decision of starting the accession negotiations with the Greek Cypriots in return for the removal of the Greek veto for the Customs Union Agreement. In 1999, Turkish authorities did not strongly criticise the EU decision that it would decide on the accession of Cyprus without seeing the solution of the Cyprus problem as a condition in return for the EU's granting candidate status to Turkey. Now, it was speculated that Turkish authorities would not raise objections to the completion of the accession process of the Greek Cypriot side in return for the EU decision to start accession negotiations with Turkey. This possibility gained weight especially in the light of the claim that Turkey would not able to launch radical actions such as the integration of the northern Cyprus into the mainland in the face of strong reactions of the USA and the EU. On the other hand, it was a fact that the EU and the USA wanted to see Turkey as their partners in protecting their interests in critical regions and in facing new threats. Therefore, they would not easily choose to alienate Turkey by imposing their own solution in the Cyprus issue. It was expected that they would try to encourage the sides to find a solution, which would be acceptable to all concerning parties.

The thinking, which dominated the Turkish rulers in that period, was the following: The Cyprus issue was not a simple ethnic problem, which could be solved with outside interventions. Since it concerned relations and interests of important regional and world powers, it had to be dealt with in this context. The important thing was the sincerity of the sides in finding a solution. If one of the sides refrained from taking such an attitude by trusting in some international factors, processes and outside powers, the problem would continue to poison important relations and interests. The USA and the EU seemed to give the impression that they did not support any particular side or viewpoint, but they expected serious steps from the parties for the sake of the Western alliance. Some important criteria could be pointed out and a road map could be drawn in finding a solution. Firstly, the recent tendency in international politics was that even communities having some common characteristics decide to establish separate states by abolishing their common state mechanism. In Cyprus, there were two communities, which had definite different characteristics and which had sour relations between themselves; therefore, it was almost an impossible task to bring together absolutely different communities. Secondly, the Cypriot leaders should try to establish a common vision and agree on the final shape of their future joint state before dealing with other main aspects of the sought solution. Thirdly, the sides should respect the main viewpoint of each other without asking the other side to change its preconditions. The possible roadmap could be summarised as the following: Firstly, the sides should reconcile their main positions and should establish a partnership state, which would present both communities with a proposal on which they can agree. Secondly, they should agree on authorities and functions, which would be transferred to this state. Finally, they should agree on all the matters considered as vital. Objections might be raised against these proposals, but it was important to state that the two communities might resolve their basic disagreements by making some concessions for the sake of a better future for themselves and all the other states involved.

The Recent Atmosphere of the Problem

The Attitude of the Greek Cypriot Side

In the latest stage of the Cyprus question, the representatives of the two communities on the island had conducted intensive negotiations to find a solution to the problem before the EU summit meeting, which would be held in December 2002 and which would decide about the finalisation of the membership process of Cyprus. The Americans, Europeans and UN officials, too, wanted a quick solution to the problem in the context of the EU membership process, which was considered as the last serious chance to benefit from. However, some facts were forgotten in the emerging suitable atmosphere, which had created serious hopes for solution. The Greek Cypriots were in an advantageous position because of the certainty of their EU membership; therefore, they did not feel that it could ever be that urgent to reach a solution to the problem. Their decisive reluctance in taking no steps to reach a possible solution was not even met by any strong disapproval or severe criticism that could be articulated openly by the official spokesperson of the EU. On the other hand, the Turkish Cypriots were not comfortable in protecting their interests since they were pressurised for a quick solution with heavy threats concerning their and Turkey's future interests.

There are important reasons for the Greek Cypriots not to be sincere in inter-communal talks on the Cyprus question. They have been recognised as the official representative of the island in the international arena since March 1964. They can join and express their opinions and cast their votes in international organisations on behalf of the Cypriots. For example, they were able to apply and to become eligible for the EU membership and they have succeeded in obtaining the unconditional support of the EU members for they could very possibly make use of all the means in such a way that the Cyprus question would turn out to be complete disadvantage on the part of the Turkish side. The Greek Cypriots also have the privileges of opening diplomatic offices throughout the world and being a member of effective groupings such as the Commonwealth and the non-aligned movement. As a result, they can propagate their causes in international forums easily. By denying the same opportunities allotted to the Turkish Cypriots, the Greek Cypriot side wants to have upper hand, but this attitude cause difficulties in reaching a solution by creating an imbalance between the positions of the sides. The other side naturally tries to protect its interests by adopting seemingly a harsher stance.

Carrying their problems by means of Turkey, including the Cyprus question, to Europe has always been one of the main foreign policy aims of the Greeks and the Greek Cypriots and, indeed, they havemade their way to become successful in that. They were sure that they would gain the upper hand by obtaining the support of the Europeans. In fact, their real intention can be detected in their statements stressing a great victory in the history of Helenism. Greek Cypriot leader Glafcos Clerides demonstrated their excitement by stating that the Greek Cypriot membership in the EU was the greatest victory they had achieved since 1960.[117] Greek Prime Minister Simitis, too, was jubilant on the result and he said that the admission of the Greek Cypriot regime to the EU turned over a new leaf in the history of Helenism and that Cyprus was now with them with a single sovereignty and administration.[118] In his opinion, Cyprus was admitted to the EU without any condition thanks to the Greek government's efforts and this was a great success, from which important lessons should be derived.[119]

The Greek and Greek Cypriot side demonstrate their reluctance in reaching a solution by giving negative responses to proposals put forward on the question. Greek Cypriot leader Clerides declared that they would reject the Annan plan if changes were made to meet some demands of the Turkish side. He was sure that a solution would be found to the Cyprus question before the end of 2003.[120] The election of Papadopoulos as the president of the Greek Cypriot administrations also implies that the Greek Cypriots want to gain more concessions by holding a more adamant attitude. In fact, Papadopoulos is known as a person having a harsher stance toward the Turks with his background as an ex-member of the terrorist organisation EOKA. He had announced that he would demand important changes in key issues when he became president. Although Papadopoulos stated after the election that he would negotiate issues with the Turkish side with a good spirit, his demands were unacceptable from the Turkish point of view. They included the return of more Greek Cypriot refugees to the Turkish territory, the withdrawal of Turkish soldiers from the island, the repatriation of Turkish refugees to their homeland and the creation of a strong central sovereignty.

---

[117] http://www.msnbc.com/news/195169.asp. 1 January 2003.
[118] http://www.msnbc.com/news/193069.asp. 18 December 2002.
[119] http://www.msnbc.com/news/192569.asp. 12 December 2002.
[120] http://www.msnbc.com.tr/news/201080.asp?cp=1. 12 December 2002.

The Attitude of the European Union

The adamant position of the Greek Cypriots on the Cyprus question is supported by the European Union attitude toward the problem. First of all, the EU takes the recognition of the Greek Cypriot administration in the international arena as granted and does not want to discuss the legality of the present situation under the international law and international agreements. The Europeans do not see any necessity to debate the Turkish Cypriot argument that the Greek Cypriots have no legal or moral right to represent the whole island.[121] On the other hand, the Turkish Cypriots have difficulty in understanding the European attitude of completely disregarding the legal positions as far as the Turkish Republic of Northern Cyprus was concerned. They resent the Europeans' effectively announcing that they do not recognise the rights of the Turkish Cypriot side as stated in the Zurich and London agreements of 1959.[122] Facing this kind of attitude, Turkish Cypriot leader Rauf Denktaş believes that he is absolutely right in criticising the Europeans on not considering him as an equal counterpart in official affairs. For example, when he was criticised because of not attending the Copenhagen summit in December 2002, Denktaş stated that he was not invited by the European Union because his well-grounded thoughts were of no significance to the European Council.[123]

The attitude of the European Union on finding a solution to the Cyprus question, too, is not satisfactory for the Turkish side and has an anti-Turkish tone. At the beginning, the EU was of the opinion that the Cyprus question should be solved before the island became an EU member. The European Commission recommended in July 1993 that the accession process should follow the resolution of the problem.[124] However, the EU reversed its position soon and it saw no connection between the two factors. It also established a strong link among Turkey's accession process, improvements in negotiations held on the Cyprus issue and the EU membership of Cyprus. Turkey was required to constructively encourage the UN's attempts at finding a solution to the Cyprus dispute. The EU's new Cyprus policy included three aspects. Firstly, it would not regard the resolution of the Cyprus question as a precondition of EU membership of the island. Secondly, the EU would take all relevant factors into account when deciding on Cyprus' accession process. Finally, it would not create problems during the implementation process of the EU's internal regulations in each and every part of the island. It could be read easily that these three points were designed to please the Greek Cypriots, Turkey and the Turkish Cypriots respectively.[125] But the EU concentrated on the first approach while it ignored the other two, thus preferring to alienate the Turkish side.

The EU's stance on the final solution of the Cyprus question and the eventual

---

[121] Tuncer, "The Cyprus Issue: Recent Developments".

[122] Erol Manisalı, "What Happens if Cyprus Joins the EU without Turkey", İrfan Kaya Ülger and Ertan Efegil (eds.), *Avrupa Birliği Kıskacında Kıbrıs Meselesi*, Ankara: HD Yayıncılık, 2001, p.64.

[123] http://www.msnbc.com/news/197807.asp, 18 January 2003.

[124] H. Tarık Oğuzoğlu, "Prennial Conflict or Everlasting Peace: the European Union's Involvement in Cyprus", *Perceptions*, July-August 2002, Vol.7, No.2, http://www.mfa.gov.tr/grupa/percept/VII-2/tarik.oguzoglu.htm.

[125] Ibid.

membership of Cyprus in the EU particularly irritate the Turkish side and lead it to launch desperate efforts to protects its vital interests. The European leaders give the impression that they always find the Turkish side responsible for any failure of inter-communal negotiations though the Greek Cypriot side, too, put forward important objections to proposed plans. This European attitude can be detected in the latest developments regarding the Annan plan prepared by the UN Secretary-General. There was no evidence whatsoever on that the Greek Cypriot side accepted the Annan plan's content altogether. In contrast, the Greek Cypriots elected a person, who raised important objections to the plan, as their president. Nevertheless, the chairman of the European Parliament, Pat Cox, held Turkey and the Turkish Cypriot administration responsible for the failure in reaching a final solution. Cox further caused a deep resentment on the Turkish side by stating that Cyprus would be represented in the EU organs as a whole after the accession agreement was signed.[126] The UN Secretary-General summoned the leaders of the Cypriot communities on 10 March 2003 to receive their final response. Neither side declared that they accepted the plan as a whole, but since that time the EU has put pressures mainly on the Turkish side by declaring that Turkey will never be a member of the EU unless the Cyprus question has been solved completely. On the other hand, the EU officials do not put forward any criticism to the Greek side and they declare that the accession process of Cyprus will be finalised smoothly.

It seems that the EU will finalise the accession process of the Greek Cypriot administration without any delay. But it is highly likely that such an occurrence will bring about serious risks and dangers for all the sides involved.[127] The accession of Cyprus to the EU as a divided state with the exclusion of the Turkish Cypriots from the process might cause deep crises between the Cypriot communities as well as between Greece and Turkey by eventually threatening peace and security in the eastern Mediterranean. In such likelihood, Turkey might lose the prospect of becoming a EU member forever and another serious crisis might erupt between the EU and Turkey. But the losers will not only be the Turkish Cypriots and Turkey. The Greek Cypriots would be deprived of living in a unified Cyprus, where they could enjoy the three fundamental rights. The anti-EU forces in Turkey would increase their political powers and the emergence of radical changes in traditional Turkish policies would be a high possibility. Of course, the European states including Greece would be affected by such a development seriously. Greece would not be comfortable about its security since it would have to live next to Turkey, which was estranged from the EU. Finally, Turkey might pursue anti-EU policies in the eastern Mediterranean, the Balkans and the Middle East and thus it might ruin vital EU interests in these regions.

The Position of the Turkish Side

The Turkish side believes that the establishment of a federation with a strong government

---

[126] http://www.msnbc.com/news/193342.asp, 19 December 2002.

[127] Hüner Tuncer, "The Cyprus Issue: Recent Developments", *Perceptions*, September-November 2002, Vol.7, No.3, http://www.mfa.gov.tr/grupa/percept/VII-3/HunerTuncer.htm. Oğuzoğlu, "Prennial Conflict or Everlasting Peace: the European Union's Involvement in Cyprus".

and two weak political entities is not a viable settlement because a deep hostility and mistrust have emerged between the two communities on the island in a long history.[128] Since they were recognised as equal political partners at the beginning and since one of them gained the international recognition in the latter stage, both of them should use its free self-determination right if a true federation will be established. It is a fact that no single Cypriot nation has been created. If a superior authority with comprehensive powers is imposed on the two communities, it will violate their separate, distinctive national characteristics.[129] The use of free self-determination right to create a partnership state will be more appropriate because it will respect sovereignty and independent political personality of the two sides. In fact, the UN's last proposal of solution is in compliance with these criteria. It includes a new partnership state with a single international legal personality based on the political equality of the sides, which will have their own laws.

Nevertheless, the Turkish side has the feeling that their expectations on co-founding partnership and political equality are not met fully in the context of the Annan plan and that the central government is strengthened with the transfer of authority of taking critical decisions in such fields as foreign policy, finance and security to it.[130] The Turkish Cypriot rulers insist that the new partnership state should not be the continuity of the present state because it was established illegally with the exclusion of the Turkish Cypriots from the administration by force. The new state should also not be the mere extension of either state that presently exists on the island because it will not be possible in this way to end the old hatreds, disagreements and debates. If the two existing political entities on the island are transformed into co-founder, equal and sovereign partners of the new partnership state, this formulation will create a more viable solution.[131] In the new state, each partner state should represent only its own people and should not claim sovereignty or jurisdiction over the other. The co-founding partners should have exclusive control over their own affairs except the matters that are explicitly assigned to the partnership state. However, the Turkish side considers the proposed structure of the Presidential Council as contrary to these criteria.[132] Since the Turkish Cypriot vice president has no veto power and since the vote of one Turkish Cypriot member is sufficient for the enactment of any legal arrangement, the Turkish Cypriots feel that their affairs are hijacked in a tricky and indirect way.

The bi-zonality of the new partnership state and having a secure territorial basis are among the most important concerns of the Turkish Cypriots because they have a smaller population and they faced great sufferings, difficulties and massacres in the past because of the actions of the other community on the island. They agree to give up some part of

---

[128] Ishtiaq Ahmad, "Resolving the Cyprus Conflict Through EU Enlargement Process", Ülger and Efegil (eds.), *Avrupa Birliği Kıskacında Kıbrıs Meselesi*, p.53.

[129] Ertan Efegil and Özgen Görgünler, "A Survey on the Public Opion's Concerns About the Proposals of the TRNC, South Cyprus, the UN and the EU", Ülger and Efegil (eds.), *Avrupa Birliği Kıskacında Kıbrıs Meselesi*, p.125.

[130] Armağan Kuloğlu, "Birleşmiş Milletler Kıbrıs Çözüm Planı Çözümün Neresinde?", http.//www.avsam.org, 17 February 2003.

[131] Tuncer, "The Cyprus Issue: Recent Developments".

[132] Kuloğlu, "Birleşmiş Milletler Kıbrıs Çözüm Planı Çözümün Neresinde?"

their territory as a part of the future solution. For example, there is almost a consensus among them that the Maraş area could be given as a good will demonstration. However, the Turkish Cypriots insist on that territorial arrangements should not cause great disturbances with large scale of new dislocations.[133] In this sense, if distinct territories or cantons are created within the territory of either side, new confrontations should be expected in the future. The Turkish side also raises objections to the inclusion of Karpaz peninsula in the Greek Cypriot side and the extension of the Greek Cypriot territory as far as the north of the Lefkosa-Magusa motorway on the ground that the security depth is lost for the northern part.[134] The Turkish Cypriots also concern that with the new arrangement, the fertile part of the Turkish Cypriot territory, which also include most of the water resources of the north, (Güzelyurt) will be left in the hands of the Greek Cypriots. On the question of property, the Turkish side prefers a global exchange of properties together with compensations to meet losses. The possible return of more than 60 thousand Greek Cypriots to the north under the new arrangement is particularly irritating for the Turkish Cypriots. In this way, the population rate of the Turkish Cypriots in the north will decrease continuously, a considerable number of the Turkish Cypriots will become refugees and the size of the Turkish territory will be reduced greatly. Some Turkish statesmen point out that these changes might create serious clashes and conflicts among the Turks by provoking the Turks, whose interests will be violated, against the others.[135]

Conclusion

Turkish officials and the Turkish Cypriots are not happy with the present situation in Cyprus and have no interests at all in the continuation of the problem because they are the ones, who suffer from the non-solution because of the pressures and embargoes they face. Nevertheless, they are not in the position to sacrifice their vital interests concerning the issue by giving consent to a quick solution, which will be imposed on them with the threats of isolating them in the international arena and blocking their future membership in the EU. They rightly point to the unjust attitude and opinions of the Greeks, the Greek Cypriots and the Europeans on the issue. The Turkish side is aware that the Greek Cypriots act with the comfort that they will be accepted to the EU with a future prospect that finding a solution favouring their terms will be possible with the support of the EU countries. It is difficult from the Turkish point of view to comprehend the fact that the Greek Cypriots, who stole the Cypriot administration with their illegal acts, are not protested because of their non-conciliatory attitude in finding a solution to the problem, but the process of their accession to EU goes on slowly but surely. Facing the Greek Cypriot attitude of using the EU as a tool for their causes and declaring a victory for Helenism and enosis as a result of securing their membership in the EU, the Turkish side

---

[133] Efegil and Görgünler, "A Survey on the Public Opion's Concerns About the Proposals of the TRNC, South Cyprus, the UN and the EU", p.126.
[134] Kuloğlu, "Birleşmiş Milletler Kıbrıs Çözüm Planı Çözümün Neresinde?"
[135] http://www.msnbc.com/news/196454.asp, 10 January 2003 (the statement of the prime minister of the Turkish Republic of Northern Cyprus, Derviş Eroğlu).

becomes more determined in protecting their interests against constant heavy pressures coming from the Western institutions. Of course, they do not want to stay outside the Western structures and to give up their aim of becoming an integral part of the West, but they are not ready to sacrifice their vital interests for this sake and they expect understanding from the West for their position.

In the minds of Turkish Cypriots and Turkish rulers, the negative stance of the EU on the Cyprus question is quite clear. The EU does not question the legitimacy of the Greek Cypriot administration and does not take the claims on the legality of the Turkish Cypriot regime into consideration. The decisions of the EU institutions have always carried an anti-Turkish tone disregarding the viewpoint of the Turkish side and harmed Turkish interests while they have taken care of the Greek Cypriot concerns. The EU attitude of insisting on the membership of Cyprus before the problem has been solved, and also considering the solution of the problem as a precondition for Turkey's EU membership is also regarded by the Turkish side as an unfair approach. Of course, the Turkish Cypriots believe that the EU might contribute to the solution of the Cyprus problem if it gives supports for a loosely centralised, single-sovereign, bi-zonal and bi-commmunal federal Cyprus. However, the present EU stance and the adamant Greek Cypriot attitude encouraged by it constitute irritating headaches for the Turkish side and discourage them in pushing for a permanent solution by working together with the Greek Cypriots and the Europeans.

The Turkish Cypriots voted overwhelmingly in favour of the Annan plan in the referendum conducted on 24 April 2004 though they had serious reservations about it. On the other hand, the Greek Cypriots, who had never been subject to serious pressures on the solution of the Cyprus problem, voted overwhelmingly against the plan. Thus it has become clear that the Greek Cypriots have expected to dominate the whole island by using their membership in the EU, which they secured regardless of the result of the referendum. The Turkish government and the Turkish Cypriots have accepted to make concessions for the sake of the integration with the European Union, but the Greek Cypriots, relying on their secured membership in the EU, have chosen not to solve the problem by making some sacrifices. It can also be seen as the proof that the Greeks and the Greek Cypriots have not given up the long-lived enosis ideal (that is the long-lasted ideology developed around the annexation of the island to Greece, now in the form of unification within the framework of the EU).

12 Turkey and Russia

Victor Panin
Henry Paniev

Introduction

The end of the Cold War has changed considerably the whole system of international relations. The bipolar world order which determined the political process of the development of the mankind in the second half of the 20th century has gone into the history. The result of such fundamental changes in the international system is a very rapid process of strategic reconfiguration of the modern world which means that the old opponents are becoming if not friends than at least allies. The countries have to combine their efforts in order to react to the new threats which arise along with the new shape of the world. Such problems as terrorism can not be settled by a single even very powerful country. Ideological rivalry has gone into the past. What would be the basis of international development? Either it will be economic interests or that would be the civilizational identity, or the geopolitical interests would still prevail? There are no vivid answers to this question for the time being. On the other hand such constant parameters of any country as its geopolitical position in the world, international environment, historic heritage, and traditional areas of national interests would also play a very important role in the foreign policy. The settlement of this dualism in the system of relationship between countries is a corner stone of the foreign policy in general and for the modern Russian-Turkish relations as well.

Not long ago - just a couple of decades these countries stood on different sides of the barricade in the Cold War. Sometimes their relations were very tense. At the same time despite many controversial approaches in many spheres it is necessary to state the fact that during the last hundred years there were no serious military conflicts between them. That might be regarded as a good example to the whole world of how the countries having lots of objective differences manage to conduct their relations by peaceful means. The recent fundamental changes in the international system created new environment which should be thoroughly analyzed both by academic community and politicians in order to preserve the long standing tradition of peaceful relationship between these countries for the mutual benefits of their peoples.

As one of the results of the breakup of the Soviet Union, in some regions of Eurasia, primarily in the Caucasus, the Caspian region and Central Asia there appeared a kind of geopolitical vacuum which naturally attracts some new geopolitical actors and some traditional ones including Russia and Turkey. The "geopolitical game" over this vast territory would inevitably lead to the new strategic configuration of the region. What's going to be its shape? What would be the nature of its foundation: either it's going to be reanimation of the old rivalry or another approaches reflecting the modern tendencies in the world development based on the principles of democracy, cooperation, transparency, mutual interests and necessity to react to the mutual threats would lead to the rapid and peaceful development of the countries situated here for the benefits of their peoples? What roads of development the countries would take in the 21st century, what would be the principles of their relationship; will it be possible to settle the conflicts inherited from the past? These as well as many other questions are the matter of intensive discussion both among politicians and scientists. Due to the limited space of the chapter it's next to impossible to analyze the whole sphere of the countries' relations. That's why the presented chapter contains the analysis and the authors' vision of the answers only to some of the updated aspects of the modern and perspective Russian – Turkish relations.

New Basis for Relationship

In the modern international system the result of the long term policy towards the construction of the industrialized secular state on the one hand and successful reforms conducted in the country on the other is the fact that Turkey nowadays is becoming a powerful geopolitical actor in Eurasia. In Russia the vision of Turkey as primarily the "Southern Flank of NATO" which was true at least twenty years ago during the Cold War has gone into the past. At that time the major geopolitical mission of the country was to be the southern bridge-head in the Western defense system. For the Western block the strategic importance of Turkey was determined by its geographical closeness to the most powerful enemy – the Soviet Union.

At present time the former approaches to the security system formation have been changed considerably. In Turkey there is a growing concern towards the threats of the new generation – terrorism in particular. The same concern is shared both by Russia as well as by many other countries in the world. These countries have been becoming one of the major targets for terrorists' attacks and there are all the grounds to consider that the tension of the terrorist activities would definitely grow if some urgent collective measures are not undertaken. Both for Russia and Turkey as well as for many other countries in the world terrorism have become the major threat to their national security. This situation gives all the ground to state the fact that the present relationship between the countries is based not only on mutual interests in different spheres but on the mutual threats to their national security.

From the middle of 1990s the area of cooperation between these countries has been enlarged. Turkey has become the first NATO member country to establish effective cooperation with Russia in the military economic and military technical spheres. Even these facts indicate that Russia has got rather solid basis for economic cooperation with Turkey. It is obvious that there are some problems or points which need further discussions. But the most important thing is that they are not hidden from the public and do not constitute the major part of the foundation in the countries' relationship. The present tendencies in the interstate relations show that in the nearest future they would receive another very important positive impulse – transportation of the natural gas from Russia to Turkey. In the framework of the 25 billion US dollars "Blue Stream" project Turkey by the end of 2025 will have received 365 billion cubic meters of Russian gas with the amount of annual supplies of 16 billion cubic meters.[1]

Though Turkey hoped to get some geopolitical preferences as the consequences of the breakup of the Soviet its key economic partner in the region remains to be Russia. The character of their relationship may be even judged by the Turkish credit to Russia in the amount of 1.15 billion US dollars. Presently more than 300 Turkish companies work in Russia mainly in civil construction and agriculture. Russia is the most important Turkish trade partner out of all NIS (New Independent States). Another remarkable example is that the amount of Turkish trade with Russia is five times more than with all Turkic states put together.[2]

At the same time Turkey is one of the major Russian geopolitical rivalries and opponents in some regions of Eurasia, even including some territories of Russia, primarily in its southern parts, mainly in the North Caucasus and in the Volga region. Turkey pays some interest even to Yakutiya. The combined military power of the Turkish Navy is higher than the Russian Black See Navy. Turkish economy despite all the difficulties is rather dynamic. Along with the Turkish ambitions to be the "Big Boss" of the region the country tries to get the position of the political leader of the big number of the Turkic countries spread from Balkans to Yakutiya. The breakup of the Soviet Union and the creation of the number of the independent states on the territory of the former Soviet Union was regarded by some people in political circles of Turkey as a unique chance to implement these strategic plans into life.

The idea of the creation of the unified Pan-Turkic state which would spread from China to the Mediterranean did not go into the history and has been recently reactivated. Its reanimation may be partially explained by the weakening of the Russian positions in the Caucasus, in the Caspian and in Central Asia and would be definitely regarded in Russia as the threat to its national security. The orient vector of the Turkish geopolitical interests and inspirations includes the North and South Caucasus, Crimea and Central Asia. As the economic basis for such a Pan-Turkic integration is rather weak. Turkey prefers to use in the term of Josef Nye Jr. the so called "Soft Power": linguistic, cultural and religious identity, historical memory, etc.

After a progress made at the beginning of the 1990s towards the Post Soviet space presently Turkey comes across some difficulties in this process. The newly created states, their political leadership being charmed at the beginning by the Turkish promises, have changed their position to a more pragmatic one analyzing the real possibilities of the cooperation with Turkey in the economic sphere, the possible consequences which might arise in the result of the too close political and more of that military integration with Ankara. Due to this Turkey is to conduct a highly constituent policy towards NIS. Priority is given to the programs of transit of the Caspian and the Central Asian oil and gas through the Turkish territory which might annually give Turkey several hundreds million dollars.

Such projects especially the Baku – Ceyhan pipeline is nothing but the attempt to

---

[1] Kamaludin Gadzhiev, *Geopolitica Kavkaza*, 2001, pp.455-456.
[2] *The Independent*, June 11, 2002.

boycott the northern (Russian) rout or at least to make out of it the additional one. It has been done despite the fact that according to the expert opinion, the Turkish rout summing up the complexity of mountain topography of the area, the availability of numerous political obstacles such as Armenia—Azerbaijan conflict, Georgian potential conflict area of Akhalkalaki inhabited by Armenians, Turkish Kurdistan conflict region is three times more expensive than the northern (Russian) rout.[3] If these plans succeed Turkey would strengthen its position as the main oil and gas transport transit corridor to the world markets which in its turn would raise its geopolitical status in the region as well in the industrialized world.

The above mentioned facts give the ground to make some conclusions. First, it has become obvious that Turkey has started to play its own relatively independent game in the post bipolar world which sometimes is not coincided with the role prepared for the country both by the USA and the EU. Second, Turkey has been becoming one of the most powerful Eurasian players having possibilities and sometimes even seeking to strengthen its position or arguments by forceful means. Third, as a reaction to such a possible strong articulation of the Turkish independent position one can not exclude the possibility of the joint actions among different actors including western countries, some regional players to block too active Turkish attempts to unanimously fill in the geopolitical vacuum appeared as the result of the end of the bipolar world order or to guarantee their concerns connected with the reanimation of the policy of Pan-Turkism. The numerous unsuccessful Turkish attempts to join the European Union are a vivid example of it.

Turkish attempts to revoke among Caucasian and Central Asian nations the feeling of their national identity by means of their incorporation into the Turkic world is rather a destructive factor in the "South Polar" of Eurasia. Needless to say, that those interests of Ankara are controversial to the interests of Moscow and Teheran. Pan-Turkism in this part of the world is the ideology of confrontation which provokes the ideological rivalry which is the major basis for the numerous painful ethnic conflicts in the region. For Moscow the matter of concern is the growing alliance between Ankara and Tel Aviv. It started to be formed at the beginning of 1990s and gives lots of advantages to Turkey in the way of strengthening its position in relationship with the neighbors: Iran, Syria and Iraq. With the view of the close ties between Baku and Ankara based on "Pan Turkic solidarity" one can not exclude the possibility of Azerbaijan joining this alliance.

The further weakening of the Russian positions on the southern strategic area would lead to the strengthening positions those of Turkey not only in the Caucasus but also in the Central Asia. The unwillingness of Europe to accept Turkey as its member cooled Turkish-European relations and predetermined escalation of Turkish activities on the Middle Eastern and Caucasian directions. The beginning of exploitation of the Baku – Ceyhan pipeline will further strengthen the positions of this country in the region.

The Caucasus

One of the most important areas of intersection of the interests of Russia and Turkey is

---

[3] Geoffrey Kemp and Robert Harkavy, *Strategic Geography and the Changing Middle East*, Washington: Brookings Institution Press, 1997, pp.140-143.

the Caucasus. Historically the Caucasus is regarded as one of the most important geostrategic regions of Eurasia which separates and at the same time unites Europe and Asia, Orthodox Christianity and Islam. Traditionally it is the area of clashes and a zone of vital interests of great powers. Nowhere in the world, at such a relatively small geographic region there live such a great variety of ethnic groups, different in their religions, economic systems, number of population, social values and cultural orientations, areas of inhabitance, levels of state organization etc. The Caucasus is located in the zone of civilizational clash between the Christian and Muslim worlds. That is why it is reasonably regarded as one of the main parts of the "Southern Rim of Instability". At the same time being situated at the boarder between Europe and Asia the Caucasus is a convenient springboard for extending influence to the Middle East, Central Asia, to the basins of the Black, Caspian and Mediterranean Seas. The Caucasus is as well the main transport corridor for supply of the Caspian energy resources to the world market – this even by itself increases its strategic significance. Strategically the whole Caucasus is the area of vital interests of Russia, more of that part of it is the Russian territory. It is the particular region where the country faces the most important threats to its security.

The Caucasus is consisted of two major geopolitical sub regions: the North Caucasus and Transcaucasia or the South Caucasus. The North Caucasus with its unique geopolitical position, ethnic diversity and as the result of it – high conflict tension has always played a remarkable role in the system of Russian national security. The region is distinguished by the broad level of ethno-cultural variety.

The North Caucasus is currently inhabited by the representatives of more than 100 nationalities. The total number of population in the area is about 17.7 million people of which 74% are Russians, Byelorussians and Ukrainians; 7.6% represent Dagestan ethnic groups; 6.2% Vainachs; 4.5% are from Turkic ethnic group; 3.5% are Abkhazo-Adigs.

Being situated at the crossroad of strategic, military, economic, civilizational, religious and other routes the North Caucasus has traditionally formed the area of interests of vital importance for the most powerful countries: first of all Russia, Turkey and Iran. This fact as well as the enormous energy potential of the Caspian basin provides to the North Caucasus the special political, economic, strategic and civilizational significance. Situation in the North Caucasus influences in many aspects on stability in the whole South of Russia and ensures the state of national security of the Russian Federation in general.

A long standing economic, social, political and ecological crisis taking place in the North Caucasus has a great negative impact on the Russian security system. A wide range crisis in the North Caucasus is the result and a complication of the all-Russia crisis, disintegration process which has been taking place since early 1990s, ineffective reforms and a very slow process of construction of the civil society in the country. This situation partially explains the recent Russian President's decision to strengthen vertical structure of power in the country.

A very important factor which influences both economic and political life of the North Caucasus is availability of great oil resources in the Caspian basin and in the eastern part of the North Caucasus. Strategic importance of oil is hard to overestimate. Oil transportation routes not once in history of the region played a significant role on the situation in the area.

Conflicts of different types occurred lately in Central Asia, in the South Caucasus and in the North Caucasus awaked intensive streams of migration which blew up historically formed balance of ethnic, cultural and confessional relations, traditional ways of life in the region. High density of population, lack of agricultural land in the mountain regions, sharpening of social problems, migration especially uncontrolled one performs as one of the major factors of tension.

Due to the wide range of reasons both historically formed and connected with the breakup of the Soviet Union the North Caucasus began to possess new geopolitical and strategic significance. One of the results of it is the creation of the unusual ethnopolitical situation which can hardly be compared with other Russian regions and is characterized by the highly explosive nature. More than 30 territorial claims lead many peace keeping efforts to a dead end. The largest and most painful of them are:

- disputes between Chechens and Ingushs about control over Sunzhensk and Malgobeck regions of the Republic of Ingushetia;
- idea of creation of autonomous Cossack republic in Sunzhensk region of Ingushetia;
- disputes between Ingushs and Ossetians over control of Prigorodny district of the North Ossetiya;
- creation of the new republic of Lezgistan from the territories of Dagestan and Azerbaijan and its joining the Russian Federation;
- debates between Chechens-Akkins and Laktzs over control of Novolaktz region in Dagestan;
- demands of the Kummik ethnic group of Dagestan to create an independent republic;
- demands of the Noggays to create their independent republic on parts of lands of Dagestan, Chechnya and Stavropol territory;
- demands of Cossacks of North Ossetiya and Adigeia to separate their lands from these republics and to join Stavropol and Krasnodar territories.

In general ethno-political situation in the North Caucasus is characterized in many aspects by the complications of the armed conflicts: Chechen, Ossetiya-Ingush, Georgia-Abkhaz, Georgia-South Ossetiya, and Karabachos. This made out of the Caucasus a very unstable region with huge conflict potential. Such situation has a very negative impact not only on the neighboring Russian regions but on the whole territory of the country, where myths about the aggressiveness of Caucasians are widely spread. People's victims, destructions, hostages, terrorism, violence give birth to the moral psychological syndrome of mutual alienation which is not typical to the local ethnic groups' cultural traditions.

After the breakup of the USSR the North Caucasus became the bordering area of Russia with the vast region of Islamic world. It has become the territory of concentration of national interests of many countries. Some of them are interested in shrinking of geopolitical influence of Russia in the southern strategic area in order to foster Political

Islam further to the north. Due to this the North Caucasus may become the "weak chain" in the Russian security system through which different plans of formation of either unified Islamic state or a kind of Islamic confederation might be realized. These plans have become corner stones of the political programs of different Pan-Islamic and Pan-Turkic organizations which unite different radicals and extremists of the North Caucasus and which receive huge financial, political and moral support from abroad.

In this connection, one can observe the formidable escalation of the so called "missionary activities" of Muslim clergy from Iran, Turkey, Jordan, Saudi Arabia, Pakistan and some other Middle Eastern countries to the region of the North Caucasus. They popularize the life according sharia laws, select young people and finance their theological education in Turkey and in the Middle Eastern countries. Distribute subversive religious literature, claiming the war against non-Muslim believers, as charity gestures provide big sums of money for the construction of new and reconstruction of old mosques. Along with this in their sermons they claim to drive out representatives of non-Muslim confessions from the region.

Such activities vividly prove the fact that some foreign forces try to play out in the North Caucasus and around it a complicated multi coursed combination with the aim to strengthen their influence in the region by means of Islamic, separatists, nationalist and terrorist actions using financial, economic, religious, ethnic, military and other factors. All above mentioned have a negative influence on the state of the Russian regional security.

To a great extent such state of things has become possible due to the absence by present time of the Russian well planned and thoroughly thought out strategic policy towards the whole southern geopolitical region. It seems to be quite necessary for the Russian Federal Center to rethink and to change its policy of neglection towards the North Caucasus. Current geopolitical dynamics of the region has become the main threat to the Russian national security as the major impulse for the further disintegration of the country.

The current unstable geopolitical situation in the North Caucasus is partially the result of the communist legacy as well as a number of serious mistakes made by the Yeltsin political leadership. The main priorities of the Russian policy in the North Caucasus seem to be the following: In economic sphere it is necessary to stop the crisis and to bring down unemployment. In some regions of the North Caucasus it reaches 60-70%. The majority of all disintegrative trends come from the unsatisfactory economic situation.

In criminal sphere the level of corruption in the North Caucasus is one of the highest in the Russian Federation. It has spread through all levels of political and state structures. No one respects the laws because it is not obligatory for all members of society to obey them. In many cases the law is substituted by family or traditional clan rules. In addition there are a great number of weapons unofficially possessed by the local population.

In social sphere, after the collapse of the Soviet Union, many conflicts spread out on the whole territory of the Caucasus. Consequently, many people migrated to the North Caucasus, mainly to Stavropol, Krasnodar and Rostov regions. Such uncontrolled migration disrupted the traditional interethnic balance of the local population in favor of non-Slavic ethnic groups which worsened the criminal situation and created an additional basis for ethnic and confessional conflicts.

In confessional sphere government authorities should support in every way the representatives of traditional Islam and consolidate them in their struggle against radical extremist groups such as Wahabism. The state should assist in creating a number of higher Muslim institutions in order to train future Muslim clergy in Russia instead of abroad.

The main social pillar of support of Russia in the North Caucasus has always been and will always be the Russian population. The dangerous phenomenon which is taking place in the North Caucasus is the ousting of Russians from the North Caucasus. This tendency can be observed in every national republic of the region.

Needless to say that not everything in the Russian history ran smoothly. Unfortunately there was withstanding, wars, human victims. But all contemporary states in the modern world have been created on people's blood. It is quite important to keep in mind that at the same time there were voluntary alliances, good neighbor relations, friendship, mutual support in hard situations. Many generations of Caucasian people and Russians lived in one state and under Russian protection. To guarantee their mutual independence and freedom all of them lost millions of lives in different wars including both world ones. It would be absolutely incorrect to state that the only historical heritage in Russian-Caucasian relations was permanent resistance and wars. Even in the periods of military clashes the withstanding happened mainly among the elites but not among common people, who during the centuries of living together have created the traditional norms of good neighborhood relations which might be easily observed even in the contemporary conflicts. The majority of the North Caucasus population clearly understands that the breakup of Russia would mean the catastrophe for their identity. The last argument seems to be the main foundation for strengthening of the Russian national security in the North Caucasus.

Cooperation in the Middle East

Another region of interception of the Russian and Turkish interests is the Middle East, where Turkey tries to play a role of the regional leader and its influence has been becoming more important. Being a NATO member and an economically developed country, during the last 50 years Turkey has been the major conductor of the western interests in the region and performed as a model of a secular Muslim state. Using the words of the professor of the Massachusetts Institute of Technology Ferrous Ahmad "Turkey is Japan of the Middle East".[4] If before the 1990s Turkey strategically played a peripheral role in the region, today the situation has been considerably changed. Three major circumstances predetermined this situation. First, the breakup of the Soviet Union led to the weakening of the Moscow geopolitical influence at the southern strategic direction. Created geopolitical vacuum must have been filled in by such a state which had

---

[4] Ahmad Ferrous, "Retrospective of the Turkish Foreign Policy during the 75 years of the Republic", *Materials of the International conference on the Turkish Foreign Policy, Harvard University*, October 24, 1998.

a high level of modernization of its economy, very close civilizational ties with the population of the newly formed states. Taking into consideration that the majority of the Central Asian states and Azerbaijan are of Turkic nature, Turkey had all the preferences in this process.

The second circumstance is very complex relations of Turkey with the EU. The Turkish – European relations started to be formed during the Cold War when the countries were united by the unified interest to guarantee their security. Beginning from the 1970s when the climate of the Cold War began to become warmer the security issues were added by economic and political interests which sometimes became to be different. These particular interests forced Europe to limit Turkey's integration with the continent. One of the most important stumbling blocks here is the position of Greece which has very complicated relations with Turkey.

The third circumstance is the transportation of the Caspian oil. In general there are two major ways of its transportation: through Russia (the northern rout) and through Turkey (the southern rout). One of the very effective methods of pushing Russia back from the Middle East and from the Caucasus is the attempt of its separation from the major oil routs going from the Caspian region. If these plans succeed Turkey will receive additional preferences in its geopolitical game both with Russia and with the Middle Eastern countries.

As the result of these tendencies Turkey starts to pretend to be the only Eurasian superpower and begins to concentrate its geopolitical interests mainly in the Caucasus, the Central Asian and the Middle Eastern regions. These tendencies might be traced back in the Turkish attempts to create Islamic Common Market, in its declarations to form the State of Great Turan – a kind of a country which would unite all Turkic peoples from Balkans till China. Realization of these plans is based on the attempts of the Turkish foreign policy to force Russia to play the second role in the regional geopolitical orchestra. At least this might be traced back in the words of professor of Bilkent University Duygu Bazoglu Sezer. At the conference on the Turkish Foreign Policy held in October 1998 at the Kennedy School of Government of Harvard University she declared that "new political order in Eurasia should be constructed without Russia's influence.[5]

Turkey has got rather complex and complicated relations with the Middle Eastern countries. It might be explained by the struggle for the regional leadership, by the Kurds problem, by the distribution of the water resources of Tigris and Euphrates. One of the most complicated problems here is the clash among two strategic doctrines: Pan-Turkism and Pan-Islamism. If the majority of the Middle Eastern countries share more or less the ideas of integration on the Pan-Islamic basis, Turkey is the generator of the Pan-Turkic doctrine.

The result of the new geopolitical configuration of the region is that Turkey now finds itself at the center, rather than at the periphery, of a changing environment. It is seen by the Arab countries and Israel as a key player, both for good and ill. Its conflict with Syria

---

[5] For more details about it see, *Victor Panin*, "Islam, Russia and the North Caucasus", Roald Sagdeev and Susan Eisenhower (Eds.), *Islam and Central Asia*, Washington: Center for Political and Strategic Studies Press, 2000.

over the water issues and Kurdish territories is one of the major stumbling blocks to regional conflict resolution. On the other hand, Turkey's relationship with Israel is of great importance to both Israel and the United States. If peaceful conflict resolution prevails, Turkey could once more become a major crossroad for the physical link between Europe and the Middle East. Whether Turkey is finally admitted to the European Union or not will in large measure determine whether it can counter the appeal of radical Islam and remain secular. Alternatively, if its leadership increasingly embraces Islam, it will never be fully accepted as a member of the European Union.

Turkey's relationship with the Caucasus is also extremely important. Indeed, Turkish involvement in the South Caucasus, notably Georgia and Azerbaijan, together with its growing economic ties with Central Asia, is reflected in the new road and sea links from Turkey to the Mediterranean would further cement these close economic ties.

These reasons, together with continuing strategic importance of the Black Sea, bear directly on relations between Turkey and Russia. Turkish-Russian competition over these and other issues is likely to grow rather than decrease in the years ahead and may be compared to the geopolitical competition between Russia and Ottoman Empire during the 19th century. Whether this relationship becomes adversarial with military dimensions remains to be seen. There is no doubt that Russia views Turkey's activity – both actual and potential – very seriously. In Central Asia secular, democratic Turkey has been seen as a countering factor to Islamic fundamentalist appeal. While the importance of this aspect can be exaggerated, there is no doubt that Turkey, with its European connections and investors, offers important access for the hard-pressed economies of Central Asia.

Role of Islam

In general religious factor is one of the major forces in world geopolitics. The most dangerous aspect of Islam is the growing influence of Islamic extremism. A sizable part of the Russian population is Muslim by faith. Russia's south borders are the vast geopolitical area of the Muslim world and could easily become the target of radical Islamic movements and groups seeking to expand their influence at Russia's expense.

Turkey, according to its Constitution, is a secular state. As a result, it refuses leadership in the Islamic world. Instead, it has started to use the ideology and practice of Turkish nationalism, i.e. Pan-Turkism. Today the government body that orchestrates Turkish policy towards the Muslim states of the former Soviet Union (FSU) is the department of Turkish Regions Affairs. Turkey regularly organizes international seminars with the participation of Muslims from the FSU, and accepts young people to study in its religious universities. It popularizes the ideas of Pan-Turkism, and acts to unify all forces supporting it. Its strategic aim is to create a belt of Turkic nation states in the northern Caucasus oriented towards Ankara.[6]

These plans for example were declared by the former president of Turkey Turgut Ozal. "The XXI century would be the century of Turkey, which has the nice possibility of the new historical unification of Turkic nations of Central Asia and the Caucasus under

---

[6] These plans were revealed by the Turkey's Secret Service agent Islague Kasap at his press-conference in the capital of Dagestan (*Severny Kavkaz*, March 1999, No.10).

Turkish guidance".[7] Turkey regularly conducts international seminars with the participation of Muslims from all FSU where all ideas of Pan-Turkism are actively popularized.

For these purposes Turkey created the special foreign fund for the studies of the Turkish world; in Ankara it supports the North Caucasus Cultural Society and different nationalistic emigrant groups such as Chechen "Terek;" the Dagestani Fund named after Shamil, and others. The Pan-Turkish "Nationalist Action Party," the government-supported "Party of Great Union," and the extremist Turkish organization "Boz Kurt" (Gray Wolves) played an active role in the Chechen Conflict in 1994-1996.

In Russia the total Muslim population (including those who possess temporary residence) is estimated to be between 18 and 20 million people. Due to expected demographic shifts, in thirty years the Muslim population is expected to reach to 30-40 million. Additionally, Muslims are expected to constitute the largest segment of immigration to Russia in the 21st century. Therefore, by 2050 it is expected that the number of Muslims in Russia will be roughly equal to the number of Orthodox Russians.[8]

Islam as a political ideology plays an integrative role for its followers. But this consolidation is multi-natured, reflecting the interests of different social groups and stratums. The most extreme expression of the Muslim ideology of superiority is Pan-Islamism—the idea that Islam should become the governing ideology in the world.[9]

The most developed form of Pan-Islamism is modern Islamic fundamentalism which represents the ideology of extremist Muslim radicals who do not accept any compromise in ideology, who stand for the purity of Islam (by their standards) and who fight against "nonbelievers" using all possible methods—including force. One can observe the recent growing attention of Pan-Islamism toward the Muslim North (Russia, Caucasus, and Central Asian Countries). Pan-Islamism's strategic goal is to unite these areas with the rest of the Muslim world. Popularization of such plans on these territories themselves foments support for the creation of different radical groups and organizations which often collaborate with other separatist and nationalist forces. Fundamentalism is the most active and aggressive form of the ideals of some of Muslim clergymen and their followers; its strategic goal is to seize political power. The conditions for its growth are poorly planned and executed social and economic policies that worsen quality the life of the society and stability of the country. The collapse of the USSR, the power vacuum that followed the collapse and the struggle for power between different political forces also assists Muslim radicals in gaining power. The experience of Muslim countries shows it is virtually impossible to destroy fundamentalism completely. Like a virus it can change its form, adjusting to new situations and environments, and under some conditions, may even be reborn again.

---

[7] Fred De Pau, *Politika Turtsii v Zakazkazye*, Sporniye Granitsy na Kavkaze. M., 1996, p.78

[8] "Does PanIslamism and Islamic Fundamentalism Threaten Russia?", *Asia i Africa Segodnia*, 1996. No.2, p.2.

[9] One of the classics of Islamic fundamentalism Said Kulb wrote: "If we want Islam to become the tool of safety it must rule", *Yuri Kobishanov*, "The Place of Islamic Civilization in the Ethnocofessional Structure of Northern Eurasia of Russia", *ONS*, 1996, No.2, p.98.

The expansion of Islamic extremism leads to the formation of tension and conflicts, which are used by Wahabists to force Russia to cool its relations with the Muslim world as it will naturally support different political Muslim forces. Islamic extremism is a real and vivid threat to Russian national security. The North Caucasus in particular becomes the center of strategic interests for some of Muslim countries, first of all Turkey, Saudi Arabia due to the Caucasus geopolitical position, its natural and energy resources, the peculiarities of political formation of some of its territories, the sizable Muslim minorities within its population, the existence of many territorial conflicts, the Soviet inheritance, the current economic crisis, etc. It is regarded as the "weak chain" through which plans of forcing a withdrawal of Russia from the North Caucasus might be realized.

Perspectives of the Russian-Turkish Relations on the Civilizational Level

The regional relationship between Russia and Turkey on the civilizational level in the past, nowadays and in perspective is better to analyze in the terms of conception of "Eurasianism". This definition has become very popular among political scientists, historians and ethnologists. The term "Eurasia", "Eurasianism" is widely used both in Russia and in the NIS, formed on the territory of the former Soviet Union.

There are several explanations of this term. Along with this it is clear that both former and present meanings of this definition are closely connected with geography. Turkey and Russia and some other states which were the parts of the former Soviet Union for centuries have been communicating and cooperating with each other on the vast, geographically unified territory including in itself the eastern part of Europe and the western part of Asia. It means that basically it may be described as a historically-geographical community the content of which includes typical for this region many centuries old economic, cultural, ethnic and political ties. In the result of this long term interrelationship some times peaceful and some times conflict by nature, during its evolution there has been created a kind of a civilizational combination which may be described in the term of "Eurasianism". As basic components this combination includes European and Oriental cultures with their traditions, ways of life, religions and ideological traditions. Those who believe in this phenomenon are eager to accept the notion that of the Eurasian civilization, or at least the tendencies towards its formation. This would be the part of the human civilization consisting of the best achievements of the rapidly growing Western civilization but remaining at the same time the independent and constructive element of the world culture in general.

The notion of Eurasian lands is not of course limited by Russia. From the Middle Aged centuries at the south of Eurasia there has existed another very powerful "Melting Pot" – the vast territories of the Ottoman state. The roots of the Ottoman-Turkish "Eurasianism" might be traced in the Middle Aged Minor Asia which became to be the region of the Turkic migration from Central Asia and the area of its interrelationship with the Byzantine culture.

Nowadays, when the republics of the former Soviet Union got their independence, taking into consideration the growing influence of Turkey as a powerful regional country, it is very important to analyze the possibility (and the terms) of the civilizational incorporation in Eurasia of two historical civilizational centers – Russia and Turkey. During this analysis two aspects should be kept in mind. First, the process of this civilizational incorporation should at the same time go along with the process of active interrelationship on one hand with the Western civilization symbolizing technological progress, on the other with the Oriental civilization – the symbol of the unique cultural and spiritual traditions. Second, all possible variants of the Russian-Turkish incorporation is not an independent process, it is only the part, though very influential and important, of the broader incorporation of the whole countries of the region. The trends of this process may be seen in the creation of the Organization of the Black Sea Economic Cooperation, in activities of different Central Asian integrative groups, etc.

Now it becomes obvious that the process of the state formation in the Central Asian countries does not mean their opposition against Russia which was the first to declare its independence at the first stage of the Soviet Union's breakup. The new geopolitical environment which has been formed on the vast territories of Eurasia dictates the necessity of finding new approaches and new mutually beneficial solutions of the creation of the modern concept of "Eurasianism". Besides Russia, this process requires equal partnership of all NIS. To conduct any dialogue about the future of "Eurasianism" without their participation but on their behalf is counterproductive. Integration, based on equality, voluntar and pragmatic interests, must be the future of Eurasia. Only then it might become an effective positive factor of the development of the world economy and international relations in general in the 21st century. One of the consequences of globalization and simultaneously the reaction to its influence might become the creation of the Eurasian Union, which will have a very promising future if it is constructed on the democratic principles.

Regarding perspectives and the nature of the Eurasian cooperation the Head of the Department of Central Asia, the Caucasus, Slavic countries and Mongolia of the Ministry of Foreign Affairs of Turkey declared, that

> The end of the era of the "cold war" opened a new page in the mankind's history. The new independent states got their place in history and Eurasia appeared as a new political structure... being situated at the center of Eurasia Turkey has to concentrate its attention simultaneously at several directions – from the process of European integration and its new architecture to the newly appeared countries of the Turkic origin in the Caucasus and Central Asia.[10]

At the same time one should admit, that beginning to discover Eurasia from the Turkic world where Turkey saw itself as a kind of a "Senior Brother", nowadays Ankara is ready to include into the notion of Eurasia all its neighbors including Russia. To ignore Russia on this territory is impossible even because of the fact that the amount of the Russian-Turkish trade is more than 4 billion US dollars. The sphere of the economic cooperation between these countries is so broad and diverse that in some aspects it depicts the general picture of the economic ties in Eurasia. Not once Turkish officials declared that the sharp decrease in the cooperation with Russia would lead to the stagnation in the Turkish

---

[10] *Akyson,* November 13, 1999.

economy. Turkey is also to pay attention to the fact that economic cooperation of the newly formed states with Russia in the framework of the Commonwealth of Independent States, which, despite all the obstacles and difficulties, remains to be the economic foundation of the Eurasian cooperation.

One of the most influential organizations of the private sector of the Turkish economy - TUSIAD in one of its researches stated the fact that rather a big part of the Turkish business works in the framework of the Russian-Turkish economic cooperation. From the "channel trade" during the last 10 years Turkey earned more than 50 billion US dollars.[11] It should be also kept in mind that Turkey's business invested the biggest trade center in Moscow.[12]

There is another very important reason for the good prospects in the field of the Turkish cooperation with Russia – it provides a kind of a balance of Turkey's interests in its relations with the EU and the USA. It is well known that the Turkish interests do not always coincide with the interests of its allies. In that sense the improvement of the Turkish-Russian cooperation based on trust would serve as a sort of a counterbalance.

All above given arguments prove that Turkey and Russia together with the newly formed states of Eurasia have the real chances to become the cofounders of the Eurasian Commonwealth. Despite any differences all the countries are secular states; their final goals are democracy and market economy. The most important thing which they possess in the relationship between themselves is the serious business partnership across the vast territories of Eurasia.

Conclusion

The analysis provided in this chapter gives all the ground to argue that in the contemporary geopolitical environment there exist objective reasons to increase the sphere of cooperation between Turkey and Russia. At the same time there are some differences in the strategic interests of these countries. The perspectives of the future in the Turkish-Russian relationship would depend in great part not only on the objective tendencies in the world development and on the regional balance of power, but on the personal choices and political will of their leaders. In this respect it is necessary to mention that in all official documents or political statements the necessity and intention to further cooperation for strengthening stability and increasing security in the region is underlined.

In the newly created geopolitical environment the countries do not have the common ground borders. It means that there can not be any territorial disputes which formed the basis for many conflicts between the countries in the past. The growing economic and cultural cooperation also meets the interests of both states. A good deal of the countries partnership is based on the mutual struggle against international terrorism. Both Russia and Turkey are interested in stability and security of the neighboring areas of Eurasia.

Any attempts to push away either Turkey or Russia from the geopolitical process in Eurasia are counterproductive and won't serve to strengthening security in the region. The

---

[11] *Opportunities and Challenges in the Eurasian Area.* Panel by TUSAID. Istanbul, November 3, 1997, pp.17-21.
[12] *Komsomolskaya Pravda*, June 9, 2000.

same result would go from any attempts to interfere in the countries' traditional areas of interests. Attempts to practical realization of some irresponsible declarations to remove Russia from the Eurasian process are first of all unreal and secondly would definitely create a serious misbalance in the geopolitical process which is taking place nowadays in the region. To some extent the future of the Turkish-Russian relations would also depend on the character and direction of the reforms which are now taking place in the Russian economic and political spheres.

In general to sum up all "pro" and "contra" for the future prospects in the relations between Russia and Turkey there are all the reasons to argue that mutual economic interests, urgent necessity to conduct joint struggle against terrorism, common desire to insure stability and security in the region as well as the mutual will to go on further along the road of constructing democracy would stand for the positive progress and promising future in the relations between these two countries.

13 Turkey and the Caucasus

Zeyno Baran

Throughout the Cold War Turkey, as the southern flank of NATO, was America's strategic ally in the Caucasus region. With the collapse of the Soviet Union and the subsequent debate over NATO's continued relevance, however, Turkey faced uncertainty about its future strategic importance. The Turkish leadership at the time saw the newly-independent states of the former Soviet Union as a potential opening for continued relevance. Strong ties to these states would turn Turkey into a true 'bridge between East (Caucasus and Central Asia) and West (Europe),' which would also make it a more attractive EU candidate and a valuable American partner.[1]

Although this focus was not declared openly, Turkish foreign policy in the early 1990s concentrated on expanding the Turkish sphere of influence into nearby territories formerly part of the Ottoman Empire. Ankara's interest in the Balkans, the Middle East and Cyprus concentrated on groups with ties to Turkey as a result of prior Ottoman rule. This was a significant shift from the traditional Turkish policy of non-involvement in the fate of Turkic/Muslim people living outside Turkey's borders, a policy followed so that other countries would not interfere with the various religious and ethnic groups inside Turkey itself, especially the Kurds. The opening up of the former Soviet bloc countries and the prospect of playing a pivotal role in this region changed the parameters of Turkey's foreign policy.[2]

Turgut Ozal, president of Turkey from November 1989 to April 1993, dreamed of a new Turkish sphere of influence ranging 'from the Adriatic to the Great Wall of China.' To the east of Turkey, this vision included the former Soviet republics of the Caucasus (Armenia, Azerbaijan, and Georgia) and Central Asia (Kazakhstan, Turkmenistan, Kyrgyzstan, Tajikistan, and Uzbekistan). The Turks originally came from Central Asia, and, in fact, Kazakhstan, Kyrgyzstan, Turkmenistan, Uzbekistan and Eastern Turkistan (modern day eastern China) used to be called 'Turkistan.' With these ethnic, religious, historic, cultural and linguistic ties, Turkish leadership believed they would have great influence in this region.

Consequently, Turkey was one of the first countries to recognize the independence of these eight countries at the end of 1991, and quickly set up embassies to provide them access to the West via Ankara, instead of Moscow. Turkey and Russia have for centuries been regional rivals, and the Caucasus and Central Asia emerged as the new battleground for influence. The Russian leadership could not accept losing its 'near abroad' and adopted policies to keep these countries dependent on Russia. Turkey, on the other hand, wanted to break up Russia's monopoly in the region in partnership with the United States

---

[1] Many Turks refer to Turkey as a "bridge between East and West". This phrase so far remained a geographic description, instead of the much-desired political/economic one.
[2] Alan O. Makovsky, "Turkey", Robert Chase, Emily Hill and Paul Kennedy (Eds.) *The Pivotal States: A New Framework for US Policy in the Developing World*, New York and London: W.W. Norton, 1999, pp.88-9.

while promoting the sovereignty and pro-Western orientation of these states.

Another Turkish interest in the region was the prevention of Iran and Saudi Arabia from exporting their fundamentalist Islamic models, with the promotion of Turkey's 'secular, democratic Muslim republic' model in their place. The US and the EU, as well as the Caucasian and Central Asian countries themselves, preferred the 'Turkish model,' which has proven to be compatible with the Western world. While Ankara focused on promoting political, economic and military ties (the 'secular democracy' part of the model), it more or less avoided the religious sphere (the 'Muslim' part), leaving the area mainly to non-governmental actors.

In early 1990s Turkey did not get sufficient attention from the West, especially the US, which had a 'Russia first' policy. Turkey was not strong enough to play a 'pivotal' role in the region on its own; it needed the US as an active partner. However, American policy began to shift after the 1993 Russian announcement of a 'near abroad' policy, which was viewed in Washington as neo-imperialist. One of the best tools for expanding Turkish-American influence and providing security and economic incentives to the region to resist Russian pressure was the development of a 'Eurasian Energy Corridor' to transport oil and gas from the region via Turkey to Western markets.

While Turkish policy towards the Caucasus and Central Asia stems from similar interests and principles, this article will focus mainly on the Caucasus from 1991-2003.[3] In the Southern Caucasus, Turkey has developed especially close relations with Azerbaijan due to ties of ethnicity, language, and energy. Turkey's relations with Georgia have also grown stronger over the last decade, mainly because of Georgia's importance in the East-West energy corridor. Relations with Armenia, however, remain deadlocked, which has limited Turkey's influence in the region. Meanwhile, Turkish policy towards the Northern Caucasus republics is tied to its haphazard approach to Russia.

Looking ahead, Turkey needs to develop and implement a common vision with the US for the Caucasus region. Russia and Iran are historic competitors and will remain so for the foreseeable future. The EU has not paid much attention to the Caucasus region and even if it did so now, it is unlikely to reach out to Turkey as a strategic ally in this region. For Turkey to realize its potential as a 'bridge between East and West,' a solid partnership with the US is the best way forward.

Recognizing the Limits of Turkish Influence

Ozal had opened up Turkey to capitalism, moving the country from an import-substitution to an export-promotion mode. He saw the post-Soviet area as an excellent opportunity for expansion of Turkish business and thus Turkish influence. While Turkish businesses were not competitive in European markets, they would have huge advantages in the Caucasus and Central Asia due to linguistic and cultural ties.

In the first several years of independence, Ozal and Prime Minister Suleyman Demirel

---

[3] Key references: Bulent Aras, "Turkey's Policy in the Former Soviet South", *Turkish Studies*, Spring 2000, pp.36-58; Ziya Onis, "Turkey and Post-Soviet States: Potential and Limits of Regional Power Influence" *Middle East Review of International Affairs*, Vol.5. No.2; Gareth Winrow, *Turkey and the Caucasus: Domestic Interests and Security Concerns*, London: Royal Institute for International Affairs, 2000.

spearheaded several business-promotion initiatives in the Caucasus.[4] When visiting the region, they were accompanied by dozens of Turkish company representatives in the export-import, construction, textile and infrastructure sectors. A Turkish Cooperation and Development Agency (TIKA) was established to grant loans to businessmen interested in investing in these risky countries.

In June 1992, Turkey also founded the Black Sea Economic Cooperation (BSEC) for economic, commercial and eventually political cooperation among the countries of the Black Sea region.[5] This forum brought Turkey together with Armenia and Azerbaijan—the only platform to date on which all three governments participate. BSEC also established a Black Sea Trade and Development Bank (BSTDB), which started operating in June 1999. While on paper a good idea, BSEC has thus far not managed to significantly increase regional trade and economic cooperation, mainly because most of its members' economies are still too weak. Moreover, the countries of BSEC do not share a common vision for the 'Black Sea' as a region.

To tie the region closer to Turkey, a 'Turkic summit' was formed to bring together presidents of Turkey and the Turkic republics. By the time of the first Turkic Summit, held in Ankara in October 1992, however, the Turkic leaders already had moved on from the 'Turkic' umbrella and concluded other international agreements in order to diversify their international connections. Turkey alone did not have the economic and political resources to provide these countries with significant assistance. As Western businesses and Western governments took the lead in the region, Turkey began to focus on culture and education. Most significantly, Ankara provided satellite TV broadcasts and scholarships for students to study in Turkey.[6]

In fact, within a few years, due to the 'undeclared pan-Turkism' of some political and business leaders, Turkey had overplayed its hand and upset the newly independent republics by acting too much like a 'big brother' in the region. Moreover, some of the initial groups of Turkish businessmen that went to Azerbaijan and the Central Asian republics were only interested in making quick cash, tricking their 'Turkic brothers' into bad business. Some policymakers also treated these people as unsophisticated, assuming they were 'like the backwards Anatolian villagers.'[7] This approach backfired, as these people—some not even Turkic—did not want to come under the influence of another big brother after so many years of living under Soviet rule. Reviewing the early days of engagement with the region, State Minister Ahad Andican, who was responsible for relations with Turkic Republics in Eurasia in 1997-1998, acknowledged that Turkey had treated these countries with condescension 'as though they were part of the Third World.'[8]

Following Ozal's death in 1993, Turkish policy under President Demirel graduated

---

[4] Demirel served as Prime Minister from November 1991 to May 1993 and as President from May 1993 to May 2000.

[5] The 11-member BSEC includes Albania, Armenia, Azerbaijan, Bulgaria, Georgia, Greece, Moldova, Romania, Russia, Turkey, and Ukraine.

[6] Elizabeth Fuller, "Turkey: A Diplomatic Return To The Caucasus And Central Asia", *Radio Free Europe/Radio Liberty*, 8 September 1997.

[7] Based on author's interviews with a number of Turkish officials.

[8] RFERL Prague, 8 September 1997.

from an attempt to establish Turkey as the region's dominant force into a balanced regional partnership with the United States in the effort to keep Iran and Russia out of the region. Ankara supported the integration of the Caucasus and Central Asia into Euro-Atlantic institutions such as the United Nations and the Council of Europe and Conference for Security and Cooperation in Europe (CSCE), now known as the Organization for Security and Cooperation in Europe (OSCE). In 1994 NATO had established a Partnership for Peace (PfP) program to expand the former Soviet bloc's military and defense cooperation with NATO members. Turkey was involved in PfP, and also provided significant military training and equipment assistance to Azerbaijan and Georgia.

Turkey has also been supportive of regional formations to bring peace and stability to the region. In 1996, Georgia, Ukraine, Azerbaijan and Moldova created a regional group (GUAM) at the Conventional Forces in Europe (CFE) Treaty Conference to focus on enhancing political and economic security through regional cooperation. While Turkey is not part of GUAM, it has closely followed the group's activities.[9]

After three years of negotiations, in April 2001, Turkey Bulgaria, Georgia, Romania, the Russian Federation and Ukraine signed an agreement to establish a Black Sea Naval Co-operation Task Group (BLACKSEAFOR) to enhance 'peace and stability in the Black Sea as well as promoting regional co-operation among the Black Sea littoral states.' BLACKSEAFOR was the first formation of naval co-operation among all the littoral states in the Black Sea and has a primary focus on search and rescue, humanitarian assistance, and environmental-protection operations.

Relations with Armenia and the Nagorno-Karabakh (NK) Conflict

While Turkey has close relations with Azerbaijan and Georgia, it has no diplomatic relations with Armenia. Turkey considers Armenian policy (and the activities of its powerful diaspora groups) since 1989 to be against its national security interests and territorial integrity. Armenia's failure to recognize the Kars Agreement,[10] along with the frequent public references to eastern Turkey as 'Western Armenia,' provides a serious irritant to Turkey. The Turkish Mt. Ararat is pictured in the official Armenian state emblem, which Turkey interprets as a sign that the 'greater Armenia' vision is still very much alive.

Turkish-Armenian relations remain caught in the events of 1915-1916, in which between 600,000 and 1.5 million Armenians were killed.[11] Turks consider the killings in the context of the First World War, as a reaction to Russian provocations. While Armenians view these killings as "genocide" and have pressured the international community to recognize this label, in the Turkish view it is not applicable, due in part to the fact that Armenians elsewhere in Turkey were not targeted.

The 1988 Armenian-Azerbaijani war over Nagorno-Karabakh and subsequent

---

[9] At the 1999 NATO Summit in Washington, Uzbekistan joined this group, which became GUUAM. Following September 11, 2001, however, Uzbekistan increased political and military cooperation with the US, including the hosting of a US military base, and has reduced its involvement with GUUAM.

[10] Soviet Russia and Turkey signed the Kars Agreement in 1921 to demarcate their border. The agreement's sixth clause states Turkey is a guarantor of the autonomy of Naxcivan (in Azerbaijan) and Ajara (in Georgia).

[11] The former figure is the Turkish, while the latter is Armenian.

developments further strained Turkish-Armenian relations. At the outset of the war, Turkish sentiment was in favor of the Azeris (ethnic brethren of the Turks), but the Turkish army stayed out of the war, in order to avoid broadening the conflict to include Russia and NATO. Nevertheless, there was great resentment of the failure of the West to assist the Muslims in Azerbaijan (the subsequent failure to help Muslims in Bosnia further contributed to this feeling)

Ankara was also disappointed that the United States excluded Azerbaijan from its foreign assistance programs starting in 1992, as a result of the influence in Congress of the powerful Armenian lobby. The so-called 'Freedom Support Act' included Section 907, which forbade all assistance to Azerbaijan with the exceptions of humanitarian aid and nonproliferation/disarmament programs. Under the act, this restriction would remain in place

> [U]ntil the President determines, and so reports to the Congress, that the government of Azerbaijan is taking demonstrable steps to cease all blockades and other offensive uses of force against Armenia and Nagorno-Karabakh...

Faced with the strong Armenian influence in Western capitals, Turkey decided to sever its relations with Armenia, hoping that this would put pressure on Yerevan to leave Nagorno-Karabakh. Thus, in the midst of the war in April 1993, Turkey closed its border with Armenia and shut down land and air communications. Still, Azerbaijan had virtually no foreign assistance, and with the 1994 cease-fire, Azerbaijan had lost Nagorno-Karabakh; Armenia occupied some 20 percent of Azerbaijani territory. Since then, Turkish policy towards Armenia has been closely tied to Azerbaijan's policy towards Armenia.

With no other peaceful leverage, Turkey and Azerbaijan decided to deny Armenia integration into regional projects and access to Western markets via Turkey. The most significant loss for Armenia was the Baku-Ceyhan oil pipeline that would start from Azerbaijan and end in Turkey: instead of the route via Yerevan, a longer route via Tbilisi, Georgia was chosen, leaving Armenia out entirely. At first, Azerbaijani President Aliyev was willing to include Armenia in the energy projects in exchange for the return of Nagorno-Karabakh and a peace agreement, but Yerevan refused.[12] Consequently, Armenia's economy over the last decade suffered tremendously and became increasingly dependent on Russia and Iran. The last Armenian national census conducted in October 2001 indicated that 950,000 people have left the country since 1989, reducing the population to just over 3 million.[13]

There are two approaches in Turkey towards Armenia. One view suggests that Turkish policy is in fact 'hostage' to Azerbaijan, with the result that Turkey's ability to influence events in the region is seriously limited. The group that maintains this view, mainly represented by the Turkish-Armenian Business Development Council (TABDC),

---

[12] Admittedly, the proposal was risky for Yerevan to accept; leaving NK would be a politically difficult and irreversible act, whereas Aliyev could at any point renege on promises to include Armenia in energy policies.

[13] Armenia's National Statistics Service statement on 15 February 2002. Non-governmental assessments suggest the number might be even less than 3 million.

argues that once the border is open to trade, political issues would be easier to resolve.[14] This approach is close to the Armenian official policy of 'economics first, politics later,' contrasting with the Azerbaijani official position of 'politics first.' Armenia has, over the years, attempted to convince Turkey to focus on bilateral relations separately and not as part of trilateral relations including Azerbaijan, but the Turkish establishment would not budge.

Those on the 'engagement' side in the internal Turkish debate have been upset that, while Turkey is backing Azerbaijan against Armenia and NK, there is no reciprocity—the Turkish Republic of Northern Cyprus is still only recognized by Turkey (and not Azerbaijan.) When at times Turkey would consider ways to improve relations with Armenia, Azerbaijan would remind Turkey that the key decision over the East-West energy corridor lay in Baku. In other words, were Turkey to soften its policy towards Armenia, Azerbaijan might choose to send its oil via Russia or Iran, which would be a serious setback for Turkish interests in the region.

While aware of this leverage, some Turkish strategic thinkers have worried about the formation of two axes in the region: Turkey-Azerbaijan-Georgia-Israel-United States, versus Armenia-Russia-Iran-Greece-Syria. This group of Turks includes the military as well as civilians who believe in the necessity of gradual improvement of Turkish-Armenian relations, regardless of the historic issues. The United States has also encouraged the Turkish leadership to think along these lines, in order to prevent further regional polarization.

As a result, in 1995, Turkey decided in a show of goodwill to allow flights to Armenia to pass through Turkish airspace. Demirel then called for reciprocal gestures from Armenia. Instead, relations became even more strained. Armenian diaspora groups started to introduce resolutions to recognize the 'Armenian genocide of 1915' in European parliaments and in the US Congress. In Ankara the 'isolationist' camp became emboldened, arguing that any economic relations would be giving a gift to Armenia, a state that does not want peace in the region. This side further argued that it would be naïve to think that Armenia would ever break off relations with Moscow or Tehran.

This group in Turkey believes that many international efforts are biased in favor of Armenia, including the OSCE Minsk Group's Co-Chairs—the United States, France and Russia. Since the May 1994 ceasefire, the OSCE and, particularly the three Co-Chairs, tried to bring the Nagorno-Karabakh stalemate to a peaceful political resolution. The Azeris, and the 'isolationist' Turks, believe that this group is biased in favor of Armenia due to Armenia's strategic relations with Moscow and its diaspora's influence in Washington and Paris. To prove this bias, they point out that when Turkey, as a member of the Minsk group, wanted to increase its involvement; it was summarily rejected because it was seen as too pro-Azerbaijani.

The Armenian and Azerbaijani sides came closest to a compromise in 1997 following the consolidation of President Heydar Aliyev's power after the elections, and Armenian

---

[14] TABDC was co-established in May 1997 in Istanbul and Yerevan as the first and most effective link between the two countries.

President Levon Ter-Petrosian's (LTP) success in marginalizing the militant anti-Turkish groups. LTP was inclined to accept the Minsk Group's so-called 'step-by-step' approach, but was ousted by Armenian hardliners due to his willingness to make concessions. His successor, Robert Kocharian, was a former president of NK; as expected, he took a much harder line. A second proposal of the OSCE Minsk Group in November 1998 suggested a 'common state' for NK, but this time Azerbaijan rejected the proposal.

With Kocharian in power, Turkish-Armenian relations became even tenser. Bilateral relations reached rock bottom following the Demirel-Kocharian meeting during the 1998 BSEC conference. Demirel wanted Kocharian to focus on the future, but the latter refused, insisting on recognition of the 'Armenian genocide.' Since then there were small steps of 'goodwill gesture' on both sides, but mutual distrust remained at the core of bilateral relations. In fact, over the years more and more people in Ankara became convinced that Armenia was not at all interested in developing good bilateral relations with Turkey, as it was pursuing hostile policies towards Ankara and making history its main element of its foreign policy.

Azerbaijan and the East-West Energy Corridor

Turkish-Azerbaijani relations have had ups and downs over the years. Bilateral relations at times have been so close that leaders from both countries would call their countries 'one nation, two states.' Turkey enjoyed excellent relations with Azerbaijan's pro-Turkish president Ebulfaz Elchibey, a strong admirer of the founder of modern Turkey, Mustafa Kemal Ataturk. Elchibey proudly pointed to the Ataturk pin on his jacket when talking about Turkey. Turkey and Azerbaijan, under Elchibey's rule, became extremely close; however, Elchibey was neither a great strategist nor a strong leader. When in June 1993 the country was on the verge of civil war, Elchibey realized that he needed former Soviet operative and experienced politician Heydar Aliyev to stabilize the situation. He invited Aliyev to Baku to help stabilize the country; Aliyev did indeed bring order to the country, becoming president himself in October 1993.[15]

Turkish policymakers believed that Moscow incited the chaos in Azerbaijan in order to undermine the anti-Russian and pro-Turkish Elchibey. Turks were therefore initially suspicious of Aliyev and feared that he might draw Azerbaijan closer to Russia. Losing the close relationship with Azerbaijan would have meant losing the access to Central Asia and Caspian energy resources, too much a risk for some in Turkey. However, relations were strengthened when Demirel made a timely call to Aliyev in March 1995, warning him of an imminent coup attempt. Due in part to this move, mutual trust was developed, greatly enhancing bilateral relations.

Unlike Elchibey, Aliyev was a grand strategist and, while maintaining close relations with Turkey, developed good relations with many other countries as well. The 'risk diversification' policy is best demonstrated by the distribution of rights to Azerbaijan's oil fields. Aliyev reached deals with companies from Russia, the US, the United Kingdom, Turkey, Japan, Saudi Arabia and Norway and thus gave powerful countries a stake in

---

[15] For a detailed account of this period see Thomas Goltz, *Azerbaijan Diary*, Armonk, New York: M.E. Sharpe, 1998.

Azerbaijan's stability and in his own survival. Following several years of tough negotiations, on September 20, 1994, Azerbaijan and a consortium of foreign oil companies signed a Production Sharing Agreement (PSA) for the first Azerbaijani offshore Caspian oil field, named Azeri, Chirag, and Deepwater Gunashli (ACG). The 30-year agreement was called the 'Contract of the Century.'

Controlling the transport of the oil reserves to markets is as important as owning the shares in the Caspian. Without a safe and secure route out of the landlocked Caspian Sea, these reserves have little value. Consequently, Russia wanted all of Azerbaijan's oil to be pumped to markets via existing Russian networks, thus maintaining its monopoly control over Azerbaijan's economy. Iran and Turkey, for their part, wanted new pipelines built in their territories. The companies operating the ACG project formed the Azerbaijani International Oil Consortium (AIOC), which was interested in the cheapest option for exporting the oil to markets. In order to win the AIOC over to the Western route option, Turkey initially promoted a pipeline from Baku to Georgia's Black Sea port of Supsa. The Turkish reasoning was that once the companies started using this line, it would be easier to get them build the 'main export pipeline' from Azerbaijan to Georgia and then to Turkish Mediterranean port of Ceyhan.

In 1995 the AIOC chose the Baku-Supsa and the Baku-Novorossiysk routes as 'Early Oil' pipelines (to transport the initially produced oil to markets), thus satisfying both the Turkish and Russian interests. The US became actively engaged in the Azerbaijani pipeline projects following the celebration of the beginning of the Early Oil project in Baku on 12 November 1997. President Bill Clinton sent Energy Secretary Federico Peña to represent the United States at the official start of production from the ACG field. Along with international oil executives and Azerbaijani officials, Turkish Prime Minister Mesut Yilmaz and Russia's First Deputy Prime Minister Boris Nemtsov also attended the ceremony. The presence of American, Russian and Turkish high-level officials was a clear demonstration of the geopolitical importance of Azerbaijan's oil pipelines.

With the start of the Baku-Supsa project, the Turkish Foreign Ministry began to strongly promote the Baku-Ceyhan pipeline. One of Ankara's arguments was that with more oil coming to the Black Sea, the dangerously narrow Turkish Straits would come under serious threat from increased tanker traffic; the Baku-Ceyhan pipeline would transport Azerbaijani and later Kazakh oil to a safe, deep-sea port where large tankers would lift the crude. Ankara then tried to secure Washington's support, both to counter Russian pressure over Azerbaijan and Georgia and also to convince the oil companies to choose the Turkish route.

Following several years of discussion about Baku-Ceyhan's strategic importance, viability and evaluation of alternative options, finally, in 1998, the Clinton Administration decided to give full support to this pipeline project. The US decision came about when the Baku-Ceyhan pipeline was seen as a useful tool to achieve other US objectives in the region. In many statements the US identified four key objectives:

1. Strengthen the independence and prosperity of the new states of the Caspian region (over the years terms such as 'maintenance of their territorial integrity,' 'strengthening of democratic structures and market economy' were also used);

2. Bolster US energy security by ensuring the free flow of new sources of hydrocarbons to world markets, unfettered by regional competitors and geographic choke-points, such as the Bosporus and the Straits of Hormuz (this meant having non-Russian and non-Iranian pipelines);

3. Reestablish economic linkages among the new states of the Caspian region to mitigate regional conflicts and promote regional cooperation;

4. Enhance business opportunities for companies from the US and other countries.

In order to ensure coordination among all the US agencies and have the US speak with one voice, a Caspian Basin Initiative was launched with the appointment of a Special Advisor to the President and the Secretary of State for Caspian Basin Energy Diplomacy. This appointment also forced the Turkish Ministry of Energy and Natural Resources and Ministry of Foreign Affairs to better coordinate their policies. To provide financial support to the East-West energy corridor, the US also established a Caspian Finance Center in Ankara in 1998 where representatives of the Overseas Private Investment Corporation (OPIC), US Export-Import Bank (EXIM) and Trade and Development Agency (TDA) would provide financial assistance to projects in Turkey and the Caucasus.

Turkish-American cooperation resulted in the 29 October 1998 Ankara declaration in support of the East-West corridor, and especially the Baku-Ceyhan oil pipeline by Turkey, Azerbaijan, Georgia, and Kazakhstan.[16] The Kazakh participation was also important, because at the time it was not clear whether there was sufficient oil in Azerbaijan to justify a major new pipeline. Moreover, for Turkey, the extension of the oil pipeline to Kazakhstan would also provide Ankara a much-desired connection to Kazakhstan. A second part of the Ankara declaration was support for the Turkmenistan-Caspian-Caucasus-Turkey-Europe gas pipeline project. This project would enable Turkey to diversify its gas supplies and also turn it into a transit country for European markets.

Henceforth, Turkish-Azerbaijani relations were focused on the completion of the oil and gas pipelines. For both Azerbaijan and Turkey, the oil and gas pipeline projects meant a long-term strategic partnership with the US and inclusion into the Euro-Atlantic energy and security partnership. Neither side at the governmental level wanted political or business groups to negatively impact this long-term vision. Demirel played a key role in this period and in many visits to Azerbaijan publicly underlined the point that Turkey would not take any steps that would run counter to Azerbaijan's position, and would publicly call for withdrawal of Armenian forces from the occupied Azerbaijani territories as a condition of settling the NK conflict.

Despite Baku's and Ankara's strong commitment to Baku-Ceyhan, the AIOC was not convinced of the 'commercial viability' of the pipeline for several more years. Leading consortium member BP and other Western companies were relieved when the Baku-Supsa Early Oil pipeline became operational in April 1999, without any incidents, as the first non-Russian East-West pipeline. With the Russian threat no longer there, the AIOC

---

[16] Uzbekistan was also a signatory, but is not involved in BTC.

preferred to expand the Baku-Supsa line, instead of committing several more billions of dollars for a much larger one. With British Petroleum (BP) taking over American Amoco in April 1998, and later BP becoming the operator for AIOC mid-1999, Turkey, Azerbaijan and Georgia, as well as the US, had one main company to deal with. In fact, the strong commitment of the three countries to make the Baku-Ceyhan pipeline commercially viable, and the close engagement of the US, had a huge role in the companies' final positive decision.

A key turning point for the Baku-Ceyhan project was the signing of the Intergovernmental and the Host Governmental Agreements in November 1999. After months of tough negotiations, BP and the three countries were able to initial the key legal documents (the Host Government Agreements), along with the Intergovernmental Agreements signed by Azerbaijan, Georgia, Turkey, Kazakhstan and Turkmenistan. By this time the Baku-Ceyhan project already was called 'Baku-Tbilisi-Ceyhan (BTC)' since it was clear that the pipeline would go via Georgia and not via Armenia. President Clinton witnessed the signing of these agreements on the sidelines of the OSCE summit in Istanbul in November 1999, and later called this event his 'most important foreign policy achievement in 1999.'

In addition to the BTC, there were also agreements signed on transporting Azerbaijani and Turkmen gas to Turkey. Contrary to BP's expectations, Azerbaijan's Shah Deniz field did not contain oil reserves, but had huge gas reserves. The best market for that gas was Turkey, and the possibility of laying two parallel pipelines via Azerbaijan through Georgia and Turkey could make commercial sense. While Turkey was also interested in getting gas from Turkmenistan (via the Caspian) and also additional gas from Russia, the Shah Deniz project would be the cheapest and closest option for Turkey, it also represented another means by which the region could grow closer to Ankara.

Shah Deniz also played an important role in the recommendations of the Bush Administration's U.S. National Energy Policy.[17] This report recommends the development of 'the Shah Deniz gas pipeline as a way to help Turkey and Georgia diversify their natural gas supplies and help Azerbaijan export its gas via a pipeline that will continue diversification of secure energy supply routes' and expresses a desire 'to encourage Greece and Turkey to link their gas pipeline systems to allow European consumers to diversify their gas supplies by purchasing Caspian gas.' This gas pipeline project also fits U.S. national strategy of bringing two NATO allies (Greece and Turkey) closer together. Transporting Caspian gas to Europe via non-Russian routes was first discussed at the May 17, 2001 EU-Russia summit and has been on the agenda since then.

Turkey shares a similar vision of wanting to both solidify relations with Greece as well as to become a 'gas exporter' for the European markets. The ability to get Caspian gas and resell it to the EU fits the essence of Turkish policy of wanting to be a pivotal player in Eurasia and bringing Ankara closer to the EU. Turkey, Greece and the EU reached a preliminary agreement on a gas interconnection in the summer of 1999 for first gas delivery to Greece in 2004/2005. Turkey and Azerbaijan have also focused on Bulgaria, Romania, Italy, Hungary, Austria, and other European markets to make the 'Eurasian'

---

[17] *Reliable, Affordable, and Environmentally Sound Energy for America's Future,* Report of the National Energy Policy Development Group, May 2001.

connection a reality.

In addition to cooperation on strategic oil and gas projects, Turkey also provided military training for Azerbaijan. There even have been talks of establishing NATO bases in Azerbaijan given that there are Russian military bases in Armenia.[18] Ankara has been especially concerned about Iran's hostile actions against Azerbaijan. In July 2001, Iranian military gunboats confronted a BP research vessel exploring the Araz-Alov-Sharg field in the Azerbaijani section of the Caspian Sea, which Iran claims is its own. The Chief of the Turkish General Staff, General Huseyin Kivrikoglu, visited Baku soon after this event. While his ostensible reason for visiting Baku was the Azerbaijani military academy graduation ceremony, the timing was such that when the show team of the Turkish Air Forces (Turkish Stars) that accompanied Kivrikoglu made their air show, it was perceived as a clear signal both to Iran and Armenia that Turkey was watching their actions and standing by Azerbaijan.

Georgia: the Weak Link

Turkish foreign policy at first did not pay much attention to Christian Georgia. The military, on the other hand, considered it strategically important as a key buffer zone with Russia. Any instability in Georgia would have negative impact on Turkey's ability to get to Azerbaijan and the rest of Central Asia. Georgia was also essential to the success of the East-West Energy corridor.

For Russia, losing Georgia had been totally unbearable because of Georgia's former President Eduard Shevardnadze. Russian hardliners still have not forgotten or forgiven Shevardnadze, who as the Soviet foreign minister was a key player in both the demise of the Soviet Union and the reunification of Germany. These hardliners have mounted several assassination attempts, and are continuously looking for opportunities to destabilize Georgia.

Georgia's initial defeat was the war in Abkhazia, which started in 1992 with Georgian nationalists' attacks, and ended with the Abkhaz receiving massive Russian assistance. When a ceasefire was reached, Russia received permission to set up bases in Abkhazia. In addition to the one in Gudauta (Abkhazia), Russia also had bases in three other strategic locations: outside Tbilisi (Vaziani), in the autonomous Ajaran republic (Batumi), and in Samskhte-Javakhetia (Akhalkalaki). Moreover, Georgia accepted the basing of the Russian military center in the South Caucasus in Tbilisi.

With the presence of the Russian bases creating even more tension between Russia and Georgia, in 1995 Tbilisi tried to reach an agreement for them to be closed within 15 years, whereas Moscow insisted on 25 years. At the 1999 OSCE summit in Istanbul, Russia agreed to withdraw from the Gudauta and Vaziani bases by July 2001 and to reach a timetable with Georgia for withdrawal from the other two. Russia was late in withdrawing from the first two—there is still dispute whether they fully did so—while repeated meetings between Russia and Georgia so far failed to produce a clear timetable for withdrawal from the other two bases.

Turkey is concerned about Russian interference in Georgia and has tried to bolster the

---

[18] Former Azerbaijani Presidential foreign policy advisor Vafa Gulizade has been the leading advocate of NATO expansion to Azerbaijan.

Georgian military by training and equipping it. In January 2001, Tbilisi and Ankara signed three agreements on defense cooperation, and the Turkish army completed the modernization of Georgia's Marneuli airbase south of Tbilisi. Together with the US, the Turkish and Georgian militaries have also formed a 'Caucasus Working Group' for improved cooperation and training for the Georgian military. While the Georgian government is aware that NATO membership is not going to happen soon, it hopes that cooperation with two strong NATO allies would, at the very least, keep the Russians in check.

Georgia also considers the East-West corridor essential for its strategic relevance and this is another important area of cooperation with Turkey. While Georgia could have chosen the expansion of the Baku-Supsa route to get more revenues from the oil pipeline, it preferred Turkish investment into the region's security and stability. Moreover, Georgians know that if it were not for bad relations between Azerbaijan and Armenia, the pipeline may not have crossed Georgia, instead taking a route via Yerevan. The result would most likely have been increased Russian domination of an increasingly troubled Georgian state.

In addition to the energy corridor, Turkey and Georgia have been interested in establishing a 'railway (silk) road' that would tie Europe to China. The key missing link of this railway is from Turkey to Central Asia, and it can go via Georgia, Armenia or Iran. Turkey and Iran have been historic competitors for influence in the region and thus there would be no reason for Ankara to include Iran in such a grand project. Militarily and strategically, Turkey's preferred option is to lay the railway from its eastern town of Kars through Tbilisi and Baku. This route would grant Turkey quick access to Baku and Central Asia. The Chinese government also saw the big strategic appeal of being able to load its goods in China to be offloaded in the midst of Europe and was interested in financing part of the Kars-Tbilisi rail project. Despite many years of discussions, however, the possibility that the existing Turkish-Armenian rail link might open up has made Kars-Tbilisi non-commercial and it remains on hold.

Turkey has also provided economic and technical assistance to Georgia. In February 1993 Turkish Eximbank provided Georgia with 50 million USD of credit. When the Georgian economy suffered as a combined result of the 1998 Russian crisis, domestic political instability and overall mismanagement, Turkey rescheduled the debt. In 2000, Turkey was Georgia's largest trading partner and second in investment after the US, with 55 million USD in direct FDI in 2001. In 1995-2001, Turkey also provided over 25 million USD in humanitarian assistance.[19]

Politically, while Turkey supports Georgia's territorial integrity, it also has special relations with the autonomous republic of Ajara that borders Turkey. According to the Kars Agreement's sixth clause, Turkey is a guarantor for the borders, autonomy, and freedom to practice Islam of Azerbaijan's Naxcivan and Georgia's Ajara regions. While Ajara has many Muslims and its leader Aslan Abashidze mentions his Islamic credentials when in Ankara, he is a devout Christian back home. As a pragmatic politician, he is as close to Moscow as he is to Ankara. Nevertheless, certain Turkish businessmen and politicians have considered that Abashidze would be the best candidate to lead Georgia

---

[19] Turkish Ministry of Foreign Affairs website. http://www.mfa.gov.tr

after Shevardnadze (in part because he does not have any Armenian ethnic background as some other key players). In fact, Abashidze tried to run against Shevardadze in April 2000 presidential elections, but Demirel urged him to withdraw his candidacy and wait for a later date, maybe the 2005 elections.[20]

Another sensitive area for Turkey is Samtskhe-Javakhetia, which is a southern Georgian region that borders Armenia. In some parts of this region—Javakhetia—nearly all of the population is ethnically Armenian.[21] Feeling surrounded by hostile Turkic peoples in oil-rich Azerbaijan and NATO member Turkey, these people have drawn closer to Armenia. Some in Samtskhe-Javakhetia are even calling for autonomy. While the Armenian government opposes such separatist tendencies, there is a small, but influential Armenian group agitating for the 'greater Armenia' idea, a clear security concern for Turkey.

The expected closure of the Russian base in the city of Akhalkalaki is a further source of tension. This base is a logistical link between Moscow and Yerevan, and it is increasingly seen as a counterweight to the growing role of the Turkish military in Georgia. The base is still the main employment provider in the region. Shevardnadze had repeatedly promised to draft a new 7-10 year development economic development program but, by the time of his departure from office, nothing was done. According to the OSCE Istanbul agreements of 1999, Russia must close this base, but Moscow is relying on local Armenian opposition to prolong its stay.

The BTC pipeline is yet another ground for concern of instability in Samtskhe-Javakhetia. Initial studies done on the routing of the BTC had suggested the cheapest and shortest route for the pipeline to cross Georgia into Turkey would be via Akhalkalaki, but the Georgian government and the BTC consortium ruled out this option due to security concerns. Azerbaijan also did not want its oil to be crossing areas inhabited by ethnic Armenians: in case of a resumption of Azerbaijani-Armenian conflict, the pipeline could be hijacked, causing serious damage to Azerbaijani economy.

Ankara is also increasingly worried about the fate of the Meskhetian Turks, who might be repatriated to Samtskhe-Javakhetia. This group, which used to live in Samtskhe (also known as Meskheti), was deported by Stalin to Uzbekistan in 1944. They had to leave Uzbekistan in 1989 following interethnic hostilities, and settled mainly in Azerbaijan, Krasnodar (Russia), Kazakhstan, and Kyrgyzstan. Now many of them would like to return to Georgia, especially those in Russia that face ethnic tension. Based on the agreement with the Council of Europe, Georgia needs to have legislation adopted for the return of the Meskhetians three years from its accession to the Council—which started in April 2001. The resettlement must be complete within 10 years of legislation, but so far

---

[20] This is no longer possible. The parliamentary elections in November 2003 led to the so-called Rose Revolution, a popular uprising that led to Shevardnadze's ouster and the accession to the presidency of opposition leader Mikheil Saakashvili in January 2004. Saakashvili's first major move was to demand from Abashidze loyalty to Tbilisi, represented by a dismantling of his personal militia and an end to the crime and corruption in Ajara.

[21] Samtskhe-Javakhetia consists of six districts: Adigeni, Aspinadza, Akhalkalaki, Akhaltsikhe, Borjomi, and Ninotsminda. Akhaltsikhe and Ninotsminda are called Javakh.

the Georgian government has not began preparations. Moreover, the Armenians of Samtskhe-Javakhetia recall memories of 1915, thinking that these Turks would take away their lands and possibly kill them.

The other strategic Georgian region important for Turkish interests is Abkhazia. With more than 700,000, there are more Abkhaz in Turkey than in Abkhazia. This Abkhaz diaspora has tried to get Ankara more involved in the Abkhaz conflict, but the foreign policy establishment was too unfocused and too weak to confront the hardliners in Russia. Abkhaz Prime Minister Vladislav Ardzinba, over the years, has repeatedly urged Turkey to engage so they do not have to be pushed to Russian arms.

Turkey took the initiative to organize an international conference in Istanbul in 1999 to bring the Abkhaz and Georgian parties together in order to facilitate dialogue towards a resolution of the conflict. While this was a good first step, the follow-up did not occur, and, in the absence of other alternatives, the Abkhaz grew closer to Russia. For example, while Turkey, like many other countries, essentially respected the embargo on the Abkhaz, the Russians continued their open engagement, thus establishing and solidifying their commercial ties to Abkhazia, both legal and illegal.

Russian policy from the late 1990s has been a gradual and de-facto annexation of Abkhazia. In December 2000, Russia imposed a visa regime on Georgia, but excluded Abkhazia and South Ossetia. In July 2001, the Russian Duma passed legislation that allows regions to accede to the Russian Federation. Starting on June 1, 2002, the Congress of Russian Communities of Abkhazia has collected Abkhazians' Soviet-era travel documents and sent them to a consular department specially set up by Moscow foreign ministry officials. Their documents were returned with a new page inserted which certified Russian citizenship. By June 2002, an estimated 150,000 people in Abkhazia had acquired the new passports, joining 50,000 who already are Russian citizens.

Concerned about all these potential hotspots in Georgia, and recognizing that regional conflicts present a threat to stability and economic development of the whole region, in January 2000 Demirel and Shevardnadze proposed a 'Caucasus Stability Pact' (CSP) in Tbilisi. They argued that with many of Europe's problems resolved, it was time to solve the 'frozen conflicts' of the Caucasus region. The new model for the region was a 3+2+2 formula (Armenia, Azerbaijan, Georgia + Turkey, Russia + European Union and the US), giving Turkey a more direct role while reducing that of Russia. While a regional power, Iran would be included at a later stage, once it fulfills basic OSCE criteria.[22] The European Union and the United States would be involved at the third level and, together with their financial institutions, would help with restructuring and rehabilitation projects. This model would require more international presence in the region.[23]

Demirel took the initiative to write to the presidents of all three Caucasus republics, as well as to several European leaders and to the president of the United States. All but

---

[22] The Balkan Stability Pact (under the umbrella of OSCE) was the blueprint for the Caucasus Stability Pact.

[23] Unal Cevikoz, Deputy Director of Caucasus Department, Turkish Ministry of Foreign Affairs. "Regional Stability: Turkish View", paper presented at a Center for Strategic and International Studies conference organized by Zeyno Baran entitled *Regional Stability and Pipeline Security in the Caucasus*, December 6, 2000.

Kocharyan replied. Nonetheless, the Turkish think tank TESEV organized two brainstorming sessions for the CSP, and tried to engage Armenian NGOs. While Foreign Minister Ismail Cem was actively involved in these initiatives, and gave the keynote address in both meetings—first in February 2001 in Istanbul and second in October 2001 in Brussels—the CSP's existence remained almost entirely on paper. Moreover, the initial excitement in Ankara disappeared when Demirel left office. His successor Ahmet Necdet Sezer did not have the same degree of interest in the region. Consequently, an international, long-term strategic engagement with the Caucasus region was postponed to a later date.

Relations with Russia

Turkey's Caucasus policy cannot be understood without a brief look at its Russia policy. In 1991, while excited about the independence of the Turkic republics, Ozal also recognized the importance of Russia for Turkish businesses. Thus, while cautious of Russia's continued interest and involvement in the Caucasus, Ankara recognized that it was possible to do business both with Moscow and with the new Caucasus governments. However, some of Turkey's projects—such as gas pipelines—were in direct opposition to Moscow's interests, sending confusing signals to both sides.

Turkey signed a natural gas agreement with the Soviet Union in September 1984, and delivery started in 1987. Following the breakup of the USSR, Turkish companies were given many construction contracts as part of the new bilateral economic partnership with Russia. In return, Russians wanted to construct a long-term, large gas pipeline project to sell more gas to Turkey. The final project—Blue Stream—would enable Russia to supply Turkey with 16 billion cubic meters (bcm) of gas via a pipeline that would be laid under the Black Sea to the Turkish port of Samsun. The argument in favor of the project was that Turkey and Russia are two giant neighbors that would gain from cooperation instead of increased competition.

While the project itself may have made sense, it was in direct contrast to what the Turkish Foreign Ministry was trying to achieve with Turkey's gas diversification. It was eager to complete the East-West energy corridor, in order to make Turkey the center of Eurasian energy projects. The pro-Russian business sector and their political allies, however, preferred to focus on the Russian market. They preferred a North-South Energy Corridor, where Russia would remain a key partner in the new energy projects. They also believed that if Russia were left out of the energy development, Moscow's political reaction would lash out and create instability in the weak Caucasus region.

The plans of the Turkish state-owned pipeline company BOTAS in 1991 included transporting Turkmen gas through Turkey to European markets. Accordingly, in 1998 Turkey and Turkmenistan signed a gas agreement of 30 bcm with Turkmenistan for TCGP, of which 16 bcm would be consumed in Turkey and the rest transported to Europe. The signing of the Blue Stream agreement when the US and Turkey were actively promoting the Trans-Caspian gas pipeline was seen as a brilliant Russian move to block the Turkmen gas project since there would not be sufficient room in the Turkish market to take both supplies.

While the Blue Stream project has harmed Turkish efforts to diversify the natural gas supply, it certainly helped to improve Russian-Turkish relations; Russia thus no longer sees Turkey as a direct competitor. In the mid-1990s, Russia saw Turkey as a serious security challenge. The White Book of Russian Special Services described Turkey as an aspiring regional power that supported Muslim movements and cherished pan-Turkic ideas. It argued that Turkey might move into the geo-strategic niche in the Caucasus created by Russia's withdrawal. Soon, however, Moscow recognized that Turkey's economic and political crisis would not lead it to present a major challenge in the region—and Blue Stream made such a Turkish challenge even less likely.

For Turkey, however, Russia remained a serious security concern, as Moscow was indirectly but actively involved in all the major conflicts in the Southern Caucasus. In the Georgian civil war, Russia aided the Abkhaz in their fight for independence, and also provided assistance to the South Ossetians. In the NK war, Russia helped Armenia against Azerbaijan. The weak state structures and massive corruption in the region have also made it very easy for Russian organized criminal groups to maintain monopolies in certain business sectors.

One of Turkey's key concerns has been the Russian effort to block BTC. When former KGB agent Vladimir Putin became president of Russia in March 2001, there was serious concern that Moscow would directly or indirectly threaten the project. The 'weak link' Georgia was the main source of concern, especially when Russia cut off gas supplies in the midst of winter to pressure Georgia to accept the North-South routes. Moscow backed down only after realizing the depth of the US commitment to the East-West corridor. In fact, while accusing the US of backing the BTC for political reasons and claiming that the project has no commercial viability, the Russian government had to simultaneously reject a request by the Russian Lukoil company to join the BTC project.

Another underlying tension for decades has been the respective perceptions of the Turkish and Russian governments of each other's 'support for the separatist Chechens' and 'support for the separatist Kurds.' During the Cold War both played the other's 'ethnic card' to destabilize the other, but especially after the signing of Blue Stream, government policy in Moscow and Ankara is to play this game no longer. Nevertheless, prior to his arrest in February 1999 in Kenya, Kurdish terrorist group PKK's leader Abdullah Ocalan sought shelter in Russia. Furthermore, with leading NGO opposition voices to the BTC pipeline coming from the Kurdish groups, Ankara remains concerned that Moscow may be sponsoring such groups.

For its part, Russia believes that Turkey aided the Chechens during the 1994-1996 war and then again through indirect financial and military assistance after 1999. There are several million Turks with Caucasian backgrounds; over the last decade, the Northern Caucasus diaspora groups within Turkey have developed a strong, united, and politically active community. While Turkey does not have a 'Northern Caucasus' policy as such, since it recognizes the region as an integral part of Russia, some NGOs in Istanbul and elsewhere have become increasingly more active.

Developments Following September 11, 2001

Following the terrorist attacks of September 11, the Eurasian region came to world attention once again as all eyes turned to Afghanistan. Turkey's strategic location on the

East-West corridor from Europe to inland Central Asia, as well as its 'democratic, secular, Muslim republic' model, increased its relevance to world affairs. Many in Ankara also wanted to take advantage of Turkey's historic ties to Afghanistan and to take direct involvement in both the war and its aftermath—especially in the reconstruction of the country, within which it could promote the Turkish example. However, unlike under Ozal, Turkey did not have any visionary leader at this juncture. Furthermore, because the country was experiencing a serious economic and political crisis, it could not realize its full potential.

President George W. Bush made clear to Turkish Prime Minister Bulent Ecevit at their White House meeting in January 2002 his belief and hope that the Turkish model could become one of the best remedies against the radical militant teachings of the Taliban and terrorist groups like Al-Qaeda. While initially very enthusiastic, Ankara could not play that role. Washington was Ecevit's last foreign trip due to his frail health, and President Sezer still was not interested in global issues. In the absence of the 'democratic, secular' part of the government, the Islamic elements became more active in the region, which seriously worried the Turkish secular establishment.

In fact, the Turkish secular system had been threatened for the last decade by Turkic Islamic movements in Central Asia and Caucasus, especially the increasingly influential network of spiritual leader Fettullah Gulen. Until the mid-1990s, Gulen's messages of love, peace and tolerance were supported by top Turkish government and business leaders, and his initiatives of establishing schools in Central Asia and the Caucasus were regarded highly. Gulen's efforts were especially important given that the Turkish state did not have the resources or the interest in providing education in areas where, following the collapse of the Soviet system, the only alternatives were poor education or Saudi-backed extremist Islamic education. Over time, however, Gulen's network became so powerful that the state started fearing that it could be infiltrated by radicals who would use it for their own purposes. In 1999 Gulen and his network was put on the 'black list.'

When Gulen went to the US for cancer treatment and remained there, many conspiracy theorists in Turkey speculated that he is backed by the US as a potential leader for a moderate Islamic form of government. With Washington touting Turkey as a 'moderate Muslim country,' many of these people worried that the US might bring people like Gulen to power in Ankara. In fact, when the Islamic oriented Justice and Development Part (AKP) won the parliamentary election in November 2002, many in Ankara believed that Washington was behind this victory.

While Washington was trying to reach out to moderate Muslim groups, US policy in the region was mainly to fight terrorists with international ties (to Al Qaeda), which brought Chechnya and Georgia's Pankisi Gorge into attention.[24] Georgia is the only country bordering Chechnya, and Turkey has been worried about the spillover impact of the Chechen war, particularly the second conflict that erupted in 1999. Georgia then took in thousands of Chechen refugees and placed them along the border region in the Pankisi

---

[24] For detailed background see, Zeyno Baran's CSIS Georgia Updates http://www.csis.org/ruseura/georgia/gaupdate.htm

gorge, where thousands of Kists (Georgian citizens of Chechen origin) were living for many decades. Along with the refugees, Chechen fighters also crossed the border to find shelter, and over time some of them developed ties to international terrorist networks. Russia wanted to launch attacks against these men for years, but Georgia refused for fear of being dragged into the Chechen war. Following September 11, 2001, however, Russian pressure increased, while the United States also began to see the danger of these Chechen exiles, providing 64 million USD to the Georgian army in order to combat them.

In addition to tension in Pankisi, Russian-Georgian relations were severely strained over Abkhazia. Georgia tried to deport several hundred Chechens from Pankisi via the Kodori valley in Abkhazia back to Chechnya. It was a strange turn of events, since it was widely believed that Russia trained and sent Chechens to fight against Georgians in Abkhazia during the civil war between Georgia and Abkhazia. One of the Chechen fighters was Shamil Basaev, who later became one of the leaders of Chechen rebels fighting against the Russians.

Turkey was concerned that no matter what the Georgians did, groups in Russia would use the presence of the terrorists as a pretext to exert more military and political pressure on Georgia, and later on the entire Caucasus. President Putin's desire to develop a strategic partnership with the US, however, could keep the military hardliners in check. The test case has been Abkhazia, as Russia, believing that the deepening strategic cooperation with the United States would allow it a freer hand in Georgia, has taken a number of steps to achieve a *de facto* annexation of Abkhazia. Disregarding its international agreements, Russia has still not fully evacuated its military base in Abkhazia. The Russians are also the only international peacekeepers in Abkhazia under the Commonwealth of Independent States (CIS), which is a security umbrella created by Russia. Turkey, along with the US, is therefore interested in seeing CIS peacekeeping forces in Abkhazia replaced by international forces.

With Washington making a case that the war is against terrorism and not against Islam, maintaining sanctions against pro-US, Muslim, secular republic Azerbaijan was no longer wise for Washington. Thus Bush waived 'Section 907' of the Freedom Support Act, both to reach out further to the Muslim world and also to be able to work closely with the militaries in counter-terrorism efforts with both Azerbaijan and Armenia.[25] Moreover, closer military cooperation would enable Armenia to enjoy the benefits of cooperation with the West and provide an alternative security arrangement to Russia.[26]

For its part, Turkey continued and intensified its trilateral cooperation with Azerbaijan and Georgia. In April 2002 the three presidents met in the Turkish Black Sea town of Trabzon and issued a joint declaration for trilateral cooperation. The three interior ministers signed a cooperation agreement on oil pipeline security, terrorism, and the fight against organized crime, including drug smuggling, money laundering and illegal weapons

---

[25] The sanctions prohibited the US from providing military assistance to Azerbaijan, and in order to keep he balance of power between Armenia and Azerbaijan, the US also refrained from military assistance to Armenia.

[26] For US policy, see Zeyno Baran, "The Caucasus: Ten Years after Independence," *The Washington Quarterly*, Winter 2002, pp.221-234.

trafficking. This agreement was a concrete success of the policy envisioning closer trilateral cooperation as a result of the East-West energy corridor.

On September 18, 2002, the three presidents met once again in Baku to lay the base of the BTC pipeline, thus bringing the dream of the three countries one step closer to reality. The BTC pipeline is expected to start pumping oil in the first part of 2005.[27]

At the same time, there is growing concern that some in Azerbaijan may become further emboldened and go to war over NK, falsely believing that they enjoy Turkish and American support. Ever since Bush waived Section 907, more and more Azerbaijanis have begun seriously to consider renewing the war with Armenia. The Bush Administration decided to 'manage' the issue by bringing together Aliyev and Kocharian. In April 2001, Secretary of State Colin Powell hosted them in Key West, Florida, and despite initial positive signals, the deadlock was not resolved. In fact, Azerbaijan came closer to taking up arms against Armenians after the 'Key West' proposal—a request that Aliyev accept the loss of NK—became clear. The preparation period for the presidential elections in Armenia and Azerbaijan in 2003 made any serious progress impossible until the conclusion of the campaigns.[28]

The improvement of Turkish-Armenian relations again became important in this context. Ankara had already made some goodwill gestures such as easing the visa restrictions imposed on the Armenians following the French Parliament's adoption of the resolution in January 2001. Ankara took this decision, just prior to Ecevit's meeting with Bush in January 2002, to demonstrate that Turkey was willing to be cooperative. In the meeting, however, Ecevit reiterated that the normalization of Turkish-Armenian relations depends on the settlement of the NK conflict. 'If and when Azerbaijan and Armenia solve their problems, if the occupation on Azerbaijan territory is ended, then we will be very glad to establish diplomatic relations with Armenia.'[29]

In order to reduce the tension over the genocide resolutions, academics from Turkey and Armenia, with American support, created a Turkish-Armenian Reconciliation Committee (TARC) in July 2001; however, this soon broke down without much success. TARC's mission was to assist in the development of mutual understanding and the expression of goodwill between the Turkish and Armenian sides; however, the two sides had different expectations and motives. The Armenian side believed that Turkey was only interested in this initiative as a way to prevent or delay genocide resolutions. And the Turkish side believed that the Armenians were mainly interested in bringing the Turks to admit to genocide, and then ask for land and financial compensation. In fact, they would point to the fact that even when Kocharian publicly stated that Armenia would not seek

---

[27] The BTC Owner Group consists of: BP 30.1%; SOCAR 25%; UNOCAL 8.9%; STATOIL 8.71%; TPAO 6.5%; AGIP 5%; TotalFinalElf 5%; Itochu 3.4%; Inpex 2.5%; Phillips 2.5%; Hess 2.36%. Shareholders of the ACG field consortium consist of: SOCAR, BP, Lukoil, ExxonMobil, Statoil, TPAO, Devon, Unocal, Itochu and Delta Hess.

[28] While Kocharyan was reelected in Armenia, he does not enjoy wide legitimacy and is therefore too weak to make any serious concessions in the short term. In Azerbaijan, with Ilham Aliyev's election as President on 15 October 2003 and Heydar Aliyev's death on December 12, 2003, it will also be some time before Azerbaijan can make any significant compromises.

[29] Turkish newspapers, 17 January 2002.

land from Turkey, the hardliners in Armenia, especially the Dashnaks, claimed otherwise.[30]

The TARC initiative came to an end when the Armenian members of the group commissioned a third-party study on the genocide despite the Turkish side's objections. The International Center for Transitional Justice (ICTJ) found 'the events, viewed collectively, can thus be said to include all of the elements of the crime of genocide as defined in the Convention, and legal scholars as well as historians, politicians, journalists and other people would be justified in continuing to so describe them.' The Turkish side denounced these findings and relations returned to the same low point at which they had been for the last decade.

While there have been hints, off and on, that Turkey might try to look for an opening to improve bilateral relations, Ankara's position has remained unchanged. In fact, when Foreign Minister Yasar Yakis in December 2002 hinted at interest in improvement of bilateral relations, there was strong reaction in Ankara. His party leader (and later Prime Minister) Recep Tayyip Erdogan refuted Yakis' move during a visit to Azerbaijan January 2003, restating that as long as NK situation is not resolved, there would be neither opening in the border nor communication with Yerevan. When President Sezer later congratulated Kocharian for his March 2003 Presidential election victory, this was also seen as yet another example of the uncoordinated policies of Ankara.

Even though Turkey saw the formation of a new government following the November 2002 elections, the basics of Turkish foreign policy towards the Caucasus does not seem likely to change. The leading AKP has Islamist elements, but considers itself as a "conservative democratic' and not 'Islamist' movement. Erdogan, who took over the prime minister's job from Abdullah Gul in March 2003, is a pragmatic politician, and like his predecessors has had to immediately focus on political and economic crises as well as on the war in Iraq. At the time of writing, the AKP has not had much time to focus on the Caucasus.

However, the fact that for the first year of his term Erdogan visited Azerbaijan and Central Asian states, while avoiding close ally Georgia (a non-Turkic, non-Islamic country), raised some eyebrows in the region. Georgia and especially Armenia worried that the AKP's desire for Turkey to play a leadership role in the Muslim world might reflect wider, pan-Turkic ambitions. The verdict is not yet out on the AKP government's intentions, but Turkish policy and interests in the Caucasus are not likely to change in the short term.

Looking Ahead—Some Policy Suggestions

For Turkey to have a significant impact on the Caucasus region's developments, close continued cooperation with the US is necessary. Turkey alone is too weakened by continual economic and political difficulties. Meanwhile, the US alone is too far away and too preoccupied with global issues. It is nonetheless a hyper-power with which all the Caucasus countries want close relations, and Ankara needs to find a way to be relevant to

---

[30] For Kocharian's views, see Mehmet Ali Birand's interview with him published by the *Turkish Daily News*, 1 February 2001.

both the region and Washington.

From Washington's perspective the region is in flux. In addition to Turkey, there are many other countries—such as Poland, the United Kingdom and Ukraine—that could play a role in the stability of the Caucasus. Since early 2003, Washington is also seriously thinking about NATO expansion to the Caucasus and the development of a new approach to the Black Sea region. It is up to Turkey to make itself a constructive and relevant force in the midst of all these developments. With other countries aiming to become new 'pivotal' states, location alone will not be sufficient for Turkey to remain a 'bridge between East and West.'

What can Turkey do? First, the BTC oil and the Sah Deniz gas pipeline projects need to be completed. The East-West corridor would bring Turkey a real voice in the Eurasian region. While both projects are being carried out more or less according to schedule, there could still be political or economic developments that could endanger the success of these pipelines. Therefore, Turkey needs to keep its focus on these two internationally significant projects before embarking on new ones.

Second, Turkey needs to find a way to engage with Armenia. A Turkish-Armenian rapprochement would change the region's dynamics for the better. The growing gap between the two axes (Azerbaijan-Georgia-Turkey-Israel versus Armenia-Iran-Syria-Greece) is simply too dangerous for the region's future. Azerbaijan's initial reaction would be negative, but US President can help—the improvement of Turkish-American relations is a major US foreign policy goal. Moreover, the US wants to solve all frozen conflicts that could become terrorist breeding grounds and possibly lead to outright war; Turkish-Armenian rapprochement would help with NK as well.

Third, Turkey can also play a constructive role in Abkhazia, which is another frozen conflict that could flare up at any moment. Given its close relations with both the Georgians and the Abkhaz, Turkey needs to focus its attention on the resolution of the Abkhaz issue; this would require Ankara clarifying its Russia policy as well.

Fourth, Turkey has to prepare for regime change in Iran, which the US is determined to midwife. When Iran was left out of the region's political and energy developments, Turkey did not face serious competition. Endowed with rich oil and gas reserves and a US-friendly population that is well educated, Iran will inevitably challenge Turkey's predominant role in the region, which is currently taken for granted. Given that one-third of Iranian population is Turkic, Turkey and Azerbaijan can influence developments in Iran. At the same time, pan-Turkism needs to be avoided, as it would bring further tension with Armenia, and limit cooperation with the United States.

14 Turkey's Relations with the Turkic Republics[*]

Gül Turan
İlter Turan
İdris Bal

Introduction

The demise of the Soviet Union came at a time when major shifts in the international environment in which Turkey had been operating, were already taking place. The relations characterized earlier by hostility between the members of the Western and the Soviet blocs had given way to more temperate relationships, culminating in the disappearance of the Warsaw Pact and the growth of security cooperation through a series of treaties and organizational instruments during the 1980s. Turkey had been a participant in this process as a member of the Western defense system. New economic opportunities also seemed to be opening up both in Eastern Europe and in the Soviet Union from which Turkey anticipated to benefit. However, none had expected the Soviet Union to break up so easily and smoothly into its 'constituent units.' The emergence of countries to the East that had Turkic origins was rather sudden and caught all parties unprepared. Yet, a feeling of euphoria swept Turkey. Finally, other countries of Turkic origins with which a partnership could be established had come into being.

In this chapter, the term 'Turkic Republics' is used throughout to mean the following republics: Azerbaijan, Kazakhstan, Kyrgyzstan, Uzbekistan and Turkmenistan. In this article, initially historical background will be outlined then, evolution of relations between Turkey and Turkic republics will be analyzed.

Historical Background

Despite the reality of common cultural roots, historically, Turkey's relations with the Turkic regions of Central Asia have been limited. The ruling elite of the Ottoman Empire had not traditionally seen themselves as being Turkish, a term reserved for the Anatolian peasants. Only toward the end of the nineteenth century, when Pan-Turkist ideologies had begun to penetrate political thinking of the intellectual and the military-bureaucratic elites of the empire, had the term gained widespread acceptance.

During the 19th century when it became clear that the empire was collapsing, the

---

[*] This chapter is a revised, updated and expanded version of a chapter by Gul Turan and Ilter Turan entitled "Turkey's Emerging Relationship with Other Turkic Republics," in Libby Rittenberg, (Ed.), *The Political Economy of Turkey in the Post-Soviet Era* Westport, Conn.: Praeger, 1998, pp.177-203. In the revision of this article implemented mainly by Idris Bal, some of the material has come from his *Turkey's Relations with the West and Turkic Republics: The Rise and Fall of the Turkish Model,* Aldershot: Ashgate, 2000. Idris Bal would like to express his thanks to Meryem Kirimli for reading and commenting on the new version of this manuscript.

Ottoman elite began to search for a 'unifying element' to cease the dispersion of the Empire. Their efforts gave birth to three ideologies; Pan-Ottomanism, Pan-Islamism, and Pan-Turkism. The aim of pan-Ottomanism was to save the Empire by uniting numerous nations under the banner of Ottomanness or Osmanlı.[1] Non-Muslim nations would be free in their beliefs and language as usual, but they would also enjoy equal rights and equal status with the Muslim population of the empire, and they would be represented in the parliament. The goal of Islamism was to integrate Islamic peoples of the empire socially and politically into a single Muslim 'political' community.[2] Pan-Turkism on the other hand aimed at the unity of people of Turkic origins.[3]

During the Tanzimat period (1839-1876,) Ottomanism was adopted state policy. However, this policy failed to satisfy the non-Muslim nations of the empire who continued their separatist activities and demanded their independence. Therefore with the ascension to the throne of Abdülhamid II (1876), pan-Islamism was adopted with the aim of salvaging at least the Muslim parts of the empire. Yet the rise of nationalism among the Muslim people of the empire proved unstoppable as well. In response, pan-Turkism emerged as another integrative formula. During the First World War, it was pursued as the state policy.

Enver Pasha, the general who led the empire into the First World War, was a dedicated pan-Turkist. His policies to restore the empire to its former prominence by allying with the Germans, however, ended in total failure. After the World War I, Enver Pasha went to Turkestan and headed the Basmachi movement fighting against Russia. He was killed in an ambush in Dushanbe in 1922. The nationalist leadership that organized an effort to build a Turkish nation state from the remnants of the empire by conducting a successful independence effort against the allies, on the other hand, was committed to consolidating the new state and shied away from trans-nationalist ideologies and movements. In the case of Azerbaijan and other Turkic parts of the Soviet Union, there were compelling reasons to disavow interest. The new republic wanted to maintain friendly and peaceful relations with its neighbors, especially its more powerful neighbor to the north, with which it shared an anti-imperialist orientation.

In 1923 Turkish Republic was established. Although Mustafa Kemal was a nationalist, his nationalism was not based on ethnicity. It was confined to the boundaries of Turkey and open to all citizens.[4] It was a quick and practical solution to the need to create a new identity and a culture which would cut its ties with the non-national legacy of its past. Now the citizens of the new Republic were asked to unify around 'Turkishness', which, as defined by Atatürk, emphasized the centrality of a being a Turkish citizen, and took no account of the origins of its constituent people. Anyone, who carried a Turkish passport and called Turkey his/her homeland, was a 'Turk'. Hence being a Turk was a question of citizenship rather than race, and in theory, Atatürk's nationalism disregarded differences in race and religion. 'Proclaiming oneself a Turk'

---

[1] Yusuf Akçura, *Üç Tarz-ı Siyaset*, Ankara: Türk Tarih Kurumu Yayınları, 1991, p.19.
[2] See, Ilter Turan, *Cumhuriyet Tarihimiz*, Istanbul: Çağlayan Yayınları, 1969.
[3] W. C. Hostler, *The Turks of Central Asia*, London: Praeger, 1993, p.143.
[4] Philip Robins, *Turkey and the Middle East*, London: Pinter Publishers, 1991, p.4.

thus became a badge of pride and the key to full membership in the political community[5] and the founder of the Republic called himself Atatürk, 'Father of Turks', and cemented nationhood with the phrase 'Ne Mutlu Türküm Diyene' ('Happy is the inidividual who can call himself/herself a Turk'), a phrase still to be found on the walls of important official buildings.[6]

After World War I, the collapse of the Ottoman Empire and the establishment of the Turkish Republic, the population had become far more homogenous than the population of the Ottoman Empire. Whereas religion had served as a major bond among the Muslim population during the Ottoman Empire, in the new Republic religion and state were separated. The importance accorded to religion as a force for political bonding was reduced. Atatürk's solution to the problem was to propose a territorially defined Turkish identity and urge the citizenry to rally around it. Therefore, with the establishment of Turkish Republic, the popularity of pan-Turkism and interest the question of 'outer' or 'external' Turks declined. Furthermore, pan-Turkism was regarded as a problematical ideology from the perspective of both domestic and global politics. From the early years of the republic, Pan-Turkist movements were generally suppressed. Some of its more militant advocates were tried and imprisoned. During the World War II, Germany supported the activities of Turkish pan-Turkists to challenge the internal security of the USSR. Consequently, these movements became somewhat more assertive for a brief period under German prodding, but never achieved sufficient stature so as to influence foreign policy.

During the late 1960s, a Pan-Turkist party was finally established. This party, which excelled more in street politics than in the electoral, managed to gain representation in the Turkish Grand National Assembly and became a partner in a series of governments known as "Nationalist Front" coalitions, which ruled Turkey intermittently between 1974 and 1978. While the party may have had some, though limited, non-public links with persons and underground movements in the Turkic parts of the Soviet Union, most notably in Azerbaijan, there is no evidence that its pan-Turkist ideology constituted an important input to foreign policy-making or implementation. Rather, pan-Turkism became manifest in its anti-Communist rhetoric where references were made to "captive Turks under the Soviet yoke." In general, Turkish state establishment maintained a reserved attitude toward pan-Turkist movements and their links with 'outer' Turks, however, and viewed them to be problematical in terms of Turkey's relations with the Soviet Union until the latter's demise.

The presence of a political movement avowedly taking an interest in the 'Turks' of the Soviet Union did not mean that there existed major academic or other expertise on Turkic peoples of the East. Although the history of the Turks constituted a specialization within the departments of history at a number of Turkish universities, there was scant information and, consequently, expertise available about contemporary Azerbaijan and Central Asia. The existing historical literature was often characterized by romanticism

---

[5] Ibid., p.5.

[6] T. Hindle, "Young Turks", *The World in 1994*, London: The Economist Publications, 1993, p.59.

and a yearning for a distant and not so well known past.

Another source that kept the idea of the Central Asian connection alive was the multifarious émigré associations. There was a considerable Azeri population in Eastern Turkey, particularly in areas bordering Iran and Armenia. Almost all Central Asian groups were present, if not in large numbers, in various parts of Turkey. These communities were often organized into cultural and/or mutual assistance associations. The successive Turkish governments would not allow these organizations to engage in activities aimed at influencing foreign policy, but they were free to work toward the preservation of culture and traditions. If there was a political value to these émigré associations, it was that they were anti-Communist, an orientation that rested well with the center-right parties that usually formed the governments in Turkey. It is not unlikely that some associations as well as some individuals had links with the Turks of the Soviet Union, but these were not significant enough to belie the generalization that linkages between these populations and Turkey were almost nonexistent.

The relations with the Turkic Republics were established through Moscow. Contacts were usually limited to the cultural domain. Occasionally, a Turkish singer or actor would visit some cities in Azerbaijan or Central Asia, and, similarly, Soviet artists might come for a visit. Except for a few contracts in the Turkic republics won by Turkish Companies just prior to the break up of the Soviet Union, economic relations were almost nonexistent. Turkey's trade in general with former USSR started to increase in late 1980s.

Table 1: Turkey's Trade with Former USSR between 1988 and 1991 (Million $)

Year	Exports	Imports	Balance	Volume
1988	271.408	442.619	-171.211	714.027
1989	704.772	596.710	+108.062	1301.482
1990	531.100	1271.400	-740.300	1802.500
1991	610.600	1089.800	-479.200	1700.400

Source: İdris Bal , *Turkey's Relations with the West and Turkic Republics: The Rise and Fall of the Turkish Model*, Aldershot: Ashgate, 2000, p.80.

It is important to stress that although academics were discussing the possible collapse of the USSR in the early 1980's, Turkey was unprepared for the emancipation of the Turkic Republics as independent states. In the first meeting of the Slavic Republics in Minsk on December 8, 1991, the Commonwealth of Independent States (CIS) was established which marked the end of the USSR. The first meeting of the expanded CIS in Alma Ata on December 21, 1991 declared the former Soviet Republics as sovereign and independent, and each Republic as having full control of its own natural and local economic enterprises. Although President Demirel referring to the establishment of the Turkic Republics, pointed out that this development had been expected for a century and that Turks were waiting for this moment,[7] on another occasion he admitted Turkey's unreadyness for the emancipation of these Republics, saying "While the 1990's approached, no one could have imagined that the Soviet Union would disintegrate, and that out of it a Georgia, an Azerbaijan, a Turkmenistan, an Uzbekistan, a Kyrgyzstan, a Tajikistan and an Armenia would become independent....the disintegration of the Soviet Union was a surprise for everybody. No one was prepared for an event of this kind. Including the Republics which emerged out of this empire, no one was prepared for this."[8]

Turkish unreadyness may be explained by three factors. First, Turkey did not want to provoke the Soviet Union, a major military power with common land an sea borders with Turkey, into thinking that Turkey was undermining its security and invite reprisals. Second, after World War I, Turkish decision-makers and intellectuals had generally refrained from dealing with other Turkic people who were known in Turkey as "dış Türkler" (external Turks) for fear that such activity would challenge the status quo thereby threating domestic, regional and international peace and stability. Third, Turkish decision-makers and analysts did not have sufficient information and expert advice about the USSR and were not able to anticipate the sudden collapse of the Soviet Union.[9] For example, even in 1991 Vahit Halefoğlu (Minister of Foreign Affairs, 1987-1989) argued in an article that

The referendum held on 17 March in the Soviet Union on the subject of the new forms of links to be established between the Federal Republics and the Union, brought to light the desire of the Turkic peoples to stay attached to the Soviet Union.[10]

These facts and the expectation that the Soviet Union would continue to function in some form meant that Turkey had no well-planned strategy to give direction to its foreign policy actions when Azerbaijan and the Turkic states of Central Asia became independent. What existed was a romantic notion of distant cousins yearning to be in some kind of political community with the Turkish Republic, a desire that had so far been thwarted by the Soviets. True, as the Soviet Union lost its ability to provide for the economic well-being of the constituent republics, it had been forced to allow the latter to engage in direct economic relations with other countries, a situation that had made it possible for Turkey to sign some economic agreements with such countries as Azerbaijan and Kazakhstan,[11] but whether these were temporary or would be long-lasting could not

---

[7] *Sabah*, 3 February 1992.

[8] "Cumhurbaşkanı Sayın Süleyman Demirel'in Türk İşbirliği ve Kalkınma Ajansı'nın Üçüncü Çalışma Yılının Başlangıcında 'Günümüzde Avrasya' Konulu Toplantıda Yaptıkları Konuşma", 14 September 1994, TIKA, pp.7-8.

[9] İdris Bal, *Turkey's Relations with the West and the Turkic Republics: The Rise and Fall of the Turkish Model*, Aldershot: Ashgate, 2000, p.80.

[10] Vahit Halefoğlu, "The importance of the Soviet Union for Turkey", *Turkish Review*, Vol.5, No.24, Summer 1991, p.30.

[11] See, e.g., Oles Smolansky, "Turkish and Iranian Policies in Central Asia", Hafeez Malik, (Ed.), *Central Asia: Its Strategic Importance and Future Prospects*, New York: St. Martin's, 1994, p.293; Irina Zviagelskaya,

be easily judged.

Nevertheless, now that the Soviet Union was no more, linkages on all fronts could quickly be established. Once the Soviet Union collapsed Turkey was eager to get involved. Demirel underlined the importance of the event by saying "The collapse of communism was a great thing for us".[12] The end of the Cold War and of the Soviet Union had a great impact on Turkey because although Turkey lost its strategic position from the Western point of view as a bulwark against the Soviet Union, new opportunities were opened for her. In six of the newly independent states of the former Soviet Union, the majority of the population was Muslim and five of these republics (Azerbaijan, Kazakhstan, Kyrgyzstan, Turkmenistan and Uzbekistan) were regarded as Turkic Republics. This new situation affected Turkish politicians, the intellectual and bureaucratic elites and the public deeply for a variety of reasons. With the end of Cold War and USSR, the issue of outer Turks became popular. Almost everyone in Turkey welcomed emergence of Turkic republics enthusiastically.

Importance of the Region

In general Central Asia and Turkic republics were important for all regional as well as global powers. With the end of Cold War, a power vacuum has been created in Eurasia. Eurasia, especially Central Asia is still important for Turkey and other regional as well as global politics. Central Asia is not an ordinary region in the world. For instance, Halford Mackinder put forward that the state that could control the Eurasian landmass between Germany and central Siberia would be able to control the world. He expressed it in this way:

> *Who rules East Europe commands the Heartland*
> *Who rules the Heartland command the World Island*
> *Who rules the World Island commands the world*

According to the theory "Central Asia is the "heartland" and the "world island" is Eurasia plus Africa – in all, over two thirds of the world's surface land area."[13] According to Mackinder, region has vital geo-strategic importance for world politics. The power that controls the Eurasian land mass and especially center of this land Central Asia, will control the whole World. In other words, the power that governs and develops the center of Eurasia will dominate entirely world politics.[14] Because of developments in technology, communication and transportation, the validity of Mackinder's theory is, of course, open to discussion. Central Asia is still important, however, for other reasons.

"Central Asia and Transcaucasia: New Geopolitics", Vitaly V. Naumkin, (Ed.), *Central Asia and Transcaucasia: Ethnicity and Conflict*, London: Greenwood Press, 1994, p.137.

[12] *The Washington Post*, 9 February 1992.

[13] Graham Evans and Jeffrey Newnham, *The Penguin Dictionary of International Relations*, London: Penguin Books Ltd., 1998, p.219.

[14] Bilgin Erdoğan, "ABD'nin Orta Asya Siyaseti", Mim Kemal Öke (Ed.), *Orta Asya Türk Cumhuriyetleri*, İstanbul: Alfa Yayınları, 1999, p.230; Also see, Sami Karamısır, *Türkiye'nin Siyasi Meseleleri*, İstanbul: Osmanlı Araştırmaları Vakfı, 1994, pp.187-194; Gerald Robbins, "Post-Sovyet Anayurdu", *Avrasya Etüdleri*, Vol.1, No.3, Winter 1994.

First, it is located in the heart of Eurasia, neighboring important countries, such as China, India, Iran, Pakistan and Russia. Especially China, Russia and India are major powers important for regional as well as global politics owing mainly to their nuclear capabilities, military power, natural resources, and economic and demographic potentials. Second, a number of soft security threats for both regional and global powers such as drug trafficking, terrorism and Islamic fundamentalism emanate from Central Asia and neighboring regions. The 9/11 terrorist attacks on the USA and subsequent US led operation in Afghanistan, underline importance of region for global security. Third, Central Asia is rich in energy resources as well. Apart from strategic importance of the region, newly discovered oil and gas resources in Central Asia and Caspian Sea are enough to make the region still important for both the regional and the global economy and therefore politics since for most of the 21st century, carbohydrates are still expected to be the main source of energy. New oil and gas resources in the region direct the attention of regional and global powers towards the area. So, political and security reasons have combined with presence of major natural resources to promote competition between regional and global players to be present and influential in the area. Though the reasons may have changed over time, the region is still of vital importance in world politics and carries a special importance for Turkey.[15]

With the end of Cold War, Turkey appeared to lose her strategic importance for the Western alliance and the US as a bulwark against the Communist threat. This presented a problematical security environment for Turkey but it also created new opportunities to become a 'pivotal' state in the global context. In this context, both the emergence of friendly states in Balkans and the emergence of Turkic republics in Caucasus and Central Asia provided Turkey new opportunities for cooperation.

Stages of Evolution in the Turkey-Turkic Republics Relationship

Having the benefit of hindsight, it may now be proposed that the relations between Turkey and Azerbaijan and the Turkic states of Central Asia went through three stages. These stages are not marked by specific events in the instance of all countries; rather they reflect transformations of the outlooks that have given direction to the relationship. Therefore, they should be construed not as being discrete but as fluctuations on a continuum. The first stage is marked by high levels of optimism and expectations about the future. The second comprises the period of the mutual discovery of constraints that helped define the limits of the relationship. The third stage can be described as the routinization of the relationship. We use these stages as an organizational scheme in the following analysis.

The Period of Optimism

As the constituent republics of the Soviet Union began to declare their independence from the center in the fall of 1991, a feeling of excitement swept Turkey. It was felt that the coming of independence to the Central Asian states would open the way to the

---

[15] İdris Bal, "Rise of Shanghai Cooperation Organization (SCO) in Eurasia: Is it an Effectivre Toll in a New Big Game", Ertan Efegil, (Ed.), *Geopolitics of Central Asia in the Post-Cold War Era*, Haarlem: SOTA, 2002, pp.272-273.

construction of a Turkic world in which Turkey would occupy a leading role. Accordingly, Turkey was the first state to extend diplomatic recognition to Uzbekistan, Kazakhstan, Kyrgyzstan, Turkmenistan and Azerbaijan. Shortly afterward, starting with Nursultan Nazarbayev of Kazakhstan in September 1991, within a short interval, the presidents of the Turkic Republics all paid visits to Ankara. Saparmurad Niyazov (now Turkmenbashi) of Turkmenistan, Islam Kerimov of Uzbekistan and Askar Akaev of Kyrgyzstan stopped in Ankara in December, while Ayaz Muttalibov of Azerbaijan came in January 1992.[16]

Table 2: Major Indicators

Country	Population Million (2003 est.)	Area (square Km)	Inflation (Annual in %) 1992 1995 2002	GDP growth rate (%) 1992 1995 2002	Per Capita Income (Dollars) 1992 1995 2002 (purchasing power parity)	Total Exports (TE) of (billion $) 1995 2002 est.	Total Imports (TI) of (billion $) 1995 2002 est.
Azerbaijan	7.8	86,600	1350 412 2.6	-22.6 -17. 2 10.6	2228 1223 3700	0.547 2	0.632 1.8
Kazakhstan	16.8	2,717,300	1513 176 9.5	-13 -8.9 6	3612 2271 7200	4.974 10.3	3.742 9.6
Kyrgyzstan	4.9	198,500	855 43 2.1	-15. 9 -6. 9 5.3	2014 1228 2900	0.409 0.488	0.522 0.587
Tajikistan	6.9	143, 100	1157 884 12	-3 – 12.4 9.1	1287 815 1300	0.749 0.710	0.799 0.830
Turkmenistan	4.8	488,100	493 1262 5	5.3 -9.3 21.1	2683 1610 6700	1.736 2.97	0.72 2.25
Uzbekistan	26	447,400	4671 305 26(2001)	-10.6 -1.2 4.2	2068 1989 2600	3.1 2.8	2.9 2.5

Source: Compiled from various Issues of the EIU s (Economist Intelligence Unit) Country Reports, and IMF's Direction of Trade Statistics Yearbook and State Statistical Institute of Turkey's Annual Statistical Yearbooks, and http://www.cia.gov/cia/publications/factbook/geos/aj.html

The optimism regarding the evolution of a Turkic world as an important region and an autonomous actor in the world system was reflected in the speeches of Turkish political leaders and in the official statements made by the government. For example, President Turgut Özal frequently alluded to the idea that the twenty-first century would be a "Turkic century",[17] while the then Prime Minister Süleyman Demirel pointed to the birth of the Turkic world that extended from China to the Adriatic Sea, intimating that Turkey was ready to take on major responsibilities in this region.[18] On their part, the leaders of

[16] Cengiz Çandar, "Değişmekte Olan Dünyada Türkiye'nin Bağımsızlığını Yeni Kazanan Yeni Türk Cumhuriyetleriyle İlişkileri," Sabahattin Şen, (Ed.), *Yeni Dünya Düzeni ve Türkiye*. İstanbul: Hava Harp Okulu, 1992, pp.63-64.
[17] Çandar, *Değişmekte Olan Dünyada Türkiye'nin Bağımsızlığını Yeni Kazanan Yeni Türk Cumhuriyetleriyle ilişkileri*, p.64.
[18] Smolansky, *Turkish and Iranian Policies in Central Asia*, p.283.

the newly independent states of the Turkic world also appeared to be interested in developing links with Turkey, as evidenced by their visits to Turkey and their willingness to respond favorably to Turkish offers of cooperation.

Diplomatic Cooperation

Some areas of cooperation immediately came to the fore. The newly born states did not have well-developed diplomatic services, since external relations were not a responsibility of the constituent republics during the Soviet era. For the same reason, they did not have a corps of diplomats trained under the Soviets who might assume responsibility for developing a ministry of foreign affairs. Yet, the new countries were hard-pressed to become involved in the workings of the international system, not only to consolidate their newly won independence but also in order to reach sources of economic assistance and support that they desperately needed. It is in this context Turkish offers of diplomatic guidance and support were, therefore, welcome. For example, very quickly a training program for diplomats was initiated by the Turkish Foreign Ministry. Turkey assumed the role of guide in promoting the participation of the Central Asian States in international forums such as the Conference on Security and Cooperation in Europe (CSCE) and the United Nations. Through Turkish efforts, Azerbaijan was included in the Black Sea Economic Cooperation (BSEC), which came into being in February 1992.[19] Similarly, Turkish efforts were indispensable in getting the five Turkish states to join (Kazakhstan as an observer) the Economic Cooperation Organization (ECO), which was originally established to promote economic, cultural, and technological cooperation between Turkey, Iran, and Pakistan at the end of 1992.

Turkey soon became aware that some institutional capability was needed to promote and coordinate closer, multidimensional relations between itself and the new Turkic states. Turkish Cooperation and Development Agency (TİKA), operating under the auspices of the Ministry of Foreign Affairs, was given this responsibility. This agency has been one of the driving forces in the development of relations.

Communications and Transportation

Another area where the need for cooperation was immediately felt was in the field of communications. Although there were high hopes on the part of Turkey to become a builder and a key member of the Turkic world, it soon became apparent that communications with the new states were very difficult, impeding from the start the realization of such an aspiration. Before extensive new communications systems could be established, which would inevitably take a long time, the Turkish government proceeded to donate digital telecommunication exchanges to each of the five Turkic republics. These had the capacity to accommodate 2500-3500 subscribers,[20] which facilitated communications between Turkey and these countries, as well as communications of the

---

[19] Şükrü Elekdağ, "Karadeniz Ekonomik İşbiliği", Sabahattin Şen, (Ed.), *Yeni Dünya Düzeni ve Türkiye*, İstanbul: Hava Harp Okulu, 1992, p.125.

[20] Umut Arık, "Türkiye'nin Azerbaycan ve İç Asya Devletlerine İnsani, Ekonomik ve Teknik Yardım Politikaları", Erol Manisalı, (Ed.), *Türk Cumhuriyetleri Arasında Politik ve Ekonomik İşbirliğ*, İstanbul: Kıbrıs Araştırmaları Vakfı, 1993, pp.35-36.

latter with the rest of the world. Based in part on this experience, Turkish telecommunication companies later won contracts to improve and develop further the telecommunication systems in some of these countries.

When Azerbaijan and the Central Asian Turkic republics became independent, there was no way to reach them by air except through Moscow. In anticipation of meeting growing needs as well as demonstrating the political importance Turkey was according to its linkage with the new states, Turkish Airlines initiated direct flights, first to Baku, Tashkent, and Almaty in mid-1992.[21] Later, while these were rendered more frequent, new flights were added to Ashgabad and Bishkek. Even today, some of the most convenient and reliable connections to Baku and the Turkic capitals of Central Asia are served by the Turkish Airlines. As these states have developed their own national air carriers, all have started to offer flights to Istanbul, such that air travel to and from them to Turkey is easy and frequent.

Land transport, in contrast to air transport, could not be improved with similar ease. With the opening of the East, Turkey opened a border crossing at Sarp into the Ajaristan region of Georgia and improved the road leading to it. This made it possible for trucks to go through Georgia into Azerbaijan, where they would then take the truck ferry from Baku to Krasnovodsk (now Turkmenbashi) in Turkmenistan. From there, all points in the Central Asian republics could be reached. There also existed a sea-land combination going through Russia. Shipments could be made by boat to Novorossisk on the Black Sea coast, where the loads would be transferred to trains that would go to such places as Almaty and Bishkek. The port of Novorossisk was overcrowded, however, and there were complaints that Turkish exports were given low priority in rail transport. A third way of reaching the Central Asian markets was through Iran. Here again, the roads were not good, and Iranian cooperation was less than satisfactory. Rail links between Iran and Turkmenistan, on the other hand, did not exist until 1996. Finally, it would have been possible to have highway access into Azerbaijan and then on to Central Asia through Armenia, but the use of this option could not be entertained until the Azeri-Armenian dispute over Nagorno-Karabagh and the termination of the Armenian occupation of some twenty plus percent of Azeri territory was settled to the satisfaction of both parties. In the initial years, all routes, whether they were highways or railways, suffered from security problems. Merchandise was often stolen or damaged, and security had to be purchased by paying fees to local gangs. Although conditions have somewhat improved, transportation of goods to Central Asia continues to be difficult.

Helping Develop Manpower Resources

Aware of the importance of elite ties in the development of long-lasting relationships between countries and recognizing that well-trained individuals, particularly in the fields of economics, banking, management, accounting, diplomacy, and other similar fields were needed in the new countries in order for them to develop a reliable public service system while, at the same time, making the transition to market economies, Turkey initiated a

---

[21] Philip Robins, "Between Sentiment and Self Interest: Turkey's Policy Toward Azerbaijan and the Central Asian States," *Middle East Journal*, Vol.47, No.4, 1993, p.604.

program through which a total of 10,000 students, two thousand from each of the five republics, would be awarded scholarships to study at Turkish universities. Already in early 1993, 7557 students from Turkic states had enrolled at a variety of Turkish educational institutions, a majority of them at universities.[22] Though not without problems such as insufficient preparation on the part of the incoming students to pursue university studies in the Turkish system and insufficient scholarship money on the part of the Turkish government, the scholarship program is still continuing. Police Academy and War Academy have also invited students from Turkic republics and students are currently studying in these universities as well.

Table 3: Distribution of Students Who Came to Turkey for Education During the Period 1992 to 1993

Country	Higher Education	Secondary Education
Azerbaijan	1,293	310
Kazakhstan	1,109	169
Kyrgyzstan	384	344
Uzbekistan	1,124	270
Turkmenistan	1,185	519
Other Turkic Groups	408	24
Total	5,095	1,634

Source: Ali Arslan, *Türk Cumhuriyetleri ve Türk Topluluklarından Türkiye'ye Gelen Öğrenciler (1992-93)*, Istanbul: Yay Ofset, 1994, p.5.

Table 4: Distribution of Students Who Came to Turkey for Education (according to 20.09.2002 records)

Country	Secondary Education	TOMER (Center for Teaching Turkish)	Pre-License (÷n Lisans) (two year University Education)	Graduate (Lisans)	Master	Ph.D.	Total
Azerbaijan	-	54	51	294	173	44	616
Kazakhstan	-	83	14	397	101	22	617
Kyrgyzstan	-	79	67	377	128	48	699
Uzbekistan	-	-	-	3	-	-	3
Turkmenistan	-	55	-	693	71	3	822
Total		271	132	1764	473	117	2757

Source: The information in this table has been provided by the Turkish Ministry of National Education.

Turkey also undertook to open an elite public high school in each of the republics, a commitment that has already been achieved. These schools, modeled after elite public schools in Turkey, in addition to teaching students standard Turkish, which would enable them to "connect with" Turkey, teaches English, which constitutes the critical instrument through which these countries can relate to the world without the intermediation of

---

[22] Arık, *Türkiye'nin Azerbaycan ve İç Asya Devletlerine İnsani, Ekonomik ve Teknik Yardım Politikaları*, p.34.

Russia. In 1992, a Kazakh university in the city of Turkestan, the Hodja Ahmed Yesevi University was reorganized into a Turkish-Kazakh University, aiming to offer education to young people from the region.

In recent years, a proliferation of private institutions of Turkish origins, offering secondary education, has also occurred. These also offer both English and Turkish to their students, filling a foreign languages gap that the local educational system is, apparently, not able to provide.[23] Larrabee and Lesser emphasize importance of Turkish private institutions as follows;

> *The followers of Fetullah Gülen, the Turkish Religious leader from the Nurcu Sect, also play an important unofficial role in promoting Turkish interests in Central Asia. Gülen's followers have founded more than 300 schools around the world, the majority of them in the newly independent Turkic states of the Soviet Union. These schools promote a philosophy based on a synthesis of Turko-Ottoman nationalism rather than Islam. They have played a major role in transmitting Turkish cultural values in these countries. Indeed, their influence may be even greater than that of official Turkish policy.*[24]

Table 5: Number of Schools and Courses opened by Turkish State (according to 20.09.2002 records)

Country	Number of Schools	Students (TR. Citizens)	Students (Others)	Number of Courses Centers	Number of People Attending Courses	Number of Teachers (TR Citizens)	Number of Teachers (others)
Azerbaijan	1	14	291	1	654	25	9
Kazakhstan	-	-	-	2	160	21	-
Kyrgyzstan	2	1	183	1	257	38	11
Uzbekistan	7	144	1228	1	32	92	78
Turkmenistan	2	211	413	2	580	49	9
Tajikistan	-	-	-	1	82	4	-
Total	12	370	2115	8	1765	229	107

Source: The information in this table has been provided by the Turkish Ministry of National Education.

A number of other educational activities were also initiated by Turkey in the early stages of relations. For example, a program for training Koran readers, which had been started in 1990 before the break up of the Soviet Union, was continued after Turkic republics became independent. Following independence, a revival of Islam had occurred in the Turkic Republics. They needed books on religion, and their mosques needed repairing. Although their aims were different, Turkey, Iran and Saudi Arabia began to send Korans and other religious books to the Republics, and experts were sent to teach

---

[23] See Şahin Alpay, "Türkiye'nin Orta Asya'da Kozu Eğitim," and "Cemaatten Cemiyete," *Milliyet*, November 1-2, 1996, p.20; Ali Bayramoğlu, "Orta Asya'daki Türk Misyonerleri", *Yeni Yüzyıl*, 31 October 1996, p.5.
[24] F. Stephen Larrabee & Ian Lesser, *Turkish Foreign Policy in an Age of Uncertainty*, Santa Monica: Rand, 2003, p.124; For a similar opservation see, Heinz Kramer, *Değişen Türkiye*, İstanbul: Timaş, 2001, p.173.

Islam. According to Arif Soytürk, who was the head of the Foreign Relations Department of the Directorate of Religious Affairs at the time, Turkish aid to 'outer Turks' began in 1990.[25] In Ramadan 1990, the Turkish Presidency of Religious Affairs sent four imams to the USSR. In Ramadan 1991, their number was increased to ten; four of them to Azerbaijan, four of them to the Russian Federation (Tatarstan), one to Yugoslavia, and one to Mongolia. In 1992, Turkey sent thirty-seven specialists to the Muslim Republics of Central Asia (including Azerbaijan). After 1991, students from Muslim Republics came to Turkey for religious education in the Koran schools.

Table 6: İmams Sent by the Turkish Presidency of Religious Affairs to the Turkic World in Ramadan 1992

Country	Number of Imams Sent
Azerbaijan	8
Turkmenistan	7
Kirgizstan	4
Uzbekistan	7
Tajikistan	4
Kazakhstan	7
Yugoslavia	5
Ukraine	3
Georgia	4
Russian Federation (Tatarstan)	10
Albania	9
Total	68

Source: 'Bugüne Kadar Başkanlığımızca Soydaşlarımıza Sunulan Hizmetler', an unpublished document prepared by the Directorate of Religious Affairs.

Apart from educating these students, the Directorate of Religious Affairs helped Turkic people to make their Hajj journeys. For example, in 1991 the Turkish Directorate of Religious Affairs paid expenses of 225 Azeris. In addition to this, Turkey sent tens of thousands of books to the Muslim Republics. The Directorate of Religious Affairs also planned to support mosque construction, for example; the foundations of the Ashgabad-Turkey mosque were laid on January 12, 1993.[26] Such efforts have not been limited to the Turkish state. Turkish private sector has often also been involved; businessmen have supported construction of buildings, and provided books on religion and Turkish culture.

With the initiative of Turkish Directorate of Religious Affairs, Eurasian Islamic Council was established and it meets periodically to discuss cultural and religious problems of the region.

---

[25] *Personal Interview with Arif Soytürk*, Ankara, 21 June 1993.
[26] *Bugüne Kadar Başkanlığımızca Soydaşlarımıza Sunulan Hizmetler.* An unpublished note prepared by the Directoratee on Religious Affairs, p.34.

As seen in Table.8, Turkish Religious Affairs Foundation opened Theology Faculties in Azerbaijan, Kyrgyzstan, Turkmenistan, Romania and Bulgaria. For instance, in 2000-2001 session, 569 students studied in these faculties. Students attending these faculties study two years in Turkey as a preparation, then they attend second class in these faculties. Students learn Anatolian Turkish and learn social and cultural structure of Turkey while they study in Turkey. Apart from faculties, the foundation opened Theology Colleges in the region and 1325 students are studying in these colleges (see Table.9). The foundation had also made plans to build 28 new mosques in Azerbaijan, Kyrgyzstan, Kazakhstan, Turkmenistan, Nakhichevan, Georgia, Abhazia, the Ukraine, Crimea Autonomous Republic, Turkish republic of Northern Cyprus and Albania. All these mosques have been completed and opened for worship.

Table 7: Distribution of the Students Who Came to Receive Religious Education in Turkey Between the Years 1991-1993 (According to Their Place of Origin)

Place of Origin	Number of Students
Mongolia	77
Kazakhstan	57
Bulgaria	70
Chechnya	30
Azerbaijan	6
Daghestan	13
Georgia	56
Uzbekistan	7
Tatarstan	15
Romania	22
Karachai	5
Turkmenistan	58
Meskhetian Turks	1
Bosnia-Herzegovina	5
Kyrgyzstan	6
Macedonia	7
Russia (Ufa-Kazan region)	87
Albania	85
Total	607

Source: 'Bugüne Kadar Başkanlığımızca Soydaşlarımıza Sunulan Hizmetler', an unpublished note prepared by the Directorate of the Turkish Religious Affairs.

Enhancing Cultural Linkages

Helping train and develop manpower resources, in addition to providing professional training and the acquisition of skills, has, from the very beginning, inevitably served as a channel of cultural interaction and transmission. Since the Turkish affinity to these states was based on historical ties, a common language, and common culture, developing cultural links was given attention in the first years of relations. As early as November 1991, The Institute of Turkish Studies of the Marmara University in Istanbul had convened a "Contemporary Turkish Alphabets Symposium" to examine the possibility of developing a standard alphabet for Turkish languages. A meeting with a similar theme was organized by the Turkish Ministries of Culture and Education in 1992 and the Ministry of Foreign Affairs in 1993.[27] There seems to be a consensus that if a common alphabet is to be adopted, it is going to be based on Latin characters. So far, Turkic republics except Kazakhstan have adopted the Latin alphabet. However, the transition to the new alphabet is still continues. The presence of a high percentage of Russians appears to have kept Kazakhstan away from considering changing their alphabets at this time.

Table 8: Faculties Opened by Turkish Religious Affairs Foundation and Number of Students (2000-2001 Session)

Theology Faculties	Number of Students
Azerbaijan Theology Faculty	198
Kyrgyzstan Theology Faculty	189
Turkmenistan Theology Faculty	97
Sofia High Islam Institute	57
Romania Kemal Atatürk Pedagogical College	28
Total	569

Source: Türkiye Diyanet Vakfı Yurt İçi Yurt Dışı Falliyetleri, *Ankara, p.54*

Table 9: Colleges Opened by Turkish Religiosity Foundation and Number of Students (2000-2001 Session)

Colleges	Number of Students
Theology College (Nakhichevan)	62
Baku Turkish College (Baku-Azerbaijan)	334
Kemal Atatürk Theology and Pedagogical College (Costanta-Romania)	320
Theology College (Turkmenistan)	185
Rusçuk Theology College (Bulgaria)	180
Mestanlı Theology College (Bulgaria)	124
Şumnu Theology College (Bulgaria)	120
Total	1325

Source: Türkiye Diyanet Vakfı Yurt İçi Yurt Dışı Falliyetleri, *Ankara, p.55*

In a different arena of cultural interaction, Turkey initiated television broadcasts to the

---

[27] Nadir Devlet, "Yeni Türk Cumhuriyetleri Açısından Türkiye ile (Politik, Ekonomik ve Kültürel Sahalarda) İşbirliğinin Önemi," Erol Manisalı, (Ed.), *Türk Cumhuriyetleri Arasında Politik ve Ekonomik İşbirliği*, İstanbul: Kıbrıs Araştırmaları Vakfı, 1993, p.17.

Turkic republics via satellite during 1992.[28] A new channel, called the Eurasian Channel (then TURK TV), was established by the Turkish Radio and Television, a state company, which began to broadcast programs that would presumably be of interest to Turkish-speaking audiences in the Caucasus and Central Asia. The programs, which contain depictions of life and society in modern Turkey, would also be designed to convey a sense of community among the Turkic peoples. However, this channel did not perform successfully. On the other hand, Turkish private TV Channels; Samanyolu, TGRT, Star TV, and Show TV started to broadcast to the region and they have (especially Samanyolu[29]) gained an audience in the region and are widely watched.

The emphasis the Turkish government has placed on the development of multifaceted relations with the Turkic republics of the Caucasus and Central Asia has led to the establishment of an international organization called Turk-soy. Established in 1994, the goal of this organization is to promote cultural interactions between the Turkic republics. Under the rules of this organization, the ministers of culture of the respective republics meet regularly to evaluate ongoing cultural activities and plan for future cooperation.

Economic Relations

As shall be elaborated later, independence came to the Turkic republics in the middle of an economic crisis, which was one of the major forces that also brought about the undoing of the Soviet Empire. The new states all had socialist economies closely integrated with that of the Russian Federation. Therefore, the independent Turkic states, much like others that came into being after the dissolution of the Union, faced the double problem of meeting the immediate economic needs of their populations and making a transition to market economies. The exporting of products to the world markets for cash was constrained in several ways. First, such products were limited in quantity and kind. Second, most of the marketable products had to be allocated for export to the Russian Federation in return for much needed amenities, which, under the difficult economic circumstances, could be procured only from that country. Furthermore, because of the lack of a transport system outside the Russian Federation through which these landlocked countries could reach international markets, Russia had significant leverage in influencing their economic decisions and behavior.

Turkey's economic relations with the Turkic states began to develop under the influence of these constraints. One of the first actions of TİKA, for example, was to extend humanitarian aid, comprising almost exclusively foodstuffs, to the newly independent countries. But TİKA has also constituted one of prime forces in facilitating economic relations between Turkey and the Turkic republics, organizing technical assistance programs, and encouraging private entrepreneurs to pursue trade opportunities and make investments. Economic relations have been promoted by a number of public and private organizations, such as the Turkish Exim Bank and the Foreign Economic

---

[28] Mehrdad Haghayeghi, "Islamic Revival in the Central Asian Republics", *Central Asian Survey*, Vol.13, No.2, 1994, pp.261.

[29] See, Yaşar Kalafat, "Türkiye Türk Cumhuriyerleri Kültür İlişkileri", İdris Bal, *21. Yüzyılda Türk Dış Politikası*, Ankara: Nobel Yayınları, 2004, pp.474-475.

Relations Board (DEİK), of which more will be said later.

The Turkish Model[30]

In this early stage of optimism and high expectations, there were often allusions to the idea that the newly independent Turkic states could pursue the Turkish model of development. Many observers noted that Turkey possessed certain characteristics that might appeal to the leaders of the new Turkic societies. These included "a relatively dynamic market economy, secular government, a respect for Islamic traditions, and a democratic system".[31] Similar ideas were expressed by some of the leaders of the Turkic states, such as Islam Kerimov of Uzbekistan[32] and Ebulfez Elchibey of Azerbaijan,[33] and seem to have had an appeal both in the Turkic states and in Western countries with which Turkey had close links.[34]

The interest shown in the Turkish model of development was prompted by a number of considerations. First, the Turkish experience was thought to have relevance in that Turkey had made a transition to a more market-oriented economy from an economy in which the state was the major actor, and the state economic enterprises accounted for most of the industrial production in the economy. Second, the Turkish experience was emphasized as a way of saying that the Turkic states were not interested in Islamic formulas that were being proposed by such countries as Iran and Saudi Arabia. Third, Turkey was thought to have better connections and more access to the Western world, from which economic assistance, investment capital, and new technology were expected to come. Finally, Western countries themselves felt that the Turkish model was a preferable model to follow than those being advocated by others.[35] Turkish political leaders such as President Turgut Özal and, later, President Demirel also emphasized the relevance of the Turkish model for the Turkic states.[36]

The Emergence of Linkage Infrastructure

If one were to characterize the major developments during the period of optimism that began with the independence of Azerbaijan and the Turkish states of Central Asia in late

---

[30] For a detailed discussion of "Turkish model" and its relevance to Turkic Republics see, İdris Bal, *Turkey's Relations with the West and Turkic Republics: The Rise and Fall of Turkish Model*, Aldershot: Ashgate, 2000.

[31] Leonid A Fridman, "Economic Crisis as a Factor of Building up Socio-Political and Ethnonational Tensions in the Countries of Central Asia and Transcaucasia," Vitaly V. Naumkin, (Ed.), *Central Asia and Transcaucasia: Etnicity and Conflict*, London: Greenwood Press, 1994, p.135.

[32] Smolansky, *Turkish and Iranian Policies in Central Asia*, p.299.

[33] Ali Faik Demir, "SSCB'nin Dağılmasından Sonra Türkiye-Azerbaycan İlişkileri", Faruk Sönmezoğlu, (Ed.), *Değişen Dünya ve Türkiye*, İstanbul: Bağlam, 1996, pp.227-228.

[34] Stephen Blank, "Russia, the Gulf and Central Asia in a New Middle East," *Central Asian Survey*, Vol.13, No.2, 1994, pp.273; Oral Sander, "Turkey and the Turkic World", *Central Asian Survey*, Vol.13, No.1, 1994, p.40; Raphael Israeli, "Return to the Source: The Republics of Central Asia and the Middle East," *Central Asian Survey*, Vol.13, No.1, 1994, pp.19, 22.

[35] Alexei Vassiliev, "Turkey and Iranian Trancaucasus and Central Asia", Anoushiravan Ehteshami, (Ed.), *From the Gulf to Central Asia: Players in the Game*, Exeter: the University of Exeter Press, 1994, p.132.

[36] Martha Brill Olcott, *Central Asia's New States: Independence, Foreign Policy and Regional Security*, Washington, D.C.: The United States Institute of Peace Press, 1996, pp.25-26.

1991 and lasted through 1992, one can argue that this is a period of infrastructure development on various fronts. First, Turkey had to develop its own instruments to establish multidimensional linkages with the new states. These included bolstering institutional capabilities and financial resources of government agencies such as TİKA and Exim Bank such that they would have the means to promote economic and cultural relations with the Turkic states as well as creating non-governmental organizations like the bilateral business councils established under the umbrella of DEİK. Second, Turkey helped bring the new states into regional organizations such as the Black Sea Economic Cooperation and ECO. Third, communication links and transportation between Turkey and the new Turkic republics were improved. Fourth, cultural and educational programs, such as the opening of high schools in the new countries and the training of university students that would lead to long-term ties were initiated. Finally, Turkey entered the cognitive maps of the political leaders and the populace of these states as a country that was interested in their fate to which they could turn for cooperation and assistance. Similarly, both the governments and the business communities of the countries of Western Europe as well as the United States became aware of Turkey's special interest in the new republics and its skills in establishing relations with them.

Discovering the Limitations

As optimism was continuing to characterize the relationships between Turkey and the Turkic states of the former Soviet Union, indications that there might be significant constraints in the development of more comprehensive relationships became apparent. Ironically, the initial signal came in the midst of an event that might be viewed as symbolically critical in the development of relations - the Ankara Summit, held in the Turkish capital in October 1992. The multiple intentions of the meeting included enhancing a sense of community, emphasizing the mutual benefit to be derived from operating as a community, and discussing specific projects. The declaration signed at the end of the summit did not entail very specific commitments. It contained loose political statements about strengthening security in the region and supporting peaceful resolution of conflicts and expressed economic aspirations such as cooperation in the field of communications and the realization of joint projects in oil and gas production and processing.[37] The lack of specific commitments owed much to Nursultan Nazarbayev of Kazakhstan, who, in addition to not making commitments, made it clear that such ties as would develop among the Turkic states would be pursued only to the extent they did not undermine his country's relations and commitments to the CIS, by which he clearly meant Russia.[38]

More generally, as relations between Turkey and the Turkic states began to intensify, a process of mutual discovery commenced. Within a year, all parties gradually became aware of the limitations and constraints to which their relationship would be subject.

---

[37] See also, Irina Zviagelskaya, "Central Asia and Transcaucasia: New Geopolitics," Vitaly V. Naumkin, (Ed.), *Central Asia and Transcaucasia: Ethnicity and Conflict*. London: Greenwood Press, 1994, p.138.
[38] Philip Robins, *Between Sentiment and Self Interest: Turkey's Policy Toward Azerbaijan and the Central Asian States*, p.599.

During the initial wave of optimism that a Turkic world might emerge, the importance of such constraints had not been sufficiently appreciated. As these societies began to interact, however, the presence of forces and conditions that impeded the evolution of closer relations began to become clear.

The Russian Presence

After the collapse of the USSR Russia initially gave priority to domestic affairs, and it was assumed that Russia did not want to regain physical control over the former Soviet territories. Although the break up of the Soviet Union had meant a reduction in Russian influence in the affairs of the new republics, it was far from gone. The Russian Federation has continued to view the Turkic republics primarily as its special domain and has worked to maintain a special relationship, using a variety of means.

Table 10: Ethnic Composition of Central Asian Republics and Azerbaijan According to Soviet Census Data-1989 (%)

National Groups/ Republics	Azerbaijan	Kazakhstan	Kyrgyzstan	Uzbekistan	Turkmenistan	Tajikistan
Russians	6	38	22	8	10	8
Uzbeks	-	2	13	71	9	24
Kazaks	-	40	-	4	3	-
Azeris	83	-	-	-	-	-
Tajiks	-	-	-	5	-	62
Kyrgyzs	-	-	52	-	-	1
Turkmens	-	-	-	-	72	-
Tatars	-	2	2	2	-	2
Uighurs	-	1	-	-	-	-
Ukrainians	-	5	3	-	1	-
Germans	-	6	2	-	-	-
Karakalpaks	-	-	-	2	-	-
Lezghians	2	-	-	-	-	-
Armenians	6	-	-	-	-	-
Others	4	6	7	7	6	4

Source: Daria Fane, "Soviet Census data, Union Republic and ASSR, 1989", Ian Bremmer and Ray Taras, (Eds.), *Nation & Politics in the Soviet Successor States*, New York: Cambridge University Press, 1993, pp.550-60.

After 1993, Russia began to clearly display its intention to regain political control over the former Soviet territory under what is known as the 'near abroad' policy, Russia justified her policy on economic, security and ethnic grounds. In the domain of economics, it was argued that these economies were complementary and the Russian economy depended on the other Republics (and vice versa). From a security perspective, Russia wanted to maintain its nuclear monopoly in the former Soviet territory and did not want to see a rival powers settling there. On the ethnic front, around 25 million ethnic Russians living outside Russia encouraged their mother country to have greater influence inl the former Soviet territory in order to guarantee their civil rights (as seen in Table. 10, 38% in Kazakhstan, 22% in Kyrgyzstan, 6% in Azerbaijan, 10% in Turkmenistan, and 8% in Uzbekistan are ethnic Russians according to 1989 figures. However, the number of ethnic Russians has been declining up to present time). In the case of Kazakhstan and Kyrgyzstan, the numbers are sufficiently large that the preferences of the ethnic Russian population for having reasonably close relations with their mother country cannot be ignored. That may be why Nazarbayev even today feels compelled to make sure that his actions are not misconstrued as moving away from Russia. In the case of the others, ethnic Russians are often situated in important jobs. Governments want to make sure that not all Russians leave quickly, vacating jobs that cannot be filled easily by non-Russians, despite some signs that the presence of ethnic Russians may not always be appreciated.[39]

Because the break up of the union is relatively recent, the Russians are quite familiar with the internal politics of the new states. There also continue to exist individuals and groups interested in, or willing to collaborate with the Russians to advance their own standing in domestic politics. In Azerbaijan, for example, the coup that brought the strongly pro-Turkish Ebulfez Elchibey down was realized, allegedly with Russian help from pro-Russian agent Suret Husseinov, who rebelled against the government. Prior to this coup, the Russians had given military aid to Armenia in its eventually successful effort to wrest territory from Azerbaijan, thereby weakening the government that Husseinov brought down.[40]

Economic Dependence on Russia

The fact that the new states are tied economically to Russia is too well known to elaborate here once again. The high degree of complementarity and regional specialization that had been achieved during the Soviet era had resulted in a high level of intra-regional trade. Prior to 1990, the share of intra-regional trade in the overall external trade was never below 80%. Trade among the member states of the CIS has continued to be high. In 1995, for example, the exports of the Turkic states to the CIS was 56% of their total exports. The corresponding figure for imports was 61%. However, dependency of member states to the CIS has been declining continually. For instance, in 2000, the exports of the Turkic states to the CIS was 26% of the total, and imports were 37%.[41] Such trade dependency impedes developing economic relations with others. For example, as has already been mentioned, the few exportable commodities the new countries possess are usually committed for export to the Russian Federation in order to get much needed imports in return. Such economic integration and dependence have impeded the realization of the full potential Turkey has expected from economic relations.

The Turkic states have also had great difficulty in paying for their trade with Turkey

---

[39] See, İdris Bal, *Turkey's Relations with the West and Turkic Republics: The Rise and Fall of the Turkish Model*, Aldershot: Ashgate, 2000, pp.119-126.

[40] Demir, *SSCB'nin Dağıllmasından Sonra Türkiye-Azerbaycan İlişkileri*.

[41] Meryem Kırımlı & Dilek Temiz, Soğuk Savaş Sonrası Türk Cumhuriyetleri'ne Yönelik Türk Dış Politikası", İdris Bal, *21. Yüzyılda Türk Dış Politikası*, Ankara: Nobel Yayınları, 2004, p.458.

either in cash, or, in some instances, when prearranged, in kind. Even in instances when economic opportunities have been perceived, the question of obligations to Russia has stood in the way. One of the authors, through business contacts, knows of an instance in Uzbekistan where plans for a significant investment in textile, yarn, and cottonseed oil production were not seriously entertained after the authorities indicated that they could not insure supplying the minimum amount of cotton needed for economical production after their commitment to Russia was met.

The dependence on Russia is not necessarily a relationship that only the Russians would like to maintain. Having small economies, lacking familiarity with the world of market economies, and not possessing the institutional structures that would enable them to be integrated to the world economic system, the Turkic republics of the former Soviet Union have themselves been reluctant to initiate policies that would put their special relationship with Russia in jeopardy. For example, while all countries have at first tried to reduce the inflow of Russian goods by initiating barriers so that they could reduce the deficit in their balance of payments, Kazakhstan and Kyrgyzstan have joined a customs union with Russia, something in which Uzbekistan had also expressed an interest.[42] Interestingly, Russia has, at times demonstrated less interest in this economic linkage to the extent that it might impose hardships on the Russian economy. A case in point is Russian disinterest in supporting the use of the ruble as domestic currency in these countries and its reluctance in including the interested countries in the ruble zone.[43]

The economic dependence on Russia, which the leaders would like to maintain, constrains the current leaders in making moves that would threaten their economic relationship with Russia. Such an orientation may change in the long run as the political and economic cadres of the Turkic states become more confident in operating in a market environment and as institutions of a market economy are better developed. Furthermore, the gradually transforming economies may, in time, generate more hard currency income. Of particular importance in this regard are oil and gas exports, which are expected, in the long run, to generate substantial hard currency income for Kazakhstan, Azerbaijan, and Turkmenistan.

Conflicts of Interest among the Turkic States

There had been, initially, a tendency on the part of Turkey to view other Turkic states as constituting a reasonably homogeneous whole, not harboring significant conflicts of interest among themselves. This exaggerated perception of unity derived, on one hand, from earlier lack of familiarity with the region and on the other, from projecting hopes and aspirations. Turkey soon enough discovered, however, that it was dealing with five different states each of which had its own political leaders and its own national interests to pursue. By way of example, while it is true that cultures and languages of the Turkic peoples are related, it is equally true that there are enough differences among them that a

---

[42] Paul Kubicek, "Regional Cooperation in Central Asia: Economic Imperatives, Local Nationalism, and the Shadow of Russia," Paper presented to the Joint JAIR/ISA Conference in Makuhari, Japan, September 20-22, 1996.
[43] Ibid.

Turk and an Azeri cannot understand a Kyrgyz or a Kazakh. More broadly, as a skeptical observer has put it,

> *while Turkey and the rest of the Central Asian countries ... may feel euphoric about being Turkic, there is virtually no guarantee that it alone could become a basis for cooperation.*[44]

In addition, since the new countries have existed as units for quite some time now, each has developed its own distinct sense of identity, its own political institutions and its own political cadres and leaders, a fact that only reinforces whatever ethnic and cultural differences may exist.

The ethnic compositions of the new republics are different, such that, for example, the presence of Uzbeks in Kyrgyzstan (which has generated inter-ethnic conflict in the past) is seen as a security problem by the latter. Some observers have also noted that Uzbekistan, which has the largest population, feels itself to be the natural leader of the Central Asian republics, a role that the others have not been willing to acknowledge. Or, while Turkey tends to think that they all belong in the same group, the Central Asian states do not feel Azerbaijan belongs to the same world as they.

Furthermore, each of the Turkic republics has different security concerns and, therefore, have different ideas about how it should conduct its relations with the Russian Federation. Azerbaijan, for example, has tried to keep the Russian military out for fear that it will act more as a domestic force than one that would remain within the confines of an alliance relationship. Turkmenistan has also resisted reestablishing close relations with Russia for fear that it would easily fall under Russian domination once again. Kazakhstan, on the other hand, has maintained a much more cooperative attitude toward Russia, if for no other reason than the fact that, as has already been noted, it has a sizable Russian population, and the Kazakh nature of some of its territory has already been questioned by Russian nationalists.

All countries, with the possible exception of Kyrgyzstan, are run by authoritarian regimes. Each leader has devised different formulae for legitimating his power, but nationalism has been a common theme in all. Nationalism in this case means local nationalism. Nationalism of a transnational kind is viewed negatively by all leaders as a force that might undermine their own authority. Similarly, just as the political leaderships of these countries are trying to build their new states, references to collectivities that transcend the nation-state are seen as detrimental to the state- building effort. Although Central Asian leaders have come together to discuss possibilities of economic cooperation, the creation of a common economic space, and so on,[45] the discussion of political union has been absent. Under the circumstances, the talk of a greater union by one leader may be perceived as an attempt to dominate them by the others.

In short, the differences among the Turkic republics have been a constraint in

[44] M. E. Ahrari, "The Dynamics of the New Great Game in Muslim Central Asia," *Central Asian Survey* Vol.13, No.4, 1994, p.536.
[45] Paul Kubicek, "Regional Cooperation in Central Asia: Economic Imperatives, Local Nationalism, and the Shadow of Russia", Paper presented to *the Joint JAIR/ISA Conference* in Makuhari, Japan, September 20-22, 1996.

Turkey's interaction with them. Turkey has had to devise specific policies for each of the countries and has had to be careful that what it does with one country does not generate reaction in others. But more important, Turkey has become aware that the Turkic world for which it had hoped to lay the foundations during the initial period of optimism that swept the country would not, in the short run, be easy or practicable.

Conflicts of Interest between Turkey and the Turkic States

Although Turkey has given, and continues to give, high priority to the Turkic Republics in its foreign policy, there are other important linkages that it has had to take into consideration in its relations with the latter. Similarly, as the discussion of the Russian influence in the region and the economic dependence of the Turkic republics on the Russian Federation has already demonstrated, each state may have policy preferences that deviate from those of Turkey.

Ankara has an important economic relationship with the Russian Federation that it aims to retain and develop. Turkish construction companies have had, and continue to have, major contracts in various parts of Russia. Tourism trade is large, with Russians coming to Turkey for vacations and shopping. There is extensive "suitcase trade," that is tourists taking goods back with them from Turkey to Russia to sell, which have in some years totalled $7-8 billion, according to the higher estimates. In developing and implementing its policies in the Caucasus and Central Asia, Turkey is always compelled to make sure that these do not generate significant losses in its relations with Russia. Turkey's import from Russia in 2003 was 5.420,4 million dollars which is 7,9% of Turkey's total imports. Turkey's exports to Russia in the same year was 1.363,3 million dollars or 2,9% of its total exports. On the other hand, Turkey's imports from the Turkic Republics in 2003 was 619,5 million dollars or 0,9% of its total imports. In the same year, Turkey's exports to Turkic Republics was 799,7 million dollars or 1,7% of its total exports. Turkey's trade with Russia is as much as five times (4.78 times) its trade with the Central Asian republics.[46] In practice this means that Turkey's policies can aim at political and economic cooperation and not security cooperation with the latter. As Olcott notes, for Turkey's leaders "to challenge Russia's special security relationship with all the CIS states is to risk sharp deterioration in their own relations with Russia".[47]

Currently, there is only limited security cooperation, mainly in the form of Turkey's training some military officers, and there appears to be no immediate interest, particularly on the part of the Central Asian states, to have common security activity with Turkey. The Russians have, nevertheless, found Turkey's interest in the Turkic republics to be a reason for concern and want to make sure that this does not conceal any pan-Turkist aims. Frequently, Ankara has had to give assurances that it has no such aims.

There are some specific areas where Turkey's interests and its policies contain elements of conflict in its relations with both Russia and some of the Turkic republics.

---

[46] *Main Economic Indicators, Turkey*, T.R. Prime Ministry State Planning Organization, February 2004, pp.60, 69.
[47] Martha Brill Olcott, *Central Asia's New States: Independence, Foreign Policy and Regional Security*, Washington, D.C.: The United States Institute of Peace Press, 1996, p.171.

One such area is Turkey's support for Azerbaijan in its conflict with Armenia. The Russians have generally been more supportive of the Armenians and have tried to use the Armenian occupation of Azeri territory as leverage against the Azeris, who have resisted Russian offers of sending Russian troops back into their country. The plight of the Azeris does not seem to generate the compassion and support in the other Turkic republics that it does in Turkey, for a variety of reasons. Actually, the opposite may describe the situation a little better. Turkey's active involvement in the support of Azerbaijan against the Armenians may invite a Russo-Turkish confrontation,[48] in which the Central Asian countries would not like to be involved. While we do not need to belabor the reasons behind these differences of approach and policy, it is important to note that the unity that Turkey had hoped would exist in a community of Turkic states is simply not there.

Another specific area where differences of preference and approach are manifest is in getting the natural gas and oil of Azerbaijan, Kazakhstan and Turkmenistan to the world markets. As regards oil, from the very beginning, Turkey has argued that the best way to transport the fuel to the world market is through a system of pipelines that will go through Turkey, to the Mediterranean port of Ceyhan (Yumurtalık). While a line through Azerbaijan and Armenia seems to be more direct, because of the ongoing Azeri-Armenian conflict, proposals for a slightly longer route going through Georgia have been developed. When it became apparent that the construction of such a long pipeline would have to await substantial increases in production, Turkey encouraged a pipeline that would reach the Georgian Black Sea port of Supsa, a counteroffer to the Russian proposals of shipping the so-called early production from Azerbaijan to Novorossisk. The international consortium that is producing the oil has proposed dividing the shipment between the Northern (Novorossisk) and the Southern (Supsa) lines. Because some shipment capacity already existed on lines remaining from the Soviet Union, the opening of the Northern route had received priority.

Turkey has tried to get the Turkic republics to make a commitment to support the construction of a pipeline that would carry Central Asian and Azeri oil to the Mediterranean. Support, however, has been low-key and usually not specific, despite the fact that such a development would generate high income for the producer countries as well as for those through which the lines will transit, rendering them less dependent on Russia. Just as the Turkish anxiety to have a pipeline go through Turkey as quickly as possible is understandable, so is the hesitation of the Turkic republics to make a clear and irrevocable commitment, due to fear of Russian reprisals. The Russian presence and influence, as well as the economic dependence of these states on Russia, constitutes sufficient explanation of the latter's hesitation. Suffice it to point out that the Azeri President Haidar Aliev, who had tried to accommodate Russia, has experienced no less than two, very likely Moscow- fomented coup attempts to oust him from power (as well

---

[48] Bruce Vaughn, "Shifting Geopolitical Realities Between South, Southwest and Central Asia", *Central Asian Survey*, Vol.13, No.2, 1994, p.310. Demirel argued that if Turkey supported Azerbaijan actively and took part in the war, other states would support Armenia and eventually a Muslim-Christian war would take place: see, İdris Bal & Cengiz Başak, "Rise and Fall of the Elchibey's Administration and Turkey's Central Asian Policy", *Foreign Policy*, Vol.22, No.3-4/1998, pp.42-56.

as attempts on his life) because he had not totally given in to Russian demands and had tried to pursue a somewhat independent line.[49] Eventually, with the backing of USA, Baku –Ceyhan Pipeline Project is now being realized. Construction of the project which began in September 2002 has progressed on schedule and is expectd to be completed by late 2005.

However, Baku-Ceyhan could still face problems. The pipeline construction costs could exceed the projected $2.8 billion to $2.9 billion costs. In addition, Russia could lower tariffs to undercut Baku-Ceyhan's competitiveness. Either move could endanger Baku-Ceyhan's commercial viability and reduce the willingness of investors to support the project...[50]

Finally, there may be a difference of perspective between Turkey and the Turkic states on the nature of their relationship. While Turkey has tried to view itself as a magnet for the newly independent countries, a leader that would help them get integrated into the world economic system, offer guidance in their transformation to market economies, and serve as an intermediary between them and Western countries, the Turkic republics have been reluctant to accept exclusive Turkish leadership. Although, this reluctance can be explained, in part, by what we have already talked about (Russian influence and economic dependence on Russia) and, in part, by what is to follow (a recognition of the limitations of Turkey in playing the role that it has shown an interest in playing), a third factor has also to be recognized: The newly independent republics have just left a heavy-handed union and are still trying to loosen the entanglements remaining from that association. They are probably not interested in acquiring a new big brother but "aim at greater diversification of their foreign relations".[51]

Mutual Awareness of Each Other's Limitations

It appears, in retrospect, that, initially Turkey overestimated its ability to extend assistance and support to the new republics and also misjudged the ability of the republics to bring about the necessary changes in their administration and politics so as to become integrated to the world system. Similarly, the new republics made judgments both about themselves and about Turkey that turned out to be not wholly accurate.

It may be best to explicate the problem by some examples. When the Turkic states first became independent, Turkey promised economic aid, both as grants and credits, to finance Turkish exports and investments. While these were all realized, and Turkey devoted substantial financial resources to that end, the sums involved did not reach nearly the levels initially promised. One observer, for example, argues that the Turkish financial

---

[49] Ariel Cohen, "The New 'Great Game': Oil Politics in the Caucasus and Central Asia", *The Heritage Foundation Backgrounder,* No. 1065. Washington, D.C.: The Heritage Foundation, 1996, p.5.

[50] F. Stephen Larrabee & Ian Lesser, *Turkish Foreign Policy in an Age of Uncertainty,* Santa Monica: Rand, 2003, 109.

[51] Irina Zviagelskaya, "Central Asia and Transcaucasia: New Geopolitics", Vitaly V. Naumkin, (Ed.), *Central Asia and Transcaucasia: Ethnicity and Conflict,* London: Greenwood Press, 1994, p.140; Martha Brill Olcott, *Central Asia's New States: Independence, Foreign Policy and Regional Security,* Washington, D.C.: The United States Institute of Peace Press, 1996, p.27; Bal, *Turkey's Relations with the West and Turkic Republics,* pp.185-186 for a similar observation).

promises in 1992 corresponded to 80% of the country's hard-currency reserves, a sum so high that it was necessary to renege on the promises.[52] In the instance of the export credits to be made available by Turkish Exim Bank, to cite one example, the credits made available did not reach the amounts promised. Part of the problem derived from the fact that many a Turkish governmental leader, in the excitement of visiting one or more of the Turkic republics for the first time, would make promises on the spot, that had to be forgotten later, since the means to implement the promise did not exist.

The Turkish businessmen who were expected to lead the investment effort in the newly independent countries soon discovered that they were less easily accessible and that it was harder to do business in them, than initially anticipated.[53] These polities, in contrast to the impression held by Turks that they had well-developed administrative systems, appeared less capable of delivering on their promises than was judged at first. From the perspective of the Turkic republics, Turkish investments were sufficient neither in their speed nor in their magnitude. A Kazakh academic research report, for example, judged that the relations between Turkey and Kazakhstan "remained limited because Ankara proved reluctant to invest money in the Kazakh economy."[54]

After the reciprocal visits it became obvious to the leadership of the Turkic Republics that Turkey had limitations economically and politically. After more frequent contacts with the outside world, the leaders of the Turkic republics have come to feel that "the Turkish model lagged behind that of other economies." The Turkic Republics were no longer inclined to view the Turkish standard of living as a long-term final goal.[55] On the other hand, although the Turkic Republics initially regarded the Turkish Model as a social and economic miracle, when they visited Turkey they found a country beset with inflation, unemployment and almost as many other problems as their own Republics. Therefore, in some respects they realized that they were not worse off than Turkey. In Akiner's words:

> *The Central Asians now realise there isn't as much money in Turkey as they had expected. Academics come back from Turkey and say there are few scientists of comparable quality to those at home. They see Istanbul and Ankara and then they see the Turkish villages and say 'we're not much worse off.*[56]

Same sentiments were expressed by Anvarbak Mokeev, Under-secretary at the Embassy of Kyrgyzstan in Ankara, who explained that they had realized that Turkey had its own problems and therefore they would avoid unrealistic expectations from Turkey. While accusing the Soviet system of colonialism, at the same time he emphasized high education level and development of infrastructure as positive aspects of Soviet rule. He also stressed that students who came from the Turkic Republics to Turkey for education should study

---

[52] Paul A. Goble, "The 50 Million Muslim Misunderstanding: The West and Central Asia Today," Anoushiravan Ehteshami, (Ed.), *From the Gulf to Central Asia: Players in the Game.* Exeter: University of Exeter Press, 1994, p.3.
[53] Martha Brill Olcott, *Central Asia's New States: Independence, Foreign Policy and Regional Security.* Washington, D.C.: The United States Institute of Peace Press, 1996, p.26.
[54] As quoted in Smolansky, *Turkish and Iranian Policies in Central Asia,* p.295.
[55] Olcott, *Central Asia's New States: Independence, Foreign Policy and Regional Security,* p.27
[56] *Independent,* 3 April 1992; See also, S. Akiner, *Central Asia: New Arc of Crisis?,* Royal United Services Institute for Defence Studies, London, 1993, p.57.

in fields which were not good in their native countries. He claimed that medical schools were better in Kyrgyzstan than in Turkey, and therefore Kyrgyz students in Turkey should not attend medical faculties, but rather faculties of business administration, international relations, economics, banking and hotel management.[57] Furthermore, it has also appeared to them that Turkey's access to the European decision-making centers is not as facile as they had initially come to believe.

While more examples may be offered, the point is already clear. Both parties became aware that they did not have the resources to raise the relations to the levels that might have been desired at the early stage, characterized by optimism. Policy adjustments had to be made.

Routinization: Prevalence of Economic Relations

The area of interaction between Turkey and the Turkic republics in which there is currently more intense activity than others is the field of economics. We therefore now turn to an examination of the economic links. We may begin our analysis by noting that the Turkish government has been one of the driving forces in the development of economic relations between the newly independent Turkic countries and Turkey. Implementation of policies along targets set by the government have helped Turkish private sector become familiar with the new markets and move into them. With government encouragement private organizations such as the Istanbul Chamber of Commerce (ITO) and the Foreign Economic Relations Board (DEİK) have worked to facilitate and promote the further development and the deepening of economic relations.

The Evolution of Institutional Structures

Shortly after the Turkic republics declared their independence in 1991 and were immediately extended diplomatic recognition by Turkey, Turkey proceeded, on the one hand, to establish a formal basis for economic cooperation, and, on the other hand, to build private institutional bases for enhanced non-governmental linkages. The formal bases on which economic relations would be grounded were Economic and Commercial Cooperation Agreements, which were signed with Azerbaijan (1992), Kazakhstan (1991), Kyrgyzstan (1991), Turkmenistan (1995), and Uzbekistan (1995). A similar agreement had also been signed with the Russian Federation in 1992. These agreements call for annual meetings of Joint Economics and Trade Committees in order to evaluate past performance, identify problems, and make future plans to expand relations. Those who participate in the meetings include high-ranking bureaucrats usually representing the respective treasuries, the ministries responsible for economic affairs, and the foreign ministries. Following a practice that was initiated in the late 1980s by joint committees established with other countries, private businesses or organizations representing them have also been allowed to sit in on these meetings and present their point of view. In this way, an opportunity is provided for bureaucrats of each country to get to know their counterparts and representatives of private business from the other side. In addition, interested business

---

[57] Cited from Bal, *Turkey's Relations With the West and Turkic Republics*, pp.182-183; Idris Bal's personal interview with Anvarbek Mokeev, Under-secretary at the Kirgiz Embassy in Ankara, Ankara, 28 December 1994.

representatives use these occasions to develop links with other countries. The meetings are usually held toward the end of the year and try to put together an indicative list of items that can be exported and imported during the next year. Questions regarding how to organize, sponsor, or participate in regional and or international fairs and other similar matters are also discussed. Often documents and information are also exchanged. The results of these meeting are usually published in the *Turkish Official Gazette*

The Turkish Cooperation and Development Agency (TİKA), which has been described earlier, although not oriented exclusively toward the Turkic republics and with activities not confined exclusively to economic matters, nevertheless needs to be mentioned here once again, since much of its activities and resources are expended for enhancing economic cooperation between Turkey and the Turkic republics. Similarly, the Turkish Exim Bank, again not exclusively oriented toward the new republics, has been one of the major public economic agencies that have been active in helping expand economic relations with the latter.

The private institutional basis for cooperation has usually been the bilateral business councils. These had been initiated after 1986 with a number of countries to promote economic relations. The Turkish side of these bilateral councils operates under the aegis of the Foreign Economic Relations Board (DEİK), an active, nonprofit organization responsible for improving economic relations between member countries by bringing together trade and investment partners. DEİK was founded in 1986 by nine private organizations, among them, the Turkish Union of Chambers of Commerce, Industry, Commodity Exchanges and Maritime Chambers of Commerce, the Union of Turkish Chambers of Agriculture, the Turkish Industrialists and Businessmen's Association, and the Foreign Investors Associations. It provides information for interested parties and helps organize bilateral business councils. The founding members of the councils on the Turkish side are generally companies that already have economic relations with the country with which a business council is to be established. Others join if they are interested in developing economic relations with a specific country. The counterpart organizations in the newly independent Turkic republics are usually either state trading organizations or ministries of foreign economic relations. These institutions usually have close contacts with both the private and public sectors in their respective countries.

A Turkish-Soviet Business Council was established as early as 1986. It started with thirty-five member companies, but membership had grown to 180 by 1991. This was a time when Turkish-Soviet trade was expanding rapidly. With the assistance of this business council, Turkish businessmen had an opportunity to get acquainted with how the economy operated in Russia, Ukraine, Georgia, and Azerbaijan. The representatives of the Turkish-Soviet Business Council also participated in the annual meetings of the intergovernmental Turkish-Russian Joint Economic Committee and contributed to the planning of trade and the devising of investment projects. They often traveled along with official delegations on state visits and attended official conferences. With the dissolution of the Soviet Union, the council was renamed the Turkish-CIS Business Council to reflect the new political reality.

Shortly after Azerbaijan declared its independence and before the Turkish government recognized it in November 1991, a Turkish-Azerbaijan Business Council was quickly established. Others followed suit in due time. Turkmen, Kazakh, and Kyrgyz councils were established in 1992, and the Uzbek in 1993.

Good Intentions, Difficult Relations

While the independence of the Turkic republics appeared to present economic opportunities for Turkey, Turkish businessmen got further confirmation of what they had learned during their experience with the Soviet Union. The transition from a planned, socialist economy to a more decentralized capitalist economy was proving problematical, rendering foreign entry to these markets difficult. These countries had been spared from the great politico-economic transformation waves that had swept Eastern Europe and some parts of the Soviet Union and had therefore been able to avoid the turmoil experienced by countries that had broken away abruptly from state guidance and control. But they continued to experience extreme economic difficulties in adjusting to the new economic realities. The rate of inflation in all countries tends to be high. Their economies, for the most part, are in a decline. The contribution of foreign direct investments to their economies is negligible. Public ownership of enterprises is still widespread, allowing for old work habits and practices to survive. Competitiveness of enterprises is feeble. The role of the state in the economy continues to be critical, and it has been sluggish in bringing about the required changes for transition to a market economy.

Table 11: Turkish Exim Bank Credits 1992-2000 (Million $)

Country	Allocated	Used	Paid Back	Deferred
Azerbaijan	250	92	21	75
Kazakhstan	240	213	131	152
Kyrgyzstan	75	48	23	43
Uzbekistan	375	347	324	0
Turkmenistan	163	133	83	48
Total	1.103	833	582	318

Source: Cited from Meryem Kırımlı & Dilek Temiz, "Soğuk Savaş Sonrası Türk Cumhuriyetleri'ne Yönelik Türk Dış Politikası", İdris Bal, (Ed.), *21. Yüzyılda Türk Dış Politikası*. Ankara: Nobel Yayınları, 2004, p.452; DTM (Office of the Undersecretariat for Foreign Trade) Statistics and DTM Representative Reports.

Not unfamiliar with these hazards, Turkish businesses have tried to reduce their risks by obtaining support or coverage from the Turkish government. An example is credits from the Turkish Exim Bank to finance projects and trade. As of the end of 1995, a total of $936 million had been allocated by the Turkish Exim Bank, but only 55 % of this total, or $514.8 million, had been disbursed. Of this sum, $322.1 million, or 62.5 % has gone to finance the purchase of goods, while $192.7 million, or 37.5 % has been used to finance various projects. The credit offered by Turkish Exim Bank increased to $1.103 million at the end of 2002. However, only 75,5% of this total, or $833 million, had been disbursed. As see in Table. 11, important sums had been made available to Uzbekistan ($347 million), Kazakhstan ($213 million), Turkmenistan ($133 million), Azerbaijan ($92 million) and Kyrgyzstan ($48 million). The bank has been criticized for the slowness in its disbursements. In response, bank officials have argued that delays have stemmed from lack of modern commercial practice and modern accounting techniques in these countries. One could also add to this the fact that while the government is generous with allocations, it does not make the funds available to the bank on time for prompt disbursement.

Neither of the parties is punctual and effective in dealing with the problems that arise in the economic relationship. Decision-making processes in both Turkey and in the Turkic republics operate slowly. Although agreements have been reached to remove double taxation to offer some guarantees as well as other incentives for investments, neither Turkey nor those countries with which agreements have been signed have been able to complete all procedures necessary to put these measures into force.

Trade Relations

Turkey's trade with the Turkic states is seen to have long-term potential, but currently it is limited. One of the reasons for the modest amount of trade has already been indicated. The high interdependency of trade between countries of the former Soviet Union leaves little room for other countries to enter the market. But a second reason is equally important. The volume of external trade of the new Turkic states is very modest indeed. This area of the world with its 60 million people (including Tajikistan) generated in 1995 around $11 billion worth of exports of which only $6 billion went to non-CIS countries. During the same period, they imported more than $9 billion worth of goods, of which only $3.5 billion came from the non-CIS countries. The non-CIS trade is led by the European Union (Germany, Italy, France, and U.K, in that order).

Table 12: Turkey's Exports to Turkic Republics (Million $)

Cn	1992	1993	1994	1995	1996	1997	1998	1999	2000	2001	2002
A	102,8	67,8	132,4	161,3	239,5	319,6	326,1	248	230	225	226
K	19,3	67,8	131,7	150,8	164	210,7	213	96,2	119	120	158
T	7,3	84	84,3	56,1	65,6	117,1	95,7	106,6	120	105	109
U	54,5	213,3	65	138,4	229,8	210,7	155,6	99,1	83	90	93
Ky	1,9	17,1	16,8	38,1	47	49,9	41,6	22,9	20	17	23
Tl	186	450	430	545	746	908	832	573	572	557	609

Cn:Cuntry, A:Azerbaijan, K:Kazakstan, T:Turkmenistan, U:Uzbekistan, Ky:Kyrgyzstan, Tl:Total

Source: Cited from Meryem Kırımlı & Dilek Temiz, Soğuk Savaş Sonrası Türk Cumhuriyetleri'ne Yönelik Türk Dış Politikası", İdris Bal, *21. Yüzyılda Türk Dış Politikası*, Ankara: Nobel Yayınları, 2004, p.452.

Turning to Turkey's trade with the Turkic republics (Azerbaijan, Kazakhstan, Kyrgyzstan, Turkmenistan and Uzbekistan), Turkey's exports to these countries totaled $186 million in 1992. It jumped to $450 million in 1993, $430 million in 1994, $551.2 million in 1995, $746 million in 1996, $908 million in 1997, 832 million in 1998. In following years Turkish export declined sharply; $573,6 million in 1999, $572,7 million in 2000, $557,4 million in 2001 and $619 million in 2002. In the year 2003, it increased to $799,7 million. In terms of percentages within Turkey's exports, 1% in 1992, 2.4% in 1994 and 2.5% in 1995. It had risen to 3.4% in 1998 and declined to 2.2% in 1999, 2,1% in 2000, 1,8 in 2001, 1,7% in 2002 and again 1,7% in 2003 (for the distribution of

Turkey's export to Turkic Republics see Table. 12).[58] Turkey's imports, on the other hand, were only $89 million in 1992, or less than 0.5% of Turkey's total. They rose to $190 million in 1993, $190 million in 1994, and went up again to $287 million in 1995. Turkey's import had risen to $628 million in 2000 but declined to $282,5 million in 2001 and then rose to 467,8 million in 2002. In 2003, it reached $619,5 million. So in a matter of four years, from 1992 to 1995, the share of the Turkic republics in Turkey's imports had risen from 0.4% to 0.8% in 1995 and then to 1.1% in 1999 and 1.2% in 2000. In the year 2001, it declined to 0,7%, then in the years 2002 and 2003 it was 0,9% (for the distribution of Turkey's import from Turkic Republics see, Table. 13).[59]

Table 13: Turkey's Imports from Turkic Republics (Million $)

Cn	1992	1993	1994	1995	1996	1997	1998	1999	2000	2001	2002
A	35	34	8,9	21,8	39	58,2	50,3	43,9	95,4	78	63
K	10,5	43,7	32,3	86,7	99,9	165,1	253,7	295,7	346.6	91	202
T	21,1	77	65,7	111,6	99,6	73,4	42,2	67,2	97,9	72	99
U	21	31,9	78,9	61,4	57,7	94,6	96,1	47,5	86	36	75
Ky	1,4	3,4	4,4	5,5	5,7	7,6	6,7	2,7	2,5	6	15
Tl	89	190	190	287	302	399	449	457	628	283	454

Cn:Cuntry, A:Azerbaijan, K:Kazakstan, T:Turkmenistan, U:Uzbekistan, Ky:Kyrgyzstan, Tl:Total

Source: Cited from Meryem Kırımlı & Dilek Temiz, "Soğuk Savaş Sonrası Türk Cumhuriyetleri'ne Yönelik Türk Dış Politikası". İdris Bal, *21. Yüzyılda Türk Dış Politikası*, Ankara: Nobel Yayınları, 2004, p.454; Devlet İstatistik Enstitüsü, DTM İstatistikleri, DTM Dış Temsilcilik Raporları.

The modest level of Turkey's trade with the Turkic republics becomes clearer when it is compared with its trade with the Russian Federation. The Turkish trade with Russia expanded initially during the mid-1980s as Turkey began to import substantial amounts of natural gas from the Soviet Union. After the dissolution of the Soviet Union and the collapse of the socialist system, trade expanded such that by 1995, exports totaled $1.3 billion while imports reached $2.1 billion, accounting for 5.7% of exports and 5.8% of imports, respectively.[60] In the year 2003, Turkey's exports to Russia totaled $1.36 billion while imports reached $5.42 billion, accounting for 2.9% of exports and 7.9% of imports, respectively. If only Turkey's trade with the CIS is taken as the criterion, then Russia takes 51.7% of Turkey's exports and provides 70.3% of its imports.[61] There exists between all countries of the former Soviet Union and Turkey, the so-called suitcase trade, which is not reflected in government statistics, suggesting that the trade between these countries and Turkey may be more substantial than what statistics would indicate. But observers all feel that the bulk of this trade, which is estimated to be somewhere between

---

[58] *Main Economic Indicators, Turkey*, T.R. Prime Ministry State Planning Organization, February 2004, p.69.
[59] Ibid., p.60.
[60] Undersecretariat of Foreign Trade, 1997.
[61] *Main Economic Indicators, Turkey*, T.R. Prime Ministry State Planning Organization, February 2004, pp.60, 69.

$5-8 billion annually, is with the Russian Federation.

Table 14: The Place of Turkey within the Total Imports of Turkic Republics between 1992-2002 (Million $)

Country	1992	1993	1994	1995	1996	1997	1998	1999	2000	2001	2002
Azerbaijan											
Total Imports		636	778	668	961	794	1077	1036	1172	1486	1800
Imports from Turkey	102,8	67,8	132,4	161,3	240	319,6	326,1	248	230	225	226
Ratio (%)	10,3	10,7	17	24,1	25	40,3	30,3	24	20	15	13
Kazakhstan											
Total imports	469	3887	3561	5387	6618	7176	6672	5645	5052	6363	9600
Imports from Turkey	19,3	67,8	131,7	150,8	164	210,7	213	96,2	119	120	158
Ratio (%)	4,1	1,7	3,7	2,8	2,5	2,9	3,2	1,7	2,4	1,9	1,6
Turkmenistan											
Total imports	30	501	894	1644	1388	1005	1137	1382	1382	1816	2250
Imports from Turkey	7,3	84	84,3	56,1	65,6	117,1	95,7	106,6	120	105	109
Ratio (%)	24,3	16,8	9,4	3,4	4,8	11,7	8,4	7,7	8,7	5,8	4,8
Uzbekistan											
Total imports	929	958	2479	3238	4240	3767	2717	1855	2600	2550	2500
Imports from Turkey	54,5	213,3	65	138,4	230	210,7	155,6	99,1	83	90	93
Ratio (%)	5,9	22,3	2,6	4,3	5,4	5,6	5,7	5,3	3,2	3,5	3,7
Kyrgyzstan											
Total Imports	418	430	316	531	783	646	756	547	554	468	587
Imports from Turkey	1,9	17,1	16,8	38,1	47	49,9	41,6	22,9	20	17	23
Ratio (%)	0,5	4	5,3	7,2	6	7,7	5,5	4,2	3,6	3,6	3,9

Source: cited from meryem kirimli & Dilek Temiz. "Soğuk Savaş Sonrasi Türk Cumhuriyetleri'ne Yönelik Türk Diş Politikasi", İdris Bal, 21. Yüzyilda Türk Dış Politikasi. Ankara: Nobel Yayınları. 2004, p.456.

Figures indicate that the significance to Turkey of trade with the Turkic republics continues to be modest. But due to the low volume of their external trade, the Turkic republics do not occupy an important place in the external trade of any non-CIS country. As indicated, they have some trade with the countries of the EU. Both the United States and Japan, on the other hand, have been rather slow in entering these markets. In addition to the two large hegemonic powers, Russia and China, a group of sub-regional powers, including Iran, Pakistan, Korea, India, and Turkey, have taken an interest in trade in the region, with Turkey and Iran being most active. In this context, their imports from Turkey is far from being negligible, accounting for 5.9 % of their total imports in 1995 or 14.5 % of imports from outside the CIS. In the year 2002, 13% of total imports of Azerbaijan is from Turkey. The percentage 1,6% for

Kazakhstan, 4,8% for Turkmenistan, 3,7 for Uzbekistan, and 3,9 for Kyrgyzstan (see Table.14). We may conclude that, in the long run, there is reason to expect that trade relations between Turkey and the Turkic republics will grow in parallel with the growth these economies may register.

Turkish exports to the area currently comprise mainly processed foods, textiles, machinery, and transport equipment. Turkish imports from the area, on the other hand, mainly comprise textiles and metal products. As the energy resources in these countries are developed, and the products begin to reach world markets, Turkey's imports of energy from the region will inevitably increase.

Table 15: The Place of Turkey within the Total Exports of Turkic Republics between 1992-2002 (Million $)

Country	1992	1993	1994	1995	1996	1997	1998	1999	2000	2001	2002
Azerbaijan											
Total Exports	1571	993	638	612	643	808	677	1025	1745	1873	2000
Exports to Turkey	35	34	8,9	21,8	39	58,2	50,3	43,9	95,4	78	63
Ratio (%)	2,2	3,4	1,4	3,6	6,1	7,2	7,4	4,3	5,5	4,2	3,2
Kazakhstan											
Total Exports	1398	3277	3231	5164	6292	6899	5870	5986	9139	8647	10300
Exports to Turkey	10,5	43,7	32,3	86,7	99,9	165,1	253,7	295,7	346,6	91	202
Ratio (%)	0,8	1,3	1	1,7	1,6	2,4	4,3	4,9	3,8	1,1	2
Turkmenistan											
Total Exports	908	1049	2010	2084	1692	774	614	1143	1143	2057	2970
Exports to Turkey	21,1	77	65,7	111,6	99,6	73,4	42,2	67,2	97,9	72	99
Ratio (%)	2,3	7,3	3,3	5,4	5,9	9,5	6,9	5,9	8,6	3,5	3,3
Uzbekistan											
Total Exports	869	721	3044	3475	3534	3695	2888	1843	2300	2550	2800
Exports to Turkey	21	31,9	78,9	61,4	57,7	94,6	96,1	47,5	86	36	75
Ratio (%)	2,4	4,4	2,6	1,8	1,6	2,6	3,3	2,6	3,7	1,4	2,7
Kyrgyzstan											
Total Exports	-	340	340	409	531	631	535	463	504	476	488
Exports to Turkey	1,4	3,4	4,4	5,5	5,7	7,6	6,7	2,7	2,5	6	15
Ratio (%)	-	1	1,3	1,3	1,1	1,2	1,3	0,6	0,5	1,3	3,1

Source: Cited From Meryem Kırımlı & Dilek Temiz, "Soğuk Savaş Sonrası Türk Cumhuriyetleri'ne Yönelik Türk Dış Politikası", İdris Bal, *21. Yüzyılda Türk Dış Politikası*, Ankara: Nobel Yayınları, 2004, p.458.

But more generally, future trade patterns will depend not only on how quickly these countries will be able to generate income but also on which trading routes will become available to them. Landlocked as they are, trade patterns will be closely affected by how relations with neighbors translate into access routes to world markets. Links to the East and to the West, by rail or by road, will, in the end, depend more on political, than on economic factors.

Investment and Finance

Entry and penetration into the markets of the new republics seem to have followed an identifiable pattern. In the first stage, trading has been the primary type of economic activity. At that stage, Turkish Exim Bank extended credit to exporters to promote trade. After the exporting firms achieved credibility and recognition, to sustain their trade, branching and the establishment of service networks became necessary. At this second stage, Turkish firms began to feel the need for financing to expand their business. Initially, the Turkish Exim Bank made credits available to serve this end. But later, both public and private Turkish banks have begun to operate in these markets. Sometimes establishing partnerships with local banks, these banks have offered investment loans.

Finally, in the third stage, firms have become interested in investing in sole or joint ventures. Here, firms have faced both economic and political risks. To encourage investments, Turkish Exim Bank has moved to offer guarantees against political risk. It also sought the help of the Multilateral Investment Guarantee Agency of the World Bank to co-insure the bank's investment risk and to help it develop model contracts.[62]

Turkish companies have been active as investors in the Turkic republics. After Russia, Turkey has become the chief investor in the Central Asian republics. As of 1996, Turkish investments in Turkmenistan totaled $1.6 billion, and in Kazakhstan $1.5 billion, to be followed by Uzbekistan with $928.4 million and Kyrgyzstan with $279 million.[63] Since the begening of 1997, Turkey has made more direct investment to Turkic republics. Numbers are as follows; $1.039.523.206 in Azerbaijan, $429.882.690 in Kazakhstan, $57.377.275 in Turkmenistan, $23.960.893 in Kyrgyzstan, $20.202.845 in Uzbekistan.[64] The major initial investments have been in the field of hotels, food, and textiles. But there are literally hundreds of Turkish firms established and operating in the new Turkic republics about which no reliable information is available.

Barring major political downturns, Turkish investments and financial activity in the new republics are likely to continue into the future. It may be anticipated that when the Turkic states begin to receive higher income from oil and gas exports, Turkish firms will assume a more active role in the expanding economies of these states.

Multilateral Relations

Turkey has also tried to enhance its relations with the Turkic republics by working through international organizations and by trying to develop for itself a role as the leading country with which others should cooperate in developing their economic relations with the Turkic republics.

---

[62] Akira Ida, Lecture on MIGA delivered on February 21, 1997 at the Asia-Pacific Research Center of the Faculty of Economics of Istanbul University by Mr. Ida, the executive vice president of MIGA.

[63] Didem Sezerler, "Türkiye Orta Asya'nın Yatırım Şampiyonu", *Yeni Yüzyıl*, 13 February 1997, p.12.

[64] Turkey's Direct Investment By Country, 31.03 2004, Undersecretariat of Foreign Trade, 2004, Private communication.

Reforms for strengthening economic management and programs of stabilization and structural reforms in the Turkic republics are, in most cases, supported by public and, occasionally, private multilateral donors/creditors, such as the Tacis Committee of the European Union, the European Bank of Reconstruction and Development (EBRD) and the United Nations Development Program (UNDP). The International Monetary Fund (IMF) and the World Bank, which the new republics joined within a year of their independence, have helped them formulate economic policy frameworks. Turkey has sought opportunities for cooperation with these agencies in the implementation of their economic programs, including the delivery of technical assistance. For example, in a cooperative effort between the EU, EBRD, the Turkish Treasury and the Banks Association of Turkey, a Regional Bank Training Center has been established in Tashkent in order to train bankers from the Kyrgyz Republic, Tajikistan, and Uzbekistan. There appears to be room for similar projects offering training in the fields of accounting, customs management, tax systems, compiling of economic statistics, computer programming, and the development of cadastral surveys, among others.

Turkey has also tried to impress upon the international business community that Turkey would be a good partner to work with in these markets in trade, services, or investments. To that end, DEİK and others have organized tours to the Turkic republics in which Turkish and foreign businessmen traveled together. The expression coined to describe the role Turkey would like to play between major economic actors and the Turkic republics is "bridge." The impact of this approach is not easy to measure. Turkish construction companies have, for example, been partners in consortia that have won contracts in the new republics, but that kind of cooperation between Turkish and foreign companies has existed for sometime in the Soviet Union and in Russia. There is not enough joint investment yet to infer that these have been inspired by Turkey's self-prescribed role.

Turkish businessmen have certain advantages over their Western counterparts that may expand the role of Turkey as a bridge in the future. To begin with, they have greater familiarity with an environment in which the state has been a major and an interventionist actor in the economy. Second, Turkish workers and professionals are more willing to accept the relative deprivation that foreigners experience when working in these republics. Finally, Turks adapt to local life and customs more easily, in addition to learning the local language more quickly.

Conclusion: Main Features of Contemporary Turkish Policy

Turkey has cultural, historic and ethnic ties with Balkans, Middle East, Caucasus and Central Asia. With the end of Cold War Socialist domination has ended in all regions and new republics emerged in the region. Therefore, a region from Adriatic to China was opened to Turkish influence. In contrast to the initial fears that end of the Cold War reduced the importance of Turkey, it indeed, pushed Turkey to the very centre of the World politics and forced Turkey to take active steps in international politics. Common ties and positive attitudes towards Turkey helped Turkey in her policies. However, Turkey was not able to use all opportunities because of her domestic problems such as economic crises, political instability, terrorism and so on.

After the flurry of excitement about a rapid formation of a politically and economically integrated Turkic world dwindled in the face of harsh political and economic realities, the policy of Turkey toward the Turkic republics has become stabilized. Closer political cooperation and more developed economic relations are maintained as long-range goals. It is recognized that significant transformation has to take place within the Turkic republics on the economic, political, and cultural fronts in order to come close to achieving the long-term goal. But to move in the desired direction, cultural linkages are promoted, and the intensification of linkages with the non-Russian world is supported. Educational exchange programs, training young people in Turkey, and the work toward the spread of Turkish and English as the first international languages are manifestations of this policy.

In the medium term, policies that would reduce the reliance of the economies of the new countries on Russia are promoted. These include the promotion of Turkish investments in the region as well as attempts to bring in other Western capital. The efforts to have as much of the Azeri and Central Asian oil and gas reach the world markets as possible without the intermediation of Russia can also be cited as part of an effort to reduce the ties between these economies and that of Russia.

In the immediate future, the policy is to conduct relations in a variety of fields, but most importantly in the economic domain. Without the continual links that the economic relationships provide, longer-term changes cannot be brought about.

Turkey has become increasingly aware that Russian security concerns should be taken into consideration in the making and implementation of policy. Accordingly, Turkey has emphasized not only that it has no pan-Turkist intentions in the long run but also that it values its relations with Russia. In fact, there also appears to be a subtle shift taking place in policy, though not always reflected in rhetoric. As the recognition that Russia continues to be in a position to thwart Turkey's policies toward the Turkic states becomes more widely shared, the need for cooperating with the Russians in the Caucasus and Central Asia is beginning to appear as a more rational policy. So, in the short and medium terms, we may more often observe cooperative relationships than competitive ones between the two countries. The Turkic republics may also find this suitable since, in this way, they would escape the pressures the Russo-Turkish competition brings them.

15 Turkish Model as a Foreign Policy Instrument in Post Cold War Era: The Cases of Turkic Republics and the Post September 11th Era*

İdris Bal

Introduction

With the establishment of Turkish republic in 1923 on the bases of Western values, Turkey completely turned her face towards the West, and the Western civilization was pointed out as a main goal for Turkey by the new leadership of the Republic. Therefore, Turkey hoped to be adapted into Western society of nations as an equal partner, entered Western institutions and regarded itself as a part of Western World. Turkish cooperation with the West and new reforms conducted by new leadership of Turkish republic is usually called as Turkish model. Since Turkish republic established in 1923, on several occasions Turkish model has been regarded and declared as an ideal model for whole Muslim world to take and adopt in the process of time. Especially, in the post Cold War era, Turkish model was considered as an ideal path for Turkic republics and also on some occasions it was defined as a bridge between Islamic world and Western world. After the 11 September attacks, the need for such bridge became obviously more important.

The aim of this article is first, to outline the position of Turkey during and after the Cold War era and identify what is meant by the term Turkish Model, second, focus on rise of Turkic republics with the end of USSR and analyze Western support for Turkish model, Turkish policies towards those republics and their reactions, third, to make emphasize on Turkey and Turkish model in post September 11 attacks era, and importance of cooperation between US and Turkey against terrorism.

Position of Turkey During and After the Cold War

The Cold War began after the Second World War and dominated world politics until 1980s. The Soviet demands helped Turkey's orientation towards the West, and Turkey became a member of NATO in 1952. This meant the beginning of a new orientation in strategic relations between the West, especially US, and Turkey, which have continued up till now. During the Cold War, world witnessed military, economic, ideological and almost every kind of competition between two blocks: NATO and Warsaw Pact.

---

* Most part of the issues in this article related with Turkish model and Turkic republics were cited from authors book. Therefore, for more detailed analysis of these issues see; İdris Bal, *Turkey's Relations With The West and The Turkic Republics: The Rise and Fall of the Turkish Model*, Aldershot: Ashgate, 2000.

Especially the leaders of these ideological and military blocks attempted to undermine each other in almost every aspect. The Cuban Missile Crisis in 1962 was an important case as two blocks came to the edge of a real nuclear war during the entire Cold War period.

Turkey was an important country in the competition as a defender of South Eastern flank of NATO and a direct neighbor of former USSR. Turkey was regarded as a barrier before Soviet invasion as apart from her strategic position, Turkey was feeding second largest army within the NATO, second to USA.. However, in the 1980s' Eastern Block and its leader USSR said "no" to competition as Socialist economies, especially Soviet economy, became more and more inefficient and therefore incompetent to finance the military competition with the West in particular in Star Wars project from 1983 onwards. Therefore, Eastern European countries were leaving the Soviet Block one by one and in 1991, USSR itself dissolved and fifteen republics that originally formed USSR declared their independence.

One of the obvious implications of the Cold War was that it had frozen maps in the World and there was some sort of stability even under the shadow of weapons. When the Cold War ended, it was believed that a New World Order would be established. Liberalism and human rights would arise and a peaceful world order could be established. In contrast to these optimistic expectations, regional problems emerged immediately after the end of Cold War. The ethnic and religious aspirations have found suitable political and sociological grounds to flourish and be materialized. Therefore, new conflicts and wars have taken place in the world, especially in the Middle East, Balkans and Caucasus. The end of Cold War led to the emergence of new power vacuums in different parts of the World and importance of regional powers increased. Thus, the positive expectations such as New World Order have been replaced by pessimistic worries such as the fear of emergence of New World Disorder.

In the post Cold War era, the US strengthened her position in the world politics and became the only single super power. Therefore, even some circles called US as police of the world order. The US attempted to establish New World Order and promoted liberalism, market economy and human rights. However, there were some challenges ahead. It was too difficult to fill the power vacuums created by the end of USSR, and US was not alone to fill the power vacuums. Regional and global powers were in a competition to take advantage of the new situation. The world history and natural rules suggest that one power cannot be dominant over other powers for a long time. Therefore, those who are disturbed by the present system will like to be rival of US and try to follow opposite policies. In fact, there are developments in this direction. It is possible to observe that EU, China, Japan, Russia and India appear on the international scene economically, politically and militarily. At present, some of these countries have good relations with US and some others, for example China and Russia, have some reactions to US policies and have ambiguous relations with US.[1]

---

[1] For a brief account of relations between US, China and Russia see. Idris Bal. "Rise of Shanghai Cooperation Organization (SCO) in Eurasia: Is It an Effective Toll in a New Gig Game", Ertan Efegil. (Ed.). *Geopolitics of Central Asia in the Post Cold War Era: A Systemic Analysis,* Harlem, the Netherlands: Research Center for Azerbaijan and Turkestan, SOTA, 2002.

In the post Cold War era, parameters changed and US needed new partners and US had to monitor changes in regional and global levels in order to safeguard her position in the world. During the Cold War period, Turkey was important as a bulwark against the Soviet Union for Western security. However, with the end of Soviet Union, the confrontation between East and West also ended and old hostilities motivated by ideological and military competition were replaced by new friendships. This new situation meant that Turkey was no longer an important partner for the West (including the US), as a bulwark against the USSR. However, Turkey's political leadership wanted to convince the Western powers that Turkey still occupied an important strategic position in global politics and was still important to the West. Therefore, Turkey was also anxious to try to find an agenda by means of which it could approach the post Cold War situation.

With the end of Cold War discipline, the world entered a new era and new handicaps as well as new opportunities have been created ever since. Turkey as a neighbor of former USSR, a member of NATO and located in the center of a sensitive region covered by Caucasus, Balkans and Middle East, has been affected by the end of Cold War radically. Turkey has lost some of her bargaining cards in the new era and therefore has needed new arguments.

In the 1990's, Turkish decision-makers started to be more active, searching for possibilities of co-operation in the region. There has been considerable change in Turkish foreign policy style; the traditional Turkish policy of non-interference with the Turks living outside of Turkey changed.[2] Özal, who advocated an active, if not aggressive, Turkish image, initiated this change. For example, during the Gulf War, he actively supported the international coalition against Saddam Hussein, a policy, which dismayed the Foreign Ministry and the chief of staff, who later resigned. Another example was Özal's declaration to a Greek newspaper in May 1991 that

> *the Dodecanese Islands were never Greek, they belonged to the Ottoman Empire. If I had been in İsmet İnönü's place [in 1944] I would have gone in and taken them. Turkey committed a historic error in this case.*[3]

He also proposed the Black Sea Economic Co-operation, advocated active support for Azerbaijan, and even mentioned military intervention against Armenia. Although Özal's active foreign policy understanding and his charismatic leadership was important in this changing style of Turkish foreign policy, there were other crucial factors which forced Turkey to be active and look for possible alternative co-operations. With the end of Cold War, as mentioned above, importance of Turkey for the West declined in terms of East-West confrontation and Turkey was trying to find new arguments to prove that she was still important in global politics and for Europe. Secondly, cool relations between the European Community and Turkey played a role in Turkey's search for alternative areas of co-operation and relations with new partners.[4] Thirdly, lack of support for Turkish

---

[2] Charles Warren Hostler, *The Turks of Central Asia*, London: Praeger, 1993, p.162.
[3] S. Deringil, "Turkish Foreign Policy Since Atatürk", C.H. Dodd (ed.), *Turkish Foreign Policy*, London: The Eothen Press, 1992, p.6.
[4] See, Idris Bal, "European Union, Turkic Republics and Turkish Dilemma", *Pakistan Horizon*, Vol.49, No.1, January 1996, pp.69-88.

position in international circles on crucial issues such as the Cyprus issue, Separatism in South East Anatolia and the water conflict with Syria and Iraq, encouraged Turkey to look for new allies in the international community.[5] Therefore, it is possible to argue that new change in Turkish foreign policy was more a product of impending requirements of post Cold War era rather than Turkish initiative.

During the same period, one of the contemporaneous worries on the part of the Western powers was that they were not sure of what was going to happen in the Caucasus, and Central Asia. Western policy-makers are worried that with the dissolution of the Soviet Union a power vacuum was created in Central Asia, which might be filled by radical Islamic fundamentalism sponsored by Iran, if the West did not take measures to prevent this. As a practical solution to the situation, the West especially US put forward Turkish model as a counter ideology in the region. Western promotion of the Turkish Model[6] provided Turkey with new instruments; it meant a ratification of Turkey's strategic position in the region after the Cold War, enabling Turkey to claim that it was still important for the West and world politics. Thus, Turkey was happy with the Western promotion of the Turkish Model.[7] Turkish decision-makers welcomed the emergence of the Turkic Republics enthusiastically. Whether Islamist or advertly Pan-Turkist, the nationalist backgrounds of the majority of the politicians of the time increased their enthusiasm. Now they could not only promote a Turkic World, but also do it with the approval of the world media and without being accused of pan-Turkism, an accusation, which in the past could lead to persecution even in Turkey. While the Turkish side (in general) tried to find new arguments and formulate a Turkish policy towards the Turkic Republics, Western (especially US) promotion of the Turkish Model gave an opportunity to the Turkish government and everybody in Turkey who wanted to deal with the Turkic Republics. The new situation offered a solution to the problem of finding an overall framework for Turkish foreign policy. Turkish Model therefore became an import toll in Turkish foreign policy in the post Cold War era and served for the interest of Turkey as well as especially for that of the West and US.

Turkish Model

After the disintegration of the former USSR, several politicians, academics and media commentators mentioned the 'Turkish Model' as a feasible model of government and development for the newly established, independent Turkic States. After a meeting with the Turkish Prime Minister Demirel in Washington on 13 February 1992, President Bush pointed to Turkey '...as the model of a democratic, secular state which could be emulated

---

[5] For the detailed analysis of these factors see, Idris Bal, *Turkey's Relations with the West and Turkic Republics: The Rise and Fall of the Turkish Model*, Aldershot: Ashgate, 2000.

[6] It must be noted that on some occasions before the collapse of the USSR, Turkey's successful economic transformation was mentioned by some circles as a model for the Eastern European states, which were struggling to transform their centrally planned economies to open market economies. For example; Özal mentioned the Turkish experience as a model for the rest: see, T. Ataöv, "Turkey's Expanding Relations with the CIS and Eastern Europe", C. H. Dodd, (ed.), *Turkish Foreign Policy*, London: Eothen Press, 1992, p. 89.

[7] *Guardian*, 3 April 1992.

by Central Asia'.[8] Similarly, in June 1992, Mme Catherine Lalumiére, the Secretary General of the Council of Europe, a body dedicated to the defense and propagation of European concepts of humans rights, visited the Central Asian Republics, and declared that '...Turkey provided a valid model for the development of many a newly independent country in Asia'[9] Uzbek President Kerimov also said 'I announce to the whole world that my country will go forward by the Turkish route...'[10] Mohammed Salih, the leader of Uzbek opposition party, the Erk, said 'We are a Turkic people and Turks have never been fanatics. I think religion should not intervene in politics and the only possible model is Turkey'.[11] In fact, initially all the leaders of Turkic republics regarded Turkey as a model for their own development. According to Mango, the usual implications appears to be that

> *the republic of Turkey is a model of a secular, democratic, Muslim country, aiming to achieve Western standards, in partnership with the West, by applying liberal free-market policies.*[12]

On the other hand, Akiner argued that

> *Turkey and Iran are in fact being used as symbols. When the message is decoded, what is actually being asked is the following: do the Central Asians intend to follow the path of Islamic fundamentalism or of secularism; do they intend to move to a market economy; do they intend to adopt a western democratic form of government.*[13]

The term 'Turkish Model' is used to refer to the model of development and government in Turkey whose characteristics are secularism in a Muslim society, a market economy, closeness and cooperation with the West, and a multi-party system. With the emergence of new Muslim republics in Caucasus and Central Asia, when politicians, academics and the media talked about the Turkish model, they in fact underlined these principles, and pointed out to Turkey as the only Muslim state, which featured all these principles in its system. The fact that Turkey which had risen from the ashes of an Islamic Empire had succeeded in achieving some form of democracy and had been able to set up a

---

[8] Ahmad Rashid, *The Resurgence of Central Asia: Islam or Nationalism*, London: Zed Books, 1994, p.210.

[9] Andrew Mango, "The Turkish Model", *Middle Eastern Studies*, Vol.29, No.4, 1993, p.726.

[10] *Independent*, 21 December 1991.

[11] Oral Sander, "Turkey and Turkic World", *Central Asian Survey*, Vol.13, No.1, 1994, p.40.

[12] Andrew Mango, "The Turkish Model", *Middle Eastern Studies*, Vol.29, No.4, 1993, p.726.

[13] Shirin Akiner, *Central Asia: New Arc of Crisis*, London: Royal United Services Institute for Defence Studies, Whitehall Paper Series, 1993, p.56. See also, R. Israeli, "Return to the source: the republics of Central Asia and the Middle East", *Central Asian Survey*, Vol.13, No.1, 1994, p.19; G. Winrow, *Turkey and Former Soviet Central Asia: National and Ethnic Identity*, *Central Asian Survey*, Vol.11, No.3, 1992, p.107; Gülnur Aybet, *Turkey's Foreign Policy and Its Implications for the West: A Turkish Perspective*, London: Royal United Service Institute for Defence Studies, 1994, p.27; Oral Sander, "Turkey and Turkic World", *Central Asian Survey*, Vol.13, No.1, 1994, p.40; O. M. Smolansky, "Turkish and Iranian Policies in Central Asia", H. Malik, (ed.), *Central Asia: Its Strategic Importance and Future Prospects*, Macmillan Press, London, 1994, pp. 292-293, 299, 305; W.C. Hostler, *The Turks of Central Asia*, Praeger, London, 1993, p.161; B.P. Henze, *Turkey: Toward the Twenty-First Century*, Rand Corporation, Santa Monica, 1992, p.35; Y. Söylemez, "Turkey: Western or Moslem", *Turkish Review*, Autumn, 1992, p.55; S. Demirel, "Newly-Emerging Center", *Turkish Review*, Winter 1992, pp.5-6; A. Yalçın, *Türkiye Modeli ve Türk Kökenli Cumhuriyetlerle Eski Sovyet halkları*, Yeni Forum Dergisinin 16-19 Eylül tarihinde düzenlediği sempozyuma sunulan bildirileri, Yeni Forum A.Ş., 1992, Ankara.

market economy, and most importantly had done all this very recently was important. What is more, Turkey was the closest in terms of its culture and language to some of the newly independent states of the former Soviet Union. If one did not scrutinize the ideological and cultural basis of this model of development and its cycle of maturation over the years, and the problems that the model brought to its country of origin, it did indeed look like a quick answer to the problems that the new states faced after the disintegration of the Soviet Union. The Turkish Model could be used as a 'transitional' model for development.

The Turkish Model was initially designed by Atatürk[14] between 1923-1938. The state was established on a secular basis therefore the Sultanate and the Caliphate were abolished and the principle of secularism was inserted into the 1924 constitution, with an amendment made in 1937 accompanied by various social reforms.[15] Significantly, Atatürk turned Turkey's face to the West and this became one of the basic characteristics of the Turkish Model. After the Second World War, Soviet demands pushed Turkey towards the West in real terms. Turkey joined NATO, and Turkish membership of Western institutions such as the Council of Europe, the OECD, and its associate membership of the EC, strengthened Turkey's closeness to the West.

In 1946, the Democrat Party was established, and it came to power after its victory in the 1950 election. This meant the end of the one-party rule, which had existed since the establishment of the Republic. Western states encouraged Turkey towards this change, as well as the dissatisfaction among the masses of the population with the RPP (Republican Peoples Party).[16] This was a success for Turkish democracy, and after this development the multi-party system became one of the important features of the Turkish Model.[17]

In the economic field, after the 24 January 1980 decisions, liberal economic policies were applied to the economy. This marked the end of the import substitution strategy as a means of industrialization. Instead, a free market mechanism was adopted and state intervention in the economy was reduced, and the economy opened to the outside world. With these policies, the Turkish economy was transformed from being closed, agricultural and non-competitive to being market-oriented, liberal and rapidly industrializing. Thus, in the 1990s Turkish experience in economic transformation and the market economy constituted other characteristics of the Turkish Model.

---

[14] For more information about Atatürk see, P. Kinross, *Atatürk The Rebirth of a Nation*, London: Weidenfeld & Nicolson, 1993; H.C. Armstrong, *Grey Wolf*, Harmondsworth: Penguin Books, 1939.

[15] For a more detailed account of the social and legal reforms of Atatürk, see for example; Kinross, *Atatürk The Rebirth of a Nation*, London: Weidenfeld & Nicolson, 1993; P. Robins, *Turkey and the Middle East*, London: Inter Publishers, 1991; A.S. Weekes and R.V. Weekes, "Turks, Anatolian", R.V. Weekes, (ed.), *Muslim Peoples*, Greenwood Press, London, 1978.

[16] Bernard Lewis, "Recent Developments in Turkey", *International Affairs*, Vol.27, No.3, 1951, p.320.

[17] For Opposition to Atatürk during the First Parliament, see for example; Mustafa Erdogan, "Turkiye'de Demokrasiye Gecis Deneyimi (1945-1950)", *Turkiye-Azerbaycan ve Orta Asya Cumhuriyetlerinde Demokrasi ve Piyasa Ekonomisine Gecis Sureci*, Yeni Forum Uluslararasi Ikinci Sempozyumu 16-23 November 1992, Baku Azerbaycan, Yeni Forum AS. Ankara; C. Koçak, "Siyasal Tarih", M. Tuncay, C. Koçak and others, (eds), *Türkiye Tarihi, Çağdaş Türkiye Cilt.4*; M. Erdoğan, "Türkiye'de Demokrasiye Geçiş Deneyimi (1945-1950)", *Türkiye-Azerbaycan ve Orta Asya Cumhuriyetlerinde Demokrasi ve Piyasa Ekonomisine Geçiş Süreci*, Yeni Forum Uluslararası 2. Sempozyumu 16-23 Kasım 1992, Baku, Azerbaycan, Yeni Forum A.Ş., Ankara, 1993.

Although the Turkish Model has achieved all of the above, it has handicaps as well. Although civil rulers have governed Turkey since 1983, Turkish democracy has been interrupted four times by the Turkish military (in 1960, 1971, 1980 and 1997). More importantly, since 1984 Turkey has been involved in an undeclared war in its own territory (in South-East Anatolia) because of Kurdish separatism. Turkish security forces captured leader of PKK, Abdullah Öcalan in 1999. However, this did not mean the end of organization. In 2000s, organization changed its name to KADEK (Kurdish Freedom and Democracy Congress) and strategy and trying to bring its cause to a political ground. This has certainly been the most important problem facing Turkey and the Turkish Model, because it undermined the popular image of the Turkish Model, and it negatively affected the Western attitude as well as that of the Turkic Republics towards Turkey. Unless a solution is found, in the long term, it will continue to cause new problems for domestic as well as foreign policies of Turkey. On the other hand, there are demands for more religious freedom from different parts of society. For instance female students who attend Turkish Universities are not allowed to attend classes unless they take off their headscarves. Although, at present, Alawite dissatisfaction as a religious minority group does not constitute a concrete danger for Turkey and the Turkish Model, it appears to be a potential source for crisis.[18] The Alawites are not satisfied with the Turkish Model and demand changes in it. They want recognition of their identity and state support for the continuation of their culture. Similarly, some religious circles in general demand more freedom in every aspects of life as well. All these problems point out some handicaps of Turkish Model in creating a democratic civil society.

Turkish Model as an Instrument of Foreign Policy in the Post Cold War Era: The Case of Turkic Republics[19]

In the 1990s, Turkey did not expect the rapid collapse of the USSR, and thus was not ready for the new situation. However, when the USSR disintegrated, the Turkish side welcomed its end and the creation of six new Muslim republics. Five of them Azerbaijan, Kazakhstan, Kyrgyzstan, Turkmenistan and Uzbekistan are usually regarded as Turkic republics. However, some circles in Turkey regard all Muslim republics created by the end of USSR as well as Bosnia and Turkic republics because of cultural and ethnic closeness and historical ties.[20] Turkish worm welcome to the developments was strongly affected by the fact that the Anatolian Turks and the population of the Turkic Republics are of the same origins, and there are cultural and linguistic connections. As outlined above, Turkey's position in the post Cold War era affected Turkish reactions as well; mainly, Turkish refusal by the EU, isolation on crucial issues like Cyprus and Kurdish separatism, and attempts to find new arguments proving it was still important to the West

---

[18] See, Idris Bal, "The Turkish Model: the place of the Alawites", *Central Asian Survey*, Vol.16, No.1, January 1997, pp.97-102; Idris Bal, "Türkiye Cumhuriyeti ve Alevi Halkin Talepleri (Turkish Republic and Demands of Alawits)", *Yeni Turkiye*, Vol.4, No.23-24, May-June 1997, pp.2695-2698.

[19] For the detailed account of this subject see, Idris Bal, *Turkey's Relations with the West and the Turkic Republics,* Aldershot: Ashgate, 2000.

[20] See for instance, Sabahattin Zaim, *Turk ve Islam Dunyasinin Yeniden Yapilanmasi*, Istanbul: Yeni Asya Yayinlari, 1993.

and global politics, played vital roles in the enthusiastic Turkish reaction to the end of the USSR and the emancipation of the Turkic Republics. Turkey regarded the Turkic Republics as natural allies who could support the Turkish position on international issues.[21]

Turkish politicians, parties, intellectuals, the media and public welcomed the end of the USSR. Although the Turkish left was skeptical at first, later on they changed their minds and also welcomed the developments. However, Marxists and the Kurdish left were the exception to this enthusiastic welcome. Turkish Marxists were determined to adhere to their cause, claiming that although the Soviet model had collapsed the communist ideology had not, and underlined the continuing presence of China and Cuba as socialist states. On the other hand, after the end of the USSR the Kurdish side turned completely towards separatism. The reaction of different levels of Turkish society-parties, elite, the media and public-affected each other and Western (statements of politicians and the media) support for Turkey affected Turkish society in general; for example, the enthusiastic statements of Turkish leaders about the Turkish world affected public opinion, and therefore Turkish people started to believe that a Common Market or Community of Turkic states would be established. On the other hand, the West's proposal of the Turkish Model, and interpretations by the foreign and domestic media such as a 'new Turkic world was born' or that 'Turkey is becoming a superpower' affected Turkish politicians and encouraged them to make such enthusiastic statements. Public opinion, in its turn, encouraged Turkish politicians to take active steps to solve the Azeri-Armenian conflict; furthermore, the Turkish public called for military intervention in the conflict.

The West, including the US, supported and promoted the Turkish Model to the Turkic Republics, which made Turkey extremely happy. Western and US decision-makers declared on several occasions that the Turkish Model was an ideal path for the newly independent Muslim Republics of the Caucasus and Central Asia. There were some assumptions and reasons behind this Western promotion and support for the Turkish Model.

Firstly, it was assumed that with the end of the USSR, a power vacuum had been created in Central Asia, as it was believed that Russia did not desire to control former Soviet territory and vacated the region. Who would fill this gap? In this respect Turkey and Iran were mentioned as rival powers. Iran represented an anti-Western and Islamic regime; on the other hand, Turkey represented democracy, secularism, the free market economy and more importantly closeness to the West. The Turkish Model was seen as an important asset and instrument by the West to overcome the power vacuum created by the dissolution of the USSR. Therefore, the Western fear of Islam, the presence of Iran, geographically, culturally and historically close to the region, and the fear that the Muslim Republics could adopt the Iranian model was the main reason that strongly encouraged the West to support the Turkish Model.

Secondly, although Western democracies are the origin of the Turkish Model and are still stronger than it, the West supported the Turkish Model and put it forward as an ideal

---

[21] See, Idris Bal, "Emergence of the Turkic Republics and Turkish Reaction", *Foreign Policy*, Vol.22, No.1-2/1998, pp.58-76.

path instead of putting forward Western Models, because Central Asians mostly had Turkic origins, and the assumption was that years of communism probably had not drastically altered these Turkic origins and cultures. Therefore, it was assumed that there was positive public opinion in these Republics towards Turkey. In other words, the assumption was that it would be easier for the Muslim republics to follow the path of a country with which they felt affinity and shared a common culture. Therefore, the alternatives for models would be either Iran or Turkey, but not Western democracies. The Turkish transition from monarchy to a semi-dictatorial leadership to a multi-party system was seen as the closest experience to that of the new republics as well.

Thirdly, after the collapse of the USSR, the Turkic Republics had to reform their centrally controlled economies, but they had no experience of free trade and the requirements of a market economy did not exist in the Republics. Therefore, a fresh example could be helpful for their transformation. In this sense, the Turkish experience in economic transformation after 1980 (following the 24 January decisions) was a fresh and successful example of a transformation from a centrally controlled economy to a market economy. Therefore, apart from other characteristics, Turkey's success in economic transformation was a factor, which encouraged the West to support the Turkish Model.

These were the main reasons that determined Western support for the Turkish model. However, it is difficult to interpret this support as Western confirmation of the maturity of the Turkish Model. Instead, the Turkish model was usually used as a symbol of the principles, secularism, market economy, cooperation with the West and a multi-party system as mentioned above. In turn, it was assumed that the adoption of these principles by the Turkic Republics would be in the interests of the West as well as Turkey.

After the first year of these republics' independence, Western knowledge of the region and its economic, cultural, social and strategic issues increased, and new developments took place. In turn, especially after two years of these republics' independence, the West and the US reconsidered their initial assumptions and policies and declined their support for the Turkish Model. Again there were some important reasons behind the decline in Western support for the Turkish Model.

Firstly, after understanding the real conditions in the region, the West realized that although Iran had some geo-strategic advantages in the region, it had significant handicaps as well. Primarily, although Iran was an Islamic state, in contrast to the initial Western assumptions, the effect of Iran in the Turkic Republics was very limited. This was mainly because there is a divide between Shiite and Sunni Muslims, and a hostile attitude between these two sects. Iran is a Shiite state; on the other hand, the majority of the population of the Turkic states is Sunni, except for the Azeris. Iran's influence even over the Azeri population is very limited, as Azeris are Turkic and their nationalistic feelings are strong. Also, Iran has an ethnic Azeri population of some twenty million living in the north of the country, and is worried about the possible unification of these peoples. It must also be pointed out that, maybe because it realized its limits in the region, in contrast to Western expectations, Iran did not become involved in a struggle to export its regime to the Turkic Republics. In fact, it has been looking for possible cooperation in economic fields, after being isolated by the West. Therefore, Iran's policy was pragmatic and realistic rather than adventurist. This was a surprise for the West as the danger of the Iranian model in the Turkic Republics was the main reason, which led the West to promote the Turkish Model to the region as a counter-ideology. Therefore, because of Iran's pragmatic policy, the main reason behind Western support for the Turkish Model diminished.

Secondly, after the collapse of the USSR Russia initially gave priority to domestic affairs and it was assumed that Russia did not want to regain control over the former Soviet territory. Most people therefore talked about a power vacuum created in the region by the end of the USSR. However, especially after 1993, Russia clearly announced its intention of regaining control over the former Soviet territory known as the 'near abroad' policy. Russia justified her policy in three ways. There were economic reasons for the Russian economy depended on the other Republics (and vice versa) and security reasons since Russia wanted to control nuclear power and did not want to see a rival power settled in the former Soviet territory. Around 25 million ethnic Russians living outside Russian territory also encouraged Russia to control the former Soviet territory in order to guarantee their civil rights. In 1994, Russia signed several agreements with the Turkic Republics and Russian bases were reopened in the region. This was not a terrible development for the West, which preferred to deal with one nuclear power in the region rather than four, and was seeking the stability in the region, which Russia could provide. Therefore, in contrast to Turkish expectations, the West allowed Russia to implement the 'near abroad' policy as if it were Russia's legitimate right to control former Soviet territory. Western support for Russian policy in the Turkic Republics was a negative development for Western support for the Turkish Model, as the two are irreconcilable.

Thirdly, promotion of the Turkish Model was an instrument of Western foreign policy, and after about a year it became clearer that the Turkic Republics were not adopting fundamentalism, there was, in fact, no power vacuum but rather stability in the Republics in general, as will be outlined below, all the Turkic republics welcomed the main characteristics of the Turkish Model, although in practice there were still problems. Therefore, in terms of Western policy, promotion of the Turkish Model had played its role successfully by attracting the interests of the Turkic Republics towards the West instead of the Islamic Middle East, especially Iran. This meant that since the Turkish Model had played its part there was no longer the need for further support of the Turkish Model. Furthermore, it might have side effects as well, because some Turkish policies and declarations by Turkish officials suggested that there was a danger of pan-Turkism for the West. Further support for the Turkish Model might have encouraged this trend, and therefore support for the Turkish Model declined in order to prevent the creation of a pan-Turkic union.

Finally, although the Turkish Model became popular after the end of the USSR, Turkey was involved in an undeclared war in South-East Anatolia costing several lives every day. It had negative effects on the Turkish economy and Turkish foreign policy. In addition to this, Turkey faced some demands from some Alawite and more religious circles as well. These groups demanded more freedoms and reform of the Turkish Model. These two problems are crucial for Turkey and constitute an important part of the current

Turkish political agenda. The effects of these crises on Turkey played a negative role in terms of Western support for the Turkish Model.

Turkey was not happy that the West and Turkic republics had stopped talking about Turkish model. However, Turkey attempted to improve her relations with Turkic republics in all fronts.[22] After the end of the USSR, Turkey started to take active steps and recognized the Turkic Republics-becoming the first country to do so. Although Turkey declared that it was not involved in competition with any other country, it also shared the Western view of the threat of Iranian export of its regime and therefore, as a secular, Western-oriented state, wanted to prevent Iran from doing this. The Turkish International Cooperation Agency (TICA) was established to regularize relations between Turkey and the Turkic Republics, and the first summit between the presidents of Turkey and the Turkic Republics took place in Ankara in October 1992. Although Turkish resources are limited and Turkey has internal problems, Turkey gave credits to the Turkic Republics, helped them to modernize their telecommunications, and encouraged them towards economic reforms. However, the most important developments took place in the field of cultural relations. Turkey welcomed Turkic students who attended Turkish universities. These students were regarded as a bridge for future relations between Turkey and the Turkic Republics. Turkish 'Avrasya TV' started to broadcast to the Turkic Republics. Turkish help was also important in the field of religion, as Turkey wanted to export its model of moderate Islam. The Turkish Presidency of Religious Affairs sent books and Imams to the Turkic republics; students from the Turkic world came to Turkey for religious education. These students were financed and educated by the Turkish Presidency of Religious Affairs. Apart from the state, the Turkish private sector has been active in the educational field: Turkish businessmen opened colleges in every Republic, which represented the Turkish culture, moderate Islam and the ideals of Atatürk. Turkish as well as English is taught to the students, and these colleges have been welcomed by the Turkic Republics since they offered education above regional standards. Another important issue was the adoption of the Latin alphabet in principle by the Turkic Republics. Turkey advocated that this was essential to integrate into the world and to adopt the Turkish Model. On the other hand, Iran advocated the Arabic alphabet, which was not welcomed by any of the Turkic republics; only Central Asian Republic welcomed this offer was Tajikistan.

Officially, the main objective of Turkish policy, as Acar Okan pointed out, was to help the Turkic Republics to gain and keep their independence.[23] There is no denial that Turkey, which needed support on crucial issues such as Kurdish separatism, the Cyprus issue and the water conflict with Syria and Iraq over the rivers Fırat (Euphrates) and Dicle (Tigris), assumed that the new Turkic Republics would be its natural allies in international organizations, and therefore regarded their full independence as being in its

---

[22] For the relations between Turkey and Turkic republics see. Idris Bal. *Turkey's Relations With the West and Turkic Republics: The Rise and Fall of Turkish Model*. Aldershot: Ashgate. 2000; Idris Bal. *21. Yuzyilda Turk Dis Politikasi*. Ankara: Nobel Yayınları. 2004; Faruk Sonmezoğlu (Ed.). *Turk Dis Politikasi Analizi*. Istanbul: Der Yayinlari. 2001.

[23] *Personal interview with Acar Okan*. adviser to the Prime Minister. Ankara. 1993.

interests.

Reactions of Turkic Republics to Turkey and Turkish Model

The initial reactions of the Turkic Republics to Turkey and the Turkish Model were strongly affected by the cultural environment of these Republics. Primarily Turkey has ethnic links, as a majority of the population of the Turkic Republics is of Turkic origin; linguistic links, as languages of the same family are spoken by the majority of the peoples of these republics; and religious links, as a majority of the population of the Turkic Republics believe in Islam, specifically the Sunni sect which is dominant in Turkey. Mainly because of this cultural environment, the peoples of the Turkic Republics feel ready to set up close ties with Turkey and therefore they react positively to the Turkish Model. This admiration and affinity for Turkey existed even amongst the leadership of the Republics, which initially welcomed the Turkish Model enthusiastically. On several occasions they stated that they would follow this Model, which had been promoted to them by the West and Turkey, and claimed that they would not go back on their decisiomn. Another factor that strongly affected the initially warm reaction to the Turkish Model was that when these republics declared their independence, they were to some extent unaware of the realities of the Turkish situation: because of the lack of communication with the outside world during the Soviet era, they assumed that Turkey was powerful, economically and politically perfect, had no problems and was ready to help them establish their new states. All of them welcomed the aspects of the Turkish Model related to secularism, the market economy and closeness and cooperation with the West, but the democratic aspect of the Turkish Model was generally not welcomed, especially by Uzbekistan and Turkmenistan, where opposition movements were repressed. Although the Kazak regime was not as authoritarian as these two, and Kazakhstan and Kyrgyzstan took the lead in instigating democratic reforms, in Kazakhstan, nationalist parties were not allowed to be registered, as the Kazak leadership was afraid of alienating ethnic Russians. Karimov and Turkmenbashi took the example of Atatürk, and wanted to follow the Turkish Model of 1920's, featuring single-party rule and the strong leadership of Atatürk. Both of these leaders appreciate and admire Atatürk; mainly for this reason, Niyazov adopted the name 'Turkmenbashi' (leader of Turkmens) which is very similar to that of 'Atatürk' (father of Turks). Kyrgyzstan and Azerbaijan, on the other hand, welcomed the democratic aspect of the Turkish Model as well.

However, after emotional statements and reciprocal visits by the Turkish side and the Turkic Republics, the latter realized the limitations of Turkish power and understood that the Turkish model did not operate perfectly even in Turkey. When the leaders of the Turkic Republics came to Turkey, they witnessed high inflation, unemployment, and separatist activities in South-East Anatolia and religious and sectarian demands by some circles from the Turkish state. The greatly increased access to the world at large after the first year of independence showed them how far the 'Turkish Model' lagged behind other economies. In contrast to initial assumption, the Turkic Republics understood that the Turkish standard of living could not be a long-term final goal for them, as the Turkish Model was not a social and economic miracle. There was not as much fund in Turkey as they had expected. Therefore, all the Republics wanted to establish close relations with the West, and asked the West to invest in their republics, because they realized that the developed states of the West, as well as the Pacific, were in a better position than Turkey to give economic help. After realizing that the West no longer promoted and supported the Turkish Model, Turkic republics stopped talking about the Turkish Model and their interest both in the Model and in Turkey declined. In contrast to initial expectations, instead of using Turkey as a mediator, the Turkic Republics realized that they could establish direct relations with the West and the US. The West also, very soon, realized that they did not need a third party.

The role of the Turkish involvement in Azeri domestic politics cannot be overlooked in the decline of the Turkish Model from favor. Turkish support for the opposition (the Azerbaijan People's Front) in Azerbaijan and the success of Elchibey alienated the Turkic republics from Turkey and encouraged them to approach Russia, since those in power were afraid that they might lose their posts if the opposition became strong through receiving help from Turkey. For example, related to this, Uzbekistan called most of the students who were sent to Turkey for education back to Uzbekistan, as Uzbek leadership believed that these students held meetings with the Uzbek opposition in Turkey.

Additionally, the fact that Turkey supported the opposition in Azerbaijan but in the end, failed to keep Elchibey in power, revealed to the Republics that Turkey's support or hostility was not so important as Turkey was too weak to compete against Russia in the region. Thus, Turkey's initial image as a strong, sister state was badly undermined after the fall of Elchibey. Above all these reasons, the Turkic Republics did not want to have a new big brother after just getting rid of the old one, and therefore are worried that Turkey could play the role of big brother for the new Republics own benefit. Some enthusiastic statements by Turkish politicians gave impetus to these worries, and in turn, this helped the Turkic Republics to lose interest in Turkey and the Turkish Model. Therefore, after the initial emotional welcome for Turkey and the Turkish Model, the Turkic Republics then became more realistic and skeptical, and although they have not abandoned the Turkish Model they have begun to say they want only the good aspects of the model, and to emphasize that Turkey is not perfect. Thus, their interest in the Turkish Model declined. However, in general Turkic republics are still eager to improve their relations with Turkey for several reasons such as economic, cultural, geographic and strategic. They are trying to attract foreign investments and lessen their dependence of Russia.

September 11th Attacks and Re-emergence of the Turkish Model

As outlined above, Turkish model was used as a magnet following the end of Soviet Union for Muslim republics of Central Asia and Caucasus to attract their attention to the West rather than Iran or Saudi Arabia. After achieving this, the West ended its support to the model and Turkey. People stopped talking about Turkish model and all the rhetoric was forgotten. However, radical Islamic movements around the world and ongoing disputes especially in the Middle East, Caucasus and Balkans encouraged people to talk about Turkey and the Turkish model again. For instance, before and during on his trip to Turkey in November in 1999, US president Bill Clinton pointed out that Turkey had a significant role to play in the act of shaping the upcoming century. He drew attention to the need to bridge the gulf between Europe and the Islamic World and implied that Turkey was a bridge between the Christian and Muslim cultures. These remarks mean that US regarded Turkey as a strategic ally in the post Cold War era and Turkish model was still important to World politics.[24]

There are several factors that encourage the West especially US to regard Turkey as a strategic ally and still a model. Turkey is an important country as a bridge between Asia and Europe geographically as well as culturally. Eurasia is still important to world politics and US interests in several aspects. The end of USSR created a power vacuum in Eurasia. Eight new independent republics came in to existence in Caucasus and Central Asia. Especially, Russia and China have risen as possible candidates that can fill the power vacuum in Eurasia.[25] After the Soviet defeat, Soviet troops vacated Afghanistan. However, this did not bring peace and stability to Afghanistan, furthermore Afghanistan became the center of instability in the region and globe, similar to Lebanon's position in the Middle East in the 1970's. Mainly because of lack of authority and rise of Taliban regime, Afghanistan became source of instability and training ground for terrorists and radical groups. There were other deep-rooted conflicts in the region, such as the one between India and Pakistan over the Muslim populated region Kashmir. Iran is also located in the region as an anti-American Islamic state. Since 1979 Islamic revolution, US have been trying to isolate this regime and contain Iran. Turkey and Israel as allies of US and Western European countries are also close to the region and especially Turkey has ethnic and cultural ties with the peoples of the region. Therefore, under these circumstances, the end of Cold War prepared a suitable base for a new big game in the region. There are several reasons concerning economical, political, ideological and cultural issues that stir up this game.

The countries of Caucasus and Central Asia are rich in oil and gas and they want to transport their oil and gas to the world markets. Because of Turkey's geo-strategic position in the region, US want to co-operate with Turkey and affect these developments according to its interests. For instance, Turkish proposal of Baku Ceyhan pipeline project was backed by US and project is now being realized. Another factor that encourages close co-operation between Turkey and US is related with regional disputes. In contrast to expectations of New World Order, the end of Cold War brought "disorder" in the forms of ethnic-based demands, regional disputes that used to be suppressed by the rivalry between East and West. After realizing these fragile conditions, US started to regard Turkey as a strategic ally to tackle with the problems in a region stretching from Balkans to Central Asia and Middle East. This region can also be regarded as a source of threats to the US interests and this makes Turkey most needed ally for the US. Also Turkey's position between Europe, Middle East, and Far East countries, China and India also strengthens Turkey's strategic position. These explanations do not mean that US need Turkey much more than Turkey needs US. Keeping in mind the fact that in the post Cold

---

[24] See, Idris Bal, "Rise of Turkey as a Model in International Relations in Post Cold War Era ad American Ratification", *Eurasian Studies*, No.18, Autumn-Winter 2000, pp.127-136.
[25] See, Idris Bal, "Rise of Shanghai Cooperation Organization (SCO) in Eurasia: Is It an Effective Toll in a New Gig Game", Ertan Efegil, (Ed.), *Geopolitics of Central Asia in the Post Cold War Era: A Systemic Analysis*, Harlem, the Netherlands: Research Center for Azerbaijan and Turkestan, SOTA, 2002.

War situation Turkey needs allies to have enough international support for its position in its crucial issues such as separatism, water dispute with Syria and Iraq, problems with Greece and Cyprus. Additionally, one can argue that after the end of USSR, Turkey needs new allies to balance Russia which is still a military super power, and Turkey has some doubts whether Russia gave up its historic ambitions of penetrating South to the hot waters. However, Russia is, at the same time, a new trading partner for Turkey, and Turkey almost depend on Russian natural gas for her domestic consumption. Turkey also needs US and Western help to overcome its economic problems such as souring rate of inflation and budget deficits. Therefore, Turkey needs US as much as US need Turkey and both sides, as a consequence, will benefit from this co-operation. For instance, Turkey has began to benefit from close co-operation with US, without whose help, Turkey would not have been able to manage catching Abdullah Öcalan, leader of Kurdish separatist organization (PKK).

In the post Cold War period, US have been trying to manipulate changes and preserve regional and global balances that can be regarded as a foundations of American hegemony. This was, and still is, a duty for US as otherwise she could (and can) lose her position as a superpower. In doing this, Turkey is important for US. Turkey can be an important instrument to manipulate change within EU as well as within the Eurasia. US followed developments in Eurasia with patient and co-operated with Turkey and attempted to limit Iran and Russia. On the other hand, US attempted to establish bilateral relations with China and Russia and did not want to provoke them. For a long time (until 1997) US regarded region within Russian influence. Then, US began to take some steps to limit Russia in the region, but these were not radical steps and US was cautious not to provoke Russia.

September 11 attacks realized in 2001 shocked everyone and also the parameters in international system as they started to change dramatically and have been changing since then. The US started a global war against terrorism and Taliban regime in Afghanistan, which became the first target of this campaign. Growing interests in co-operation between China and Russia and rise of SCO (Shanghai Co-operation Organization) disturbed the US, and terrorist attacks provided an excellent opportunity for the US to deal with Eurasia directly. With the Afghan operation, the US settled in the region by setting up permanent military bases; consequently, especially Russia and Uzbekistan approached to the US. However, this rapprochement should be regarded as a tactical step rather than a strategic step for Russia. Later on, it was seen that Russia was trying to take every opportunity and improve her relations with the states of "axis of evil", Iran, Iraq and North Korea. Furthermore, in Iraq war in 2003, Russia, China as well as France and Germany criticized US and therefore US was not able to get a decision from Security Council to justify occupation of Iraq. US settlement in Eurasia with the operation against Afghanistan was an important step that US took to undermine Russian-Chinese co-operation and the SCO. The US is also trying to establish close relations with India, a growing power that can balance out China, and can also be a possible member of the SCO.

In the post September 11 attacks era, security and global war against terrorism is now at the top of political agenda. However, terrorism is not an easy enemy to punish. States must act within the domestic and international law and morality otherwise they can themselves be regarded as "terrorists". The main objective of a counter terrorist strategy must be the protection and the maintenance of the liberal democracy, the rule of law and upholding the state's constitutional authority. However, there is no such self-restraint on terrorists, who have freedom of action in this regarded. The public audience is the most important actor as both the state and the terrorists address the public audience and states should not lose the public's support.

The US declared a global war against terrorism. However, Liberal States have great difficulty in implementing counter-terrorism strategies. The problem facing governments in their wars against terrorism are related to deterrence, intelligence and early warning, defense and retaliation. It is difficult to argue that terrorists can easily be deterred as they have no rational mind and they have no visible assets to be retaliated. But states that support the terrorists can be retaliated. The fundamental problem of retaliation is political. Retaliation against supporting states is a political decision. Before retaliation there must be enough evidences to prove that the state in question supports the terrorists, otherwise the political cost of retaliation can be very high. However, in most cases, the ties between terrorists and supporting countries are difficult to prove.[26]

The US is trying to punish those states that supports terrorism and as mentioned above, President Bush labeled Iran, Iraq and North Korea as "axis of evils". Two of these countries are neighbor of Turkey and their people believe in Islam. The US was trying to topple Saddam but in contrast to 1991 operation against Iraq, most of the World especially Islamic world was against such a new operation. However, US managed to topple Saddam in 2003. The end of Saddam regime did not mean the end of international terrorism. Struggling terrorism should be much more that military operations for a successful solution. Political, economic, social and cultural grounds that produce terrorism need to be studied and necessary measures should be taken. It should not be forgotten that terrorism is a weapon of the weak and therefore "peace" and "justice" should be achieved in the world. In combating against terrorism, Turkish moderate Islamic approach is obviously important. Turkish moderate Islamic approach is not a product of modern Turkey as anticipated by most of the circles, in fact, it has strong roots in Turkish history. For instance, several European countries such as France (1290), England (1392), Spain (1492) and Portugal (1497) deported Jews in the history. Some of the deported Jewish people migrated to Eastern European countries, most of them moved to Ottoman Empire as a safe heaven, which welcomed and furthermore sent ships to help them in their migration.[27] Jews as well as other nations and religious were respected in Ottoman Empire and they lived according to their religion and tradition under the umbrella of nation system (millet sistemi). That is the reason why all peoples of Balkans,

---

[26] For the problems that government face in their wars against terrorism see, Arie Ofri, "Intelligence and Counter-Terrorism", *Orbis*, Spring 1984; Lawrence Freedman, *Terrorism and International Order*, New York: Routledge Kegan Paul Ltd., 1986; Idris Bal, "Terrorism, Liberal State and International Co-Operation", *Turkish Year Book of Human Rights*, Vol.21-25, 1999-2003, pp.117-132.

[27] Tayyar Ari, "2000'li Yillarda Turkiye'nin Ortadogu Politikasi", Idris Bal, *21. Yuzyilin Eşiğinde Turk Dis Politikasi*, Istanbul: Alfa Yayinlari, 2001, p.433; Fahir Armaoğlu, *Filistin Meselesi ve Arap İsrail Savaşları, 1948-1988*, Ankara: Türkiye İş Bankası Yayınları, 1991, pp.11-12.

Caucasus and Middle East were able to keep attached to their nationalities and religions as well as their traditions. Jews celebrated their 500th anniversary in 1992. This is an example showing Turkish tolerance and moderate Islamic understanding. After bearing in mind all the problems of Islamic world especially in the Middle East, it is clear that this approach is urgently needed in all Islamic world as well as maybe in some other countries.

It is also necessary to emphasize that global war is against terrorism not Islam, or any other religion. Otherwise, the US campaign against terrorism can encourage the rise of radical movements and anti Americanism in Islamic world. In turn, these developments can cause further headaches for the West and US. Therefore, the US needs international help and co-operation. Turkey as an ally of US suffered from terrorism and more than 40,000 Turkish citizens lost their lives in combating against terrorism in the last two decades. Therefore, the US-Turkish relations, and where Turkey stands and with whom regarding the US foreign policy in post September 11 attacks era, are important issues to discuss in detail. The legendary Turkish model, therefore, becomes an instrument again to tackle with Islamic World and Turkish position as a bridge between the West and Islamic World culturally is getting more important again. This is manly because the US government is trying to undermine radical movements and encourage moderate Islamic approaches.

Although three-year-term span is over now after September 11 attacks, there are several questions, which require clear and persuasive answers. Why did September 11 attacks take place and who did plan and support them (in every aspect)? What is the message given by September 11 attacks? Are there any relations between global and regional rivalries and September 11 attacks? Are there any relations between globalization and anti-globalization fronts and 11 September attacks? What are the parameters of international system after September 11 attacks and what direction international system is being pushed? What is the philosophy of the US global war against terrorism? What are the details of the US project of global war against terrorism and problems of anti terrorism strategies? What are the handicaps of global war against terrorism? Can global war against terrorism encourage radicalism in the world (especially Islamic World)? Afghanistan was the first and Iraq was second step in the way of combating againts terrorism. What will be third and following steps? Can this process encourage rise of rival global powers against US…? It is possible to ask more questions. But it is obvious that Turkey has an important role in new international system and in US global war against terrorism. However, the question of to what extent Turkish and US interests overlap in the new era will be main handicap of these relations.

In answering these questions and in a global war against terrorism, Turkey and Turkish model seem to be important and present developments seem to bring Turkish model to the political ground to see whether it can be used as an instrument in international relations. US has prepared a plan "the Greater Middle East Initiative" to tackle problems in the Middle East. It can be argued that Turkey and Turkish model may play a vital role in this initiative.

Conclusion

The term 'Turkish Model' is used to refer to the model of development and government in Turkey whose characteristics are secularism in a Muslim society, a market economy, closeness and co-operation with the West, and a multi-party system.

The end of Cold War prepared a suitable ground for new disputes, and power vacuums occurred in the various parts of the world. Eight new republics gained their independence in Caucasus and Central Asia. Six of these republics are Muslim-populated countries. It was considered to be scary in that Iran could export her anti-western ideology to new Muslim populated republics. Therefore, as a counter ideology, Turkish model was put forward. Turkish model was an instrument to attract the attention of Turkic republics to the West and the US rather than Iran and Saudi Arabia.

One can argue that the West especially US achieved almost all its objectives by promoting the Turkish Model, as the Turkic Republics welcomed secularism, the market economy and co-operation with the West. In the case of democracy, all the republics said that they wanted to establish a democratic multi-party system, but some of them (especially Turkmenistan and Uzbekistan) are reluctant to embark on democratic reforms as they claim they need time to do so. In general, they refused the Iranian model, and there is no instability in the Turkic Republics that could pose a threat to Western business interests.

As for Turkey's part, there was a degree of success, as Turkey also wanted to stop Iran and advocated the principles noted above. The adoption of these was only a partial success for Turkey, however, as Turkey had broader expectations and wanted to expand its economic, cultural and political influence under the banner of the Turkish Model. In the cultural field Turkey has had some success, and in terms of politics it managed to co-ordinate the summits among the leaders of the Turkic Republics and Turkey. But in general Turkey was not ready for the role it wanted to play because Turkey is economically weak and it tries to attract Western investment and needs Western capital and technology, politically it is experiencing ethnic and religious minority problems. Therefore, Turkey can be regarded as partly successful, as almost all the principles advocated by Turkey and the West were adopted to a degree by the Turkic republics, despite the fact that its more ambitious projects such as Özal's initiative of a Turkic common market failed. Given the reality of the domestic political conditions and World politics, this was the natural result, and Turkish enthusiasm for 'leadership' was more utopian than realist.

With the end of Cold War and Soviet Union, parameters have changed in international system. The East-West rivalry has ended up in allowing the US to become a single superpower. However, with the September 11 attacks, the parameters in international system are changing again. There is global war against terrorism headed by US. In this war and in US foreign policy, the importance of Turkey and Turkish model is getting greater. The US is trying to undermine radical movements and Turkish model and moderate Islamic approach is important as an alternative view.

Unless Turkey creates a successful model running perfectly at home, the Turkish model with its present handicaps can only be a foreign policy instrument for the West and the US. It can only be used to refer to some principles and to attract the attentions to the West rather than other alternatives. As soon as the model fulfils its duty, it will inevitably be obsolete. However, if Turkey can create a real miracle such as a successful economy, a mature democracy, a new understanding of secularism that gives enough freedom to the pious people, sects, ethnic groups, and the like, by uniting her people around the Turkish state and create a magnet at the center. Provided Turkey can achieve all her overall goals to become a democratic country, Turkey can play a real key role in the region as well as in the World. It is very likely that a successful Turkish model will attract other Islamic countries and serve for the peace and cooperation in the world, but not as a model developed around her present-day characteristics- a far cry from the ideal.

16 Instability in the Middle East and the Relevant Role of the PKK[*]

İdris Bal

Introduction

One of the obvious implications of the Cold War was that it froze maps in the World and there was some sort of stability even under the shadow of weapons. When the Cold War ended, it was believed that a New World Order would establish, liberalism and human rights would rise and a peaceful world order would establish. In contrast to these optimistic expectations, regional problems emerged immediately after the end of the Cold War. Ethnic and religious aspirations found suitable conditions to flourish and to be materialized. The end of the Cold War was like an end of the control mechanism that prepared a suitable base for new conflicts to flourish. Therefore, new conflicts and wars took place in the world, especially, in the Middle East, Balkans and Caucasus. The End of the Cold War led to the emergence of new power vacuums in different parts of the World as well as an increase in importance of regional powers. The Middle East was not a stable place where as Iran-Iraq War and Arab-Israeli wars took place. However because of the effects of the Cold War other problems were frozen in the Middle East as well.[1]

The Middle East is one of the unstable regions of the world. Since the end of the Ottoman Empire, number of powers have tried but failed to establish stability in the Middle East. Jews and Arabs fought several times, the Iran-Iraq war lasted for eight years and then Iraq occupied Kuwait in August 1990. Kuwait was liberated in 1991 by an international coalition headed by US, and then in 2003 the US and the UK occupied Iraq and gave an end to Saddam regime. There are several conflicts and terrorist organizations shadowing Middle East politics at present. It is important, therefore, to underline the factors that prepare instability in the Middle East. In this article, firstly the factors that cause instability in the Middle East will be outlined and analyzed. Secondly, PKK's (Kurdish Workers Party) contribution to instability in the region, especially in Turkey, will be focused on.

Instability in the Middle East

There are several reasons related to cultural, social, economic, and strategic conditions of the region that create instability. These reasons can be divided into four groups. First group of reasons are related to political, strategic, social, cultural, ethnic and natural

[*] First version of this chapter was published in, İdris Bal, "Instability in the Middle East and Relevant Role of PKK", *Turkish Review of Middle East Studies*, Annual 2002, Istanbul, pp.135-156. I would like to thank my colleague, H. Bülent Olcay for reading this article.

[1] See İdris Bal, "Turkish Foreign Policy (1960-1980)", *Encyclopaedia of Turkish History, Vol.6*, Ankara: Yeni Türkiye Publications, 2002, pp.263-281.

structures of the region. These are mainly artificial maps and nations, richness in religions and sects and presence of holy places, incomplete nationalization process, presence of rich hydrocarbon reserves, scarcity of water and absence of democratic regimes in the region. Second group of reasons are related to Arab-Israeli conflict, which is central problem of the Middle East. Third group of reasons are related to the Gulf War, Iran and ideological issues. Fourth group of reasons can be regarded as potential reasons that will cause new disputes in the future. Artificial structure of the region and cool relations between Arabs and Turks constitute another group of reasons that lead to instability in the region.

Economic, Cultural, Political, Social and Ethnic Structure of the Region

First group of reasons are related to the political, geographic, social, cultural, ethnic and natural structures of the region. After the fall of the Ottoman Empire, several new states were created in the region. However, in the process of drawing maps and creating new nations, social, ethnic and cultural structure of the region were not taken into account seriously and therefore the map and nations created become artificial that prepare a suitable base for disputes and revisionist movements. Artificial borders and nations can cause further problems in the future as well. Especially when Arab Israeli dispute is over and foreign interventions and influences in the region is declined, it is highly likely that new disputes and may be new wars will take place in the region over the artificial boundaries and sharing of the natural resources of the region. Iraqi invasion of Kuwait should be regarded as an important indicator of what would happen if foreign intervention in the region declined and countries of the region gained some sort of power.

The region is rich in terms of religions and sects. After the Ottoman rule in the whole came to an end, peoples of the region established separate and sometimes confronting groups, identified themselves with their sects and/or tribes as well. Policies of new regimes and colonial powers as well as emergence of Israel as an independent state in the region gave impetus to the process of creating radical identities. The region is important for Islam, Christianity and Judaism. For instance, Jerusalem is an important sacred place for all three main celestial religions and therefore believers of these religions want to control this city.[2]

On the other hand, nationalization process has not ended and peoples in the region have not yet gone through the stage of becoming a "nation" but rather comprised of separate groups. This also maintains instability in the region. For example, population of Iraq consists of Shia people in the South, Sunnis in central region and Kurds and Turcomans in the North. These groups regard themselves first of all as a member of their groups before being a member of Iraqi nation. Strong sense of devotion to being a member of a tribe means much more than any other characteristic that they can very possibly identify themselves. This situation prepares a suitable base for the instability and it also forms a barrier standing in the way of democratization.

One of the outstanding features of the region is that although new oil reserves were

---

[2] Ahmet Davutoğlu, *Stratejik Derinlik*, İstanbul : Küre Yayınları, 2001, pp.329-330; Mehmet Atay, "Ortadoğuda Terör Savaşı ve Barış Arayışları", Ümit Özdağ and Osman Metin Öztürk, *Terörizm İncelemeleri*, Ankara: Avrasya Stratejik Araştırmalar Merekezi Yayınları, 2000, pp.203-204.

discovered in Caspian region and the Central Asia, the Middle East has still overwhelming strategic importance. The fact that nearly two thirds (65.3%) of the World oil reserves are located in the Middle East and production costs are relatively low in the region encourages outside powers to intervene in the Middle East politics. Moreover, more than one third (36.1%) of the World natural gas reserves are located in the Middle East as well. Rich hydrocarbon resources are therefore enough to make the region a center of attraction in the world.

Table 1: Distribution of Oil Reserves in the World

Regions	%
Middle East	65.3
South and Central America	9.1
Africa	7.3
Former USSR	6.2
North America	6.1
Asia Pacific	4.2
Europe	1.8

Source: BP Web Page.

Total oil reserves in the world are around one trillion and fifty billion barrels. As seen in table 1, more than sixty five per cent of the oil reserves (685.6 billion barrels) exist in the Middle East. Furthermore, world natural gas reserves are around 155 trillion meter cubic, and, as seen in table 2, more than thirty six per cent of natural gas resources (55.91 trillion meter cubic) are located in the Middle East.

Table 2: Distribution of Natural Gas Reserves in the World

Regions	%
Former USSR	36.2
The Middle East	36.1
Asia Pacific	7.9
Africa	7.2
North America	4.9
South and Central America	4.6
Europe	3.1

Source: BP Web Page

During the Cold War era, the block leaders, the USSR and the USA were involved in the Middle East politics. In the post Cold War era, mainly the USA and other Western powers were interested in Middle East politics. However, Russia has been trying to regain a ground in the Middle East politics, improving her relations with Middle East countries especially with the two members of "axis of evil" as labeled by President Bush, Iraq and Iran. They wish to exert their influence over the petrol reserves, oil production and its price. Therefore, outside powers' influence over Middle East may be considered as a negative factor as it prevents the Middle East regimes from becoming mature. The outside powers' interests cannot also coincide with the interests of the regional countries all the times. In that case, the outside interventions can encourage disputes between regional states. Therefore, one may argue that a concrete co-operation among Middle Eastern countries is not for the benefit of outside powers. This is mainly because a stable and united region will never allow outside interventions to last long. Policies originated in the region will no doubt find their way to develop and to be implemented accordingly.

Rise of revisionist or nuclear state is not welcomed in the region as well. For instance, Cheney, the Vice President emphasized that a nuclear-armed Iraq would

> *seek domination of the entire Middle East, take control of a great portion of the world's energy supplies... and subject the United States or any other nation to nuclear blackmail"*[3]

Therefore, apart from other reasons, the existence of rich petrol reserves in the Middle East is in fact a negative factor for instability in the region as it encourages outside powers to intervene in the Middle East politics.

Likewise, water or scarcity of water in the Middle East is another factor that can cause instability in the region. For example, there are problems between Turkey, Syria and Iraq over the sharing of waters of Euphrates (Fırat) and Tigris (Dicle) rivers.[4] There are similar problems between Israel, Jordan, Syria and Lebanon as well. The Nile is also a source of conflict between Egypt and Sudan. There are scenarios that will be put into effect in the future because of water not oil. It is clear that only co-operation between countries of region can prevent such kind of horrible scenarios from being realized. If countries in the region cooperate in oil, water and other natural resources, peoples of the region will benefit and this cooperation will prevent horrible scenarios from being realized. Cooperation in Europe may be an example for the Middle East. For instance, although Germany and France fought twice in twenty century, they managed to cooperate under the umbrella of Coal and Still Community and this process ended up with the creation of EU.[5]

Furthermore, there are no democratic regimes in the Middle East. There are usually dictatorial or elite rules and limited numbers of people control the regimes in the Middle East Arab countries. Islamic movements form main opposition to the existing regimes. However, these movements were forced to act wholly or partly in underground and supporters of these movements are being radicalized step by step because of undemocratic regimes.[6] Therefore, stability and strength of the regimes in the region are open to discussion. Several revolts have taken place in the region. Regimes usually isolate

---

[3] William Saletan, "Cheney vs. Scowcroft, How to duck the arguments against attacking Iraq", *Slate, Msn*, Posted Tuesday, August 27, 2002, at 3:21 pm PT.
[4] See for instance, Vefa Toklu, "Türk Dış Politikasında Su Sorunu", İdris Bal (ed.), *21. Yüzyılda Türk Dış Politikası*, Ankara: Nobel Yayınları, 2004, pp.791-808.
[5] See Veysel Bozkurt, *Avrupa Birliği ve Türkiye*, Bursa: Vipaş AŞ. 2001; Cihan Duru & Hayriye Atik, *Avrupa Birliği Gümrük Birliği ve Türkiye*, Ankara: Nobel Yayınları, 2003.
[6] Ersin Kalaycıoğlu, "Yeni Demokratikleşme Dalgası ve Ortadoğu", Sabahattin Şen, *Su Sorunu Türkiye ve Ortadoğu*, İstanbul: Bağlam Yayınları, 1993, p.85.

themselves from their peoples and regard their peoples as potential dangers to the existing regimes. The main problem is how to integrate opposition into the system peacefully. Some disputes and conflicts have been seen in the past. For instance, Syria bombarded her own people (Islamic opposition) destroying her own cities called Hama and Hums; Algeria was once face-to-face with a civil war that was about to break out. This is another aspect of the instability in the region. If the opposition was not integrated into the system, we might likely to see more examples in the region similar to Algerian example.

Another aspect of the problem is that deficiency of democratic regimes is a negative factor and a barrier before international co-operations in the region. This is mainly because these regimes, first of all, desire to control their own people, keep holding the power in their hands and they refrain from international co-operation, as they are frightened into panic due to great loss of power. They are afraid of the fact that international co-operation can help rise the opposition or strengthen oppositions by preparing a suitable environment for them to flourish. Stability of the Middle East depends on the ability of the present regimes in integrating Islamic or secular oppositions into the system peacefully.[7] If opposition is integrated into the system peacefully, obviously this will be a positive development for democratization process and stability in the region. The US is trying to encourage democratization in the Middle East countries. For instance, president Bush reminded Syria, Iran and US allies in the region; Egypt and Saudi Arabia of the necessity to overthrow Saddam in Iraq as it was a prerequisite for establishment of global democratic process, and he warned them to adopt democratic traditions and realize democratic reforms.[8]

To deal with the poverty, ignorance, violation of human rights, despotism, etc., in the region, the US has prepared a "Greater Middle East Initiative" and will announce it in G-8 summit in June 2004.[9] However, there are some doubts about democratization in the Middle East. For instance, Peter Ford, British Ambassador to Damascus, gave a speech entitled 'Syria in the Post-Iraq Middle East' in Harvard University. In response to my question pertaining to democratization in Syria, he replied that although he admitted minority ruled majority in Syria, he claimed that if present regime changed in Syria, a despotic Sunni regime would come in power and therefore he would prefer the existing political system.[10] This situation indicates complicity of democratization and different approaches of Western states and US. Furthermore, apart from domestic barriers before democratization, there are global barriers, doubts and unwillingness of some global powers concerned with the democratization process in the Middle East.

---

[7] Cemil Oktay, "Soğuk Savaş Sonrasında Ortadoğu'yu Okumak", Sabahattin Şen, (ed.), *Su Sorunu Türkiye ve Ortadoğu*, p.100.

[8] David E. Sanger, "Bush Asks Lands in Mideast to try Democratic Ways", *The New York Times*, November 7, 2003.

[9] Paul Rogers, "The "Greater Middle East Initiative": vision or mirage?", 12.2.2004. www.opendemocracy.net/about/index.jsp

[10] Peter Ford, British Ambassador to Domascus and former WCFIA Fellow, "Syria in the Post-Iraq Middle Esat", *Middle Esat Seminer*, Jointly sponsored by the Weatherhead Center for International Affairs and the Center for Middle Esatern Studies, Harvard University.

Arab ñIsraeli Conflict

Second group of reasons are related to Arab-Israeli conflict. Central problem of the Middle East is Arab-Israeli dispute.[11] Since Israel was founded in 1948, Arabs have fought several losing battles, which encouraged them to get armed. Arabs lost the Six Days War against Israel in 1967 became pessimistic. After realizing that they would not be able to beat Israel in a regular war, some Arabic groups adopted terrorism as an instrument and used it as an effective weapon against Israel and later they began to use the same weapon against the other states as well. The West, especially USA has been usually criticized in the Middle East because of their help to Israel up till now. The western world, especially the US citizens and assets have therefore sometimes become targets of some terrorist attacks. Most of the hijackers in September 11 attacks originated in the Middle East. However, it does not mean that only these people were responsible for the attacks. There may be several other aspects of the attacks, and there may also be several other groups or even states that took part in the attacks in one form or another.

Terrorism is a weapon of the weak[12] and therefore some groups in the Middle East preferred this method. 1968 was the year in which international terrorism was born in the Middle East. The seeds of 1968 led to the formation of the present terrorist groups and terrorist activities.[13] Guerrilla groups' involvement and activities made a very negative effect on the Middle East stability. These developments forced Israel to develop a strong intelligence service and counter terrorism strategies. Although both sides had their own justifications, Israel made several clandestine operations that would fall into the activities considered to be 'terrorism', in a nutshell. Therefore, the Arab-Israeli dispute can be regarded as the most important problem in the region that prepares a suitable base for instability. In order to stop terrorism, apart from military solutions, democratic and equitable administrations and justice in international relations are of urgent necessities to help establish stability in the region. Cultural, economic and social bases that prepare favorable conditions for terrorism to flourish should also be considered.[14]

Gulf War, Iran and Ideological Issues

Third group of reasons are related to the Gulf War, Iran and ideological issues. Before 1979 Islamic takeover, Iran was an ally of the USA in the Middle East. However, with the revolution in 1979, Iran became a representative of anti-Western and anti-US front in the world and formed one of the factors that caused a suitable base for instability. After the Islamic revolution, Iraq attacked Iran in 1980 and the West supported Iraq against Iran in order to undermine Islamic revolution. The war lasted for eight years. Because of the Western and the US help during the war against Iran, Iraq became an important

---

[11] İhsan Gürkan. "1989-1990 Demokrasi Devrimi ve Soğuk Savaş Dönemi Sonrasında Ortadoğu ve Türkiye". Sebahattin Şen. (ed.). *Su Sorunu, Türkiye ve Ortadoğu*. p.56.

[12] See. Idris Bal. "Terrorism, Liberal State and International Co-Operation". *Turkish Year Book of Human Rights*. Vol.21-25, 1999-2003, pp.117-132.

[13] Sabahattin Şen. "Ortadoğuda Terör". Sabahattin Şen. (ed.). *Su Sorunu Türkiye ve Ortadoğu*. p.260.

[14] Idris Bal. "Terrorism, Liberal State and International Co-Operation". *Turkish Year Book of Human Rights*. Vol.21-25, 1999-2003, pp.117-132.

military power of the region, and in turn, Iraq posed a threat to the regional balances as well. The Gulf war against Iraq in 1991 helped Iran since Iraq considerably lost her military power and got economically weakened, which relaxed Iran to a certain extent. Iran preferred to take no sides in the Gulf War in 1991, and in turn, got involved in the bilateral talks to persuade Saddam Hussein to surrender some disputed territory, and to release Iranian prisoners she had been holding since Iran-Iraq war in the 1980s. Iraq entrusted to Iran to save a hundred warplanes from the US bombardments during the Gulf War. However, Iran refused to hand them over.[15] Additionally, Iran did not refrain from supporting and encouraging Shiite groups in the South of Iraq.

There has been struggle between Iran and the West. In this struggle, it is claimed that Iran used terrorism as an informal method of influence apart from diplomacy. For instance, it was claimed that Iran used some terrorist groups to kidnap some important citizens of US, UK, France and some other countries to use these hostages as a bargaining card.[16] It was believed that especially during the Khomeini regime, Iran was trying to export its regime to the other Muslim populated Middle Eastern countries. Therefore, Iran supported radical groups in these countries and pursued propaganda to achieve this end. This, in turn, resulted in the isolation of Iran in international arena economically and politically. On the other hand, all these created more instability in the region. Then, Iran's policy changed and Iran began to put national interest before the ideological interest. Iran is now following a pragmatic policy and trying to integrate into the world.[17] In May 1997, Hatemi became president in Iran and the world community was expecting a change in Iran. However, apart from some steps that helped Iran to gain some positive image, a radical change did not take place. This indicated that political power did not solely belong to Hatemi, but also to the religious leader Hameney since he was absolutely influential in the decision making process, and always played an important role. Iran regards Israel and US as important threats. During Hatemi era, armament efforts rose to the peak, and Iran implemented new policies to increase cooperation with Russia and China. Weapon sale and nuclear weapon technology appear to be important subjects in this cooperation. For instance, Hatemi's visit to Russia in March 2001 resulted in agreement on the sale of Russian weapons to Iran, which was worth seven billion dollars. Iran is also in cooperation with China to import nuclear technology as well. This situation can also be regarded as a negative development for the stability in the region.

In the post Cold War era, the US strengthened her position in the world politics and became single superpower. On the other hand, former superpower USSR, leader of the Socialist block, left the competition and disunited. The United States attempted to establish New World Order and promoted liberalism, market economy and human rights. However, there were some challenges ahead. It was too difficult to fill the power vacuums

---

[15] *The Economist*, August 17-23rd 2002, p.46.

[16] Şen, *Ortadoğuda Terör*, p.262

[17] İdris Bal, *Turkey's Relations with the West and the Turkic Republics, The rise and fall of the Turkish Model*, Aldershot (UK): Ashgate Publishing Limited, 2000, pp.118-120; For details see Edmund Herzig. *Iran and the Former Soviet South*, London: Royal Institute of International Affairs, 1995.

created as a result of the disintegration of the USSR, and the US was not alone to fill them. Regional and global powers were in a competition to gain advantage in the new situation.[18] In the post Cold War era, to maintain international peace, the US and the Western world aimed to undermine regional power centers, prevent spreading of nuclear technology and limit development of regional threat factors.[19]

Iran-Iraq war lasted for eight years and then Iraq occupied Kuwait in August 1990. After the occupation, the US formed and headed an international coalition against Iraq. Most of the countries of the region supported international coalition against Iraq including Turkey, Syria and Saudi Arabia. Turkey became one of the supporters of the American–led United Nations coalition which first imposed sanctions and waged war on Iraq in January 1991. Turkey's support for the coalition, which involved stopping all the traffic to Iraq and cutting the flow of oil through pipelines in Turkey was very much the personal policy of the late president Özal. He gave the Americans the right to use their major military bases in Turkey, İncirlik airbase to the east of Adana, for bombing raids on Iraq. Eventually, anti-Iraq coalition headed by US punished Iraq and liberated Kuwait. However, this was not the end of the problem and one may argue that the problem then had already begun. Iraq was divided into three parts: North of the 36th parallel, south of the 32nd parallel and Iraq between the 36th and the 32nd parallels. Iraq could not exercise its authority in the North and South. In the South, Shia opposition close to Iran was dominant while in the North, Kurdish groups: KDP (Kurdish Democrat Party headed by Mesud Barzani) and KPU (Kurdish Patriotic Union headed by Jalal Talabani) controlled the region, which resulted in a *de facto* state. Turcomans close to Turkey were trying to gain a grant in the North as well. There was an embargo imposed on Iraq by the UN Security Council. This embargo led to the downfall of Iraq's economy, which paved the way for the deterioration of the economies of the neighboring countries doing business with Iraq on a large scale. Therefore, not only Iraq, but also other countries like Turkey were also punished, and the international community has not so far, for instance, made up for Turkey's loss incurred because of the embargo.

The US and the UK toppled Saddam in 2003. However, there are some handicaps ahead such as 'who will be the next leader of Iraq or what kind of regime will be established after all. Will new regime be able to unite all country? Can Kurds in the North take the opportunity and establish an independent state? How will Shia majority will act, and so forth?' In general, the unstable Iraq may cause new problems in the region unless a stable new regime is established immediately. Iraq has ten percent of world oil reserves. Neighbors of Iraq are rich in petrol reserves as well. Therefore instability in Iraq will disturb not only the region, but countries which need oil will be disturbed by the instability in Iraq as well. If new regime cannot unite Iraq, conflicts similar to that of Afghanistan can take place between Sunnis, Shiites, Kurds and Turcomans. If Kurdish groups establish an independent state in the north, this move can encourage nationalism

---

[18] See, Idris Bal, "Rise of Shanghai Cooperation Organization (SCO) in Eurasia: Is it an Effective Toll in a New Big Game", Ertan Efegil, (Ed.), *Geopolitics of Central Asia in the Post Cold War Era: A Systemic Analyses*, Harlem: The Research Center for Azerbaijan and Turkestan, SOTA, the Netherlands, 2002.
[19] Oktay, *Soğuk Savaş Sonrasında Ortadoğu'yu Okumak.*, p.96

and ethnic unrest in Turkey, Syria and Iran, where there are citizens of Kurdish origin.

Deficiency of authority in the region is another source of instability in the region. Understanding the position of Lebanon in the region is important to analyze. Lebanon is a country in name but has no state authority over the homeland. In fact, guerrilla groups control some of the territory of the country. Lebanon's weakness prepares a suitable base for the terrorist groups who use this territory as a safe heaven. Lebanon is divided in terms of religion, sect, politics, ideology and terror factors. Some of the Lebanon territory is under Syrian occupation and under the influence of Iran and Palestinian Liberation Organization (PLO) and some other groups.[20] Civil war began in 1975 in Lebanon. Israeli troops occupied south Lebanon in 1982. A bomb installed in his helicopter in 1987 killed Rashid Kerami, the prime Minister of Lebanon. Then, in 1989, Rene Moawad, the president of Lebanon was killed in an assassination.[21] The devastating 16-year civil war ended in Lebanon in 1991. Since then, Lebanon has made progress toward rebuilding its political institutions. Under the Ta'if Accord--the blueprint for national reconciliation--the Lebanese have established a more equitable political system, particularly by giving Muslims a greater say in the political process while institutionalizing sectarian divisions in the government. Although some positive developments have taken place such as most of the militias have been weakened or disbanded. Israel withdraw from its security zone in southern Lebanon in May 2000, and the Lebanese Armed Forces (LAF) have extended central government authority over about two-thirds of the country, Hezbollah, the radical Shi'a party, retains its weapons and Syria maintains about 16,000 troops in Lebanon, based mainly in the east of Beirut and in the Bekaa Valley. The Arab League legitimized Syria's troop deployment in the Ta'if Accord and allowed it during Lebanon's civil war.[22] Lebanon is still an instable part of the Middle East and prepares a suitable base for the continuation of instability in the region. In order to achieve stability in the Middle East, one of the steps necessary be taken is that power vacuum in Lebanon should be filled. If this is achieved, terrorist groups will not be able to use the territory as a safe heaven and training base.

Likewise, another misfortune of the region is that some countries of the region regard terrorism as a foreign policy instrument. Since 1950's Syria, Iraq and Libya and others obtained financial and military aid from the USSR.[23] During the Cold War era, Syria for instance, was in co-operation with the USSR and the region housed some terrorist groups. In the post Cold War era, she continued to support these terrorist groups as well. Its activities in the region helped the instability in the region and undermined the efforts of co-operation among the countries of the region. Syria tends to use these groups as leverage and as an instrument for her foreign policy. For instance, as will be further discussed below, Syria used the PKK (Kurdish Workers Party) against Turkey as a bargaining card for water. PKK and radical groups were supported by both Syrian and

---

[20] İhsan Gürkan, "1989-1990 Demokrasi Devrimi ve Soğuk Savaş Dönemi Sonrasında Ortadoğu ve Türkiye", Sabahattin Şen, (ed.), *Su Sorunu Türkiye ve Ortadoğu*, İstanbul: Bağlam Yayıncılık, 1993, p.55.

[21] Faruk Sönmezoğlu, *Uluslararsı İlişkiler Sözlüğü*, İstanbul: Der Yayınları, 2000, pp.485-486.

[22] http://www.cia.gov/cia/publications/factbook/geos/le.html

[23] Gürkan, *1989-1990 Demokrasi Devrimi ve Soğuk Savaş Dönemi Sonrasında Ortadoğu ve Türkiye*, p.50.

Iranian governments. Relations between Turkey and Syria have been repaired quite recently. This is a positive development for the peace and stability in the region. Arabs encourage Russia to take part Middle East actively. They are trying to balance Israel and US by Russia. Especially after the Putin administration, Russia is willing to take part in Middle East politics. Russia is getting closer with China and Iran and is in dialogue with EU especially with Germany. This situation disturbs USA.[24] This development can make Middle East politics even more complicated.

End of Cold War and the Role of Turkey

Forth group of reasons can be regarded as potential reasons that can cause new disputes and here the role of Turkey should be underlined as well. The Cold War had frozen the map in the Middle East like elsewhere. Apart from Arab-Israeli wars and Iraq-Iran war in the region, boundary disputes did not lead to the war. However, Iraqi invasion of Kuwait in 1990, underlined importance of boundary disputes and irredentism in the region.[25] Baath movement refused artificial country maps in the region. Although Arab countries usually unite against Israel, in fact they have some territorial claims in cost of each other. Kuwait case was an example to these territorial claims. Arab-Israeli dispute shadows the fact that there are problems between Arab states over many issues. The ambiguous relations between Lebanon and Syria illustrate an example.[26]

Another aspect of the instability in the region is related to Turkey. Most of the countries in the region fall within the Ottoman hinterland and therefore, there are historical ties between Turkey and the countries of the region. However, because of the events in the history, the other powers' and new regimes' propagandas against the Ottoman Empire, there has been a cool attitude towards Turkey in Arabic World, and this stirs up the instability and prevents a real rapprochement between Turkey and her Arab neighbors. Besides, Turkish public opinion has also some doubts and vexation towards Arab people as Turkish people cannot forget the fact that some Arabs sided with the enemy, the British, in the first World War and several uprisings against the Ottoman Empire took place at a time when the Ottomans were most vulnerable. Most of the Turks regard these events as being stabbed from the back by the Arab brethren. This psychological condition and unwillingness of the Turkish and Arab sides to get rid of these kind of negative factors help the instability in the region. However, cultural, historical, geographic and economic reasons encourage Turkey and countries of the region to sustain close cooperation.[27]

The presence of Turkey as a successor of the Ottoman Empire as a relatively developed and democratic country can be regarded a positive factor. However, the region is one of the most

---

[24] See İdrisBal, "ABD'nin Orta Asya Politikasına Yön Veren İç ve Dış Dinamikler", *Stratejik Analiz*, No.12, April 2001.

[25] Oktay, *Soğuk Savaş Sonrasında Ortadoğu'yu Okumak.*, p.98.

[26] Ibid., p.98.

[27] For Turkey's relations with Middle East see articles in Idris Bal, *21. Yuzyilda Turk Dis Politikasi*, Ankara: Nobel Yayinlari, 2004, pp.643-822. For a brief account of these relations see, Tayyar Ari, "Geçmişten Günümüze Türkiye'nin Orta Doğu Politikası'nın Analizi ve İlişkileri Belirleyen Dinamikler", Idris Bal (Ed.), *21. Yuzyilda Turk Dış Politikası*, Ankara: Nobel Publications, 2004, pp.667-700.

problematic areas of the world, and the rise of the PKK in Turkey greatly has contributed a lot to instability and consequently undermined Turkey in every respect.

PKK's Role in the Regional Instability

Abdullah Öcalan founded the PKK in November 1978. Despite the military regime's measures, the leadership of the PKK managed to flee from the country. In September 1980, Öcalan settled in Damascus and with the help of the Syrian government, established training camps for his followers in the Beqa'a valley. In July 1981, the first official congress of the PKK was held on the Syrian-Lebanese border. The PKK began its guerrilla activity in the southeast Turkey in 1984. Gradually, the scale of the PKK activities increased. In 1989, the PKK concluded an alliance with a number of extreme left wing urban guerrilla groups (Dev Sol, TİKKO, DHKP-C and others), which increased its ability to strike in Turkey's big cities.[28] Clashes between the PKK and the Turkish security forces cost loss of lives of more than 40.000 people. In general, economic problems in the region, military coups and some mistakes that Turkey has made such as banning Kurdish language made negative affects on Kurdish problem and strengthened the PKK's hand to justify its terrorist counter actions and its separatist propaganda. Abdullah Öcalan was captured in 1999 while he was hiding in Greek embassy in Kenya. Although capture of Öcalan has affected the PKK in negative way, it is the fact that PKK is still an important organization and trying to carry its struggle onto the political ground. To this end, the PKK changed its name to KADEK (Kurdish Freedom and Democracy Congress) in order to get rid of the PKK's negative image at home and abroad and to portray a more positive and civilized image.

The PKK had negative effects on Turkish and regional stability in several ways. The first and most important of all, it should be underlined that when the PKK was born as a terrorist group in the region and found a suitable environment to grow. Because of power vacuum in Lebanon, she was a ready safe haven and a training base for the terrorist groups. States of the region like Syria had also experience in manipulating terrorism in their foreign policies. Under these circumstances, the PKK grew rapidly and became ruthless killing machine.

There were terrorist groups in the region mainly based in Lebanon and used by some states against Israel and other states. In an unstable Middle East, the PKK became an independent actor that furthered instability. It had thousands of men, trained for guerrilla warfare. PKK began to fill in power vacuums emerged in the region. From 1982 onwards, the Iran-Iraq war gave Kurdish organizations in Northern Iraq, Mesud Barzani's Democratic Party of Kurdistan and Jalal Talabani's Patriotic Union of Kurdistan, a free hand, because Iraq needed its troops on the front in the South. The Relations between the Marxist PKK and Barzani's rather conservative KDP were never cordial, but the latter nevertheless allowed Öcalan's followers to operate from the KDP controlled areas and the south of the Iraqi-Turkish border. This gave the PKK two routes of infiltration into Turkey, directly from Syria and over Iraq.[29]

The Gulf War of January 1991 undermined Baghdad's control over Kurds in Iraq;

---

[28] Erik J. Zürcher, *Turkey A Modern History*, London: I.B. Tauris & Co Ltd Publishers, 1994, pp.312-314.
[29] Ibid., p.313.

Barzani and Talabani were still controlling the area. A power vacuum was created in the north of 36th parallel and this enabled the PKK to establish bases and training camps in the northern Iraq.[30] This region was very suitable for the PKK to be organized and to infiltrate into Turkey, as there are high mountains in the region. Therefore, the northern Iraq can be regarded as an area more suitable for the PKK activities than the area along the Turkish Syrian boundary to infiltrate into Turkey.[31] There was a *de facto* Kurdish state in the northern Iraq. After the US occupation, if new regime in Iraq cannot unite Iraq and Kurdish groups can get international support and recognition, in turn, this Kurdish state will eventually provoke Kurds in Turkey, Iran and Syria for independence. In that case, this situation will be a supplement to the instability in the Middle East and will cause new problems and disputes. If a Kurdish state is established in the northern Iraq, some states would like to use it as instruments for their foreign policies. This will certainly create further problems and disputes. It is obvious that power vacuum in the northern Iraq helped the PKK and any Kurdish state will further help the PKK too. Turkey's unwillingness to play an active role and support for USA in the latest Gulf War (in 2003) helped Kurds in Iraq to play a vital role in the reformation of new Iraq.

Turkey is successful in combating against PKK. Ocalan was captured, power of PKK was undermined and its terrorist operations were stopped. However, the PKK badly undermined Turkey in many aspects. In general, the Turkish image and Turkish model were weakened in international arena. Thus, attraction of Turkey in the region declined, which made a negative effect on other countries' policies towards Turkey. It gave an impression that Turkey could not pursue a stable policy as it was on the verge of the separation, a kind of social, political and even geographical disintegration, so to speak.Turkish foreign policy was also undermined. While the US and the EU tend to approach the issue from the human rights perspective, Central Asian states regard the issue as an indicator of the weakness of Turkish power and Turkish model.[32] Turkey spent its limited resources in fighting with terrorism, so that the cost of PKK was more than 100 billion US $.[33] If successive effects of the problem are taken into account, cost of the problem is obviously much greater than this amount. On the other hand, combating against terrorism for a long time compelled Turkey to create active armed forces and to keep keenly critical eye on every little detail concerning possible terrorist activities in the future. After its success against PKK, Turkey is now recovering her positive image in the region and World in general.

In fact, Turkey could be (and can be) a hope for stability of the region. Turkey is located right in the center of three problematic regions, the Balkans, the Caucasus and the

---

[30] Ibid., p.314.

[31] İhsan Gürkan. "1989-1990 Demokrasi Devrimi ve Soğuk Savaş Dönemi Sonrasındsa Ortadoğu ve Türkiye", Sabahattin Şen. (Ed.). *Su Sorunu Türkiye ve Ortadoğu.* İstanbul: Bağlam Yayıncılık. 1993, pp.53-60

[32] See for Turkish Model. İdris Bal. *Turkey's Relations with the West and the Turkic Republics, The rise and fall of the Turkish Model.* Aldershot (UK): Ashgate Publishing Limited. 2000.

[33] For detailed explanations about PKK see. Nihat Ali Özcan. *PKK (Kürdistan İşçi Partisi).* Ankara: ASAM. 1999.

Middle East. All these regions have ethnic, cultural and historic ties that form a suitable base for Turkey to play a key role in regional co-operation. Turkey still remains a unique country in Islamic world. It has experience in westernization and it advocates cooperation and closeness with the West. It also has a democratic system and a market economy. Therefore, Turkey could, and in fact should be regarded as an example for the Islamic world in establishing peaceful relations and integrating with the West.

The then US president Clinton underlined Turkey's role model for the Muslim world as a bridge in 1999, during his speech at the Turkish Grand National Assembly. However, the PKK terrorism devastated Turkish democratization process by encouraging the Turkish Army's pressure to continue. Terrorism occupied the top of the domestic and foreign policy agenda of Turkey and more important issues and new opportunities were put behind and lost. If there was no problem regarding the issues discussed so far, the country could have focused on more productive issues like developing relations with the former Soviet republics, searching for other partners for alternative co-operations and/or doing business with countries that have more stable, promising bright future in every respect. Turkish sources were scarce and limited judging by the efforts made to reach all the political economical and social objectives set in advance.

Furthermore, the PKK exported instability to Europe through migrants. The PKK encouraged and helped Turkish citizens of Kurdish origin to migrate to Europe in order to be more powerful there. Several demonstrations and clashes took place in Germany and Holland where ethnic Kurds and Turks live. The PKK also financed all the anti-Turkish activities through these people. The PKK collected tribute from those people usually by threat of violence. The PKK has also managed to establish effective lobbies to change European public opinion about Turkey in a negative way. Moreover, PKK became a foreign policy instrument for the states concerned and also for the groups intending to weaken Turkish Administration. Some countries hold the PKK as a bargaining card. While Russia attempted to use PKK against Chechnya, Syria used PKK against Turkey to bargain over water issue.[34]

Fragile relations between Turkey and Arabs have been further undermined by the rise of the PKK. Some Arab states began to use the PKK as an effective bargaining weapon against Turkey. As mentioned above, there are already cool attitudes between Turks and Arabs because of bad memories of the First World War and before. With the explicit supports of some Arab countries for the PKK such as Syria, these cool attitudes can worsen the relations and turn into being hostilities. Therefore, this situation creates a psychological barrier for the future Arab-Turkish possible co-operation. For instance, if Syria had not handed over Abdullah Öcalan to Turkey or expelled him from Syria, it would have deteriorated all the possible relations, and a Syrian-Turkish war or an Arab-Turkish war would very possibly break out. Therefore, the PKK formed a new barrier before Turkish-Syrian relations, in particular and Turkish-Arab in general.

There are two main reasons that encourage Syria to support the PKK: Hatay (Alexandratte) and water issues. Syria tried to put pressure on Turkey by supporting the

---

[34] Şen, *Ortadoğuda Terör*, p.264.

PKK members who were allowed to assault from Syria to the Turkish territories. The implied bargain was that she would finish off the PKK if guarantees about the water supply were received.[35] After 1998, Greece and Greek Cypriots started a process of collaboration with the PKK and the ASALA and Greek Cypriots allowed these terrorist groups to open camps in Greek part of Cyprus. The roles given to the PKK by different countries may be contradicting, and this situation can also be regarded as destabilizing factor for the region.

In order to finance its activities the PKK became an important actor in drug smuggling, weapon smuggling, kidnapping and homicide. Likewise, the PKK attacked places known as tourism centers in Turkey and set fire to the forests in order to undermine Turkish power. The PKK planted bombs on the beaches and kidnapped some tourists to shift world opinion to Turkey to imply that this country was not a safe place to visit, and in this way, aimed to undermine the Turkish economy. PKK attempted several times to destroy the Kerkuk-Yumurtalık pipeline. The PKK meant that Turkey was not the right place in terms of security to invest in and start projects like the Baku-Ceyhan Pipeline Project.[36]

One of the by-products of the PKK terrorist activities was the rise of the Kurdish nationalism in Turkey. Not only intellectuals but also ordinary Kurdish citizens even, who are illiterate, began to adopt Kurdish nationalism because of the PKK's constant propagandas and activities. This is very important issue to consider since Turkey can face new problems in the region because of the strength of nationalism. Turkey has to carry out counter-propaganda in the region in order to gain public support if she wants to put an end to this unfavourable trend.

Conclusion

There are several factors that create instability in the Middle East, which can be divided into four groups. First group of reasons are related to political, strategic, social, cultural, ethnic and natural structures of the region. These are mainly artificial maps depicting a number of nations, diversity of religions of that particular area, a number of sects of these religions adding more to the diversity of religious teachings, holy places making the region quite extraordinary in terms of beliefs, incomplete nationalization process creating chaos and adding more to the turmoil mixed with terrorist attacks, which becomes usual atmosphere of the region, rich hydrocarbon reserves making the region more problematic rather than a land of peace and tranquility, shortage of drinking water, and absence of democratic regimes in the region. The presence of these factors prepares a suitable and fertile ground for the regional disputes, international interventions, and consequently instability.

Second group of reasons are related to Arab-Israeli conflict, which is central issue of the problem of the Middle East. This problem has several by-products such as sharp rise observed in the number of terrorist attacks, race in armament in the region that certainly prepares a suitable ground for instability.

---

[35] Zürcher, Turkey A Modern History, p.316.
[36] About this project see, Nejdet Pamir, *Bakü-Ceyhan Boru Hattı*, Ankara: ASAM, 1999.

Third group of reasons are related to the Gulf War, Iran and ideological issues. These are mainly due to the rise of Islamic regime of Iran in 1979, its war against Iraq, the Gulf War, power vacuum in northern Iraq, presence of Lebanon with limited authority over her territory, and presence of the long-lasting tradition of using terrorism as a "foreign policy instrument". Iran-Iraq war and subsequent Gulf war created power vacuums in the region that are being filled by some military and terrorist groups and the region becomes more vulnerable day by day.

Fourth group of reasons can be regarded as potential reasons that will cause new disputes in the future. Artificial structure of the region constitutes a suitable ground for the future disputes. At present, the Arab countries usually unite against Israel; meanwhile, there are problems and claims amongst themselves. Problems between Kuwait and Iraq, and Syria and Lebanon are examples of these disputes. If Arab-Israeli conflict is over, more disputes among the Arabic countries will appear.

Turkey is an important keynote actor because of her strategic position, and cultural, ethnic and historic ties with the region. It also has close relations with the West for its established multiparty system and market economy. Turkey is defined as a model for the rest of the Islamic world. However, its problematic relations with Arab states constitute important barriers for regional co-operation. Meanwhile, international community should help Israel and the Arabs to find a fair solution about their conflicts that will please all sides.

For a sincere cooperation, psychological barriers and bad memories of World War I. should be overcome. If Turkey can get rid of her handicaps and initiate a co-operation in the region and support democratization process in the region, that will open the gate for international co-operations and integrating radical groups into the societies. Despite negative effects of the PKK, in comparison with other regional countries, Turkey could be regarded as a peaceful country.

It can be argued that because of the presence of deep and complex problems in the region, it is too difficult to find an acceptable solution in short term. Above all, the presence of rich hydrocarbon resources in the region encourages outside interventions and regional conflicts. Therefore, discovering alternative energy resources and maintaining cooperation between regional and global powers can help sustain stability in the region.

17 Turkey's Middle East Challenges: Towards a New Beginning?

Meliha Benli Altunışık

Turkey's foreign policy towards the Middle East has entered into a new phase in the 1990s. After the fall of the Berlin Wall and the dissolution of the Soviet Union, unlike its NATO allies Turkey did not experience a sense of increased security, but on the contrary especially perceived threats from the Middle East. This development signaled a significant change in Turkey's relations with this region, which previously occupied a relatively minor position in Turkish strategic and foreign policy thinking. Although during the Cold War years Turkey's importance for NATO originated to some extent from its location as a buffer between the oil-rich Middle East and the Soviet Union, Turkish foreign policy makers were—with the exception of the 1950s—generally reluctant to get involved directly in the affairs of the region. Among the policy circles as well as with the opinion makers the conflict-ridden region was considered as a 'swamp' that Turkey should remain aloof. In any case Turkey's Western orientation put Turkey also ideologically apart from the region as since the establishment of the republic Turkey became much more determined to become a member of the West and did not identify itself with the Middle East.

This reluctance did not prevent Turkey to develop its economic relations especially with the oil-rich countries. Turkey also sought to develop political ties with the pro-Western countries in the region in the context of multidimensional foreign policy. Turkey's increasing support for the Palestinians in the 1970s eased some of the tensions that were very much part of the early Cold War years. Nevertheless limitations remained. The Ottoman legacy put strains on Turkey's relations with Arab nationalist regimes in the region. Whereas with Iran, either during the monarchy or after the revolution, a sense of rivalry between two major regional powers prevailed. The Islamic revolution of 1979 in Iran added an ideological bent to that rivalry.

The Emergence of Hard Security Threats

Turkey began to redefine its relationship with the region in the 1990s. The most important factor in this redefinition was the Kurdish issue. The separatist Kurdish organization, the PKK (Kurdish Workers' Party), had been waging a war against Turkey since 1984. This war entered into a new phase as a result of the Gulf War of 1991 and the subsequent developments in Iraq. The Iraqi Kurdish uprising in northern Iraq after the war and its suppression by the Saddam Hussein regime created a refugee problem of enormous proportions and put the plight of the Kurds into the international agenda. The Operation Provide Comfort (OPC) formed in January 1991 and composed of the forces of the US, the UK and France, made use of the Turkish territory first to realize the safe return of the refugees and later to enforce a no-fly zone over the 36th parallel.[1] As a result of such activity in October 1991 Saddam Hussein withdrew the central government administration from some Kurdish populated areas and thus led to a creation of a Kurdish enclave, which went below the 36th parallel in the northeastern part of the country. Thus began a new era in Iraqi history: the central government lost its effective control over the mostly Kurdish-populated areas in the north where a no man's land was created. Over the next twelve years, till the Iraq War of 2003, a Kurdish self-rule was allowed to flourish under the US and UK protection, as France withdrew from the OPC in the meantime. Within this context elections were held in 1992 and a regional government was organized. The stability in this part of Iraq was disturbed between 1994-1997, however, as a result of in-fighting between the two main Kurdish factions, namely the Kurdish Democratic Party (KDP) of Masoud Barzani and the Patriotic Union of Kurdistan (PUK) of the Celal Talabani. In the process, the KDP even allied itself with Saddam regime and fought against the PUK, invaded Sulaimania, which eventually led to US personnel and their local allies to leave the area in 1996. Realizing that Baghdad could reinstute its control over the north, Washington brokered an agreement between the two Kurdish factions in 1997. The two parties began to govern the area in relative peace afterwards, but only through an establishment of two separate administrations: The PUK was based in Sulaimania and governed the area that runs along the Iranian border. The KDP was based in Erbil and governed the northern part of the enclave. Thus effectively two parallel administrations were created. Financially the enclave depended on its share of the oil-for-food program and the cross-border trade with Turkey.

The developments in northern Iraq presented a very complex challenge to Turkey. First, there were conventional threats to its security. The PKK making good use of the developments in northern Iraq had established itself a base there. The organization thus gained a momentum especially in the first part of the 1990s. In addition the Kurdish self rule heightened the concerns of a possible disintegration of Iraq and the establishment of a Kurdish state with irredentist claims over Kurdish populated regions of neighboring countries including Turkey. Finally the involvement of the major external powers in the issue seemed to bring back the traumatic experiences of the disintegration of the Ottoman Empire, the war of independence, and the establishment of the republic of Turkey. Thus, the embedded tensions between Turkey's experience with the West resurfaced. These tensions go back at least to the 19th century where the Ottoman reformers were trying to reorganize the state and to some extent the society along Western lines, while at the same time dealing with increasing Western economic and political encroachment. Similarly narrative of the war of independence always underlined that it was a war "against the

---

[1] The humanitarian emergency due to the Iraqi Kurdish refugee crisis led the UN Security Council to adopt Resolution 688 which called for measures to end human suffering which was also regarded as a threat to international peace and security. The Resolution in fact made a reference to Chapter 7 of the UN Charter. Thus it can be considered as the first example of humanitarian intervention, a new modality that started to be used by the UN within its newly-defined post-Cold War roles. The US, the UK and France interpreted this resolution to create a safe haven in northern Iraq and thus formed a military force, OPC, to enforce it. The Turkish Grand National Assembly extended the mandate for the OPC in every six months.

West" with the ultimate aim of "being part of the West" as it represented the "contemporary civilization". These tensions that were frozen during the Cold War resurfaced mainly as a result of the Iraqi issue. Ankara on the one hand acted with its allies in the Gulf War and in the post-War developments in the Iraqi issue. Yet some groups within the state continued to have suspicions about the intentions of its allies as regards to Iraq and even as regards to Turkey. The images of the Sevres treaty, which was imposed on the Ottoman Empire after World War I and allowed the creation of a Turkish state only over a small portion of central Anatolia, were evoked. These concerns were also reflected in the debates about the extension of the mandate of the Operation Provide Comfort (later renamed Northern Watch in 1997).[2] In the meantime Turkey's regional identity was started to be a subject of debate as being a member of NATO was no longer enough to make Turkey as part of "the West". The rejection of Turkey's bid for membership in the European Community (EC) in 1987 further underlined this confusion about regional identity. The domestic identity of the regime also came under pressure when political Islamists and Kurdish nationalists began to challenge its secular and unitary nature respectively.

The Kurdish issue dominated Turkey's relations with its other two Middle Eastern neighbors: Syria and Iran. Especially with Syria the conflict as regards to Syrian support to the PKK culminated in a crisis in October 1998. Turkish-Iranian relations too were effected from time to time by the accusations of Turkey that Iran was also giving support to the PKK.[3] Thus the Kurdish issue had become an Achilles heel for Turkey as Syria and Iran, having their own sensitivities about their Kurdish minorities, did not refrain from using this issue against Turkey. Especially for Syria support for the PKK became a trump card to be used in its water conflict with Turkey.[4] Furthermore, in the context of general insecurity felt by Turkish policy makers in that period and specifically rising challenge of the political Islamists, the ideological conflict with Iran also intensified more so than it existed in the first decade of the revolution.

Thus in the 1990s Turkey's foreign policy towards the Middle East was largely formulated through the lens of the Kurdish issue. Due to the fact that the war with the separatist PKK intensified largely as a result of the direct and indirect support provided to it by Turkey's Middle Eastern neighbors, traditional power politics approach dominated Turkey's relations with the region. The 'referent object' of security became Turkey's

---

[2] Meliha Benli Altunisik, "Turkish-US Security Relations: The Middle East Dimension", Mustafa Aydın and Cagrı Erhan (eds) *Turkish-American Relations: 200 Years of Divergence and Convergence*, London: Routledge, 2004.

[3] Kemal Kirisci, "The Future of Turkish policy toward the Middle East," Barry Rubin and Kemal Kirisci (Eds.), *Turkey in World Politics: An Emerging Multiregional Power*, Boulder and London: Lynne Rienner Publishers, 2001, pp.125-126.

[4] Water conflict with Syria and Iraq emerged in the mid-1980s over the utilization of the waters of Euphrates and Tigris rivers. Both Syria and Iraq threatened by the launching of Turkey's multi-billion dollar ambitious Southeastern Anatolian Project (GAP), which consists of network of dams and irrigation schemes. For more on the water issue see, Ayşegül Kibaroğlu, *Building a Regime for the Waters of the Euphrates-Tigris River Basin*, The Netherlands: Martinus Nijhoff, 2002.

territorial integrity.[5] Ankara redefined its strategy and identified the Middle East as the number one source of threat to Turkey. Casting of the issue as one of an existential threat called for extraordinary measures beyond the traditional policy means.[6]

Turkey adopted a multifaceted policy in Iraq. On the one hand it tried to end the PKK presence there through the use of military force. During those years the Turkish Armed Forces staged regular incursions into the northern Iraq. A few of them like the one in March 1995 were quite big operations. Such operations both inside Turkey and in northern Iraq constituted an important reason for the military's support for the OPC, despite harsh criticisms from politicians such as Bülent Ecevit. In addition to its benefits like preventing another refugee flow to Turkey, the army valued its cooperation with the OPC as it allowed Turkey's operations in northern Iraq.[7] Eventually Turkey even established a permanent presence of special forces in northern Iraq in mid-1990s. As part of its strategy in Iraq Turkey also cultivated relations with the Kurdish groups in northern Iraq both to enlist their support against the PKK and also to have leverage over the developments there. Turkey provided diplomatic passports to both Barzani and Talabani and became their link to the outside world. In addition to allowing for border trade, Ankara even provided economic aid to them. Most importantly, however, by allowing the US and the UK forces to use İncirlik airbase Turkey was key for the continuation of the north's de facto independence from Baghdad. Finally, Turkey hoped to increase its cards in future developments in Iraq by actively supporting the cause of the Turkmens there. Iraqi Turkmens constitute the third ethnic group in Iraq, who are part of the educated middle class and largely dispersed as a result of Saddam regime's policies. As with other groups in Iraq there are no dependable figures as to their numbers, although the estimates vary from 600,000 to 3 million. Turkey began to establish contacts with the Turkmens and to support their organization in the 1990s.

In the Turkish-Syrian relations Turkey did not refrain from using the threat to use force. The relations between the two countries had been escalating for some time. On January 23, 1996 Turkish Foreign Ministry send a memorandum to Damascus asking Syria to cease its support to the PKK and if not, declaring Turkey's "right to respond with any measure it deems appropriate at an appropriate time." The Syrian regime did not respond and Turkey froze all its relations with Syria.[8] There were even limited border skirmishes in that year. The two consecutive governments that came to power between 1996 and 1998, however, made last ditch efforts to solve the issue diplomatically. The Welfare (Refah) Party, the senior coalition partner of the government from July 1996 to June 1997, put the improvement of Turkey's relations with Syria, together with Iran and Iraq, on the list of priorities.[9] Similarly, the government under Prime Minister Mesut

---

[5] Barry Buzan et.al. *Security: A New Framework for Anaysis*, Boulder, London: Lynne Rienner Publishers, 1998, p.20.
[6] Ibid.
[7] Hasan Cemal, *Kürtler* (Kurds), Istanbul: Doğan yayıncılık, 2003, pp.286-7.
[8] Şükrü Elekdağ, "Suriye'ye karşı strateji yokluğu", (Lack of strategy against Syria) from "Dünyaya Bakış" (A Glimpse at the World) column, *Milliyet*, 21 September 1998.
[9] *Hürriyet*, 1 July 1996.

Yılmaz, leader of the Motherland (*Anavatan*) Party, made an effort to solve Turkey's problems with Syria diplomatically through especially the initiatives of Foreign Minister Ismail Cem.[10] However, these efforts also failed. The National Security Council meeting in September 1998 approved a plan of action. As a result, the tension between Turkey and Syria quickly escalated in late 1998 when Ankara issued an ultimatum and reinforced its troops in its Syrian border. The crisis was finally resolved as Abdullah Öcalan, the leader of the PKK, left Damascus and the representatives of the two countries met in Adana, Turkey, and signed an agreement in which Damascus agreed to stop all its support to the PKK.

Another response given by Ankara to increasing threats coming from its immediate Middle Eastern neighbors was to emphasize the security aspect of Turkish-Israeli relations that had been normalizing since the beginning of the 1990s as a result of the Arab-Israeli peace process. Turkey, which had been reluctant to involve in open security cooperation with Israel, began to reconsider this policy in the mid-1990s. As a result, Turkey and Israel established close ties in security related matters and signed two military agreements to further their relations in this area.[11]

Turkey's new policies led to general deterioration of Turkey's relations with the region in general. The burgeoning ties with Israel represented a bold initiative on the part of Turkey. For the first time in the republican history Turkey openly engaged in a strategic alignment with Israel and felt no restraint to publicize this relationship. Because of its deepening ties with Israel, Turkey became a focal point of criticism from several regional states. In contrast to earlier policy of balancing, this time Ankara seemed like not paying much attention to the problems in the Arab-Israeli peace process and largely disregarded the criticism coming from the regional states. The timing of Turkey's increasing military ties with Israel was especially problematic for the Arab states as during the government of Benjamin Netanyahu in Israel the peace process stalled. The Arab states, therefore, perceived Turkish-Israeli relations as a development that would drastically change regional balance of power in favor of Israel. The regional states were also concerned about the fact that Turkish-Israeli alignment also gave Turkey an additional leverage in the region. However, Ankara's perception of threats coming from its immediate Middle Eastern neighbors took precedence over other issues in the Middle East and what they were basically concerned was to offset those threats. There was widespread consensus on Turkey's new Middle East policy at home. For instance, except the Islamist Welfare (*Refah*) Party,[12] all parties with different ideological backgrounds supported the policy. Domestically the military was successful in the 1990s in establishing an alliance with different segments of the Turkish society on the basis of "threats to Turkey's secularism and its territorial integrity". These "internal threats" were openly linked again by the

---

[10] *Yeni Yüzyıl*, 18 Mart 1998.

[11] Military Training and Cooperation Agreement and Defense Cooperation Agreement both in 1996.

[12] Before coming to power *Refah* (Welfare) Party was very critical of Turkish-Israeli relations. Several RP officials were threatening to tear up the agreements that were signed between the two countries. Yet once in power RP did little to prevent further development of relations. See Altunışık. *Turkish-US Security Relations: The Middle East Dimension*, pp.68-70.

military to Syria and Iran. Therefore, relations with Israel were presented and largely perceived within this context, and thus supported by the members of this domestic alliance formed around the military.

However, under close scrutiny the new Middle East policy showed some nuances. Ankara was trying to make it clear that it was not really taking sides in the Arab-Israeli issues, but yet aiming to defend itself from the threats coming from the region. Therefore, during this period Turkey made sure to have good relations with Jordan and the Palestinian National Authority (PNA). With Jordan Turkey also developed military relations, however, especially because of Jordanian sensitivities, these relations were not advertised. Jordan also participated as an observer in the joint naval exercises in the Mediterrannean by the US, Israel and Turkey.[13] Furthermore, Ankara placed a lot of emphasis on explaining its new policy to Egypt. High-level contacts between presidents Süleyman Demirel and Husni Mubarak became a vehicle of this approach. Turkey made the point that it did not treat all Arab countries as a monolith and, in fact, countries like Jordan, Egypt, Algeria, Tunisia and the Gulf countries had good relations with Turkey. Although this was true, because of inter-Arab balances, Syria, which led the opposition towards Turkey, swayed the Arab world. Interestingly Turkey had good relations bilaterally with several Arab countries, and yet its relations with the Arab world in general remained problematic. This was reflected most in the Arab League meetings where Turkey was frequently criticized for its ties with Israel, its water problems with Syria and Iraq, and its Iraq policy. The strong sense of Arab regional identity was a factor that limited Turkey's efforts to develop better relations with the Arab countries.

Yet overall hard security considerations dominated Turkey's foreign policy towards the region throughout most of the 1990s. Especially in the context of the armed conflict with the Kurdish separatist PKK Turkey's policy was very much influenced by its concerns and sensitivities in this issue.

Limited 'Desecuritization'[14] of Turkey's Middle East policy

At the end of the 1990s there appeared some signs of a new opening in Turkey's Middle East policy. The most important development in that respect was the October 1998 crisis with Syria, resolving of which created a thaw in Turkey's Middle East policy. Since the Adana Agreement Turkish-Syrian relations have improved considerably. There were immediate developments in sesurity area. The measures that were called for in the Adana agreement, such as regular security meetings, hotline, the appointment of four special security officials to each other's diplomatic missions were put into place. As a result of this security cooperation, PKK's training camps in Syria were closed and the logistical support to the organization stopped.[15] Since then the two countries have escalated their

---

[13] For Turkey's relations with the PNA and Jordan see, Kemal Kirişçi, "Turkey and the Muslim Middle East", Alan Makovsky and Sabri Sayarı (Eds.), *Turkey's New World: Changing Dynamics in Turkish Foreign Policy*, Washington. DC: The Washington Institute For Near East Policy, 2000, pp.48-50.

[14] This conceptualization belongs to Barry Buzan et. al. where it is defined as moving issues out of "threat-defense sequence and into ordinary public sphere." Buzan et. al. *Security: A new Framework for Anaysis*, pp.23-24 and 29.

[15] Sami Kohen, "Apo neden (baştan) Suriye'den istenmedi?" (Why didn't Turkey ask for Apo's extradition

efforts to look for ways to increase cooperation and dialogue. Even a military cooperation agreement that is based on mutual exchange of military personnel, mutual invitations for monitoring war games, and military training was signed. Turkish President Ahmet Necdet Sezer's attendance to Hafiz al-Asad's funeral represented a turning point. Syrian vice-president Abdul-Halim Khaddam's visit to Turkey followed it in November. In July 2003 Syrian Prime Minister Mohammed Mustafa Miro became the first Syrian prime minister to visit Turkey in 17 years. Three agreements on health, oil and natural gas, and custom matters were signed during this visit to further enhance cooperation between the two countries. At the same time visits at ministerial and technical levels intensively conducted on a reciprocal basis to further social and economic cooperation. Trade between Turkey and Syria reached the $1 billion benchmark in 2002. As a sign of improving ties, Turkish companies established 12 investment projects in Syria in 2003, especially in the textile and oil industries. In 2001, both countries agreed to open two borders check points for their citizens to visit their relatives and exempted them from border fees. The improvement in relations culminated in the visit by Syrian President Bashar al-Assad in January 2004 –the first official visit by a Syrian head of state in 57 years—during which specific measures were taken to improve economic relations as well as coordination and consultation on regional issues, especially the situation in Iraq.

The Adana agreement and later the capture of Öcalan in Kenya in February 1999 after a long odyssey largely freed Turkey's policy towards the Arab world from being a hostage to this issue. After the crisis with Syria there appeared new possibilities of normalizing relations with the region as a whole. For instance, relations with Egypt improved after 1998. President Demirel's visit to Cairo on July 1999 was a turning point in that respect. During that visit for the first time since the signing of Turkish-Israeli agreement in February 1996, there was no mention of Turkish-Israeli relations.

There were improvements in Turkish-Iranian relations as well. The election of Muhammed Khatami and the fall of the Islamist Welfare Party government in Turkey put an end to the crisis between the two countries and led to a gradual improvement. The two countries started a process of security cooperation against the PKK, which eventually led to the signing of a memorandum of understanding in January 2000. In the meantime, in Turkish-Israeli relations there was transition form hyperactivity to normal ties. Unlike in the mid-1990s, Ankara opted to play low-key in its relations with Israel. Ankara's attampts to improve its ties with other regional powers largely removed Turkish-Israeli relations from the regional agenda.

In addition to the changing nature of relations with Syria that brought a general thaw in Turkey's relations with the Middle East, there were other factors that led to the relative desecuritization of Turkey's policy towards the region.

First of all, there were some regional developments that paved the way for a slight shift in Turkey's policy. One was the coming of power of Ehud Barak government in Israel. As an opposition leader Barak had frequently giving the Syrians the message that they need not be concerned with Turkish-Israeli military cooperation and was, in general,

---

at the beginning?) from "Yorum" (Comment) column, *Milliyet*, 5 December 1998.

showing his apprehension about possible negative effects of Turkish-Israeli relations.[16] During the election campaign Barak also stressed his objective of making peace with Syria soon. This once again increased Ankara's concerns about being left out with its problems with Syria. The timing of the Turkish-Syrian crisis can be to some extent explained by these concerns. On the other hand, Barak's declared commitment to sign peace treaties in all tracks seemed to force Turkey to prepare itself for a post-peace environment. In such an environment it was clear that Turkey could not just rely on its ties with Israel. On the Arab front too there were changes. Egypt seemed to be concerned about the post-peace order in the Middle East and in that environment those who argued for including Turkey rather than alienating it gained an upper hand. Some Egyptian analysts even began to consider Turkey as one of the core countries in the future establishment of a Middle Eastern security cooperation framework.[17] Syria also might have wanted to strengthen its hand against Israel and thus engaging Turkey in cooperation rather than in conflict after October 1998 crisis. In the case of Iran the strengthening of the reformists in Iranian politics paved the way for normalization in relations between the two countries.

More importantly, however, there were some domestic changes in Turkey that brought a new approach in Turkey's Middle East policy: First of all, in the military, the most vocal advocates of Turkish-Israeli military ties left the army. It is safe to argue that their absence at least changed the style of handling Turkey's relations with Israel. This, together with the resolution of the main problem with Syria gave Democratic Left (*Demokratik Sol*) Party, the main coalition partner that also held the Foreign Ministry, to implement its program of "regionally-based foreign policy". Such an approach was based on the argument that Turkey should develop good relations in all its regions, and thus play an important role in these regions independent of its ties with the West. In fact, in line with this argument, even during the height of Turkish-Israeli relations the Foreign Ministry was thought to warn for caution and advocated a slower pace in improving relations with Israel. The other senior coalition partner, ultra-nationalist National Action (*Milliyetçi Hareket*) Party, also was an advocate of improving relations especially with Baghdad to be able to control the negative implications of the developments in Iraq for Turkey.

Nevertheless, the most important development that led to a limited desecuritization was decreasing sense of insecurity in Ankara during this period. Some developments in the domestic front eased the urgency of "internal threats" and thus created a possibility of easing of tensions in Turkey's Middle East policy. The capture and subsequently the trial of Abdullah Öcalan, the PKK's decision to call off its 15-year war and the declarations of the military victory over the PKK on the one hand, and the closure of the Welfare Party and the weak showing in the elections of the Virtue (*Fazilet*) Party, on the other hand, decreased the sense of insecurity. In the meantime the improvement in Turkey's relations with the EU increased confidence in Turkey. At the December 1999 Helsinki Summit the

---

[16] *Ha'aretz* (English Edition), 16 June 1998.
[17] Personal contact, October 2000.

EU finally decided to accept Turkey's candidacy for membership. Since 1987, all of its previous applications to join the EU had been rejected, thus this decision boosted the self-confidence. Turkey's increased military strength by the late 1990s was another factor that led to confidence and thus eased the concerns about the threats. In fact, the Turkish military modernization began to give Turkey capabilities that far outstrip those of its Middle Eastern neighbors. As a result, same analyst began to consider Turkey as becoming an independent security actor.[18]

However, despite such attempts to desecuritize Ankara's relations with the Middle East the uncertainty surrounding Iraq continued to put constraints on Turkey's Middle East policy. During this period Turkey also added a new element to its Iraq policy; that is to improve its relations with Baghdad. This policy was specifically justified by increasing losses of Turkey from the embargo and consequently rising criticism of the UN sanctions regime in Turkey. Being aware of the financial difficulties the embargo imposed on the already weak economy of southeastern Turkey and thus its impact on rising Kurdish nationalism, for many years Turkey and the UN turned a blind eye to the illegal trade based on export of cheap crude oil from Iraq through tankers to Turkey. However, due to increasing oil company protests this trade became limited in the late 1990s. In response local interest groups, such as the Turkish-Iraqi Friendship Association, started to increase their pressure on Ankara for the lifting of sanctions. There was in general increasing criticism of the UN sanctions regime also because of its negative political and strategic implications. Prime Minister Bülent Ecevit has long been uneasy about the US policy towards Iraq and its implications for Turkey. Finally, the fact that more and more countries began to challenge the US policy on Iraq both inside and outside the region gave Turkey an opportunity to make some changes in its Iraq policy. After the easing of the oil-for-food program for Iraq in December 1999 with UN Resolution 1284, Turkey as well began to seek opportunities for improving economic relations with that country. State Minister's visit to Iraq with 100 export companies was touted as "a new page" in Turkish-Iraqi relations; several Turkish humanitarian aid planes were sent to Baghdad; and Turkey restored the diplomatic ties with Baghdad at an ambassadorial level in January. There was also talk of opening a second border with Iraq and to build a natural gas pipeline from Iraq to Turkey. In the meantime, the rail link between the two countries was reopened in April.

George W. Bush Administration's policy of getting though on Iraq limited Turkey's opening up to Baghdad. Ankara identified the possible division of Iraq as a major security threat. However, the reintegration of that country under the Saddam regime could also present challenges. Ankara already had several problems with Baghdad before the Gulf War and concerned about facing a more hostile one in the future. The Turkish government already accused Iraq for harboring the PKK since 1998.[19] Therefore, the Iraqi issue was full of minefields for Turkey.

---

[18] Michael Robert Hickok, "Hegemon Rising: The Gap Between Turkish Strategy and Military Modernization", *Parameters: US Army War College*, Vol.30, No.2, 2000, pp.105-110.
[19] *Radikal*, 16 February 1999.

The Iraq War of 2003

Since the Gulf War of 1991 Turkey's foreign policy towards the Middle East has been very much influenced by the developments in the Iraqi issue, which presented Turkey with complex challenges. On the one hand Turkey acted with the US, but on the other hand, all the way Turkey was very much concerned about what the US policy meant in terms of the future of Iraq and Turkey's interests there. Therefore, from the beginning there was an ambiguity in Turkey's policy towards Iraq. Within this ambiguity, Turkey tried to develop coherent policies to deal with this complexity. Overall however there was a lot of frustration about the Iraqi issue throughout the 1990's in Turkey, widely shared by the policymakers and the public at large. According to this view, Turkey had suffered in two main ways as a result of this war: First, the war and the international sanctions against Iraq had cost Turkey economically. The estimates of Turkey's economic loss varied from US\$ 40 billion to US\$ 60 billion, including indirect costs. Second, and maybe more importantly, was the security challenges that emanated from what happened in Iraq after 1991. Turkey's experience in the 1991 Gulf War and the way this experience has been read in the country was omnipresent in Turkey's interpretation of the recent Iraqi crisis and the war, again both at the public and the policy-making levels.

Therefore the re-emergence of conflict between Iraq and the US intensified the ambiguity in terms of Turkey's policy. On the one hand, it was seen as a way to resolve this situation: the status quo was seen as detrimental to Turkey's interests. Nevertheless, on the negative side there was an increased uneasiness about the situation: Turkey was concerned about possible political, strategic and economic ramifications of such a war. Turkish policy-makers seemed to be daunted by the enormous scale of post-war challenge and possible instability that could emerge in Iraq after such an operation. In addition, there were concerns about a potential upsurge in Kurdish nationalism that could accompany the war, which could in turn have implications for Turkish national security. In fact, the Prime Minister Bülent Ecevit on numerous occasions articulated these concerns quite openly when he said in a CNN interview for instance that an attack on Iraq could lead to the portioning out of Iraq, which could create problems for Turkey and for Turkey's territorial integrity.[20] That was a very clear expression of the concerns in Ankara at that time. In fact, the government and several parties in opposition frequently voiced their displeasure with the developments in northern Iraq, such as the announcement of a constitution for a federal Kurdish region with Kirkuk as the regional capital. In that atmosphere Ankara even went as far as declaring the establishment of a Kurdish state and the expansion of Kurdish control to oil-rich Kirkuk as *casus belli*.

The problems came to surface when the Bush administration decided to start a war against Iraq and sought Turkey's support. Washington's highly comprehensive list of requests created a debate in Turkey as to the level of Turkey's involvement in the possible war. The ambiguities in the Iraqi issue and US-Turkish relations with respect to Iraq came to the fore in this atmosphere. The newly elected AKP (*Justice and Development Party*) government, already overwhelmed by economic crisis, Copenhagen Summit of the

---

[20] *CNN.com,* 16 October 2002.

EU and the Annan Plan for the resolution of the Cyprus problem, engaged in an intense bargaining with the Bush administration.

The background of the earlier bargaining between the two countries framed to some extent the latest negotiation process. Turkey's bargaining position was largely affected by the commitment to "not to repeat the mistakes of the past". The belief that Turkey has suffered significant economic losses due to the Gulf War of 1991 led the government to insist on clear commitments and large financial compensation from the US. In addition the Turkish foreign and security elite was anxious about possible political and security implications of such a war and seeking commitments to prevent any unwanted consequences such as the establishment of a Kurdish state. After a hard bargaining an understanding was reached and the AKP government took that to the parliament for approval. The TGNA voted on March 1, 2003 264 to 250 in favour of the motion but was three votes shy of a constitutionally mandated simple majority since there were 19 absentees.

One very important factor was the role of public opposition to the War and Turkey's participation in it. This opposition grew over the course of the negotiations and reached to about 90 percent. The newly established AKP, which got an impressive 35 percent votes in its first election, was especially sensitive to such an opposition as its main strength within body politic lies with the public support. The party's Islamist core especially became quite vocal in its critique of the war. Lack of international support for the US also strengthened the hand of those who opposed the war and complicated Turkey's position. Finally, the ambiguities of the military and the foreign policy bureaucracy clearly played a role in facilitating Turkey's reluctance to get involved in the war. The US administration attitude throughout the negotiation process and its increasing ties with the Kurdish opposition in Iraq were problematic from their perspective. The exclusion of Turkmens, ethnic Turks in Iraq, from the Iraqi opposition meeting sponsored by Washington in northern Iraq on 26 February-1 March 2003 only helped to substantiate these concerns.

Turkish parliament's rejection of the deal that would have allowed the US to move 62,000 troops through Turkish territory to open a northern front in the war created a major crisis in Turkish-American relations. Determined to start a war against Iraq and topple Saddam Hussein regime, Washington was forced to change its war plans. Already frustrated by Ankara's tough bargaining the Bush administration seemed to feel let down by Turkey. At the end of March the Turkish parliament adopted a new bill, which was passed by 332 votes to 202 that granted over flight rights to US. This motion clearly left most of the US military requests unfulfilled. Washington was not even permitted to use airbases, including for refuelling. Furthermore the new bill led to another crisis in relations between the two countries as it also authorised the entry of the Turkish troops into Iraq if necessary. The possibility of unilateral incursions alarmed the Bush administration, which openly talked about its concerns related to the intentions of the Turkish army and a complicating possibility of a Kurdish-Turkish war in Iraq. That crisis was resolved when Turkey gave assurances that it would only intervene in the case of tide of refugees from Iraq or an establishment of a Kurdish state, both of which was not going to happen anyway according to the Bush administration. Secretary of State Colin Powell's visit to Ankara in April 2003 was a successful attempt to heal the rift. Despite some improvement in the relationship, the instability inherent in terms of their positions in Iraq once again highlighted when 11 Turkish soldiers, part of the Turkish contingent in northern Iraq, which was permanently stationed there since the mid-1990s, were took into custody by the US forces in July 2003 over an alleged plot to harm Iraqi Kurdish civilian officials, a claim denied by Turkey. After a weekend of intense negotiations between Ankara and Washington the soldiers were returned. However, the incident created uproar in Turkey. Turkey's chief of staff Hilmi Özkök characterised the incident as a major crisis of trust between Turkish and US armed forces and maintained that 'I don't think this is US armed forces policy, but I have a great difficulty in seeing it as a local event.'[21]

In the meantime the elements of Turkey's policy towards Iraq were once more reiterated. The first one was the concern about keeping Iraq's territorial integrity intact. That has been the corner stone of Turkish foreign policy towards this issue from the beginning and after the war the ensuing chaos in some parts and the difficulty of the US in controlling Iraq, exacerbated the concerns about the territorial integrity of Iraq. A related concern has been the presence of PKK/KADEK in Iraq. Another consideration has been Turkey's limited military presence in Iraq. Ankara has been arguing that as long as the PKK/KADEK remains in Iraq, it should be able to keep its military presence there. However, as the Suleimania incident has shown there may be future tensions as to their existence.

Another aspect of Turkey's Iraq policy has been the concern about the nature of the future Iraqi regime. Turkey initially was opposing to a federal structure. Later Ankara readjusted its position to argue that Turkey did not favor federalism based on ethnicity or sectarian differences, but rather supports a form of administrative federalism. Within that context Turkey adamantly opposed to Kurdish control of Kirkuk because of the importance of that region for oil wells and how that could contributed to eventual consolidation of Kurdish control over these areas and maybe eventual disintegration of Iraq. Turkey has also been calling for a census before elections in Iraq. The last dependable census in the country took place in 1957. It is clear that espacially for constructing a new Iraq based on representation of ethnic and sectarian differences a new census is essential. Finally, Turkey's policy towards Iraq has been emphasizing Turkmens, especially what is called the protection of political rights of Turkmens in future Iraq.

Thus Turkey has wanted to have a say in Iraq so that it can prevent developments that it considers to be against its interests. As to the means to achieve this overall objective initially there was much more emphasis on military means. Those who supported the failed motion that called for Turkey's involvement in the Iraq war, including the Prime Minister Tayyip Erdoğan himself, were justifying their positions by emphasizing that this could be a way for Turkey to have a say in the post-war Iraqi scene. A second attempt to achieve Turkey's objectives through the use of military came when the US and Turkey

---

[21] *Hürriyet*, 5 July 2003.

came up with the idea of sending approximately 10,000 Turkish troops to Iraq as a Stability Force. On October 7, 2003 the Turkish Grand National Assembly passed a motion authorizing the deployment of troops in Iraq. Turkish troops were going to be deployed in the "Sunni traingle" where the US forces were facing the fiercest resistance. However that initiative failed because the US backed down when it faced opposition from Iraqi Governing Council. The Kurdish groups opposed the presence of Turkish troops, which would inevitably use northern Iraq not only to enter the country but also as supply routes. The Arabs on the other hand argued for non-involvement of the neighbors of Iraq.[22] Thus the debate over means inevitably has shifted to non-military means of being part of Iraqi reconstruction, which means that Turkey in a way, at least for now, has to rely on the US to address its security concerns in Iraq.

There is now a discussion under way in Turkey as to political and economic means to which Turkey can become part of reconstruction in post-War Iraq. The Turkish foreign ministry seems to be working for increased economic ties with Iraq while at the same time Turkey is trying to be part of the political developments as well. Yet there are serious limitations in that regard, particularly when considering the perspective of most of the groups in Iraq regarding Turkish involvement. Even there are limitations in Turkey's involvement in economic reconstructing. Foreign Ministry has launched an initiative with the public and private companies to support especially Turkey's involvement in food and construction sectors as well as the revitalization of transportation business in southeastern Turkey.[23] Turkey's economic involvement in Iraqi reconstruction was supported by the US. Nevertheless the problem of insecurity in Iraq continues to limit such an involvement. Similarly the Kirkuk-Yumurtalik oil pipeline has not been in full operation for a sustained period of time, again due to the problems of security.

There are still uncertainties as to what will happen in Iraq and Turkey is trying to develop strategies to deal with that uncertainty on a subject that is considered as vital to Turkey's interests. Within this context Turkey has also been engaging in regional countries to discuss regional developments and the Iraqi issue in particular with the perspective of initiating regional alternatives. Turkey's Middle East Initiative to galvanize the country's neighbors on the Iraqi crisis started before the war. To that end then Prime Minister Abdullah Gül began a tour of Middle East countries. However, that initiative largely failed as most of the countries in the region, despite their concerns about the war, did not want to be seen as opposing to the US and did not want to explain to their public their inaction in the face of Turkey's activism in this regard.[24] Yet Turkey's efforts continued after the war Turkey launched the regional states initiative in January 2003. The fifth foreign ministers' summit of Iraq's neighbors and regional states was held in Kuwait on February 14-15, 2004. In the meantime Turkey continued its consultation with Iran and Syria, the two countries equally sensitive about a possible disintegration of Iraq, as regards to the developments in that country. Ankara, however, tries to balance its

---

[22] Ibrahim al-Marashi, "A New Chapter in Iraqi-Turkish Relations? Examining Iraqi and Arab Reactions to the Turkish Deployment to Iraq," *Insight Turkey*, Vol. 6, No. 1, January-March 2004, pp. 119-128.
[23] *Hürriyet*, 4 May 2003.
[24] Personal contact with a Turkish Foreign Ministry official.

regional initiatives with its relations with the US and acts carefully not to give the impression of a counter-alliance to US policies.

Conclusions

In the 1990s Turkey's Middle East policy was based on traditional security threats. Turkey's domestic war with the Kurdish separatist PKK intermingled with the regional developments to create a sense of vulnerability and threat perception in Ankara. Turkey responded to this new environment by increasing use of military force in addition to diplomatic means including fostering new alignments.

However, there has been a limited desecuritization of Turkish foreign policy towards the Middle East since the end of the 1990s due to several internal and external reasons. The uncertainties as regards to Iraq prevented total desecuritization. In addition long-term issues limited Turkey's options in the region. Historical legacy, the domestic uncertainties and ongoing debates about Turkey's international and domestic identity, all made it difficult for the political elite to develop a coherent Middle East policy based on a long-term vision. The general lack of understanding and the appreciation of the complexities of the region further complicated the problem. Interestingly this is also true for the Islamists that have generally been ardent supporters of good relations with the Middle East. Their vision of Turkey's relations with the region is based on various forms of what came to be termed as Neo-Ottomanism, which is obviously quite disturbing and patronizing from the perspective of the Arab states. Furthermore, their Islamist ideology is also considered a problem for many Arab regimes, which are struggling with their own Islamists. Finally, there were several limitations to Turkey's policy towards the region, emanating from the region itself. First, the Arab world's perception of Turkey is still very much colored with their Ottoman experience, Turkey's secularism, Cold War alliances and Turkey's desire to be part of the West rather than the Middle East. Second, there is no agreement or clarity on how to engage Turkey. On the one hand, Turkey is sometimes criticized for its "disinterest in the Middle East" and "severing its ties with the region". On the other hand, when Turkey is active in the region there are apprehensions about its role. It is either considered as a "Western stooge" or "trying to impose a hegemony", political, military and economic.[25] Third, despite Turkey's desire to consider the Arab world not as a monolith and improve its bilateral ties, the existence of strong sense of regional identity makes this quite difficult and from time to time, Turkey, as a non-Arab country, plays the role of bringing the Arab world together.

Several recent developments seem to suggest increasing possibilities for relieving Turkey from narrowly-defined security focus in its foreign policy towards the region. First of all, Turkey's non-involvement in Iraq militarily paved the way for increasing emphasis on non-military means. Secondly, the re-emergence of Turkey as a "model", a predominantly Muslim country with a secular system, having a democratic experience since 1946, an economic transformation since 1980 and long institutional links with

---

[25] For Arab perceptions of Turkey's new role in the Middle East in the 1990s see Ofra Bengio and Gencer Özcan, "Changing Relations: Turkish-Israeli-Arab Triangle", *Perceptions* (Ankara), Vol.5, No.1, 2000, pp.134-146.

Europe and the United States also opens up the possibilities for Turkey to emerge as a soft power in the region. This is irrespective of Turkey's promotion within the context of such external projects as the US's Greater Middle East Initiative. Turkey is already emerging as an interesting case for the regional countries. Especially Turkey's recent reform experiences with respect to its relations with the EU are closely watched by the reformers in the region. Thirdly, the progress in Turkey's relations with the EU are crucial in further desecuritization of Turkish foreign policy in the region. Especially if Turkey can start accession negotiations with the EU that will start a process in which Europeanization of Turkish foreign policy will take place, which would mean more emphasis on non-military means of foreign policy. Furthermore the consolidation of democratic process in Turkey would contribute to the further resolution of Turkey's internal problems and thus decrease the vulnerabilities in that respect. It was largely the juxtaposition of Turkey's relations with the Middle East within the context of domestic debates and struggles in Turkey that put limitations on formulating policies towards this region. In the long run internal resolution of these conflicts will decrease the opportunities for the regional states to manipulate Turkey's internal problems and thus produce security for Turkey in its foreign policy towards this region.

18 Politics of the Euphrates and Tigris Waters

H. Bülent Olcay

The general aim of this section is to consider the purpose of Turkey's water management projects and their influence on relations with her neighbors, the effect of water on Turkey's position in the Middle East and other important foreign policy matters among the riparians of the Euphrates and Tigris rivers. The shift 1997 Convention[1] made to international water law has also been discussed.

Ambiguities and confusion regarding Turkey's place and role in the Middle East have an important impact on the nature of relations between Turkey and the surrounding countries. Water has been a conflict-laden component of both the domestic and external politics of the region's main actors. Geographic relationships, linkages between policy areas, the concern for "image," the concern for sovereignty, as well as the concern of own agendas of related riparians political leaders are important. Relations among actors are based not only on power and economic interests, but also on past actions and events, customs, values and beliefs.

Water issues are irritated by political tensions and rising consumption. All parties to the water conflicts try to assess the issue and interpret the facts and figures according to their own political preferences. However, the trans-boundary rivers signify a natural bond of interdependence by their physical, hydrological and ecological factors.

In developing countries, riparian relations are strained due to unilateral considerations and lead to disputes over management of shared water resources. Large-scale hydro-facilities probably restrain conflicts; yet if attacked, they seriously aggravate it.

Non-Navigational Use

Despite the 1997 Convention, international law on the use of shared water resources is still subject to interpretations. International law on the non-navigational use of international waters has been developed relatively recently. Most bilateral or multilateral treaties drawn up in the nineteenth and early twentieth centuries regulated only freedom of navigation. The correct terminology has long been awaited, i.e., whether watercourses flowing across territorial boundaries should be referred to as 'international' or 'trans-boundary' rivers or 'international river basins' or 'international river systems' or 'trans-boundary watercourse systems.'

When rivers cross the territory of one or more states, then they are called "successive" or "trans-boundary rivers" such as the Euphrates and Tigris. Developments, natural and man-made, affecting the water resources in one section of a water system, have the potential to change the quantity, quality, or attainable benefit from the water sources in

---

[1] Convention on *the Non-Navigational Uses of International Watercourses*, 1997. (hereinafter 1997 Convention)

another selection. However, geo-politics has contributed to two extreme claims depending on the geographic location of a riparian, i.e. the absolute territorial sovereignty, claimed by an upper riparian state, and the absolute territorial integrity, claimed by a lower riparian to secure undiminished natural flow of the river.

Downstream states have, naturally, always opposed the 'territorial sovereignty' doctrine and have pressed theories either requiring their consent to acts to be performed upstream that produce adverse downstream effects or calling on co-riparians to share the benefits of an international river. Almost every assertion, by words or by action, of such unrestricted freedom by upper-basin states has been vigorously contested or protested by lower-basin states.

> *The theories manifest a shift from a traditional extreme concept of sovereignty towards a more liberal and pragmatic approach.[2] Despite the difficulty in identifying rules of customary law of international validity regarding international water resources, there are at least four rules that are accepted as such equitable utilization of shared water resources; duty of prior consultation; prohibition of management practices likely to cause substantial and lasting injury to other states; duty to cooperate and to negotiate with a genuine intention of reaching an agreement.[3]*

As in the case of Euphrates and Tigris watercourse system, the quantity or quality of the water is such that all the competing uses or claims cannot be satisfied. The doctrine of 'equitable utilization' or 'equitable apportionment' has emerged as the most acceptable juridical method of adjustment. A number of international agreements directly or impliedly have adopted this concept "which may be seen as evidence of the force of the principle in customary international law."[4]

In practice, states must inform one another prior to water development plans and projects which may have a significant harm on their respective interests. The duty to inform and to consult, and then to work out a solution that impedes the predicted significant harm is the fundamental principal.

The 1997 Convention states that nations have an obligation to notify and inform other nations of any activities on shared watercourses that will affect them. Such notification permits the affected state to negotiate mitigation or to protest, and, perhaps, modify or prevent the action. However, the "Prior Appropriation (notify and inform) rule" requires the 'appropriation' well before the water development plans and projects are carried out.

Three months prior to taking action of filling process of the reservoir behind the Atatürk Dam on the Euphrates River in 1991, Turkey notified the downstream nations effectively reduced the flow in the river to zero for approximately one month. For a compensation of the loss of the downstream countries, Turkey had released more water between September and December 1990. Therefore Ankara argued that its commitment of

---

[2] See *Legal Aspects of Hydroelectric Development of Rivers and Lakes of Common Interests,* prepared by Sevette, UN Doc. E/ECE/136-E/ECE/EP/98 Rev.1, pp. 81-93.

[3] D. Caponera, *Principles of Water Law and Administration: National and international,* Rotterdam, 1992, p.190.

[4] UN Doc. A/CN.4/348, Third Report of Mr. Schwebel, in *YILC (1982),* Vol.II, Part One, p. 75, para. 41.

500 cum/s flow to Syria had been met. Whether Turkey's obligation to notify under the principles of international water law was met at such short notice and following compensations is debated. Not only Syria and Iraq, but also some other Arab countries, have still been accusing Turkey of its 'inappropriate' action.

The other basic rule reflected in treaty practice is that a state may not, through its actions affecting an international watercourse, significantly harm other states.[5] The maxim, "*sic utere tuo ut alienum non laedas*" -use your property in a way not to injure others- is often cited. A state is responsible for preventing actions inside of its borders that would harm the activities or property of another state. This principle permits harmful actions put requires compensation or mitigation as acceptable alternatives to avoidance. A major complication in applying this principle is the difficulty in quantifying downstream environmental and economic impacts and in determining the extent of responsibility for those impacts resulting from upstream activities.

An effective application of the "no harm rule" in international river disputes is largely dependent on the meaning of "injury." The term "injury" has been often qualified as substantial, permanent, material, appreciable, considerable, significant etc.[6]

The limits, rather, hinge upon the good will of states, on their readiness to negotiate and on the good relations between them. The fact that river waters are one of the best carriers of trans-frontier harms implies that a state has to be cautious while utilizing them.

The obligation to share data is reaching widespread acceptance, but the most important barrier to gathering information on water plans, use and its availability in certain countries is that most states treat water data as on a par with military intelligence. It is considered that such strategically valuable and politically useful information might be used in legal arguments against them by potential rival claimants for the same river.

Efforts or even plans by later-developing upstream countries to begin to utilize their water resources often give rise to strenuous objections by their downstream neighbors. The downstream countries often take the position that they have acquired rights to the quantity (and perhaps quality) of the water they have used in the past. Thus, any use by the upstream state that would interfere with these rights would be unlawful.

The later-developing upstream countries typically take the position that they have not previously had the need or the capability to develop their water resources, or that the technologies for such development simply did not exist while the lower riparian country was developing its dependence on the water (as in the case of hydroelectric facilities). They rely upon the principle of equitable utilization and point out that a strict rule against causing harm to other riparian states forecloses, or at least unreasonably limits, development.

These controversies are typically resolved (i) when the states concerned otherwise

---

[5] "No Harm (to other interests) Rule" This principle is reflected on many of the treaty provisions concerning successive watercourses cited in Stephen McCaffrey, *Second Report on the Law of the Non-Navigational Uses of International Watercourses*, 38th Session of the ILC 1976 *Yearbook [1974] of the International Law Commission*, UN, New York, vol. 11, part 1, p.88.

[6] UN Doc. A/CN.4/367, YILC (1983), Vol.II, Part One, pp.172-3, para. 100.

enjoy good relations with each other, (ii) where one of the states is clearly more powerful than the other but wishes to end the dispute or (iii) where it is otherwise in the mutual interest of the states concerned to do so. Otherwise the dispute remains unresolved.

The 1997 Convention on the Law of the Non-navigational Uses of International Watercourses defines and refers to terminology of the subject such as 'international watercourse' and 'watercourse states.'[7] These states must use water in an 'equitable and reasonable manner' to attain 'optimal and sustainable utilization thereof', and cooperate on the basis of mutual benefit and ecological protection. The combined impact of all these deliberations has been the emergence of the 1997 Convention and such regulations will only come into force if ratified by states. The Convention provides in part that where there is a conflict between uses of an international watercourse by different states, that conflict is to be resolved in accordance with the principle of equitable utilization and the obligation not to cause significant harm to co-riparian states. In order to evaluate the conflict in the Euphrates and Tigris rivers dispute, applicability of the related articles of the Convention, as a frame of reference, will briefly be reviewed.

The Application of the 1997 Convention

The Convention may be used as a framework agreement. It provides the states with "general principles and rules governing the non-navigational uses of international watercourses in the absence of a specific agreement among the states concerned and provide guidelines for the negotiation of future agreements."

Turkey defines those rivers as "trans-boundary," a term which reflects its national, rather than international character, nevertheless the river system qualifies for inclusion in the framework agreement provided by the Convention. The both rivers are watercourses according to the definition provided by the Convention Art.2., par. (a). Since both rivers flow through more than one state, they fall within the definition of "international watercourse" established by the Convention [Art. 2. par. (b)]. Both rivers are located on part of the territory of each of the riparian states; thus each state qualifies as a "watercourse state" [Convention Art. 2. par. (c)]. Any of the three riparian states may invoke the Convention. Absolute territorial sovereignty and absolute territorial integrity cannot be reconciled with the demands of the Convention.

National security concerns, rivalries, and other parochial interests will prevent optimal utilization of the river until the basin states negotiate a watercourse agreement. The fears and insecurities of the various states have stymied negotiations. The existing regime of watercourse agreements or accords (i.e., 1987 Accord between Syria and Turkey; 1946 Agreement between Turkey and Iraq) would continue to exist within a framework agreement, until the riparians negotiated new agreements. The potential obstacles which may be expected to prevent the realization of a watercourse agreement accepted by all the riparians should be sought at the political relations of the riparian states.[8]

Turkey allocates water from the Euphrates River to irrigate land in the south-eastern Anatolia. Nevertheless, that land does not lie outside the physical confines of the

---

[7] 1997 Convention, Article 2 (b) and (c).
[8] H. Bülent Olcay, Hydropolitics Among the Riparians of the Euphrates and Tigris Watercourse System. *Unpublished Ph.D. Thesis. Leicester University*, 1997, pp.130-203.

Euphrates and Tigris river basin. Rather, it is exactly between the two rivers. The term watercourse, as defined by the Convention, includes diverted waters. Thus, Turkey's removal of the water from the Euphrates River does not take the water outside the scope of the Convention.

The Euphrates River system is unable to satisfy the water demands of all its watercourse states. This conflict of uses finds its resolution in Articles 5, 6 and 7. Article 6 is the basis used to determine whether Turkey's use of the Euphrates River water is equitable and reasonable. Each of the seven factors is pertinent to the Euphrates and Tigris river system. Factor (a) calls for consideration of "geographic, hydrographic, hydrological, climatic, ecological and other factors of a natural character," including consideration of quantity and quality of the water. The total water resource of the Watercourse System is approximately 32 billion cubic meters (BCM),[9] and the quality of the water deteriorates as the river flows south. The qualitative and quantitative demands of Turkey, Syria and Iraq exceed the capacity of the river. Factor (a) represents the basis of the problem and weighs heavily in the scale balancing the equity and reasonableness of Turkey's use.

Factor (b) commands riparians to consider the "social and economic needs of the watercourse states concerned." Both Turkey and Syria rely heavily on the resources of the Euphrates River system, whereas Iraq enjoys the abundant Tigris River waters as well. Firmly imbedded in the principle of equitable and reasonable utilization is the goal of attaining optimal utilization. Factor (c) requires consideration of the population dependent on the concerned watercourse in each watercourse state. Factor (d) seems heavily against Turkey and Syria in terms of their upstream positions, when it considers "the effects of the use or uses of the watercourse in one watercourse state on other watercourse states." Factor (e) calls for an appraisal of "existing and potential uses of the watercourse." This factor leads to two different considerations. If an existing use carries more weight, then Iraq and Syria may argue for more water because they have used it for centuries. On the other hand, if potential uses outweigh existing uses, then upstream states Turkey and Syria will prevail. In fact, denying upstream users the opportunity to develop their portions of the river (the Euphrates and Tigris) waters simply to maintain Iraq's as well as Syria's historical supremacy seems quite irrational.

While according conditional priority to existing beneficial uses is generally recognized in customary water law, it is rejected in the Convention. The Article 6 (1) (e) refers to both existing and potential uses as relevant considerations in the allocation process "in order to emphasize that neither is given priority." The Convention adopts the equitable utilization standard without requiring either the maintenance or precedence of existing uses. This demonstrates a preference for redistribution over maintenance of the status quo. A middle course must be taken, one that gives conditional priority to existing beneficial uses.

Factor (f), on the other hand, relates to the "conservation, protection, development and economy of use of the water resources of the watercourse and the costs of measures taken

---

[9] John Kolars, "Hydro-Geographic Background to the Utilization of International Rivers in the Middle East", *Proceedings of the 1986 Annual Meetings of the American Society of International Law*, Washington DC, *The American Society of International Law; Water Issues Between Turkey, Syria and Iraq, the Turkish Foreign Ministry publication*, Ankara, June 1996.

to that effect." Turkey has expended a great deal of time, effort, and finance to develop its huge GAP projects which cover many dams and irrigation canals, to supply water to its irrigable land and produce electricity. To deny the legitimacy of that use would impose a great hardship on Turkey's social and economic life. On the contrary, the Convention does not recognize any use as essentially superior to any other. Turkey's investment in its water distribution system and its efficient irrigation techniques to some extent justify that this factor is in Turkey's favor.

Turkey refuses to recognize any limitation on its utilization of the Euphrates and Tigris waters originating in its territory.[10] This assertion of absolute territorial sovereignty stands against the spirit and letter of Article 5, para.1, which imposes on all riparians the duty "to utilize an international watercourse in an equitable and reasonable manner." Moreover, Article 5, par. 2, requires riparians to "participate in the use, development and protection of an international watercourse in an equitable and reasonable manner." Whereas the principle of equitable and reasonable utilization recognizes Turkey's right to share in the benefits and the uses of the both waters, it also requires that Turkey abstain from depriving other riparians of their rights to equitable utilization.

The other point is that Article 7 obligates states "not to cause significant harm," thus limiting Turkey's right to exploit the waters of the Euphrates as well as the Tigris. The Article prevents Turkey from exercising its control over the waters within its territory in a way that causes damage to downstream riparians.[11] According to the Commentary, Articles 5 and 7 are complementary principles.[12] Any use that causes significant harm to another riparian may not be justified by claiming that the use causing the harm is equitable. Uses causing harm are regarded as '*prima facie*' inequitable.[13]

Both of the lower riparians' argument relies on their historical utilization of the rivers. The lowest riparian, Iraq, regards its utilization as a custom, and thus its argument carries some force. Nevertheless, Convention Article 10, paragraph 1 states that "no use of an international watercourse enjoys inherent priority over other uses." Long established use of the concerned waters by Iraq and Syria neither allows nor denies other watercourse states the opportunity to utilize their portions of the Euphrates or the Tigris. Reliance of Turkey's downstream countries Syria and Iraq on custom is justified to the extent that there is no "conflict between uses."[14] Complete acceptance of downstream reasoning, however, would effectively freeze any significant utilization by upstream watercourse states, including Syria (in position to Iraq) and Turkey. This issue, which is a "conflict" in the terminology of the Convention, must be apprised under Article 10, paragraph 2 "be resolved with reference to articles 5 to 7." The argument of the downstream watercourse states, Syria and Iraq, taken to its extreme, would violate Article 5's mandate that watercourse states "utilize an international watercourse in an equitable and reasonable manner." The Commentary to paragraph 1 of Article 5 states that "a watercourse state has the right, within its territory, to a reasonable and equitable share, or portion, of the

---

[10] For the Turkish justification see Turkish Foreign Ministry, *Water Issues*, Ankara, June 1996.

[11] For Commentary, see *[1988] YILC, 22, pp.35-36.* UN Doc. A/CN.4/SER.A/1988/Add.1 (part 2).

[12] *[1988] YILC*, 22, p.36. UN Doc. A/CN.4/SER.A/1988/Add.1 (part 2).

[13] *[1988] YILC*, (part 2).

[14] *The 1997 Convention* Article 10, para. 2.

uses and benefits of an international watercourse."[15] No watercourse state can deprive a fellow watercourse state of its right to equitable utilization.

In Article 5 as a whole, the most "equitable and reasonable" outcome would tend to fall on the side of the vast untapped potential available to the uppermost watercourse state, Turkey. Whereas, "optimal and sustainable utilization" does not necessarily correspond to "maximum use," the most technologically efficient use, or the most monetarily valuable use, denying the upper watercourse state the opportunity to develop its equitable portions of the Euphrates and Tigris waters simply to maintain Syria and Iraq's historical pre-eminence would be irrational.

Article 6 requires that "all relevant factors and circumstances" be taken into account in determining whether a watercourse state's utilization is equitable and reasonable. It sets forth a non-exclusive list of seven factors to guide the determination. These factors, as well as other relevant factors, must be weighed in applying the "general and flexible" principle of equitable and reasonable utilization.

Syria's utter dependence on the Euphrates River is the primary point in its favor. Without the water provided by the Euphrates, Syria will not be able to survive. Therefore, Article 6, para.1 (a), which calls for consideration of "geographic, hydrographic, hydrological, climatic, ecological and other factors of a natural character," clearly favors a substantial amount of water portion for Syria. Factor (b) enjoins watercourse states to consider the "social and economic needs of the watercourse states concerned." This is applicable for all parties' claims, and is therefore not to be considered. Factor (c) considers the population who are "dependent on" the concerned watercourse in each country. Factor (d) considers "the effects of the use or uses of the watercourses in one watercourse state on other watercourse states." This does not support downstream riparians' unqualified assertions that upstream countries have the right to utilize the waters of the concerned rivers without prior approval.

If this theory were accepted, downstream watercourse states would have a veto power over projects of upstream watercourse states. Nevertheless, under Part III of the Convention, downstream countries do have the right to demand exchange of information and negotiation with upstream watercourse states if they believe their planned measures may have "possible effects."[16] Factor (e) calls for an appraisal of "existing and potential uses of the watercourse." Evaluation of this factor could lead to two widely divergent conclusions. If existing uses carry more weight, then mainly downstream users will prevail since they utilized it even before Turkey utilized it. If, however, potential uses outweigh existing uses, then the upstream watercourse states, Turkey and Syria, will prevail.

As a whole, the Convention gives an advantage to states that developed their uses early. By enshrining prior appropriation, the Convention places a premium on early, but not necessarily rational, development of the watercourse system. The Convention also

---

[15] The Law of the Non-Navigational Uses of International Watercourses. [1987] 2 YILC., p.31. UN Doc. A/CN.4/SER.A/1987/Add.1 (Part 2)

[16] The Commentary defines "possible effects" which has been used in Article 11, as "all potential effects of planned measures, whether adverse or beneficial." *[1988] YILC, 22, p.45.* UN Doc. A/CN.4/SER.A/1988/Add.1 (part 2).

provides a pragmatic foundation for cooperation on condition that states leave their provincial viewpoints for the sake of an opportunity to attain optimal utilization of the international watercourse.

The foregoing considerations lead to the conclusion that any division of the waters must take into consideration the needs of each basin state. This, naturally, calls for some compromise on the part of all basin states. Although Turkey seems to have the physical power to cut off all the water within its jurisdiction, however, the exercise of such a power to the detriment of interest of lower states would not be tolerated. Furthermore, downstream states Syria and Iraq could not be permitted to require Turkey to give up its power altogether in order that the river might come down to it undiminished. All three states have real and vital interests in the Euphrates River that must be reconciled as best as they may be.

The role of the law has generally been only one factor influencing the outcome of major international water controversies. States have rarely shown a disposition to defy generally accepted principles of international law, and indeed, usually rely on those principles in their diplomatic exchanges. Further, the more concrete and generally accepted the applicable legal principles become, the more likely it is that they will play a major role in the resolution of international water controversies.

In the nineteenth and twentieth centuries, a large number of water related treaties, agreements, conventions, etc., were concluded by states of the Middle East. However, many of these treaties were concluded between a Middle Eastern state and a stronger European state (bordering on the Middle East or controlling an area thereof), reflecting Western concepts. Meanwhile, there are no priority categories of water use in Middle East conventional law, such as the ones existing in European and American international agreements.[17] No attempt is seen to judge one type of water utilization as more deserving or important than another, the matter being left entirely to the option of the country concerned.

The 1946 Turkey-Iraq Treaty of Friendship and Neighborly Relations was an example of an upstream state waiving to some extent its territorial sovereignty to enable a downstream state to benefit in its territory from the waters of successive international rivers. The two countries recognized the importance of conservation works on the Tigris and Euphrates and their tributaries, and the need for the maintenance of a regular water supply, the regulation of the water flow with a view to avoiding floods during the annual periods of high water.

The elaborate treaty regime established by Syria and Iraq in 1975, with respect to the international watercourses they share all along their lengthy common frontier, has failed as a result of the belligerent behavior of the two states. During April–August 1975 period, Iraq claimed that the flow reaching its territory was "intolerable" and asked that the Arab League intervene in its dispute over this with Syria. The Syrians claimed that less than half the river's normal flow was reaching its borders that year, and after a barrage of mutually hostile statements, an Arab League technical committee that had been

---

[17] Hirsch, A. M., 1956, "Utilization of International Rivers in the Middle East: A Study of Conventional International Law", *The American Journal of Law*, pp.81-100.

formed to mediate the conflict pulled out. In May 1975, Syria closed its airspace to Iraqi flights, and both Syria and Iraq reportedly transferred troops to their mutual border. Only mediation on the part of Saudi Arabia broke the increasing tension.

Even though an accord between Syria and Turkey was reached in 1987, whereby Turkey is willing to let a minimum 500 cum/s flow into Syrian territory, Syria still looks for a permanent international agreement governing the use of "*sharing*" of the water resources. Meanwhile Ankara never accentuates the word 'sharing' of waters; it prefers to use another word: '*allocating*.'

The interstate water problems are seriously related to the larger political questions among the parties. Foreign policy is often drawn on the basis of the need to ensure access to the waters of the rivers concerned.

After the Cold War and the Gulf War, the only superpower was more involved in pushing conflicts in the region beyond certain limits or allowed the conflicts to get out of control. The invasion of Iraq has proved that the US has not been careful on the whole to draw boundaries round its respective behaviors so as not to push the system into instability.

The Tigris and Euphrates river valleys are coming under increasing population, irrigation, and energy pressures. In political conflicts that escalate to military aggression, water resource systems have regularly been the targets of war. The usual tools of conflict are military weapons of destruction, though the use of water and water resources systems as both offensive and defensive weapons also has a long history. Most recently, dams, desalination plants and water conveyance systems were targeted by both sides (Iran and Iraq) during the Persian Gulf War. In early 1993, Saddam Hussein poisoned and began to drain the water supplies of southern Shiite Muslims in his efforts to quell the opposition to his government.[18]

During the war between Iraq and the multinational force in early 1991 it was suggested[19] that Turkey might try to reduce the flow of water from the Tigris to Iraq in order to increase pressure on Saddam Hussein's regime. Yet, any thought of switching off the river totally as part of the UN sanctions programme or as a leverage of an upstream country like Turkey is not feasible. The water would need to be stored and the obvious storage area, the Atatürk Dam lake, has already been filled. Furthermore, any geo-politically inspired denial of water would irreparably damage relations among the riparians and even lead a war. Not only for that, but also for the sake of cultural and historical reasons Turkey has to avoid such exercises and speculations.

Despite advance warnings of Turkey of the temporary cut-off during the filling process of the Atatürk Dam, Syria and Iraq both protested against Turkey, accusing her of using water as a "weapon" that could be used against them. It is impossible to keep the management of the Euphrates River non-political.

Water Availability

In the Tigris and Euphrates watercourse system, hydrologists and water-resources

---

[18] *BBC Geographic Magazine*, July, 1993, London, p.12.

[19] That suggestion came from the coalitional states against Iraq and then Turkish Energy and Natural Resources Minister Kamran Inan reiterated that Turkey would never use water in the near future as a tool of political or military pressure. Reported from London. *BBC/SWB*. February 16, 1991.

specialists must collect and more widely broadcast data on the supply and use of shared water resources. Environmental issues are not seen to lead conflicts in the Middle East, at least until real issues on utilizing or sharing of them is resolved.

The lack of consensus on irrigable land potential, demonstrates the need for more comprehensive work to be done to clarify the existing situation. The collection of all relevant data and its dissemination to all concerned may serve to allay apprehension. The disagreeing parties should endeavor to predict objectively the consequences and ramifications of the alternative courses of action in the light of the available data.

Turkey, Syria, Iraq and Iran are the riparians of the Euphrates and Tigris basin region. Iran shares a very small portion of the Euphrates just before it empties into the Gulf. Turkey's South-eastern Anatolia Project (GAP, Güneydoğu Anadolu Projesi, hereinafter the GAP) is regarded as the most comprehensive one. However, Syria and Iraq too have been carrying out projects to use the waters of the Euphrates and Tigris and their tributaries for irrigation and have initiated large-scale dam projects.

Syria and Iraq have been claiming that due to the GAP of Turkey, the flow of both rivers has been substantially reduced. The uppermost riparian state Turkey, despite its disputes with downstream neighbors, has been completing the GAP project as planned. The hydro-political implication of the GAP is claimed to pose a threat to regional stability. The problem is that development is not easily digested by the downstream countries of Turkey. With the realization of the GAP project, the outcry seems to be heard more than ever.

The basic functions of the dams which Turkey is currently constructing on the Euphrates River are to regulate the flow of water for the irrigation for 1.7 million hectares of land, and for hydroelectric power which will produce 27 billion kilowatts of energy. The downstream countries are also expected to benefit from the water regulation functions of the concerned dams without their financial involvements.

Map: Euphrates-Tigris Watercourse System

The Euphrates and Tigris Rivers comprise 28.5 per cent of Turkey's overall flowing water potential.[20] The amount of water that flows in the Euphrates River can drop down to 100 cubic meters per second in summer months while it reaches over 7000 cubic meters during the months when snow thaws. In fact, it shows the importance of the dams. Otherwise, downstream countries would face a drought in summer, and floods in spring as were the case prior to major dams. The both rivers have seasonal periods of high water followed by periods of extremely reduced flow. At high flow season, which is spring, the Euphrates has 28 times as much flow as its minimum amount, and the Tigris River nearly 80 times as much. The water becomes abundant when need is relatively limited and poor when need is great.

Linked with its tributaries, the Euphrates drains a basin 444,000 square kilometers (170,000 square miles) in area. The total length of the Euphrates is about 2,800 kilometers. The total length of the Tigris is about 1,890 kilometers. The average annual discharge of the Euphrates at the Turkish-Syrian border is 30.377 km^3 and 31.8 km^3 at Hit in Iraq. The average annual discharge of the Tigris at the Turkish border is 16.8 km^3, 18.5 km^3 at Mosul. Over 98 per cent of Euphrates flow, including the main tributaries of the Khabur, Sajur and Balikh rivers, originates in Turkey, although Turkey accounts for only 28 per cent of the basin area. Turkey also contributes 45 per cent of the flow of the Tigris.

Syria

Syria is either an upstream or downstream country on the Yarmuk, the Orontes (Asi) and the Euphrates. Thus, any legal position Syria chooses to defend with regard to the Jordan or the Yarmuk could potentially affect its ability to dispute its rights *vis-à-vis* Lebanon on the Orontes or Turkey on the Euphrates. The Orontes River, which rises in Lebanon and flows through Syria into the Hatay region of Turkey, presents quite a complicated issue. Ninety per cent of the average annual discharge of the Orontes is used by Syria. The situation of this river is the inverse of the Euphrates and Tigris Rivers. The upstream state is Syria and its irrigation schemes have virtually halted the flow of the river into Turkey's Hatay province, which is claimed by Syria.

Syria plans irrigation development along the Euphrates as well as the Khabur to cover 773,000 acres of land. It has built two major dams on the Euphrates. The larger one, the Tabqa Dam, with six of its eight turbines in operation, provides 60 per cent of Syria's electricity, though much of its production depends on the flow of water from Turkey. Syria's vast new irrigation projects, would certainly disquiet Baghdad. However, Syria intended to proceed slowly and reclaim and develop at the rate of 20,000 hectares per year of the projected total of 640,000 hectares of new arable land.[21] Syria has been

---

[20] John Kolars, "The Future of the Euphrates River", *World Bank Workshop*, Washington DC, June 1991; also see J. Kolars, & C.Mitchell, *The Euphrates River and the South-East Anatolia Development Project*, Carvondale: University of Southern Illinois Press, 1991.

[21] Zohurul Bari, "Syrian-Iraqi Dispute over the Euphrates Waters", *International Studies*, Quarterly Journal of the School of International Studies, Jawaharlal Nehru University, Vol.16, No.2, April-June 1977, p.235.

demanding to be allowed to develop its use of the Euphrates waters, claiming it is not yet using the share that it deserves.

The dams and power plants in Syria are inappropriate to the region's needs. The Tabqa Dam power plant is situated above the earth; therefore, the dam must always be full to get maximum output from the power plant. Syria plans to press ahead with land reclamation targets to increase the irrigated area to 1.4m ha by 2010, which in the light of Turkish utilization of the Euphrates as well as existing management difficulties seems somewhat unrealistic.

Iraq

Until the US invasion in 2003, the government of Iraq viewed agricultural self-sufficiency as a cornerstone of its national security policy, and so poured large sums of money and manpower into its agricultural projects. Iraq uses the Euphrates relatively minimally. Iraq mainly uses the Tigris by the Tharthar Canal, which compensates for the increased reduction in Euphrates flow by connecting the two rivers. This strategy has helped to prevent any real conflict with Turkey or Syria over Euphrates resources.

Iraq has serious problems with water management and soil salinity and these have dogged irrigation projects throughout the history of Mesopotamia. Successive governments have undertaken a number of water management schemes on the Euphrates, notably the Qadisiyya Dam (1985, 6.4 km^3 storage capacity) to irrigate 1 m ha. The waters of the Tigris are used to irrigate 2.2m ha, mainly using the Saddam Dam (10.7 km^3). The Shatt al-Arab was used to irrigate 105,000 ha, but the current picture is uncertain in the light of extensive economic disruption caused by the 1990-1 Gulf War. Before the Gulf War, Iraq was implementing a number of hydraulic projects on the major rivers and their tributaries, notably the Tharthar canal project to divert water from the Tigris into the Tharthar depression and thence, if necessary, into the Euphrates.

In the war with the multinational force in 1991, several dams were hit in the bombing campaign. The destruction of dams and pumping installations, water purification plants and power stations has had serious consequences for energy and food production, and for the provision of clean drinking water. Restoration of such installations to proper functioning became a major priority of its post-war reconstruction programme, as did restoration of drinking water supplies and sewerage systems in Baghdad and other major cities.

Iraq is rich in land: 433,000 square kilometers, all of it cultivable.[22] Even partial fulfillment of development plans by Turkey and Syria will make it difficult for Iraq to meet its own irrigation needs on the Euphrates. But the bulk of Iraqi agriculture, along with most of its population, is located in the southern and central regions of the state. Further expansion therefore requires extensive population relocation, and the retention of northern Tigris waters.

The US Involvement

The US may not willingly agree to continue spending billions of its taxpayers' money to

---

[22] *EIU Country Report* 3rd quarter 1996, p.11.

attempt to solve the problem of the Middle East. Developments in the aftermath of the September 11 show that the Americans have a desire for a long-term intervention and ready to undertake its cost. America's major interest lies in ensuring the continued flow of Gulf oil to the industrialized world. Nevertheless, third party resolution of water disputes is quite prominent in conventional river law. Professional bodies could help to resolve water questions; their expertise is essential in the juridical decision making process, but a mere technical approach may not be effective unless boosted by political acceptance or legal formulations.

When disagreements develop with regard to utilizing trans-boundary water resources, riparians should first try to settle their differences by consultation and negotiation. These are the most frequently used methods for the pacific settlement of international disputes. Resort to negotiation is rather a duty imposed on all state parties to a dispute. The International Court of Justice has, in many cases,[23] declared that the parties were under an obligation to negotiate, and the Permanent Court of International Justice stated that the parties to a dispute must 'not only enter into negotiations but also pursue them as far as possible with a view to concluding agreements even though there was no obligation to reach an agreement.'[24]

As in the Euphrates and Tigris Rivers controversy, riparians generally prefer to take care of their disputes without the assistance of disinterested third parties. However, if consultations and negotiations fail to produce a solution, then the concerned riparians face the question of whether or not they should request third parties to help in resolving the problem. In reality, this necessity is rather imposed by third parties, especially institutions and academics of the third parties, on behalf of the "injured" sides.

As a consequence of the end of the Cold War, the US is regarded as the only state with sufficient power to deal with any aggressor. The US government has a strong history of involvement in Middle East water resources development. In 1987, M. Peter McPherson[25] noted that the "development of water resources is a critical foreign policy issue for the US."[26] By investing substantial sums of money and committing the combined expertise of its various bureaus and departments, the federal government has emerged as a powerful force in shaping development trends in the region. The US Department of State has a long involvement in regional water issues. The Johnston Plan of the early 1950s exemplifies its capabilities and commitment.

The most important obstacle to US involvement in a water solution is on the public relations side. None of the three riparians want to be associated publicly with an agreement that the US single-handedly brokered, financed and researched, regardless of whether or not it was under UN auspices. As Starr suggests, the region's water future requires "extraordinary leadership and vision, not the salvo offer of American or United

---

[23] *International Court of Justice Reports*. 1969. pp.3, 48.

[24] In its advisory opinion on the Railway Traffic Between Poland and Lithuania, *Permanent Court of International Justice*, Series A/B, No.42.

[25] The then administrator of the USAID and later Under-Secretary of the Treasury.

[26] Joyce Starr, "Water Wars", *Foreign Policy*, No.82, Spring 1991, p.32.

Nations troops."[27]

It is quite extraordinary that there is a particular *"hadith"*[28] of the Prophet Muhammad, on the Euphrates River, stating that in modern times the Euphrates will be a source of conflict. According to the *hadith*, "the Euphrates is soon to uncover a treasure of gold, but those who are present must not take any of it."[29] It is commonly interpreted in the Islamic World that "a treasure of gold" is the water of the Euphrates.[30] Although Islamic Law explains procedures for water use and water sharing procedures,[31] however, laws of the three countries are strictly secular. Therefore, in a short term, neither establishing a religious basis for an agreement on using the waters of the Euphrates and Tigris watercourse system, nor the understanding of the meaning of that hadith by the conflicting riparians seems quite possible.

Transporting schemes

In a broader perspective, in order to resolve the Middle East water puzzle, projects such as Turkey's "Peace Pipeline" and "Manavgat River Project," may be feasible provided that the political obstacles can be removed. On paper, the ambitious plans seem simple and convincing to the concerned parties; however, importing water schemes (i.e., by tanker) is only a short term solution, and inter-basin transfers must be considered a viable alternative once the appropriate conservation and management strategies are in place. Transport of water from source to end-user by pipeline or tanker is a common method.

International water transfers by pipeline, though, have significant potential, but to date have not become operational. The reason the international water carrier has not become operational is their perceived strategic vulnerability. These fears have been given substance by the consequences of the Arab initiative in the early 1960s to prepare for the transfer of water from the Banias spring, one of the major springs feeding the Jordan's irrigation schemes in the Jordan Valley. The military intervention of Israel interrupted the construction.

Syria and Iraq as well as the Gulf states suspect that Turkish offers for exporting water, are not altruistic gestures that will be of mutual benefit, but are parts of a nefarious plot to reassert Turkish hegemony over the region. International agencies have encountered resistance even to taking the seemingly neutral first step of getting the parties to agree to collect and fully share all necessary hydrological data.

Physical obstacles can be overcome, like threats from terrorist actions, but political objections are likely to be far more substantial. The vulnerability invited by obtaining even part of the national drinking water supply from an outside source might well prove

---

[27] Joyce Starr, "Covenant Over Middle Eastern Waters: Key to World Survival", Henry Holt & Co, New York, 1995, p. 187.

[28] A hadith is a narration of the life of the Prophet Muhammad.

[29] Reported by Abu Hurairah (a companion of the Prophet). Quoted from *Sunan-i Abu Daud*. Chapter 1599, Hadith No. 4299, p.1201.

[30] The Commentary of that hadith quoted from the Turkish daily *Zaman Gazetesi*, Akademi Sayfasi. August 7, 1993. p.7.

[31] For a very useful bibliography for an interested reader. Dante A. Caponera. FAO, 36 *Water Law in Muslim Countries*, Roma, 1973.

unacceptable. As a commodity of low value which is required in bulk, water, other than for drinking, could not be imported economically over large distances. The strategic consideration, resulting from the dependence on a foreign source for such a vital commodity, leads to a strong preference for self-sufficiency at whatever cost.[32]

The Manavgat River Project

The Manavgat River Project was first unveiled in the Israeli press.[33] Interestingly, the scheme was kept secret in Turkey under the order of the late president Özal, and it was only brought into public in the summer of 1994. Since then, the Israeli government has been considering the use of giant water bags towed by tugs to make two trips a month to bring water from Turkey to Israel, to make Israel independent of Jordan water. During a visit to Israel in March 1996, Turkish President Süleyman Demirel confirmed that a sales agreement had been reached in principle and that exports would start within two years.[34] Turkey has meanwhile pressed ahead with the construction of water export facilities, including submarine pipelines leading to single-point mooring facilities offshore.

Figure: Water export scheme from Manavgat River

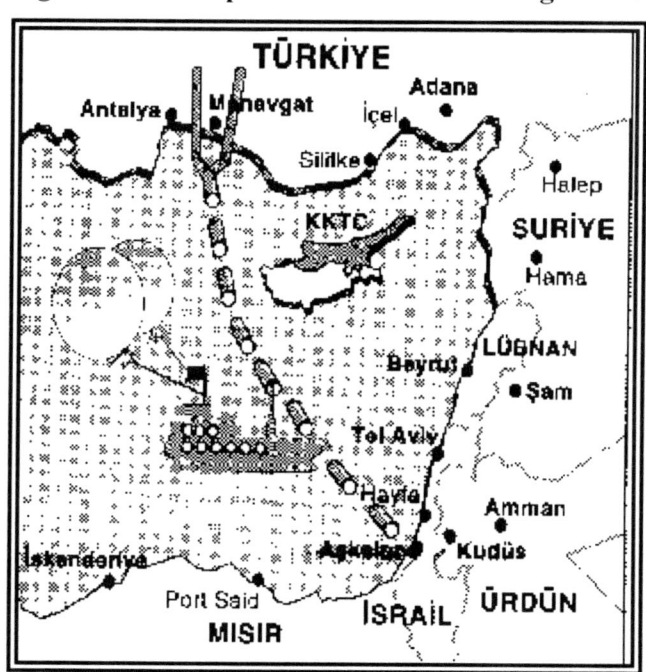

---

[32] Clive Agnew and Ewan Anderson, *Water Resources in the Arid Realm*, London: Routledge, 1992, p.206.

[33] On October 20, 1989. Quoted in major Turkish Newspapers on October 22nd.

[34] Turkish Foreign Trade Undersecretary Nejat Eren noted that "Israel wanted to purchase water from Turkey and that Demirel said that Turkey could give 150 million cum. of water in two years time." *Sabah Gazetesi*, March 13, 1996.

Turkey's reliability as a source of water is the most critical issue. For Israel, among the positive changes in Turkish-Israeli relations are that they have been raised to the ambassadorial level, and bilateral cooperation in military, intelligence, tourism and other areas is openly developing. Furthermore, Jordan and the Palestinians are interested in obtaining Turkish water, and Arab objections might be undercut further in time with the settlement of Iraq's new regime.

Changes in the composition of the Turkish government considerably affect Turkey's basic foreign policy. One typical example is the offer of the Islamist prime minister, Necmettin Erbakan, to sell Turkey's water to Libya. Erbakan, indifferent to Libya's pariah status in the West, apparently saw Manavgat as a way of strengthening political ties.[35] Ironically, in spite of his efforts to improve Turkey's relations with the Islamic World, Erbakan has made little progress in coping with the dispute with Baghdad and Damascus over the GAP project.

The nature of the objection to selling water to Israel arises more from emotional animosity toward Israel, rather than from a tendency to conserve national water resources. How secure even this will be if Palestinian-Israeli clashes escalate further, and if Israel's relations with the relatively moderate Arab states further worsen as a consequence?

The Peace Pipeline Project

In the face of the grave situation in the Middle East, Turkey has come up with a partial solution for the region. The solution involves the pumping of about 6 mcm. of water a day to the Arab Mashreq. The project is called the "Peace Pipeline." The Seyhan and Ceyhan Rivers, which both originate in the Anatolian heights and flow into the Mediterranean, carry approximately 39.17 mcm. of unpolluted, good quality water a day. Turkey intends to use 23.4 mcm. of it for its planned needs. The basic idea is to provide drinking water through two pipelines, to Syria, Jordan, Saudi Arabia and other Gulf States at a price that is a fraction of the cost of desalinated water.

The project is to divert water to Jeddah in the west and Muscat in the east of the Arabian Peninsula. The western pipeline will take water through the Noor mountains by tunnel, via Aleppo and Homs to Damascus, Amman and Medina. Pumping stations will pipe it from Medina to Jeddah, Mecca and Yanbu.

Extensive development in the watersheds of the two rivers has already occurred and many dams have been constructed. The proposed scheme entails building a branched pipeline to supply about 6 mcm. or 1,320 million gallons of water a day. This is well in excess of the present installed desalination capacity in the six Gulf states. Though estimates vary, according to a feasibility study, desalinated water can cost as much as $5 a cubic metre; on the other hand the maximum cost of the water pumped along the Peace Pipeline would be the highest at $1.07 a cubic metre.[36]

---

[35] John Barham, "Water everywhere and not a drop of profit", *Financial Times*, 3 October, 1996, p.3.
[36] The feasibility study of the US company Brown & Root's, held at the Ministry of Energy and Natural Resources, Ankara.

Figure: Possible Routes for the Peace Pipeline

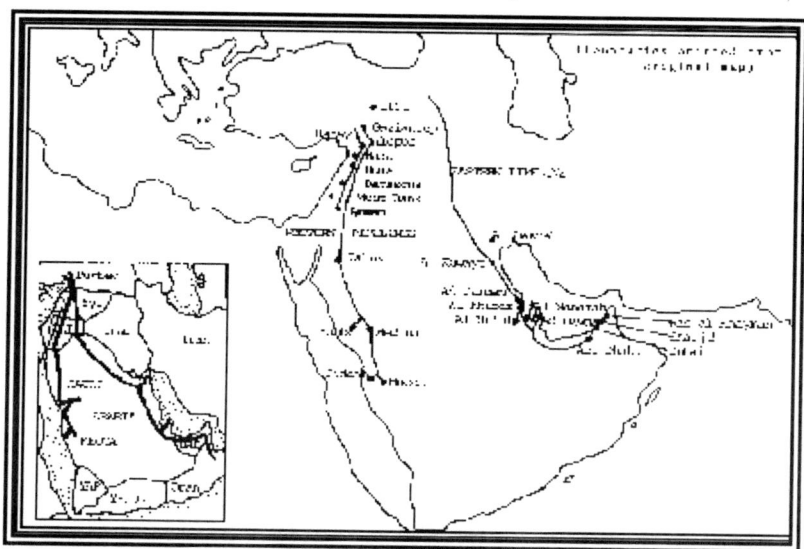

Source: J. Kolars and C. Mitchell, (1991), p.290. Devlet Su İşleri (DSİ) Bülteni, Ankara, 1992; Cumhuriyet, 8 June, 1988

Table: Technical Information on the Peace Pipeline

	Western Pipeline	Eastern Pipeline
Length	2700 km.	3900 km.
Capacity	3.5 million m³/day	2.5 million m³/day
Expenditure	8.5 billion $US	12 billion $US
Price of 1 m³	1.07 $US	1.07 $US

Source: DSI, Brown & Roots Feasibility Reports, Ankara

The pipelines with their attendant structures such as pumping stations present obvious targets in any level of conflicts. Moreover, if they are damaged, the economic results will be felt almost immediately. In strategic terms, every one of the Gulf states is strategically vulnerable to full attack or sabotage on their desalting capability as well. The consumer countries would always be vulnerable to supply cut-offs. The Saudi Arabian and Turkish cutting off of Iraq's oil pipelines, during the Gulf crisis, demonstrates how unreliable such a dependency is. It can be argued though that should the Turkish Peace Pipeline come to fruition, the number of countries potentially at risk would be very large and the mutual vulnerability would be so great that it would tend to militate against unilateral action.

The political attitudes of Turkey's neighbors towards the project have been cautious. Some of the Arab countries have been worried that, with the water pipeline, Turkey could take Arab countries "hostage" by controlling the water supply. This argument which is advanced by some Arab commentators,[37] emerges from historical misperceptions of

---

[37] *Arab Times*, Kuwait, March 22, 1988.

Ottomans among the Arab nationalists.

Treaty obligations will enforce compliance among the different states of the basin, offering 'carrots' for cooperation, and 'sticks' for strife. Concerns that Turkey might wield too much influence over a given downstream state are unfounded because, as one passes southward, various political allegiances change with borders so that allies may lie downward from the pipeline, below potential enemies. The over-arching goal will be to configure the regime so that alliances will not be able to marshal their forces to strangle one state or another of the water so precious to development. There is ample evidence of successful cooperation between states which was begun to foster not only closer economic ties but to forge closer political links between countries. The hydroelectric dam that strides the Brazilian-Uruguayan border is an example.

As a country which aspires to join the European Union, Turkey cannot allow itself to be perceived as the 'town bully' and it may be within this framework of image building that one has to look at the Turkish proposal for the 'Peace Pipeline Plan' which presents Turkey as a co-operative state, for a price, ready to share precious resources with its neighbors.

The "Three-Staged Plan" of Turkey

Apart from its Peace Pipeline and Manavgat River projects, Turkey has made other suggestions such as the 'Three-Staged Plan' for the usage of water resources with its co-riparians. However, Syria and Iraq believe that any cooperation on water should be based on the division (*sharing*) of water resources in accordance with their own needs. If a meaningful cooperation cannot be developed in the region today on the issue of water, then it is necessary to be aware of and to accept the fact that it is as a result of the pursuit of unilateral and narrow interests by the riparians. The natural basis for such cooperation is the creation of models and adoption of procedures which will enable the maximum usage of water resources.

The "three-staged plan for optimum, equitable and reasonable utilization of the trans-boundary watercourses of the Euphrates and Tigris Basin" was first introduced by Turkey, at the fifth meeting of the Joint Technical Committee between 5-8 November 1984. In time, it has been fully developed and reaffirmed up to 1993. The Plan has following features:[38]

1. The Euphrates and the Tigris have to be considered as forming one single transboundary watercourse system. They are linked not only by their natural course when merging at the Shatt-al-Arab, but also because of a man-made Tharthar Canal connection between the two rivers in Iraq. Consequently, all existing and future agricultural water uses need not necessarily be derived from Euphrates. Irrigation water for areas fed by Euphrates, may also be supplied from the Tigris River.

2. The inventory of water and land resources should be drawn up and evaluated jointly since the methods used in each country for data collection, interpretation and evaluation show disparities from country to country and are not readily

---

[38] Turkish Ministry of Foreign Affairs, Dept. of Regional and Transboundary Waters, *Water Issues Between Turkey, Syria and Iraq*, June 1996, Ankara, pp.21-23.

applicable to transboundary watercourses.

3. Finally, necessary means and measures should be determined to attain the most reasonable and optimum utilization of resources on the basis of the above mentioned studies. Turkey suggests that an equitable, rational and optimum utilization of water resources can be achieved through a scientific study which will determine the true water needs of each riparian country.

The Three-Staged Plan actually does not respond to the claims of the downstream countries for two reasons. First, it is highly subjective in terms of the terminology used and the solution suggested for another water source for Syria. While Turkey suggests diverting of Tigris waters to Syria, it does not address the probable reactions of Iraq. The second reason is that, with regard to the suggestions for joint action to end water data disparities, Ankara behaves like a mediator rather than a party in the dispute. Therefore, the plan, though it sounds highly logical and idealistic, may well be regarded as quite a good diplomatic way of doing nothing or a time gaining exercise until the GAP is completed. The "Three-Staged Plan" was rejected by the Syrian and Iraqi delegates, during the meeting held at ministerial level in June, 1990, in Ankara.[39]

The issue is intertwined with other issues, such as nationalism, economic development, foreign policy, ideology, and internal politics. Hence, solving a water conflict might be a precursor or a means to establishing confidence-building measures that would help in paving the way for settling other seemingly unmanageable conflicts in the basin. The Euphrates water dispute so far has proven intractable because the decisive forces for co-operative behavior inside the water arena can be found in geopolitical, social and economic factors which lie outside the province of water and have to do with countries' foreign and internal policies. That makes discussion of water allocation an unnegotiable multi-faceted issue.

As far as protecting their supply of water from the shared source is concerned, downstream states can choose between two basic strategies. They can seek to engage their upstream neighbors in co-operative arrangements, or pursue a variety of blocking manoeuvres aimed at preventing upstream states from going ahead with their plans.

As in the Euphrates and Tigris case, usually every negotiant wants a liberal safety margin. Then, the total demand exceeds the available quantity. In such a river water dispute, if every country wants to have what it hopes to use, what it potentially can use and then a safety margin on top of it all, there will never be enough water. Safety margins can be reduced by only psychological means, by increasing trust and minimising fears.

Turkey has an absolute advantage. In addition to being the upstream riparian, it is also militarily the strongest. Given its hegemonic status in the basin, it is not immediately obvious why it should support the creation of a water regime with Syria and Iraq. Without a regime, it is able to enjoy the maximum advantage; with a regime, its maneuverability would be constrained. Evidently, Syria and Iraq could gain considerably

---

[39] A paper presented by the Turkish Foreign Ministry, Ankara, 1994, p.19. For more information on three staged plan see Gün Kut, "Ortadogu Su Sorunu: Çözüm Önerileri", Sabahattin Sen (Ed.), *Su Sorunu, Türkiye ve Ortadogu,* Istanbul: Baglam Yayincilik, 1993, pp. 478-479.

from a basin-wide accord.[40]

A water regime cannot be built on current practices of water management. New criteria need to be built on what Falkenmark & Lundqvist[41] term "a new water ethic." Yet it is clear that it will only be possible to convince both sides of the reasonableness of a set of norms, rules and procedures if they are convinced it satisfies their security needs.

The interpretation of security has slowly-but perceptibly-been changing in the post-Cold War era. In the framework of development issues the concept of human and environmental security is gaining currency. Helmut[42] suggested a basin-wide plan by assuming that there are no frontiers between Syria, Iraq and Turkey for the planning purposes and that utilization of shared resources be balanced. A decision would then be taken for the area as an integral whole, instead of a piecemeal approach as is the case today. Such a plan would use the land, water and resources in the most efficient fashion, giving optimal benefit to all three countries. After developing this plan which allows the optimal and equitable use of the water, borders would be put back on the negotiating table and the distribution of projects would be discussed. This offer is too platonic and it may lead to new territorial disputes. Moreover, it is too late for planning when projects have already been completed over the two rivers.

The key to achieving the establishment of a technical infrastructure for hydro-policy is to address the problem at two levels: basin and regional. The parties involved in the Euphrates and Tigris case should find a way to arrange tripartite meetings for development planning, which could become a model for regional institutions to cooperate on development as well as security issues. Specifically, this would involve the establishment of two interrelated types of water institutes:

- An institute for the Euphrates and Tigris River basin,
- A comprehensive Middle East Water Institute or Authority.

Wolf and Ross[43] argue that scarce water resources are actually inextricably related to regional conflict, having led historically to intense and sometimes armed competition, but also to occasional instances of cooperation between otherwise hostile players. Throughout the 45 years of hostilities, water issues have been the subject of occasional secret talks and even some negotiated agreements between the states in the Middle East. In the future, cooperation on regional water planning or technology might actually help provide momentum toward negotiated political settlements. A cooperation cannot be achieved

---

[40] Failing that, the two downstream states would benefit from bilateral cooperation to counterbalance Turkey, whose relative power is growing. It, however, would require a favourable political climate. As in the Euphrates basin, in three-party games bilateral cooperation through the formation of a "cooperative cluster" could be more favourable than each state "going it alone." As a result, Syria and Iraq would achieve relative gains collectively. See, "International Cooperation Among Relative Gains Maximizers," *International Studies Quarterly* Vol. 35. 1991.

[41] Falkenmark & Lundqvist., 1995. p.179. Quoted in Jeroen Warner, *Kicking the water habit: Israel, Palestine and the new water order*, Amsterdam: Amsterdam Middle East Papers, No. 8, December 1996.

[42] Helmut van Edig. "Strengthening the Regional Cooperation-The German View" in Ali Ihsan Bagis. 1994, pp.441-2.

[43] Aaron Wolf and John Ross. "The Impact of Scarce Water Resources on the Arab-Israeli Conflict", *Natural Resources Journa*, Fall, 1992. Vol.32, p.919.

unless the dominant power in the basin has accepted it, or has been induced to do so by an external power.

In the Euphrates and Tigris basin it is not easy to see a way forward that would lead to an agreement about water allocation. All three countries involved in the dispute appear to have taken up entrenched positions from which they are unlikely to be easily moved. The three riparians have had difficulty in collaborating on the use of the Euphrates River. This was observed when Turkey announced its GAP project, which indeed was unilaterally designed, without comprehensive Syrian and Iraqi consultation.

The established Trilateral Technical Joint Commission on the Euphrates River, whose members were Turkey, Syria, and Iraq, only discussed technical matters such as river flow and rainfall data. When the Commission felt that it was unable to make any progress, it left the issue to the diplomats. Further, because Turkey regards the area of the Euphrates and Tigris rivers as one basin and Iraq views the rivers and their basins as separate entities, the difference could prove to be an obstacle in finalising any future water agreement. Both Syria and Iraq remain extremely vulnerable to water shortages as a result of Turkey's actions. The ambitious Turkish GAP project certainly affects the flow into Syria and Iraq, and thus is of immediate concern to both; however, no cooperative water-sharing agreement has been secured between the two against Turkey.

The changes in Turkey's foreign environment are provoking vigorous argument over the country's identity and role in the world.[44] For all three of her neighbors Iran, Iraq and Syria, Turkey is perceived as a rival in the struggle for regional control and in the expansion of their interest into new domains, particularly Central Asia and the Caucasus. For Syria, the closer relationship with the US and Israel, which predated the Gulf War also accentuates a rivalry over influence and support beyond the immediate region.

The anxieties surrounding Turkey's GAP project must be put in perspective. The project is intended primarily as a means of boosting economic development in Turkey's least developed areas, mainly the Kurdish populated region, and has raised expectations of economic transformation. As a consequent, the flows of the Euphrates and Tigris downstream have been reduced. Meanwhile, Iraq and Syria are constructing additional water storage facilities to offset likely depletions. The extent to which water becomes an instrument of foreign policy and an item in international relations in this area depends principally on Turkey's security concerns and objectives.

Turkey denies having excess water, even though it has sufficient enough water resources. Problems unrelated to the Arab-Israeli conflict will continue to beset regional tranquillity. The Middle East is not likely to be more stable since the risks of an Arab-Israeli military confrontation not faded away.[45]

It is unlikely that disputes between Turkey and Syria, Turkey and Iraq, or Syria and Iraq over exploitation of the Tigris and especially the Euphrates rivers would escalate

---

[44] For the picture of the region's strategic interests dilemma, see Daniel Pipes and Patrick Clawson, "Ambitious Iran, Troubled Neighbors" *Foreign Affairs*, Vol. 72, No.1, 1993, pp. 124-141; Heinz Kramer, "A Changing Turkey", Brookings Institution Press, 2000.

[45] For likely reshapings in the Arab World see Khair el-Din Haseeb, *The Future of the Arab Nation, Challenges and Options*, London, 1993.

beyond diplomatic protests. Water issues occupy a relatively minor position on the Turkish security agenda. Ankara prefers to participate in joint hydrological projects and to continue regular exchanges of hydrological data, rather than to have multilateral quota-based water sharing.

Turkey's reluctance is partially explained by its insistence of sovereignty over water resources originating in its territory, and partially by Syria's own ambiguous position on the rights and obligations of riparian states. Syrian exploitation of the Yarmuk, and particularly, the Orontes (Asi) River, is hardly cooperative. Syria appears to have awarded itself the kind of upstream rights of sovereignty over these rivers which it vigorously denies to Turkey on the Euphrates or Tigris.

Conclusion

Water related disputes are a consequence, rather than a primary cause, of deteriorating relations between the riparian states. The actual conflict over water is the unilateral appropriation or diversion of a shared water course by upstream riparians without due consultation. Cooperation in the exchange of hydrological data, flood forecasting, joint HEPP and water-recovery ventures, can dampen regional tension and contribute to stability.

The Euphrates possesses some of the elements of a legal regime. Syria and Iraq have at least sometimes agreed to Soviet arbitration and have accepted Saudi Arabian mediation; there is the 1946 Turkish-Iraqi Agreement to consult on water issues; there are similar old Franco-Turkish agreements on sharing the Euphrates which still bind Syria and Turkey, and there appear to be on-going technical discussions involving the three riparian states, the Turkey-Syria protocol, 1987, in this regard. The central problem is the territorial and ideological conflict among the three states. Second is the over-estimated demand for water. In the next 25 years, however, the total demand may well outstrip the water available.

How the dispute among the riparians of both the Euphrates and Tigris Rivers will be solved, if at all, remains uncertain. As a dominant power, Turkey has no interest in basin-wide cooperation with its superior riparian position. Direct negotiations, as pursued since the 1980's, have not produced concrete, stable results. Proposals such as the "Peace Pipeline Project" may represent the most feasible solution to the various conflicts over water in the Middle East. The Peace Pipeline project has now been emphatically rejected by all Arab states who will depend on non-conventional waters in their territory including seawater desalination. In the meantime, it is up to neighboring countries to work out mutually agreeable water-sharing terms and treaties.

Water scarcity represents a security issue for all countries. Overdrafts or cut-offs on existing water resources, reducing quality below usable levels as a linkage to other matters obviously make water a dominant concern. As the uppermost riparian, Turkey is in a position where it has to demonstrate its political will to negotiate and must follow a forward-looking rather than reactive policy; not only in the basin but also in the region.

19 Opening the Closed Window to the East; Turkey's Relations with East Asian Countries

Deniz Ülke Arıboğan

The grand ambitions of Wilsonian idealism, along with the inadequate compromises of the Versailles settlement, proved unequal to the challenges of revolution, disintegration, and the creation of successor states in the aftermath of the First World War. Following World War II, the remaining imperial European powers gradually relinquished their colonial possessions and directed their energies inward, toward creation of a Common Market to facilitate European political unity. In a sense, internecine quarrelling, hot or cold, was left to the United States and the Soviet Union, the two superpowers that emerged from the war. During the Cold War, the main challenge facing the United States and her allies was containment of the threat of Soviet military power and communist expansion. As a member of NATO (North Atlantic Treaty Organization), Turkey's situation on a west-south axis ideally positioned her to mobilize forces against any hint of aggression by the Socialist Block. From the standpoint of Turkish foreign policy makers, the implementation of strategies contrary to Soviet ambition was desirable as they adhered to the country's domestic, social and economic concerns, entirely Western in orientation. This was when enemies and friends stood out clearly. While 'West' was the symbol of beauty, 'East' was the Beast.

The collapse of communism and disintegration of the former Soviet Union engendered an optimistic and idealistic atmosphere, similar to that immediately following the First World War, a radical change of environment for which neither politicians nor academicians were prepared. This emotional and optimistic attitude toward new developments held sway for a short time, briefly overcoming previous indifference toward rising challenges to international peace. The emergence of a political vacuum in the wake of Soviet hegemony soon gave way to a multitude of ethnic, religious and nationalistic claims around the globe. Turkey has been faced with the difficulties of adapting to the challenges in this post Cold War environment. The collapse of the Soviet Union, whose existence represented a continual threat to Turkish sovereignty, carried a mixed blessing as long suppressed ethnic, irredentist and nationalist sentiments emerged on Turkey's borders and, at times, within Turkey itself.

Currently Turkey faces a variety of ethnic and religious difficulties that alternatively might hold potential as assets. Nationalist claims considered a threat to Turkey's territorial integrity, for example, may function equally as a source of solidarity and political power linking Turks of the Balkans, Anatolia and the Caucasus to the China Sea. Religion, another element deemed threatening to the secular Republic's stability, might equally promote bonds of solidarity between Muslims of Africa, Europe and Asia up to Indonesia and Malaysia. These twin characteristics grant Turkey a uniquely privileged status in the new geopolitical arena, which assumes that inhabitants of a territory, sharing in common such traditions as a like history, cultural heritage, language or expectations are more important than the geographical location of the territory itself. The new geopolitics, while activating the psychological and cultural dynamics among nations, also builds new perceptions, sentiments and aspirations concerning group identity and solidarity. In this context Turkey's ties both to Muslim societies and Turkic speaking communities become more important than Turkey's geographical location. As Graham Fuller noted, "it's language and myth, not rivers, mountains or raw materials that link the Turkish shores of the Mediterranean to the shores of Lake Baikal over the rivers of Western China- in the real political sense".[1] Therefore, at this present moment Turkey seems poised to regain its former geopolitical importance by virtue of its historical, cultural and moral background. While these assets provide Turkey with a very favorable strategic position, it would not be a mistake to argue that Turkey is not only a key to open the doors of the Muslim Middle East or the Muslim-Turkic Caucasus, it also is a fulcrum and a stepping stone to reach the Muslims and Turks of eastern and southern Asia.

In the wake of changing geopolitical environment, Turkey's potential to fulfill its new global role is increasingly apparent, yet the Turkish academic community remains reluctant to consider this issue, a reluctance shared for the most part by the international academic community. The reason for this lies mainly in the trends of Cold War ideology, which stemmed from the geo-strategic perceptions of the period and the limits to the definition of the threat to international peace prevalent in the Cold War era. Turkey's strategic role in preserving the stability of the international system' was also restricted by Cold War terminology and Turkey was regarded solely as a buffer state to the Soviet threat. But this perspective was inadequate in indicating who was the enemy and who was the ally. Because in simply defining the Soviets as the only threat to international peace and Turkey as the weak ally lying along the south-eastern flank of Europe, it ignored or overlooked the iron curtain, which prevented academics, politicians, and strategists from seeing the turmoil that lay behind its repressive cover. Now, those previously concealed problems form the cleavage lines of today's international conflicts.

The Cold War was an imaginary war, but the new system might be prone to a real one as asserted by Samuel Huntington in his 'clash of civilizations'.[2] Far East Asia includes at least three of Huntington's distinct groups. China and other countries form the core of Confucian civilization, Indonesia, containing the world's largest Muslim population is Islamic, along with Malaysia. Japan remains as an entirely separate culture. Thus, this region is a very critical place where three civilizations meet and interact. Considering the growing importance of these countries in terms of economic development, it does not seem fruitless to suggest 'this region might be a laboratory to test whether the peaceful co-existence of different cultures can be sustained in a so-called pacific century.

Poised on the brink of this pacific century, Turkey has yet to build adequate relations with countries in the region for a number of reasons. Firstly, there is a psychological

---

[1] Graham Fuller, "The New Mediterranean Security Environment: Turkey, the Gulf and Central Asia", Ian Lesser and Robert Levine (Ed.), *The RAND Institute Conference on the New Mediterranean Security Environment: Conference Proceedings*, Santa Monica, CA, RAND, 1993, p.45.
[2] See Samuel Huntington, "The Clash of Civilizations", *Foreign Affairs*, No.72, Summer, 1993.

factor limiting Turkey's vision and isolating Far East Asia as distinct and distant, from the specific region in which Turkey is situated. 'One should not hesitate to go as far as China to equip oneself with scientific knowledge' is a very popular saying -a traditional *hadith-* in Turkey. In addition to the literal meaning of these words, there is the implication of China's geographic remoteness, of a place beyond the normal reaches of travel or interaction. Yet now that, even the longest distances may be covered in a short span of time, Turkey is the closest European power in the western alliance for protecting the new international security structure against lately emerging threats.

Second, political reality positions the West as the most civilized and developed model for Turkey. In support of this, there is a perception afoot that the East is the embodiment of static, underdeveloped and uncultured societies. This bias traces back to the early Turkish enlightenment and remains surprisingly valid on a large scale. The argument was particularly popular among Turkish intelligentsia who led the push toward modernization. Efforts aimed at adopting western modes of life- took root in the Ottoman period in the mid eighteenth and nineteenth centuries under the reigns of Sultans, Mahmut II and Selim III, each of whom attempted to create a westernized Ottoman Empire. Following the Empire's collapse, Mustafa Kemal Atatürk, sought to build a republican-style nation-state with a secular constitution adhering to international rules of law and human rights, rather than to the Islamic sharia. This effort included a western-oriented institutional 'perestroika', which exchanged a set of social reforms aiming at the application of western standards, for oriental modes of social conduct. In formulating these goals as the main principles of the new republic, the founders tried to use the latent antagonism between eastern and western values heavily promoting the West to the detriment of the East. From a strategic perspective 'Turkey's political elite felt the need to protect the domestic order predicated on western ideas and models of socio-political organization against any turbulence, or worse yet from direct challenges from the outside...The narrowly defined priorities of Turkey's external orientation were primarily a function of domestic exigencies'.[3] Promoting westernization policies both domestically and as an international security tool, and isolating herself from the Islamic East, Turkey could neither look to the Far East as a separate entity nor differentiate between her interests in the Near and Far East.

Third, the predominant strategic and military concerns in the post-World War II era focused Turkey's attention locally, fostering regional rather than global interests. In addition to sharing her northeastern border with the former Soviet Union, Turkey's physical location at the crossroads of three continents -Asia, Europe and Africa-meant facing several threats to her territorial integrity. With the breakup of the Soviet Union, she is surrounded by regional instability and reshuffling in the Balkans, Middle East and Caucasus. As Turkish foreign policy makers have their hands full with these concerns, they have little time to deal with events in the Far East. However, this does not preclude awareness of the transformation in the balance of power from a formerly European

---

[3] Duygu Bazoğlu Sezer, "Turkey in the New Security Environment in the Balkan and Black Sea Region". Vojtech Mastny and R. Craig Nation (Ed.), *Turkey Between East and West; New Challenges for a Rising Regional Power*, Boulder Colorado, Westview Press, 1996, p.78.

centered order to a decentralized multi-polar system. Therefore development of new strategies must include a systemic analysis and should indicate a shift in approach, acknowledging the interaction of local and global concerns.

Creating an objective and multi-dimensional view towards Far East Asia without using chauvinist or religious claims should be a *sine qua non* strategy not only for improving analysis in Turkey's relations with East Asia, but also for understanding the inherent problems posed by Turkish-Western interaction. An objective attitude will also prevent a reactive oriental radicalism, which might be a serious threat both to Turkey's traditional foreign policy orientations and the interests of her western allies. This article aims at providing a new dimension, an Asiatic vision as it were, to Turkish foreign policy, emphasizing Turkey's advantages in building effective relations with Far East Asian countries.

Historical Ties with the Far East

Despite several hundred years of diplomatic, commercial, and social interactions, historians have shown little interest in relations between the Ottoman Empire and Muslim countries in Far East. The sixteenth and the seventeenth centuries were witness to the peak of Ottoman expansion and power. The Empire's territories ranged from Hungary in the west, to the Caucasus and the Middle East in the east, and from Crimea in the north, to North Africa and the Arab peninsula in the south. The Ottomans controlled most of the territories around the Mediterranean and the Black seas, but the area of their influence was even more extensive, ultimately reaching to the Muslim societies of the Far East. Traveling south and east through Asia, Turkish merchants and seamen during the fifteenth and sixteenth centuries engaged in voyages of 'discovery', parallel to the oceanic voyages of their western counterparts. Despite the alien aspect of various cultures the travelers encountered, they worked to build good relations among the inhabitants of these lands. In particular the territories of the Muslim Atjeh Sultanate appealed to many merchants (Turkish as well as Arabian and Persian) who preferred to settle where they could freely maintain their religious affiliations and cultural traditions.[4] The Atjeh Sultanate reigning in the north of Sumatra established diplomatic relations with the Ottomans in the sixteenth century. Although the two Muslim powers sought to build upon their initial contacts, distance remained as a barrier to strengthening relations until the Atjeh governors asked for Ottoman support in fending off Portuguese invaders. The Atjeh Sultan Alaeddin el- Kahhar sent a diplomatic mission to Sultan Suleyman I seeking help in protecting the Atjeh territories against colonialist attacks. As the Atjeh mission took almost two years to reach Istanbul, however Sultan Suleyman was deceased when they arrived. The new Sultan, Selim II (1566-1574) received the mission, willingly granting assistance to a friendly Muslim country against the Portuguese colonial incursions. His decision was in keeping with Ottoman claims of precedence, regardless of boundaries or distances, in defending territories falling within the domain of Islam. Selim II dispatched Hızır Pasha to defend the Atjeh Sultanate. Unfortunately a rebellion in Yemen sidetracked

---

[4] James T. Siegel, *The Rope of God: A Study of Religious Symbolism in Atjeh, An Islamic Community in Indonesia,* Los Angeles: Berkeley, 1969, p.37.

the mission, as the Pasha's first duty lay in securing Ottoman territories. Despite the failure of this Ottoman mission to reach Atjeh lands, the Sultan was subsequently able to send 2 warships and 500 soldiers to the aid of Atjeh.[5] In 1567, an agreement between the Atjeh Sultanate and the Ottoman Empire rendered the Sultanate an Ottoman protectorate. Relations between the two powers remained friendly although the Ottoman ability to defend Muslim territories diminished over time. By 1873, when the Atjeh governors requested Ottoman help against Dutch aggression in accordance with the 1567 agreement, the weakened Empire could only respond by sending a note stating that Atjeh was under its protection.[6]

Despite the diminishment of virtual authority in the last decades of the Ottoman Empire, the caliphate retained a political authority that Sultan Abdulhamid II (1876-1909) was ambitious to exploit in territories falling within the purview of Islam. Concomitant to the accession of Abdulhamid II, the international political order of the late nineteenth century experienced a tectonic shift, affecting the already weakened position of the Ottoman Empire. Between 1870 and 1900, the race for colonial possessions reached its height and the British Empire, supported by her Navy, emerged as the leading power. The unification of Germany in 1871 introduced a new European power to the international political arena, contributing to the upset of the previous balance. In addition, the depth of infirmity revealed by the Ottoman defeat in the Russo-Turkish war of 1877-78 influenced British Imperial policy toward the Ottoman Empire. This policy altered from the preservation of Ottoman 'territorial integrity', thereby safeguarding the road to Indochina, anticipating the demise of the 'sick man of Europe'. Thus Abdulhamid's advocacy of pan-islamism seemed inevitable as virtually the only potentially powerful instrument at his disposal in an Islamic zone extending from the Mediterranean to the Pacific Ocean. His influence as Caliph over Muslim communities suffering from imperialist attacks would not only affect the Russian Empire but also British interests throughout that region. Consequently, Abdulhamid restructured the caliphate into a centralized, universal Muslim institution, taking upon himself the role of defender of the religious rights of all Muslims. "Once more the Turks asserted their role as the defenders of Sunni-Orthodox Islam but did not leave the caliphate to others (as in 1051) or give it a relatively neutral status (as in post 1517-20), but rather, revitalized and politicized it in the role of representative for the entire Muslim community".[7]

The political power represented by Islam was an important asset for the Ottomans. As different elements tried to make use of it in the international struggle for power, so too, the Ottomans employed it as a bargaining and balancing chip. For instance during the Spanish-American war over the Philippines in 1898, the United States government sought the Caliph's support in order to manage the Muslim communities inhabiting the islands

[5] Affan Seljuk, "Osmanlı İmparatorluğu'nun Malay-Endonezya Takımadalarındaki Müslüman Krallıklarla İlişkileri", trans. İsmail Hakkı Göksoy, *Türk Dünyası Araştırmaları*, No.94, Şubat 1995, pp.115-16

[6] Seljuk, "Osmanlı İmparatorluğu'nun Malay-Endonezya Takımadalarındaki Müslüman Krallıklarla İlişkileri", p.116

[7] Kemal Karpat, "The Ottoman Empire and the Beginning of the Reform Movement", *Turkey's Politics-The Transition to a Multi-Parti System*, Kemal H. Karpat, Princeton University Press, 1959, p.29

primarily, in the north east of Borneo. Abdulhamid issued a decree to the people of the territory to support the United States of America, which the Muslim population promptly accepted.

Abdulhamid's policy differed markedly from that of his predecessors in wielding the religious authority of the caliphate as a political sword against Europe, in general and the British Empire in particular.[8]

Everybody is aware that one word of mine as a caliph will suffice to jeopardize the British hegemony in Indo-China. There is no need to be a genius to realize this. If Germany, France and Russia had asked for it during the Boxer Rebellion, they would be able to demolish the pseudo castle of the British Empire in Indo-China with my help. However, they lost this opportunity, as they did not react on time.[9]

Abdulhamid sent envoys to Far East, attempting to persuade Muslim sheiks and sect leaders to recognize the sovereignty of the Caliph in Istanbul. One of the most important attempts was the mission led by Enver Pasha in 1901. Muslim communities all along the route welcomed this mission on its journey into China. Despite the challenge presented to such diplomatic sorties by the British Empire, with its frequents calls for Muslim allegiance to the Crown, Ottoman influence ultimately proved more effective as Chinese Muslims preferred to recognize the Caliph as their spiritual leader. During this competition for political influence in the Far East, Kaiser Wilhelm II of Germany supported the Ottomans to further relations already strengthened through cooperation on the Anatolia-Baghdad railway project.[10] Kaiser Wilhelm asked the Caliph to send agents to China to organize the Boxer rebellion. A German newspaper 'Der Ostasiastische Lloyd' stated that the Muslim communities were preparing to authorize the Caliph in their internal political affairs as well.[11] In 1908, the 'Beijing- Hamidiye University' was opened in Beijing with the Ottoman flag hanging to symbolize Chinese Muslim respect for the Ottoman Caliph. France also supported the Ottomans venture in the Far East hoping thereby to neutralize Ottoman power in North Africa. With the backing of two such considerable European powers the Ottoman Empire managed to remain an effective influence in the Far East until World War I.[12]

In addition to advocating a religious fraternity, Abdulhamid sought alliances with Japan and other East Asia countries that might prove useful in counteracting western encroachments, particularly on the part of Russia. For the Japanese, an alliance with the Ottoman Empire seemed a useful step toward eliminating, or at least withstanding, colonialist pressures. Forced to accept foreign trade and interactions after maintaining a

---

[8] İsmail Hami Danişment. *İzahlı Osmanlı Tarihi Kronolojisi.* C.4. İstanbul: Türkiye Yayınevi. 1972. p.352.

[9] Selçuk Günay. "İkinci Abdülhamid Dönemi'nde Güney ve Güneydoğu Asya Osmanlı Politikasından Bazı Örnekler", *Atatürk Üniversitesi Edebiyat Fakültesi Araştırma Dergisi,* No.18. Erzurum, 1990. p.134

[10] For Ottoman-German relations and information about the historical Anatolia-Baghdad railway see Murat Özyüksel. *Osmanlı- Alman İlişkilerinin Gelişim Sürecinde Anadolu ve Bağdat Demiryolları.* İstanbul: Arba, 1988.

[11] İhsan Süreyya Sırma. "Sultan II. Abdülhamid ve Çin Müslümanları", *İslam Tetkikleri Enstitüsü Dergisi,* İstanbul. IÜEFY. 1979. C.7. Cüz 3-4. p.201

[12] Sırma. "Sultan II. Abdülhamid ve Çin Müslümanları". p.204.

policy of strict isolation for 250 years, the Meiji government scrambled to modernize and achieve parity with the West, adopting western technology along with some political institutions. At the same time, the Japanese sought alliances with countries under similar threat from imperial colonialism. The Ottoman Empire, also facing the double threat of western imperial interests and physical proximity to Russia, was a logical choice. After the initial visit by Japanese foreign ministry officials in 1871, the Japanese envoys traveling to Europe first broke their journey in Ottoman territory. However, the Meiji government's spectacular success in transforming Japan into a technologically sound imperial power led the Ottomans to question their bilateral relations, especially in light of subsequent Japanese demands capitulation within the Ottoman Empire. The Ottomans also entertained doubts concerning Russian reaction to an Ottoman-Japanese alliance not wishing to escalate the already existing tension with Russia, as emphasized by Abdulhamid. "In order to maintain the peaceful coexistence both with our friends and enemies, it is necessary to keep the bilateral relations at a certain level, so that we should not be the victim of the other's hostility while strengthening the relations with our friends".[13]

Following the first visit by Fukuchi Genichiro from the Japanese foreign ministry in 1873, the two governments proceeded to exchange a number of official visits over the next quarter of the century[14]. During one such exchange, a tragedy involving the frigate Ertugrul, sent by the Ottomans to visit the Japanese ports, provided dramatic reinforcement to already burgeoning diplomatic relations. In 1878, the Japanese squadron 'Seiki' arrived in Istanbul en route to a training mission in Europe. The Ottomans welcomed the ship and hosted its crew. Then in 1881, Prince Kato Hito visited the Ottoman Empire in an effort to conclude agreements relating to trade and wartime status, but concern regarding the possible Russian reaction caused Abdulhamid to hesitate over signing the agreements. However following the visit of Prince Komatsu in 1887 bearing a message of friendship from the Japanese Emperor, the Sultan responded in kind. The frigate Ertugrul, a training ship carrying some 600 young naval officers, was dispatched to Japan with a return message of friendship and presents. Unfortunately, by the closing years of the Nineteenth century the Ottoman navy was in poor condition and the frigate was ill prepared for a long arduous journey. During the passage, which took almost a year, the ship suffered several accidents, but continued to sail along its route to Japan, making stops at Bombay, Colombo, Singapore, Saigon and Hong Kong. The Ertugrul was well received by Muslim communities along the route, and its arrival in Japanese waters likely induced some sense of solidarity among the Japanese for the Muslims of the Far East, despite the strong disapproval of the British government. Emperor Meiji received the frigate's crew, who presented to him a letter from the Sultan along with the highest decoration of the Ottoman Empire. The crew then spent three months in Tokyo until they received a message recalling them to Istanbul. Although Japanese officials repeatedly warned them of terrible weather conditions, they insisted on departing with all

---

[13] Sultan Abdulhamid, *Siyasi Hatıratım*, İstanbul: Dergah Yayınları, 1987, p.136.
[14] Hee-Soo Lee ve İbrahim İlhan, *Osmanlı Japon Münasebetleri ve Japonya'da İslamiyet*, İstanbul: Türk Diyanet Vakfi Yayınları, 1989, p.24.

possible speed. In September 1890, the Ertugrul sank south of Honshu Island during a violent typhoon in which 581 of the young naval officers on board drowned. Japanese fishermen managed to rescue only 69 officers. News of tragedy caused great sorrow in the Ottoman Empire as well as in Japan. The Meiji Emperor ordered his government to assign the warships Hiei and Kongo to return the survivors to Istanbul. The Ottoman government welcomed them, extending their gratitude to the Japanese government both for their rescue efforts and sympathetic treatment of the remaining officers. Thus, Japanese conduct throughout this tragedy worked to strengthen already friendly relations between the two powers. Today, there stands a graveyard in the southeast grounds of Kashinozaki lighthouse built for the crew of the frigate Ertugrul, drowned in that disaster.[15]

The strength of relations between the Ottoman Empire and Japan steadily increased in the years leading up to World War I, despite the disturbance to both Russian and British Empires. With the outbreak Russo-Japanese War, Abdulhamid professed "the victory of Japan will make us (the Ottomans) happy, because their victory means our victory. Such a victory will also help us by enforcing the Russian government to send their troops to the Far East and reduce its forces in the Black Sea".[16]

Apparently, promotion of a so-called 'pan-islamic' policy did not prevent Abdülhamid from forming an alliance with a non-Muslim country. Fully aware of the Empire's weakened condition he attempted various methods of securing Ottoman territories against colonialist depredations. Abdulhamid sought to create a 'balance of terror' system, threatening the hegemony of both Russia and the British Empire in Asia, while continuing to exercise the influence he wielded as Caliph among the Muslims of the Far East. From the standpoint of the Japanese government, the Ottomans were the only possible ally among the western states as their traditional, 'oriental' culture exhibited characteristics similar to the more conservative, non-western Japanese society. Following the Sino-Japanese war in 1894 and, more importantly, the Russo-Japanese war in 1904, Japan emerged both as an important international power in her own right and a potentially destabilizing factor to Western interests in the Far East. In light of this circumstance friendship between Japan and the Ottoman Empire presented a threatening development to western hegemony and interests in Asia.

Relations with the Far East in the Republican Period

By the close of the First World War, the previous century's absorption with powers equilibrium, ententes, and alliances altered irrevocably (though not permanently) to accommodate an archetypal political system based on Wilsonian principles. The collapse of three great empires, Austria-Hungary, Russia and the Ottoman Empire, paved the way for the introduction of the Twentieth-century nation-state as a distinct political entity.

---

[15] For more information about the Ertuğrul Disaster see Erol Mütercimler, *Ertuğrul Faciası ve 21. Yüzyıla Doğru Türk Japon İlişkisi*, İstanbul: Anahtar Kitaplar, 1993; Çetinkaya Apatay, *Ertuğrul Firkateyninin Öyküsü*, İstanbul: AD Kitapçılık, 1998; Kaori Komatsu, *Ertuğrul Faciası ve Bir Dostluğun Doğuşu*, Ankara: Turhan Kitapevi, 1992.

[16] Sultan Abdulhamid, *Siyasi Hatıratım*, p.165.

Though the British Empire emerged from the War victorious and even expanded, the days of the imperial colonial system were clearly numbered. The founders of the new Turkish Republic realized that any overt adherence to the heritage of the Ottoman Empire would cause considerable difficulty in the emergent international system. Therefore the Turkish Republic proclaimed itself a secular state in the modern European national mold, adopting western norms and customs and abolishing the Caliphate, perhaps the singular most significant act of westernization. Such a radical action, though it found favor in government circles, sent shock waves rippling through the Muslim societies of Far East Asia. Muslim communities in China and India, having recognized the Caliph as their spiritual leader were particularly disappointed. Not surprisingly, there resulted a slight diminishment in the enthusiasm and sympathy displayed towards Atatürk, despite his status as a national hero and campaigner against colonial powers. In Malaysia, for instance a distinct lack of interest prevailed towards the Turkish Revolution apart from young Malays for whom Kemal Atatürk embodied a successful Asian challenge to imperialist western powers and the chief concerns regarded future conditions for the pilgrims who regularly visited Ottoman lands.[17] The reaction was most positive in Japan, which undertook similarly inclusive reforms during the Meiji period. Japanese intelligentsia closely monitored the developments in Turkey regarding the Turkish war of independence as an Asian victory against Europe. Members of the Japanese elite even proposed establishing a pan-Asian Union,[18] though this proposal stemmed from a misperception concerning the ultimate aims of the Turkish revolution. In fact, the Turkish revolution not only directed itself toward integration with the western world, it also aimed at breaking with its oriental Asiatic roots.

Differing from the Ottomans in the conduct of domestic social, economic and political matters, the foreign policy range of the new Turkish Republic also differed from that of its predecessor. The Ottoman Empire was a global empire, maintaining an international vision even throughout its prolonged decline, whereas the Turkish Republic was a regional state with a necessarily limited scope in foreign policy activity. Yet, though Turkey treated Far East issues with studied indifference and concentrated on Western Europe, the government did undertake a few initiatives in an eastern direction.

Turkey's first diplomatic relations with Far East countries were established with Japan, despite the fact that the two states opposed one another during World War I. Having concluded the Lausanne Treaty in 1924, Japan accredited its first ambassador to Istanbul in the following year. Turkey, in turn, opened her embassy in Japan in 1931 and bilateral relations gradually intensified until World War II. By 1927 Turkey maintained 27 diplomatic missions world wide, but only one of them, Japan, was located in a Far Eastern country.[19] Despite the fact that Japan was one of the victorious countries of the First World War, their expansionist claims in Asia continued in contravention, as it were,

---

[17] A.C. Miller, "Türk Devriminin Malezya'daki Etkileri", İskender Gökalp ve François Georgeon (Ed.), *Kemalizm ve İslam Dünyası*, İstanbul: Arba Yayınları, 1990, pp.188-189.

[18] Yuzo Nagata, "Türk Devriminin Japonya'daki Yankıları", *Studies on the Social and Economic History of the Ottoman Empire*, İzmir: Akademi Kitabevi, 1995, p.33.

[19] Kemal Girgin, *Osmanlı ve Cumhuriyet Dönemleri Hariciye Tarihimiz (Teşkilat ve Protokol)*, Ankara: Türk Tarih Kurumu Basımevi, 1994, p.122.

of Wilsonian policy. Japan's growing hegemony over the region rapidly changed the balance of power in Far East Asia. In 1932, the declaration of 'Manchuko' under a Japanese mandate gave rise to an environment of increasing distrust between Japan and other powers with interests in the region, such as China, the United States, Great Britain and Russia. During this time, however, Japan sought to maintain cordial relations with Turkey, as evidenced by use of the slogan 'there is Turkey in the west of Asia while there is Japan in the east of it'.[20]

Turkey's official contacts with China date from 1925. The first diplomatic mission in Nanking was established in 1929. During the Nineteenth and the early Twentieth centuries these two Empires were each dubbed 'sick men of the East', with 'China as the sick man of the Far East and the Ottomans the sick man of the near East'. Sharing similar positions in foreign policy in addition to somewhat shaky constitutions, the Chinese were understandably interested in events leading to the establishment of a secular Turkish Republic in 1923, following an anti-imperialist war for independence. There were those among the Chinese who viewed political and social developments in Turkey with admiration, considering Mustafa Kemal Atatürk, a brilliant example of political leadership who could be taken as a model for China as well.[21]

Until the communist takeover in 1949 there were no problems concerning relations between China and Turkey. After the Chinese revolution Turkey officially maintained its relations only with the government of what is now called the Chinese Taipei. Mao Zedong and Zhou Enlai, the men responsible for shaping Chinese foreign policy for most of the period from 1949 through 1976, sought to preserve China's autonomy while enhancing its security within the framework of the Cold War. From 1949 through 1960 Mao guided the People's Republic to 'lean to one side', the Soviet side, while Turkey leaned to the other, namely, the United States of America. When Sino-Soviet relations broke down over controversies relating to security, sovereignty and ideology, China preferred to remain autonomous and became a member of the non-aligned movement established in Bandung-Indonesia in 1955. Although Turkey participated in the Bandung Conference, the government's policy of leaning toward American support and friendship placed the Turkish mission in an untenable position. In his speech, the Turkish foreign minister Fatin Rüştü Zorlu emphasized the communist threat and while discrediting the non-aligned movement, defended NATO as the only preserver of world peace. This speech found little favor among the participants in the conference, especially India and China. Both Zhou Enlai and Nehru brought counter arguments against Turkey, with Nehru declaring Turkey's membership to NATO an unacceptable humiliation for an Asian country.[22] Henceforth, Turkey failed to build sufficient relations with nonaligned countries and in many of the international conflicts in which Turkey subsequently found herself involved, these countries generally took positions unfavorable to Turkey.[23]

---

[20] Nagata, "Türk Devriminin Japonya'daki Yankıları", p.33

[21] William Eberhard, "Yeni Türkiye ve Çin, Atatürk Bibliyografyasına İlave", *Belleten*, Cilt.V, I.Teşrin, Sayı 20, 1941, p.627.

[22] Mehmet Gönlübol, (Ed.), *Olaylarla Türk Dış Politikası (1919-1973)*, Cilt.1, Ankara: A.Ü., SBF Yayınları, 1982, p.284.

[23] For voting behaviors of both Turkey and the nonaligned countries see Faruk Sönmezoğlu, "Kıbrıs Sorunu, Bağlantısızlar ve BM Genel Kurulu'ndaki Oylamalar/Kararlar", Faruk Sönmezoğlu (Ed.), *Türk*

During the inter-war period Turkey worked to transform herself into a contemporary nation-state capable of assuming membership among the ranks of the modern western community. After the death of Mustafa Kemal Atatürk, his successor İsmet İnönü took office and continued to support the single party system, aimed at creating a secular/civilized society isolated from its Islamic and Ottoman heritage. Efforts to integrate with the West forced Turkey along a uni-dimensional, euro-centered policy path, resulting in an ever-widening information rift as the country turned away from consideration of Asian affairs. Until the outbreak of the Korean War in 1950, Turkey remained markedly unaware of political developments in Far East Asia. In keeping, however, with her determination to win acceptance to NATO, Turkey voluntarily sent troops to Korea to indicate her willingness in assisting international peacekeeping efforts. The government took the decision to send the troops without first laying the matter before the Turkish National Assembly, as Turkey was sensitive, throughout this period, concerning the Soviet threat bordering her territory. Though the political opposition decried this decision as unlawful, it was heavily supported by the public, thereby ensuring its tenancy.[24] In the end Turkey sent 4500 troops to Korea, the second largest contribution overall and lost 878 soldiers with 2246 injured.[25] Turkey's involvement in the Korean War stemmed not from any direct interest in the region but, rather, from determination to carve for herself a niche as 'equal partner' in relations with the West. The Chinese government, on the other hand, with a definite interest in regional security, sought volunteers to fight with the North Koreans. For the next three years the Chinese sustained large losses, both from the battle and from the brutal winters, before they succeeded in stalemating the Korean conflict providing Mao with a safe northeastern flank.[26]

Turkey's effort in the Korean War was an expression of her desire to enter the western alliance of powers in the post-World War II system. The effort was rewarded and Turkey was chosen as a member of the UN Security Council for the first time in 1951. As the most popular ally of the West, Turkey became a member of NATO in 1952 followed by membership in the other international organizations created by the Western powers during the 1950s and 1960s. However, the results of the Korean war motivated Turkey to reevaluate relations with the Asian powers, and, after concluding an agreement with Japan in 1951, Turkey began establishing diplomatic relations with some of the countries of the region. By 1953, Turkey had diplomatic missions in China (Taipei), India, Japan and Pakistan.[27] Turkey also signed a trade agreement with Indonesia in 1958.

Indonesia was an Asian country with which Turkey was relatively unfamiliar until the late 1950s, a condition that did not apply in reverse. Indonesian political history was influenced by developments in the Turkish democratization and secularization process,

Dış Politikasının Analizi, İstanbul: Der Yayınları, 1994, pp.441-81.
[24] İsmail Soysal, *Soğuk Savaş Dönemi ve Türkiye; Olaylar Kronolojisi (1945-1975)*, İstanbul: ISIS Yayıncılık, 1997, pp.99-100.
[25] Soysal, *Soğuk Savaş Dönemi ve Türkiye; Olaylar Kronolojisi (1945-1975)*, p.179
[26] John R. Faust and Judith F. Kornberg, *China in World Politics*, Boulder, Colorado: Lynne Rienner Publishers, 1995, p.35.
[27] Girgin, *Osmanlı ve Cumhuriyet Dönemleri Hariciye Tarihimiz (Teşkilat ve Protokol)*, pp.140-41.

and the Indonesian leaders long debated the Turkish Revolution as a pattern for their state building endeavors. During the 1940s Turkish secularization formed the main topic of discussion between the reformist leader Sukarno and Islamist leader Natsir. Sukarno propounded the Turkish model, which completely segregated issues of religion and state. In contrast, Natsir suggested that a single party system with no respect for freedom of thought and belief was not a democracy, and criticising Atatürk's policies he added that the reform in Turkish Islam was neither progressive nor liberalizing up, but merely a new form of colonization by the western powers.[28]

Far East Asia resumed a prominent position in Turkey's political agenda during the Vietnam War. Although Turkey was not involved in the war, the Turkish government declared its support for the United States of America on several occasions. The Turkish foreign minister İhsan Sabri Çağlayangil emphasized that the steps taken by the American government would facilitate a solution to the problem in Vietnam and reiterated his belief that Richard Nixon's presidency would prove beneficial toward building a peaceful environment in the region.[29]

The basic motivation underlying Turkey's political attitude during the 1960s and 1970s was containment international communism. Bordering the Soviet Union, Turkey felt strongly the ever-present threat of communist expansion, perhaps overestimating the danger, but both in domestic and foreign policy implementation. Turkish governments gave priority to the struggle against socialism and communism. Since China was also considered a potential threat, supporters of Mao and communist China in Turkey were put under pressure by the government, resulting in a fundamental clash of political ideologies. The 1970s in Turkey formed the framework for almost a decade of civil war, marked by chaos and terror, as the very fabric of society was rent by division between socialist and anti-socialist forces.

Turkey-Far East Asia Relations in Recent Times

The ideological polarization of the 1970s resulted in a military coup détat in 1980. The leaders of the political parties were arrested and new political, economic and social policies were put into force. Under the leadership of Turgut Özal, import substitution policies were set aside, and Turkey adopted an export promotion policy, simultaneously liberalizing its economic activities for integration into the global capitalist market.

To a certain degree, economic imperatives achieved supremacy over military and political considerations as Turkey began to pay special attention to economic alliances and trading partners. Increasingly, she turned toward the East as there existed a vast potential for economic cooperation and trade between Turkey and the countries of Far East Asia, many of whom had succeeded in adopting models of development without investing in heavy industry, achieving considerable and sustainable growth rates. The aggregate trade volume within the whole region surpassed $3.5 billion, and despite the effects of the Asian crisis in the late 1990s, economic relations remained lively.

Given the current state of affairs, it seems natural to speak of Far East Asian countries

---

[28] François Georgeon, "Kemalizm ve İslam Dünyası (1919-1938); Bazı İşaret Taşları", *Kemalizm ve*, pp.41-42
[29] Yılmaz Altuğ, *Vietnam*, Istanbul: Çantay Kitabevi, 1998, pp.113-14.

as trading partners. During the 1970s, however, Japan was the only Asian country Turkey felt she could trust, as there were no ideological rivalries between the two powers, and Japan was regarded as the 'western state of the East'. While the trade volume between the two countries increased from $44.3 million in 1970, to $376 million in 1976, giant projects were undertaken, such as the Pendik maritime arsenal and the Afsin-Elbistan thermal station. The Japanese Eximbank provided a credit of $166 million for promoting trade with Turkey and until Turkey reached a bottleneck in providing foreign exchange in the late 1970s, economic relations developed rapidly. In 1979 the trade volume dropped down to $148.2 million, and the Japanese government halted some of the bilateral economic activities until the mid 1980s. In 1983 a Japanese foreign minister, Shintaro Abe, paid a historical visit to Turkey to negotiate both on political issues such as Middle East affairs and the Iran-Iraq war, and on economic issues facing Turkish government. Following the visit, a loan agreement of $65 million was signed between Turkey and Japan a vital support for the new Turkish government.[30] During the election campaigns Turgut Özal promised to transform Turkey and to create a 'Japan of the Middle East'. After Özal, the most popular Turk in Japan,[31] took office, relations rapidly improved. In 1985, when the Iraqi government declared that it would begin a non-limited bombing campaign in Iranian territory, Turkey sent two aircrafts to remove Japanese citizens from Iran, thereby strengthening the relations between the two countries. Throughout the Özal period the Turco-Japanese relations were harmonious in the economic as well as in the political sphere. The volume of trade between Japan and Turkey increased from $234 million in 1980 to $ 615.4 million in 1989 and in 1990 Turkey was among the top ten recipients of Japanese aid.[32] In the 1990s with economic ties growing and the volume of trade reaching more than $1579 million in 1995,[33] the two countries worked to emphasize and improve their social and political relations. In the early 2000s the trade volume between the two countries stabilized at around $1.5 billion.

From a security perspective, Japan needs good relations with Turkey in order to access the tremendous stores of energy available in the Middle East and the Caucasus and Turkey needs good relations with Japan to access a prominent international *entrepot*. The breakup of the Soviet Union was followed by the emergence of several new republics with Muslim populations. With a total population of over 50 million Turkish speakers, these countries provided Turkey with a new geopolitical and geo-strategic role. Equally, emerging security concerns in North East Asia led Japan into assuming a larger and more active role in regional affairs. Political uncertainties in Russia, China and the Korean peninsula, intermix with territorial disputes among the countries of the region, including Japan, to sustain tensions and the occasional conflict. In addition to territorial disputes with Russia, Japan recently developed tensions with South Korea over the latter's use of

---

[30] Hiranao Matsutani, *Japonya'nın Dış Politikası ve Türkiye*, İstanbul: Bağlam Yayınları, 1995, p.108.

[31] Matsutani, *Japonya'nın Dış Politikası ve Türkiye*, p.108.

[32] Danny Unger, "Japan's Capital Exports: Molding East Asia", in Danny Unger and Paul Blackburn (Ed.), *Japan"s Emerging Global Role*, Boulder, Colorado: Lyenne Rienner Publishers, 1993, p.157.

[33] *Foreign Trade Statistics, State Institute of Statistics*, Prime Ministry, Republic of Turkey, Ankara, 1997, p.48.

the waters around the disputed northern territories, as well as with China and Taiwan over the Senkaku Islands, located north of Taiwan.[34] Although Japan regards itself as a power of 'pacific times', an economic rather than a military giant, the financial retrenchment leading to the decline of the American military's presence in the region forced Japan to step into the breach. Recently the responsibility of maintaining the balance of power in the Far East devolved on Japan. As this more active role may potentially lead to a Sino-Japanese rivalry, the US-Japan Security Treaty takes on increasing importance, and closer dialogue on security matters between these two countries seems essential. In the light of the assumption that 'as security is a global issue, there is no regional security', contributions from other American allies such as Turkey, Israel or Great Britain would prove equally beneficial.

By the same token, the Sino-Turkish relations might also be considered a matter of global security, certainly of potential economic value to both countries. Since the Far East again appeared on Turkey's political and economic agenda in the post Cold War period, the measure of relations between Turkey and China has grown significantly. Although relations normalized with Turkey's recognizing the People's Republic of China as the sole representative of the Chinese nation in 1971, relations between Turkey and China failed to develop as successfully as they should have. There were two important reasons for this condition. Firstly each power felt that the other belonged to an ideologically diametrical order, China being communist and Turkey, liberal capitalist. Second their relations developed primarily from without, heavily influenced by the American initiatives. Once the US administration actively pursued a policy of improving American relations with China in the late 1960's, China assumed a place on the agenda of the Turkish foreign policy. Following the Sino-Soviet border clashes in 1969, the American government altered its strategic position in Asia, and shifting China's status to that of a de facto ally in countering Soviet power in Asia.[35] The opening of bilateral relations between the US and China in the 1970's, caused the Turkish government to change her policy towards China as well. After the recognition of the Republic of China, a civil aviation agreement (1972), a trade agreement (1974) and a trade protocol (1981) between the two countries were signed in order to both establish and cement economic and political ties. But for Sino-Turkic relations to strengthen, it was necessary to wait until the early 1980s. Kenan Evren, the seventh president, was the first Turkish head of state to visit China, in May 1982. The then prime minister, Turgut Özal, visited Beijing in 1985, giving a strong impetus to bilateral relations. The Chinese senior leadership reciprocated these state visits. The intensified diplomatic traffic was sustained in the 1990s. The result of these official exchanges of visits was two-way trade approaching $429 million in 1995 and $1105 million in 2002, as compared to $98 million in 1985.

As China continues to develop its economic and political potential, transforming itself into a formidable Twenty-first century mercantile power in the Far East, Turkey must build new, multidimensional strategies for dealing with her Asian partner. The strategic

---

[34] Masashi Nishihara, "North East Asia and Japanese Security", *Japan's Emerging Securiy Role*, p.95

[35] Tan Qingshan, *The Making of U.S. China Policy*, Boulder, London: Lynne Rienner Publishers, 1992, p.3.

center of gravity is also shifting towards China and other dynamic Pacific-Rim nations, ushering in fundamental changes to traditional balance of power equations. Turkey and China are situated at opposite ends of Asia, but linked by the vast Eurasian landmass, strive toward the creation of a Twenty-first century version of the ancient Silk Road that linked China to the Middle East and Europe through Central Asia.[36] Considering that both are great powers with important strategic assets at their disposal, their relationship should be based on a critical assessment of their respective positions in the modern world.

The two countries may cooperate as well as compete in the economic and political arenas. Some Turkish strategists liken China to an uncontrolled cascading river and perceive it as a threat to all Muslim and Turkish speaking communities in Asia. According to them there is nothing to prevent the Yellow Sea from overflowing its banks into Mid-Asia and the West, so one must not underestimate the Chinese threat.[37] In contrast, other strategists suggest that the relationship between China and Turkey diversify beyond traditional issues, in recognition of the growing economic and geo-strategic significance of the region. They think that the presence of Turkic and Muslim minorities in China's Xinjiang/Eastern Turkistan Uygur autonomous region may be considered an asset in rejuvenating relations between the two countries.[38] However, the region actually encompasses one of the most disputed sections of Chinese territory, with more than 10 million ethnic Turks inhabiting the area.

Historically the region traces back to the late Ottoman ages, when Yakup Khan, the founder of the Kasghar Khanate established in that specific region in 1865, asked the Ottomans for help in his struggle against both Russian pressure and Chinese attacks. The Ottoman government responded by sending military specialists to train the new Kasghar army and the two countries established diplomatic relations soon after. But the valuable natural resources of the region attracted the attention of the British Empire as well, and to ensure its safety, the Kasghar Khanate accepted the status of protectorate within the Ottoman Empire. In 1870 they recognized Sultan Abdülaziz as their Caliph, minting coins with his image and delivering the special sermon (*hutbe*) in the mosque citing his name. Unfortunately, this measure was not equal to eradicating the instability of the Khanate, and the Chinese attacks grew increasingly violent. After the death of Yakup Khan in 1877, the Kasghar territories were invaded by the Chinese army. One year later China captured the whole of the Xinjiang/Eastern Turkistan region, but the Ottoman government was too weak to confront the Chinese in the aftermath of the Russo-Turkish War.[39] Following the episode, the ethnic Turks within Turkistan attempted twice more to establish sovereign states, but neither the first Republic of Eastern Turkistan, which declared its independence in 1933, nor the second one, in 1944, were able to maintain

---

[36] Mehmet Öğütçü, "Turkey and China", http://www.egemenlik-ulusundur.org/ustat/ulastra/ ogutcu1.htm., p.1 also printed in *Perceptions, Journal of International Affairs*, Vol.1, No.3, Sept.-Nov. 1996

[37] Muzaffer Özdağ, "Taşan Sarı Okyanusun Yarattığı Tehdit", *Avrasya Dosyası*, Vol.2., No.2. Summer 1995, p.74

[38] Öğütçü, "Turkey and China", p.10.

[39] Rıfat Uçarol, *Siyasi Tarih, (1789-1994)*, İstanbul: Filiz Kitabevi, 1995, pp.271-72.

their existence.[40] In the 1950s, Mao's argument on 'China's political and cultural integrity' and his declaration that 'Xinjiang was a part of China for over 2000 years' led to strict control over the people in the region. During the Cultural Revolution assimilation policies and the forced settlement of Chinese 'Han' ethnic groups in this particular region succeeded in altering the population distribution, with the 'Han' population figures increasing by almost 8% every year.[41] According to Chinese official data, the Chinese population has reached to 5.287.000 million in 1983, from 324.000 before 1949.[42]

Today the Xinjiang/Eastern Turkistan province comprises the most fertile land in China as well as tremendous energy and material potential, earning it the occasional sobriquet of the 'Chinese California'. In addition its growing strategic importance intensified the conflict of interests over the region, as the province borders the ex-Soviet Turkish speaking Republics of Kazakhistan, Kırgızistan and Tajikistan. The non-Han residents of Xinjiang province have far more in common with their brethren, both in the new Republics and in Turkey, than they do with the Chinese leaders in Beijing. The common historical and ethnic background linking the people of these different countries may prove advantageous to China in approaching the Central Asian Republics as a trading partner, or ally, or even a hegemonic power. Equally, this same-shared heritage may prove disadvantageous to China's territorial integrity. So too, Turkey, as successor to the Ottoman Empire, might claim a critical voice in the region by virtue of the ethnic and religious background it shares in common with the people of the region. With this potential connection in mind, the Chinese president, Jiang Zemin, warned the Turkish prime minister, Bülent Ecevit in 1998 that the anti-Chinese activities by the Uygur people living in Turkey might disturb political relations between China and Turkey.[43] Turkey's response will determine whether she will serve as a moderator between the Chinese government and the Turkic speaking people within the province and surrounding territories or as an agitator, provoking the people against China, in order to undermine Chinese authority in the region and parry China's hegemonic claims. Currently, Turkey's choice seems that of a moderator in the Balkans, the Middle East, in Central Asia, and, in fact, in all the regions inhabited by Muslim populations. After taking steps to create a Balkan Pact in the West, the Turkish president, Süleyman Demirel, proposed a 'Stability Pact' throughout the Caucasus in February 2000. This seems a promising initiative designed to secure Central Asia from different hegemonic attacks and to neutralize the region by eliminating external influences and interests, so that neither Russia, China nor the United States of America may involve themselves in internal factions or conflicts.

Turkish pro-Chinese strategists believe that another opportunity for strengthening relations with China lies in the Turkish Southeast Anatolia Project (GAP),[44] designed to

[40] Ahat Andican, "Türkistan Cumhuriyetleri, Rusya ve Çin Üçgeninde Doğu Türkistan", *Avrasya Dosyası*, Vol. 2, No.2, Summer 1995, p.82.
[41] Andican, "Türkistan Cumhuriyetleri, Rusya ve Çin Üçgeninde Doğu Türkistan", p.82
[42] *Doğu Türkistan*, Doğu Türkistan Göçmenler Derneği Yayını, İstanbul, no date, p.17
[43] Mehmet Öğütçü, *Geleceğimiz Asya'da mı?Yaralı Asya, Çin ve Türkiye*, İstanbul: AD Kitapçılık, 1999, p.164.
[44] Öğütçü, "Turkey and China", p.11.

contribute to China's food supplies and agri-industrial requirements beyond the year 2000. Current projections indicate that China will suffer severe food shortages in the first quarter of the Twenty-first century. There are also indications that she will require upwards of 568 million tons of grain by the year 2030, transforming the country into a major future importer. The GAP project, initiated in 1983 with an intended completion date 2006, includes the massive Ataturk Dam, which will prohibit periodic flooding, generate electricity, and provide irrigation for dry, cultivated lands in the southeastern portions of Turkey. The whole project includes thirteen smaller projects, seven on the Euphrates and six on the Tigris rivers and involves an area of 74000 square kilometers with 4,5 million inhabitants. The area to be irrigated is 1.6 million hectares that will double Turkey's production of cotton, oil and grains.[45] Thus, some strategists believe that Turkey and China can mutually benefit from this project, and success would certainly afford Turkey an opportunity to further amicable relations with China.

Looking to the future, Turkey's relations with China seem promising. In April 1999, Chinese leader, Li Peng, paid an official visit to Turkey, where he met with a group of Turkish businessmen and urged an increase of exchanges with their Chinese counterparts to further economic cooperation. Political results were also important as it was noted in the meeting that 'there were no fundamental conflict of interests between China and Turkey and the two had similar and identical views on many major and regional issues'. The warming of relations and the bilateral demands for cooperation resulted in a security cooperation agreement in February 2000. The agreement, which is composed of 12 articles declared the bilateral cooperation of China and Turkey in combating cross-border crimes. It also stressed that necessary measures would be taken against separatist activities targeting the territorial integrities of both countries. In January 2001 another step was taken by the foreign ministers of the two countries and an "action plan" was signed to increase cooperation and consultations between the ministries.

However, other Far East Asian countries maintain doubts regarding China's hegemonic ambitions, and the ethnic problems in the Xinjiang Uygur autonomous region are still unresolved. Consequently, Turkey needs to design strategies for possible future conflicts with China as well as the other Asian powers. Territorial disputes between China and her neighbors clearly serve to increase tension in the region, making escalation to armed conflict a likely possibility. Ultimately, China must determine whether to promote stability in East Asia or pursue a policy of pure self-interest in the region, with latter choice likely leading to a further escalation of violence and bloodshed. The security role of China in Asia will be one of the most important components in international politics in the near future.

Turkey's relations with the other Far East Asian countries have also accelerated during the last decade and Turkey's Far East strategy developed a new dimension in the mid 1990s, after the Islamic party took office. The leader of the Islamic Party, Necmettin Erbakan, began an initiative in 1996 called the D-8 (Developing 8) among the Muslim

---

[45] Michael Schulz, "Turkey, Syria and Iraq: A Hydropolitical Security Complex", Leif Ohlsson (Ed.), *Hydropolitics; Conflicts Over Water as a Development Constraint*, London: New Jersey, Zed Books, 1995, p.99.

countries: Turkey, Bangladesh, Egypt, Iran, Pakistan, Nigeria, Indonesia and Malaysia. With a total population of almost 800 million, the member countries of D-8 represent a significant portion of world population. They control an equally significant portion of the world land with 7,5 million km2. Thus, the Turkish ex-prime minister attempted to create an alternative to Turkey's ceaseless westernization efforts, with a pan-Islamic, non-Arab call to the other seven Muslim countries. The first meeting, in which the D-8 organization was formally established, was held in June 1997. After the second meeting, held in March 1999, the organization was declared as a south-south dialogue and the Dakka Declaration was concluded. Iran's proposal for calling 2000 'the year of intercultural dialogue' was accepted by consensus. In addition, the D-8 countries approved liberal trade regimes within the framework of WTO (World Trade Organization) guidelines. The charged atmosphere of the initial meetings proved illusory, however, with few concrete developments in the intervening period.

Turkey's strategy in the 1990's consisted of evaluating the region as a whole, and creating multidimensional partnerships among different groups of countries. During the last decades Turkey established new embassies throughout Asia and by 2000 she had embassies in China, Indonesia, Philippines, India, Japan, Republic of Korea, Malaysia, Singapore, Thailand and Vietnam. Official visits to Asian countries have increased, and in recent years the government has attempted to remedy the diplomatic rift that developed between Turkey and Far East Asia. Officially, the Turkish foreign ministry is preparing to send diplomatic missions so as to establish formal relations with countries with whom she has no prior diplomatic interaction such as Taiwan and North Korea.

Promoting Turkey as an economic, political and cultural bridge between East and West became a principal objective for Turkey's foreign policy makers. For example, during his official visit in May 1995 to the Far East (India, Pakistan, China, Hong Kong and Indonesia), President Süleyman Demirel proposed an active bridging role for Turkey in the modern day Silk Road from China to Europe. This bridge metaphor was used by the statesman on several occasions as Turkish leaders held forth on the vision of a community of Turkic peoples and made great efforts to develop links with the external Turks in Turkey's near abroad stretching from the Adriatic to the borders of China.[46] According to Samuel Huntington, however, 'a bridge... is an artificial creation connecting two solid entities but is a part of neither. When Turkey's leaders term their country a bridge, they euphemistically confirm that it is torn'.[47] One is reluctant to concur with Huntington as bridges are built of necessity where paths are lacking, making them an integral connection between solid entities. Therefore their function confers a measure of solidity. They are constructed for reasons of security, commerce, interaction, and connection, and, as such, have ever been symbolic of integration, communication, and future prosperity.

Under the light of the September 11 attack, it seems that it is vital to construct well-designed bridges between conflicting cultures, in order to convince them of becoming co-

---

[46] Samuel Huntington, *Clash of Civilizations and the Remaking of a World Order*, New York: Simon and Schuster, 1996, p.146
[47] Huntington, *Clash of Civilizations and the Remaking of a World Order*, p.149.

operating civilizations. Otherwise it will be too costly to afford creating a sustainable peace, for all sides of the conflict.

Conclusion

Given the preceding assessment, it is critically important for strategists to follow the rising Far East phenomenon, and map strategies to strengthen Turkey's ties with the East Asian countries. It will be a grave mistake if foreign policy makers insist on maintaining a Euro-American approach without taking into account Far East Asia as a region of future international importance.

Even though Turkey is a regional state with limited external scope for its national interests, the changing international political environment assigned Turkey a role on the world stage. Carrying the ethnic and religious mantle of the Ottoman Empire, Turkey plays an important role in Far East Asian politics. She may seek to foster relations with Islamic communities as a rightful, albeit secular, member of House of Islam. Equally, she may pursue relations from ethnic standpoint as a member, albeit determinedly non-ethnic, of the Turkic-speaking communities of the region. These two conditions may eventually outweigh or at least counterbalance Russian and Chinese influences in Far East and Central Asia. Turkey possesses the potential to become the 'holder of the balance' though she has not enough potential to impose hegemony upon the region. By building moderate relations and maintaining a trustworthy profile, Turkey can build a perfect bridge between East and West, between Turks and Asians and between Muslims and non-Muslims, creating an accord rather than a clash among civilizations.

20 Post- September 11 Impact: The Strategic Importance of Turkey Revisited

Hüseyin Bagci
Saban Kardas

The aim of this chapter is to analyze the debate surrounding Turkey's increasing strategic importance in the wake of September 11 terror attacks on Washington and New York. Traditionally, Turkey has been considered an important country because of its geographic location between Europe, the Middle East and Asia, which gives it easy access to strategically important regions and major energy resources. Moreover, thanks to its character as a modern Muslim country, culturally, Turkey stands as a bridge between Western and Islamic civilizations. The conventional importance attributed to Turkey's strategic value became more visible following the events of September 11, and consequently, Turkey has come under the spotlight. As a result, Turkey and Turkish foreign policy started to receive a great interest, and the mood in the discussions about Turkey and Turkey's strategic importance was usually optimistic. However, the discourse was mainly a historic, temporal and isolated from reality, and the focus was very narrow. Therefore it was often lost in the debate that, seen in a wider perspective, there are a number of other factors to be taken into account that indicate that a more cautious and balanced approach is necessary. In this sense, the tone in this article will be rather critical and skeptical. What we are going to do is, first, to briefly summarize the central arguments that are used to emphasize an enhanced strategic role for Turkey in the new era. After each argument, we will try to approach this argument critically and underline the inconsistencies and shortcomings of the argument under consideration. The chapter concludes with an attempt to develop a more balanced interpretation of the effect of post-September 11 developments on Turkish foreign policy.

Growing Acceptance of Turkish Theses on Fight Against Terrorism, or You See "We Were Right!" Syndrome

The first effect of September 11, which can be said to have contributed to Turkey's position, was alleged growing acceptance towards the Turkish approach to the fight against terrorism in international relations. Turkey itself had long struggled against separatist terror and political Islam in domestic context. Since the 1970s, Turkey has been engaged in fighting against terrorism and continues to be one of the major targets of terrorist activities, both at home and abroad. Turkey's first encounter with international terrorism was political assassinations carried out by ASALA (Armenian Secret Army for the Liberation of Armenia) against Turkish diplomats abroad in the 1970s. During the last two decades, particularly the Kurdish issue and the terrorist activities of PKK

(Kurdistan Workers' Party) involved cross-border aspects and became of international concern.[1] Therefore, one part of the Turkish strategy to deal with this problem was to seek international cooperation in fighting against terrorism. In this regard, successive Turkish governments endeavored to generate an international concern against terrorism. In particular, they worked hard to convince European countries to limit the activities of various separatist, leftist and Islamic organizations. As part of its activities, Turkey even tried on some occasions to bring the terror issue onto NATO's agenda.[2]

Besides trying to raise the terror issue in several political and diplomatic fora, Turkey did not hesitate to resorting to the military instruments as well. To meet the rising challenge of separatist terror in South Eastern Anatolian region, Turkey employed a stubborn, and at times harsh, policy based on heavy reliance on military measures in order to, first stop the terror activities carried out by the PKK, and then root out the formation of terrorist groups and their support bases. In a similar vein, emphasis on the use or threat of force outside its borders as part of the fight against terrorism was a logical correlation of this policy. Numerous instances of Turkish incursions into northern Iraq are cases in point. The authority vacuum emerged after the imposition of no-fly zone in the Northern Iraq enabled PKK to use the region as a rear base to conduct terrorist attacks inside Turkish territory. Based on a somewhat complicated mixture of the notion of 'hot pursuit' and an expanded interpretation of the norm of self-defense, Turkish armed forces were dispatched into Northern Iraq to destroy PKK guerillas and training camps or prevent PKK from planning and executing subversive attacks on Turkish soil.[3] While some of those operations were limited in scope, some were large-scale involving thousands of troops –at times Turkish soldiers crossing the border reached 35.000-, backed by tanks, artillery, and helicopters.

The relations with Syria as far as its support to PKK terrorism is concerned, is another case in which Turkey resorted to essentially military means. By mid-1998, the PKK came to maintain its existence almost entirely on Syrian support; Abdullah Ocalan, the PKK's leader, had been given a sanctuary by the Syrian government, and Syrian territory was a safe route for PKK militants in their journey between PKK training camps in Lebanon's Syrian-controlled Bekaa valley and the Turkish border. Indeed, during the Turkish Syrian crisis of October 1998 Turkey used a coercive diplomacy backed up by a credible threat of force against the Syrian regime to end its support to PKK and give up providing shelter to Ocalan. It is worth noting that, in the meantime, Turkey had already

---

[1] For more information on the PKK, see the extensive analysis provided in: Nihat Ali Özcan, *PKK (Kürdistan Isci Partisi): Tarihi, Ideolojisi, ve Yöntemi*, Ankara: ASAM Yayinlari, 1999; for the international dimension in PKK's emergence and operations, in particular see, pp.222-325; Michael Radu, "The Rise and Fall of the PKK," *Orbis*, Vol.45, No.1, Winter 2001, pp.47-63; Kemal Kirisci and Gareth Winrow, *The Kurdish Question and Turkey*, London: Frank Cass, 1997.

[2] But, it must be underlined that in order not to internationalise PKK issue, and keep the PKK from becoming an interlocutor Turkey was cautious in those endeavours. Therefore, it mainly tried to include terror as a whole into NATO statements.

[3] An extensive analysis can be found in: Ümit Özdag, *Türkiye, Kuzey Irak ve PKK: Bir Gayri Nizami Savasin Anatomisi*, Ankara: ASAM Yayinlari, 2000; also see, Ümit Özdag, *The PKK and Low Intensity Conflict in Turkey*, Ankara: ASAM & Frank Cass, Ankara Paper.5, 2002.

strengthened its military ties with Israel to exert pressure on Syria from the south. Turkey's threat of force accompanied by military maneuvers undertaken close to the Syrian border bore fruits; faced with overwhelming power of Turkish military Syrian government complied to Turkish demands and had asked Ocalan and the PKK to leave the country which constituted the first step in a chain of events that led to the capture of Ocalan in Kenya. Following their expulsion from Syria, PKK forces relocated in northern Iraq, yet, and a subsequent Turkish incursion into the region dealt a severe blow to their military capabilities, and the PKK collapsed militarily.[4]

As a matter of fact, Turkish activities to this end, be it diplomatic or military, were hardly welcomed by its neighbors, nor by its Western partners; as a result, Turkey could not raise the necessary international support in its own fight against terrorism. To the contrary, these issues have constantly been a point of tension and disagreement in Turkish foreign policy throughout the 1990s and Turkey came under severe international criticism. Assertive Turkish foreign policy towards the Middle East region added to the already troubled relations with the Arab neighbors. Likewise, it was in this context that from time to time Turkey's relations with its Western partners deteriorated due to the problems stemming from Turkey's struggle with terrorism, and that issue has been a major impediment to Turkey's will for a closer integration into the European Union. In particular, the charge that Turkey's approach to the issue of terrorism and the way Turkey tackles with this problem was a major source of human rights violations and the limitations of individual rights and liberties at home was often raised against the country at several international platforms. Therefore Turkey was always under a European pressure to undertake domestic reforms to ameliorate the situation. As far as foreign policy is concerned, with its principally military-oriented security strategy, in stark contrast to 'civilian' European approach, Turkey's assertiveness in the region was seen as an indication that Turkey was a 'security consuming' or 'insecurity provider' to the European security, thus an actor to be treated with a certain reservation.[5]

Against this background, it is obvious that Turkey was one of the main beneficiaries of the new international atmosphere. At last, the phenomenon of terrorism and the threat of terrorist activities were formally recognized as an international concern and an international consensus on the issue seemed to be emerging. The challenge posed by terrorism to international security was considered so acute that it was even enough a justification for the North Atlantic Council to invoke NATO's Article 5, for the first time ever. From the United Nations to the OSCE, several other international and regional organizations captured the prevailing mood and adapted similar revolutionary resolutions or decisions to express their willingness to respond to the perils of terror at international

---

[4] See, Svante E. Cornell, "The Kurdish Question in Turkish Politics," *Orbis*, Vol.45, No.1, Winter 2001, pp.31-46.

[5] This somewhat extremely critical interpretation of Turkey's place in European Security architecture can be found in Dietrich Jung, *Turkey and Europe: Ongoing Hypocrisy?*, Copenhagen Peace Research Institute: Working Paper 35, September 2001, pp.1-21; for a counter view: Meltem Müftüler-Bac, "Turkey's Role in the EU's Security and Foreign Policies", *Security Dialogue*, Vol. 31, No. 4, 2000, pp.489-502.

level. It did not take so long that the Turkish side grasped this opportunity; thus the president, the prime minister, the foreign minister and other officials representing the country gave their full and unqualified support to those international initiatives.[6] This was in fact more than an expression of international solidarity with the U.S. and the victims of those startling attacks. Beyond that, there was a golden, god-given opportunity for Turkey to utilize. Turkish elites and intellectuals just did this, by, after reminding in each declaration or speech that Turkey itself had suffered from terrorism, repeatedly emphasizing that the events of September 11 proved the validity of Turkish arguments. They went on by expressing their hope that Turkey's European partners would also realize their past mistakes in criticizing Turkey, and eventually readjust their policies vis-à-vis Turkey in the face of the new realities out there proving Turkey's rightfulness: President Ahmet Necdet Sezer was maintaining that those attacks should be a lesson for the European countries and was calling for a change in their attitude and state of mind towards terrorism. After pointing out that terrorism was a crime committed against all humanity, he went on saying,

> *that's why we have always repeated in all international platforms that international cooperation in the fight against terrorism should be improved. The attacks on the US have shown how correct Turkey is in her stance against terrorism. I guess the attitudes of European countries have begun to change too.*[7]

This was so because, in Turkish view, the European countries misinterpreted the balance between the concepts of human rights and terrorism, a point emphasized by a senior Turkish Foreign Ministry official:

> *The United States was very well aware of the concerns raised by Turkey regarding terrorism. However, the Europeans did not understand this and the concept of human rights was raised by our European colleagues when we made references to terrorism at international gatherings. And now, it is clearly seen that a balance between the concepts of terrorism and human rights is necessary.*[8]

Moreover, in a similar line, Turkey paid a special attention to stress that terrorism is a global issue and thus must be fought globally. This point was also repeatedly emphasized by the government officials as well as columnists and civil society organizations. Foreign Minister Ismail Cem, in his address at the Organization of Islamic Countries Summit was referring to the same point:

> *Terrorism does not have geography, it is the same terrorism, which manifests itself in several countries, in the West and in the East, in all geographies, all over the world... Therefore, terrorism is a global phenomenon that crosses borders and the*

---

[6] See several Turkish dailies from September 12-13, 2001. Also, for a collection, see, *Newspot*, No.29, September-October 2001.
[7] *Cumhuriyet*, 13 September 2001; "Sezer: I Reckon Western Countries are Going to View Terrorism Differently from Now on", *Turkish Daily News*, 13 September 2001.
[8] "Shifting of International Perceptions on the Agenda; A New Role for Turkey", *Turkish Daily News*, 13 September 2001; for more on initial Turkish position, see, Baki Ilkin, "Combating Terrorism and Rebuilding Afghanistan: The Turkish Perspective", *Foreign Policy-Ankara*, Vol.27, Nos.3-4, 2002, pp.3-9.

fight against it requires effective international cooperation.[9]

In this sense, NATO's decision to invoke Article-5 was a welcome development for Turkey, as expressed by Ambassador Onur Öymen, Turkey's Permanent Representative to NATO:

We have always called for terrorist activities to be included within the Article 5... we have always stated that an attack does not only mean a country's intrusion into another country's territory but it also covers terrorist attacks which is an international problem. That's why NATO's invoking of Article 5 is very important for us.[10]

Furthermore, some Turkish analysts did not even hesitate to announce the advent of a "global February 28."[11] While challenging the rise of political Islam, the particular conditions and characteristics of Turkey were used as a justification to limit the individual rights and democratic freedoms by the secular elites, backed by the powerful military, during the 28 February process. In a similar vein, it was argued that the U.S. and Western countries may embark on a similar policy at a global scale so as to wipe out several international networks, irrespective of whether they are moderate or radical, which were supposedly behind the terror attacks of September 11. As part of this new strategy, in particular, the U.S. would be less willing to criticize non-democratic practices in the Islamic world for the sake of assuring their cooperation in the global war against terrorism. That could, the argument goes on, in return, hint at the emergence of a new "precedent" justifying the Turkish way of dealing with terrorism, and in effect, relieving Turkey of some of the external pressures it had encountered in the past.

The first observation about these arguments is that they were, to a large extent, self-propaganda. It was not possible to hear, from outside, a corresponding appreciation of the Turkish theses, except perhaps some American commentators.[12] To name one, Radu was a very vocal supporter of Turkish position on that matter. He argues,

Europeans, at least before September 11, were playing games in the name of 'human rights' –particularly for terrorists, who were protected at home and even against the vital security of non-EU countries... Let us hope that once the US and Turkey, to mention just two cases, are finally seen as equally victimized, the EU response will be similar... That revision also includes a new look at Turkey's anti-PKK and anti-Islamic policy –not as anti-democratic, but as protective of the Muslim world's only

---

[9] Ismail Cem, *Statement to the Press at the Organization of the Islamic Conference*, Doha: 10 October 2001, reprinted in *Newspot*, No.29, September-October 2001; "Turkish Top Officials Call for Increase in International Cooperation against Terrorism," *Turkish Daily News*, 13 September 2001; Similarly see, Mustafa Balbay, "Terör Sinir Tanimiyor," *Cumhuriyet*, 12 September 2001; Turkish Industrialists and Businessman Association (TUSIAD) also stated that the events that terror attacks exposed the dimensions of international terrorism and that there is a need for international cooperation and solidarity to fight against international terrorism, *Milliyet*, 13 September 2001.

[10] *Cumhuriyet*, 14 September 2001; "Ankara Backs Activating Article 5," *Turkish Daily News*, 14 September 2001.

[11] Rusen Cakir, "Global 28 Subat Süreci Basladi," *Hurriyet*, 15 September 2001.

[12] For a similar view see, Murat Belge, "Jeopolitik," *Radikal*, 22 January 2002.

truly secular democracy.[13]

The optimistic mood and Turkish discourse, therefore, largely remained wishful thinking.

The main problem with this argument was that Turks chose to interpret these developments in such a way that this new 'precedent' justified whatever Turkey did in the past to fight against separatism and political Islam, a point very well illustrated by Ismail Cem:

> *For years, Turkey has kept on explaining to the international community what terrorism is, the consequences of it, the importance and the need for international cooperation in struggling against it, and have kept on making proposals at international platforms methods of a collective struggle against terrorism. September 11 has proved how right Turkey's sensitivity on this issue was. What everyone is trying to do collectively today is no different to that which Turkey has strived to achieve for years.*[14]

However, it is unlikely that the Turkish arguments will be entirely accepted by the West in general and Europeans in particular, without any reservations. For instance, if we take Turkey's warm welcome to NATO's activation of Article 5, one has to bear in mind the particular conditions in which NATO took that decision, and the unique position of the U.S. in shaping decisions in NATO; thus its value as an almost automatic precedent remains an open question. Even if one accepts that Article 5 could be activated against terror attacks, what is less clear is whether it will be applicable to the threats or attacks coming from an organization established in one's own country. Last but not least, when the time comes to the implementation of Article 5, there might be possibly divergences over identifying the concrete source of terror threat, or how to respond to that particular threat.[15]

Another limitation to Turkey's optimism is exerted by differing views on terrorism. Particularly in regards to the Kurdish issue, broadly speaking, the European view is that it cannot be simply confined to fighting against terrorism. Although official Turkish discourse preferred to view the Kurdish issue as originating from socioeconomic conditions of the southeastern Anatolia, and aggravated by the problems posed by terrorism that is largely aroused by outside support of those trying to undermine Turkey, in European eyes, it is rather very much related to political and cultural rights and democratization.[16] Thus, the well-known analogy: one's terrorist might be independent

---

[13] Michael Radu. "The War on Terrorism is not an American War," *Insight Turkey*. Vol.3, No.4, October-December 2001, pp.52.54.

[14] "Cem: Turkish Model is Paradigm of Civilization," Interview given to *Turkish Daily News*, 7 January 2002.

[15] For an early skeptical approach by Sadi Erguvenc, see: Lale Sariibrahimoglu, "Turkey Should be Cautious on Article 5," *Turkish Daily News*, 14 September 2001; however Özdag underlines that although it may not act as an automatic trigger, NATO's invocation of Article-5 might be used as a precedent, "Interview with Ümit Özdag," *2023*, No.6, 15 October 2002, p.23.

[16] On different perceptions of the issue in Turkey and Europe, see, Cornell, *"The Kurdish Question,"* p.31; for an analysis approaching Kurdish issue through a human rights and democratization perspective see, H. Ayla Kilic, "Democratization, Human Rights and Ethnic Policies in Turkey," *Journal of Muslim Minority*

fighter in others' eyes. And there is reason to expect that this will remain the case, despite Turkish initial optimism to the contrary.[17] Moreover, large Kurdish populations in Europe are acting as a strong pressure group and limiting the maneuverability of Western governments. As it is claimed rightly, Kurdish issue has also been a European one for it affects the Turkish and Kurdish migrants living in Europe, and the host countries.[18] Furthermore, there is a fundamental difference between the EU and Turkey in regards to the problem of terrorism. Even if one accepts the reality of terrorism, the ways to tackle this problem are differently perceived. The Turkish approach is closer to the United States than the EU.[19] As we observe, the EU and the United States have been differing on many issues, including the question of how to identify the causes and sources of terrorism as well as the means to be used in fighting against it. The EU has stressed the importance of preventive measures and prioritizing the political and economic instruments, and has questioned the effectiveness of punitive military measures. Considering that the Europeans were even critical of the United States, expecting that they would welcome Turkish activities without any reservations is hardly tenable.[20]

Therefore it is hard to be very optimistic and expect a major breakthrough that would bring about a substantial shift in Western responses to Turkey's approach to combating terrorism.[21] Moreover, Turkey's hope that the new emerging consensus on terrorism will relieve it of European pressures on the Kurdish issue is difficult to sustain. The Europeans would resist subsuming this wider problem under the rubric of terror and maintain their demands from Turkey to continue with the necessary domestic reforms in political and cultural aspects of the issue, even after the September 11. Thus, Kurdish issue will not cease as one of the hurdles Turkey has to face on its journey towards the European Union. The discussion about the list of terrorist organizations prepared by the EU within the context of forging an international coalition against the sources of terrorism was illustrative of this point, and one can expect similar differences in the future as well. The story developed as follows:

Turkey has started an intensive diplomatic initiative in the wake of the September 11 attacks to utilize the international environment to convince EU members to include 10 Turkish organizations on its list of terrorist organizations. The inclusion of an

---

Affairs, Vol.18, No.1, April 1998, pp.91-110.

[17] For an optimistic view that after September 11, PKK issue would no longer be considered within the context of ethnic conflict or independence movement see, S. Rana Sezal, "Kimlik Politikalari, Terör ve Etnik Catisma Kavramlari: 11 Eylül Sonrasi Türkiye'nin Terör Sorunu," *Stratejik Analiz*, Vol.2, No.20, December 2001, p.100.

[18] See for instance: Gülistan Gürbey, "Die Europaesierung des Kurdenkonflikts," *Blaetter für Deutsche und Internationale Politik*, 4:99, p.404.

[19] Ali L. Karaosmanoglu, "Afganistan Savasi'nin Transatlantik Iliski Boyutu," *Zaman*, 27 November 2001, p.10.

[20] For an argument to the effect that Turkey could capitalize on U.S. interpretation of terror and thus solve its own PKK problem see, Damla Aras, "Minareyi Calan Kilifi Hazirladi: Bir Baska Acidan 11 Eylul," *Stratejik Analiz*, Vol.2, No.24, April 2002, p.39.

[21] Ali Nihat Özcan, a Turkish expert on terrorism, also points out that the selective response to terror in Europe would limit Turkey's utilization of the new conditions. "BM Karari ve PKK," *NTV: Arka Plan*, 03 October 2001, for transcript of this TV interview see, http://www.ntvmsnbc.com/news/110594.asp.

organization on the list means that its assets will be frozen, its offices closed and its activities traced. However, this may not automatically translate into the extradition of its members to their country of origin, particularly if the country is not a EU member and still practices the death penalty. Despite Turkey's efforts, the EU included none of the terrorist organizations on its list, which was declared on December 27, 2001. Especially the exclusion of the armed militant groups from the first version of the list, such as the outlawed Kurdistan Workers Party (PKK) and the Revolutionary People's Liberation Party-Front (DHKP-C), which are active in some European countries under different banners, drew Turkish reaction and that problem remained on the agenda for some time.[22] Turkish diplomacy and lobbying worked; thus, on May 2, 2002 the two organizations were finally added to the modified EU list. This decision was seen by many as a Turkish victory.[23] Yet, to be able to assess the effectiveness of those measures, one has to wait and take into consideration a couple of other factors.

First, in the meantime, the PKK announced in April that it would cease all activities and regroup under a new name, the Kurdistan Freedom and Democracy Congress (KADEK).[24] KADEK said it was ending its armed struggle to campaign peacefully for greater rights for Kurds in southeastern Turkey, but without disbanding its armed wing. The Turkish government has termed the name-change meaningless.[25] Yet, in spite of Turkey's demands, KADEK is not included on the EU list. The EU countries prefer to wait to be able to judge whether to include KADEK as well.

Second, these EU norms need to be transformed into national legal orders, and in some of the EU member states, the national legal norms are not enough to effectively limit the activities of these terrorist organizations, and this point has been utilized by the operatives of those organizations. This is especially true as far as Belgium is concerned.[26] Third, most of these organizations have been active in Europe for decades and they know the ways to circumvent such legal barriers. For instance, a spokesman for the DHKP-C has claimed that these decisions will not substantially affect their activities.[27] What the EU member states can do, is to freeze their bank accounts, but they have no money in banks. The same source further claimed that the name DHKP-C is on the EU list, but that the registered name of their organization is the DHKP and DHKC, and mentioning the fact that they have been working in the United Kingdom for many years, although the DHKP-C was outlawed there. They may have some more ways to find loopholes in legal norms as well. Therefore, Turkey still has to work hard in order to ensure the effectiveness of this initiative.

---

[22] Selcuk Gültasli, "The Opportunity and the Principle," *Turkish Probe*, Issue 479, 31 March 2002.

[23] "Türkiye Brüksel'de Zafer Kazandi," *www.ntvmsnbc.com.tr* news portal, 3 May 2002.

[24] Mehmet Ali Birand, "PKK or KADEK," *Turkish Daily News*, 2 April 2002.

[25] Ali Nihat Özcan, Ö.Rengin Gün, "PKK'dan KADEK'e: Degisim mi Takkiye mi?", *Stratejik Analiz*, Vol.2, No.25, May 2002, pp.5-20.

[26] "DHKP/C and PKK on EU Terrorist List," *Turkish News*, 03 May 2002; "Belgian Judicial Officials: There is not Much to Do against the PKK and DHKP-C," *Turkish Daily News*, 6 May 2002.

[27] "DHKP-C: The List did not Affect Us," *Turkish Daily News*, 10 May 2002.

Caught Between 'Islam' and 'Terrorism': Turkey as a 'Role Model' for the Islamic World?

The second development regarding Turkey's growing strategic importance was the increasing reference to Turkey as a model for the Islamic world. The war against the Taliban and the al-Qaeda was, in a political and intellectual sense, also a war against a militant, reactive, anti-Western, or anti-American, interpretation of Islam. The protests against American operations and support for bin-Laden in some parts of the Islamic world created fears that the developments might lead to a so-called "clash of civilizations," or a "Christian-Muslim confrontation." Therefore, the American administration strived to use every opportunity to prevent such a negative interpretation of the American role and to deliver a message that this was not a war against Islam. As a concrete proof of this policy, the inclusion of certain Muslim countries into the international coalition appeared to be necessary, especially when it later came to using force in Afghanistan.[28] Within this light, Turkey emerged as a valuable asset for American policy.

No doubt, Turkey offered all assistance in its capability to the international coalition from the very beginning, through allowing the use of its territory and air space for logistical support, or through its contribution to international peacekeeping force in Afghanistan. But, this was more than a practical military/strategic contribution in the long-term war against the forces of terrorism and fanaticism. Hence, the fact that Turkey is the only Muslim country with a secular governing system, which is also member of NATO and other European institutions, was repeatedly expressed not only by the Turkish policy makers themselves, but also by the international observers, and U.S. officials. As such, as the argument goes, Turkey would play a perfect role model for the Islamic world. The 21st conference of the American-Turkish Council (ATC) held in Washington in March 2002 was an important venue where those arguments were often heard. A few days before the conference, Deputy Defense Secretary Paul Wolfowitz was underlying that supporting moderate Muslims who abhor terrorism and extremism was a key to winning the war on terrorism. "To win that war against terrorism, we have to reach out to the hundreds of millions of Muslims who believe in tolerance and moderation... By helping them to stand up against terrorists, we help ourselves." Therefore, the anti-terrorism campaign was not just a military fight but also "a battle for hearts and minds as well"; and within this context Turkey, "can be an example for the Muslim world" of a country that reconciles Islam with liberal democracy.[29] According to US President George W. Bush, Turkey was a hope-provoking alternative against radicalism and religious intolerance. In his message sent to the ATC conference, he stressed that Turkey with its

---

[28] "With Turkey's Pledge, U.S. Coalition Gets its First Muslim Troops," *International Herald Tribune,* November 2, 2001.
[29] Matt Kelley, "America Must Support Moderate Muslims to Win War on Terror. No.2. Pentagon Official Says," *Turkish Daily News,* 11 March 2002; also see: United States Department of Defense, "Bridging the Dangerous Gap between the West and the Muslim World," *Remarks Prepared for Delivery by Deputy Secretary Paul Wolfowitz at the World Affairs Council,* Monterey, CA, 3 May 2002.

Muslim beliefs and its embracing of the democracy ideals of Atatürk set an example.[30] In his address at the conference, U.S. Deputy Secretary of State Marc Grossman was also underlying that one of the few things that had not changed after September 11 was:

> *Turkey is once again highlighted as a model for those countries with an Islamic heritage who choose to be -and work to be- modern, secular, democratic, and true to their faith simultaneously. Those of us who have admired Turkey for this vision for years now find we are not so alone in wishing that your great endeavor succeeds.*[31]

However, the very fact that the terrorist activities were undertaken by an organization, justifying its actions by reference to Islam, was a serious moral challenge many Muslim countries had to respond.[32] There was a considerable effort on the part of the statesmen and intellectuals in the Islamic world to stave off linking terror in general, and September 11 terror attacks in particular to Islam and Islamic groups. Perhaps, nowhere was this concern more visible than in Turkey, a country that, while orienting itself towards Western norms and values, at the same time maintained its ties with Islam and Islamic world. Indeed, it was this duality that put enormous pressure on Turkey to call the world to draw a distinction between Islam and terror. Turkish political leaders and intellectuals, like their counterparts in other Islamic countries, took pains to emphasize that Islam was a religion of peace and a distinction between Islam and terrorism must be drawn. While the Prime Minister was calling equating Islam with terror unjust,[33] the Foreign Minister was saying:

> *terrorism does not have a religion, geography and there can be no justification for terrorism under any circumstances... To identify terrorism with any religion is an insult to all religions. We strongly condemn those who have used the name of our holy religion to define some terrorists. Following the tragedy in the USA, Turkey conferred with some fellow members of the OIC and urged her NATO allies as well as the EU members to avoid such misuse.*[34]

In this regards, the OIC-EU Summit, which was held in Istanbul in 12-13 February, was an expression of Turkey's determination to assume its responsibility through a policy of bridging the East and the West, and calling for harmony, rather than conflict between two civilizations. The Forum turned out to be a useful platform for an intensive exchange of views between representatives of international organizations, high-ranking politicians, opinion-makers, intellectuals from EU-member countries, OIC-member countries and observer countries, and mutual compliments filled the air although it remains to be seen

---

[30] "Turkey a Model Secular Country: Bush," *www.ntvmsnbc.com.tr* news portal, 18 March 2002; also see, "21st ATC conference held in Washington," *Turkish Daily News*, 19 March 2002.

[31] U.S. Department of State, "Grossman: Change in the Value of Enduring Alliances." *Remarks to the American Turkish Council by U.S Under Secretary of State for Political Affairs Marc Grossman*, Washington, D.C., March 19, 2002.

[32] See, Anas Malik, "Selected Reflections on the Muslim World in the aftermath of 9-11." *Alternatives: Turkish Journal of International Relations*, Vol.1, No.2, Summer 2002, pp.201-225.

[33] "Ecevit'ten Teröre Karsi Dayanisma Cagrisi," *Hürriyet*, 12 September 2001; "ABD'nin Yanindayiz," *Hürriyet*, 13 September 2001; For several Turkish intellectuals' response: "Linkage to Islam rejected," *Turkish Daily News*, 14 September 2001.

[34] Cem, *"Statement to the Press."*

what it will bring about in concrete political terms.[35] Nevertheless, organizing such a conference, and bringing together EU member states and Muslim countries around the same table had a symbolic meaning and it was seen as the start of the new Turkish role.[36] Ismail Cem's views on the conference were reflective of this:

An example of what Turkey could do [to play a bridging role between the Islamic World and the Western Christian World] can be seen in the forthcoming meeting of the OIC and the EU. For the first time these two organizations will be coming together for a political exchange of opinions. Besides, in the aftermath of September 11 we are strongly opposed to the wrong perception of placing terrorism and Islam side by side. I had spoken with many of my Western colleagues and drew their attention to the sensitivity of wording used... In correcting such mistakes and in establishing some sort of a harmony, Turkey has a pioneering place that is provided to it by its history, culture and modern identity. We have to act in awareness of that responsibility.[37]

This argument, to conclude, implied at least two interrelated aspects: First, Turkey's support for the coalition was instrumental in defusing the charge that the war was a Muslim-Christian confrontation.[38] This point was very well expressed by Foreign Minister Cem:

This is the fight between democracy and terrorism and the struggle between the wise and fanatic. We believe that this fight will be won by our side. Turkey will be the biggest obstacle before those who want to divert this fact to a wrong path such as a fight between the religions.[39]

Second, the Turkish model was offered as an alternative to a Taliban version of Islam. That means, Islam and modern values are compatible with each other, and it is possible to reconcile Islam within a modern, Western-style, democratic and secular system. In the words of Dale F. Eickelman,

Turkey can only offer the world an example of a nation in which Western democratic values and Islam converge in an increasingly strengthened civil society in which the state and religion are not seen as adversaries. 'Western' societies, like 'Islamic' ones, have no place for either militant secular extremism or militant religious extremism.[40]

In practical terms, Turkey's taking part in the Western-led coalition was expected to

---

[35] For the coverage of the Forum in Turkish Press see, http://www.byegm.gov.tr/on-sayfa/oic/oic.htm; also see the information provided on Turkish Ministry of Foreign Affairs' webpage: http://www.mfa.gov.tr/OIC_EU_cdrom/index.htm.
[36] Elif Ünal, "West and East Attempt to Bridge Differences in Turkey," *Turkish Probe*, No.473, 10 February 2002.
[37] *"Cem: Turkish Model is Paradigm"*.
[38] In a sense, this was a duty on Turkey see, Karaosmanoglu, *"Afganistan Savasi'nin Transatlantik Iliski Boyutu"*.
[39] "Bu, Demokrasi ile Terörizmin Kavgasi," *Hürriyet*, 14 September 2001.
[40] Dale F. Eickelman "Turkey between the West and the Rest," *Turkish Probe*, No.474, 17 February, 2002.

facilitate other countries' adapting counter-terrorist stance and cooperation with the US.[41] Seen from another perspective, it was also argued that this "geo-cultural" dimension, in addition to the geopolitical position, could constitute another asset for Turkey in its relations with Western world, particularly as far as its quest for becoming a full member of the European Union concerns.[42]

Yet the argument that Turkey could be a role model for Islamic world is also controversial in some aspects. First, Turkish ambitions in this direction are not new and we have enough evidence to judge how they are perceived in other parts of the Islamic world. Turks themselves are proud of being the only secular country in the Islamic world; and from time to time, Turkey is offered as a role model from the outside as well. Yet, it is also equally true that Turkey's perception of itself as a model could not go beyond being an illusion, and those Western ideas promoted by Turkey have hardly penetrated into other Muslim societies. Arab countries' criticism of the secular Turkish model, and other problems dominating Turkish-Arab relations are no secret. In this sense, any fundamental shift in the perceptions of other Muslim societies, which would ease the objections to adapting a Turkish style system, cannot be observed. On the contrary, considering the growing anti-American feelings it is hard to expect that such a role for Turkey would be welcomed. Moreover, American way of dealing with terror through primarily military means or through supporting the existing non-democratic regimes in the Islamic world may hinder the burgeoning reformist movements in those countries and set fallbacks to the natural transformation of those societies, with a result that radicalism in the Islamic world could be given a new impetus. In this sense, Turkey's attempts to carry the Western values into the region might even widen the existing gap between Turkey and other Islamic societies.

Second, the main problem with this argument is the question of whether it is possible at all to transform a society from the outside. As long as domestic enthusiasm for reform is lacking, the international pressures or influences to change a society's nature, structure, laws, and political, economic and social cultures to make them conform to certain models have limited effect. To be able to influence a society from outside, international actors must have strong linkages, which would enable them to exert pressures stimulating a change in the behavior of the domestic actors. For instance, if we remember Turkish-EU relations, despite the existence of strong linkages, there is still a resistance to change coming from the Turkish establishment. Considering the lack of linkages, societal differences and geographical distances between Turkey and other Muslim societies, prospects for Turkey's influencing other Muslim countries remain limited. Likewise, democratic regimes and other practices cannot be established overnight, nor can they be taken granted. It took Turkey decades to reach its current level, and this was no doubt a painful process. That also dictates against transplanting Turkey's experience into other societies, which have not followed a similar path. On the other hand, even if one assumes

---

[41] See, Ilter Turan, "Short Term Pains for Long Term Pleasures," *Private View*, Spring 2001, p.10.

[42] Orhan Gökce and Birol Akgün, *Degisen Dünya Politikasinda Türkiye'nin Rolü: 11 Eylül'ün Getirdigi Firsatlar, Riskler ve Tehditler*, Paper Presented at First METU International Relations Conference, Ankara, 3-5 July 2002, p.14.

that Islamic world wants and needs change, there is nothing to suggest that that be imposed from Washington in line with its own political agenda.

A Turkish Zone of Influence in Central Asia and the Caucasus?

Let us move to the third area where Turkey's influence is supposedly growing, and a similar Turkish role is expected. The war against Afghanistan and terrorism brought the Central Asian, Caspian and Caucasus regions once again into the locus of interest. Some countries in the region, which are mostly ruled by former Communist leaders in an authoritarian manner, were also under pressure from domestic opposition. Since this opposition was mixed with some elements of Islamic radicalism, particularly in the case of Central Asian states, such as Uzbekistan, the regimes became active supporters of the international coalition against the Taliban and al-Qaeda. Moreover, the prospect of American involvement in the region offered a good chance to those countries for balancing the Russian dominance through assuring American backing. Consequently, they did not hesitate to respond to American demands and they provided the United States with access to their air space and military bases.[43] The U.S. willingness to widen the international coalition against terrorism diminished concerns for human rights and democratization, and resulted in a situation where human rights violations and anti-democratic practices by the governments in the region might be overlooked. Once being an impediment to more proactive U.S. engagement in the region, disappearance of human rights considerations in effect facilitated the U.S. cooperation with the Central Asian countries.

In developing this relationship, Turkey's special ties with the region again appeared to be an important asset for the U.S. policy. Turkey had a lot to offer: Not only did Turkey have strong political, cultural and economic connections with the region, but it had also accumulated a significant intelligence capability in the region. Moreover, the large experience Turkey accumulated in fighting terrorism would be made available in expanding the global war on terrorism to this region.[44] As a result, after the locus of interest shifted to a possible operation against Afghanistan, and then to assuring the collaboration of the countries in Central Asia, Turkish analysts soon discovered that Turkey's geo-strategic importance was once again on the rise. It was thought that, thanks to its geography's allowing easy access to the region, and its strong ties with the countries there, Turkey could play a pivotal role in the conduct of U.S. military operations in Afghanistan, and reshaping the politics in Central Asia:

> *Turkey is situated in a critical geographic position on and around which continuous*
> *and multidimensional power struggles with a potential to affect balance of power at*
> *world scale take place. The arcs that could be used by world powers in all sorts of*

---

[43] for more on the motivations and contributions of those countries see. Alec Rasizade. "The New 'Great Game' in Central Asia after Afghanistan." *Alternatives: Turkish Journal of International Relations*, Vol.1. No.2, Summer 2002, pp.132-134.; for Uzbekistan see. Nermin Güler. "Özbekistan Dis Politikasinda Dönüm Noktasi: 11 Eylül," *Stratejik Analiz*, Vol.2, No.20, December 2001, pp.59-65; for the contribution of those countries to the U.S. operations see. Department of Defense (DOD). *International Contributions to the War Against Terrorism*, Fact Sheet: 7 June 2002.

[44] See the next section on Afghanistan.

conflicts pass through Turkey. Turkish territory, airspace and seas are not only a necessary element to any force projection in the regions stretching from Europe and Asia to the Middle East, Persian Gulf, and Africa, but also make it possible to control its neighborhood... All these features made Turkey a center that must be controlled and acquired by those aspiring to be world powers... In the new process, Turkey's importance has increased in American calculations. With a consistent policy, Turkey could capitalize on this to derive some practical benefits... Turkey has acquired a new opportunity to enhance its role in Central Asia.[45]

Growing international interest in the region had further implications on the energy resources in the Caspian basin and Central Asia. Already before the September 11 events, there had been much talk about a new 'great game' in the making on the chessboard of Central Asia and Caucasus.[46] After the war in Afghanistan, there was a growing belief among many analysts that the centuries-old great game was entering a new phase.[47] According to this line of reasoning, the US military operations in Afghanistan were not simply a response to the attacks of September 11. Rather,

the plans for the American offensive in Afghanistan were not formulated in response to September 11, but existed prior to the terrorist attacks in the USA. Therefore, it could be argued that the attacks on September 11 provided the US with the opportunity to enter Afghanistan to further extend a project that had already started months, if not years, earlier.[48]

This was attributed to the special geostrategic significance of Afghanistan. Because,

Afghanistan occupies a strategic position in the geopolitical landscapes in general, and the geopolitics of the oil and natural gas resources in particular. Afghanistan has been in an extremely significant location spanning South Asia, Central Asia, and the Middle East... the US administration has significant political/ military and economic reasons to try to turn Afghanistan into a base for American military operations in the region. There can be no doubting Afghanistan's strategic importance to the US.[49]

Even one analyst goes as far as claiming that "The hidden stakes in the war against terrorism can be summed up in a single word: oil."[50] This reading of post-September 11 developments in the region found a large support among many Turkish analysts, and a number of studies raised the same argument, with the implication that those developments contributed to Turkey's strategic position.[51]

---

[45] Osman Nuri Aras, "Yasanan Yeni Sürecte Avrasya Enerji Kaynaklarinin Yeri ve Önemi," *2023*, 15 November 2001, No.7, p.38.

[46] M. E. Ahrari with James Beal, *The New Great Game in Muslim Central Asia*, Washington, D.C.: National Defense University, Institute for National Strategic Studies, McNair Paper 47, 1996; Zbigniew K. Brzezinski, *The Grand Chessboard: American Primacy and Its Geostrategic Imperatives*, New York, NY: Basic Books, 1997.

[47] Rasizade, *"The New 'Great Game'"*, p.125.

[48] Bülent Gökay, "The Most Dangerous Game in the World: Oil, War, and U.S. Global Hegemony," *Alternatives: Turkish Journal of International Relations*, Vol.1, No.2, Summer 2002, p.48.

[49] *Ibid*, p.49.

[50] Frank Viviano, *San Francisco Chronicle*, 26 September 2001, quoted by *ibid*, p.61.

[51] See for instance: Editorial, "Türkiye, Hazar, ve Afganistan Ekseninde Petro-politik," *2023*, 15

The construction of alternative pipelines to transport oil and gas from the region to the world markets was the crux of the issue, because the Caspian resources are landlocked. The methods and the routes through which the oil and gas are carried to world markets have direct geopolitical effects. But it had long been on the agenda, without a definite answer. Turkey had been pressing for the Baku-Tbilisi-Ceyhan pipeline project. The developments in the wake of September 11 turned out to strengthen Turkey's hand in this issue. The U.S. threw its weight on Turkey's side and the construction of the pipeline is scheduled to start around September 2002, and finish by the end of 2004.[52]

Against this background, within Turkey there is a growing optimism that the cumulative effect of these developments will strengthen Turkey's position within the region and promote a Turkish zone of influence. However, this argument has, among others, the following limitations. A proactive Turkish engagement with Central Asia and the Caucasus is not a new concept.[53] After they gained independence with the collapse of the Soviet Union, the newly emerged Turkic states looked toward Turkey as a model. There was also a corresponding great enthusiasm in Turkey for closer relations with the region, as well as Western support to promote the 'Turkish model' that embedded secularism in a predominantly Muslim society, adapted capitalist-market economy, and a multi-party system, and prioritized Western orientation. For Turkey, this region was to offer a new area to expand Turkish influence and boost Turkey's geo-strategic value to the West. Turkish ambitions, however, remained largely unrealized, and soon that model started to decline in the face of the political realities of the region and changes in Western perceptions over time.[54] In Turkey itself, the demise of Turkish model was mainly due to Turkey's own constraints: the lack of enough financial and economic resources to meet the expectations of these countries. Given that the structural obstacles Turkey confronted in trying to enhance its influence in the region –the compatibility of Turkish model, the receptivity of the target governments, the role of other players, particularly Russia, and the constraints set upon Turkish foreign policy by domestic problems- remained unaltered, then expecting acceleration by the post-September 11 developments is difficult to sustain. Particularly, considering that Turkey is itself struggling to overcome its own economic and financial problems, the question arises as to how she will be able to engage in an active new role in the region.

Yet, the developments so far imply that Turkey's relations with the region in the new era are seen differently. Previously, Turkey was perceived as a model for the economic, social and political transformation of these countries. This time, the role expected from Turkey is limited to military and strategic field. In addition to the existing ones, Turkey

---

November 2001, No.7, pp.8-15; Nadir Biyikoglu, "Afganistan Gercegi ve Büyük Oyun'a Dönüs," *2023*, 15 November 2001, No.7, pp.16-21; Aras, "Yasanan Yeni Sürecte".

[52] "Bush Voices Support for Oil and Gas Pipelines Leading from Caspian to Turkey," *Turkish Daily News*, 5 June 2002.

[53] Graham E. Fuller, "Turkey's New Eastern Orientation," in Graham E. Fuller and Ian O. Lesser, *Turkey's New Geopolitics: From the Balkans to Western China*, Boulder, CO: Westview/RAND, 1993, pp. 7–97.

[54] Idris Bal, *Turkey's Relations with the West and the Turkic Republics: The Rise and Fall of the 'Turkish Model'*, Aldershot: Ashgate, 2000.

has concluded several new military cooperation and education agreements with these countries. After September 11, Turkey shifted its military assistance to Uzbekistan[55] and Kazakhstan,[56] and to a lesser extent to Kyrgyzstan,[57] by supplying arms and military equipments and offering military training for the modernization of the military capabilities of these nations. Moreover, after those countries allowed the U.S. to use their airspace and military bases before the military campaign in Afghanistan started, Turkish Air Force Command personnel conducted site surveys for possible airfields in Tajikistan, Kazakhstan and Kyrgyzstan to be used in air operations.[58] Likewise, post-September 11 developments and ensuing U.S. interest in the region had spillover effects in the Caucasus and provided an added impetus to the Turkish activism in the region. Besides the positive steps taken in the issue of pipeline projects and Turkey's close relations with Azerbaijan, Turkish-Georgian cooperation in the military field remarkably accelerated. Turkey had already started providing military assistance to Georgia in 1997. After the U.S. decision to establish military presence in Georgia,[59] Turkey's cooperation with Georgia became particularly important.[60]

Aside from those military contributions, Turkey tried to raise a common concern for terrorism in the region through bilateral visits, as well as on multilateral platforms. On 29-30 April 2002, the Presidents of Turkey, Azerbaijan and Georgia held a summit meeting in Turkish city of Trabzon and signed an agreement to work together against terrorism, and also promised cooperation on the pipelines to bring the energy-rich region's resources to the West. The summit was completed with a joint press conference of the three leaders after the signing of the agreement of "The Struggle Against Terrorism, Organized Crime and Other Important Crimes".[61] Likewise, on June 4, 2002, the "Summit for Cooperation and Confidence-Building Measures in Asia" held in Kazakhstan's capital Almaty brought together heads of state of Turkey, China, Russia, India, Pakistan, Palestine, Israel, Egypt, Iran, Mongolia, Tajikistan, Kazakhstan, Kyrgyzstan, Uzbekistan, Afghanistan and Azerbaijan. The leaders signed a "Declaration

---

[55] "Turkey Equips, Trains Uzbek Military," *Turkish Daily News*, 7 March 2002; "Kivrikoglu Visits Uzbekistan, Signs Deal for Military Assistance," *Turkish Daily News*, 19 March 2002;.

[56] RFE/RL *Central Asian Report*, Vol. 2, No. 11, 21 March 2002.

[57] "Turkey, Kyrgyzstan Aim at Strategic Partnership," *Turkish Daily News*, 22 February 2002.

[58] DOD, *International Contributions*, p.12.

[59] "U.S. Military in Georgia Will Increase Baku-Tbilisi-Ceyhan Pipeline Security," *Turkish Daily News*, 7 March 2002; for the effects of this new development on the region, see: Kamil Agacan, "ABD'nin Gürcistan'a Asker Göndermesi: Terörle Mücadelede Üçüncü Cephe mi, Yoksa Köprübasi mi?," *Stratejik Analiz*, Vol.2, No.24, April 2002, pp.69-76.

[60] "Turkey Donates Vehicles, Communications Equipment to Georgian Military," *Turkish Daily News*, 7 March 2002; "Turkey Gives Military Aid to Georgia," *Turkish Daily News*, 12 June 2002; it should also be noted that the U.S. policy towards Azerbaijan also changed. In December 2001, Section 907 of the Freedom Support Act, preventing U.S. from direct U.S. government assistance to Azerbaijan was revoked.

[61] "Caucasus Cooperation Agreement against Terrorism Signed," *Turkish Daily News*, 1 May 2002; an agreement was reached on holding the summit regularly in the coming years, *Disisleri Güncesi*, April 2002; However, it was criticized because it failed to include other key players of the region, notably Russia, Armenia and Iran see, Yusuf Kanli, "A Summit with Missing Key Players," *Turkish Daily News*, 1 May 2002; for more on the impact of the summit on the region see, Hasan Kanbolat, "Türkiye-Azerbaycan-Gürcistan Zirvesi ve Bölgedeki Ortak," *Stratejik Analiz*, Vol.3, No.26, June 2002, pp.52-57.

Aimed at Eradicating Terrorism and for Supporting a Dialogue between Civilizations", as well as an accord that included regulations, principles and commitments for establishing a comprehensive security mechanism.[62] Moreover, the celebration of the tenth anniversary of the Black Sea Economic Cooperation organization (BSEC) on 25 June 2002 in Istanbul was another occasion where terrorism was discussed at a regional scale.[63]

All these imply that what is required from Turkey is for it to play a "subcontractor" role in the region, thus facilitate an American presence there within the wider context of the war on terrorism, rather than creating a genuine independent Turkish zone of influence, or promoting Turkish model once again. Therefore Turkey's ambitions and maneuverability are very much limited by international interests in the region. Moreover, a policy based primarily on limited contributions in military field, as long as lacking in economic dimension would be flawed. It is bound to remain temporary and once the conditions have changed, and the region returns to normalcy, the underlying realities may resurface and this policy may leave Turkey in a disadvantaged situation in political and economic terms.

This observation is strengthened by a parallel development in the way this region is treated by the international power centers. These countries are geographically landlocked with no direct connections to open seas. Moreover, they are also far from the prosperous Western markets. In the short run, they would not be able to attract significant foreign capital, except energy investments. They will probably be seen as "raw material suppliers," rather than as "emerging markets"; in other words, they will not be Asian tigers or Central and Eastern European Countries, but new Gulf states. For this reason, in the foreseeable future, the prospects for these countries to be part of the global market economy and move towards democratic pluralistic regimes are limited. They will be approached from a strategic perspective, and it is against this background that Turkey's pivotal role in the region can be better comprehended. In this context, as far as the optimism surrounding the launching the construction of Baku-Ceyhan pipeline is concerned, it must be kept in mind that a number of other developments might diminish the benefits of the pipelines to Turkey. Particularly the high pipeline construction costs, the possible developments that may come about concerning the alternative routes, such as Afghanistan,[64] and the tactics to be employed by other players could have adverse affects on the feasibility of the project.

A more definite reality, which speaks against Turkish ambitions in this region, is the changing shape of U.S.-Russian relations. Under Putin, Russia has chosen a non-confrontational type of relationship with the United States. Moreover, Putin has already

---

[62] *Newspot*, No.33, May-June 2002; In his address at the Summit, President Sezer reemphasized Turkey's experience in fighting terrorism and the importance of international cooperation in tackling with this issue. President's Press Office, *Asya'da Isbirligi ve Güven Artirici Önlemler Konferansi Zirve Toplantisi'nda Yaptiklari Konusma*, 4 June 2002.

[63] "Black Sea Economic Cooperation Tackles Energy and Terrorism," *Turkish News*, 26 June 2002.

[64] "Afghanistan is on Agenda again as Energy Route," *Turkish Daily News*, 24 May, 2002; for an analysis on the impact of the war on BTC pipeline see, Cenk Pala, "Afganistan Savasi'nin Hazar Boru Hatti Projelerine Etkisi: 'Kirmizi Kalem' bu Kez Kimin Elinde?," *Stratejik Arastirmalar Dosyasi*, Vol.3, No.11 2002, pp.17-24.

come a long way toward restoring Russian power and influence in the region, and cementing Moscow's primacy, without being opposed by Washington.[65] In this regard, following September 11, Russia cooperated with the United States and did not resist U.S. military deployment in Central Asia and the Caucasus. At the same time, partly in return for its concurrence with U.S. engagement in the region, Russia also tried to utilize the international atmosphere and use the discourse of fighting against terrorism to justify its own activities in the region, thus strengthened its position.[66] Based on these developments, there are also some arguments that a U.S.-Russian rapprochement might better provide security and stability in this region, therefore the United States should also recognize Russian interests there. If events follow such a course, that will clearly create some problems for Turkey, since Turkey and Russia have been competing with each other in this area.[67] Nevertheless, it must be noted that many analysts refer to prospects for cooperation between the countries. Throughout the 1990s, contrary to earlier expectations, both sides had prioritized the economic interests and Turkish-Russian relations developed cooperatively.[68] Similarly it is argued that cooperation, rather than competition might be the case also after the September 11, and this cooperation might be extended beyond bilateral relations and includes multidimensional partnership in Eurasia.[69]

What Role in Afghanistan?

As it was made clear so far, Turkey emerged as one of the leading actors in the fight against terrorism, hence it rigorously supported the international coalition against the Taliban and the al-Qaeda. When it became clear that the September 11 attacks had originated from Afghanistan and a military campaign was inevitably going to take place, the government was quick in obtaining a parliamentary authorization in October 2001 to

---

[65] F. Stephen Larrabee, "Russia and Its Neighbors: Integration or Disintegration," in Richard L. Kugler and Ellen L. Frost, (eds.), *The Global Century, Globalization and National Security, Volume II*, Washington, D.C.: National Defense University Press, 2001, pp. 859–874.

[66] For an analysis of the new developments see, Elnur Soltan, "Bush-Putin Zirvesi: Soguk Savas'in Ikinci Bitisi," *Stratejik Analiz*, Vol.2, No.20, December 2001, pp.5-24; However Özdag notes that rather than a willing consent to U.S. deployment in Central Asia, Russia had to bow to U.S. pressure see, Ümit Özdag, "Terörizm, Küresel Güvenlik ve Türkiye," *Stratejik Analiz*, Vol.2, No.19, November 2001, p.8.

[67] For an early warning that Turkey's 'bridging role' may shift to Russia, see: Mehmet Binay, "Ankara Köprü Rolünü Devrediyor," *www.ntvmsnbc.com.tr* newsportal, 5 October 2002.

[68] See, Duygu Bazoglu Sezer, "Turkish-Russian Relations a Decade Later: From Adversary to Managed Competition," *Perceptions*, Vol. 6, No.1, March–May 2001, pp. 79–98.

[69] This is justified by referring to a document, called the Eurasia-Action Plan, signed in November 2001 by the foreign ministers of the two countries, see, Karaosmanoglu, *"Afganistan Savasi'nin Transatlantik Iliski Boyutu"*; In his New Year's address, Foreign Minister Cem was also underlining that Turkey perceived Russia more as a partner than competitor. *Disisleri Güncesi*, January 2002; likewise, Turkey's reaction to U.S.-Russian rapprochement was positive: "Turkey Pleased with US - Russian Rapprochement," *Turkish Daily News*, 29 May 2002; even a change in Russia's attitude towards Baku-Tbilisi-Ceyhan pipeline was also noted. For the evolution of Russian position, see, Sinan Ogan, "Kremlin ve Lukoil Arasinda Rusya'nin Baku-Ceyhan Politikasi," *Stratejik Analiz*, Vol.3, No.26, June 2002, pp.68-76.

contribute troops to the U.S. campaign. The bill, which was met with public opposition,[70] also authorized the government to allow the stationing of foreign troops on Turkish territory and permit the use of Turkish airspace and airbases.[71] However the former Chief of Staff Kivrikoglu and other top officials expressed their hope that the scope of the conflict and Turkey's direct contribution would be limited. Reflecting the overall ambivalance of Turkish elite, while maintaining that Turkey cannot remain aloof to the developments in Afghanistan, Kivrikoglu at the same time called for a limited Turkish role leaving out active Turkish contribution to combat operations.[72] Turkish government however decided to contribute to the campaign by sending a unit of special forces to work with U.S. troops in humanitarian operations and train Northern Alliance fighters. Turkey also hinted that it could make its experience in guerilla warfare available, and it could help carve out a coalition between various Afghan factions against Taleban. Moreover, the U.S. benefited from Turkish airspace, used Incirlik airbase as a transport hub for the campaign, and according to some reports, was supplied intelligence by Turkey.[73] The rapid collapse of Taleban rule however made the possible role of Turkish soldiers in actual combat phase unclear, but soon a new rationale emerged. When the Taliban rule in Afghanistan came to an end, it became possible to launch international initiatives to rebuild the country, and the role of Turkey was again undeniable. Although it was not able to make a significant contribution in terms of financial and economic reconstruction aid, Turkey actively participated in the International Security and Assistance Force (ISAF), charged with assisting the newly formed interim Afghan authority and with providing order and stability in the capital, Kabul. Within the framework of the ISAF, Turkey contributed to the training of a national Afghan police and military force and providing military aid and equipment, as well as patrolling Kabul and its environs. Moreover, in June 2002, when the British mandate was over, Turkey assumed the lead-nation role and took over the command of the ISAF.[74]

Based on these developments, it is claimed by most analysts that Turkey is going to become a more assertive power, not only in its immediate neighborhood, but also "out of area." In Turkish reasoning, its active support for the U.S. military campaign was a logical corollary of its position on fighting international terrorism. According to Primer Minister Ecevit, it was natural that Turkey joined a war against terror because the U.S. always stood behind Turkey, and he emphasized that the war had to be fought to the end until Taleban regime was wiped out.[75] For Turkey, at the same time, capitalizing on U.S.-

---

[70] "Majority Opposes Attack on Afghans," *Turkish Daily News*, 4 October 2001.

[71] Turkey had already provided the U.S. with overflight rights in September shortly after attacks: "Turkey Opens Airspace to US," *BBC News Online*, 22 September, 2001.

[72] see Turkish dailies from 03 October 2001; for different reactions see, "Asker Gönderme Icin ne Demislerdi?," *www.ntvmsnbc.com.tr* newsportal, 2 November 2001; this initial ambivalence and 'passivism' was however criticized by some analysts, see: Özdag, *"Terörizm, Küresel Güvenlik,"* pp.10-11.

[73] "Analysis: Turkey's Pivotal Position," *BBC News Online*, 18 October, 2001.

[74] For the Turkish debate on ISAF see, Saban Kardas, "Dilemmas of Peacebuilding: Reflections on Turkey's Drive for ISAF Command," *Features – Turkish Daily News*, 19 April 2002.

[75] "Basbakan Sayin Bülent Ecevit'in TBMM'de Yaptiklari Konusma," *Disisleri Güncesi*, 10 October

led war on terrorism was a useful instrument to enhance its influence in Central Asia. By taking the strategic decision and taking active part also in military realm, Turkey sought to have a say in the future political landscape of not only Afghanistan, but also Central Asia. As regards active participation in ISAF, it was in line with its policy on peace operations, as it evolved in the post Cold War era. Turkey has been involved in several U.N. and NATO peacekeeping missions, from Somalia to Bosnia and Kosovo. This time, through participating actively in the ISAF and commanding this multinational force, it could show its military capabilities and ability to project power abroad, and thus expand the Turkish sphere of influence.[76] More concretely, Turkey sought compensation for its military support in economic field.[77] Turkish economy, which was already undergoing a severe crisis and was under an IMF program, was hit by the September 11 shock badly. Turkish Economy Minister Kemal Dervis, after claiming that Turkey must support the international fight against terrorism because it had suffered a lot from similar threats, hinted that there might be a price. According to him, "Turkey's strategic importance for the European Union and NATO is increasing and within this strategic framework Western allies should consider the cost that Turkey will have to bear."[78] A similar reasoning was used by Ecevit for justifying assistance to the U.S.[79] In practical terms, that meant delay of loan payments, and when necessary provision of new IMF loans, as well as direct U.S. assistance.[80]

At the same time, similar to the general arguments regarding Turkey's being an example to the Muslim world, discussed earlier, it was also claimed that Turkey could become a model for Afghanistan as well. That a war against Afghanistan offered the possibility to replace the fundamentalist Taleban regime, which Turkey had been consistently opposed, was an important reason behind Turkey's support for American war. Prime Minister Ecevit was one of the vehement supporters of this view, and during his correspondence with President Bush he underlined that a military operation on Afghanistan should include the toppling Taleban regime.[81] He went on stating that the model to be introduced had to be one similar to Turkey's secular democratic model for peace, stability, and tranquility in Afghanistan. Here, at times, the discussions sometimes ran into an emotional mood. The deep historical ties between the two countries have been

2001; also see, "Basbakan Sayin Bülent Ecevit'in CNN International Televizyonu'na Verdikleri Mülakat," *Disisleri Güncesi*, 12 October 2001.

[76] "Leadership to Test Turkish Military Might," *Turkish News*, 03 May 2002.

[77] For more on Turkey's motives see, "Afganistan Politikamizi Ulusal Cikarlarimiz ve Tercihlerimiz Belirliyor," Interview with Hüseyin Bagci, *2023*, November 2001, No.7, pp.22-27; Mehmet Seyfettin Erol, "Firsatlar ve Zorluklar Ikileminde Türkiye-Afganistan Iliskilerinde Yeni Dönem," *Stratejik Analiz*, Vol.2, No.23, March 2002, pp.77-85; Alan Makovsky, "Turkey's Unfinished Role in the War on Terrorism," *Insight Turkey*, Vol.4, No.1, January-March 2002, pp.44-45; Hugh Pope, "Turkey's Role in Afghanistan Presents Opportunity," *Wall Street Journal*, June 6, 2002, p.A16.

[78] "Turkey Rattled by Conflict Fears," *BBC News Online: Business*, 17 September, 2001.

[79] "Turkey Promises Troops for Afghan Campaign," *Insight Turkey*, Vol.3, No.4, October-December, 2001, p.180.

80 "US Delegation Suggests Rethink of Turkey's $5 Billion Military Debt," Turkish News, October 2, 2001.

[81] Fikret Bila, "Ecevit'ten Bush'a: 'Taliban Devrilmeli'," *Milliyet*, 26 September 2001.

continuously repeated to underline the 'necessity' of Turkey's support for Afghan people: Afghanistan was the first country to recognize the new Turkish Republic; Turkey helped Afghanistan in its modernization efforts; Ataturk - the founding father of the modern Turkish Republic - put special emphasis on Afghanistan, and so on.[82] Some proponents of a proactive Turkish foreign policy went as far as maintaining

> *the first country to recognize Kemal Atatürk's revolution and adopt the Turkish model was Afghanistan in 1921. Under the right political reformulation, to which Turkey will undoubtedly contribute, Afghanistan could be the first model in the post Cold War period to rehabilitate itself through the methods and means provided in the historic Turkish national experiment.*[83]

However, Foreign Minister Cem, though acknowledging the universal validity of Turkish model, called for caution in that Turkish model

> *is not one that could be forced upon from the outside. What kind of a model they want, what kind of a model they need, and to what kind of a model they are ready are something to be decided upon by the Afghan people themselves.*[84]

From American perspective, as discussed above, Turkey's support and participation into the coalition was useful to rebut allegations that the U.S. was engaged in a war against Islam. Therefore, similar to Turkish arguments, there were extensive references to Turkey's constituting a model for Afghanistan as well.[85] Moreover, besides its military contributions, as stated, Turkey had important linkages in the country and the region that could facilitate the U.S. presence there. As for peacekeeping phase, Turkey has a large standing army with accumulated experience in special operations and peacekeeping and as such it could spare its troops for such a mission.[86]

Yet, prospects for heightened expectations regarding region is difficult to substantiate.[87] First, Turkey's interest to Afghanistan is similar to the sudden discovery of Central Asia and Caucasus after the collapse of the Soviet Union. Therefore, because of the lack of any previous strategic perspective towards the country and the region, except for the Atatürk era, raising the expectations conjecturally is highly problematic. Second, as was discussed earlier, Turkey's potential for becoming a model for the Muslim world is highly limited. In the case of Afghanistan, this is further limited by the particular characteristics of this war-torn country: The people of the country are illiterate and very closed-off from the world; the society is very much fragmented and economically collapsed. Considering that even in relatively more developed Muslim countries Western liberal values are not welcomed by the people, one may wonder how Turkey would be

---

[82] See, for instance Prime Minister's address at party group. *Hürriyet.* 9 November 2001, also for the coverage of Foreign Minister Cem's visit to Kabul on 17 December 2001, in which he made extensive references to historical ties as facilitating factor of cooperation, see Turkish dailies from 18 December 2001.

[83] Paul M. Wihbey and Sule Kilicarslan, "A Turkish Strategic Window of Opportunity," *Insight Turkey.* October-December 2001, Vol.3, No.4, p.21.

[84] *"Cem: Turkish model is Paradigm".*

[85] "Powell: Atatürk Afganistan Konusunda Hakliydi," *Hürriyet.* 06 December 2001.

[86] See, Makovsky, *"Turkey's Unfinished Role,"* pp.42, 44.

[87] for a critical account see, Kardas. *"Dilemmas of Peacebuilding"*; also for a careful approach see, Erol. *"Firsatlar ve Zorluklar Ikileminde".*

able to carry these values to Afghanistan.

With regard to military contributions and assuming the ISAF command, for sure they will give an important impetus for Turkey's role in the region, and international standing. However, if they are not backed by other economic and political incentives in the medium and long-term, their practical benefits could be severely limited. Particularly, if we judge based on the past experience about Turkey's earlier expectations regarding Central Asia, geographical distance and lack of enough means could further limit transforming this engagement into political influence. The effect of geographical distance and the global reach of the U.S. therefore should be carefully evaluated. As the empirical evidence about Central Asia suggests, although Turkey sees itself as a bridge to open up these countries to the West, the West was in fact able to establish direct contacts with these countries. Similarly, in a military sense, particularly during the preparation and conduct of the Operation Enduring Freedom, the U.S. was able to get the support of other regional powers, notably Pakistan, and as such minimized the role of Turkey in the overall operation.[88] Last but not least, the dynamism of U.S. foreign policy in the new era and whether Turkey can keep pace with it - how many such other engagements Turkey can sustain- should be taken into consideration in evaluating the impact of Afghanistan engagement on Turkish foreign policy. In this line, any shift of international interest away from the Central Asian region, especially if one considers the U.S. intentions to expand the war on terrorism, could also result in a situation where the novelty of the "strategic importance of the region" might wear off. In such a situation, this out-of-area role might lose the wider political context in which it takes place and turn out to be another sporadic short-term engagement.

A Breakthrough in Turkish-EU Relations?

Another area of activity in Turkish foreign policy was observed in Turkish-European Union relations. The basic Turkish argument could be summarized as follows: because the events of September 11 have proven Turkey's value, not only to the Americans but also to the Europeans, Turkey could now "anticipate a warmer West."[89] Turkey therefore tried to utilize this opportunity so as to cement its relations with both the U.S. and Europe by emphasizing its role as a significant pro-Western power in such a critical juncture. Moreover, there was a strong Turkish belief that in the new era opened up by September 11 events, because the concern for fighting international terrorism was going to be the major leitmotiv, the international system would be increasingly dominated by security-oriented considerations. That would, the argument goes, inevitably enhance the role of

---

[88] There were even speculations that in the planning and conduct of military campaign in Afghanistan U.S. central command could be situated in Turkey, yet they turned out to be unsubstantiated exaggerations of Turkey's role. Based on this prospect, some analysts even had gone as far as arguing that moving the central command to Turkey could revitalize Turkey's strategic importance and could create a counterbalance against the growing influence of the EU/Germany in Eastern Mediterranean in view of the accession of Cyprus into the EU. "Prof. Dr. Osman Metin Öztürk'le Söylesi." *2023*, October 2001, No.6, pp18-19.

[89] "Bozkir (Vice Secretary-General for European Union Affairs): 'Turkey Can Anticipate a Warmer West,'" *Turkish News*, 3 October, 2001.

powerful security actors –such as the U.S. and NATO- at the expense of less powerful ones –EU members, and CFSP. By this way, the urgency of Turkey's relations with CFSP/ESDP was expected to diminish.[90] In this vein, besides the hope that Turkey's renewed importance would boost Turkish-European relations, there was therefore an additional impetus in the Turks' viewpoint: in the context of the growing American-Turkish strategic partnership, the Turks felt confident that the U.S. would not leave Ankara alone and would press the EU to satisfy Turkish demands. Therefore, the EU should appreciate the Turkish position in some of the problems dominating Turkish-European relations for some time.

The Turkish expectations that the EU and European countries would be more receptive to Turkey's position in fighting against terrorism have been already elaborated. Other issues which were supposedly going to be solved in a manner favorable to Turkey's interests included the Cyprus issue; the deadlock in the ESDP (European Security and Defense Policy); and Turkey's troubled EU membership process. There were indeed some initial positive steps in all those areas and a sense of optimism was inserted.[91] There appeared a chance to overcome the squabble over the ESDP-NATO relations and over what place Turkey would have in the development of the ESDP. In the run up to the Laeken Summit in December 2001, a consensus, called Ankara Document, was reached between Turkey, the United Kingdom and the U.S. Moreover, after a long pause, the dialogue between the leaders of the two communities on Cyprus was resumed. Both achievements were viewed as success by the Turkish politicians,[92] and the U.S. was said to have given stimulus to those developments.[93]

Without discussing all these issues in detail, at the risk of simplification, we would suggest that there are some fundamental challenges to Turkey's arguments, which would limit a sudden breakthrough in Turkish-EU relations. The main weakness of the Turkish discourse could be identified as follows. The initial rhetoric seemed to have perceived the West as a monolithic bloc.[94] Although this seemed to be true at the immediate aftermath of the September 11 terror attacks and all European powers expressed that they were united with the U.S. against the dangers of terrorism, after the novelty of the slogans of solidarity with the U.S. faded away, the underlying divergences in the transatlantic relations over a wide range of issues resurfaced. This was exacerbated by another feature of the approach taken by Turkey, which was to rely on U.S. pressure in its dealings with the EU. Those developments slowly put Turkey in an awkward position. First, because

---

[90] For an assesment of the effects of the war in Afghanistan on CFSP/ESDP see, Saban Kardas. "Afganistan Operasyonu'nun AGSP'ye Olan Yansimalari," 25 November 2001, http://www.liberal-dt.org.tr/guncel/Kardas/sk_afganistan.htm.

[91] "Rays of Light: For the First time in a Year, Turks are Seeing Some Flickers of Hope," *Economist*, 15 December 2001, Vol.361, No.8252.

[92] "No Concessions on ESDI and Cyprus: Ecevit", *www.ntvmsnbc.com.tr* newsportal, 7 December 2001.

[93] Particularly Colin Powell's visit to Ankara was the indicator of U.S. support: "Powell to Push for Cyprus Settlement," *Turkish Daily News*, 3 December 2001; Jim Kapsis, "Beyond Geopolitics for Cyprus," *The Washington Times*, 5 December 2001; for a Turkish view see, Cengiz Candar, "11 Eylül Jeopolitigi ve Kibris'ta Son Tango," *www.haberturk.com* newsportal, 06 December 2001.

[94] see for instance the quotation from Economy Minister Dervis, above.

EU-U.S. relations were increasingly characterized by disagreements over several issues, and, transatlantic relations were more occupied with how to find a solution to those problems than with Turkey, in fact the urgency of Turkey's problems in the eyes of the U.S. was far away from meeting the Turks' expectations.[95] Even if one assumes that the U.S. would be inclined to support Turkey, it would approach Turkish-EU relations from a strategic perspective, and that may not be compatible with the actual realities of Turkey-EU relations and the expectations of the EU from Turkey. This reasoning applies largely to democratization and human rights priorities of the EU vis-à-vis Turkey, –the famous analogy of "democratic and stable Turkey versus stable and democratic Turkey." That could in turn lead to the next problem. Perhaps, this 'tactic' of using the relations with the U.S. as a leverage vis-à-vis the EU is likely to cultivate a mood of distrust between Turkey and the EU, as well as a friction between the EU and the U.S. Instead of creating a healthy dialogue with the EU, Turkey's use of its strategic ties with the United States and the U.S. lobbying as a stick against the EU was increasingly perceived as 'a kind of low-intensity threat' against Brussels. In the long run, Ankara therefore hinders the creation of a strong channel of trust with the EU, and thus isolates itself. Against such a picture, it was no surprise that soon Turkish elite started to question Turkey's membership process into the EU. This was paralleled by another debate on whether Turkey should make a choice between the EU membership and strategic partnership with the US.[96]

Moreover, Turkish political elite's perception of the country as an actor indispensable to the West, particularly in political and strategic realm, is a cause for further problems. It is true that Turkey's role in the European security architecture is very vital, but a security-dominated discourse that lies at the basis of Turkish perceptions of the relations with Europe has an impact not only on the way Turkey values itself, but also on the actual course of the developments. At times, this leads to robust attitudes towards the EU and asking for concessions or a different treatment in a way to further hamper the integration process. More importantly, capitalizing on the strategic importance diverts the attention away from real problems and reduces the urgency for introducing and implementing economic, political, and cultural reforms demanded by the European integration process. The more Turkey is focused on its indispensability to the West, the less the country will be willing to undertake the necessary transformation on its journey towards EU membership. Therefore, the EU representatives were quick in making their positions clear against Turkey's attempts to capitalize on strategic importance and de-

---

[95] It suffices, in this regard, to remember that during a U.S.-EU summit in May 2002 Turkey was barely on the agenda: "EU-US Summit Starts Today: Turkey's EU Membership is not on the Agenda," *Turkish Daily News*, 3 May 2002.

[96] Tuncer Kilinc, Secretary-General of the National Security Council, who, with his statement on March 7, 2002, shocked observers and stimulated an intensive discussion by maintaining that Turkey would never be accepted by the EU, hence it should rather seek alternative allies. "Turkey Will Never be Accepted by the EU: Kilinc." *www.ntvmsnbc.com.tr* news portal, March 7, 2002; Ihsan Dagi, "Kritik Karar: ABD ya da AB," *Radikal*, 12 March 2002; Ihsan Dagi, "Competing Strategies for Turkey: Eurasianism or Europeanism?", *Central Asia and Caucasus Analyst*, SAIS Biweekly Briefing, Wednesday, May 8, 2002; M.Ali Birand, "Will Turkey Choose the EU or the USA?," *Turkish Daily News*, Opinion: 19 April 2002 .

emphasize membership criteria. EU Commissioner responsible for enlargement, Gunter Verheugen, maintained that Turkey should meet the hard criteria to be a member of the EU; otherwise, the 'whole European Integration Project' will lose its credibility. He went on saying "(w) e will soften the conditions of Turkey's membership. In return, Turkey will give us the guarantee of strategic aid. We cannot make such a bargain."[97] Given that there were even initial expectations that, similar to Turkey's entry into NATO following its contribution of troops to Korean War, Turkey's participation into military campaign in Afghanistan could pay the way for Turkey's membership into EU, this warning is quite telling.

Last but not least, remembering that the underlying merit of the problems, which have so-far dominated Turkish-EU relations, is unlikely to disappear all of a sudden, even after September 11 we are further called to be cautious. The continuation of the Greek veto on the Ankara Document, which, from Turkey's side,[98] resolved the tension over ESDP, and Turkey's futile attempts to force the EU to set a deadline for the start of membership negotiations are some of the examples.[99] Therefore, a fundamental shift in the EU's policy towards Turkey just for the sake of Turkey's enhanced strategic importance is hard to expect. Rather, the determination to carry out the transformation on the domestic scene, and the speed with which Turkey delivers those changes in this process would continue to remain the single most important determining factor of Turkey's relations with the EU.

Turkish-American Relations: Revival of Strategic Partnership?

Having said that, we can move on to Turkish-American relations. As it has been underlined so far, from American point of view, Turkey came to be seen a critical country whose support and cooperation was essential. First, there was a strong belief in the United States that supporting moderate Muslim countries, which oppose terrorism and extremism, was the key to winning the war against terrorism. The Turkish model, which embeds Islam within a secular system, appeared to be the best candidate to fit this role. Moreover, Turkey's geographical location and experience in fighting terrorism made its cooperation essential to the international coalition against terrorism. Furthermore Turkey was more than willing to contribute to U.S. agenda in Afghanistan by dispatching troops to the peacekeeping force. As a result, Turkish-American relations, which were characterized by up-and-downs throughout the 1990s, started to receive renewed interest. As mentioned above, on several occasions, many American statesmen liked to call Turkey "a steadfast partner in war on terrorism."[100] The changed mood was observed not only in

---

[97] "Türkiye'yi Kaybederiz," *Milliyet*, 22 October 2001.

98 "ESDI is completed from our point of view: Cem," www.ntvmsnbc.com.tr newsportal, 13 December 2001.

[99] Similarly, despite initial optimism, the results of Laeken Summit were far from meeting Turks' expetations see, A.Seda Serdar, "Belcika'nin Kazanclari ile Türkiye'nin Tavizleri: Laeken Zirvesi Sonuclari," *Stratejik Analiz*, Vol.2, No.21, January 2002, pp.40-45.

[100] U.S. Department of State, *"Grossman: Change in the Value of Enduring Alliances"*; "Turkey Called the 'shining crown jewel' amid Unstability: US Team Hails Turkey for its Important Role," *Turkish Daily News*, 2 October 2001; U.S. Ambassador to Turkey was also underlining that the U.S. could have no better ally than Turkey in the war on terrorism see, Robert W. Pearson, "The United States and Turkey: A Model of Sustained Engagement," *The Fletcher Forum of World Affairs*, Winter-Spring 2002, pp.53-62; Annie

the declarations of American politicians, but also in the titles of articles written on the issue, which were at times heavily emotional. Here is an example: "Turkey and the US: A partnership rediscovered."[101]

From Turkey's perspective, the revival of strategic relations with the U.S. implied several potential advantages, and consequently the Turks expected more rigorous U.S. assistance in a number of areas: U.S. support in the campaign against PKK terrorism; the promise of enlarged exports to American markets; the removal of obstacles to military transfers to Turkey; U.S. backing of Turkish command of Afghan peacekeepers and Baku-Ceyhan pipeline project; American support for further IMF loans; and American support for Turkey's other foreign policy issues, such as Cyprus, the ESDP and EU membership. Another repeated theme in the Turkish arguments was that, contrary to the Europeans, the U.S. had always been more supportive and sensitive to Turkey's demands in most of those contentious issues, thus it was a partner to be relied on. As a result, after September 11, Turkish-American relations that were characterized as 'strategic partnership' by President Clinton in 1999 have been further deepened.[102] In this regards, the Prime Minister Ecevit's visit to Washington On January 14-19 was a climax, which provided an important occasion to cement the strategic partnership.[103]

Indeed, in principle, it is hard to ignore that American-Turkish relations converge to a large extent. It was this convergence of interests and shared strategic vision that constituted the basis of some common policies towards a number of issues and regions, such as Balkans, and Caucasus. Nevertheless, one should not underestimate some limitations, which force us to take a more cautious stance. To start with, growing references to Turkey's renewed strategic importance in the wake of September 11 attacks inevitably reproduces the basic nature of Turkish-American relations, which were heavily security-dominated. Because there are mutual security-related concerns in several issues and regions, this is of course understandable. However, as in the past, this situation leaves Turkey very much depended on the shifting American strategic priorities. Because it remains the passive receiver of the external conditions in this partnership, Turkey is deprived of the ability to form the shape and direction of this partnership according its own agenda and priorities.

Such considerations in mind, after September 11, there were in fact serious attempts to diversify the relationship and give it a more solid standing. However given that the U.S. foreign policy is itself going to be largely driven by a "security first" discourse, and some underlying problems are still there, one has to wait to judge whether a major step towards diversification could be realized. Among others, the most attractive attempt towards diversification one was the proposal to increase trade volume between Turkey and the United States. The idea of increasing economic ties with the U.S. is in fact not new, and

---

Pforzheimer, "The United States and Turkey: A Post –September 11 Model of Sustained Engagement," *Polis Bilimleri Dergisi*, Vol.4, No.1-2, January-June 2002, pp.1-8.

[101] Steven A. Cook, "US-Turkey Relations and the War on Terrorism," *Insight Turkey*, Vol.3, No.4, October-December 2001, pp.37-48.

[102] Ismail Cem's New Year's address, *Disisleri Güncesi*, January 2002.

[103] "Ecevit's Washington Visit Highlights Turkey's Increased Value," *Turkish Daily News*, 15 January 2002; "Turkish-US Relations," *Newspot*, No.31, January-February 2002; *Disisleri Güncesi*, January 2002.

has been on the agenda since the Gulf War. To compensate Turkey's losses in the war, there was a discussion about how the U.S. could help Turkey. Then president of the country, Turgut Ozal, was also raising a similar argument by saying: "we don't want direct financial aid, what we need is more trade with the United States. For this, the United States should abolish textile quotas and other barriers to trade." Yet once the war was over, Turkey's demands were forgotten and Turkey was left alone to deal with its economic problems.

This time, following Prime Minister Ecevit's visit to Washington in mid-January, the strengthening of Turkish-American trade relations and adding an economic dimension to the strategic partnership came once more on the agenda.[104] At a press conference in Washington, Ecevit said the outcome of his contacts deserved the highest marks: "adding economic partnership to political and military alliance with the United States is an event that deserve 10 marks."[105] To this end, a Turkish-American Economic Partnership Commission was established to handle all economic and trade related issues between Turkey and the U.S.[106] It had its first meeting in Ankara in February.[107] Yet, the conclusions of these meetings were far from meeting Turkish expectations. Moreover, the plan to establish Qualified Industrial Zones (QIZ) was also criticized due to the fact that instead of establishing a direct relationship between the U.S. and Turkey, the American side preferred a quick-fix solution and tried to incorporate Turkey into the existing QIZ between Israel and the U.S.[108] This small example is indicative of the fact that the Bush administration was not ready to take the painful step and go to the Congress in order to seek a legislation to establish closer economic relations with Turkey because of the opposition in Congress. Therefore, in assessing Turkish-American relations, one has to bear in mind the fact that U.S. policies can shift easily because of different factors affecting U.S. policy making, such as lobbying, Congress and internal American debates on how to conduct U.S. foreign policy. At the moment, there are many supporters of Turkey in the Bush administration but this cannot be taken for granted forever, and there is still strong opposition within Congress against Turkey.[109] The expectation of full, unqualified U.S. support for all the issues mentioned above is therefore overly optimistic, and the developments so far prove this observation.

Moreover, as a matter of fact, despite the convergence of priorities at strategic level –

---

[104] "The Target is More Trade with America: Ecevit," *www.ntvmsnbc.com.tr* newsportal, 14 January 2002.
[105] For this and other reactions see, Elif Ünal, "PM Ecevit Earns High Marks with U.S. Visit," *Turkish Probe*, No.470, 20 January 2002.
[106] "U.S. Ready to Discuss Turkish Trade," *Associated Press*, 17 January 17 2002.
[107] "Turkish-US Commission Meets over Heavy Agenda," *Turkish Daily News*, 27 February, 2002.
[108] "Türkiye, ABD-Israil anlasmasina katilacak," *www.ntvmsnbc.com.tr* newsportal, 27 February 2002; "Hopes Dim after First Round of Turkey-US Economic Partnership Commission," *Turkish Probe*, No.475, 3 March 2002; The Chairman of Turkish-US Business Council, Akin Öngör, was critical of the conclusions of the meeting: "ABD Türkiye'yi Ihmal Ederse Uyuyamaz", *Hürriyet*, 17 March 2002; "US Leaves out Several Sectors from Turkish QIZs," *Turkish Daily News*, 27 June 2002.
[109] Although there was optimism that most of the Congressional opposition to Turkey would dimish, on certain issues it did in fact persist: "Inan: Armenian Lobby has no Chance against Turkey," *Turkish Daily News*, 8 May 2002; compare: "Obstacle From the Greek Lobby to Helicopter Purchase," *Turkish Daily News*, 12 June 2002.

having concurrent interests on broad issues and regions-, divergence might be the case at the practical level. In addressing certain tangible issues, the approaches to be taken might not be always mutually agreeable. Likewise, even when both countries' positions overlap on a certain case, that should not lead to overlooking the fundamental characteristic of this relationship which stem from the relative positions of the partners towards each other: the concerns of Turkey and the U.S. are guided by entirely different sets of foreign policy priorities, a global hegemony versus regional power. Therefore, the possibility that there could be diverging, even conflicting, interests and priories on certain issues is always there. Over-activism observed in the U.S. foreign policy in the new era is likely to further amplify this problem.

In this regard, as it was underlined, though the issue of terrorism might be a common concern to both Europe and America, when it comes to dealing with it there might appear some diverging opinions. A similar reasoning does in fact apply to Turkish-American relations. Turks repeatedly liked to argue that the US war against terrorism is a policy parallel to that of Turkey. As Turkish Ambassador to the U.S. Osman Faruk Logoglu underlined: "we are at the forefront of the war, as a friend, as an ally, and in reciprocation for the United States' understanding of our own fight against terrorism."[110] But, in reality, soon it became clear that there exist some fundamental differences, as well as diverging interests. The controversy over a possible military operation against Iraq is the case in point, which is also illustrative of the perils Turkey's geo-strategic importance may at times cause.

Turkey's geographical location was its main asset, but at the same time, it also produced Turkey's greatest headache: Iraq. In an effort to root out the sources of international terrorism, the U.S. shifted its focus to the so-called rogue states, and President Bush took this one step further by declaring Iraq, Iran and North Korea as the axis of evil. Even before this speech, extending the military operations against Iraq was on the U.S. agenda. Following developments such as the supposed Iraq-al-Qaeda links, the anthrax cases and the dispute over U.N. arms inspections in the country, made Iraq the next potential target for the U.S. fight against terrorism. This inevitably brought Turkey to the fore anew, due to its strategic value in a future war against Iraq.

However Turkey strongly opposed to a possible extension of war against Iraq. Before September 11, the Turkish government had been trying to normalize relations with Iraq despite U.S. opposition in order to compensate for the economic losses resulting from the UN-imposed embargo on Iraq. Therefore, the U.S. determination to intervene in Iraq was an unwelcome development. Yet, the real problem lies somewhere else.[111] There is a fear that the operations against Iraq and the turmoil created by post-Saddam political developments might have serious repercussions for Turkish security. Turkey is worried that the war against Iraq might end up with the breakup of Iraq and the establishment of a

---

[110] "Turkish Ambassador to US Speaks at Fletcher," 14 March 2002, http://www.tacsne.org/Past%20Activities/Fletcherhaber.htm.
[111] For Turkish worries concerning Iraq, see Armagan Kuloglu, "11 Eylül Sonrasi Degisen Dengeler Cercevesinde Türkiye'nin Irak Politikasi," *Stratejik Analiz*, Vol.2, No.23, March 2002, pp.5-22; "The Fears of a Muslim Ally: Turkey doesn't Want to Prove its Worth to the West by Fighting a War with Neighboring Iraq," *Newsweek*, 28 January 2002.

Kurdish state in the northern part of Iraq. Such a possibility would, from the Turkish perspective, encourage Kurdish separatist elements within Turkey. For this reason, Turkey's main priority is that an operation against Iraq should be avoided to the extent possible; and if it is going to take place anyway, Iraq should remain one nation. Yet, it appears that once an operation against Iraq starts, it would be almost impossible for Turkey to keep itself outside. In such a situation, the nightmare is that the Turkish army might be forced to occupy northern Iraq to prevent the emergence of an independent Kurdish state there, and affect the post-Saddam political developments in Iraq. Such a policy may not be compatible with the U.S. agenda in Iraq, and Turkish-American interests could move towards sharpened divergence.

Indeed, it was persuasively argued by some Turkish analysts that managing divergence and reaching a common position on Iraqi issue could be the 'test case' for Turkish-American partnership. In a critical account of the optimism following Ecevit's Washington visit, Cengiz Candar puts it blatantly:

> *Turkey's protection by America on 'political and economic platforms' depends to a large extent Turkey's ability to act in tune with America on the issue of Iraq. I mean, as Turkey, you would oppose to an American operation in Iraq; but at the same time you would become a 'strategic partner' with the U.S., and you would rely on U.S. 'economic assistance' to Turkey unreservedly. That won't happen. Cannot happen... Saddam is the 'gist' of the calculations on Turkish-American relations and 'strategic partnership'.*[112]

Moreover, everything comes with a certain price. It is therefore noted that the deepening of strategic partnership and the generous support Turkey receives from the U.S. administration, ironically, intensifies Turkey's dependence on the U.S. with the effect that the burden of being a 'strategic ally' limits the room of maneuver for Turkey.[113] However, given the obvious divergence of positions towards Iraq, that situation only adds to the complexity of Turkey's uncomfortable partnership with the U.S.

Last but not least, one should also bear in mind that Turkey's willingness to engage in active policies on several fronts simultaneously is likely to confront it with the problem of having the necessary capabilities and setting the priorities. Particularly, the wish to enhance the relations with Europe, while at the same time moving towards a deepened 'strategic partnership' with the U.S. and engaging in a proactive policy in Eurasia, would be increasingly difficult to reconcile. Perhaps, as was discussed in the previous section, the debate over whether to choose between membership into the EU and strategic partnership with the U.S. was just an early indicator of the dilemmas of a 'multi-dimensional' assertive foreign policy.

An End to the Cycle of Economic Crises?

Now, let us change the course from the foreign policy issues, and talk about the impact of post-September 11 developments on Turkey's domestic economic problems. Since early 2001, a severe economic crisis has been hitting the Turkish economy. The crisis

[112] Cengiz Candar, "'Stratejik' degil 'aday ortak'....," *Yeni Safak*, 22 January 2002.
[113] Kemal Balci, "US Ties Turkish Government's Hands," *Turkish Probe*, No.470, 20 January 2002.

devastated the industrial sector, lowered living standards, raised unemployment and jeopardized Turkey's international financial solvency.[114] In dealing with the crisis, Turkey received a significant amount of IMF credits, which in total amounted to more than $30 billion. American support was crucial for Turkey getting this IMF aid. Because Turkey emerged as a critical ally and the 'best model' for the Islamic countries in the new era, from American perspective, Turkey had to be supported economically. By this way the U.S. could not only assure Turkey's cooperation but also send a strong message that it would never leave a U.S. ally and Muslim country alone, when it is in need. The remarks by a U.S. Congressman, Robert Wexler, are quite telling: "An economic collapse in Turkey would be disastrous for America... America has got to treat the economy of Turkey as if is the economy of New Jersey."[115]

Although the Turkish side repeatedly claims that the IMF credits were provided to Turkey without any political concessions, there is a perception, both at home and abroad, that without the war in Afghanistan and the Turkish support in the campaign against terrorism, the IMF would have never given such a huge amount of money to Turkey. Even according to some analogies, Turkey could have had a catastrophe similar to what happened in Argentina.[116] As quoted above, Turkish Economy Minister Dervis, who took over the Turkish economy in March 2001, and Prime Minister Ecevit made strong linkages between Turkey's support for the international fight against terrorism and economic assistance to Turkey.[117] Similarly, representatives of Turkish private sector were more than willing to argue on strategic grounds. According to the Chairman of Turkish-US Business Council, Akin Öngör, if the Americans do ignore Turkey and fail to support it economically, they would not be able to go to bed in safety.[118]

Whatever the exact motives behind the IMF decisions might be, the fact is that with IMF help Turkey was able to control the economy in the short term and avert a catastrophe. Yet, in the long-term this situation may have some negative consequences. As long as the economic and political system remains decayed and structural problems cannot be remedied, the injection of foreign capital into the economy is bound to have a short-term effect. There is growing speculation by financial analysts that Turkey's total debts, which now exceed its gross national product, may create serious problems in the servicing and repayment of the growing debts.[119]

---

[114] "Kriz, OECD Liginde Küme Düsürdü," www.ntvmsnbc.com.tr newsportal, 19 May 2002; Bülent Aliriza, "Turkey and the Global Storm," *Insight Turkey*, Vol.3, No.4, October-December 2001, p.25.

[115] "Congressman Wexler: US Must Throw all Support behind Turkey," *Turkish Daily News*, 21 February 2002.

[116] on this famous analogy, see two contributions to *Turkish Policy Quarterly*, Vol.1, No.1, Spring 2002: Cem Akyürek, "Argentina's Experience: Any Lessons for Turkey?"; Ümit Kumcuoglu, "Turkey vs. Argentina: A Comparative Analysis with a Long Term Perspective"; also see, Murat Ücer, When You Cry for Argentina, Should You Cry for Turkey too?," *Private View*, No.1, Summer 2001, pp.56-59.

[117] Indeed, although Dervis' negotiations with IMF at the end of September 2001 did not bear fruits, by mid-November the IMF announced the release of further US$ 11 billion loans. In the meantime, Dervis visited Vice President Cheney and brought his case directly to him. It seems, the U.S. influence paid off. See, Aliriza, "*Turkey and the Global Storm,*" p.33.

[118] "ABD Türkiye'yi Ihmal Ederse Uyuyamaz," *Hürriyet*, 17 March 2002.

[119] Aliriza, "*Turkey and the Global Storm,*" p.33.

In assessing the performance of an economy and the issue of foreign assistance, perhaps, what is more important than receiving direct aid is the amount of foreign investments flowing into a country. In this regard, Turkey does not have a promising picture. According to a recent report conducted by the United Nations Conference on Trade and Development, between 1998-2000, Turkey ranked 122nd among 137 countries in terms of foreign capital inflow.[120] The reasons behind why foreign investors did not prefer Turkey mainly included macroeconomic instability, widespread corruption and the complex nature of the transactions that needed to be fulfilled. As a result, later Turkey decided to take steps towards reforming its foreign investment rules, as part of its IMF-backed reform process.[121] Another study reveals the other side of the coin: The amount of Turkish capital, which is invested abroad, especially in Switzerland and Luxembourg, is estimated to be $70 billion. Most of this money left Turkey after the economic crises for the purpose of securing the money abroad, since domestic investors lost their reliance on the Turkish economy.[122]

Here is the real paradox of Turkey: With a new crisis in the region, Turks think that the country has become strategically important. Yet, in political and economical terms it is considered to be a 'risky' place to invest, because its economic system is not stable and possible conflicts in the region pose threats to the country. If everybody is convinced that an operation against Iraq is inevitable, and if the deputy prime minister of the country maintains that an operation would destabilize the whole region, then, one wonders how international and domestic investors could be convinced that it is reasonable to invest in Turkey.

Moreover, the belief that "they cannot ignore us! They have to help us economically and financially, because we are strategically important" is not a good one. First, this mood would hinder domestic determination and the ability to solve the country's problems on its own. Moreover, this would result in taking the economic reforms not so seriously, and, in turn, diminish the self-discipline and self-control necessary for economic transformation. Therefore, how Turkey will be able to solve the vicious cycle of economic crises remains an open question.

Those economic problems, in turn, limit the country's ability to act independently in its foreign policy, as was observed in discussions about a possible operation against Iraq. On a TV show on America Fox-News channel, to the severe annoyance of many Turks, even one American analyst, former Clinton adviser Dick Morris, was claiming "Turkey has to support us; because the owner of Turkey is the IMF, and the IMF has already paid Turkey for this service."[123] This 'dependency' applies to other cases as well. Many American analysts did not hesitate to make references to American support for further IMF aid to Turkey in arguing for the relevancy of the 'dependent alliance' between Turkey and the U.S. Daniel Nelson, for instance, argues,

Turkey needs American and the US needs Turkey. Aside from a Republican

---

[120] "Yabanci Hala Inat Ediyor," *Radikal*, 29 April 2002.
[121] "Turkey Overhauling Foreign Investment Procedures," *Turkish Probe*, No.487, 26 May 2002.
[122] "Türkiye'nin 70 Milyar Dolari Disarda," *www.haberturk.com* newsportal, 15 November 2001.
[123] "ABD'li Yorumcu: IMF Türkiye'yi Satin aldi," *www.ntvmsnbc.com.tr* newsportal, 2 April 2002.

administration in Washington, Turkey hears only criticism of human rights record, and sees ongoing exclusion from Europe. Without Washington, US$ 10 billion in further IMF loans would have been impossible, and the image of an Argentina catastrophe would loom. Without Washington, Athens' place in the EU would mean intensified pressures to back away from the Turkish Republic on Cyprus. America has been a better friend than any alternative.[124]

On the other hand, there is a fundamental contradiction in the interplay between economics and strategic importance in the new era. The increasing strategic importance and the requirements of the new activism stemming from it, in fact, do not coincide with Turkish economy's needs and priorities. Whereas Turkey is undergoing a severe economic crisis and experiencing shortage of capital, the new engagements as part of Turkish contribution to international fight against terrorism, which are no doubt costly, do require a solid economic backing. For instance, although Turkey was more than willing to contribute actively and assume the command of ISAF in Afghanistan, the financial burden of this operation delayed the negotiations.[125] For a long time, Ankara's worries for the financial repercussions of Turkish contributions and the funding issue could not be met by the U.S. and U.K. Turkey's repeated demands for western funding of the ISAF fell on deaf ears for a long time. It was reported that Washington was reluctant to provide extra financial support for Ankara on ISAF because billions of dollars in IMF loans had already been provided to Turkey to help its recovery from the financial crisis.[126] There were even some speculations that Turkey could give up its quest for ISAF leadership, based on financial and other considerations.[127] However, after prolonged discussions, at the end, it was only American assurances that Turkey was able to accept to lead the force.[128] Similarly, because Turkey is keen on power projection beyond its borders, in order to sustain her military engagements abroad, there is a willingness to spend further on military procurement in the aftermath of September 11. For instance, one of the biggest Turkish defense projects came to a realization stage, and Turkey successfully concluded the negotiations for the purchase of four AWACS early warning aircraft from the Boeing. The financial cost of that project to Turkey is expected to be around US$ 1.1 billion.[129] One has to wait and see how it will be possible to reconcile those strategic calculations requiring heavy military spending with the current needs of Turkish economy.

Before concluding this section, it must be underlined that the interplay between economics and Turkey's strategic importance is problematic also in other aspects. Turkey's over-emphasis on its geo-strategic position and its strategic value to the West,

---

[124] Daniel N. Nelson, "The Dependent Alliance," *Insight Turkey*, Vol.4, No.1, January-March 2002, p.62.

[125] "Turkey Wants Assurances before Taking ISAF Command," *Turkish Daily News*, 27 February 2002.

[126] Elif Ünal, "Playing 'World power' Role may Cost Turkey," *Turkish Daily News*, 3 March 2002.

[127] "Türkiye ISAF Liderliginden Vazgecebilir," www.ntvmsnbc.com.tr newsportal, 11 March 2002.

[128] "Türkiye'nin ISAF Faturasini ABD Ödeyecek," *Hürriyet*, 18 March 2002; "Turkey to Take over Afghan Mission," *Associated Press*, 29 April 2002; however, the U.S. aid was also delayed due to Congressional approval, "Turkish Troops in Afghanistan, US Aid is Delayed," *Turkish Daily News*, 12 June 2002.

[129] "AWACS Negotiations Complete," *Turkish Daily News*, 5 June 2002.

and the determination to transform this into tangible economic benefits could work at the time of crises. However, it must be kept mind that such a policy could also turn out to be self-defeating in the long run. One cannot take the geostrategic value granted; rather it may change over time and depending on the case under consideration. Therefore, if Turkey is serious in solving its economic problems, it has to focus on structural remedies, rather than conjectural external developments. More importantly, using its politico-military contributions to Western security so as to gain leverage in economic realm may diminish the trust between itself and its allies, and in the longer run that may affect the relations or partnerships adversely.

Concluding Remarks

In light of the activism observed in the fields discussed so far, the dominant view is that the post September 11 events have contributed to Turkey's strategic importance, thus have helped reshape Turkey's relations with the United States and Europe, as well as with the countries in its neighborhood. As expressed by Foreign Minister Cem, "the unfortunate events of September 11, 2001 and ensuing developments have confirmed and consolidated some fundamental preferences of the Turkish foreign policy. Besides, they have boosted Turkey's strategic importance."[130] It might even, according to these arguments, stimulate the long-delayed redefinition of Turkey's role in the post Cold War world. Here is an excellent example of such arguments:

> *What is required in the current circumstance is for Turkey to seize the strategic initiative, with bold political leadership that articulates Turkey's national security aspirations within the new regional context. An historic window of opportunity exists for Turks, with Western support and encouragement, to emerge from their bunker mentality and assert themselves in shaping a positive historical trend outside their borders... Turkey is ready... What remains is for the West, and specifically the United States, to help Turkey mobilize its potential.*[131]

Although overall it is true that Turkey's international standing has been visibly enhanced, as it has been made clear so far, there is however need for a more cautious approach in assessing the post-September 11 developments on Turkish foreign policy. We would argue that the best way to discus the Turkish role is to analyze it in the context of regional power. Turks have ambitious and, at times, over-exaggerated expectations about their country's international position, but in reality, Turkey is mainly acting as a pivotal power. This can be best observed in the discussions regarding the Turkish role in Afghanistan, and Turkey's relations with Central Asia and the Caucuses. For example, on the one hand, Turkey is trying to lead the ISAF, but on the other hand it is asking the United States to pay its financial expenses and provide Turkey with the necessary transport, intelligence and logistic facilities. This is exactly the dilemma the country as is facing as a pivotal state. This necessarily brings us to the issue of the mismatch between the capabilities and foreign policy vision. One has to admit that, as the things stand, the gap between Turkey's capabilities and its expectations is difficult to bridge in the short-

[130] *"Cem: Turkish Model is Paradigm".*
[131] Wihbey and Kilicarslan, *"A Turkish Strategic Window,"* pp.22-23.

run. As a result, Turkey's ability to act as an independent actor initiating its own projects is severely limited by, or depends on, the degree to which it will be successful in managing balancing its own priorities with external factors. That means, Turkey could act in cooperation with other global and regional powers, and mobilize their support in the areas of converging interests. By this way, Turkey can both advance its own interests and contribute to the agenda of its partners. However to the extent that Turkey's interest will diverge from those of its partners it will be increasingly difficult to follow an independent course. If this is chosen, the growing divergence may run the risk of confrontation. This point, which many advocates of Turkey's strategic importance fail to see, must be the basis of any assessment on Turkish foreign policy. That dictates that Turkey should seriously get engaged in a comprehensive and in-depth debate on its role in the world and in the region, what capabilities instruments are at its disposal, what foreign policy vision it envisages, and what are its priorities. Such a debate should be conducted by leaving aside the influence of short-term, conjectural developments, and focusing more on setting long-term structural priorities. The responses to those questions are of vital importance for the successful resolution of not only foreign policy but also domestic problems the country is facing.

This segues into our next observation regarding post-September debate on Turkey's strategic importance. The arguments raised for Turkey's enhanced strategic importance are very similar to those employed at the beginning of the 1990s, following the Gulf War and the collapse of the Soviet Union. Yet, remembering that the euphoria of the 1990s remained largely unrealized and diverted the country's attention away from more important policy objectives, it would be legitimate to argue that it is high time for Turkey to see the facts in a more realistic manner. First, that means, the foreign policy issues that are on Turkey's agenda will evolve according to the actual realities of the issue under consideration, rather than altered strategic conditions. It is true that increased strategic value of the country may have positive effects on its international standing but in such contentious issues as the relations with Europe or America, the underlying sources of cooperation or divergence will not vanish. Therefore it would be wrong for Turkey to choose the easier way of capitalizing on its strategic importance and downplaying the necessary steps it needs to take in its foreign and security policies.

Second, the need for a more realistic vision on Turkish foreign policy has also implications on domestic realm. Whatever model it follows in its foreign policy, or whatever priorities it sets for itself, be it EU membership, leadership in Eurasia, or strategic partnership with the US, Turkey's international performance will depend above all its capability to solve problems internally and reach economic and political peace and tranquility. In this respect, a rational assessment of the country's international role would help avoid unnecessary external adventures and enable it to direct its attention to necessary domestic transformation. The economic, political and diplomatic problems facing the country are structural and fundamental; they cannot be solved through a simple redefinition of Turkey's strategic role in the new conjuncture. Engaging in ambitious external projects or relying on the tempting idea of Turkey's indispensability to its Western partners would diminish the urgency for reform and take the focus of the country away from economic and political modernization. Economic reforms, political transformation and human rights and democratization issues would receive less attention compared to the life-and-death problems of national sovereignty and national security. A choice is, therefore, being forced upon Turkey. Either it will aspire to become a so-called "stable" regional or pivotal power willing to project power beyond its borders, by maintaining and reproducing the current political culture, which is dominated by military and security considerations, or it will choose to become an ordinary, but "democratic" and self-sufficient state, by focusing on the necessary economic and political reforms and restructuring and transformation of its system.

This is definitely not an easy task. To be sure, Turkey's geographical location offers many advantages. Yet, the very same reality is also a source of problems for the country. Whether one likes it or not, we are living in this volatile region, characterized by several actual and potential crises. For instance, two states that belong to the so-called 'axis of evil' are Turkey's neighbors; and any development in the surrounding regions forces Turkey to get involved in one way or another. This is the reality in which we are living. If we cannot escape this reality, then what we can do is to act in a rational manner with a long-term perspective, based on carefully elaborated priorities, instead of being dictated by self-propaganda, conjectural calculations and short-term gains.

Contributors

Meliha Benli Altunışık is Associate Professor at the Department of International Relations, Middle East Technical University, Ankara. She was a Fulbright scholar in 2003-2004 and she spent her sabbatical at the Middle East Institute in Washington DC. She is the author of numerous publications on the Middle East politics, Caspian oil and Turkey's relations with the Middle East.

Deniz Ülke Arıboğan is Professor of Istanbul Bilgi University, Institute of Social Sciences, International Relations Department, Istanbul. Specialties; international politics, security and strategy.

Hüseyin Bağcı is Professor of International Relations at Middle East Technical University in Ankara and Vice Chairmen of the Center for European Studies. He was quest researcher at the German Society for Foreign Affairs (DGAP) in Bonn, and Senior Fellow at the Center for European Integration Studies (ZEI) in Bonn and at the Landesverteidigungsakademie und Militarwissanschaftliches Büro des Bundesministeriums für Landesvorteidigung in Vienna. He has published several books and large number of articles on Turkish Foreign Policy and Turkish German relation.

İdris Bal is Assistant Professor of International Relations at the Faculty of Security Sciences, Police Academy, Ankara. He was a Fulbright Scholar at Harvard University in 2003-2004. He has published several books and large number of articles on Turkish Foreign Policy, Turkish-US-EU relations, Eurasian political and economic developments, Islam, World Politics, hydrocarbon resources and energy issues and terrorism.

Zeyno Baran, is director of International Security and Energy Programs, The Nixon Center Washington DC-USA. Specialties; Eurasian political and economic developments; political Islam; Caspian energy; US-Turkish-EU relations.

Fulya Kip Barnard is Assistant Professor of International Relations at Middle East Technical University in Ankara. Main interests; EU and Migration.

Erol Bulut is Research Assistant in Department of Economics, Gazi University and University of Aberdeen.

İbrahim S. Canbolat is Professor of Uludag University, Department International Relations, Görükle-Bursa. Working and interest fields; European Union, Turkish Foreign policy, German foreign Policy, the global conflicts and politics, The Third World or developing countries in the international politics, Balkan countries.

Şaziye Gazioglu is Associate Professor in the Middle East Technical University, Ankara-Turkey and University of Aberdeen, Unite Kingdom. She is a specialist in International Economics. Her interest includes dynamic Macroeconomics, Financial Markets, Risk Management and Financial Crises.

Ramazan Gözen is Associate Professor and Lecturer in the Department of International Relations at Atilim University in Ankara. He has published several books and large number of articles on Globalisation, Turkish foreign policy, NATO, ESDP, Middle East; For instance, *Turkey's Delicate Position between NATO and the ESDP*, Ankara: Center for Strategic Research, 2003.

Saban Kardas is currently a PhD student in political science at the University of Utah, Research Assistant at METU and Sakarya University (Turkey). His research interests include international relations theory, human rights and international relations/foreign policy; humanitarian intervention; peace operations; European Security and Defense Policy; Transatlantic relations and Turkish foreign policy.

H. Bülent Olcay is Associate Professor of International Law and Diplomacy at the Faculty of Security Sciences, Ankara. Research interests; hydropolitics, enlargements of NATO & European Union, Islam and Democracy, Diplomacy in Islam.

Cengiz Okman is Professor at the Department of International Relations, Işık University, İstanbul. Specialties; Turkish Foreign policy, EU, Diplomatic history.

Henry E. Paniev is a Ph.D. student in Political Science at the Pyatigorsk State Linguistic University, Russia. The sphere of his scientific interests is international relations, Turkish foreign policy, Geopolitical interests of Turkey in the Caucasus, Turkish-Russian relations.

Victor Panin is the director of the Center for the North Caucasus Studies and the professor of political sciences at the Pyatigorsk State Linguistic University, Russia (PSLU). He is the vice-president of the North Caucasus Independent Institute for Strategic Studies. Specialties; international relations, foreign policy, strategic policy, security problems, conflict management, geopolitics, U.S.-Russian relations, Russian-Turkish Relations, the Middle East and the Caucasus.

Dirk Rochtus is Associate professor in Diplomacy at the Lessius Hogeschool Antwerpen and the University of Antwerpen (Belgium). Publishes on Federalism, German politics, Turkey. In 2002 he co-edited the book "Turkije: Springstof voor de Europese Unie?" (Garant, Antwerpen/Apeldoorn).

Faruk Sönmezoğlu is Professor of Department of International Relations, Faculty of Political Science, Istanbul University. Main interests; international politics and foreign policy analysis, Turkish foreign policy, diplomatic history. Specific interests; Cyprus question, Caucasian and Central Asian affairs.

Gül Turan is currently adjunct professor of Economics at Koc University. She has served as professor of Economics at Istanbul University 1967-2001. She has held visiting appointments in the United States and France. Her interests and works are in the area of international political economy, and money and banking.

İlter Turan is Professor of Political Science and the former president of Istanbul Bilgi University. He has previously taught at Istanbul and Koc Universities and has frequently held visiting appointments at various American universities. His works in English and in Turkish have been on Turkish politics and institutions, and Turkish foreign policy. His recent writings have been on the Turkish parliament and on the domestic and international politics of water.

Mustafa Türkeş is Associate Prof of Department of International Relations, Middle East Technical University, Ankara, specialized on the Politics in the Balkans.

Nasuh Uslu is Assistant Prof. Dr. the University of Kirikkale, the Faculty of Economic and Administrative Sciences, the Department of International Relations. Specialized on Turkish-American relations, the Cyprus question, Turkish foreign policy.

Index

Printed in the United States
68987LVS00003B/9-12